Law Enforcement Ethics

Law Enforcement Ethics

CLASSIC AND CONTEMPORARY ISSUES

Brian D. Fitch
EDITOR

Los Angeles | London | New Delhi
Singapore | Washington DC

Los Angeles | London | New Delhi
Singapore | Washington DC

FOR INFORMATION:

SAGE Publications, Inc.
2455 Teller Road
Thousand Oaks, California 91320
E-mail: order@sagepub.com

SAGE Publications Ltd.
1 Oliver's Yard
55 City Road
London EC1Y 1SP
United Kingdom

SAGE Publications India Pvt. Ltd.
B 1/I 1 Mohan Cooperative Industrial Area
Mathura Road, New Delhi 110 044
India

SAGE Publications Asia-Pacific Pte. Ltd.
3 Church Street
#10-04 Samsung Hub
Singapore 049483

Acquisitions Editor: Jerry Westby
Associate Editor: MaryAnn Vail
Editorial Assistant: Nichole O'Grady
Production Editor: Laura Barrett
Copy Editor: Matthew Sullivan
Typesetter: C&M Digitals (P) Ltd.
Proofreader: Eleni Georgiou
Indexer: Judy Hunt
Cover Designer: Michael Dubowe
Marketing Manager: Terra Schultz
Permissions Editor: Jennifer Barron

Copyright © 2014 by SAGE Publications, Inc.

Printed in the United States of America

Library of Congress Cataloging-in-Publication Data

Fitch, Brian D.

Law enforcement ethics : classic and contemporary issues / Brian D. Fitch.

p. cm.
Includes bibliographical references and index.

ISBN 978-1-4522-5817-1 (pbk.)

1. Law enforcement—Moral and ethical aspects—United States. 2. Police ethics—United States. 3. Police misconduct—United States. 4. Police training—Moral and ethical aspects—United States. I. Title.

HV7924.F576 2014
174′.936323–dc23   2012041595

This book is printed on acid-free paper.

13 14 15 16 17 10 9 8 7 6 5 4 3 2 1

Brief Contents _____

Detailed Table of Contents_____

Preface _____

In the United States, as well as in other democratic societies, police officers are accorded an extraordinary set of powers and responsibilities available to few others (Chappel & Piquero, 2004; Kappeler, Sluder, & Alpert, 1998). Police officers have the power to search and seize personal property, to detain and make arrests, and to apply varying levels of coercive force, up to and including deadly force, in the pursuit of their legal mandates. While police officers may have considerably more authority and, by extension, more opportunities to abuse that authority, there is no evidence to suggest that law enforcement professionals are any better equipped than the general public to make moral decisions (Cohen & Feldberg, 1991). Moreover, evidence suggests that law enforcement professionals are not necessarily any less likely to commit criminal offenses than the average citizen—findings that are further complicated by the fact that police officers are, for the most part, free to come and go with little, if any, oversight or supervision (Kappeler et al., 1998).

Nonetheless, society has tremendous expectations of law enforcement and very low tolerance for unethical behavior (Boles, 1995). Officers are expected to adhere to a strict and unwavering code of ethics and to conduct themselves accordingly at all times, both on and off duty. As a result, law enforcement agencies face serious implications when unethical behavior or criminal activities are exposed, including damaged public trust, jeopardized criminal investigations, and costly, often unnecessary, litigation (Dunn & Caceres, 2010; Kappeler et al., 1998). Nonetheless, it seems that one does not have to look very far these days to find myriad examples of police misconduct, corruption, and abuse in the media. Rodney King, Abner Louima, Antoinette Frank, and, most recently, Kelly Thomas—a schizophrenic homeless man who was bludgeoned to death with the butt of a Taser at a bus stop in the city of Fullerton, California—have become household names.

Indeed, the harm caused by the increasing number of high-profile cases of abuse, misconduct, and corruption may be responsible for the growing number of internal affairs units found in many large law enforcement agencies, whose role it is to investigate citizen complaints, as well as potential violations of department rules identified by supervisors (Cohen & Feldberg, 1991). While there is a lack of data regarding the scope of law enforcement misconduct, it is likely that virtually every police agency has witnessed some form of corruption, abuse, or scandal (McCafferty, Sourynal, & McCafferty, 1998). Although scholars, educators, and practitioners often disagree on the precise mix of factors responsible for misconduct, it is probably safe to assume that law enforcement corruption and abuse are influenced by a number of individual, collective, contextual, and organizational variables, some of which are more difficult to study and address than others. This collection of essays is the result of the collaborative efforts of a diverse taskforce with a vested interest in law enforcement ethics. The contributors represent practitioners from local, state, and federal law enforcement agencies; faculty from university departments, including criminal justice, political science, psychology, sociology, medicine, and law; professional oversight bodies; and centers devoted to the study and teaching of ethics.

This volume comprises 18 chapters, organized around four broad categories. Part I, *Ethical Foundations*, contains five chapters. In Chapter 1, J. J. Klaver provides an overview of law enforcement ethics. The author explores the individual, organizational, and environmental factors that may contribute to law enforcement misconduct. The issues of organizational structure, departmental policies and procedures, social influences, and organizational culture and their relationships to misconduct are also considered. Chapter 2 highlights the need for proper psychological screening of law enforcement applicants. Ana Gamez and Gary Collins discuss the importance of a partnership between the evaluating psychologists and agency management in selecting potential law enforcement candidates. Chapter 3, presented by Brian D. Fitch, Christine H. Jones, and Luann P. Pannell, argues for a new model of law enforcement ethics training. This includes a discussion of many of the problems associated with traditional lecture-based models of instruction, as well as strategies for incorporating the latest findings from the field of adult education to enhance learning, memory, and retention. In Chapter 4, Brian D. Fitch, Randy B. Means, and Gregory Seidel investigate the management of police ethics. The authors outline the need for clear policy, effective supervision, and proper consequences in influencing officer behavior. The final chapter is this section considers issues of policy, supervision, and oversight in the United Kingdom's 43 police services. Attilio R. Grandani discusses the minimum international standards affecting the United Kingdom's statutes and structures, Police and Criminal Evidence (PACE) Act 1984, inspections, audits, and the current complaint system.

Part II, *Ethical Perspectives*, is composed of five chapters. In Chapter 6, Theron L. Bowman and Daniel T. Primozic offer a forensic examination of the "will" by charting the internal pathology of morality and irrationality. This includes a study of the classic philosophical arguments presented by Aristotle, as well as those offered by Robert J. Steinberg, as a strategy for attenuating police misconduct. Chapter 7 confronts the ways officers' values, beliefs, and behaviors are influenced by social learning, including beliefs about misconduct. Brian D. Fitch and Christine H. Jones discuss the essential propositions of social learning theory, as well as how these tenets function as a general theory of police misconduct. In Chapter 8, Aaron D. Conley and Bryon G. Gustafson address fundamental questions about group failings and organizational and institutional responses to those failures. This includes questions about how standards of behavior come to be and what law enforcement organizations should do when institutional standards are violated. Chapter 9, written by Paul T. Zipper and Tina Adams, presents the psychology of marginality. The authors investigate the emotional, psychological, and organizational causes of marginality, while highlighting the importance of early intervention by management and mental health professionals in addressing marginal behavior in all its forms. Chapter 10 outlines the need for greater awareness of the causes, symptoms, and treatment of PTSD among members of the law enforcement community. Amir Hamidi and Patrick Koga examine the symptoms and onset of PTSD, including the neurophysiological correlates of PTSD, biological responses to fear, and subclinical PTSD. The chapter also includes an investigation of current treatments available for PTSD, including cognitive processing therapy (CPT) and mindfulness-based stress reduction (MBSR).

Part III, *Ethical Professionalism*, presents four chapters. In Chapter 11, Kevin A. Elliott and Jocelyn M. Pollock take an in-depth look at the ethics of force. This includes an examination of pertinent case law, policy, and training, as well as the damage to public trust caused by highly publicized incidents. Chapter 12 focuses on the use of trickery and deceit in criminal interrogations. James L. Ruffin explores the effects of case law—more specifically, the U.S. Supreme Court case of *Miranda v. Arizona* (1966)— on interrogation practices, as well as arguments commonly found in the courts, social sciences, and philosophy. The chapter includes a discussion on the emergence of Investigative Interviewing in the United Kingdom and other democratic nations, while concluding with an overview of research on the attitudes of American police officers toward the use of trickery and deceit. Chapter 13, authored by Alexandro Villanueva, explores the question of why law enforcement officers cheat in a variety of settings, including promotional exams. The chapter offers a typology of cheating and a brief theoretical background of the civil service system, and concludes with recommendations to address cheating, while creating more fair and equitable standards throughout the promotional process. In Chapter 14, Bernard E. Harcourt confronts the problem of racial profiling among American law enforcement agencies by examining the arrest of Henry Louis Gates Jr. and the rationale behind racial profiling. He further offers strategies to combat this phenomenon while increasing the overall effectiveness of law enforcement.

Part IV, *Ethical Challenges*, features four chapters on emerging issues facing today's law enforcement leaders. Chapter 15 looks at how leadership, ethics, professionalism, and accountability have assumed prominent roles in academic, government, and public discourse since the events of 9/11.

Presented by Kelly W. Sundberg, this chapter focuses on the increasing importance of professionalism and ethical policing, especially among federal agencies, while outlining many of the challenges associated with recruiting highly skilled officers capable of adapting to diverse new political mandates. In Chapter 16, Cyndi Banks takes a penetrating look at the concept of democratic policing in three developing nations: The Philippines, Nigeria, and Sierra Leone. Topics of discussion include the ways norms affect "best practices," how local policing customs continue to survive into the postcolonial period, and challenges associated with transforming current models into modern democratic policing practices. Chapter 17 discusses the destructive consequences of off-duty misconduct to officers, their agencies, and the public at large. The author, David Massey, explores the implications of stress, culture, and other factors associated with misconduct, as well as offers suggestions about what leaders can do to proactively address the problem in our modern, media-driven age. Chapter 18, written by Jarret Lovell, explores the impact of citizen journalism and social media on contemporary policing. The author outlines the ways changes in media technology bring new information about police practices to the public sphere, often leading to strategic and organizational change. This includes a discussion of how contemporary law enforcement must learn to work with citizen journalists, while recognizing the technology of social media as a positive force for enhanced police professionalism and accountability.

References

Boles, M. L. (1995). *Institutionalizing ethics for the next century* (Senior Leadership Program Research Papers 3). Tallahassee: Florida Department of Law Enforcement.

Chappel, A. T., & Piquero, A. R. (2004). Applying social learning theory to police misconduct. *Deviant Behavior, 25*(2), 89–108.

Cohen, H. S., & Feldberg, M. (1991). *Power and restraint: The moral dimension of police work*. Westport, CT: Praeger.

Dunn, A., & Caceres, P. J. (2010, Spring). Constructing a better estimate of police misconduct. *Policy Matters Journal,* 10–16.

Kappeler, V. E., Sluder, R. D., & Alpert, G. P. (1998). *Force of deviance: Understanding the dark side of policing* (2nd ed.). Long Grove, IL: Waveland Press.

McCafferty, F. L., Souryal, S., & McCafferty, M. A. (1998). The corruption process of a law enforcement officer: A paradigm of occupational stress and deviancy. *Journal of the American Academy of Psychiatry and Law, 26*(3), 433–458.

PART ONE

Ethical Foundations

1

Law Enforcement Ethics and Misconduct

An Introduction

J. J. Klaver

We who enforce the law must not merely obey it. We have an obligation to set a moral example which those whom we protect can follow.

Louis Freeh, Director of the FBI, 1993–2001

The following public press release was issued by the U.S. Attorney's Office, Eastern District of Pennsylvania, on August 18, 2011:

FORMER PHILADELPHIA POLICE OFFICER SENTENCED TO 16 YEARS FOR DRUG CONSPIRACY

PHILADELPHIA—Mark Williams, 28, of Philadelphia, was sentenced today to 16 years and three months in prison for his role in a drug conspiracy in which a phony arrest was orchestrated in order to steal drugs from a drug dealer. At the time of the crime Williams was a Philadelphia Police Officer assigned to the 39th District. The theft scheme, orchestrated by then-officer Robert Snyder and his wife Christal, involved a phony arrest by Williams and another co-defendant, then-officer James Venziale. After the phony arrest, the defendants distributed the heroin to a person they thought was a drug dealer and money launderer, but who was actually an undercover Special Agent from the Drug Enforcement Administration.

Co-defendants Robert and Christal Snyder and James Venziale pleaded guilty to charges and were sentenced in May. Robert Snyder is serving 13 years and one month in prison; Venziale is serving three years and six months in prison; Christal Snyder is serving 10 years and six months in prison.

In the second scheme, the defendants attempted to rob someone they believed was a member of the "Mafia," but who in reality was an undercover FBI agent. Ortiz believed that the "Mafia" member routinely collected large amounts of gambling proceeds from individuals in Pennsylvania and New Jersey and then delivered those proceeds to be laundered by who they believed was a drug dealer and money launderer, but who in reality was an undercover Special Agent with the DEA. A scheme was developed whereby defendant Williams and Robert Snyder, abused their positions as Philadelphia Police officers, by planning to have defendant Williams conduct a vehicle stop while defendant Ortiz was in possession of the United States Currency and a small amount of narcotics. After finding the narcotics and United States Currency, Williams would make it appear as if he was arresting Ortiz and seizing the money and drugs. To ensure that the "Mafia" member believed that the seizure was legitimate police activity, defendant Williams provided Ortiz with a Philadelphia Police Department property receipt.

On June 25, 2010, Williams was placed on restricted duty by the Philadelphia Police Department. As a result, he was not permitted to wear a police uniform, not permitted to carry a weapon on or off duty and was not permitted to take any police action. Additionally, Williams was required to, and did, turn in his Police Department issued weapon. Despite these restrictions, an attempt to commit the robbery took place on July 9, 2010. Williams recruited another person who drove a vehicle equipped with strobe lights, to pretend to be an undercover police officer to assist in the vehicle stop. Williams then, while off duty and on restricted duty, armed himself with his personal handgun, and took, without authorization, a Philadelphia Police Department vehicle from the 39th Police district. After meeting with Ortiz and discussing the final arrangement, Williams and the other person took their positions to await the arrival of the "Mafia" member. The "Mafia" member was, in reality, an undercover Agent, and the robbery was not allowed to occur.

This chapter provides an introduction to many of the central issues of law enforcement ethics, paying particular attention to the individual, organizational, and environmental factors that may play a role in the ethical lapses that contribute to patterns of corruption or individual acts of official misconduct or abuse by law enforcement officers. The issues of misconduct, abuse, and corruption have most often been examined within the context of individual or personal deviancy; however, organizational structure, departmental policies and procedures, social influences, and the nature of the ethical climate within organizations have been shown to influence individual behaviors and actions. Therefore, factors such as employment screening and recruitment, training and continuing education, disciplinary practices, and the presence and effectiveness of both internal and independent oversight elements are examined with respect to their relationships to and influences on law enforcement corruption, abuse, and misconduct.

The Study of Law Enforcement Misconduct

Law enforcement professionals throughout the United States are bestowed with great authority and power to carry out their assigned and expected duties and responsibilities. The citizens of organized and structured societies give up the right to personally enforce the law or take the law into their own hands to redress wrongdoing against them, and instead vest substantial authority in the law enforcement to handle such issues (Peak, Stitt, & Glensor, 1998). Because of this, the citizenry expect and deserve a high degree of accountability and trustworthiness from their law enforcement public servants (Seron, Pereira, & Kovath, 2004) and demand that these organizations display a high degree of institutional integrity (Conditt, 2001). This integrity, in many ways, is gauged and measured by the actions of individual organizational members as they perform their day-to-day duties and conduct themselves in their official capacities. Any form of malfeasance or deviant misconduct by law enforcement officers in the performance of their official duties undermines the organization's ability to fulfill its mission and erodes the public's confidence in the organization and its members (Palmiotto, 2001).

From a practical standpoint, the law enforcement "mission" is a multifaceted concept encompassing protection and service aspects; however, from a theoretical perspective, the underlying role of law enforcement in a democracy is the production of moral products—that is, "helping to secure those conditions in which the citizenry can enjoy the pursuit of human flourishing and avoiding the worst consequences of human limitations and liabilities" (Adlam, 1998, p. 139). From this perspective, success depends on law enforcement organizations and their members remaining separate from the "limitations and liabilities" they are helping the society at large avoid by not engaging in the types of behaviors and actions that they are charged with addressing. This is, in some senses, the basis of the higher standard that law enforcement officers are held to in the conduct of their official, and often personal, actions. To effectively enforce the law, one must first and always obey the law (Conditt, 2001). "Public service is a public trust that obligates civil servants to operate on a 'higher ethical plane' and according to more stringent standards and expectations" than the citizenry at large (Rothwell & Baldwin, 2006, p. 218).

Law enforcement is, at its core, about the rule of law, fairness, protection of individual and collective civil liberties, and due process. Corruption and other forms of deviance undermine the legitimacy of the law enforcement organization and, by implication, the wider collective state apparatus (Punch, 2000). Not surprisingly, research suggests that a majority of citizens place great emphasis on these concepts of fairness and due process by law enforcement officers, and have the expectation that officers will perform their duties within a set of fair, public, and accountable guidelines (Seron et al., 2004). At the same time, policing is a phenomenon that often allows the ends to justify the means, even if the means are viewed as questionable or in violation of accepted ethical and behavioral guidelines. Policing exists in a culture judged on its outcomes, due in part to the attitude of the wider society, which primarily judges the effectiveness of policing on the achievement of measurable goals, such as reductions in crime rates and other quality of life measures (Mills, 2003).

The issues of law enforcement misconduct, abuse, and corruption have most often been considered within the context of individual deviancy or examined within the socio-psychological disciplines as a form of deviant behavior supported by normative influences within the subculture of the group (Haarr, 1997). While individual psychological or collective behavioral influences can not, and should not, be ignored in any analysis of the root causes of law enforcement misconduct, abuse, or malfeasance, there is a larger organizational component to this issue that can also be important. While there can be recognition that individual characteristics alone are insufficient to explain moral and ethical behavior, there is also increasing acknowledgment of the impact of social and organizational factors on individual behavior (Victor & Cullen, 1988).

While situational factors may be at least as important as individual characteristics in explaining unethical or deviant conduct, the interaction or combination of individual factors and organizational context may more accurately explain ethical lapses than either element alone (Adams, Tashchian, & Shore, 2001). "The research on individual versus organizational impacts on ethical behavior suggests that organizational context is an overriding influence on individual moral decisions made in organizations" (p. 201). Sechrest and Burns (1992) acknowledge this reality specifically for law enforcement in noting that corruption of police officers can arise out of both individual factors and socio-structural factors specific to the characteristics of law enforcement organizations. Nelligan and Taylor (1994) also note that it is well established that law enforcement deviance is best understood not as an individual pathology, but rather as a product of the social organization of police work.

The position of legal authority that law enforcement officers occupy requires them to engender and maintain the public's trust that the exercise of that authority will be fair, just, and equitably exercised. "Reports of misconduct by police officers often result in citizens losing their confidence in the police" (Palmiotto, 2001, p. 344).

A Historical Perspective

The genesis of modern law enforcement structure in the United States can, in some ways, be traced back to the very birth of the nation itself, when the country's founders fled the tyranny of centralized autocratic leadership. In establishing the legal and societal boundaries of the new country's functioning, specific measures were taken to decentralize political and physical power to avoid development of the conditions that had been left behind. "Early American policing was greatly influenced by the choice that policing and public safety were to be the responsibility of local government" (Johnson & Cox, 2004, p. 71). The very nature of policing, however, which is dominated by the power of discretionary coercive authority and the mandate to use force when deemed necessary, combined with decentralized local control and oversight by local politicians, often resulted in early American law enforcement agencies becoming extensions of the political machinery that appointed them to their positions and controlled their professional fates. "Political machines maintained control of the police by appointing people loyal to them. Professionalism and competence took a backseat to political loyalty" (p. 71).

Even early on in the history of modern policing, this connection between law enforcement authority and political power was recognized as problematic. A collection of chiefs from around the country gathered in Chicago in 1893 and formed the National Police Chiefs Union, now known as the International Association of Chiefs of Police (IACP, 2007). While the original purpose was primarily to apprehend and return wanted persons who fled local jurisdictions, the collective group of chiefs drafted the beginnings of what would eventually become the Law Enforcement Code of Ethics. This code (Table 1.1, below) established for the first time, in writing, that the

Table 1.1   Basic Law Enforcement Code of Ethics, IACP, 1893 (adapted from IACP, 2007; Johnson & Cox, 2004)

To serve the community
To protect lives
To save the weak from those who would use intimidation
To keep an officer's private life separate from his official duty
To be courageous and show resolve when faced with the possibility of death
The badge symbolizes not only authority, but also acts as an image of public faith
The officer will maintain confidentiality
The conduct of the officer will always be ethical and consistent with department regulations and the law (added in 1992)

basic responsibilities and duties of a professional police officer included fair, equitable, courageous, and confidential service always within the limits of constitutional rights and guarantees.

Despite this early attempt at professionalizing law enforcement, the empirical and academic support for any concept of an ethical component to decision making in the execution of police work was slow to develop. While the issue of law enforcement corruption garnered much public attention, comparatively little emphasis was placed on the development of a comprehensive code of professional ethics, and that effort was fragmented at best (Loewenthal, 1981).

In the 1970s, as Heffernan (1982) notes, well-publicized and pervasive scandals involving large groups of law enforcement came to light in several major U.S. cities, and practitioners in the field agreed that ethics training for all officers should be implemented to "professionalize" the occupation of policing and stem the tide of what was perceived as increasing corruption. "Professionalism implies a multifaceted value orientation, including trust by clients that is based on the professional's schooled expertise and commitment to rules of ethical behavior" (Seron et al., 2004, p. 669). The approach that would yield the greatest benefit, however, could not be agreed on with such ease.

Today, training in ethical issues has become fairly widespread in law enforcement officer training and education (Pollock & Becker, 1996; Schafer, 2002). The purposes of such training include providing practical behavioral guidance, increasing awareness of the moral and ethical dilemmas faced by law enforcement officers as they conduct their official duties, and satisfying the concerned public constituency that law enforcement officers swear under oath to serve and protect (Conditt, 2001; O'Malley, 1997; Pollock & Becker, 1996).

The Study of Organizational Ethics

While the theoretical concepts identifying the existence of organizational work climates has been empirically accepted for some time, Victor and Cullen (1987, 1988) introduced the specific concept of ethical climate as a means of explaining and predicting individual ethical conduct within the organizational context.

Organizational climate researchers intended for the understanding of work climates to be instructive of how individual human behavior reflects and incorporates organizational practices, policies, and procedures. Victor and Cullen (1988) narrowed in on the "prevailing perceptions of typical organizational practices and procedures *that have ethical content* [emphasis added]" as constituting the ethical work climate of the organization (p. 101). This ethical climate serves as a guide for, and influence of, employee behavior in the workplace when the individual is faced either consciously or unconsciously with the Socratic question, "What *should* I do?"

While the potentially devastating effects of both serious individual acts of misconduct and organizationally systemic and endemic patterns of deviance are easily recognized and measured, there exist no real, quantifiable prescriptions for preventing their occurrences. From a theoretical perspective, official misconduct and manifestations of professional deviance by law enforcement officers likely exist due to the complex interrelationships among contributing factors, such as individual and personal proclivities; the nature of the law enforcement position, which inherently manufactures opportunities to engage in misconduct; organizational factors; and larger societal and social influences that can include a strong emphasis on results and "success" by the law enforcement measured in low or decreasing crime rates (Ivkovic, 2003; Johnson & Cox, 2004).

Each and every day as law enforcement officers fulfill their professional duties, they are faced with situations and dilemmas that demand quick decisions and sound judgments based on ethical principles, legal prescriptions, public expectations, administrative regulations, and procedural guidelines. "The outcomes of those dilemmas will be determined by the tradition, character, ethical system, and training of the agency" (Peak et al., 1998, p. 33), and will be framed within the confines of the organizational contexts in which they occur.

While there certainly would never be any way to assign specific and unequivocal causality to any individual act or incident of deviant misconduct, or to identify specific contributory factors always present in the analysis of such activities on larger scales, there do exist opportunities in the empirical realm to more narrowly isolate pieces of the larger puzzle in the hope of providing support for theories that contribute to the understanding of how and why deviant misconduct occurs in law enforcement organizations by law enforcement officers, and how its occurrence can be, at best, prevented and, at least, minimized or reduced.

Policing, as Haarr (1997) notes, is recognized as a diverse enterprise; across the nearly 18,000 state and local law enforcement departments in the United States, there is remarkable diversity in mission, duties, style, and membership. There are many references, both colloquially and in academic literature, to the "police culture"; however, early concepts of a single unified occupational culture of law enforcement that maintains a homogeneous belief system have largely been replaced by an alternative conceptualization of diversity, variation, and contrast within law enforcement organizations and the occupation as a whole (Haarr, 1997). Despite this diversity, the common aspects of the policing roles—that is, those of the three functional roles of enforcement of the laws of society, social order maintenance, and public service (Perez & Moore, 2002)—provide for some common and identifiable themes (Ford, 2003).

Law Enforcement Misconduct

Misconduct has been a problem that has hindered law enforcement organizations since their inception. It has undermined their effectiveness in performing their assigned duties, diminished the morale of law enforcement employees, and harmed their relations with the citizens whom they serve. Misconduct has an extremely negative impact on the abilities of law enforcement organizations to carry out those duties (order maintenance, crime control, and public service) for which they were created (Hunter, 1999).

Due to the nature of the phenomenon of law enforcement misconduct and deviancy, and the effect that the incidences of its occurrence has at both the micro and macro levels of analysis (i.e., at the individual and societal levels), much of the literature on the topic is generally focused on (1) establishing typologies and definitions to aid in development of explanatory theories for the purpose of clarifying understanding and awareness; (2) its etiology for the purpose of generating prescriptions and recommendations for its prevention; and (3) moral or ethical defects in individuals as explanations for the occurrence of incidents of misconduct.

Serious and academically rigorous studies into the issues of law enforcement misconduct, abuse, and corruption began only recently in the social sciences, mostly as a result of the civil unrest and the violent nature of encounters between law enforcement agencies and the public during the early civil rights movement of the late 1950s and 1960s (Bolton, 2002). The lack of theoretical examination of law enforcement misconduct and ethics is due in part to difficulties not only in defining the concept of misconduct, but also in gathering historical and contemporary relevant data (Chappell & Piquero, 2004).

One of the principal difficulties in academically examining or measuring the issue of law enforcement misconduct lies in the very nature of the concept itself. "The secretive nature of corrupt transactions and the lack of incentives to release information about them render obtaining accurate measurements—the actual number of corrupt incidents and offenders, and the actual losses arising from corruption—a very difficult task" (Ivkovic, 2003, p. 600). While the logical sources of information about corruption are the very individuals involved in the acts of its commission, that is, law enforcement officers themselves, one major obstacle to obtaining accurate and useful information is the motivation of organizational members and leaders to conceal or hide the nature of existing problems and the fact that deviant conduct and corruption by officers are generally private, obscure, and unusually difficult to observe (Chappell & Piquero, 2004; Haarr, 1997).

Additionally, the very nature of the law enforcement mission and the authoritarian and protective structure of the police role within society makes penetrating the veil of secrecy surrounding official misconduct by those outside the law enforcement role or community potentially problematic (Kingshott, Bailey, & Wolfe, 2004). "The problems arising from the clannish nature of police officers can be aggravated further by a dangerous us-against-them mentality" (O'Malley, 1997, p. 21). Law enforcement professionals are tasked with maintaining order and protecting citizens in a society that often is chaotic and violent. They work in a stressful environment where quick decisions that may have life-or-death consequences are later subjected to intense scrutiny under a complex set of legal rules. In such circumstances, even well-intentioned officers motivated by a desire simply to catch criminals may become frustrated and vulnerable to an ends-justifies-the-means mentality (O'Malley, 1997).

Rothwell and Baldwin (2007) and Kingshott et al. (2004) also note that the characteristics of the law enforcement working environment—including dangerous missions, a sometimes hostile public, and excessive scrutiny of actions by administrators and outsiders—can contribute to a cohesive and isolationist solidarity that excludes participation or influence by outsiders seeking information for the purposes of scrutiny or reform. Loyalty to fellow officers becomes a key feature of the overall culture of policing (Skolnick, 2002), and informal enforcement mechanisms have been shown to exist to encourage cohesive solidarity and silence in the form of social and professional sanctions (Benoit & Dubra, 2004).

Factors that make examining and ultimately controlling or limiting official misconduct difficult, particularly misconduct engaged in for the purpose of personal financial or other gain, include the reluctance of officers to report corrupt activities by fellow officers through a recognized "Blue code of silence" or air of secrecy that develops around police activities (Hyatt, 2001; Westmarland, 2005), the reluctance of police administrators to publicly acknowledge or identify the existence of individual or systemic corruption in the organizations they are responsible for overseeing, the benefits of certain types of corruption for the parties involved, and the lack of available victims willing to report on or admit their involvement in corruption (Klockars, Ivkovic, Harver, & Haberfield, 2000).

An important distinguishing feature of policing in the United States is that it operates under restrictions characteristic of the limits of government established to ensure our free democratic civil society (Loewenthal, 1981). The individual civil rights of citizens are both protected by and protected from the coercive law enforcement authorities, and this very paradox can create some reluctance to take actions that, while reducing misconduct and corruption, may at the same time make police less productive. This reluctance can serve as tacit acceptance of misconduct.

Defining Misconduct

While there is not one single all-encompassing definition of official law enforcement misconduct, a generally well-established understanding is that any instance of the exercise of an officer's public authority or official discretion for private, personal, or self-interested gain is considered misconduct or corruption, in that self-interest or gain undermines the very purpose of public service (Barker, 1996; Kleinig, 2002).

Roebuck and Barker (1974) derived an empirical typology of law enforcement corruption based on a content analysis of the relevant literature for the period 1960 through 1972, and along with work by Loewenthal (1981), Punch (2000), Barker (1996, 2002) and Grant (2002), Table 1.2 provides an overview of the broad typology of official law enforcement misconduct considered here.

Table 1.2 Typology of Misconduct (adapted from Barker, 1996, 2002; Grant 2002; Loewenthal, 1981; Punch, 2000; Roebuck & Barker, 1974)

	Type of Misconduct	Examples of Behaviors
1	Corruption of authority	Seeking or receiving material gain by virtue of position without violating the law per se (e.g., free meals, merchandise, or other gratuities not afforded to others outside the position)
2	Abuse of authority/ violation of civil liberties	Physical abuse or use of excessive physical force, psychological abuse through verbal assault or ridicule, and legal abuse involving violation of constitutional or civil rights
3	Kickbacks/bribes	Monetary gain for referrals to particular individuals or companies (such as towing companies, repair shops, lawyers)
4	Opportunistic theft	Theft of property from crime scenes, crime victims, detainees, etc.
5	Shakedowns	Solicitations or acceptance of bribes for particular actions (such as not writing a ticket, not effecting an arrest, not impounding a car)
6	Protection of illegal activities	Protection from enforcement action for those committing illegal activities (such as gambling operations, drug dealers, auto thieves)
7	Fixing arrest or prosecution	Intervening in and undermining criminal proceedings, such as investigations or prosecutions
8	Direct criminal activities	Outright criminal activity by law enforcement officers, in direct violation of both agency guidelines and legal statutes
9	Internal payoffs	Special prerogatives or benefits available to officers, such as working holidays for extra pay, overtime shifts, shift allocations, promotions, are bartered or sold
10	Disclosure of information	Furnishing confidential information, such as criminal records, the identities of confidential sources, or information concerning ongoing investigations to those without a legitimate law enforcement interest
11	Discrimination	Harassment of, taking action against, or failing to take proper action because of an individual's personal characteristics (race, gender, creed, religion, national origin, or sexual orientation)
12	Falsification/lying	Planting incriminating evidence at crime scenes or on individuals to "strengthen" weak criminal cases or artificially enhance perceived productivity, or falsifying official reports

In a broad sense, law enforcement corruption and deviance can be considered as any type of proscribed behavior engaged in by officers within the scope or purview of their official capacities that contradicts established normative systems, undertaken with the expectation of an actual or potential unauthorized material reward or gain (Roebuck & Barker, 1974). Normative systems can include legal statutes, procedural guidelines, administrative requirements, and behavioral role expectations embodied in the oath of office sworn to when law enforcement powers are granted. Discretion is central to the successful execution of law enforcement authority by the officer on the street (Seron et al., 2004), and the deployment of that discretion is very often unrelated to specific laws or formal organizational mandates (Ford, 2003).

Organizational Elements and Control

Traditional attempts at reducing corruption have historically involved the control of law enforcement agencies and their officers through the use of paramilitary systems with bureaucratic hierarchical structures (Brown, 2001) and repressive measures (Punch, 2000). Ethics, as applied to the law enforcement role, has been viewed generally as the attempt, through methods and practices within these control structures, to ensure proper conduct and behavior from law enforcement officers (Johnson & Cox, 2004). It is not enough to be reactive and reactionary in the face of misconduct, but rather control systems must include an investment in motivating organizational members to stay in compliance with laws and professional standards of conduct. Corruption and misconduct are not simply "individual aberrations of an incidental character that can be effectively banished by temporary, repressive measures," but rather are persistent and recurring dangers that are generated by a combination of factors, including the nature of the work, the nature of the organizations, and the position of policing in the wider society (Punch, 2000, p. 321).

In many senses, the approaches necessary for the prevention and reduction of the incidence of official misconduct and corruption by law enforcement involves management of the risk and control of the contributory factors (Walker & Alpert, 2002). Managing the risks within the policing role and law enforcement organization can require implementation and execution of multifaceted strategies within the entire life cycle of the law enforcement career, starting from the hiring process, through training, and into ongoing monitoring and supervision of employees (Sechrest & Burns, 1992).

Police officers themselves, in an attitudinal survey conducted by Hunter (1999), overwhelmingly support (1) restrictive selection and screening of applicants, (2) better training, (3) strict and fair disciplinary practices, (4) clear written policies and procedures, (5) professional ethical standards and codes, (6) investigation of allegations by internal affairs units, and (7) review of incidents by external entities such as civilian review boards, as means of regulating police behavior and reducing misconduct.

Recruitment and Screening

While research efforts have failed to identify law enforcement recruit characteristics that differ significantly from those of the general population before being hired (Ford, 2003), there is empirical support for psychological screening used to identify potentially high-risk applicants and officers in need of intervention or further scrutiny (Chappell & Piquero, 2004). The primary goal of personnel selection should be the consideration of any characteristic that may be detrimental to later performance, and for this very reason, criteria used in the selection of law enforcement candidates is of critical importance (Sechrest & Burns, 1992). There are specific psychometric measurement tests that can assess antisocial behavioral tendencies and conscientiousness traits, both of which have been shown to be valid predictors of future police job performance (Arrigo & Claussen, 2003).

The intention of prescreening applicants for law enforcement positions is twofold, in that it is a combination of looking for warning signs as predictors of potential future problems and looking for key traits or characteristics that are positively related to future performance in the job. "Acting ethically or unethically is ultimately an individual choice, and it is important to know which factors individuals say influence that choice" (Frank, McConkey, Huon, & Hesketh, 1995, p. 1). Good moral character and a clear ethical understanding of the requirements of the job are essential components of law enforcement competence, for officers are often faced with situations involving conflicting interests and often make discretionary decisions that must take into consideration the meaning of justice, community standards, and social morality (Perez & Moore, 2002).

Arrigo and Claussen (2003) and others have identified a series of antisocial characteristics that have been shown to be related to an individual proclivity to engage in antisocial or deviant conduct, and that could be particularly troublesome in the context of the law enforcement profession. These characteristics include a lack of guilt, a callous disregard for the rights of others, irresponsibility, egocentricity, impulsivity, and a lack of conscience. One of the obvious intentions of pre-employment screening should be the consideration of such antisocial characteristics, as they are potentially detrimental to the performance of the law enforcement role (Arrigo & Claussen, 2003; Arrigo & Shipley, 2001; Martens, 2000).

Vicchio (1997) delineates a list of core professional individual virtues, or personality traits, deemed integral for the attainment of organizational goals, that, taken together and integrated into behavioral attributes, represent a measure of professional integrity and serve to bring about the service and protection goals of the law enforcement profession. These virtues include

(1) prudence, or the practical ability of deliberation or discernment, meaning the ability to resolve conflicts while deciding what action (or inaction) is deemed most appropriate; (2) trust in the context of the nature of the relationship between a law enforcement officer and citizens, a law enforcement officer and other officers, and a law enforcement officer and his supervisors; (3) effacement of self-interests and the elevation of the protection and service mandates above the individual's power, prestige, or profit; (4) courage, both physically and mentally, to place oneself in situations of stress or danger while maintaining the fortitude to persevere through to a conclusion; (5) intellectual honesty, taken as the ability to recognize and admit the limitations of one's knowledge; (6) justice, in fairly and evenly providing those individuals being served with what they are due according to the mandates of law and society; and (7) responsibility, exhibited in the understanding of what is right, the intent to do what is right, and cognizance of available alternative actions.

The underlying assumption in the formulation of screening strategies and protocols is simply the recognition that some individuals lack the requisite skills, character, personal commitment, and integrity to fulfill successfully the roles demanded of the law enforcement position (Perez & Moore, 2002). The appropriate individual moral and ethical framework that is attempting to be ascertained during prehiring procedures is, in many ways, just as important as demonstrating possession of the requisite physical agility or intellectual ability needed to perform the job of a law enforcement officer (Crank & Caldero, 2000).

While it is not suggested that possessing any or all of the above attributes indicates some empirical measure of potential performance as a law enforcement officer, the suggestion is that identification of such attributes through a screening process may contribute to an overall ability to reduce misconduct and deviancy within law enforcement organizations (Palmiotto, 2001). Resisting temptations to behave unethically has been demonstrated to be associated with distinct individual and situational factors (Frank et al., 1995), and the intent of any type of prescreening and continued monitoring of organizational members is to identify and monitor a selected portion of these factors. Rigorous hiring standards are seen as one component of managing for ethics within organizations, and the applicant selection process represents a critical component of law enforcement ethics programs by ensuring applicants' compatibility with the organization's ethical philosophy (O'Malley, 1997).

Preservice and In-Service Training

It is a fair assumption that an academic knowledge of ethical issues serves to, in the least, sensitize individuals to these issues prior to actually encountering them in "real-world" occupational situations, and the concepts of ethical decision making can help law enforcement officers navigate the often murky waters of discretionary authority (Pollock, 1993). Law enforcement officers, as a result of the authority vested in their position, can have tremendous power over people's lives and their individual freedom and even, in certain circumstances, over life and death. For this very reason, it is important that adequate training "contribute to a sense of professionalism and help to ensure a recognition of the public trust inherent in criminal justice positions that involve decisions about people's liberty" (p. 378).

Despite this recognized need, the majority of law enforcement academy training in the United States devotes only a relatively small amount of time to ethics and the role of ethical decision making in the day-to-day activities of police officers. Perez and Moore (2002) note that a nationwide study of law enforcement academy training revealed that state regulations require an average of only three and one-half hours of ethics training in an entire police academy curriculum. "Given the gravity of the problem of police misconduct and the opportunities and enticements to misbehave faced by every officer on the street, this amount of discussion is woefully inadequate" (p. 8).

Ethics education for law enforcement officers should fulfill several functions: (1) It should stimulate moral awareness and reasoning by posing difficult ethical dilemmas and various, differing solutions; (2) it should encourage the recognition of ethical issues and how they are applied in the context of job performance; (3) it should aid in the development of abstract analytical skill sets; (4) it should elicit a sense of moral obligation and instill a duty to personal responsibility in the exercise of authority; (5) it should provide greater understanding of the morality associated with the coercive authority granted with the job, and; (6) it should contribute to a tolerance for the ambiguity that is inherent in the discretionary decisions faced by law enforcement officers (Sherman, 1981).

Education in ethics and ethical issues, as part of the overall training experience, represents one important piece of the entire socialization process of new law enforcement officers, and training at various stages of a law enforcement officer's career should concentrate, in part, on developing an awareness for the need for and importance of integrity (Simpson, 1977).

Policies and Practices

Policy is defined by Barker (1996) as the principles and values that guide the performance of departmental activities, and that should be followed in order to attain some departmental goal or objective. Policy is not intended to be a directive as to how to act in any given situation, but rather is the framework for drafting procedures, rules, and regulations. The rules and regulations that arise from the underlying policy statements refer to the specific requirements or prohibitions that are intended to prevent deviations from policies or procedures; that is, policies are intended to form attitudes and guide judgments, while rules are designed to form and govern behavior.

There is historical support in the relevant literature for the application of external codes of prescribed values as a means of combating the social, organizational, and opportunity-based influences that can contribute to incidences of misconduct or occupational deviance by law enforcement professionals (Simpson, 1977). The effectiveness of any code of ethics, however, is directly related to how seriously and completely it is incorporated into training, supervision, and daily departmental decision making. "Only by keeping it constantly within the thoughts and vision of each officer will it be eventually incorporated into their actions" (Brown, 2001, p. 20).

While a written code of conduct represents a formalized representation of the value system of the organization, informal codes of conduct can be established and maintained by hiring ethical and trustworthy individuals and by providing periodic ethics refresher training (Conditt, 2001).

Accountability

Crank and Caldero (2000) identify law enforcement accountability as general efforts to control police behavior, and note that it has been one of the central problems of policing in the United States since the turn of the 20th century.

Accountability for the actions or misdeeds of law enforcement officers is accomplished through the application of a variety of control and review systems, such as executive modeling and moral leadership, direct supervisory management and oversight, internal affairs investigative units, and external law enforcement or civilian reviews of allegations of misconduct (Perez & Moore, 2002). External reviews of allegations of misconduct, performed either by other law enforcement agencies or by community civilian review boards, are intended to introduce independent, outside perspectives to the problem of investigating incidents of law enforcement misconduct. While the issue of independent civilian review of allegations of misconduct is frequently met with resistance by those within law enforcement agencies, studies indicate there is no significant difference in the outcome of cases in municipalities that have parallel civilian and police controlled investigation and review systems (Lynch, 1999).

In general, disciplinary programs in place in law enforcement organizations consist of four general elements: (1) established codes of conduct; (2) investigations of allegations of misconduct; (3) adjudication of substantiated findings; and (4) public reporting on disciplinary processes (Conditt, 2001).

Organizational Ethics and Influences

Studies of ethics, ethical conduct, and misconduct within organizations have largely centered on sociological examinations of cultural and climatic elements, and how these constructs impact and influence the behaviors and actions of individual and collective group members. "There is a growing belief that organizations are social actors responsible for the ethical or unethical behaviors of their employees" (Victor & Cullen, 1988, p. 101). This responsibility, as Victor and Cullen (1987, 1988) note in their seminal work on the topic, stems from the specific and identifiable ethical climate that exists within each organization and that, in conjunction with individual moral development, serves to influence how and even why individuals engage in a variety of behaviors.

Climates within organizations refer to the shared perceptions of organizational practices, policies, and procedures that members of those organizations have, and that provide some indication of the institutionalized normative systems that guide individual behavior (Grojean, Resick, Dickson, & Smith, 2004). There are a variety of factors, both internal and external to the organization, that influence the perceptions of individual members as to the norms and expectations of ethical conduct, including exposure to objective structural factors, selection, screening, and monitoring criteria that tend toward the selection and retention of individuals whose personal ethical standards, values, and beliefs are in congruence with those of the larger organization, and socialization and training processes which serve to teach and indoctrinate individuals to the norms of behavior that are expected and accepted (Grojean et al., 2004).

The ethical climate, then, as a perception of how policies, rules, and procedures define and influence proper behavior within the organizational context, serves as the mechanism by which organizational values are translated into actions by individual members. "Ethical climate not only influences which issues organization members consider to be ethically pertinent, but it also determines the moral criteria members use to understand, weigh, and resolve such issues" (Martin & Cullen, 2006, p. 177). The ethical climate provides the guidance to organizational members as to what factors (i.e., internal rules, external laws, individual self-interest, etc.) are more or less important as criteria for ethical decision-making (Appelbaum, Deguire, & Lay, 2005).

Nielsen (2003) offers that the root causes of unethical behavior in organizational contexts lay in a framework of factors at the individual, organizational, and environmental levels. Victor and Cullen (1987) assert that individual characteristics alone are insufficient as an explanation of moral and ethical behavior, and that organizational social and structural factors exert a measurable and identifiable influence on individual moral behavior. "Since deviance is defined in terms of departure from organizational norms, this would seem to provide further support for the possibility that deviant behavior in the workplace may be predictable from the climate of the organization" (Peterson, 2002a, p. 50). Deviance in the workplace setting is generally defined as voluntary behavior that is in conflict with the norms of the organization, and as such threatens the well-being of the organization as a whole or its individual members (Appelbaum et al., 2005).

Organizational Policies and Procedures

Bourne and Snead (1999) build on the construct of ethical climate by focusing on the component of environment within the typology of ethical climates of organizations. Environment, in this context, includes both the community environment external to the organization and the structural dimensions of the intra-organizational environment. With respect to the internal organizational environment, Bourne and Snead note that factors that have been shown to be significantly and consistently positively related to ethical behavior include written codes of conduct, ethics training, organization size, and the individual's position or level within the organizational hierarchy.

Vardi's (2001) study of the relationship between organizational attributes and work-related misbehavior did positively correlate certain portions of Victor and Cullen's ethical climate typology with unethical or deviant workplace behavior. There is support for the contention that ethical climate has some positive effect on the incidence of misconduct by organizational members, and Vardi's results do infer that achieving higher levels of person–organization fit, that is, screening applicants to determine their ethical fit with the climate and structural components of the organization, can potentially serve as a mitigating factor reinforcing positive behaviors and reducing or discouraging negative activities. Mills (2003) also notes the potential effectiveness of recruitment strategies for weeding out those individuals whose prior behavior is deemed ethically unacceptable or an indicator of unacceptable ethical belief systems.

There is likewise empirical support for the negative relationship between an organizational code of ethics, as a component of the overall ethical climate, and the incidence of unethical behavior within the organization (Peterson, 2002a; Trevino, Butterfield, & McCabe, 1998). Peterson's (2002b) specific study demonstrated that regardless of the ethical climate of an organization, as measured by the Ethical Climate Questionnaire originally developed by Victor and Cullen (1987), it may be possible to reduce unethical behavior by implementing a clear and written code of ethics to serve as a guide for employee behavior and decision making. Peterson's study replicated that of Trevino et al. (1998) in demonstrating that ethical climates are more strongly associated with observed unethical behavior in organizations that do not have written codes of ethics, and that ethical climates are measurably different in organizations with written and enforced codes than in organizations without them.

Wotruba, Chonko, and Loe (2001) studied the influence of ethics codes within organizations on both attitudes and behaviors of organizational members, with the assumption that codes of ethics serve several important purposes. Codes serve to institutionalize ethical values in the organization, they represent a public demonstration of a concern for ethics by the organization, they transmit the underlying ethical values of the collective organization to individual members, and they positively impact the ethical decision making and overt behavior of organizational members. "As the content of such codes translates into institutionalized behavior, these codes become a significant factor influencing the organization's ethical climate" (p. 61).

Several key factors concerning the effectiveness of ethics codes in influencing behavior have been demonstrated, including that organizational members must be familiar with and understand the content and intent of a written code of ethics and they must properly perceive the usefulness of the code (Wotruba et al., 2001), the code must become part of the fabric of the organization such that it aids in the socialization of new employees (Adams et al., 2001), and the strictures of the code must be firmly and consistently enforced across all levels of the organization so that the ramifications of disregarding its guidelines are clear and understood (Trevino et al., 1998).

Mills (2003) notes, with respect to ethical codes of conduct in law enforcement agencies, that they likely are not effective as merely stand-alone instruments separate and apart from the fabric of the decision-making process, but rather their measurable and recognizable effect comes about when they are supported by appropriate education, training, and development programs. When viewed as a component part of the overall organizational climate that is created, "there is the opportunity to heighten understanding and awareness of ethical issues, to engage in meaningful debate and hopefully for members of the organization to internalize the values underpinning the code" (p. 333).

Adams et al. (2001) determined through their study that formalized ethics codes within organizations impact employee perceptions and behaviors in several important ways. The very presence of a code signals to employees that ethical behavior is an organizational value by representing a concrete and visible manifestation of that core value, and thus serves as psychological support for behaving in an ethical manner. It can also serve as a form of advanced warning, via the threat of negative sanctions or punishment, that violation of the codified principles of behavior will not be tolerated or accepted by the organization. The code can also serve to influence behavior by fostering dialogue among employees about ethical issues and dilemmas faced, and can provide clear guidance in resolving those issues when they arise. "A code of ethics provides a context for behavior by contributing to an organizational climate in which ethical behavior is expected and encouraged" (p. 208). Ethics codes can be an important component of accountability for personal decisions and actions by providing operational guidance and clear standards of conduct that are expected (O'Malley, 1997).

Ethics Training

Luthar and Karri (2005) examined the linkage between ethics education or formal academic training and ethical behavior in organizations to support earlier evidence indicating that education in ethics and ethical issues can influence the development of moral perspectives among students (Rest, 1988). While the literature on the effectiveness of education to impact adult ethical development and decision making indicates mixed results, some scholars have postulated that education and training can be a powerful force in shaping the assumptions and understandings that exert an influence on how and what individuals view as right and wrong (Luthar & Karri, 2005). If moral development and ethical cognition are viewed as fluid psychological constructs, then the assumption is that "people can continue enhancing and developing their sense of ethics at any age due to life experiences as well as through proper training, education, and guidance" (p. 357). Formalized training in ethics can serve to heighten ethical awareness and awareness of the role ethical dimensions play in everyday conduct by addressing topics such as personal character and organizational values that are the foundation of ethical codes of conduct (Peak et al., 1998).

Within law enforcement agencies, the empirical support for the connection between formalized ethics training in the academy setting and later performance as officers is ambiguous; however, there appears to be potential value in such training if it is rigorous and emphasizes critical thinking and reasoning skills, reasoning ability, and problem-solving techniques (Vicchio, 1997).

O'Malley (1997) points to empirical support for formal education reinforcing already established personal ethical values, and for organizational commitment to learning as a characteristic common to organizations rated as highly ethical. Formal training programs are thus considered part of a strategy of managing for ethics, in that they ensure that organizational members understand the code of ethics and the related behavioral expectations that it engenders, they elevate the perceived importance of ethics and ethical behavior throughout the organization by underscoring management support, and they can provide specific and practical guidance in determining appropriate decision-making criteria.

Organizational Leadership

The issue of guidance by organizational leaders in affecting the ethical behavior of organizational members is one that is composed of a variety of mechanisms (Grojean et al., 2004). Values-based leadership involves not only setting an example through the modeling of actions and behaviors, but also the establishment of clear expectations of ethical conduct through the creation and implementation of policies, practices, and training that "clearly and unequivocally communicate the accepted and expected standards of ethical conduct" (p. 229). Formal socialization processes, ethics training, coaching and support, recognition and reward of behaviors that support organizational values, and insuring the proper fit of individuals to the organization and its environment are all mechanisms that support this objective.

In the context of law enforcement organizations, the manifestation of these concepts can include such practices as proper screening of applicants through background reviews and polygraph examinations, formalized academy and field training programs, mentoring, internal disciplinary programs, continuing-education programs, and monitoring of employee actions and behaviors (Conditt, 2001).

Ethical behavior relies, in some respect, on an individual's awareness of the moral ramifications of their actions and their ability to consider the effects of their actions on others (VanSandt, Shepard, & Zappe, 2006). There is empirical support for the contention that overall ethical climate is a primary predictor of organizational members' degree of moral awareness (p. 425), which in turn can directly impact the rates of misconduct engaged in by those members. Ethical functioning within organizations is a dynamic interaction between individual and group values, behaviors, and organizational structures (Nicholson, 1994).

Connor (2006) stresses that one key component in achieving the desired organizational and individual outcomes with respect to ethical behavior is the issue of alignment and consistency among the diverse elements of the organizational structure.

> An ethical organization is a function of individuals of principle, making effective decisions about applying those principles in real situations . . . and having the will to be consistent in applying those principles, even in the face of opposition and obstacles. (p. 149)

If it is accepted that the ethical climate of an organization is based on the system of values and beliefs that compose the culture of the group, then ethical behavior among the individual group members becomes, in part, a function of their ability to integrate the principles of those shared values and beliefs into their cognitive decision-making processes and ultimately their behaviors.

While law enforcement organizations would be expected, through their rhetoric and mission, to score high in ethical expression, research suggests that law enforcement agencies can and do vary widely in their overall environments of ethical integrity (Klockars et al., 2000; Maguire, 2004). Nicholson (1994) notes the danger that can exist when ethical expression becomes dislocated from the reality of enacted forms of action, particularly when internal arrangements, rules, or practices are not designed to effectively detect and correct lapses and deviations by organizational members. Simply stated, it is not enough to merely espouse ethical behavior in the context of law enforcement operations, but rather organizations and the members within them must be personally and collectively committed to ensuring high ethical standard of professional performance, and an organization's structural components must be in place that support this objective.

Summary

There is no argument about the devastating effects that law enforcement misconduct, abuse, and corruption can have on law enforcement agencies, communities, and society as a whole. Law enforcement officers exercise great power and authority over civil liberties, and this authority must be wielded within an overarching framework of fairness, justice, and impartiality. "If we are going to think of policing as a profession then we must assume the level of responsibility that a professional life entails. The profession should require more from its members than we expect from the general population" (Vicchio, 1997, p. 13).

There is not one magic solution or one single policy or procedure that if adopted would eliminate or even reduce the incidence of law enforcement misconduct, abuse, and corruption. Rather, the issue of law enforcement misconduct and corruption must be addressed through a comprehensive strategy and with coordinated initiatives. Management of and control over the organizational environment in which policing occurs should be part of this strategy.

The approach to reducing corruption and misconduct must include both reactive responses and proactive approaches. Departments must first ensure that they are selecting the best individuals in which to entrust law enforcement responsibilities, must adequately train and prepare these individuals for the difficulties and stresses associated with the policing profession, and must put adequate organizational structures and policies in place to effectively oversee and control individuals and groups within those organizations. Allegations of misconduct must be adequately and comprehensively addressed, and independent outside oversight, such as that afforded by civilian review boards, can be an important component of the overall process. External review or involvement in the process of handling official misconduct affords a level of necessary transparency, and contributes to the public's trust of its important and powerful law enforcement components.

It is important to remember in the context of any examination or discussion of official misconduct, abuse, or corruption that even the most widely publicized and egregious cases of malfeasance represent only a miniscule proportion of the devoted law enforcement professionals engaged in dedicated public service every day. When a law enforcement officer is charged with the very same criminal offenses he is sworn to enforce, when he conspires with other officers to engage in organized and egregious criminal behavior, or when he joins forces with those criminals he is charged with investigating and arresting, it should not be allowed to unduly tarnish the reputations of his fellow officers. Former Philadelphia Police Officers Mark Williams, Robert Snyder, and James Venziale were convicted and given lengthy federal prison terms. These prison sentences represent "punishment" for their specific crimes; however, the broader effects that these crimes have on the police department, on their fellow officers, and on the community as a whole that the department serves, remain long after the sentences have been handed down.

While the effects of corruption or misconduct can have devastating personal and societal effects for all those involved or even tangentially connected, these relatively isolated incidents should not be allowed to detract from the immeasurable positive contributions made by the overwhelming majority of this country's 970,000 sworn law enforcement officers serving in the approximately 14,254 total law enforcement organizations in operation in the United States today.

Discussion Questions

1. How does official misconduct detract from the mission of law enforcement agencies?

2. What are the types of factors that contribute to misconduct by law enforcement officers?

3. What are some difficulties associated with identifying and preventing law enforcement misconduct, abuse, and corruption?

4. Identify organizational policies or procedures that can help reduce the incident of official misconduct by law enforcement officers.

5. Explain how organizational environment or climate can influence the incidence of official misconduct within law enforcement agencies.

References

Adams, J. S., Tashchian, A., & Shore, T. H. (2001, February). Codes of ethics as signals for ethical behavior. *Journal of Business Ethics, 29*(3), 199–211.

Adlam, R. (1998). Developing ethics education for police leaders and managers: Action research and critical reflection for curriculum and personal development. *Educational Action Research, 6*(1), 131–151.

Appelbaum, S. H., Deguire, K. J., & Lay, M. (2005). The relationship of ethical climate to deviant workplace behaviour. *Corporate Governance: The International Journal of Business in Society, 5*(4), 43–55.

Arrigo, B. A., & Claussen, N. (2003). Police corruption and psychological testing: A strategy for preemployment screening. *International Journal of Offender Therapy and Comparative Criminology, 47*(3), 272–290.

Arrigo, B. A., & Shipley, S. M. (2001). The confusion of psychopathy (I): Historical considerations. *International Journal of Offender Therapy and Comparative Criminology, 45*(3), 325–344.

Barker, T. (1996). *Police ethics: Crisis in law enforcement.* Springfield, IL: Charles C. Thomas.

Barker, T. (2002). Ethical police behavior. In K. M. Lersch & M. L. Dantzker (Eds.), *Policing and misconduct* (pp. 1–26). Upper Saddle River, NJ: Prentice Hall.

Benoit, J. P., & Dubra, J. (2004, August). Why do good cops defend bad cops? *International Economic Review, 45*(3), 787–809.

Bolton, K., Jr. (2002). Historical perspectives of police misconduct. In K. M. Lersch & M. L. Dantzker (Eds.), *Policing and misconduct* (pp. 27–53). Upper Saddle River, NJ: Prentice Hall.

Bourne, S., & Snead, J. D. (1999, October). Environmental determinants of organizational ethical climate: A community perspective. *Journal of Business Ethics, 21*(4), 283–290.

Brown, A. M. (2001). Police as symbols of government and justice. In M. P. Palmiotto (Ed.), *Police misconduct: A reader for the 21st century* (pp. 15–31). Upper Saddle River, NJ: Prentice Hall.

Chappell, A. T., & Piquero, A. R. (2004). Applying social learning theory to police misconduct. *Deviant Behavior, 25*(2), 89–108.

Conditt, J. H., Jr. (2001, November). Institutional integrity. *FBI Law Enforcement Bulletin, 70*(11), 18–22.

Connor, K. T. (2006). Assessing organizational ethics: Measuring the gaps. *Industrial and Commercial Training, 38*(3), 148–155.

Crank, J. P., & Caldero, M. A. (2000). *Police ethics: The corruption of the noble cause.* Cincinnati, OH: Anderson.

Ford, R. E. (2003, March). Saying one thing, meaning another: The role of parables in police training. *Police Quarterly, 6*(1), 84–110.

Frank, M. G., McConkey, K. M., Huon, G. F., & Hesketh, B. L. (1995). *Individual perspectives on police ethics: Ethics and policing—study 2.* Payneham, South Australia: National Police Research Unit.

Grant, J. K. (2002, December). Ethics and law enforcement. *FBI Law Enforcement Bulletin, 71*(12), 11–14.

Grojean, M. W., Resick, C. J., Dickson, M. W., & Smith, D. B. (2004). Leaders, values, and organizational climate: Examining leadership strategies for establishing an organizational climate regarding ethics. *Journal of Business Ethics, 55*(3), 223–241.

Haarr, R. N. (1997). "They're making a bad name for the department": Exploring the link between organizational commitment and police occupational deviance in a police patrol bureau. *Policing, 20*(4), 786–812.

Heffernan, W. C. (1982). Two approaches to police ethics. *Criminal Justice Review, 7*(1), 28–35.

Hunter, R. D. (1999, May). Officer opinions on police misconduct. *Journal of Contemporary Criminal Justice, 15*(2), 155–170.

Hyatt, W. D. (2001). Parameters of police misconduct. In M. J. Palmiotto (Ed.), *Police misconduct: A reader for the 21st century* (pp. 75–99). Upper Saddle River, NJ: Prentice Hall.

International Association of Chiefs of Police (2007). *History of the IACP.* Retrieved from http://www.theiacp.org/Foundation/AboutUs/Ourhistory/tabid/528/Default.aspx

Ivkovic, S. K. (2003). To serve and collect: Measuring police corruption. *The Journal of Criminal Law and Criminology, 93*(2–3), 593–649.

Johnson, T. A., & Cox, R. W., III (2004, Winter). Police ethics: Organizational implications. *Public Integrity, 7*(1), 67–79.

Kingshott, B. F., Bailey, K., & Wolfe, S. E. (2004, June). Police culture, ethics and entitlement theory. *Criminal Justice Studies, 17*(2), 187–202.

Kleinig, J. (2002). Rethinking noble cause corruption. *International Journal of Police Science & Management, 4*(4), 287–314.

Klockars, C. B., Ivkovic, S. K., Harver, W. E., & Haberfield, M. R. (2000, May). The measurement of police integrity. *National Institute of Justice: Research in Brief,* 1–11.

Loewenthal, M. A. (1981). Police professionalism: Law and ethics. *Journal of Contemporary Criminal Justice, 2*(1), 10–13.

Luthar, H. K., & Karri, R. (2005). Exposure to ethics education and the perception of linkage between organizational ethical behavior and business outcomes. *Journal of Business Ethics, 61*(4), 353–368.

Lynch, G. W. (1999). *Human dignity and the police: Ethics and integrity in police work.* Springfield, IL: Charles C. Thomas.

Maguire, E. R. (2004, August). Ideas in American policing: Police departments as learning laboratories. *Police Foundation, 6,* 1–16.

Martens, W. H. (2000). Antisocial and psychopathic personality disorder: Causes, course, and remission. *International Journal of Offender Therapy and Comparative Criminology, 44*(4), 406–430.

Martin, K. D., & Cullen, J. B. (2006). Continuities and extensions of ethical climate theory: A meta-analytic review. *Journal of Business Ethics, 69,* 175–194.

Mills, A. (2003, April). Ethical decision making and policing: The challenge for police leadership. *Journal of Financial Crime, 10*(4), 331–335.

Nelligan, P. J., & Taylor, R. W. (1994, March). Ethical issues in community policing. *Journal of Contemporary Criminal Justice, 10*(1), 59–66.

Nicholson, N. (1994, August). Ethics in organizations: A framework for theory and research. *Journal of Business Ethics, 13*(8), 581–596.

Nielsen, R. P. (2003, January). Corruption networks and implications for ethical corruption reform. *Journal of Business Ethics, 42*(2), 125–149.

O'Malley, T. (1997, April). Managing for ethics. *FBI Law Enforcement Bulletin, 66*(4), 20–27.

Palmiotto, M. J. (2001). Can police recruiting control police misconduct? In M. J. Palmiotto (Ed.), *Police misconduct: A reader for the 21st century* (pp. 344–354). Upper Saddle River, NJ: Prentice Hall.

Peak, K. J., Stitt, B. G., & Glensor, R. W. (1998). Ethical consideration in community policing and problem solving. *Police Quarterly, 1*(3), 19–34.

Perez, D. W., & Moore, J. A. (2002). *Police ethics: A matter of character.* Cincinnati, OH: Copperhouse.

Peterson, D. K. (2002a, Fall). Deviant workplace behavior and the organization's ethical climate. *Journal of Business and Psychology, 17*(1), 47–61.

Peterson, D. K. (2002b, December). The relationship between unethical behavior and the dimensions of the ethical climate questionnaire. *Journal of Business Ethics, 41*(4), 313–326.

Pollock, J. M. (1993, Fall). Ethics and the criminal justice curriculum. *Journal of Criminal Justice Education, 4*(2), 377–390.

Pollock, J. M., & Becker, R. (1996, November). Ethics training. *FBI Law Enforcement Bulletin, 65*(11), 20–28.

Punch, M. (2000, September). Police corruption and its prevention. *European Journal on Criminal Policy and Research, 8*(3), 301–324.

Rest, J. R. (1988, Winter). Can ethics be taught in professional schools? The psychological research. *Ethics: Easier Said Than Done, 1,* 22–26.

Roebuck, J. B., & Barker, T. (1974). A typology of police corruption. *Social Problems, 21*(3), 423–437.

Rothwell, G. R., & Baldwin, J. N. (2006, September). Ethical climates and contextual predictors of whistle-blowing. *Review of Public Personnel Administration, 26*(3), 216–244.

Rothwell, G. R., & Baldwin, J. N. (2007, February). Ethical climate theory, whistle-blowing, and the code of silence in police agencies in the State of Georgia. *Journal of Business Ethics, 70*(4), 341–361.

Schafer, J. A. (2002). Community policing and police corruption. In K. M. Lersch & M. L. Dantzker (Eds.), *Policing and misconduct* (pp. 193–218). Upper Saddle River, NJ: Prentice Hall.

Sechrest, D. K., & Burns, P. (1992, September). Police corruption: The Miami case. *Criminal Justice and Behavior, 19*(3), 294–313.

Seron, C., Pereira, J., & Kovath, J. (2004, December). Judging police misconduct: "Street-level" versus professional policing. *Law and Society Review, 38*(4), 665–710.

Sherman, L. W. (1981). *The teaching of ethics in criminology and criminal justice.* Chicago: Joint Commission on Criminology and Criminal Justice Education.

Simpson, A. E. (1977). *The literature of police corruption: Vol. 1. A guide to bibliography and theory.* New York: John Jay Press and McGraw Hill.

Skolnick, J. H. (2002). Corruption and the blue code of silence. *Police Practice and Research, 3*(1), 7–19.

Trevino, L. K., Butterfield, K. D., & McCabe, D. L. (1998, July). The ethical context in organizations: Influences on employee attitudes and behaviors. *Business Ethics Quarterly, 8*(3), 447–476.

VanSandt, C. V., Shepard, J. M., & Zappe, S. M. (2006). An examination of the relationship between ethical work climate and moral awareness. *Journal of Business Ethics, 68,* 409–432.

Vardi, Y. (2001, February). The effects of organizational and ethical climates on misconduct at work. *Journal of Business Ethics, 29*(4), 325–337.

Vicchio, S. (1997, July). Ethics and police integrity. *FBI Law Enforcement Bulletin, 66*(7), 8–13.

Victor, B., & Cullen, J. B. (1987). A theory and measure of ethical climate in organizations. *Research in Corporate Social Performance and Policy, 9,* 51–71.

Victor, B., & Cullen, J. B. (1988, March). The organizational bases of ethical work climates. *Administrative Science Quarterly, 33*(1), 101–125.

Walker, S., & Alpert, G. P. (2002). Early warning systems as risk management for police. In K. M. Lersch & M. L. Dantzker (Eds.), *Policing and misconduct* (pp. 219–230). Upper Saddle River, NJ: Prentice Hall.

Westmarland, L. (2005, June). Police ethics and integrity: Breaking the blue code of silence. *Policing and Society, 15*(2), 145–165.

Wotruba, T. R., Chonko, L. B., & Loe, T. W. (2001, September). The impact of ethics code familiarity on manager behavior. *Journal of Business Ethics, 33*(1), 59–69.

2 Psychological Evaluations of Law Enforcement Applicants

The Search for Ethical Officers

Ana M. Gamez and Gary G. Collins

John was a 26-year-old, single, military veteran who, by the time he applied for his dream job as a police officer, had already experienced three deployments overseas. In each case, he was exposed to combat, resulting in short-lived post-traumatic stress symptoms. Shortly after his most recent deployment, John experienced nightmares for approximately three months, was emotionally distant from family and friends, and was more easily upset. By the time he applied for the sworn position, he had reportedly adjusted well to his return home to the extent that he was no longer experiencing symptoms. John's history did not indicate any issues with alcohol, drugs, blackouts, criminal behavior, credit, ethics, or Article 15 (nonjudicial punishments). John was sent by the agency to be evaluated for the sworn peace officer position.

During the psychological interview, John was charismatic and physically fit, presented well, and reported being mentally prepared for the academy. Data from the psychological testing, however, indicated that John might be too aggressive and too assertive for a sworn position in law enforcement. The results further suggested that John might not be adaptive enough for law enforcement, as well as evidence for low levels of empathy and moderate emotional detachment. Nonetheless, the agency decided to hire John for a lower position, one with limited peace officer powers. John performed well in his new assignment—so well, in fact, that within several months, he was promoted to the peace officer position (without being required to undergo a new psychological examination) and sent to the academy. A few years later, John was terminated after the agency discovered a pattern of unreported excessive force.

This chapter explores the importance of selection and hiring standards for peace officer applicants. It begins with a review of the contributions of pre-employment psychological suitability recommendations. Next, the authors investigate the personality factors, character traits, and personal values believed to contribute to success in policing. This is followed by a discussion of commonly used psychological inventories in pre-employment screenings. The chapter concludes with recommendations to improve selection and hiring practices in an effort to identify the most ethically qualified applicants.

Ethics in Law Enforcement

Ethics is defined as the standards of individual or group conduct that define what is morally right and wrong (Johnson & Cox, 2005). As public perceptioins of law enforcement are linked with the ethical conduct of officers, the selection and hiring standards of peace officers are an integral component in the effective functioning of all police organizations. According to International Association of Chiefs of Police (IACP) (1950), the role of peace officers is to "serve mankind; safeguard lives and property; protect against deception, the weak against oppression or intimidation, and the peaceful against violence or disorder; and to respect the Constitutional rights of all to liberty, equality, and justice" (as cited in Josephson, 2009, p. 9). In law enforcement, the expectation of compliance with the agency's mission and core values is made clear, irrespective of personal values and ethics (Josephson, 2009). Law enforcement officers are expected to follow their department core values with professionalism, even when compliance conflicts with personal values or self-interests.

Because peace officers are held to high standards, their behavior is continuously scrutinized by the media and public, irrespective of whether the conduct occurs on or off duty. When the media features a story highlighting alleged misconduct or corruption by a law enforcement officer, the integrity of the agency is called into questioned, as are the agency's selection and hiring standards. In an effort to establish clear guidelines for ethical conduct, a number of law enforcement associations have developed codes of ethics. For example, the IACP's code of ethics states the following:

> With no compromise for crime and with relentless prosecution of criminals, I will enforce the law courteously and appropriately without fear or favor, malice or ill will. I will never act officiously or permit personal feelings, prejudices, animosities or friendships to influence my decisions. I will never employ unnecessary force or violence. (as cited in Josephson, 2009, p. 29)

In addition to codes of ethics, standards in the selection and hiring of law enforcement officers have gradually become the accepted practice among most agencies throughout the United States (Borum, Super, & Rand, 2003;

Hargrave & Berner, 1984; Hartman, 1987; Hiatt & Hargrave, 1988). While good psychological health and adjustment, increased functionality, and the absence of psychopathology are all qualities that typically increase an applicant's probability of success, an applicant may still be ill-suited for a career in law enforcement for any number of reasons, including poor decision-making skills, prior unethical or criminal conduct, or a predisposition toward violence.

Selection and Hiring Trends

Law enforcement agencies rely on a number of standardized procedures (e.g., background investigation, medical assessment, structured interview, psychological evaluation, drug screening, physical fitness testing, and polygraph examination) to select the most suitable candidates (Cochrane, Tett, & Vandecreek, 2003). Indeed, the use of appropriate criteria is critical to the identification and selection of psychologically, emotionally, and physically healthy officers. Poor selection methods, on the other hand, can yield a range of organizational problems, including poor performance, unsatisfactory quality, high turnover rates, or the presence of other problematic behaviors that hinder the accomplishment of the agency's mission and goals. Unlike other professions, an ineffective police officer can negatively impact the well-being and safety of an entire community (Castora, Brewster, & Stoloff, 2003). Officer misconduct, corruption, and abuse can have even more devastating results—diminishing agency morale, creating costly litigation, and reducing public support for the law enforcement mission (Tully, 1998). Thus, the cornerstone of effective policing is the ethical conduct of officers, at all levels of the organization, in all facets of their job performance (Peak, Stitt, & Glensor, 1998).

In the past, candidates were often selected who were "tough, young, aggressive, politically favored, and/or popular"; unfortunately, many of these same candidates were perceived as "uneducated, brutal, quick to attack, and slow to reason" (Blau, 1994, p. 17). The selection practices of law enforcement agencies have shifted as a result of changing trends in criminal activity, community expectations, financial liability, and court decisions addressing police practices (Blau, 1994). Moreover, there is an increased level of public awareness in the idea that a few "bad apples" may slip through the cracks. These unsuitable candidates are often the same officers who abuse their police powers; violate the public trust; lack integrity, honesty, loyalty, professionalism, respect, and accountability; and violate the law.

Pre-employment screening serves a number of important functions by considering a host of factors, including collateral information, job analysis, research knowledge, and legal standards of employment. Together, these factors allow examiners to determine the suitability of an applicant, thus allowing for the most informed and appropriate recommendation to the hiring agency. Ultimately, it is the agency that makes the decision to hire an applicant, not the evaluating psychologist. Rather, the psychologist's goal is to assist the agency in the selection of applicants who possess the attributes necessary to succeed as peace officers (Lorr & Strack, 1994; Lough & Ryan, 2006; Mills & Bohannon, 1980; Yarmey, 1990). The purpose of a psychological evaluation, then, is to provide an objective, evidenced-based assessment of an applicant's suitability to perform the required duties of a peace officer (Ben-Porath et al., 2011; IACP, 2009; Palmiotto, 2001). However, in addition to identifying desirable characteristics, properly administered evaluations can help to recognize behavioral or psychological characteristics that may contribute to problematic behavior in the workplace (Hargrave & Hiatt, 1989).

Peace officers are tasked with enforcing laws judiciously and ethically, while requiring professionalism and respect for all those with whom the officer comes in contact. Unfortunately, not everyone who is hired will be a successful officer or exhibit ethical behavior throughout the course of their career. One challenge in the selection process is the complex, multidimensional nature of job behavior (Gregory, 2011). In addition to the multitude of variables that contribute to the success of an employee, there are often extraneous variables that are difficult to capture, many of which impact the successful prediction of job performance (Gregory, 2011; Ones, Dilchert, Viswesvaran, & Judge, 2007). This does not, however, negate the fact that there is great benefit in having personnel selection systems within organizational settings.

Because of the high stakes involved, law enforcement organizations expend tremendous resources in recruiting, hiring, and training only the most qualified applicants. The reasons for the increased focus on psychologically healthy applicants include minimizing payouts resulting from lawsuits and operational costs for employees who are off work because of administrative investigations (Baker, 1995); screening out of individuals with known psychopathology (Blau, 1994; California Commission on Peace Officer Standards and Training [CA POST], 2008; "California Law," 2008; Hargrave & Berner, 1984), minimizing corruption (Arrigo & Claussen, 2003), eliminating the use of unjustified force (Castora et al., 2003), and enhancing the overall quality of officers (Rubin & Cruse, 1973), especially in light of the fact that law enforcement agencies can be held liable for the actions of their employees (e.g., *Bonsignore v. City of New York*, 1981; Flanagan, 1986; Ostrov, 1986).

While employers are responsible for screening potential employees entering health and safety-type professions (Borum et al., 2003; *McCabe v. Hoberman*, 1969), the manner in which agencies accomplish this is influenced by, among other concerns, a host of federal employment laws that dictate equity in hiring practices. For example, in the selection of law enforcement applicants, the methods of measurement that employers use to qualify or disqualify applicants must be empirically validated to avoid discrimination (Pallone, 1992). Furthermore, hiring practice must comply with state and federal laws that prohibit discrimination, as well as determine the manner in which pre-employment evaluations are conducted.

Americans With Disabilities Act (ADA) 1990

State and federal standards have been developed to ensure that employers provide job applicants with equal opportunity to employment. More specifically, such statutes prohibit discrimination on the basis of race, color, sex, national origin, religion, or age (e.g., Americans With Disabilities Act [ADA]) (U.S. Department of Justice, 1990). State and federal regulations also help dictate the manner in which pre-employment evaluations are performed. The ADA, for example, prohibits employers from discriminating on the basis of disability, as defined by a physical or mental condition the employer should reasonably accommodate for an otherwise qualified applicant, unless doing so imposes undue hardship on the operation of the employer's business (U.S. Equal Employment Opportunity Commission, 2010). The ADA (1990) has further impacted the way that pre-employment evaluations are conducted by limiting the types of questions that employers can ask applicants prior to a contingent offer of employment.

In the past, pre-employment evaluations were conducted early in the hiring process, often prior to the completion of a background check or polygraph examination. In contrast, pre-employment evaluations are now completed at the end of the hiring process, only after an initial offer of employment has been extended to an otherwise qualified applicant (U.S. Equal Employment Opportunity Commission, 2010). In other words, a contingent officer of employment is extended to an otherwise qualified applicant prior to a medical or psychological examination being conducted (IACP, 2009; Lowmaster & Morey, 2012). The term *qualified* means that the applicant has likely passed the criminal background check, polygraph examination, and physical requirements of the job. This change in procedure is often beneficial to the hiring agency because applicants who have passed the initial employment criteria prior to a psychological screening are often better adjusted and, therefore, more likely to be ultimately hired as law enforcement officers (Lowmaster & Morey, 2012).

The Role of Personality and Psychological Screenings in the Workplace

Within the past several decades, there has been increased interest in understanding the personality characteristics of individuals drawn to law enforcement (Aamodt, Brewster, & Raynes, 1998; Aamodt & Kimbrough, 1985; Biggam & Power, 1996; Hennessy, 1999; Hogan, 1971; Hogan & Kurtines, 1975; Johnson & Hogan, 1981; Lester, Babcock, Cassisi, Genz, & Butler, 1980; Tong et al., 2004). An individual's personality is composed of several factors, including character traits, states, values, and attitudes, as well as cognitive and behavioral styles (Cohen & Swerdlik, 1999). The assessment of personality is important in law enforcement because, simply put, not all applicants are suitable for the profession.

Personality characteristics are typically evaluated through the use of assessment techniques, often in the form of self-report questionnaires (Cohen & Swerdlik, 1999; Graham, 1993).

As previously discussed, an important aspect of pre-employment screenings is the identification of psychopathology or other mental health symptoms that are likely to impact an officer's job performance negatively, as well as the recognition of factors that may cause a candidate to demonstrate inappropriate performance during stressful situations (e.g., officer-involved shooting, vehicular pursuit, or altercation) (Borum et al., 2003). The California Penal Code, for example, states that "peace officers must be physically, mentally, and morally fit" (Section 13510 [a]), and the California Government Code mandates that peace officers be "free from any physical, emotional, or mental condition that might adversely affect the exercise of their powers as a peace officer" (Section 1031 [f], 2008). In addition to identifying psychopathology or other undesirable traits, pre-employment evaluations attempt to identify individuals who possess the kinds of desirable characteristics that increase a potential candidate's chances of performing the job well (Bartol & Bartol, 2012; Ben-Porath et al., 2011).

According to Barrick and Mount (2005), "[E]ven modest effects from personality meaningfully contribute to a selection decision, even after one accounts for other important differences" (p. 362). In fact, with particular job classifications, it may be important that certain personality characteristics be matched with the skills and knowledge base required for the job. Other researchers who have examined the role of personality within organizational settings have concluded that self-report personality measures not only provide useful information about job success but also provide information about the applicants' attitudes, such as job satisfaction and organizational behaviors (Ones, Viswesvaran, & Dilchert, 2005).

Studies suggest that the type of candidate most likely to be successful as an officer is someone who demonstrates good ethical reasoning, moral intelligence, psychological health, emotional stability, cognitive, flexible, and cultural sensitivity (Palmiotto, 2001). Certainly, identifying the specific qualities that make an individual a good officer is complex given that human behavior is multifactorial and not the result of any single variable. Nonetheless, a number of desirable traits have been identified in the literature, including those of good judgment, decision-making skills, ability to function under stress, effective communication, and leadership capabilities (Yarmey, 1990). The California Commission on Peace Officer Standards and Training (CA POST, 2009) approved the following psychological characteristics to assist evaluators in identifying desirable characteristics of applicants believed to contribute to success in policing:

- Social competence
- Teamwork
- Adaptability and flexibility

- Consciousness and dependability
- Impulse control and attention to safety
- Integrity and ethics
- Emotion regulation and stress tolerance
- Decision making and judgment
- Assertiveness and persuasiveness
- Avoidance of substance abuse and risk-taking behaviors.

Use of Personality Instruments in Suitability Evaluations

As early as 1950, psychological testing for the purposes of police selection and the prediction of employment success began to emerge (Humm & Humm, 1950; Kenney & Stewart, 1990). In 1954, the Los Angeles Police Department (LAPD) implemented psychological screening procedures, as well as a testing battery, for the evaluation of peace officer applicants (Blau, 1994). The use of personality measures for psychological testing has grown considerably since their introduction. As a tool, personality measures, when used in conjunction with corroborating information, provides important information about personality traits, characteristics, psychopathology, personality disorders, and test-taking attitudes (Inwald, 1987). While these measures provide information about a candidate's psychological profile, psychological testing must be conducted by a practitioner licensed and trained in the psychometric properties of the tests being administered, including the purpose of the exams, validity and reliability of the instruments, strengths and limitations of each measure, and test norms (Hargrave & Berner, 1984; Ben-Porath et al., 2011).

A number of psychological measures have been used historically to screen law enforcement applicants. Some of these instruments assess for normal personality traits found in the general population, while others examine the presence of psychopathological markers. The IACP Police Psychological Services Section (PPSS) recommends that evaluators use a written test battery that includes a minimum of two measures of personality that have been validated with police populations (Ben-Porath et al., 2011). Also, with pre-employment screenings, objective psychological tests are preferred over the use of projective measures (Hargrave & Berner, 1984). This is because objective measures have been found to provide better forms of reliability and information about reporting styles, such as over or underreporting of symptomatology and defensive style of responding (Hargrave & Berner, 1984; Hartman, 1987).

Discussed below are some of the most commonly used personality measures in selection screenings (Bartol & Bartol, 2012; Hargrave & Berner, 1984; Hartman, 1987). Each of the instruments listed are objective, valid, and reliable personality measures that provide information about reporting or defensiveness styles, rule-breaking, or risk-taking behaviors (Butcher,

Dahlstrom, Graham, Tellegen, & Kaemmer, 1989; Green, 2000; Hathaway & McKinley, 1940). These include

- Minnesota Multiphasic Personality Inventory-Revised (MMPI-2)
- Personality Assessment Inventory (PAI)
- California Psychological Inventory (CPI)
- NEO Personality Inventory-Revised (NEO-PI-R)
- Sixteen Personality Factor Questionnaire—Fifth Edition (16PF)
- Inwald Personality Inventory (IPI)

Minnesota Multiphasic Personality Inventory-Revised (MMPI-2)

According to Hathaway and McKinley (1940), the MMPI-2 is a 567-item self-report, objective personality measure that was designed specifically to assess personality and psychopathology characteristics (Butcher et al., 1989; Green, 2000; Groth-Marnat, 2003; Hathaway & McKinley, 1940; Nichols, 2001). The literature on the use of the MMPI-2 in pre-employment screenings suggests that it continues to be one of the most frequently used personality measures in pre-employment screenings (Bartol & Bartol, 2012; Borum & Stock, 1993; Dantzker & Freeberg, 2003; Weiss, Davis, Rostow, & Kinsman, 2003; Weiss et al., 1999; Weiss, Serafino, & Serafino, 2000). The MMPI-2's validity scales have been found useful in analyzing response patterns, including minor defensiveness to overt deception (Borum & Stock, 1993). The MMPI-2's validity scale L (Lie) has been found to predict job performance (Weiss et al., 2000), as well as problematic behaviors in officers and termination from the law enforcement (Weiss et al., 2003).

Empirical literature examining the MMPI-2 has consistently found that candidates tend to present in a positive light, to show fewer depressive symptoms and less anxiety, and to be more assertive and energetic in comparison to the normative sample (Carpenter & Raza, 1987; Kornfeld, 1995) even when gender, race, tenure, or department are considered (Detrick, Chibnall, & Rosso, 2001). Researchers have found that it is not atypical for even the most psychological healthy applicants to attempt to minimize weaknesses in an effort to be hired by an employer (Kornfeld, 1995).

Several criticisms have emerged with respect to the use of the MMPI-2 in pre-employment screenings, including a low correlation with police performance and the fact that it was not designed to evaluate job performance or suitability for hire, it underestimates minority groups and females, it elicits sexual orientation and religious attitudes, and it fails to measure the construct of conscientiousness, found to be a predictor of job performance (Claussen-Rogers & Arrigo, 2005). However, there may be continued value in using the MMPI-2 in pre-employment evaluations in a manner that capitalizes on the instruments' intended purpose. According to Bartol and Bartol (2012), given that the MMPI-2 was designed to assess personality and psychopathology characteristics, it may be more effective in selecting out undesirable applicants than selecting in desirable characteristics. Another benefit of the MMPI-2 is the extensive research and test norms that have been developed with law enforcement populations (Bartol, 1991).

Personality Assessment Inventory (PAI)

The PAI is another instrument that has been used in pre-employment selection screenings of law enforcement personnel. The PAI is a self-report objective personality measure that was developed in 1991 (Morey, 2007) The PAI consists of 344 items, measured on a four-point scale designed to screen for symptoms of psychopathology in adults. Morey (2007) states that the PAI is similar to the MMPI in that it, too, assesses psychopathology and has sound reliability. According to this author, the PAI may be an alternative to the MMPI. Several studies have examined the usefulness of the PAI with law enforcement populations. For example, Lowmaster and Morey (2012) examined the usefulness of the PAI to predict job performance and problematic behaviors in a group of police applicants. These authors found the PAI to be modestly but statistically related to job performance, integrity problems, and the tendency of employees to abuse disability statuses. These authors also found the PAI to be similar to the MMPI in the positive distortion or defensiveness in reporting and further note that prediction of job performance is enhanced when applicants are forthcoming with their responses. While defensiveness in reporting may limit the PAI's ability to predict job performance, it nonetheless highlights important findings among law enforcement personnel.

Lowmaster and Morey (2012) also found that applicants with difficulty forming attachments in their personal lives would likely exhibit difficulty establishing attachments with peers or supervisors. These authors discovered that individuals with average levels of reported psychological distress were less likely to demonstrate integrity-related concerns at work in comparison to those who reported a complete lack of distress. Lowmaster and Morey further learned that disability problems after hire were related to somatic concerns, perceived current stress, and distress from psychological trauma during the pre-employment screening. According to these authors, this type of profile is suggestive of an employee who may be susceptible to stress responses in the workplace.

California Personality Inventory (CPI)

A third personality measure that has been found useful with law enforcement populations is the California Personality Inventory (CPI) (Gough, 1957). The CPI, which assesses normal personality characteristics, was originally published in 1956 and revised in 1987 (Hargrave & Hiatt, 1989; Meyer & Davis, 1992). It contains 462 true-false self-report items and has 20 scales that are divided into four classes of scales, referred to as "folk concepts" (Hargrave & Hiatt, 1989; Meyer & Davis, 1992). Some of the characteristics assessed by the CPI include interpersonal styles, sense of responsibility, values, maturity, achievement, and personal manners of relating to others in various settings (Meyer & Davis, 1992). The CPI has also been found useful in identifying characteristics that may contribute to job problems.

Varela, Boccaccini, Scogin, Stump, and Caputo (2004) conducted a meta-analysis examining the validity of personality measures as predictors of police officer job performance. These authors found the CPI predicted job performance followed by the MMPI and Inwald Personality Inventory. In another study, Hargrave and Hiatt (1989) found that law enforcement graduates who were rated as unsuited by their instructors had lower CPI profiles than those rated psychologically suitable for police work. The suitable group had elevated CPI scores on self-confidence, poise, maturity, self-control, personal values, and achievement potential. Overall, more elevated CPI scores have been found to be associated with fewer job related problems (Hargrave & Hiatt, 1989).

NEO Personality Inventory-Revised (NEO-PI-R)

The NEO Personality Inventory-Revised (NEO-PI-R) has also been used within organizational settings (Costa & McCrae, 1992). The NEO-PI-R is a 240-question self-report measure that assesses normal personality using a five-point scale. The instrument contains five personality factors, each of which contains six facet scales (Costa & McCrae, 1992; Gregory, 2011). Researchers have found that the "Big Five" traits of conscientiousness and emotional stability are good predictors of job performance (Barrick & Mount, 2005). In another study, Ones and colleagues (2007) summarized meta-analytic research on the relationship between the "Big Five" personality dimensions and behaviors in organizational settings. In their review, the personality traits of emotional stability, agreeableness, and conscientiousness were most predictive of job performance in law enforcement organizations. Claussen-Rogers and Arrigo (2005) suggest that using the NEO-PI-R to assess conscientiousness and the Inwald Personality Index to assess antisocial personality traits would likely enhance the identification of suitable law enforcement applicants.

Sixteen Personality Factor Questionnaire—Fifth Edition (16PF)

The 16PF is yet another instrument used with law enforcement populations. The 16PF is a self-report personality measure originally developed by Raymond Cattell that consists of 185 items (Russell & Karol, 1994). The 16PF has 16 primary scales and five global factors. Drew, Carless, and Thompson (2008) used the 16PF to predict turnover of police officers and found that officers were more likely to quit their jobs if they were emotionally affected or easily upset, tender minded, or venturesome. These authors discussed their findings in terms of the public expectation of law enforcement, namely, that officers are expected to be emotionally stable, tough-minded, focused on the job, and nonimpulsive. Individuals with those characteristics were less likely to quit their employment.

Inwald Personality Inventory (IPI)

The Inwald Personality Inventory (IPI) is a 310-item true-false self-report measure that was originally developed in 1979 to assess behavioral and personality characteristics in law enforcement applicants (Inwald, 1982, 2008; Inwald, Knatz, & Shusman, 1983). Some of the constructs assessed include guardedness, substance use, rule breaking, nonconformity, and risk taking (Inwald, 2008). A revised version of the IPI was developed to address future problematic behaviors (e.g., violence), impulsivity, and poor job performance. Researchers have examined the usefulness of the IPI in predicting job performance among law enforcement officers (Shusman, 1987). In a comparative study between the IPI and the MMPI, the IPI was found to be more robust in the assessment of behavioral patterns (e.g., substance use, legal violations, and prior job performance) that affect future job performance than the MMPI.

The instruments briefly described above are some of the more common personality tests used by pre-employment psychologists. Over the past decade, there has been continued interest in improving the screening methods of applicants entering law enforcement to select individuals who will perform the job well and who will not engage in problematic behaviors in the workplace (Schmidt & Hunter, 1998). The Matrix-Predictive Uniform Law Enforcement Selection Inventory (Davis & Rostow, 2008) is an example of a recently developed instrument that was created to assess suitability among law enforcement applicants. According to the test developers, this instrument measures attitudes and behaviors that are relevant to law enforcement populations (Williams, Davis, & Rostow, 2011). Psychological assessments, however, are only part of the picture. To make an objective, informed recommendation, a pre-employment interview is often conducted to further assess the applicant's suitability. The interview provides the evaluator with an opportunity to obtain information about the applicant's use of judgment in past situations, ability to modulate behavior, tendency to engage in impulsive behaviors or high-risk behaviors, and issues with honesty or trustworthiness among other areas of concern.

Pre-Employment Interviews

Pre-employment psychological screenings for peace officer positions require an analysis of the applicant's characteristics, behavioral history, job analysis, and best practices for the profession (Borum et al., 2003; Crosby, 1979; Hargrave & Berner, 1984; Hartman, 1987; Hiatt & Hargrave,

1988; McGinnis, 1987). Psychological testing provides information about personality traits and characteristics found in normal and clinical populations, but they are only one piece of an entire process. Pre-employment interviews are another piece of the puzzle that provide important information. Interviews offer evaluators the opportunity to ask follow-up questions that address specific concerns from the testing, such as behavioral history (e.g., criminal misconduct), judgment and decision making in various situations, substance abuse or dependence, financial or relational problems, driving habits or rule-breaking practices, and employment problems, including motivation, job performance, attendance, termination, and coworker conflict (Borum et al., 2003). Psychological interviews are an important facet of the pre-employment psychological process when a recommendation not to hire an applicant will be made based on the applicant's mental or emotional state or when test data has yielded inconclusive, invalid, or marginally valid information (Hargrave & Berner, 1984). Pre-employment interviews are also important when the applicant will be recommended for hire.

Researchers have identified levels of employee suitability, including suitable, marginally suitable, and unsuitable (Borum et al., 2003). According to these authors, a finding of suitability is indicative of no identifiable psychopathology and no behavioral problems or patterns, whereas a determination of marginal suitability is indicative of possible symptoms of psychopathology or some behavioral tendencies that evidence the presence (or severity) of a problem that is insufficient to disqualify an applicant. An unsuitability recommendation would likely be made when the applicant exhibits symptoms of psychopathology or behavior problems significant enough to impact job performance (Borum et al., 2003; CA POST, 2008). These may include impaired judgment and decision making, poor problem-solving abilities, and difficulties with communication, as well as a lack of any of the following: integrity, self-control, dependability, assertiveness, flexibility, responsibility, or courage (Borum et al., 2003; California POST, 2008).

Nonetheless, there are limitations that exist with regard to pre-employment screenings, including the fact that pre-employments screenings are time sensitive and provide a limited snapshot of the applicant's suitability at the time of the evaluation. Also, they may be better predictors of officers' short-term job behaviors than of long-term performance (Scogin, Schumacher, Gardner, & Chaplin, 1995). Over time, the predictors of effective functioning may be impacted by any number of things, such as exposure to trauma or vicarious trauma, critical incidents, officer-involved shootings, organizational stressors, conflicting supervisory expectations, inconsistencies in disciplinary actions, pressure from peers, and culture of the law enforcement agency. An officer's behavior may be further impacted by an imbalance between personal and professional lives, a shift in personal priorities, peer pressure, stress, or other factors (Ellison, 2004).

Focusing on Ethical Standards

In their discussion on ethical dilemmas in policing, Peak and colleagues (1998) suggest that agencies that want to foster high moral standards must recruit individuals who possess a good moral compass. Although not everyone who applies for a peace officer position will possess strong morals, they do need to care enough to do what is right. Evidence suggests that ethics and morals are learned and reinforced throughout the course of a lifetime, with early formative years being particularly pivotal in the shaping of behavior. And while a person's moral character and ethics are malleable throughout the course of a lifetime, change is a conscious choice (Peak et al., 1998). The responsibility to uphold and enforce integrity and sound ethical practices belongs to both the officer and the agency. This implies that, once hired, officers have the personal duty and responsibility to uphold ethical principles and the core values of the hiring agency, but the agency has the responsibility to make sure this is occurring.

According to Peak and colleagues (1998), improper work behavior is learned on the job and influenced by peers and job pressures. Not everyone who is exposed to transgressions will exhibit behavioral drifts, but when ethical violations occur, the organization has the ultimate responsibility to take corrective action (Martin, 2011). What is not beneficial, however, is when agencies conform to an employee's behavioral drift—that is, accept or adapt to transgressions in moral conduct. Thus, at the pre-employment psychological phase of the hiring process, it is advised that evaluators conduct a thorough psychological screening that adheres to the best practices of the specialty, while simultaneously meeting the needs of the organization.

In terms of maximizing the probability of selecting and hiring suitable applicants, good communication between the agency and the evaluating psychologist is essential. Communication between the agency and evaluator is important for developing standards and procedures relevant to issues of confidentiality pertinent to the evaluation itself (Ben-Porath et al., 2011). In addition, ongoing discussions between the agency and the evaluating psychologist about the agency's goals, selection and hiring expectations, most prevalent ethical problems faced by the agency, and other areas of concern may add to the quality of the psychological screening and ultimately impacting who is hired. It might even be helpful to provide training about the psychological screening process to background investigators.

Additionally, both the agency and the evaluator should remain connected to their respective state peace officer standards and training organizations, while staying abreast of current research and competency standards. Furthermore, once an employee is hired, the agency should develop ways to help shape the officer's professional identity through mentorship and training that is embedded within the job and not peripheral to their duties.

Formal training should focus on ethical dilemmas, while emphasizing organizational values and increasing ethical awareness (Peak et al., 1998). An example of an active way of learning is through the use of scenarios that address ethical dilemmas. In fact, the use of scenarios may also be helpful at different junctures of the pre-employment process to get the applicant to articulate the processes they use to solve ethical problems, make judgments, and formulate decisions.

Summary

Several key points have emerged in this chapter. First, ethics are an important component in the functioning of law enforcement given that officers are hired to serve and protect the community. Selection and hiring procedures have become standard practice among organizations throughout the United States (Ben-Porath et al., 2011; Hargrave & Berner, 1984; Borum et al., 2003). Law enforcement agencies have a vested interest in hiring officers who will have a positive impact on the organization, while increasing public trust. Several agencies have developed standards that guide and, in some cases, even regulate the selection and hiring of candidates (e.g., CA POST, IACP). These guidelines and regulations ensure that no discrimination occurs in the selection process but also that the most suitable applicants are hired. Psychological pre-employment screenings are an important aspect of the total selection process. As such, a number of psychological measures have been developed for use in pre-employment psychological screenings. These instruments are tools that can be used to assess suitability for hire as a peace officer (Hargrave & Berner, 1984; Inwald, 2008; Lowmaster & Morey, 2012; Varela et al., 2004; Weiss et al., 2000; Weiss et al., 2003).

In the case presented in the beginning of the chapter, the applicant appeared to be a good candidate based on his behavioral history. The "red flag" of temperament identified during testing and, subsequently, addressed during the interview yielded a recommendation of unsuitability for hire. Ultimately, the final decision to hire an applicant is made by the interested agency. In this case, the applicant had a strong positive profile that made him a competitive candidate for peace officer. The agency decided to take a chance, which sometimes occurs. The applicant was hired into a different position with limited peace officer powers for a brief time. The applicant was subsequently sent to the academy without a new psychological evaluation. In this case, requiring the applicant to participate in a new evaluation would have provided insight into how well the applicant had adjusted to the organization, how well he had adapted to changes in life circumstances, and how well he was coping with his new-found responsibilities—possibly saving the agency considerable time, money, and embarrassment.

Discussion Questions

1. Why is psychological evaluation important in determining a police applicant's suitability for hire?

2. If someone has worked successfully for a police agency in a non-sworn (not a police officer) capacity and the person applies for a sworn position, do you believe a psychological evaluation is necessary?

3. When did the psychological evaluation of police officer applicants first begin?

4. How do personality instruments aid in the selection of police officers?

5. At what point during the hiring process should a psychological assessment be conducted?

6. Why is pre-employment psychological interview important?

References

Aamodt, M. G., Brewster, J. A., & Raynes, B. L. (1998, September). *Is the "police personality" predisposed to domestic violence?* Paper presented at the FBI Conference on Domestic Violence by Police Officers, Quantico, VA.

Aamodt, M. G., & Kimbrough, W. W. (1985). Personality differences between police and fire applicants. *The Journal of Police and Criminal Psychology, 1,* 10–13.

Arrigo, B. A., & Claussen, N. (2003). Police corruption and psychological testing: A strategy for pre-employment screenings. *Journal of Offender Therapy and Comparative Criminology, 47*(3), 272–290.

Baker, S. A. (1995). *Effects of law enforcement accreditation: Officer selection, promotion, and education.* London: Praeger.

Barrick, M., & Mount, M. K. (2005). Yes, personality matters: Moving on to more important matters. *Human Performance, 18* (4), 359–372.

Bartol, C. R. (1991). Predictive validation of the MMPI for small-town police officers who fail. *Professional Psychology: Research & Practice, 22*(2), 127–132.

Bartol, C. R., & Bartol, A. M. (2012). *Introduction to forensic psychology: Research and application* (3rd ed.). Thousand Oaks, CA: Sage.

Ben-Porath, Y. S., Fico, J. M., Hibler, N. S., Inwald, N. S., Kruml, J., & Roberts, M. R. (2011, August). Assessing the psychological suitability of candidates for law enforcement positions. *The Police Chief,* 64–70.

Biggam, F. H., & Power, K. G. (1996). The Personality of the Scottish police officer: The issue of positive and negative affectivity. *Personality and Individual Differences, 20*(6), 661–667.

Blau, T. H. (1994). *Psychological services for law enforcement.* New York: Wiley.

Bonsignore v. City of New York. 521 F. Supp. 394 (1981).

Borum, R., & Stock, H. V. (1993). Detection of deception in law enforcement applicants: A preliminary investigation. *Law and Human Behavior, 17*(2), 157–166.

Borum, S., Super, J., & Rand, M. (2003). Forensic assessment for high-risk occupations. In A. Goldstein & I. Weiner (Eds.), *Handbook of psychology* (Vol. 11, pp. 133–147). New York: Wiley.

Butcher, J. N., Dahlstrom, W. G., Graham, J. R., Tellegen, A., & Kaemmer, B. (1989). *MMPI-2: Manual for administration and scoring.* Minneapolis: University of Minnesota Press.

California Commission on Peace Officer Standards and Training (CA POST) (2008). *Overview of peace officer selection standards.* Retrieved from http://www.post.ca.gov/overview-selection-standards.aspx

California law. (2008). California Government Code: Division 4, chapter 1, article 2, section 1031 f. Retrieved from http://www.leginfo.ca.gov/cgi-bin/displaycode?section=gov&group=01001-02000&file=1020-1042_

Carpenter, B. N., & Raza, S. M. (1987). Personality characteristics of police applicants: Comparisons across subgroups and with other populations. *Journal of Police Science and Administration, 15*(1), 10–17.

Castora, K., Brewster, J., & Stoloff, M. (2003). Predicting aggression in police officers using the MMPI-2. *Journal of Police and Criminal Psychology, 18*(1), 1–8.

Claussen-Rogers, N. L., & Arrigo, B. A. (2005). *Police corruption and psychological testing. A strategy for pre-employment screening.* Durham, NC: Carolina Academic Press.

Cochrane, R. E., Tett, R. P., & Vandecreek, L. (2003). Psychological testing and the selection of police officers: A national survey. *Criminal Justice and Behavior, 30*(5), 511–537.

Cohen, R. J., & Swerdlik, M. E. (1999). *Psychological testing and assessment: An introduction to tests and measurement* (4th ed.). Mountain View, CA: Mayfield.

Costa, P. T., & McCrae, R. R. (1992). *NEO-PI-R: The Revised NEO Personality Inventory.* Odessa, FL: Psychological Assessment Resources.

Crosby, A. (1979). The psychological evaluation in police selection. *Journal of Political Science and Administration, 7,* 215–229.

Dantzker, M. L., & Freeberg, D. (2003). An exploratory examination of pre-employment psychological testing of police officer candidates with a Hispanic surname. *Journal of Police and Criminal Psychology, 18*(1), 38–44.

Davis, R. D., & Rostow, C. D. (2008). *Matrix-Predictive Uniform Law Enforcement Selection Evaluation (M-Pulse) Inventory: Technical manual.* Toronto, Canada: Multi-health Systems, Inc. Retrieved from http://media.post.ca.gov/PersonalityTestInformation/Questionnaire/Multi-Health_Systems_Inc/MPULSE_Inventory/

Detrick, P., Chibnall, J. T., & Rosso, M. (2001). Minnesota Multiphasic Personality Inventory-2 in police officer selection: Normative data and relation to the Inwald Personality Inventory. *Professional Psychology: Research and Practice, 32*(5), 484–490.

Drew, J., Carless, S. A., & Thompson, B. M. (2008). Predicting turnover of police officers using the sixteen personality factor questionnaire. *Journal of Criminal Justice, 36,* 326–331.

Ellison, K.W. (2004). *Stress and the police* (2nd ed.). Springfield, IL: Charles C. Thomas.

Flanagan, C. L. (1986). Legal issues between psychology and law enforcement. *Behavioral Sciences & the Law, 4*(4), 371–384.

Gough, H. G. (1957). *Manual for the California Psychological Inventory.* Palo Alto, CA: Consulting Psychological Press.

Graham, J. R. (1993). *MMPI-2: Assessing personality and psychopathology.* New York: Oxford University Press.

Green, R. L. (2000). *The MMPI-2: An interpretive manual* (2nd ed.). Boston: Allyn & Bacon.

Gregory, R. J. (2011). *Psychological testing: History, principles, and applications* (6th ed.). Boston: Allyn & Bacon.

Groth-Marnat, G. (2003). *Handbook of psychological assessment* (4th ed.). Hoboken, NJ: Wiley.

Hargrave, G. E., & Berner, J. G. (1984). *POST psychological screening manual.* Sacramento: State of California, Department of Justice.

Hargrave, G. E., & Hiatt, D. (1989). Use of the California Psychological Inventory in law enforcement officer selection. *Journal of Personality Assessment, 53*(2), 267–277.

Hartman, B. J. (1987). Psychological screening of law enforcement candidates. *American Journal of Forensic Psychology, 5*(1), 5–10.

Hathaway, S., & McKinley, J. C. (1940). *The MMPI manual.* New York: Psychological Corporation.

Hennessy, S. M. (1999). *Thinking cop feeling cop: A study in police personalities.* Gainesville, FL: Center for Applications of Psychological Type, Inc.

Hiatt, D., & Hargrave, G. E. (1988). Predicting performance problems with psychological screening. *Journal of Police Science and Administration, 16*(2), 122–135.

Hogan, R. (1971). Personality characteristics of highly rated policemen. *Personnel Psychology, 24,* 679–686.

Hogan, R., & Kurtines, W. (1975). Personological correlates of police effectiveness. *The Journal of Psychology, 91,* 289–295.

Humm, D., & Humm, K. (1950). Humm-Wadsworth temperament scale appraisals compared with criteria of job success in the Los Angeles Police Department. *Journal of Police Psychology, 30,* 63–75.

International Association of Chiefs of Police (IACP) (2009). Pre-employment psychological evaluation guidelines: Ratified by the IACP police psychological services section. Denver, CO: Author.

Inwald, R. E. (1982). *Inwald Personality Inventory (IPI) technical manual.* New York: Hilson Research.

Inwald, R. E. (1987). Use of psychologists for selecting and training police. In H. W. More & P. C. Unsinger (Eds.), *Police managerial use of psychology and psychologists* (pp.107–139). Springfield, IL: Charles C. Thomas.

Inwald, R. E. (2008). The Inwald Personality Inventory (IPI) and Hilson Research Inventories: Development and rationale. *Aggression & Violent Behavior, 13*(4), 298–327.

Inwald, R. E., Knatz, H., & Shusman, E (1983). *Inwald Personality Inventory manual.* New York: Hilson Research.

Johnson, T. A., & Cox, R. W. (2004–2005). Police ethics: Organizational implications. *Public Integrity, 7*(1), 67–79.

Johnson, J. A., & Hogan, R. (1981). Vocational interests, personality and effective police performance. *Personnel Psychology, 34,* 49–53.

Josephson, M. (2009). *Becoming an exemplary peace officer: The guide to ethical decision making.* Los Angeles: Josephson Institute.

Kenney, D. J., & Stewart, W. (1990). Intelligence and the selection of police recruits. *American Journal of Police, 9*(4), 39–64.

Kornfeld, A. D. (1995). Police officer candidate MMPI-2 performance: Gender, ethnic, and normative factors. *Journal of Clinical Psychology, 51*(4), 536–540.

Lester, D., Babcock, S. D., Cassisi, J. P., Genz, J. L., & Butler, A. J. P. (1980). The personalities of English and American police. *The Journal of Social Psychology, 111,* 153–154.

Lorr, M., Strack, S. (1994). Personality profiles of police candidates. *Journal of Clinical Psychology, 50*(2), 200–207.

Lough, J., & Ryan, M. (2006). Psychological profiling of Australian police officers: A longitudinal examination of post-selection performance. *International Journal of Police Science & Management, 8*(2), 143–152.

Lowmaster, S. E., & Morey, L. C. (2012). Predicting law enforcement officer job performance with the personality assessment inventory. *Journal of Personality Assessment, 94*(3), 254–261.

Martin, R. (2011). Police corruption: An analytical look into police ethics. *FBI Law Enforcement Bulletin, 80*(5), 11–17.

McCabe v. Hoberman. 33 AD 2d 547-NY: Appellate Div. (1969).

McGinnis, J. H. (1987). Police careers: Assignments, assessment, and development. In H. W. More & P. C. Unsinger (Eds.), *Police managerial use of psychology and psychologists* (pp. 141–170). Springfield, IL: Charles C. Thomas.

Meyer, P., & Davis, S. (1992). *The CPI applications guide: An essential for individual, group, and organizational development.* Palo Alto, CA: Consulting Psychologists Press.

Mills, C. J., & Bohannon, W. E. (1980). Personality characteristics of effective police officers. *Journal of Applied Psychology, 65*(6), 680–684.

Morey, L. C. (2007). *Personality Assessment Inventory (Professional Manual).* Lutz, FL: Psychological Assessment Resources.

Nichols, D. S. (2001). *Essentials of MMPI-2 assessment.* New York: Wiley.

Ones, D. S., Dilchert, S., Viswesvaran, C., & Judge, T. A. (2007). In support of personality assessment in organizational settings. *Personnel Psychology, 60,* 995–1027.

Ones, D. S., Viswesvaran, C., & Dilchert, S. (2005). Personality at work: Raising awareness and correcting misconceptions. *Human Performance, 18*(4), 389–404.

Ostrov, E. (1986). Police/law enforcement and psychology. *Behavioral Sciences & the Law, 4*(4), 353–370.

Pallone, N. J. (1992). The MMPI in police officer selection: Legal constraints, case law, empirical data. *Journal of Offender Rehabilitation, 17*(3–4), 171–188.

Palmiotto, M. J. (2001). Can police recruiting control police misconduct. In M. J. Palmiotto (Ed.), *Police misconduct: A reader for the 21st century* (pp. 344–354). Upper Saddle River, NJ: Prentice Hall.

Peak, K. J., Stitt, G., & Glensor, R. W. (1998). Ethical considerations in community policing and problem solving. *Police Quarterly, 1*(19), 19–34.

Roulette v. Department of Central Management Services 141 Ill. App. 3d 394, 490 N.E.2d 60 (1986).

Rubin, J., & Cruse, D. (1973). Police behavior (part II). *The Journal of Psychiatry & Law, 1*(3), 353–375.

Russell, M., & Karol, D. (1994). *16 PF fifth edition: Administrator's manual.* Chicago: Institute for Personality and Ability Testing.

Schmidt, F. L., & Hunter, J. E. (1998). The validity and utility of selection methods in personnel psychology: Practical and theoretical implications of 85 years of research findings. *Psychological Bulletin, 124*(2), 262–274.

Scogin, F., Schumacher, J., Gardner, J., & Chaplin, W. (1995). Predictive validity of psychological testing in law enforcement settings. *Professional Psychology: Research and Practice, 26*(1), 68–71.

Shusman, E. (1987). A redundancy analysis for the Inwald personality inventory and the MMPI. *Journal of Personality Assessment. 51*(3), 433–440.

Tong, E. W., Bishop, G. D., Diong, S., Enkelmann, H., Why, Y., Ang, J., et al. (2004). Social support and personality among male police officers in Singapore. *Personality and Individual Differences, 36,* 109–123.

Tully, E. J. (1998, June). *Misconduct, corruption, and abuse of power: Part II. What can the officer do?* National Executive Institute Associates. Retrieved from http://www.neiassociates.org/misconduct-corruption-abuse/

U.S. Department of Justice (1990). *Americans With Disabilities Act of 1990, as amended.* Retrieved from http://www.ada.gov/pubs/ada.htm.

U.S. Equal Employment Opportunity Commission (2010). *Laws enforced by EEOC.* Retrieved from http://www.eeoc.gov/laws/statutes/

Varela, J. G., Boccaccini, M. T., Scogin, F., Stump, J., & Caputo, A. (2004). Personality testing in law enforcement employment settings: A meta-analytic review. *Criminal Justice & Behavior, 31*(6), 649–675.

Weiss, W. U., Davis, R., Rostow, C., & Kinsman, S. (2003). The MMPI-2 L scale as a tool in police selection. *Journal of Police and Criminal Psychology, 18*(1), 57–60.

Weiss, W. U., Serafino, G., & Serafino, A. (2000). A study of the interrelationships of several validity scales used in police selection. *Journal of Police and Criminal Psychology, 15*(1), 41–44.

Weiss, W. U., Serafino, G., Serafino, A., Willson, W., Sarsany, J., & Felton, J. (1999). Use of the MMPI-2 and the Inwald personality inventory to identify the personality characteristics of dropouts from a state police academy. *Journal of Police and Criminal Psychology, 14*(1), 38–42.

Williams, K. M., Davis, R. D., & Rostow, C. D. (2011, August). *Comparing the M-Pulse Inventory and MMPI-2: Degree of overlap and predicting misconduct in 7,161 law enforcement officers.* Paper presented at the 37th Annual Conference of the American Psychological Association, Washington, DC.

Yarmey, A. D. (1990). *Understanding police and police work: Psychosocial issues.* New York: New York University Press.

3

Rhetoric Versus Reality

Why Ethics Training Fails—and How to Fix It

Brian D. Fitch, Christine H. Jones, and Luann P. Pannell

"What we teach is how we teach"

John McArthur, Harvard University

Berkeley police Chief Michael Meehan was already under intense scrutiny when the *Oakland Tribune* featured a story involving his use of department resources to locate his son's missing iPhone (Bender, 2012). The incident began on January 11, 2012, when Meehan's son, a freshman at Berkeley High School, found that his iPhone, equipped with the Find My iPhone tracking software, was missing from his unlocked gym locker. The boy alerted his father, and Meehan pulled out his own cell phone and showed a property crimes detective sergeant the real-time movement of the stolen phone.

Given the active signal of the stolen phone, the detective sergeant took his team to try to locate it. As the signal was moving into the city of Oakland, the detective sergeant called the drug task force to ask for some additional assistance, said Sgt. Mary Kusmiss, a department spokeswoman. However, a police report about the theft of the iPhone was never written, and the Oakland Police Department was never notified that officers on the department's drug task force were in North Oakland knocking on doors looking for the phone. Three detectives and a sergeant each logged two hours of overtime.

Controversy over the search comes at a time when the city is spending $20,000 to make sure its police department's media policies are up to speed after the chief was widely criticized for sending a sergeant to a reporter's home about 1 a.m. on March 9 to ask for changes to an online story. The Berkeley police union criticized the move, saying Meehan's actions "do not represent the will, spirit or sentiment of the membership of the Berkeley Police Association," and called for an independent investigation.

Chief Meehan's conduct is simply one of myriad examples of poor ethical judgment and decision making found at all levels of law enforcement. Clearly, society demands the highest standards of ethical conduct from its guardians of justice. Poor ethical decisions can damage the public trust, jeopardize investigations, and create unnecessary and, in some cases, costly litigation. Thus, it is imperative that law enforcement officers receive the ethics, critical thinking, and decision-making skills necessary to maintain the highest levels of public trust. However, Scott (2000) observes that both the quantity and quality of formal training in most contemporary policing models is lacking. Hundersmarck (2009) maintains, "Academics should focus on encouraging critical thinking skills using problem-based learning techniques more reflective of the complex nature of police work, such as changing laws, using technology, and responding to crises" (p. 2).

Despite the obvious need for a new model of law enforcement training, Bradford and Pynes (1999) observe that police academy training has changed little in the past several decades, with most agencies still failing to incorporate recent advances in the fields of psychology, education, and learning. In this chapter, the authors outline many of the problems associated with the traditional practices of law enforcement training, including attention, absence of student involvement, lack of emphasis on prior learning, and failure to address the affective dimension of learning. The authors further discuss the philosophy and principles of active learning; how active learning strategies can be used to increase student attention, motivation, and retention; and the components of an effective ethics training program. The chapter concludes with suggestions for aligning ethics training with the tenants of active learning.

Pedagogy and Practices of Law Enforcement Training ____

Law enforcement training has relied traditionally on lecture-based methods of instruction that require recruits to sit passively and take notes while more experienced instructors and subject matter experts lecture on the core curriculum. According to this pedagogical model, learning is assumed to be the product of machine-like processes, similar to those reflected in foundational behavioral learning theory (Bruning, Schraw, Norby, & Ronning, 2004). Teachers disseminate knowledge, while students listen attentively, take copious notes, and demonstrate proficiency by parroting information on multiple-choice exams (Brooks & Brooks, 1999). A rigidity of thinking is reinforced, as learning is reduced to nothing more than a "mimetic" activity, a process that involves students doing little more than repeating, or miming, newly presented information (Jackson, 1986), while field application for much of the curricula is left up to each recruit or student to discover while on the job. Further, field application is heavily influenced by the experience and guidance of one's training officers.

The didactic model of pedagogy found in law enforcement academies has a long history in education. According to Swanson and Torraco (1994), lecture emerged as a formal teaching process centuries ago that began with a duteous reading of important passages from the text by the master, followed by the master's interpretation of the text. Despite opportunities provided by changing technology and educational research, surveys indicate that the use of lecture as the dominant method of instruction throughout institutions of higher education and beyond has changed very little (Benjamin, 2002; Costin, 1972; Gunzburger, 1993; Karp, 1983), a finding that holds true in law enforcement training as well, where lecture has become the default approach for training with a number of topics, including criminal law, search and seizure, crimes in progress, communication, problem solving, and ethics. The continuing popularity of lecture is not difficult to understand. Lecture offers the advantages of decreased training costs, efficient use of instructor time and talent, judicious use of resources, and standardization of the educational experience (McLeod, 1998). Moreover, many students enjoy the nonthreatening format offered by lecture, while others fear that the use of less traditional methods of instruction will not allow sufficient time to cover the required test materials, negatively impacting their chances for a passing grade (Bonwell & Eison, 1991; Qualters, 2001).

In spite of the continued popularity of lecture, a growing body of evidence suggests that "learning is not just a spectator sport" (Chickering & Gamson, 1987, p. 30). Even the best students are unable to listen effectively for long periods of time, regardless of how motivated or skillful. Human attention requires considerable cognitive resources and energy, with most students unable to focus their attention for periods of longer than about 15 minutes before confusion and boredom begin to set in, significantly decreasing the possibility of meaningful learning and memory (DiCarlo, 2009; Penner, 1984; Solomon & Solomon, 1993; Sousa, 2001). For example, a study at the University of California at Berkeley found that college students only remembered 20% of what they heard from a traditional lecture or demonstration several days after class, ostensibly because the students were too busy taking notes to internalize the information. The results further indicated that, in a large lecture, fewer than 15% of learners are paying attention to what is being presented at any one time, not counting the first eight minutes of class when a much higher percentage of students are following the discourse (Angelo, 1991). Moreover, there appears to be only a weak association between lecture attendance and course grades (Hammen & Kelland, 1994). Thus, the effectiveness of lecture fails to correlate with its popularity, especially for complex cognitive topics, such as critical thinking, decision making, and ethics.

Problems With the Didactic Model

There are a number of factors that appear to contribute to the low rates of attention and learning associated with traditional classroom lecture. To begin with, human attention is restricted by the limitations of working memory, the component of memory most often associated with thinking, recall, and the manipulation of new information into useable concepts and ideas (Willington, 2009). Because space in working memory is limited, the average student can hold no more than five to seven pieces of information at any given time, a finding that lies in stark contrast to the deluge of facts that students are often required to memorize for "test purposes." DiCarlo (2009) maintains that instructors, rather than concentrating on covering content, should focus on how they teach by reducing the amount of factual information that students are required to memorize, while emphasizing the importance of problem solving and independent learning.

A second problem associated with passive lecture is the lack of student engagement and participation. In traditional lecture, most of the effort is devoted to filling the student's mind with fact and figures rather than preparing and developing it (DiCarlo, 2009). Teachers are viewed as containers filled with knowledge who actively transmit learning to students; students, on the other hand, are seen as vessels wanting to be filled with information, but who play little more than a passive role in their own learning. Not surprisingly, interaction between the student and teacher, typically in the form of student questions, is characteristically limited in scope and effectiveness (Brooks & Brooks, 1999). In a study of questioning in colleges and universities involving 40 full-time undergraduate faculty instructors at both small and large institutions, Barnes (1983) found that the mean total percent of class time spent with students answering questions was less than 4%. Of those questions, 63% focused on simply memory or recall, while another 19% concerned routine administrative inquires. Even more disturbing, however, was the fact that nearly 33% of the questions asked failed to generate a student response.

A third complication related to lecture is the lack of emphasis on prior learning. Students do not enter the classroom *tabula rasa*, subject only to the learning conditions offered by their immediate environment (Bruning et al., 2004). Rather, each student brings a rich tapestry of prior experience, learning, interests, attitudes, and goals—factors that significantly influence how students understand, apply, and retain information. The effects of prior learning are especially important in light of the proliferation of law enforcement themes in the media, including television, movies, news, and radio, where reality and fantasy are regularly merged for entertainment value. Thus, trainers must assume that new recruits, and, in some cases, veteran officers, will be filled with preconceived biases and misperceptions from media exposure. Law enforcement ethics training, then, must not only convey new information but also correct faulty thinking and reasoning as well.

In a review of 183 studies, Dochy, Segers, and Buehl (1999) found a strong relationship between prior learning and performance. Almost all the studies investigated (91%) reported a positive effect of prior knowledge on performance, and, in some circumstances, what the learners knew about the topic prior to instruction predicated as much as 60% of the variation in student test scores. Hence, it appears that instruction should provide learners with a collaborative experience in which they have both the means and opportunity to construct new understandings by relating current problems to past learning (Tam, 2000).

A fourth difficulty linked to passive lecture is the failure of many educators to acknowledge the affective dimension of learning. According to Ledoux (1994, 1996), emotions drive attention, enhance retention, and have their own memory pathways. Recent findings in neurophysiology suggest that the limbic brain formations associated with emotion are active during every function of the cerebral cortex and R-complex. When new information from the senses enters the brain, it passes first to the thalamus, where it travels simultaneously on pathways to the higher brain centers of the neocortex, as well as to the limbic formations, where it is processed for emotional content and survival value (Damasio, 1994; Goleman, 1994; Hart, 2002). Because every experience includes an emotional dimension, an affective reaction is a natural part of each student's subjective learning response. Thus, learning and memory of a new experience include not only facts and information but also the feelings and emotions that accompanied the original event. These facts provide evidence for a strong relationship between emotion and learning (McGaugh, 1993; Phelps & Sharot, 2008), a phenomenon that signifies the necessity of emotional engagement during learning to maintain motivation, enhance learning, and increase retention (Ferro, 1993; Wlodkowski, 1985).

The final hurdle within law enforcement training is the overreliance on fear, humiliation, and punishment as tools for learning. In many cases, this is done to observe whether or not recruits can "handle" the stresses of training—often viewed as a proxy for one's ability to handle the stresses an officer is likely to encounter in the field. Research has demonstrated the positive effects of moderate stress on performance (Hardy, 1999; Humara, 1999; Robazza & Bortoli, 2007). For example, stress exposure training, in which individuals are exposed to simulated stressors and forced to perform target skills, can build familiarity with potential stressors, teach individuals strategies to maintain performance under stress, and contribute to task mastery, overlearning, and increased self-confidence (Deikis, 1982; Driskell & Johnston, 1998; Saunders, Driskell, Johnston, & Salas, 1996). However, continuously high levels of stress—or, in some cases, a single highly stressful or emotional event—can lead to emotional exhaustion, lower organizational commitment, and increased turnover intentions (Cropanzano, Rapp, & Bryne, 2003).

Evidence on the relationship between stress and performance suggests an inverted-U shape (Humara, 1999). Thus, individual performance on a given task will be lower at high and low levels of stress and optimal at moderate levels of stress. At moderate levels of stress, performance is likely to be improved by the presence of enough stimulation to keep the individual vigilant and alert, but not enough to divert or absorb his energy and focus (Kavanagh, 2005). At low levels of stress, in contrast, activation and alertness may be too low to foster effective performance, while at high levels of stress arousal is too high to be conducive to task performance. These findings suggest that most training is best conducted under conditions of moderate stress, while avoiding the dangers of boredom or excessive emotional arousal.

While the best way to prepare officers for high-stress encounters (e.g., officer-involved shooting, vehicle pursuit, or application of force), in many cases, is to train under high-stress circumstances, law enforcement trainers must be careful in their application of stress. In addition to problems associated with emotional exhaustion and lower organizational commitment, difficulties can arise when students begin to perceive training as a "game." At this point, training actually does little more than reinforce individual survival—that is, developing strategies to survive the exploits of the most experienced people in the room (instructors). Through this style of training, law enforcement has frequently reinforced that it is important to do the right thing when others are watching, but that is very different than the internalization of values that are fully lived out when no one is watching (Horner, Pannell, & Yates, 2011).

Unfortunately, the pervasive use of lecture and, in some cases, fear has left many recruits ill-prepared to handle dynamic interpersonal situations, apply problem-solving skills, and ensure ethical decisions and conduct in the community (Birzer, 1999; Horner et al., 2011). The changing societal needs and the demand for more democratic management in implementing contemporary models of policing have begun raising the awareness that traditional, lecture-based methods are deficient in serving either officers or the public. The era of producing physically strong, rigid officers to reactively enforce the law has become limiting, less sophisticated, and antiquated. In place of a uniform crisis response approach, there has been a gradual recognition documented in the police literature that officers need to be trained in emotional intelligence skills, such as effective communication, decision making, critical thinking, leadership, creative thinking skills, and ethics (Birzer, 2003; Birzer & Tannehill, 2001; Codish, 1996; Dwyer, & Laufersweiler-Dwyer, 2004; Horner et al., 2011; Marenin, 2004; Vicchio, 1997) in ways consistent with the tenets of active learning.

Active Learning

Lecture-based pedagogy has historically been the method of choice for law enforcement training (Flosi, 2011). This practice was assumed to be applicable to all learners, including adults, at all times. Regrettably, the current lecture-based (and sometimes fear-infused) model offers few opportunities for cognitive or emotional growth, while often downgrading complex topics, like ethics, to monochromatic issues of right and wrong. Teaching nonmechanistic skills such as critical thinking, decision making, communication, and ethics requires a more active approach to learning—that is, a methodology more consistent with how the brain naturally processes, evaluates, and remembers information (Sousa, 2001). However, the importance of a pedagogical model focused on active learning is not new. The eminent Harvard psychologist B. F. Skinner (1968) argued more than 40 years ago that a learner "does not passively absorb knowledge from the world around him but must play an active role" (p. 5).

Knowles (1984), often cited as a major contributor of modern adult learning theory, or *andragogy*, introduced key assumptions of the learning process that differentiate adults from children, articulating that adults, unlike children, are self-directed, are self-motivated, and take responsibility for learning decisions (Knowles, 1980). Based on his empirical work focused primarily on "middle-class" learners (Merriam & Cafarella, 1999; Tough, 1983), Knowles concluded that adults need to know the purpose of learning specific information, as well as to learn experientially by drawing on personal experiences. Adults, moreover, learn best when information can be applied practically and immediately, such as opportunities to solve contemporary problems similar to those found in real-world settings.

Conducting police academy training using a holistic and collaborative adult learning model not only improves learning and memory, but also better aligns recruit training with public demands for a more community-oriented policing philosophy, enhanced accountability, and improved public safety. This is due, at least in part, to the fact that the andragogical model makes it possible to teach the more sophisticated, softer skills of ethical police work deemed necessary for effective community policing, for example, problem solving, mediation, resource referrals, and communication (Birzer & Tannehill, 2001). The andragogical model also resonates with democratic values (Brown, 2004) and better adheres to the value-based social contract between the public and the police.

Rather than focusing on content, instructors should emphasize learning strategies that stress problem solving, skill development, and higher order thinking, while significantly reducing or, in some cases, eliminating the role of lecture (Brooks & Brooks, 1999; DiCarlo, 2009; Jensen, 2005). If the topic of ethics becomes self-evident to the student in the classroom environment, it is more likely that the student will respond in a socially prescribed and approved manner. Several areas of active learning warrant further discussion, including the roles of the facilitator, the student, content, context, affect, and assessment.

Role of the Facilitator

In the traditional classroom, the roles of teacher and student are clearly defined and understood. Studies, however, suggest that not only do a significant number of individuals have learning styles best served by the tenets of active learning, but also that students actually prefer strategies that promote active learning to traditional lecture (Bonwell & Eison, 1991). This requires law enforcement instructors to supplant outdated methods of passive lectures with active learning strategies that involve students in doing things and in thinking about what they are doing, while creating a supportive intellectual and emotional environment that encourages risk (Bruning et al., 2004).

In contrast to the teacher-centric approach found in traditional classrooms, instructors who engage their students in active learning serve as facilitators by creating opportunities for discussion, checking periodically for understanding, and challenging learner assumptions by posing contradictions, presenting new information, and asking thought-provoking questions that focus on deep understanding (Barrows, 2000). This focus on reflective thought provides students with the tools necessary not only to comprehend the material but also to become active, motivated, self-regulated, and self-reflective learners capable of effectively regulating their own thoughts and actions (DiCarlo, 2009). However, most importantly, the facilitator acts as an expert learner—that is, someone who is able to model good strategies for learning and thinking (Hmelo-Silver & Barrows, 2006).

Consistent with the idea of teacher as facilitator, research has identified the quality of discourse as one of the most critical elements in effective learning (e.g., Calfee, Dunlap, & Wat, 1994; Chinn, Anderson, & Waggoner, 2001; Kuhn, Shaw, & Felton, 1997; Nystrand & Gamoran, 1991; Wiencek & O'Flahavan, 1994). As participants strive to understand and participate in discussions, they are forced to relate, reorganize, and reevaluate what they know (Bruning et al., 2004). A good discussion, however, requires considerable preparation, thoughtful implementation, and a supportive environment. Among other duties, the facilitator is responsible for selecting suitable topics for discussion; designing appropriate queries; managing the physical environment, including group size and composition; establishing suitable norms; and monitoring group progress (Bonwell & Eison, 1991).

Much of this lies in contrast to the "military model" of instruction found in many law enforcement training sessions, especially basic academy training, where the emphasis is on respect and discipline, rather than on higher order thinking and decision-making skills. While law enforcement's mission is very different from that of the military, it is not difficult to understand the attraction of the discipline and respect honed through military service. Nonetheless, the myth of the military model is just that—a myth (Cowper, 2000). Military instructors do not simply apply arbitrary stressors; the military services have had decades to research and perfect their training models with every exercise and assignment precisely arranged to achieve a particular set of learning objectives. Therefore, to be effective, facilitators must learn to separate their role as drill instructor from their role as facilitator, where their primary responsibility is teaching the decision-making and critical thinking skills necessary to make sound, ethical decisions.

Role of the Student

A clear understanding of students' beliefs and motivation is critical to effective facilitation and meaningful learning. Every student enters the classroom with a wealth of information, education, and life experiences that have led the student to presume certain truths about the world (Bruning et al., 2004). While some of these presumptions can be said to reflect reality accurately, others do not. Understanding these assumptions is critical because what students already know has a profound influence on subsequent learning, memory, and performance (DiCarlo, 2009). Teachers who operate without awareness of their students' prior points of view often doom learners to dull, irrelevant experiences, and, in some cases, even failure (Brooks & Brooks, 1999; Hunt & Sullivan, 1974). Unfortunately, the didactic lecture-based methods found in traditional classrooms often fail to provide the tools necessary to uncover many of these assumptions.

Achieving an appreciation of students' prior learning, as well as how these assumptions impact current performance, requires opportunities for learners to share their experiences in a safe, supportive, and structured environment (Brooks & Brooks, 1999). Students are continuously searching for how the materials being learned in the classroom are applicable in their daily lives, a fact that is especially important for adult learners. By offering students opportunities to apply prior knowledge, facilitators not only maximize attention and learning, but also provide the opportunity for students to assume responsibility for their own learning (Bonwell & Eison, 1991).

Despite the advantages of adult learning methods, students learn very quickly what to expect and how to behave in a class filled with traditional lectures. Thus, students being exposed to facilitated discussion, small-group learning activities, and other active learning methods may be initially uncomfortable (Bonwll & Eison, 1991). Preference for a particular method of instruction should not be confused with the actual learning and application of material—the ultimate goals of any training session. Therefore, facilitators will need to role model the kinds of interactive learning strategies they are attempting to foster in students while remaining patient with the initial discomfort that many students will doubtless experience. While some students may be satisfied with just the "facts," memory and retention are significantly facilitated when students are able to connect new learning to real-world future events (Sousa, 2001). Thus, the facilitator needs to monitor continuously students' energy levels and interest to assess the best learning strategies to reinforce the usefulness of material at any given time.

Role of Content

Knowles (1984) advises that training should rely primarily on interactive and relevant methods, such as case studies, role-plays, and real-world contextualized simulations. Examples and case studies can be pulled from the personal experiences of recruits, current events, or the media, including movies, magazines and radio. The examples provided can be either negative or positive, but it should be made clear that exemplary performance, not perfection, is the goal (Robinson, 2008). The application of new knowledge in the context of problems is critical because it helps foster the transfer of such concepts in ways that allow students to identify, understand, and solve similar problems in the future (Bradford & Pynes, 1999).

If students are going to be expected to perform well in the field with ethical challenges, then ethical training (e.g., ethical dilemmas) should be woven in to the design of other topics and resources (Bradford & Pynes, 1999). Ethical training should be fully integrated throughout the course content, rather than merely waiting until the final days of a recruit's basic academy training, as though ethics is merely a suggestion. Doing so implies that ethics is somehow less important than other "real" law enforcement topics, such as tactics, fitness, survival skills, and firearms. To be effective, training must emphasize the critical thinking, decision making, and ethical reasoning necessary to protect an officer, the agency, and public from the start.

In support of Knowles's recommended methods, Hundersmarck (2009) found in his study with academy recruits that lecture-based classes were viewed as less relevant and less valuable when contrasted with more real-life police scenarios or hands-on training. Similarly, White (2007) contended that the realities of police encounters need to be incorporated into the academy through critical discussions, role-plays, and interactions between the recruits and instructors. Johnson, Johnson, and White (2005) echo similar beliefs, suggesting that trainees need to work with practical ethical experiences to comprehend the concepts and to transfer learning to the real world. It is not enough for students to acknowledge that something is wrong. Discussions need to be conducted to elicit the answers to why something is wrong and the consequences of the unethical behavior (DiCarlo, 2009). Facilitators who press for critical thinking and emphasize self-reflection will better equip officers to make ethical decisions in any situation they may encounter in the future.

One problem with cultivating critical thinking and ethical decision-making skills in law enforcement is the self-evident nature of the content. Many students understand clearly what is expected of them during an "ethics" course—and answer the questions and scenarios appropriately. It is probably safe to conclude that few recruits lack a complete social understanding of law enforcement responsibility. Thus, facilitators should not be surprised when a student can provide the right answers. As a result, training tends to occur at the lowest levels of Bloom's taxonomy (Atherton, 2011; Bloom, 1956), simple knowledge and comprehension—as opposed to the higher levels of application, analysis, synthesis, and evaluation associated with improved levels of retention and learning. Moreover, this approach fails to replicate the complicated and challenging environments where real ethical decisions occur.

To maximize learning, teachers need to present complex problems, ask relevant questions, and pose ethical dilemmas that require students to apply what they have learned in real world contextualized scenarios (Pollack & Becker, 1996). During this process, constructive feedback and reinforcements should be used to deepen understanding. Recruits should be asked to integrate past experiences into classroom activities to build intrinsic meaning and motivation. This model when applied correctly should generate a collaborative, open environment where communication, consultation, leadership, and human relation skills can be practiced with both classmates and instructors to maximize the retention and transfer of learning (Barrows, 2002).

Role of Context

Effective educators recognize that context influences both the form and quality of learning, and that the social activities that occur in the classroom are fundamental to the cognitive development necessary to identify, evaluate, and solve the kinds of problems that students are likely to encounter in the real world (Bruning et al., 2004). Therefore, facilitators encourage students to engage in dialogue—both with the instructor and with one another—by providing opportunities to share personal knowledge, fostering multiple viewpoints, emphasizing relevant problems, and checking for understanding (Slavin, 1990).

A meta-analysis of 500 experimental studies on the teaching of writing found that structured classes with clear objectives and interaction that focused on specific problems that students were likely to encounter in the real world were more effective than classes dominated by teacher talk in which students played little more than a passive role (Lewis, Woodward, & Bell, 1988). Similarly, in a study comparing student learning in four small lecture classes with one large class characterized by active learning, the greater the number of higher order questions posed by the facilitator, the higher the student scores on the posttest, leading the researchers to conclude that it is the instructional method, rather than the size of the class, that seems to influence learning (Lewis & Woodward, 1984). Therefore, training that relies on a philosophical and structural design that reflects the foundation of the adult learning model can benefit the learning outcome.

Facilitators must also consider the important roles played by practice and feedback. Certainly, no recruit would be deemed ready for field operations after a simple lecture on firearms. Proficiency with a firearm requires continuous practice and feedback. The same finding holds true for training in ethics, critical thinking, and decision making—they all require continuous practice and feedback. One does not learn to recognize, assess, and act in ethical situations without the practice and feedback necessary to develop the requisite skills set (Bruning et al., 2004). Thus, the challenge for police trainers is to integrate ethical training throughout the law enforcement curriculum, including ample opportunities for practice and feedback involving real-life scenarios that imitate what an officer is most likely to encounter in the field. Absent the necessary application, it is highly unlikely that classroom conversations on ethics will be able to translate to desired results in the field.

Role of Affect

In basic police training, emotions are often dismissed or devalued. Reece and Walker (2005) argue that since thoughts, feelings, and actions are interconnected, people respond holistically and not in parts. Therefore, individuals should be trained as "total organisms." Vodde (2008) argues that the affective component of learning is as important, if not more important, than the cognitive component when instilling the ethical philosophy and corresponding soft skills necessary for effective policing. To deliver effectively a more holistic approach, academy training should induce emotions with ethical scenarios or simulations that include realistic factors, such as accurate language and supervisor presence. Ethical training can fail when it fails to simulate affective experience, that is, "the pit in the stomach" that comes with an actual ethical dilemma. If students have to struggle, identify, and overcome ethical dilemmas during training, they are more likely to replicate those responses in the field.

Kasher (2008) asserts that emotions play an important role in ethics training, and that ethics education needs to appeal to the emotional brain, as well as the rational brain. The ethos of an ethical police organization can be emotionally transmitted through pervasive and seductive traditions that include distinctive uniforms, rank, ceremonial rituals, insignia, customs, etiquette, repetitive drills, police language, and the familiar grounds of police headquarters. Recruits who are exposed to this dominant cultural force eventually begin to identify emotionally with these symbols. As they resonate more and more with these symbols, their loyalty, obedience, and group conformity can be expected to increase (Haslam, Reicher, & Platow, 2011). This powerful transformation can positively shape attitudes and behaviors if the organization consistently links law enforcement with ethics and professionalism. Hundersmarck (2004) remarked that identity is closely associated with many aspects of learning, particularly for police officers. In this way, constant symbolic reminders and rituals that imbue ethics will help officers maintain congruent attitudes that reflect the pride felt from belonging to a value-based organization.

In addition to identity, Goleman (1994) maintains that individuals with emotional intelligence have well-formed social skills and use this emotional awareness to direct their actions. Exposing recruits to real-world scenarios, naturally impacts their total self (i.e., thoughts, emotions, and behavior), guiding emotional reactions and evaluations of their performance. Holistic training offers officers a greater range of emotional intelligence tools accessible for use when addressing suspects, witnesses, community relations, ethical dilemmas, crises, critical incidents, and supervisors, as well as one's spouse and family. The longer-term benefit of a holistic approach is its ability to address the unrealistic image of a super masculine warrior who views emotions as a hindrance, both to himself and to others. It helps law enforcement professionals better understand the importance of emotions when making decisions (Damasio, 1994), while giving officers permission to stop being emotionally detached. Consequently, instructors can teach recruits to access their wise emotions and cognitions to help navigate the dangers of policing.

Role of Assessment

In the traditional classroom, learning is predominately assessed through multiple-choice or short-answer tests. Such examinations focus on what students can remember and repeat, with students often committing information to memory just long enough to pass the assessment (Brooks & Brooks, 1999). Thus, both the content and the method of instruction found in traditional classrooms nullify the chances of students developing the higher order thinking and problem-solving skills necessary to successfully apply what they have learned to the challenges they are likely to encounter in the real world. In contrast, active learning focuses on what students can demonstrate, generate, and exhibit, not what they can repeat (Bonwell & Eison, 1991).

Traditional instructional methods break wholes into parts and then focus independently on each segment. While this greatly simplifies the construction of lesson plans and assessment, it makes it difficult for students to understand how the parts work together to form an integrated whole—in other words, the "big picture" (Brooks & Brooks, 1999). Imagine attempting to teach a student to drive an automobile by lecturing on the "design and development of the steering wheel." This could be followed by similar lectures on "the history of the rear-view mirror," and so forth. Each lecture would be accompanied by a multiple-choice examination. What are the chances that a student who received a passing grade on every test would be able to drive? Why, then, do law enforcement instructors continue to evaluate topics like ethics, communication, and decision making using multiple-choice examinations when such topics are best assessed through demonstration?

In an active classroom, facilitators assess student learning in the context of daily instruction. This is based on the idea that learning is not simply about committing a set of facts to rote memory, but the ability to use resources to locate, evaluate, and apply information to genuine problems (DiCarlo, 2009). Active assessment begins with building lesson plans and learning activities around "big ideas," as opposed to more traditional clusters of small, seemingly disconnected units. Students work together in small groups to define and evaluate problems, share knowledge, and construct solutions that reflect their understanding (Brooks & Brooks, 1999). Rather than evaluating student understanding as a separate activity, the memorization of information is subordinated to student problem-solving activities and discussions. Accordingly, ethics instruction would focus less on traditional lecture, while replacing it with discussions centered on the identification, evaluation, and solution of problems, including the affective learning domain and its impact on student values, attitudes, and beliefs.

The Need for a New Model of Training

According to Birzer and Tannehill (2001), the need for more and improved law enforcement training is gathering increasing momentum as we enter the 21st century. It is through training that change, protocol, and philosophies are first introduced to law enforcement personnel. Thus, the application of the andragogical model is theorized to better facilitate the learning, educative, and training goals for police officers. Vodde (2008) believes that the application of the andragogical model will, in turn, influence the police agency, its mission, and the delivery of services. Kennedy (2003), also in favor of implementing the adult learning model in police training, states,

> The field of adult education has been emerging steadily as a discrete field of social practice in the United States since the founding of the American Association for Adult Education in 1926. Since that time, research has produced many new concepts about the learning processes of adults and the motives that direct and influence an adult's ability to acquire new knowledge and skills. Recognition and application of these concepts are the keys to more effective law enforcement training programs. (p. 1)

Massey (1993) stresses a similar argument, believing that it is insufficient to train officers based strictly on a code of conduct. Although many police agencies have a code of conduct written for their officers, it is not necessarily a code that lives and breathes in daily operations. He further advocates for a model of ethics training that emphasizes the theoretical basis of moral decisions in ways that allows officers to apply independently their ethical reasoning to any situation in the field. Developing this specific skill would likely be a hedge against an overreliance on situational ethics and police corruption. However, the creation of such a prototype requires a realignment of ethics training in ways that are consistent with the tenets of adult learning, including the development and delivery of curricula.

Realigning Law Enforcement Ethics Training With Active Learning

According to a report by the International Association of Chiefs of Police (IACP) Ad Hoc Committee on Police Image and Ethics (1997), police academies, in general, offer ethics programs that are isolated, instead of being incorporated into the context of a larger training curriculum. In 2005, a decade after the Ad Hoc Committee convened, Trautman and Prevost (2005) observed that there has been little change in the state of affairs on ethics, while underscoring the need for agencies to do more. He believed that law enforcement's greatest training need was in ethics. The IACP committee reported that the majority of departments (70.5%) conducted ethics training for four hours or less, a finding that is complicated by the fact that most ethics training consists of little more than a lecture or sermon, often presented in a threatening or offensive tone. And while there has been consensus among law enforcement administrators, academicians, and member of the general public that ethics is important, there has not been enough change in providing adequate training in this area.

Despite the fact that morality has consistently been identified as integral to police work (Delattre, 1996; Miller, Blackler, & Alexandra, 1997) and among police agencies (IACP, 1997), the patchy, haphazard implementation of ethics training remains little more than a knee-jerk reaction to police abuse or corruption that has been publicly exposed. Addressing quality ethics in democratic policing must begin in the academy, when recruits are first introduced to their professional identity, as well as the cultural philosophy of the organization. Building moral consciousness and moral reasoning skills in impressionable recruits requires a significant cultural shift in the design and curricula used to deliver ethics training. Instead of imposing predominantly militaristic control in the pedagogical delivery of training, law enforcement academies should employ the adult learning philosophy and corresponding training curricula that emphasize the critical thinking, decision making, emotional intelligence, and other soft skills necessary to empower officers to behave ethically (Kennedy, 2003).

Van Slyke (2007) states, "It is essential that police ethics training utilize teaching modes that complement the adult learning process" (p. 1). Rather than teaching only a code of conduct, law, and department policies to address ethics in policing, it would be more substantive to build additional skills that address the daily ethical dilemmas faced by officers (e.g., being able to recognize and reflect on the crossroads of loyalty and immorality, and problem solving the social psychological behavior such as conformity). Applying the adult learning model to draw out these additional ethical tools would better prepare recruits for working in the community and in the police culture. Covey (1991) asserts that the challenge facing today's leaders has less to do with how to manage and control their people and more to do with ways to develop value-centered leaders who resonate the character that the police field demands. One way of accomplishing this is to challenge students with ethical scenarios that can only be solved with higher order ethical thinking (Kohlberg, 1981). As students struggle to identify, understand, and solve these complex dilemmas, their critical thinking and moral reasoning skills will grow accordingly, effectively enhancing retention, learning, and application.

Kleinig (2002) states that "morally responsible decision-making is more than a matter of 'following the rules'" (p. 287). As a result, ethical behavior requires more than the rote memorization of rules and policies. Ethics training in the academy must interactively comprehend the purpose of each society having a police agency. Empirical research has, in fact, demonstrated that transfer from the classroom to the field is most likely to occur when a person understands the underlying principles (Brown, 2004). Moll (2007) suggests the need for recruits to understand the framework of policing in terms of social contract theory. According to this theory, the authority and legitimacy exercised by law enforcement professionals are derived from the people via a social contract. The government's noble duty, then, is to further protect the natural rights possessed by the people—those of life, liberty, and property. As part of this agreement, citizens agree to relinquish the power to protect their own rights to the police and trust that the police will use its powers to protect the welfare of the public (Kappeler, Sluder, & Alpert, 1998). If the government agency fails to meet its obligation, citizens are no longer bound by the terms of the contract. Integrating the social contract theory using the interactive andragogical learning model can help provide officers with a deeper understanding of their responsibility to the citizenry, while better equipping officers to make ethical decisions across different dilemmas.

Benchmarks of Ethical Policing

Josephson (1995) describes ethics as being a code of values that helps guide our decisions and actions that paves the course for our future. Rather than describing ethics as a written code, he argues that ethics are best represented by an individual's choices and actions. Ethics is not simply about what someone believes but also about how their values translate to behaviors.

According to Kooken (1947), the benchmarks that signify ethical policing include due process, justice, equal protection of the laws, checks and balances, separation of power, right to bear arms, freedom of speech, religion, press, protection against unreasonable searches and seizures, protection against self-incrimination, right to a lawyer, and right to a speedy trial. Ethics training should help recruits accept the operating social contract system and use it to guide them in their work. In fact, more than 160 years ago, Sir Robert Peel (cited in Reith, 1948), generally recognized as the father of modern police work, stated that the police are the public and the public are the police; thus, an us-versus-them, or the strong-versus-weak, mentality poisons the reality that we are all citizens of the same republic. Imbuing recruits with a humanistic approach that emphasizes the importance of a social contract better reflects the democratic ideals that officers are supposed to embody within a just, equitable, and democratic society (Marenin, 2004).

While many scholars agree on the importance of ethics training, they often disagree about its content. Moll (2007), for example, believes that comprehensive ethics training needs to include information on what is right and what is wrong. Expecting recruits to navigate the ethically complex pressures and temptations of police work by drawing exclusively on their personal values, religious principles, or common sense only increases their vulnerability in misjudging situations. Pollack and Becker (1996), however, disagree with the implementation of abstract theoretical training. They believe that the application of ethical principles should be taught by drawing from practical examples that are common to police work.

Kasher (2008) believes that individuals need to be taught what is required of them to properly meet the ethical standards established by their professional identity. Therefore, recruits require training on what it means to be law enforcement professionals in a democratic republic. Bushway (2004) goes a step further by proposing that every officer should be challenged to strive to be the same individual in both private and public life. Officers should be encouraged to carry their solidified morality from their personal lives into their professional lives to avoid moving ethical lines, as is often the case with situational ethics. Academy instructors can help recruits better align their personal and professional lives by drawing examples from students that demonstrate adherence to moral virtues, while introducing common themes and ethical dilemmas in policing that challenge their belief systems and future behaviors.

Davis (1991) expands the discussion of police ethics by going beyond the self. He addresses the content of ethics training by proposing the use of a code of conduct to teach officers that being a professional means being moral, as well as being responsible for helping one's fellow officers do the right thing. Swope (1998) makes a similar argument, asserting that officers must be taught that ethical behavior is in their personal best interest, while policing their own is the only reasonable option for maintaining the ethical standards required of law enforcement by the public they are entrusted to serve. This internal standard of checks and balances creates a double layer of protection—the individual and partners looking after one another by applying appropriate peer pressure—that ensures appropriate standards of ethical conduct are continuously communicated and honored throughout the agency. Ideally, immediate supervisors would offer a third layer of protection to correct any ethical drift.

Summary

Law enforcement training has been traditionally dominated by lecture. Instructors disseminate knowledge, while learners focus their resources on replicating what they have learned. Regrettably, the traditional didactic model discourages student cooperation, requires students to work in relative isolation, and focuses on low-level skills, rather than on higher order reasoning and problem solving (Brooks & Brooks, 1999). Teaching the higher order thinking and reasoning skills necessary to police effectively in today's complex, multicultural societies requires a more active and holistic approach—more specifically, a methodology that is consistent with how the brain naturally processes, evaluates, and remembers information (Sousa, 2001). Training in law enforcement ethics, decision making, problem solving, and critical thinking requires facilitators who understand the importance of prior learning, appropriate questions, checking for key assumptions, and involving students in the learning process.

Considering the growing body of research linking active learning with improved retention, memory, and performance, the chapter concludes with suggestions for improving current ethics training.

Reduce or Eliminate Lecture

This chapter has outlined a number of problems associated with traditional lecture, including the limits of human attention (Willington, 2009), lack of student involvement (DiCarlo, 2009), effects of prior learning (Bruning et al., 2004), failure to acknowledge the affective dimension of learning (Ledoux, 1994, 1996), and the debilitating effects of chronic stress (Kavanagh, 2005). Considering these problems, law enforcement facilitators would be well served to minimize or, whenever possible, eliminate the role of lecture altogether. Instead, facilitators should focus on learning exercises that engage students in critical thinking and problem-solving exercises. Learning should center on exercises that prompt students to identify, diagnose, and solve real ethical dilemmas in a collaborative, supportive learning environment that encourages risks.

Incorporate Active Learning Strategies

Active learning strategies are teaching methods that engage students in doing things and thinking about what they are doing (Brooks & Brooks, 1999). The human mind is limited in the amount of information that can be retained or processed in short-term memory at a given time, a finding exacerbated by stress or other strong emotions. Rather than focusing on content, facilitators should emphasize learning strategies that stress problem solving, skill development, and higher order thinking (DiCarlo, 2009). This includes small-group learning activities, facilitated discussions, case studies, role-plays, and other activities intended to inquire about learner understanding, encourage student dialogue, test assumptions, and stimulate critical thinking.

Emphasize Prior Learning

All students enters the classroom with a wealth of information, education, and life experience that have led them to believe certain truths about the world (Bruning et al., 2004). Many of these assumptions have a significant impact on how students understand, process, and remember new information. Students are continuously searching for how the materials being taught in the classroom connect to prior experiences and learning. By offering students opportunities to apply what they already know, test assumptions, and assimilate new knowledge into existing belief systems, facilitators maximize attention, learning, and retention in important ways (Bonwell & Eison, 1991). Nonetheless, many students may be initially uncomfortable with facilitated models of learning. As a result, facilitators must continuously monitor student attention levels, energy, and interest to ensure the best learning experience possible.

Connect With the "Real World"

Adults are self-directed, self-motivated, and take responsibility for their own learning (Knowles, 1980). Moreover, most adults are busy, thus their time is valuable. As a result, adults need to know the purpose of the training—and, more specifically, how they can apply what they are learning in the classroom to become more effective in the real world. Facilitators can best demonstrate the applicability of classroom learning by engaging students in problem-solving activities, facilitated discussions, and case studies that best represent the kinds of problems that students are most likely to encounter while on the job (DiCarlo, 2009). Thus, the ethical problems and scenario used to instruct ethics must be relevant, that is, they should simulate the types of real-world ethical dilemmas that officers can expect to face in the performance of their daily activities.

Serve as Facilitator

Rather than lecturing while students sit passively, law enforcement ethics instructors should assume the role of facilitators by creating opportunities for discussion, checking periodically for understanding, challenging learner assumptions, and asking thought-provoking questions designed to stimulate higher order problem solving and critical thinking (Barrows, 2000). Unlike traditional teacher-centric methods that focus almost exclusively on content, the facilitator's job is to create a supportive learning environment. Thus, the facilitator stimulates learning by selecting suitable topics for discussion, designing appropriate questions, managing the physical environment, establishing suitable norms, and monitoring group progress (Bonwell & Eison, 1991), while students solve problems and engage in meaningful dialogue.

Integrate Affect

Emotions drive attention, enhance retention, and have their own memory pathways (LeDoux, 1994, 1996). When new stimuli from the senses enters the brain, it is processed for emotional and survival significance, as well as information value. As every experience includes an emotional dimension, affective reactions are part of each student's subjective learning experience. As Sousa (2001) suggests, the learning and memory of new information includes not only facts and information but also feeling and emotions that accompany the event. Therefore, student role-plays, case studies, and other exercises should be designed to include an affective component—that is, learning activities that stimulate the emotional brain, as well as the rational brain.

Model Behavior

Finally, facilitators should model the kinds of learning strategies they are attempting to impart on their students. In other words, facilitators should act as expert learners in the classroom and in the field. They should deliberately and purposely model good strategies for thinking and learning that include asking open-ended questions, remaining open-minded, exploring alternative theories, checking for understanding, examining key assumptions, and working collectively with students toward solutions (Hmelo-Silver & Barrows, 2006).

Ethics, critical thinking, and problem-solving skills are critical to the success of today's law enforcement professionals. Unlike traditional didactic models of instruction, active learning activities involve students in the learning process and impart important learning strategies, while enhancing learning, retention, and memory (DiCarlo, 2009; Sousa, 2001). The use of active learning also makes students responsible for their learning, as well as allowing them to better understand the purpose of learning by connecting new knowledge with prior experience (Knowles, 1980). By adopting these recommendations, law enforcement trainers should be better suited to assist students in meeting the demands imposed by our increasingly complex societies—including a realization of the high standards of ethical conduct expected by the citizenry. Moreover, improving ethics training in ways that focus on real-world problem solving may help tomorrow's law enforcement professionals avoid the flawed decision-making process that led a police chief to assign valuable resources to search for a stolen iPhone without so much as a police report.

Discussion Questions_____

1. What are the roles of the teacher and student in traditional lecture-based classroom?

2. Describe three problems associated with lecture-based methods of instruction.

3. What is active learning?

4. How does the role of facilitator differ from the role of lecturer?

5. Explain the relationship between stress and learning.

6. What should be included in the content of ethical instruction?

References

Angelo, T. A. (1991). Ten easy pieces: Assessing higher learning in four dimensions. In T. A. Angelo (Ed.), *Classroom research: Early lessons from success* (New directions for teaching and learning No. 46) (pp. 17–31). San Francisco: Jossey-Bass.

Atherton, J. S. (2011). *Bloom's taxonomy.* Retrieved from the Learning and Teaching website:http://www.learningandteaching.info/learning/bloomtax.htm#ixzz20U2Any00

Barnes, C. P. (1983). Questioning in college classrooms. In C. L. Ellner & C. P. Barnes (Eds.), *Studies of college teaching* (pp. 61–81). Lexington, MA: Lexington Books.

Barrows, H. S. (2000). *Problem-based learning applied to medical education.* Springfield: Southern Illinois University Press.

Barrows, H. S. (2002). Is it really possible to have such a thing as dPBL? *Distance Education, 23*(1), 119–122.

Bender, K. J. (2012, May 21). Berkeley Police Chief calls on officers to track down son's stolen iPhone in Oakland. *Oakland Tribune.* Retrieved from http://www.berkeleyside.com/2012/05/21/berkeley-police-chief-sent-10-officers-on-hunt-for-sons-iphone/

Benjamin, L. T., Jr. (2002). Lecturing. In S. F. Davis & W. Buskist (Eds.). *The teaching of psychology: Essays in honor of Wilbert J. McKeachie and Charles L. Brewer* (pp. 57–67). Mahwah, NJ: Erlbaum.

Birzer, M. (1999). Police training in the 21st century. *FBI Law Enforcement Bulletin, 68*(7), 16–19.

Birzer, M. (2003). The theory of andragogy applied to police training. *Policing: An International Journal of Police Strategies and Management, 26*(1), 29–42.

Birzer, M., & Tannehill, R. (2001). A more effective training approach for contemporary policing. *Police Quarterly, 4*(2), 233–252.

Bloom, B. S. (Ed.) (1956). *Taxonomy of educational objectives, the classification of educational goals: Book 1. Cognitive domain.* New York: McKay.

Bonwell, C. C., & Eison, J. A. (1991). *Active learning: Creating excitement in the classroom* (ASHE-ERIC Higher Education Report No. 1). Washington, DC: The George Washington University, School of Education and Human Development.

Bradford, D., & Pynes, J. (1999). Police academy training: Why hasn't it kept up with practice? *Police Quarterly, 2*(3), 283–301.

Brooks, J. G., & Brooks, M. G. (1999). *In search of understanding: The case for constructivist classrooms.* Alexandria, VA: Association for Supervision and Curriculum Development.

Brown, G. (2004). Studies of student learning. In *How students learn: A supplement to the RoutledgeFalmer Key Guides for Effective Teaching in Higher Education series* (pp. 32–33). London: Routledge. Retrieved from http://www.routledgeed ucation.com/resources/pdf/how_to_learn.pdf

Bruning, R. H., Schraw, G. J., Norby, M. M., & Ronning, R. R. (2004). *Cognitive psychology and instruction* (4th ed.). Upper Saddle River, NJ: Pearson Education.

Bushway, S. (2004, May). The ethics of policing. *Police Department Disciplinary Bulletin*, 1–2.

Calfee, R., Dunlap, K., & Wat, A. (1994). Authentic discussion of texts in middle grade schools: An analytic-narrative approach. *Journal of Reading*, 37(7), 546–556.

Chickering, A. W., & Gamson, Z. F. (1987, March). Seven principles for good practice. *AAHE Bulletin*, 39(7), 3–7.

Chinn, C. A., Anderson, R. C., & Waggoner, M. A. (2001). Patterns of discourse in two kinds of literature discussion. *Reading Research Quarterly*, 36(4), 378–411.

Codish, K. (1996). Putting a sacred cow out to pasture. *The Police Chief*, 63(3), 40–44.

Costin, F. (1972). Lecturing versus other methods of teaching: A review of research. *British Journal of Education*, 3(1), 4–31.

Covey, S. R. (1991). *Principle-based leadership*. New York: Free Press.

Cowper, T. J. (2000). The myth of the "military model" of leadership in law enforcement. *Police Quarterly*, 3(3), 228–246.

Cropanzano, R., Rapp, D., & Byrne, Z. (2003). The relationship of emotional exhaustion to work attitudes, job performance, and organizational citizenship behaviors. *Journal of Applied Psychology*, 88(1), 160–169.

Damasio, A. (1994). *Descartes' error: Emotion, reason, and the human brain*. New York: Penguin.

Davis, M. (1991, Summer–Fall). Do cops really need a code of ethics? *Criminal Justice Ethics*, 10, 14–28.

Deikis, J. G. (1982). *Stress inoculation training: Effects of anxiety, self-efficacy, and performance in divers*. (Unpublished doctoral dissertation). Temple University, Philadelphia, PA.

Delattre, E. (1996). *Character and cops: Ethics in policing* (3rd ed.). Washington, DC: The AEI Press.

DiCarlo, S. E . (2009). Too much content, not enough thinking, and too little fun! *Advances in Physiological Education*, 33(4), 257–264.

Dochy, F., Segers, M., & Buehl, M. M. (1999). The relationship between assessment practices and outcomes of studies: The case of research on prior knowledge. *Review of Educational Research*, 69(2), 145–186.

Driskell, J., & Johnston, J. (1998). Stress exposure training. In J. Cannon-Bowers & E. Salas (Eds.), *Making decisions under stress* (pp. 191–217). Washington, DC: American Psychological Association.

Dwyer, R. G., & Laufersweiler-Dwyer, D. L. (2004). The need for change: A call for action in community-oriented policing. *FBI Law Enforcement Bulletin*, 73(11), 18–24.

Ferro, T. R. (1993). The influence of affective processing in education and training. In D. D. Flannery (Ed.), *Applying cognitive learning theory to adult learning* (pp. 25–33). San Francisco: Jossey-Bass.

Flosi, E. (2011). Curriculum development for law enforcement: Pedagogy versus andragogy. *Police One*. Retrieved from http://www.policeone.com/Officer-Safety/ articles/3773478-Curriculum-development-for-law-enforcement-Pedagogy-versus-Andragogy/

Goleman, D. (1994). *Emotional intelligence: Why it can matter more than IQ*. New York: Bantam Books.

Gunzburger, L. K. (1993). U.S. medical schools' valuing of curriculum time: Self-directed learning versus lectures. *Academic Medicine, 68*(9), 700–702.

Hammen, C. S., & Kelland, J. L. (1994). Attendance and grades in a human physiology course. *Advances in Physiology Education, 12*(1), 105–108.

Hardy, L. (1999, October). Stress, anxiety, and performance. *Journal of Science and Medicine in Sports, 2*(3), 227–233.

Hart, L. A. (2002). *Human brain and human learning* (3rd ed.). Covington, WA: Books for Educators.

Haslam, S. A., Reicher, S. D., & Platow, M. J. (2011). *The new psychology of leadership: Identity, influence, and power*. New York: Psychology Press.

Hmelo-Silver, C. E., & Barrows, H. S. (2006). Goals and strategies of a problem-based learning facilitator. *Interdisciplinary Journal of Problem-based Learning, 1*(1), 21–39.

Horner, D. H., Pannell, L. P., & Yates, D. W. (2011). Creating a culture for leading and performing in the extreme. In P. J. Sweeney, M. D. Matthews, & P. B. Lester (Eds.), *Leading in dangerous situations* (pp. 313–332). Annapolis, MD: Naval Institute Press.

Humara, A. (1999, September). The relationship between anxiety and performance: A cognitive-behavioral model. *Athletic Insight, 1*(2), 1–14. Retrieved from http://www.athleticinsight.com/Vol1Iss2/CognitivePDF.pdf

Hundersmarck, S. (2004). *Sixteen weeks and a year: The generalization of knowledge and identity between the police academy and police field training* (Unpublished doctoral dissertation). Michigan State University, East Lansing, Michigan.

Hundersmarck, S. (2009). Police recruit training: Facilitating learning between the academy and field training. *FBI Law Enforcement Bulletin, 78*(8), 26–31.

Hunt, D. E., & Sullivan, E. V. (1974). *Between psychology and education*. Hinsdale, IL: The Dryden Press.

International Association of Chiefs of Police (IACP). (1997). *Ethics training in law enforcement: A report by the ethics training subcommittee of the IACP ad hoc committee on police image and ethics*. Retrieved from http://www.theiacp.org/PoliceServices/ExecutiveServices/ProfessionalAssistance/Ethics/ReportsResources/PoliceOfficerEthicsASelfAssessment/tabid/194/Default.aspx

Jackson, P. W. (1986). *The practice of teaching*. New York: Teachers College Press.

Jensen, E. (2005). *Teaching with the brain in mind* (2nd ed.). Alexandria, VA: Association for Superior Curriculum Development.

Johnson, T., Johnson, D., & White, J. (2005). *Organizational roadblocks to prevent public misconduct*. Paper presented at the Ethics and Integrity Governance: A Transatlantic Dialogue Conference, Leuven, Belgium, June 2–5, 2005.

Josephson, M. (1995). Police corruption. In D. Close & N. Meier (Eds.), *Morality in criminal justice* (pp. 285–313). New York: Wadsworth.

Kappeler, V. E., Sluder, R. D., & Alpert, G. P. (1998). *Forces of deviance: Understanding the dark side of policing* (2nd ed.). Long Grove, IL: Waveland Press.

Karp, H. J. (1983). The use of Keller's personalized system of instruction. *College Student Personnel Abstracts, no. 0298-19, 19*(1), 146.

Kasher, A. (2008). Teaching and training military ethics: An Israeli experience. In N. D. Lee, D. Carrick, & P. Robinson (Eds.), *Ethics education in the military* (pp. 133–146). Burlington, VA: Ashgate Publishing.

Kavanagh, J. (2005). *Stress and performance: A review of the literature and its application to the military*. Santa Monica, CA: RAND Corporation.

Kennedy, R. (2003). Applying principles of adult learning: The key to effective training programs. *FBI Law Enforcement Bulletin, 72*(4), 1–5.

Kleinig, J. (2002). Rethinking noble cause corruption. *International Journal of Police Science and Management, 4*(4), 287–314.

Knowles, M. (1980). *The modern practice of adult education: From pedagogy to andragogy* (2nd ed.). New York: Association Press.

Knowles, M. (1984). *Andragogy in action*. San Francisco: Jossey-Bass.

Kohlberg, L. (1981). *The philosophy of moral development*. San Francisco: Harper & Row.

Kooken, D. L. (1947). Ethics in police service (continued). *Journal of Criminal Law and Criminology, 38*, 172–186.

Kuhn, D., Shaw, V., & Felton, M. (1997). Effects of dyadic interaction on argumentative reasoning. *Cognition and Instruction, 15*(3), 287–315.

Ledoux, J. (1994). Emotion, memory, and the brain. *Scientific American, 270*(6), 50–57.

Ledoux, J. (1996). *The emotional brain: The mysterious underpinnings of emotional life*. New York: Simon & Schuster.

Lewis, K. G., & Woodward, P. (1984). *What really happens in large university classes?* Paper presented at an AERA Annual Conference, April, New Orleans, Louisiana. Retrieved from ERIC database. (ED245590)

Lewis, K. G., Woodward, P., & Bell, J. (1988). Teaching business communication skills in large classes. *Journal of Business Communication, 25*(1), 65–86.

Marenin, O. (2004). Police training for democracy. *Police Practice and Research, 5*(2), 107–123.

Massey, D. (1993). Why us and why? Some reflections on teaching ethics to police. *Police Studies, 16*(3), 77–83.

McGaugh, J. L. (1993) *Memory and emotion: The making of lasting memories*. New York: Columbia University Press.

McLeod, N. (1998). *What teachers cannot do in large classes* (Research Report No. 7). Leeds, UK: Leeds University.

Merriam, S. B., & Cafarella, R. S. (1999). *Learning in adulthood* (2nd ed.). San Francisco: Jossey-Bass.

Miller, S., Blackler, J., & Alexandra, A. (1997). *Police ethics*. St. Leonards, Australia: Allen and Unwin.

Moll, M. (2007). Improving American police ethics training: Focusing on social contract theory and constitutional principles. *Forum of Public Policy, 3*, 1–14.

Nystrand, M., & Gamoran, A. (1991). Instructional discourse, student engagement, and literature achievement. *Research in Teaching of English, 25*(3), 261–290.

Penner, J. G. (1984). *Why many college teachers cannot lecture*. Springfield, IL: Charles C. Thomas.

Phelps E. A., Sharot T. (2008) How (and why) emotion enhances the subjective sense of recollection. *Current Directions in Psychological Science, 17*(2), 147–152.

Pollock, J. M., & Becker, R. F. (1996). Ethics training using officers' dilemmas. *FBI Law Enforcement Bulletin, 65*(11), 20–27.

Qualters, D. (2001). Do students want to be active? *The Journal of Scholarship and Learning, 2*(1), 51–60.

Reece, I., & Walker, S. (2005). *Teaching, training, and learning* (5th ed.). Oxford: Business Education Publishers Limited.

Reith, C. (1948). *A short history of the British police*. London: Oxford University Press.

Robazza, C., & Bortoli, L. (2007). Perceived impact of anger and anxiety on sporting performance in rugby players. *Psychology of Sport and Exercise, 8*, 875–896.

Robinson, P. (2008). Ethics education in the military. In N. D. Lee, D. Carrick, & P. Robinson (Eds.), *Ethics education in the military* (pp. 1–14). Burlington, VT: Ashgate.

Saunders, T., Driskell, J. E, Johnston, J. H., & Salas, E. (1996). The effects of stress inoculation training on anxiety and performance. *Journal of Occupational Health Psychology, 1*(2), 170–186.

Scott, M. (2000). *Problem-oriented policing: Reflections on the first 20 years*. Washington, DC: U.S. Department of Justice, Office of Community Oriented Policing Services.

Skinner, B. F. (1968). *The technology of teaching*. Englewood Cliffs, NJ: Prentice-Hall.

Slavin, R. (1990). *Cooperative learning theory, research, and practice*. Englewood Cliffs, NJ: Prentice-Hall.

Solomon, R., & Solomon, J. (1993). *Up the university: Recreating higher education in America*. Reading, MA: Addison-Wesley.

Sousa, D. A. (2001). *How the brain learns* (2nd ed.). Thousand Oaks, CA: Sage.

Swanson, R. A., & Torraco, R. J. (1994). History of technical training. In L. A. Kelly (Ed.), *ASTD technical and skills training handbook* (pp. 1–47). New York: McGraw-Hill.

Swope, R. E. (1998). Ethics in law enforcement: The core-virtue bell curve. *The Police Chief, 2*(1), 37–38.

Tam, M. (2000). Constructivism, instructional design, and technology: Implications for transforming distance education. *Educational Technology & Society, 3*(2), 50–60.

Tough, A. (1983). Self-planned learning and major personal change. In M. Tight (Ed.), *Adult learning and education* (pp. 141–152). London: Croom Helm.

Trautman, N. E., & Prevost, A. (2005, June). *Police ethics training state-of-the-art now more effective and comprehensive*. Retrieved March 5, 2011 from http://www.ethicsinstitute.com/EthicsTraining.htm

Van Slyke, J. M. (2007). *Police ethics training: Preferred modes of teaching in higher education law enforcement* (Unpublished doctoral dissertation). The University of Texas in Austin, Texas.

Vicchio, S. J. (1997, January). Ethics and police integrity: Some definitions and questions for study. In National Institute of Justice (Ed.), *Police integrity: Public service with honor* (pp. 11–17). Washington, DC: U.S. Department of Justice.

Vodde, R. (2008) *The efficacy of an andragogical instructional methodology in basic police training and education* (Unpublished doctoral dissertation). University of Leicester, London, England.

White, M. D. (2007). *Current issues and controversies in policing*. Boston: Pearson Education.

Wiencek, J., & O'Flahavan, J. F. (1994). From teacher-led to peer discussions about literature: Suggestions for making the shift. *Language Arts, 71*(7), 488–498.

Willington, D. T. (2009). *Why don't students like school? A cognitive scientist answers questions concerning how the mind works and what it means for your classroom.* San Francisco: Jossey-Bass.

Wlodkowski, R. J. (1985). *Enhancing adult motivation to learn: A guide to improving instruction and increasing learner achievement.* San Francisco: Jossey-Bass.

4

The Role of Supervision in Motivating and Maintaining a Culture of Ethics

Brian D. Fitch, Randolph B. Means, and Greg Seidel

Officers Davis and Contreras arrived for their shift briefing five minutes late. Officer Davis nodded to the sergeant, took his customary seat at the back of the room, and put his feet up on a table. In contrast, Officer Contreras apologized to the sergeant, took a seat at the front of the room, and opened his field notebook to write down any important information gleaned from the briefing. Officers Davis and Contreras both joined the agency seven years ago. Both officers had worked similar assignments, had similar levels of police experience, and had similar disciplinary histories. However, it was common knowledge throughout the department that Davis and the sergeant were personal friends who spent much of their off-duty time riding motorcycles together. At the end of the briefing, the sergeant turned to Officer Davis, held up his hands, and stated, "Try to be on time tomorrow." Davis laughed, got up from his seat, and left the room. Next, the sergeant focused his attention on Officer Contreras. "Look, you can't show up late to briefing; it sets a bad example," he said. "Follow me to the sergeant's office, so that I can document this in your performance log." "Hold on, Sarg," Contreras complained, "this isn't fair." As Contreras followed the sergeant down the hall, he declared, "If we were both late, why am I the only person being written up?" Contreras signed the performance log entry and left the office;

however, several days later, the sergeant was summoned to the chief's office to explain the write up. Officer Contreras, it seems, had filed a formal grievance for disparate treatment.

This scenario illustrates the adverse legal effects, poor working conditions, and just plain confusion that can result when supervisors fail to enforce organizational policy fairly and equitably. This chapter focuses on effective organizational and supervisory practices in motivating and managing a culture of ethics. The authors begin by examining the need for clear, concise policies and directives, as well as suggestions for developing and implementing effective rules and guidelines. Next, the chapter outlines the role of supervision in confronting and correcting poor performance, including a discussion of performance counseling. The chapter concludes by investigating the fundamental legal requirements of workplace equity, as well the importance of developing and implanting an employee recognition system.

Introduction

In simplest terms, police misconduct is defined as wrongdoing committed by a police officer in relation to his official duties (Palmiotto, 2001). This includes engaging in misconduct that an officer knows or should reasonably know is improper, immoral, or illegal, as well as failing to do something that an officer knows or should reasonably know is required. One popular remedy for misconduct suggests that the key to organization ethics lies in hiring good people (Guthrie, 2008). According to this theory, if an agency invests the time, resources, and monies necessary to identify, select, and train only the most qualified candidates, misconduct should all but disappear. The idea that good people will behave ethically, regardless of the circumstances or situational pressures, is based on the notion that a person's behavior is a reflection of their character. Proponents of character-based approaches argue that certain officers engage in misconduct, abuse, or corruption simply because they lack the requisite moral character for police work (Josephson, 2009).

While an officer's character is certainly important, there is, however, a problem with this thesis—namely, that law enforcement agencies go to great lengths to identify, select, and train candidates with a demonstrated history of good moral behavior. To be considered for a law enforcement position, applicants must complete a lengthy background process, including a physical fitness assessment; polygraph examination; written test; medical health screening; background interview; credit review; and interviews with family members, friends, and previous employers (Fischler, 2001). Moreover, there is evidence to suggest that moral values, education, and religiosity often have little impact on behavior. In other words, despite the best of intentions, good people often do bad things by engaging in unethical, immoral, or illegal conduct. For example, a 2002 national study of 12,000 high school students reported the following: 74% admitted cheating on an exam at least once in the past year; 38% admitted shoplifting at least once in the past year; and 37% admitted that they would lie "in order to get a good job" (Josephson, 2002).

The fact that many otherwise good people will cheat when provided an appropriate opportunity (Ariely, 2012) is further complicated by the finding that no profession is more susceptible to "noble cause" corruption than law enforcement. Certainly, the idea of making the world a safer place by "doing something about bad people" is a powerful temptation to do whatever is necessary to accomplish the mission (Crank & Caldero, 2000). Nonetheless, scholars, educators, and practitioners have identified a number of "best practices" available to law enforcement supervisors, managers, and senior leaders to address and, in some cases, prevent misconduct in workplace. This includes the development and enforcement of clear policy, proper supervisory practices, effective performance counseling, and the proper use of discipline and rewards. The remainder of this chapter examines each of these variables in greater detail.

Policy

Organizations throughout the United States, including law enforcement, have begun to recognize the importance of being explicit about the types of behaviors that are ethically acceptable and those viewed as unacceptable (Grojean, Resick, Dickson, & Smith, 2004). Today, most law enforcement agencies build ethical standards into their system of written directives—that is, the policies and procedures, as well as the state and federal laws, that prescribe the standards of conduct that an agency expects from its members (Schroeder, Lombardo, & Strollo, 2006). Theoretically, then, all a police organization has to do to achieve the desired ethical standards is get officers to follow the rules. The same construct applies to the law. Unfortunately, as the all-too-familiar litany of law enforcement misconduct cases featured in the media will testify, this is not always the case.

One argument is that, while officers understand the policy and the law involved, they choose to behave unethically by weighing the expected value (cost versus benefits) of their behavioral options. According to this theory, often referred to as the *rational model of decision-making*, a person decides on a course of action by: identifying the problem, generating possible solutions, and selecting the best outcome (Robbins, 2005). In other words, an officer chooses to behave ethically because the expected rewards of doing so (value) outweigh the cost of misconduct. Conversely, when an officer engages in misconduct, he does so because the expected utility for doing so (value) is greater than the expected value for behaving ethically. This representation of human decision making, however, rests on a number of fundamental assumptions, most notably that the individual recognizes the ethical nature of the situation, understands fully the consequences of each choice, decides on a course of action based on the rationale consideration of expected value, and possesses the requisite moral motivation to pursue that choice of behavior (Chen, Sawyers, & Williams, 1997; Josephson, 2009; Robbins, 2005).

Despite the continued popularity of this model, there is considerable empirical data to suggest that human beings are not the rational, objective decision makers they were once believed to be (see, e.g., Kahneman, 2011). Rather, it appears that human reasoning, decision making, and behavior are more often the product of emotion than logic. In many cases, the short-term emotional gratification of misconduct serves as a powerful motivator, especially in those cases where the probability of punishment is low. Evidence suggests that in many day-to-day decisions, the emotional brain (limbic system) reaches a conclusion long before the more logical neocortex has fully processed the information (Goleman, 1994). Once a judgment has been reached, the higher centers of the brain construct a plausible narrative of the logic supporting the decision, effectively allowing the individual to maintain a belief that their decision was the product of logic and reason, rather than emotion (Gazzaniga, 2011). The human preference for emotion can be especially troubling during high-stress incidents, such as vehicular pursuits, physical altercations, or officer-involved shootings.

Ethical conduct and accountability begin with the development and implementation of policies and procedures that provide officers with clear, consistent expectations. The presence of appropriate guidelines empowers officers to work in ways that establish accountability to professional standards, while avoiding a range of pitfalls, including disciplinary action and civil litigation (Alpert & Smith, 1994; Wasserman, 1982). However, despite widespread agreement on the importance of policy, experts often disagree on the amount of specificity or detail required—that is, whether policy manuals should contain specific rules or general guidelines.

Rules Versus Guidelines

A *guideline* is defined as a statement or other indication of policy or procedure used to determine a particular course of action (National Association of EMS Physicians, 1989). In contrast, a *rule* is a managerial mandate that either requires or prohibits certain behavior (Alpert & Smith, 1994). Proponents of guidelines argue that it is impossible to develop and implement rules that could apply properly to every conceivable set of circumstances an officer might encounter. In light of the potential number of scenarios to which a rule might be applied, many organizational managers also worry about the notion of being tethered to a particular position (Clawson, Martin, & Hauert, 1994). This debate has been further complicated by attorneys who suggest the inadvisability of implementing hard and fast rules, as doing so might adversely impact an agency's ability to defend against potential litigation (Means, 2008b).

In either case, the key issue is employee performance—in other words, officers performing their duties in a manner consistent with established policy (Clawson et al., 1994). One way of resolving the issue is the conspicuous presence of the following wording at the beginning of a policy manual:

> This manual contains both policies and procedures, both rules and guidelines. Employees are expected and required to adhere to the provisions of this document. However, no policy manual could ever anticipate all of the infinite fact situations that an employee could face in the course of organizational and human affairs. In the event that an employee reasonably and honestly believes that to follow a policy or rule in this manual would cause an illegal, unjust, or significantly inappropriate outcome, the employee may be excused from adherence to the policy or rule in question. In the event that an employee perceives that such a situation exists and consequently chooses to deviate from the requirements of this manual, the burden will be on the employee to prove that the circumstances he or she faced made it unreasonable to follow policy or rule. If the employee can establish that such was the case, the employee's deviation from the policy or rule will be excused. (Means, 2008b)

A related issue is the concern regarding policy length—that is, whether policy should be lengthy and detailed or relatively short and general (Alpert & Smith, 1994). Arguments in favor of short, general policies typically involve rationale similar to that historically used to promote guidelines rather than rules. For example, no amount of policy detail could ever address all the possible questions that could arise in the imponderably broad scope of law enforcement involvement. However, short, general policies present their own set of challenges. Most notably, short, general policies tend to be vague and nonspecific in application (Wasserman, 1982). According to Means (2008b), effective policies proscribe general duties and obligations, as well as how those standards are applied. Put differently, officers need to know not only the policy itself, but how the policy should be practiced in the real world.

Alpert and Smith (1994) suggest that law enforcement policies and regulations should

1. be workable in real-world situations;

2. be adaptable to training;

3. be written in a positive manner;

4. refer to or incorporate relevant laws;

5. be pretested to assure that all officers understand the specific intent and consequences for noncompliance;

6. include in-service training, as a matter of record, for all officers and supervisors; and

7. provide proactive examples of behavior.

As a response to the inconsistencies among law enforcement policy throughout the United States, the International Association of Chiefs of Police (IACP) established a National Law Enforcement Policy Center (1991). The center has developed a comprehensive compilation of model policies concerning some of the most difficult issues facing law enforcement, including the use of force, deadly force, and pursuit driving. These model policies were developed to provide general guideline to agencies based on commonalities for high-risk activities. For example, the model policy regarding "use of force" includes the following:

A. Purpose

B. Policy (statement of philosophy)

C. Definitions

D. Procedures
   a. Parameters for the use of deadly force
   b. Parameters for the use of nondeadly force
   c. Training and qualifications
   d. Reporting use of force
   e. Department response (investigation, documentation, and administrative review)

Once officers are familiar with organizational expectations, supervisors at all levels must proactively enforce those directives. This includes confronting and correcting poor performance through appropriate performance counseling, implementing protocols for investigating misconduct, and documenting all incidents of deviant behavior in ways that make the information available to managers at all levels in the organization (Trautman, 2000). This should include the type of misconduct, the personnel involved, and the measures used to address the problem.

Supervision

Law enforcement supervisors ensure proper compliance with policy by confronting and correcting the behavior of officers who violate organizational directives, and recognizing and rewarding the conduct of officers who adhere to those same mandates (Fitch, 2011). Supervisors have a range of proactive tools at their disposal, including audits, inspections, early warning criteria, and employee recognition awards (Newham, 2002). Fortunately, most officers support the organization, work hard, and follow department directives. When problems do arise, they are usually solved quickly, typically requiring little more than an informal discussion (Fitch, 2011). Nonetheless, performance problems, including policy violations and misconduct, invariably arise. The ways supervisors handle these challenges can have a profound impact on organizational culture, employee motivation, and future incidents of misconduct (Governor's Office of Employee Relations, 2010). While many supervisors do a competent job rewarding good behavior, they often hesitate to address performance problems, particularly the failure of officers to follow policy, because they lack the necessary tools, training, and resources to do so effectively.

Supervisors are responsible for ensuring that all officers under their command are familiar with organizational policies and procedures, as well as state and federal laws, by verifying that officers are properly trained—and documenting the results of those sessions. Too often, supervisors assume that employees understand the requirements, missing important opportunities to mentor officers, address substandard performance, and mitigate misconduct (Grote, 2006). Once a supervisor becomes aware of unethical conduct or poor performance, he has a responsibility to confront and correct the officer's behavior, including an appropriate level of documentation and, if necessary, discipline. In many instances, however, a properly conducted performance counseling session may be all that is required to correct inappropriate behavior.

A performance counseling session is a discussion about an employee's work-related performance, typically focused on a particular aspect of the officer's performance that fails to meet organizational standards. The goals of the discussion are

- to communicate the organization's performance expectation in clear, objective, and measurable terms;
- to determine the reason for the employee's actions;
- to outline a specific plan for improvement or development; and
- to improve the employee's performance.

Performance Counseling

Setting limits, holding officers accountable, and confronting poor performance can be difficult for many supervisors. Absent the proper skills and training, most supervisors fall naturally into one of two categories—they either attempt to coerce employees into performing appropriately or they try to avoid problems altogether (Grote, 2006). In the first instance, the supervisor relies on formal authority to compel acceptable performance. Supervisors using this approach often fail to employ basic leadership skills, such as building relationships and rewarding appropriate behavior (Kouzes & Posner, 2007). While this approach is often effective at producing short-term results, it seldom motivates the type of long-term behavioral change necessary to correct chronic performance issues. In contrast, supervisors who rely on the second strategy tend to avoid problems because they are uncomfortable confronting employees. Unfortunately, when supervisors fail to address poor performance, the problem officer seldom improves and, in many instances, the behaviors in question only get worse (Daniels, 2007).

One reason that supervisors stumble in their efforts to address poor performance is their failure to prepare adequately for the session. To begin with, supervisors should focus their attention on objective, quantifiable behaviors, not intangibles like feelings, beliefs, or attitudes (Daniels, 2007). The discussion should focus on the performance expectation or policy the officer has violated, the agency's standard, and the necessary behavioral change. If an officer has a "poor attitude," for example, but performs the job well, there is often little need for performance counseling, although the supervisor may opt to send the employee to leadership or human-relations training. One effective way of preparing for a performance counseling session is to create an outline highlighting the main points of the meetings. Preparing ahead of time can significantly increase a supervisor's chances of success by enhancing confidence, insulating against manipulation, and providing appropriate references (Grote, 2006).

The basic philosophy behind performance counseling in any law enforcement agency is the same: Each individual officer must be responsible for his own performance (Miller, 2006). Thus, supervisors preparing for a performance counseling session should focus on the following areas of concern:

Investigate the Problem

As an old adage suggests, "Failing to prepare is preparing to fail"—and nowhere is this more accurate than performance counseling. Prior to meeting with an employee, the supervisor should research the details of any instance in question (Phil Varnak Associates, 2008). For example, if an officer has received a string of discourtesy complaints, the supervisor should be armed with the dates, times, and specifics of each incident. Performing the necessary research will, among other things, enhance the supervisor's credibility, keep the conversation focused, and lay the groundwork for a successful resolution (Governor's Office of Employee Relations, 2010).

Describe the Required Performance

When discussing performance, the supervisor should be as specific and objective as possible, being especially careful to avoid vague or fuzzy statements of performance, such as "I want you to be more positive" or "I want you to enjoy your job." The supervisor's statement of desired performance should explain the organizational standard in clear behavioral terms that can be easily understood, observed, and measured (Daniels, 2007). Because supervisors often fail to develop a concise behavioral definition of organizational objectives or proper behaviors, they speak in general, abstract terms. Yet if a supervisor expects an officer to understand precisely what is expected of him, he must describe the desired performance clearly and objectively (Governor's Office of Employee Relations, 2010).

Outline the Reasons

Absent a compelling reason, no performance discussion should ever take place. Preparing and presenting a list of reasons helps the officer understand why his conduct is inappropriate, as well as why it needs to be changed (Governor's Office of Employee Relations, 2010). More importantly, however, it can help to gain the officer's cooperation in solving the problem. Officers, like most people, tend to do better with the "what" if they understand the "why." While this process is not very difficult for most supervisors, it is critical to the success of any meaningful outcome.

Discuss the Consequences

Regardless of an officer's reasons for poor performance, the meeting should include a discussion of the logical consequences that will follow should the employee choose to continue his poor performance (Garber, 2004). This is not to suggest that a supervisor should threaten an officer, but merely to highlight the natural implications of any future conduct—either positive or negative—for the employee. Because it is ultimately the officer who will decide whether or not to improve his performance and who will endure the consequences of that decision, the employee should understand under no uncertain terms precisely what is at stake (Fitch, 2011).

While there are no specific guidelines as to when performance counseling is necessary, a session is generally appropriate when an officer fails to meet agency standards, violates policy, or otherwise demonstrates poor or unsafe performance (Miller, 2006; Phil Varnak Associates, 2008). It is also important to note that once a supervisor has identified the need for counseling, the session should be conducted promptly before a pattern of problematic behavior is allowed to develop. Employees may interpret a supervisor's failure to address performance problems promptly as tacit approval, essentially encouraging the behavior to continue. Furthermore, supervisors should document the session, including a statement of the reason for the meeting, date and time, and clear expectations for future performance (Governor's Office of Employee Relations, 2010). If personal problems are interfering with the employee's performance, the supervisors should recommend the services of an employee assistance program. Finally, it is paramount that supervisors demonstrate consistency and fairness when enforcing organizational policy, counseling employees, and documenting rule violations.

Consistency

Consistency begins with the understanding that all members of the organization are accountable to the same standards of conduct (Chen et al., 1997; Grojean et al., 2004). According to Stoner (1989), consistency occurs on two levels: consistency throughout the organization and consistency through a variety of situations. First, consistency throughout the organization asserts that the types of behaviors demonstrated at one level of the organization are the same as those accepted at other (typically lower) levels. In other words, senior leaders live by the same set of rules as line officers. Perhaps even more important is that the behaviors of first-line, middle-level, and upper-level leaders are consistent. Consistency in a variety of situations, on the other hand, asserts that the company adheres to the same ethical standards of behavior regardless of the situation or stressors.

One important facet of consistency concerns the rules requiring supervisors to document and report misconduct (IACP, 2006). If organizations require that only major misconduct be documented, this can create inconsistency in determining the types of actions that must be reported. This is not to suggest that senior leadership should personally handle minor problems. Obviously, there are a variety of concerns that should be handled by first-line supervisors that include arriving late to work, abusing sick time, or minor traffic incidents. Rather, it implies that consistency in handling misconduct must be monitored and managed to assure the required levels of fairness (Trautman, 2000).

It is important to note, however, that supervisors must not only be consistent with those whom they supervise; they must also be consistent with each other. To achieve the necessary consistency among supervisors, the organization must develop protocols that govern the handling of critical matters, like abuse, corruption, or misconduct—and enforce those rules across all levels of the organization (Newham, 2002). Fairness and equity dictate that one employee cannot receive a stern warning for the same behavior that eventually results in the suspension or termination of another employee. Most employees have an innate sense of fundamental fairness, while violating those beliefs can have a negative impact on officer morale, job satisfaction, and misconduct.

Fairness

Fairness is concerned with how individuals evaluate and react to differences in treatment. Equity theory (Adams, 1965) proposes that people are motivated by fairness in social exchanges (Miles, Hatfield, & Husmen,

1989). Employees consider how they are treated by supervisors—relative to the way salient others are considered under similar circumstances—to decide if they are being handled fairly or not. Equity theory suggests that employees weight what they put into a job (input) against what they get from it (output), and compare that ration to the input–output ratio of other workers. Input characteristics include the qualities and characteristics that an employee possesses, such as age, gender, seniority, social status, education, effort, skill, and ability. Employees tend to be happiest when their input–output ratio is equal to that of others in the same referent group. If the ratio is unequal, the employee tends to view himself as being under- or over-rewarded (Adam, 1965).

An employee's perceptions of fairness within a given social exchange are important to the development and maintenance of motivation, job satisfaction, and performance (Kohn, 1986). If an employee perceives the exchange between input (effort) and output (reward) as unfair, he may engage in a variety of misconduct, including corruption, theft, and bribery, in an effort to resolve the inequity (Adams, 1965). Greenberg (1990), for example, found that employees whose pay was reduced without explanation corrected the imbalance by engaging in high levels of employee theft. In contrast, if the employee perceives the exchange as fair, he is more likely to maintain his current level of performance—and, in some cases, go beyond the normal dictates of the job.

Notions of equity and fairness in matters of supervision and discipline play key roles in several measures of job-related performance. If an officer believes that he is being treated equitably and fairly, he will be more likely to accept corrective actions, maintain a positive attitude toward the organization, and feel less alienated (IACP, 2006). In contrast, when an officer views discipline as unfair, unpredictable, or unjust, he is less likely to accept corrective actions. The officer is also more likely to undermine the process, develop a negative attitude toward supervision, and feel alienated. It can further be argued that a perception of unfair discipline may support the development of a "code of silence" among officers, while undermining the legitimacy of the disciplinary process itself (Trautman, 2000).

Legal Requirements

Equity is more than a social phenomenon. It is a legal obligation: Employees are protected by certain entitlements created by specific laws (U.S. Equal Opportunity Commission, 2009). When an employer (or the employer's agent) treats one employee differently than another without good cause, particularly when these scenarios involve differences in race, ethnicity, gender, age, religion, or other protected class, it likely prohibited discrimination and illegal. In other instances, where state or local governments create, by force of law, a reasonable expectation of continued employment (as contrasted with "at will" employment), employees are protected by Fourteenth Amendment "property interests" in their pay and career (Means, 2011). In such cases, employees are entitled to due process of law in matters concerning salary, benefits, and employment. Due process comes in two types: procedural and substantive.

Due Process

Procedural due process involves things like rights to hearings and to receive timely notice of exactly what one is accused of doing wrong (Merriam & Sitkowski, 1998). Substantive due process involves fundamental fairness, which is just that. For example, when an employer treats one employee differently than another, absent a compelling legal justification, in matters affecting pay or the job itself, such treatment is fundamentally unfair and illegal, irrespective of race or gender issues (Means, 2011). When such disparate treatment involves people of different classifications by race, age, gender, national origin, or religion, it is likely to be prohibited discrimination and even more illegal. Whether or not it's actually illegal, it is bad practice because it's ethically and morally wrong.

As mentioned, one kind of notice involves an employee's right to hearings, including time and place (Merriam & Sitowski, 1998). While failures in this area can lead to litigation, a bigger problem involves a more subtle ethical question: Has the employer provided the employee with clear notice of expectations—in particular, requirements and prohibitions? If an employee has a "property interest" in his salary and employment, and the employer is attempting to take away one or both, the employer must prove that the employee was on notice of the rule he is accused of violating (Trautman, 2000). Thus, if an organization wishes to proscribe certain types of association, the agency must create a rule prohibiting such conduct. In many cases, a rule prohibiting "conduct unbecoming an officer" will not suffice because it fails to provide employees with clear notice of the prohibited behavior (Means, 2008b).

Proportionality

In matters of employee discipline, *proportionality* refers to the fact that the punishment must fit (be proportionate to) the "crime." Any form of discrimination, unfairness, or inequality in the treatment of employees can expose the agency to potential litigation (Brown & Welch, 2002), as well as damage an employee's respect for the organization (Felton, 2009). Thus, it would be fundamentally unfair, for example, to fire a long-tenured, exemplary employee for being five minutes late to work one time.

Law enforcement agencies have tried a variety of methods to ensure consistent, effective discipline. One method has been to adopt a matrix system

(IACP, 2006). Under a rigid matrix system, any employee who violates a rule receives the level of punishment assigned to that rule, regardless of the circumstances, the severity of the violation, or the employee's disciplinary history. Other agencies have adopted a variation of the rigid matrix system that assigns different punishments (or a range of punishments) to rule violations depending on a given set of factors that, if present, may modify the punishment within a certain range. For instance, an employee with no prior history of discipline who violates a rule may receive a written reprimand, while another officer who violates the same rule, but who has a history of discipline for similar offenses, may receive a suspension. A third method is best described as comparative discipline. Under such a system, a chief will generally consider the facts of the particular incident, the significance and severity of the violation, the employee's record, and the potential exposure for liability before deciding on a course of action (Risher, 2005).

Clearly, employees want to know that their punishment is consistent with the punishment received by other officers for similar acts of misconduct. To be consistent, the punishment for one officer's act of misconduct must be the same or closely similar to the punishment given other officers who committed the same or similar acts (IACP, 2006). Properly employed, a disciplinary matrix can help eliminate perceptions of unfairness by eliminating an officer's gender, race, seniority, and other characteristics from the process.

Regardless of the type of system an agency employs, consistency and proportionality are critical to perceptions of fairness, equality, and effectiveness (Risher, 2005). This requires that agencies maintain a well-planned and well-designed tracking system to ensure that all supervisors are familiar with the facts of all alleged cases of discipline and the corrective measures taken in each instance. Additionally, agency leaders must ensure that they can articulate the basis for any disciplinary differences or disparities if a discrimination issue arises. For example, if an agency awards substantially more discipline to a female officer than to a male officer for a similar violation, the administrator must be able to articulate the specific basis for the discipline, as well as be able to demonstrate that, despite the fact that it appears the agency is treating the female officer differently than her male counterpart, the additional discipline was warranted given the totality of the circumstance, and the same amount of discipline would have been awarded to a male officer with the same disciplinary history (*Shaw v. Stroud*, 1994).

Timeliness

The last legal consideration, timeliness, is an important aspect of fairness. Supervisors and managers must provide employees with timely notice of their failure to meet organizational expectations (Trautman, 2000). This provides employees with an opportunity to improve their deficiency in performance before it becomes a bigger problem. To meet the requirements of timeliness, all supervisory counseling sessions that address issues of performance should be documented (Felton, 2009). Documentation not only provides employees with important opportunities to address performance deficiencies; it offers a vital record in the event the employee later challenges some form of disciplinary action taken against him as a result of poor performance or other behavioral issues. Without such documentation, it is not possible to ensure disciplinary consistency for the same officer or other employees who have engaged in similar misconduct, nor is it possible to respond effectively to potential disciplinary appeals (IACP, 2006). It is important to note that documentation applies equally to all disciplinary measures, including verbal reprimands and counseling.

Finally, any disciplinary action that is forthcoming should be delivered as soon as the matter can be rightly decided (Denver Police Department, 2008). Officers should not be left uninformed about the possibility of disciplinary action for any longer than it takes to gather the facts, conduct an investigation, and decide on an appropriate outcome. Even if an officer is placed on administrative leave with pay, he will no doubt believe that lengthy delays in the process are fundamentally unfair.

Employee Motivation

The final factor to consider is the supervisor's role in employee motivation, including the application of rewards and punishments in shaping appropriate behaviors. In simplest terms, motivation is defined as the inner force that compels individuals to accomplish personal and organizational goals (Lindner, 1998). It is the driving force that helps explain why people pursue certain goals, how they attempt to accomplish those goals, how hard they will work to do so, and the degree of adversity they are willing to overcome. Employees are typically motivated by a combination of external (i.e., pay and benefits) and internal (i.e., commitment and positive affect) factors. Of the two types, internal motivation is most significantly correlated with measures of employee performance, including organizational commitment, job performance, absenteeism, and turnover (Chatman & Malka, 2003; Tella, Ayeni, & Popoola, 2007).

Supervisors' beliefs, attitudes, and leadership skills play an important role in enhancing officer performance (Engel, 2003; Pelletier & Vallerand, 1996). Because supervisors sometimes believe that officers are motivated primarily by pay and benefits, they can feel powerless to influence their subordinates. However, as most administrators know from personal experience, there can be significant differences between the motivation and productivity of employees working for the same organization but for different supervisors. These differences are often the result of effective and ineffective supervisory practices (Engel, 2003; Engel & Worden, 2003). A supervisor's behaviors and attitudes have a direct impact on the ways officers perceive their roles and responsibilities, how strongly they identify with the agency's values and mission, and how valuable officers believe they are to their organizations, coworkers, and communities.

One facet of workplace motivation is the extent to which officers believe the agency cares about their contributions and welfare (Eisenberger, Cummings, Armeli, & Lynch, 1997). This construct, commonly termed *perceived organizational support*, is especially important for supervisors to understand because officers' beliefs are, to a large extent, based on the actions of their immediate managers. Because most officers have only limited contact with senior leadership, the administration's credibility often depends on the conduct of first-line supervisors. Officers view the behaviors of their immediate supervisors as signs of their value by the larger agency—that is, an indication of the agency's commitment to its officers. If officers believe that the department cares about their welfare, goals, and career aspirations, they are more likely to see the agency in a positive light (Eisenberger, Huntington, Hutchison, & Sowa, 1986; Levinson, 1965). On the other hand, when officers feel that the agency is not concerned with their welfare, they perceive little organizational support, which can generate negative emotions and lower performance.

Not surprisingly, officers believe that being valued by their agency is likely to result in a variety of benefits, including approval, respect, and promotion. To the extent that officers and their departments value the relationship, they rely on the norm of reciprocity to meet their needs (Settoon, Bennett, & Liden, 1996). As long as officers believe that their efforts are being rewarded, they will be satisfied with their agency (Homans, 1958; Wayne, Shore, & Liden, 1997). However, when the department fails to reward officers for their hard work and commitment, it can have a negative effect on morale and productivity. Supervisors should also remember that employees' goals help determine the direction, intensity, and persistence of their behavior. The organizational goals that officers select are based on the anticipated rewards or punishments associated with those choices (Skinner, 1974). Officers who believe that their efforts on behalf of the department will be rewarded are more likely to pursue the agency's goals. In contrast, when officers feel that their work will go unrecognized or unrewarded, they are less likely to identify with their agency's objectives (Truckenbrodt, 2000; Wayne et al., 1997). Thus, supervisors, managers, and senior leadership should take every opportunity to reward and reinforce appropriate behavior, including the development of formal recognition systems.

Reward Systems

Law enforcement agencies are traditionally organized in a paramilitary structure with a specific chain of command (Alpert & Smith, 1994). This type of arrangement suggests a strong need for control-type management, with many supervisory practices based on the negative reinforcement of behavior. Indeed, police policies are regularly stated negatively, often leading to micromanagement by limiting behavioral alternatives through the strict enforcement of rules, policies, and procedures. Rather than reward officers for their application to duty, management focuses on disciplining officers for their misconduct. While the implementation of fair and consistent discipline is critical to the success of all law enforcement organizations, this philosophy runs contrary to decades of research demonstrating the effectiveness of positive reinforcement in shaping behavior (Kazdin, 2001).

Behavioral scientists generally recognize two types of reinforcement: (1) positive and (2) negative (Catania, 1998; Kazdin, 2001; Ormrod, 2008). Positive reinforcement occurs when an officer is rewarded for performing the correct behavior. In contrast, negative reinforcement occurs when some unwanted condition—a supervisor yelling, for example—is removed once an officer completes the desired task. Or, put another way, positive reinforcement rewards officers for performing a given behavior, while negative reinforcement motivates officers to do just enough to avoid something they don't want, such as discipline. Both positive and negative reinforcement, if used properly, increase the frequency of a behavior (Skinner, 1974). While negative reinforcement usually produces little more than grudging compliance, with officers doing no more than is necessary to avoid a supervisor's wrath, that can be all that is required in certain circumstances, such as an officer obeying the dictates of the agency's sexual harassment policy.

The third consequence, punishment, decreases the frequency of behavior when applied properly (Skinner, 1953). Punishment occurs when an officer either gets something that he does not want (reprimand or suspension) or loses something of value that he does want (pay or promotional opportunity). Unlike reinforcement, punishment is used to remove unwanted or dangerous behaviors on the assumption that those actions are less likely to be repeated in the future. To be effective, punishment should be applied fairly, consistently, immediately, and, in most cases, only after an officer has received notice of the job requirements and consequences for violating the standard (Ormrod, 2008).

It is worth recognizing that consequences have no inherent, intrinsic value in and of themselves. In other words, consequences are neither good nor bad. The effectiveness of a consequence is measured simply by its effect on behavior (Skinner, 1971). While some consequences are positive and rewarding—increasing the probability that a behavior will be repeated—others can be negative and punishing, decreasing the likelihood that a particular action will reoccur in the future under similar circumstances. How well an officer learns and demonstrates a particular activity is influenced by the strength of the relationship between the behavior and its consequence (Anderson, 2000). Simply put, the greater the number of times a particular action is paired with a reinforcing outcome, the more likely an officer is to perform the behavior under similar circumstances in the future (Ormrod, 2008).

Common Mistakes

While the basic application of consequences appears straightforward enough, even the best intentions of supervisors can fall short. Behavioral psychologists have identified four critical factors that tend to influence how effective consequences will be at shaping behavior:

Perception

Human beings vary widely in their likes and dislikes. What is positive for one officer may not necessarily be rewarding to another. The same principle applies to punishment: What one officer finds punishing, another may not. One common mistake among supervisors is the belief that others should value the same things that they do. To be effective, supervisors must get to know their officers, recognize their likes and dislikes, and apply rewards and punishments accordingly (Daniels, 2000).

Contingency

The effective use of reinforcement also depends heavily on how incentives are delivered. Contingency refers to the relationship between a behavior and a consequence (Skinner, 1971). Rewards can be either contingent or noncontingent on behavior. If an officer must perform a particular behavior before receiving an incentive, the reward is contingent on the activity. In contrast, if he receives a reward without completing the appropriate task, the reinforcer is noncontingent. Performance management is only successful to the degree that supervisors make rewards contingent on appropriate behaviors (Daniels, 2000).

Timing

As a general rule, the greater the delay between a response and its consequence, the slower the learning (Ormrod, 2008). When a supervisor reinforces what an officer is doing while the employee is doing it, the behavior will almost certainly be strengthened. In contrast, any time a supervisor reinforces an action after it has stopped, he runs the risk of strengthening some other behavior the officer is performing at the time. When supervisors apply immediate reinforcement, officers stand a better chance of understanding precisely which behaviors are being emphasized (Catania, 1998).

Consistency

Contrary to conventional wisdom, rewarding or punishing one instance of performance rarely results in a lasting change in behavior (Daniels, 2000).

In fact, psychologists have found that shaping a particular behavior can require hundreds—and, in some cases, thousands—of reinforcements before any lasting change can be expected to occur. It is only through the contingent, timely, consistent application of meaningful consequences that supervisors can expect any lasting change to occur (Skinner, 1971).

Research has demonstrated that the ethical behavior of employees is significantly related to the reinforcement and support offered by the organization. For example, the 2003 National Business Ethics Survey found that approximately 40% of those surveyed would not report misconduct if they observed it for fear of reprisal from management (Ethics Resource Center, 2003). Thus, law enforcement organizations must work to create systems that reward ethical conduct, while punishing misconduct swiftly, fairly, and appropriately (Kaikati & Label, 1980). This includes rewarding and valuing those employees who demonstrate appropriate moral conduct, adhere to policy, and follow the law, even when doing so reflects negatively on statistical measures of effectiveness, such as arrests and citations (Stoner, 1989).

The basic principles of reward and reinforcement are constantly at work in all law enforcement organizations. In fact, virtually everything an officer says or does receives some type of reinforcement—positive or negative, intentional or unintentional (Skinner, 1974). Rather than relying on luck or happenstance, good supervisors look for ways to reward ethical performance by continuously scanning the work environment for examples of ethical conduct (Fitch, 2011). This includes employees who adhere to organizational policy, obey the law, and set a positive example for others to follow. Similarly, effective leaders are quick to confront and correct poor performance, investigate allegations of misconduct, and document their findings.

Recognition

Means (2008a) suggests that a proper reward system for law enforcement professionals should include recognition for an officer's ability to demonstrate proficiency in a number of core competencies, such as knowledge and policy, human relations and interpersonal skills, physical fitness, and tactical and driving abilities. A system might include ten criteria for evaluation, with a "star" awarded for each category, provided the officer is able to meet certain standards.

Knowledge

The first rating requires an officer to demonstrate an appropriate level of knowledge in proper decision making and appropriate actions. At a minimum, this should include knowledge of law, policy, and other critical professional information.

Human Relations Skills

The second category represents the presence of good human relations skills. Interpersonal communication abilities are arguably the most important skill set an officer can possess, and proper evaluation requires measurement of those skills. The assessment of such skills might involve graded role-play performance, similar to firearms proficiency tests.

Physical Preparedness

The third measure represents an officer's level of physical preparedness to perform the essential physical functions of law enforcement, many of which may not occur during a particular rating period. Thus, similar to human relations skills, this rating should require the officer to demonstrate competency in each area assessed.

Tactical Skills

The fourth criterion applies to the tactical competencies critical to officer safety. This might include searching and handcuffing, weaponless defense, firearms, and driving skills in view of their obvious (often life and death) importance to safe and effective law enforcement work.

Reliability

This rating would be earned by demonstrated reliability, including adherence to policies, procedures, and laws. This category would be especially important, as higher rating would likely be correlated with lower instances of misconduct.

Attitude

This sixth area represents attitude. While attitude is not everything, it is one of the most valuable attributes an officer can bring to the workplace.

Productivity

This category would be awarded based on an officer's productivity in a given performance period. The key to proper measurement of productivity is careful recognition of the differences in officer work types, work areas, geographic assignments, work shifts, and, in some places, even seasons of the year.

Quality

This criterion represents not the amount but the quality of work performed during the rating period. Focusing only on results can send the wrong message to officers—a message that says quantity (arrests and citations) is more important than quality (following policy and law). Thus, the inclusion of this rating is a critical component of preventing misconduct.

Education

Education is generally valued positively in society at large and in professional workplaces in particular. Most law enforcement agencies show at least some preference in both hiring and promotion processes for those who have achieved certain levels of academic attainment.

Community Involvement

The final rating reflects an officer's level of community involvement outside his normal duty requirements. Working with youth programs, helping the elderly, assisting the disabled, and other similar initiatives all tend to show police officers in a favorable, humanitarian light and tend to improve police–community relations.

Summary

Creating a culture of ethics begins by providing rules, regulations, training, and structured accountability to control the broad discretionary powers of officers. However, those policies are only effective to the degree that supervisors enforce organizational mandates fairly and consistently. Among their other responsibilities, supervisors are accountable for the performance of subordinate personnel (Schroeder et al., 2006). This requires supervisors to confront and correct poor performance in all its forms, including misconduct. The responsibility for reporting misconduct, however, should not be restricted to supervisory personnel. Indeed, all employees—regardless of rank, status, or title—have a vested interest in the ethical functioning of the organization, including the unethical behavior or poor performance of individual officers. Thus, all employees should be required to report any form of misconduct of which they have personal knowledge, as well as to intervene in instances of clearly illegal behavior by other officers (Newham, 2002).

In the case of Officer Contreras at the beginning of this chapter, the sergeant treated Contreras' violation of policy differently than Officer Davis' disobedience of the same mandate. The sergeant's disparate treatment resulted in Contreras filing a formal grievance with the agency. Failure to enforce policy fairly and equitable can damage employee morale, lower productivity, increase misconduct, and expose the organization to civil liability. This chapter highlighted a number of organizational and supervisory practices for motivating and maintaining a culture of ethics. To avoid many of the problems described in the opening story, supervisors must enforce policy fairly and consistently, address misconduct and poor performance, counsel employees appropriately, and award ethical behavior.

Discussion Questions

1. Why are policies and procedures important in creating an ethical culture?

2. What role does supervision play in enforcing policy?

3. Explain the legal requirements for fairness and consistency.

4. Why is timeliness an important legal requirement?

5. When is performance counseling appropriate?

6. Describe the common mistakes that supervisors make when attempting to shape an officer's behavior.

References

Adams, J. S. (1965). Inequality in social exchange. In L. Berkowitz (Ed.), *Advances in experimental psychology* (Vol. 2, pp. 267–299). New York: Academic Press.

Alpert, G. P., & Smith, W. C. (1994). Developing police policy: An evaluation of the control principle. *American Journal of Police, 13*(2), 1–20. Retrieved from http://criminology.fsu.edu/transcrime/articles/DevelopingPolicePolicy.htm

Anderson, J. R. (2000). *Learning and memory: An integrated approach* (2nd ed.). New York: Wiley.

Ariely, D. (2012). *The (honest) truth about dishonesty: How we lie to everyone—especially ourselves.* New York: HarperCollins.

Brown, R. F., & Welch, T. S. (2002). Legal issues for supervisors. Richardson, TX: Brown & Hofmeister, LLP. Retrieved from http://www.docstoc.com/docs/18331768/Legal-Issues-For-Supervisors

Catania, A. C. (1998). *Learning* (4th ed.). Upper Saddle River, NJ: Prentice Hall.

Chatman, J. A., & Malka, A. (2003). Intrinsic and extrinsic work orientation as moderators of the effect of annual income on subjective well-being: A longitudinal study. *Personality and Social Psychology Bulletin, 29*(6), 737–746.

Chen, A. Y. S., Sawyers, R. B., & Williams, P. F. (1997). Reinforcing ethical decision making through corporate culture. *Journal of Business Ethics, 16*(8), 855–865.

Clawson, J. J., Martin, R. L., & Hauert, S. A. (1994, October). Protocols vs. guidelines: Choosing a medical dispatch program. *Emergency Medical Services.* Retrieved from http://www.emergencydispatch.org/articles/protocolsvsguidelines1.htm

Crank, J., & Caldero, M. (2000). *Police ethics: The corruption of noble cause.* Cincinnati, OH: Anderson.

Daniels, A. C. (2000). *Bringing out the best in people: How to apply the astonishing power of positive reinforcement.* New York: McGraw-Hill.

Daniels, A. C. (2007). *Other people's habits: How to use positive reinforcement to bring out the best in people around you.* Atlanta, GA: Performance Management Publications.

Denver Police Department. (2008). *Discipline handbook: Conduct principles and disciplinary guidelines.* Retrieved from http://www.denvergov.org/Portals/338/documents/Handbook%206-4-08%20-%20FINAL%20with%20appendix.pdf

Eisenberger, R., Cummings, J., Armeli, S., & Lynch, P. (1997). Perceived organizational support, discretionary treatment, and job satisfaction. *Journal of Applied Psychology, 82,* 812–820.

Eisenberger, R., Huntington, R., Hutchison, S., & Sowa, D. (1986). Perceived organizational support. *Journal of Applied Psychology, 71,* 500–507.

Engel, R. S. (2003). *How police supervisory styles influence patrol officer behavior.* Washington, DC: National Institute of Justice.

Engel, R. S., & Worden, R. E. (2003). Police officers' attitudes, behavior, and supervisory influences: An analysis of problem solving. *Criminology, 41*(1), 131–166.

Ethics Resource Center. (2003). *National business ethics survey.* Retrieved from http://www.ethics.org/resources/2003-national-business-ethics-survey-nbes

Felton, T. (2009, January). Best practices in documenting employee discipline. *Workforce.* Retrieved from http://www.workforce.com/article/20090115/NEWS02/301159997

Fischler, G. L. (2001). Psychological fitness-for-duty examinations: Practical considerations for public safety departments. *Law Enforcement Executive Forum, 1,* 77–92.

Fitch, B. D. (2011). The two roles of supervision in performance counseling. *FBI Law Enforcement Bulletin, 80*(3), 10–15.

Garber, P. R. (2004). *Giving and receiving performance feedback.* Amherst, MA: HRD Press.

Gazzaniga, M. S. (2011). *Who's in charge? Free will and the science of the brain.* New York: Ecco.

Goleman, D. (1994). *Emotional intelligence: Why it can matter more than IQ.* New York: Bantam Books.

Governor's Office of Employee Relations. (2010). *Supervisor's guide to counseling* (3rd ed.). New York: Authors. Retrieved from http://www.delhi.edu/administration/human_resources/Supervisors_Guide.pdf

Greenberg, J. (1990). Employee theft as a reaction to underpayment inequity: The hidden cost of pay cuts. *Journal of Applied Psychology, 5,* 561–568.

Grojean, M. W., Resick, C. J., Dickson, M. W., & Smith, D. B. (2004). Leaders, values, and organizational climates: Examining leadership strategies for establishing an organizational climate regarding ethics. *Journal of Business Ethics, 55,* 223–242.

Grote, D. (2006). *Discipline without punishment: The proven strategies that turn problem employees into superior performers* (2nd ed.). New York: AMACOM.

Guthrie, S. D. (2008, June). Police ethics (Part II). *Law Enforcement Journal.* Retrieved from http://www.in.gov/ilea/2420.htm#Police_Ethics_-_Part_II

Homans, G. C. (1958). Social behavior as exchange. *American Journal of Sociology, 63*(6), 597–606.

International Association of Chiefs of Police (IACP). (2006, October). Employee disciplinary matrix: A search for fairness in the disciplinary process. *The Police Chief*. Retrieved from http://www.policechiefmagazine.org/magazine/index .cfm?fuseaction=print_display&article_id=102006

Josephson, M. (2002). *Report card 2002: The ethics of American youth*. Los Angeles, CA: Josephson Institute of Ethics. Retrieved from http://charactercounts .org/programs/reportcard/2002/index.html

Josephson, M. (2009). *Becoming an exemplary police officer*. Los Angeles, CA: Josephson Institute of Ethics.

Kahneman, D. (2011). *Thinking, fast and slow*. New York: Farrar, Straus, and Giroux.

Kaikati, J. G., & Label, W. A. (1980, October). American bribery legislation: An obstacle to international marketing. *Journal of Marketing, 44*(4), 38–43.

Kazdin, A. E. (2001). *Behavior modification in applied settings* (6th ed.). Belmont, CA: Wadsworth.

Kohn, A. (1986). *No contest: The case against competition*. New York: Houghton Mifflin.

Kouzes, J. M., & Posner, B. Z. (2007). *The leadership challenge: Becoming a better leader* (4th ed.). San Francisco: Jossey-Bass.

Levinson, H. (1965). Reciprocation: The relationship between man and organization. *Administrative Science Quarterly, 9,* 370–390.

Lindner, J. R. (1998). Understanding employee motivation. *Journal of Extension, 36*(3). Retrieved from http://www.joe.org/joe/1998june/rb3.php

Means, R. B. (2008a, July). Evaluation and recognition systems. *Law & Order*. Retrieved from http://www.hendonpub.com/resources/article_archive/results/ details?id=2653

Means, R. B. (2008b, August). Rules versus guidelines. *Law & Order*. Retrieved from http://www.hendonpub.com/resources/article_archive/results/details?id= 2593

Means, R. B. (2011, November). Keys to fairness in dealing with employees. *Law & Order*. Retrieved from http://www.hendonpub.com/resources/article_archive/ results/details?id=1200

Merriam, D. H., & Sitkowski, R. J. (1998, Summer). Procedural due process in practice. *Planning Commissioners Journal, 31,* 5–9. Retrieved from http://www .umass.edu/masscptc/pdfs/Procedural%20Due%20Process%20Article.pdf

Miles, E. W., Hatfield, J. D., & Husmen, R. C. (1989). The equity of sensitivity construct: Potential implications for worker performance. *Journal of Management, 15,* 581–588.

Miller, B. C. (2006). *Keeping employees accountable for results: Quick tips for busy managers*. New York: Amacom.

National Association of EMS Physicians. (1989). Position paper: Emergency medical dispatching. *Pre-hospital and Disaster Medicine, 4*(2), 163–166.

National Law Enforcement Policy Center. (1991). *A compilation of model policies*. Arlington, VA: National Law Enforcement Policy Center.

Newham, G. (2002, June). *Tackling police corruption in South Africa*. Johannesburg, South Africa: Centre for the Study of Violence and Reconciliation. Retrieved from http://www.csvr.org.za/wits/papers/papoli14.htm

Ormrod, J. E. (2008). *Human learning* (5th ed.). Upper Saddle River, NJ: Pearson Education.

Palmiotto, M. J. (2001). Police misconduct: What is it? In M. J. Palmiotto (Ed), *Police misconduct: A reader for the 21st century* (pp. 32–41). Upper Saddle River, NJ: Prentice Hall.

Pelletier, L. G., & Vallerand, R. J. (1996). Supervisors' beliefs and subordinate intrinsic motivation: A behavioral confirmation analysis. *Journal of Personality and Social Psychology, 71*(2), 331–340.

Phil Varnak Associates. (2008). *Employee relations for managers and supervisors.* Aurora, CO: Authors. Retrieved from http://www.pvarnak.com/ER%20Sample.pdf

Risher, J. (2005, September). Chief's counsel: Fairness and consistency in disciplinary action. *The Police Chief.* Retrieved from http://www.thepolicechiefmagazine.org/magazine/index.cfm?fuseaction=print_display&aarticle_id=92005

Robbins, S. (2005). *Essentials of organizational behavior* (8th ed.). Upper Saddle River, NJ: Prentice-Hall.

Schroeder, D. J., Lombardo, F., & Strollo, J. (2006). *Management and supervision of law enforcement personnel* (4th ed.). Binghamton, NY: Gould Publications.

Settoon, R. P., Bennett, N., & Liden, R. C. (1996). Social exchange in organizations: Perceived organizational support, leader-member exchange, and employee reciprocity. *Journal of Applied Psychology, 81,* 219–227.

Shaw v. Stroud, 13 F 3d 791, 798, 4th Cir. (1994).

Skinner, B. F. (1953). *Science and human behavior.* New York: The Free Press.

Skinner, B. F. (1971). *Beyond freedom and dignity.* Indianapolis, IN: Hackett.

Skinner, B. F. (1974). *About behaviorism.* New York: Vintage Books.

Stoner, C. R. (1989, Summer). The foundation of business ethics: Exploring the relationship between organizational culture, moral values, and actions. *Sam Advanced Management Journal, 54,* 38–43.

Tella, A., Ayeni, C. O., & Popoola, S. O. (2007). Work motivation, job satisfaction, and organizational commitment of library personnel in academic and research libraries in Oyo State, Nigeria. *Library Philosophy and Practice.* Retrieved from http://www.webpages.uidaho.edu/~mbolin/tella2.htm

Trautman, N. (2000, October). *Police code of silence facts revealed.* Paper presented at the Annual Conference of International Association of Chiefs of Police, San Diego, CA. Retrieved from: http://www.aele.org/loscode2000.html

Truckenbrodt, Y. B. (2000, Summer). The relationship between leader-member exchange and commitment and organizational citizenship behavior. *Acquisition Review Quarterly,* 233–244. Retrieved from http://www.au.af.mil/au/awc/awcgate/dau/truck.pdf

U.S. Equal Opportunity Commission. (2009). *Federal law prohibits job discrimination questions and answers.* Annapolis Junction, MD: Authors. Retrieved from http://www.eeoc.gov/facts/qanda.html

Wasserman, R. (1982). The government setting. In B. Garmine (Ed.), *Local government police management* (2nd ed., pp. 30–51). Washington, DC: International City Management Association.

Wayne, S. J., Shore, L. M., & Liden, R.C. (1997). Perceived organizational support and leader-member exchange: A social exchange perspective. *Academy of Management Journal, 40,* 82–111.

5

Ethics and Accountability

Policy and Oversight in the United Kingdom

Attilio R. Grandani

On April 22, 1993, Stephen Lawrence, an 18-year old Black man, was stabbed to death by a gang of White youths in Eltham, southeast London. Within hours, Luke Knight, David Norris, Gary Dobson, and brothers Neil and Jamie Acourt were identified as suspects. Almost from the start, the case was mired in controversy, with three of the five suspects acquitted of murder charges after a private prosecution collapsed at the Old Baily in 1996 (Weaver, 2009). The case, as well as its wider implications, was investigated by a former high judge, Sir William Macpherson, who concluded the police investigation was "marred by a combination of professional incompetence, institutional racism and a failure of leadership by senior officers" (Macpherson, 1999, p. 317). The report went on to recommend a series of 70 measures intended to subject the police to greater public control, enshrine rights for victims of crime, and extend the number of offenses classified as racist.

In the years following Lawrence's death, the London Metropolitan police was plagued by allegations of institutional racism and corruption, including the suggestion that Clifford Norris, the gangland father of one of the prime suspects, might have paid former detective sergeant John Davidson to stay one step ahead of the investigation—an accusation that ultimately appeared as part of a 2006 *BBC* documentary (Weaver, 2009). These and other charges continued to plague the department for years, eventually culminated in the arrest of a former police constable and a serving member of the Metropolitan police staff for allegedly withholding evidence from the original murder inquiry.

Although two of the five suspects (Gary Dobson and David Norris) were ultimately convicted and ordered to serve sentences of 15 and 14 years, respectively, for Lawrence's murder, the verdicts came at a price. Fallout from the Lawrence murder investigation—including the findings outlined in the Macpherson report—brought about a series of major changes to policing, the law, and politics (Laville & Dodd, 2012), many of which are discussed in detail throughout this chapter. As the Lawrence case illustrates, law enforcement organizations, as well as the individual officers who constitute those agencies, must be held accountable for their actions, including the quality of investigations, treatment of victims, and handling of the media and public.

This chapter examines the importance of accountability in relation to police services in the United Kingdom (UK), as well as associated ethical issues. The fact that there are so many policing areas calls into question the need for a multilateral agreement to ensure that the various UK police agencies and, of course, the ever-extending policing family are held accountable to the general populace. The chapter begins with a study of the minimum international standards that influence the UK's statutes and structures, as well as how those standards have been set. Next, the tripartite structure of the UK police, which significantly impacts the ways officers conduct themselves, is discussed. This chapter, then, outlines the introduction of the Police and Criminal Evidence (PACE) Act 1984, which established important guidelines concerning how those who come into contact with the police can expect to be treated. This is followed by an analysis of the need for inspections of each constabulary, the official audit of those examined, and measures for ensuring that police services provide "best value." The chapter concludes with an overview of the current complaint system used to ensure accountability and ethics throughout all of the UK's 43 police services.

The Importance of Accountability

To comprehend the complex environment of police accountability within the Metropolitan Police Service (MPS) in the UK, it is necessary to examine the three separate jurisdictions that influence the 43 police forces as a whole, as well as to highlight several themes. By identifying the different policing areas within the UK and exploring many of the important changes in legislation, the author hopes to demonstrate how the use of stringent rules and regulations has influenced the operational procedures of UK's police forces and the conduct of individual officers, and helped to ensure that police agencies and individual officers are held accountable for their actions.

It is imperative from the outset to provide a clear and transparent appraisal when referring to the UK police service, as it should not be regarded as a unitary body. Moreover, it should not be considered similar to other national police forces that exist in so many other parts of the world. England and Wales have 43 forces and undertake territorial policing on a geographical basis (Ayling, Grabosky, & Shearing, 2009). This is in stark contrast to service in Scotland, where there are only eight regional police forces in existence. In November 2001, and following the recommendations of the Patten Commission, which observed the troubles in Ireland, the police service of Northern Ireland (PSNI) was created (Newburn, 2007). It replaced the Royal Ulster Constabulary, which itself had been in operation since 1922.

Additionally, there are a number of police agencies regarded as non–Home Office forces that operate under a specific remit and exercise their authority throughout the UK. These include the British Transport Police, the Ministry of Defence police, and the Civil Nuclear Constabulary, or, as it was formerly known, the United Kingdom Atomic Energy Authority Constabulary, which is the only routinely armed police force in England and Wales (Wilkinson, 2007). The Jersey, Guernsey, and Isle of Man police are separate organizations that carry out policing on those islands, and, as such, have their own powers (Mawby, 1999). Unlike the police forces in England and Wales, their policing areas are divided into parishes rather than boroughs. Although policing responsibilities often differ depending on the area, one fundamental fact remains: The primary role of the police is to uphold the law.

At this point, it may seem obvious that referring to the UK police services as a single, unitary entity should be discouraged. It is axiomatic, therefore, that with so many police forces in existence, the arrangements for police accountability are nothing less than complex. Indeed, police accountability has been a consistent and, at times, fiercely debated political issue. This was particularly evident during the 1980s when police accountability in England and Wales became a topic of considerable national debate (Joyce, 2011). The primary concerns involved how best to control the police (if, in fact, they should actually be controlled at all) and whether or not they were beyond any form of democratic influence. Debatably, these issues are still in existence today, even though they may have lost some of their controversy. This may be due to a paradigm shift emphasizing accountability, performance, and effectiveness, which has been heavily debated within the political sphere.

Public Trust

Many critics have duly noted that trustworthiness remains a significant subject in relation to policing accountability (Kappeler & Gaines, 2009). More recently, the need for public trust has affected a shift away from a "cloak-and-dagger" image to one of increased transparency. There are several factors that may have played some part in the aforementioned shift, including a need to mitigate the unwarranted exercise of coercive power by the police in an effort to enhance trust and achieve community support. Clearly, there is little doubt among those in the political sphere that the effective use of power contributes to the legitimacy of the police in some way.

Policing can also be regarded as an extension of political power in many instances, as the police are seen to exercise the laws handed to them by the politicians and lawmakers responsible for creating them (Newburn & Jones, 1996). In this sense, it can be suggested that there exists a need for law enforcement to be held accountable for their use of public resources, especially when there are vast amounts of public funds involved. Politicians are often required to explain to voters and other political factions exactly how and why the police used public monies, as well as demonstrating the received value for those monies (VFM) in relation to enhanced public safety. The UK Taxpayers Alliance closely monitors the expenditure of taxpayer funds, especially considering the current fiscal restraints imposed by the Chancellor of the Exchequer, George Osborne, and the government per se (Toynbee & Walker, 2008). While the financial budget varies from one policing area to another, it is worth noting the total expenditure for the MPS during the fiscal year 2011–2012 was £1,127,735,964 (Home Office, 2011), which had been taken from the UK policing budget for the same period, which was £4,808,807,759 (Directgov, 2011).

Although policing of the UK involves three separate systems based on geographic and legal divisions, this chapter focuses primary on England and Wales, which is home to some 90% of all UK residents (Jones & Norton, 2010). Where significant differences exist in the policing systems operating in Scotland and Northern Ireland, which also fall under the authority of the UK, these will be highlighted. Additionally, other agencies and groups that are responsible for policing will be discussed.

International Standards

There are numerous identified mechanisms that have considerable relevance to the UK police, such as the International Standards on Policing and Accountability. The United Nations (UN) Universal Declaration on Human Rights in 1948 is a fundamental source of "legislative and judicial methodologies and corporate practices" (Devine, Hansen, Wilde, & Poole, 1999, p. 1). It provides principles and standards that clearly underpin the need for law enforcement accountability, especially in relation to the restraints imposed by the existence of the current Human Rights Act (HRA) 1998.

The European Convention for the Protection of Human Rights and Fundamental Freedoms, which were created in 1951, supports the UK (Devine et al., 1999). These rules are endorsed in principle by the UN declaration. The articles of the Convention simply reaffirm the fundamental freedoms in a democratic system of government. The UK law gave effect to the Convention in the HRA 1998, and as the UK police are regarded as a public authority under the act, they have a responsibility to abide by the Convention.

The HRA 1998 provides "mediation" by the UK domestic courts and for the award of compensation, especially in cases where public authorities have breached the Convention rights (Elliott & Quinn, 2011). Complainants are able to take cases that UK domestic courts are unable to resolve to the European Court of Human Rights, which sits in Strasbourg, France (Colvin & Cooper, 2009). This powerful legislative structure makes the UK police particularly accountable for their actions. The Independent Police Complaints Commission (IPCC)—as well as, in Northern Ireland, the Police Ombudsman—is, therefore, well served to take notice of the HRA 1998, especially when investigating allegations concerning police misconduct (Anthony, 2008).

The HRA 1998 has a deep-rooted influence on offences taken into consideration (TIC), as well as the processes, policies, and standard operating procedures associated with it (Grandani, 2009b). This is due primarily to the fact that Article 6 of the HRA 1998 refers to persons entitled to a fair trial (Fenwick & Phillipson, 2007). It could be argued that by not informing every prisoner brought into police custody in England and Wales of TIC procedures—as well as providing offenders with an opportunity to admit to other crimes—that those offenders may, in fact, be denied a fair trial if they were to admit to other offenses that could be TIC by a criminal court and later arrested for those crimes.

Nonetheless, there is sufficient evidence to suggest that human rights issues continue to challenge the criminal justice system in the UK. In recent years, disquiet has continued over diverse issues, including members of the public being shot by armed police officers, deaths occurring while in police detention, and the questionable intransigence and proficiency of certain investigations into murders of members of various ethnic minority communities, including the Stephen Lawrence case (Macpherson, 1999). The topic of race relations continues to run through many of these problem areas despite the raft of government and police self-imposed reforms embarked on following the Macpherson inquiry. In light of these and other issues, it is highly probable that human rights issues will continue to test the systems of police accountability and associated ethics in the UK for many years to come.

Accountability and Bureaucracy

Although there are concerns regarding the overall effectiveness and clarity of accountability, systems, structures, and policies, the main issue appears to be that while welcoming the government's police reform programs, there is a real danger that over-bureaucratic measures may sabotage otherwise good intentions. Additionally, the proliferation of agencies, including the Crime and Disorder Reduction Partnerships and Local Strategic Partnerships, and the new performance monitoring processes, such as the Police Performance Assessment Framework (PPAF), may contribute to an environment of substituted accountability, especially if it obscures the chief constable's role as operational commander. This is mainly due to the fact that responsibility must be clear and unequivocal. In this environment, the clarity of liability is no longer pure, and chief constables must distinguish between accountability and the broader demand for information.

Additional measures that provide specific guidance for the UK police with respect to conduct are found in the UN Code of Conduct for Law Enforcement Officials 1979 (Kleinig & Zhang, 1993). The code sets forth the basic principles for all police forces the world over, including the UK. These principles apply to all law enforcement officers who exercise their powers of arrest and incarceration and are suspected of violating the law. Needless to say, there is a real need to ensure that not only UK police forces, but all police authorities, recognize the rights set out in the UN Universal Declaration and other international conventions (Kleinig & Zhang, 1993), especially issues surrounding the use of force. It is clear that the police should only use reasonable force when necessary and that the amount of force must be proportionate to the situation.

The problem that is patently obvious is that in England and Wales, what is actually regarded as reasonable force has never been clearly explained (Casciani, 2009). This issue has been left for the courts to decide, based on the facts of individual cases. This has led to inconsistencies, such as irrational sentencing of offenders, failings in the CJS, and, in some instances, miscarriages of justice (Walker & Starmer, 1999). Until lawmakers in England and Wales define reasonable force, the onus for deciding what is, and what is not, "reasonable" will continue to fall on an already overburdened CJS; thus, society should well expect to witness more of the previously mentioned inconsistencies.

United Kingdom Statutes and Structures

The police have to be held accountable for not only what they do but also how they do it, which must, in all cases, be deemed legally, ethically, and morally correct. It is, therefore, imperative to ensure that strict rules and regulations exist to provide sufficient guidance and minimum standards of behavior. In 1979, the Council of Europe Declaration on the Police defined the rules of conduct. These rules govern those police agencies that are part of the member states of the Council of Europe, which obviously includes the UK (Neyroud & Beckley, 2001). These rules were designed specifically to assist and promote the protection of human rights, as well as to improve the overall status of all police officers and, therefore, all police forces in Europe.

The basic minimum standards for law enforcement agencies to act legitimately are provided not only in the UN Code of Conduct, but in the Code of Police Ethics as well (Neyroud & Beckley, 2001). It is worth noting that neither the UN Code of Conduct nor the Code of Police Ethics are regarded as law, although they should be regarded as guides that indirectly inform the practices of policing and accountability within the UK (Neyroud, 2003).

The statutes and structures recognized by the 43 UK police agencies exist to ensure that "police forces are held accountable" for their actions (Wilkinson, 2007, p. 66). As previously mentioned, the UK police are subject to the rule of law, which has been enacted by the government. Although the judicial process and, in particular, case law, may influence the ways legislation is interpreted (a process usually guided by the executive branch), the UK police derive their power from the legislative branch of government. In this sense, they are subordinated to the law and to the law alone. This lies in stark contrast to a variety of policies and dictates, as the majority of the public powers, which stem from the government, are vested ministers who are deemed servants of the Crown. The UK police also have an allegiance to the Crown that supplants the state as the central organizing principle of the lawful government (Sanders, Young, & Burton, 2010). This means accountability is not restricted to those regarded as subordinates to government officials, nor simply the government of the day; instead, a far more intricate and complex system is used to ensure accountability throughout the police services.

The 43 police forces of England and Wales are held accountable under a tripartite structure. The MPS is the largest and most diverse police force in Europe (Sanders et al., 2010) and is responsible primarily for policing the whole of London, the capital of England. There is one square mile in the heart of this vast policing area that is policed by another force, the city of London Police. All 43 police forces are held accountable for their own policing area and day-to-day business.

The Tripartite Structure

The current system of holding the 43 police forces of England and Wales accountable has been characterized as the tripartite structure of police accountability. The tripartite system was established following the deliberations of the 1962 Royal Commission on the Police (Grieve, Harfield, & MacVean, 2007). The tripartite structure and its associated processes govern the methodology for distributing responsibilities between the Home Office, the local police authority, and the chief constable of the force. The tripartite arrangements have been endorsed through the passing of legislation, namely the Police Act 1964, the Police and Magistrates Court Act (PAMCA) 1994, and the Police Reform Act 2002 (Grieve et al., 2007).

In England and Wales, the responsibility for policing policy and key priorities sits within the remit of the Home Secretary; responsibilities afforded them via the tripartite processes and systems (Oliver, 1997). The key priorities are formalized within the National Policing Plan. Chief constables are required to respond to circulars and policies set out by the executive, a body containing the Home Office and Her Majesty's Chief Inspector of Constabulary. Debatably, the independence of chief constables is limited predominantly by the current arrangements, even though case law has made it abundantly clear that police are servants of the law in terms of their operational discretion and, therefore, not subject to administrative or political direction in this respect. If this argument is true, however, then it begs the question as to why the police are subject to statistical targets at the commencement of each financial year or when a new government is voted into power. Some have argued that this arrangement is tantamount to Statistically-Led Policing (SLP), as police forces are likely to concentrate their resources on the specific areas of business currently being used to assess performance at the expense of other enforcement efforts (Grandani, 2009a).

The primary objective of the PAMCA 1994 is to reinforce the ability of local police authorities to function correctly (Grieve et al., 2007). This has been achieved by providing them with additional powers, which includes involving them in the development of local policing plans. The police authorities should engage with the chief of police for their local area and ascertain the best policing methodology, that is, the strategies best suited to address the specific problems and areas in questions. It is worth noting that the Police Reform Act 2002 was the catalyst for a shift toward the "center," resulting in the introduction of the Home Secretary's "rolling three-year National Policing Plan" (Joyce, 2011. p. 77).

It was mentioned earlier that even though the UK police have many different forces, it must also cater to Scotland, which, unlike England and Wales, and prior to the Police Act created in 1964, was already in possession of a tripartite system of governance with the local authority acting as the local police authority (Grieve et al., 2007). The reforms in England and Wales followed similar routes with the passage of the Police (Scotland) Act 1967 acting as the primary catalyst. This meant that Scottish Ministers retain overall responsibility for all aspects of policing policy, while police authorities and joint police boards are responsible for setting police budgets and ensuring that best value is attained for public finances. Chief constables, on the other hand, are responsible for the operational aspects of policing within their particular force areas (Eriksson, 2009).

Similarly, the role of the policing board in Northern Ireland is to take on the responsibility of, and act as, the police authority (Eriksson, 2009). It is responsible for ensuring the delivery of an efficient police force and for assisting the PSNI to fulfill its statutory obligation to meet the minimum standards of the HRA 1998. The board's most prominent power, however, is the ability to initiate inquiries into any and all parts of the PSNI's work, with no requirement to seek the agreement of the chief constable. This clearly provides the policing board with a more active role in the management of PSNI and certainly more power than is afforded to other local police authorities.

Accountability and Guidance 1984

The police forces in England and Wales are not only accountable to the tripartite structure and its associated legislation and processes, but to the Police and Criminal Evidence Act (PACE) 1984 as well (Carrabine, Cox, Lee, Plummer, & South, 2009). The CJS is designed to ensure that all persons apprehended by police officers, who are subsequently charged with a criminal offence, have the right to a jury trial in serious cases, and are provided an opportunity to seek legal representation. Under the UK system, legal representation is impartial and free. The CJS also ensures that the police have conducted themselves in accordance with the correct procedures, for example, those established by the PACE 1984. Failure to comply with these rules can, and often does, result in absolute failure to secure a conviction (Home Office, 2005). This is primarily due to the fact that courts increasingly use exclusionary rules to render inadmissible any evidence that has not been legally and fairly obtained. The application of this principle means that entire cases can fail when the rules have not been followed with important repercussions for police effectiveness and, of course, public confidence.

The MPS and, therefore, the 32 London Borough Operational Command Units (BOCUs) have stringent guidelines and protocols in place to ensure that certain criminal offences are brought to the attention of the Crown Prosecution Service (CPS) prior to charging a detainee with a criminal offence (Moreno & Hughes, 2008). This is particularly evident when allowing for offences considered suitable for the TIC processes. It is worth mentioning that the CPS acts as the prosecuting agency for the police forces in England and Wales; however, the CPS is not measured or held accountable in the same ways as the police services (CPS, 2005). The CPS's performance is measured via conviction rates at court, as opposed to the UK police who are measured on detection rates for crime.

Due process dictates that all admissions be conducted via a PACE compliant interview when questioning an offender in relation to offences TIC. Failure to adhere to this policy is considered a breach of process, while undoubtedly rendering any information or evidence gleaned in relation to offences TIC inadmissible, typically resulting in acquittal (Home Office, 2005).

Consultation and Monitoring

Consultation and monitoring continue to be two important strands of accountability with some aspects enjoying statutory support, which places a high reliance on contributions from individual volunteers. Both consultation and monitoring are carried out through the various police community consultative groups established under paragraph 106 of the PACE 1984 (Home Office, 2005). The purpose of local consultative committees is simply to promote communication and consultation between local policing commanders and the communities they serve. Research suggests that committee meetings are nonadversarial, poorly attended, and non-representative or reflective of the overall communities alluded to. Additionally, these committees possess no power; rather, they tend to be regarded as forums for the police to explain their activities and governing policies.

Details regarding the PACE 1984 can be found in the Codes of Practice and are not restricted to police personnel. In fact, any member of the public can enter a police station in England or Wales and request to see a copy of the codes. The Codes of Practice was created under the act governing cautioning procedures, identification parades, and a range of other responsibilities, including stop and search, entry to premises, search and seizure of property, arrest, and the detention and questioning of suspects, which are all outlined by the PACE 1984 (Home Office, 2005). The codes may not be regarded as constitutional, although any breach of their requirements will amount to a disciplinary offence. Moreover, any such contraventions of the codes are deemed admissible in evidence during a criminal or civil proceeding against the police force.

Inspections of Constabulary

Examining strict compliance and other processes falls within the remit of Her Majesty's Inspectorate of Constabulary (HMIC) for England and Wales (HMIC, 1999).

Contrary to popular belief, HMIC is not a recent creation; in fact, it has been in existence for some considerable time. The first inspectors of constabulary were appointed under the provisions of the County and Borough Police Act 1856 (HMIC, 1999). The inspectors enjoy independent status, being servants of the Crown and not Home Office employees. In particular, Section 38 of the 1964 Police Act specifies clearly the inspectors' role and provides them with the power to inspect and report to the Home Secretary on the efficiency and effectiveness of each and every police force. The role of HMIC has since been laid out in the Police Acts of 1994 and 1996 and, relating to best value, the Local Government Act 1999 (HMIC, 1999).

As stated, the inspectorate's role is primarily to promote the "efficiency and effectiveness" of policing in England, Wales, and PSNI, which is achieved through inspection of police organizations and functions (Eriksson, 2009, p. 52). These inspections are conducted to certify that agreed standards are not only achieved but also maintained. They also serve to spread good practice and, therefore, ensure that performance is improved. Additionally, the inspectorate can provide advice and support to the tripartite partners that include not only the Home Secretary and Police Authorities, but the concerned local agency as well. As such, they play an integral and vitally important role in the development of future leaders by ensuring that protocols are addressed to reflect modern-day society.

In terms of inspections, HMIC conducts reviews of forces and of any geographic Basic Command Unit, referred to within the MPS as BOCUs, of which there are currently 32 (HMIC, 1999). It also conducts inspections that focus on specific areas of policing, such as corruption, integrity, visibility, reassurance, and diversity. This is due to state concerns that unless public confidence is maintained and professionalism upheld, apathy may ensue, ultimately leading to civil unrest and possibly anarchy. Furthermore, the police could be accused of lacking ethics. When working in partnership with the Audit Commission, HMIC also conducts VFM or Best Value inspections to ensure that the allocated policing budget is being used to good effect (Audit Commission, 1988).

Inspections by HMIC are usually preceded by formal notice. One of the primary functions of such inspections is to ensure that a valid sample of raw data is collected on a regular basis of the individual forces. This methodology helps identify error at the earliest opportunity, allowing for timely correction and organizational learning. HMIC will announce, in advance, the areas of business to be inspected, while expecting that any and all data and related correspondence be available on request. This includes tangible documents, as well as those retrievable and stored on electronic devices (Audit Commission, 1988). The time period for inspections tends to vary across the spectrum, although HMIC will not comment on findings until their report is completed. Arguably, this may be considered by some as another bureaucratic mechanism to test not only the efficiency of police services, but also the ethical methodology deployed when executing their duties.

Audit Commission

The police service within England and Wales has been heavily analyzed by the Audit Commission, which began reviews in 1983 (Audit Commission, 1988). The Local Government Finance Act (1982) established the Audit Commission as an independent body. They were initially assigned several tasks that included monitoring and promoting the economy, as well as overseeing the efficiency and effectiveness of local government. It was not until 1988 that the Audit Commission first focused on the police forces. Early reports suggest that the commission scrutinized the financing of police funding and budget allocation; however, reports that followed appear to focus more on operational matters, such as crime management and patrol work. Even though the commission's recommendations are not prescriptive, they are commonly implemented, which is considered no mean feat.

Best Value Program

The issue of VFM or Best Value program was introduced in April 2000 and placed a statutory duty on all local authorities to deliver services in compliance with clear standards via the most effective, economic, and efficient means possible (Cowan & Halliday, 2003). Local law enforcement authorities are also included as best value authorities and, as such, police forces in England and Wales are required to demonstrate VFM. Accordingly, police forces must report against a series of Best Value Performance Indicators. As previously alluded to, if the Home Office, government, and society as a whole observe those measures as indicators of success or failure, then it is prudent to suggest that resources should be directed to focus on those areas. This supports the theory of SLP. Caution, however, needs to be observed, as other areas of business could easily suffer, which would not only undermine the influence that policing has on societal control but other criminal offences that are not being measured may increase as well.

Minimum Standards

The Police Standards Unit (PSU) commenced work within the Home Office in July 2001, but it was not formally established until the introduction of the Police Reform Act 2002 (Gilling, 2007). It has become increasingly influential in its role to identify good policing practice and the best means of dissemination. The PSU typically plays an intervention role that it is able to employ if a police force has been identified as requiring remedial action. By intervening, it is able to highlight issues and suggest methods to improve performance. In this capacity, the PSU works closely with HMIC.

In April 2004, the Home Office developed the Police Performance Assessment Framework (PPAF). The PPAF was created as the result of liaising with the Association of Chief Police Officers (ACPO) and Association of Police Authorities (Newburn, 2008) to enhance the overall effectiveness and clarity of accountability, systems, and structures throughout the various UK police forces. The creation of PPAF provides an effective structure for comparing police performance and provides a firm basis for effective performance management. It is, therefore, intended to be both a means of holding individual police forces accountable for their performance and of comparing the performance of various forces against each other. Bureaucratic influences and protocols are supposed to hold chiefs accountable for each of the 43 policing areas. The fact remains that no two policing areas are the same; therefore, only certain performance indicators can be used to provide a comparable entity.

According to the Home Office, in addition to focusing on operational effectiveness, the PPAF provides measures of satisfaction and overall trust and confidence in the police, as well as computes performance in the context of efficiency and organizational capability (Brain, 2010). In line with the government's desire to enhance policing accountability at local levels, performance against national and local priorities is reflected in the framework. HMIC published its first baseline assessments of each force in England and Wales midway in 2004, which led to much debate in the media, public, and political circles concerning the comparative performance of forces and press speculation over whether chief constables rated as poor could, or even would, be dismissed. Parties from all factions across the political spectrum observe that access to information is a key to encouraging public scrutiny of the police. Like most topics within the policing and social spheres, everything is subject to change; therefore, PPAF has now become the Assessment of Policing and Community Safety (APACS) (Brain, 2010).

The recognized difference between PPAF and APACS is that the latter attempts to support a realistic balance between nationally and locally identified priorities. APACS covers policing and community safety issues in a balanced way that reflects relative seriousness. The benefits appear to include a lean toward simpler and clearer messages about performance and far less bureaucracy with better joint delivery. It has taken considerable time to arrive at this sensitive juncture in policing and social terms and it has not been without its struggles and politics along the way. This additional scrutiny, however, helps emphasizes the ethical ways that police are held accountable for their actions and leads to real trust in the ability of officers to complete their duties.

Fiscal Responsibility

During the 1980s, the government applied its public sector Financial Management Initiative to police service (Fielding, 2005). The initiative included specific audit techniques related to financial accountability with respect to public finances. The National Audit Office has produced many reports in relation to VFM in policing and district auditors have been empowered to undertake all audits in relation to the finances of public sector organizations, which obviously include police services.

It is self-evident that the introduction of the PAMCA 1994 changed the overall system of police funding in ways that theoretically provide greater control to the local police authority and greater devolution of budgeting within law enforcement agencies. Since the 1994 act, each local police authority receives a financially limited grant from the Home Office that is supplemented by funding from the local authority raised through revenue supporting grants, nondomestic rates, and council taxes (Grieve et al., 2007). The police forces are also permitted to seek out a relatively small proportion of funding through sponsorship arrangements (Brain, 2010). Strict caution must be adhered to, as not every sponsor is suitable for police service. The overall image of the service must not be threatened in any way, thus strict guidelines established for potential sponsors must be honored. The local police authority and the chief constable, rather than the Home Secretary, must decide on the allocation of funds, which are shared between police officers and civilian staff. This needs to take into account the cost of equipment, upkeep of buildings, and the purchase and service of vehicles. Therefore, while the home secretary retains control of the total amount of the grant, police authorities and chiefs have greater freedom within the budget.

Organizational Responsibility

Despite the importance of accountability, there are instances when it may, in fact, be considered a false piety. The mere fact that the police service portrays an image of accountability without being totally accountable for all measurable functions might appear hypocritical. In a vain attempt to address this imbalance while demonstrating some form of accountability, a wide range of agencies have been developed. Critics, however, are still concerned that certain aspects of the system lack transparency and, therefore, do not reflect a true and independent report, a finding that undermines any suggestion of legitimate accountability. This places greater pressure on police services as they attempt to report their findings in an ethical manner. A prime example is the procedure used to handle public complaints, which has in the past, more often than not, caused insecurities within minority communities (Waseem, 2005). The IPCC was established as an independent entity, separate from the police services, with the intent of investigating potential allegations in the most autonomous, impartial, and ethical manner possible, regardless of the agency involved.

In addition to complete, timely, and impartial investigations, law enforcement agencies in the UK have known for considerable time that working in partnership with local communities is one of the best ways of ensuring the delivery of appropriate police services (Waseem, 2005). This is evidenced by the ways police services attempt to reassure the public of their abilities, especially in relation to reducing crime and disorder—all part of the National Reassurance Policing Programme, a government-led curriculum. The ACPO firmly supports the principles of the program, which has been adopted by individual police forces across the UK (Brain, 2010). The primary objective appears to be the creation and maintenance of reassurance policies aimed at the general public. Furthermore, the clarification and promotion of public confidence can greatly assist in unifying the police and public.

Observing issues of accountability at corporate and organizational levels appears consistent with the hierarchical "military style" structure employed by most police organizations, including an individual officer's role and rank (Cowper, 2000). Arguably, this framework is designed to produce a disciplined, ethical, and answerable police service.

Officer Accountability

In addition to the oversight already mentioned, all police officers are subject to a disciplinary code that enables the service to punish offences, such as failure to comply with lawful orders, many forms of discreditable conduct, racially inflammatory and discriminatory behavior, and any suggestion of falsehood. The alleged offences are investigated internally and judged at disciplinary hearings. Punishments vary according to offense, but include reprimand, fine, and dismissal from police service (Newburn & Jones, 1996). It is worth mentioning that a breach of the code may, in some cases, constitute a criminal or civil offence, which, of course, could result in the officer being summoned to court. Although an officer may be initially arrested or summoned to court for an offence, this does not negate the fact that the officer could still face a disciplinary board once the trial is over.

Police officers in England and Wales, up to and including the chief inspector, can call on the support of the police federation, generally considered as the official police union (Brain, 2010). The federation is available 24 hours a day, seven days a week, and can provide advice and guidance on all aspects of disciplinary matters.

It is worth noting that while police officers can be held accountable for any number of responsibilities their primary duty is to uphold the law (Barnett, 2010). Dealing with criminal investigations of reported crimes is arguably the main activity in relation to reactive policing. If the police fail to investigate all reasonable lines of inquiry, they may find themselves subject to disciplinary proceedings. This is, at least in part, due to the fact that behind every allegation of reported crime is a victim; therefore, failure to investigate correctly may result in an offender remaining free to possibly commit further offenses with additional victims. Furthermore, in high profile cases, failure can result in the local or even national populace feeling betrayed (Barnett, 2010).

Complaints System

Despite the existence of the IPCC, the majority of complaints continue to be investigated by internal investigators assigned to individual forces, a process guided by the Home Office. Consistent with the practices of many large metropolitan law enforcement agencies, police forces in the UK monitor complaint patterns for individual officers. Those with higher than average numbers or worrisome patterns are identified and inquiries made into their conduct (Sanders et al., 2010). Moreover, a number of police authorities retain complaint subcommittees responsible for monitoring trends, which, it may be argued, is tantamount to the police actually policing the police. There is probably sufficient cause for concern from certain sections of the community who clearly believe that the police are less than ethical in their actions; thus, there is a need for deeper research and closer scrutiny of the system as a whole.

The police complaints system in the UK has historically attempted to establish credibility and boost public confidence by ensuring that those who are punished are named and shamed (Freeman, 2011). This helps to ensure the general public that police officers can and should be trusted. As previously discussed, the PACE was established in 1984, the same year that saw the introduction of the Police Complaints Authority (PCA). The PCA was created to oversee the investigation of complaints against police officers and followed widespread criticism about the ways complaints were dealt with in the past (Freeman, 2011). While the PCA has achieved some measure of credibility, it has struggled to achieve and sustain public acceptance. This has been due partly to continued questions regarding its declaration of independence. The IPCC replaced the PCA in April 2004 under the Police Reform Act 2002 (Sanders et al., 2010). This new complaints system was the result of numerous calls for change from many areas of government and society. Perhaps the most prevalent call originated from the Macpherson Inquiry into the murder of Stephen Lawrence, which involved the PCA, police services, various community and complainant groups, and the Home Affairs Select Committee. The IPCC claims independence on the basis that it is an entirely separate public body, wholly disconnected from the police services in England and Wales. It has vast powers and the findings of their investigations can only be overruled by a court of law. The IPCC is not part of the government or any of its departments.

The IPCC consists of 18 commissioners, who, by law, must not have worked previously for the police service. They also have their own investigative teams (Sanders et al., 2010). This enables the commissioners to investigate incidents of alleged misconduct absent any formal allegation or complaint. In Scotland, there is no agency comparable to the IPCC, thus all complaints of police misconduct continue to be investigated by the police themselves, effectively providing another example of the police policing the police (Audit Scotland, 2004). There is a right of appeal regarding the way investigations are conducted to HMIC in Scotland. The same can be said for Northern Ireland, where, yet again, there is no parity to the IPCC in existence. Instead, the responsibility for investigating complaints against the police rests squarely at the door of the Police Ombudsman, which possesses the authority to initiate misconduct hearings (Anthony, 2008). This is a reasonable example of the fact that although the UK police service is sometimes referred to as a unilateral force, this should clearly be discouraged.

Despite this intricate web of accountability with its checks, balances, and separation of powers, police accountability has always been, and remains, a contentious issue of public and political debate (Newburn & Jones, 1996). Thus, despite the efforts previously discussed, there exist some recurring problems of police accountability in the UK, including issues of power in the tripartite agreement, consultation and monitoring, and media-fueled debates.

Multilateral Agreement

The tripartite system rests on the separation of powers, but there have been enduring debates concerning the balance of authority between the three associates. At the time of the enactment of the PAMCA 1994, there was no requirement to reinforce the relative position of the local police authority (Grieve et al., 2007). The PAMCA 1994 and other subsequent legislation, which includes the Police Reform Act 2002, have simply strengthened the relative position of the Home Secretary. This has debatably been to the detriment of local democratic accountability. The government of the day and subsequent powers have moved to draw the balance of control toward the center. Interestingly, it has also been highly critical about the apparent lack of local community involvement in policing, a tactic seen as an essential ingredient in building on the confidence of communities in general and, in particular, the adverse impact on ethnic minority communities in these modern times.

Agency Monitoring

To ensure that the police service delivers VFM in an appropriate manner, it seems self-evident that it needs to be monitored. The very way in which the police conduct their roles must also be scrutinized. In view of this, the *Home Office Circular 12/86* refers to the layperson or visitor's scheme (Kemp & Morgan, 1990). This is a prime example of how the government and the police attempt to demonstrate transparency in the ways police go about their business. While visitors' schemes provide ample opportunity for accountability, it has been recommended that structures be implemented for the lay inspection of police station custody suites, although the actual arrangements are left to local police authorities. The lay visitors, who are actually members of the public, arrive unannounced, observe the conditions under which the detainees are held, and report their findings to the local police authority (Davies, Croall, & Tyrer, 2010).

The Independent Advisory Group (IAG) encourages observations of lay visitors as a way of ensuring that non-police viewpoints are presented. The practice is also influenced by the Macpherson Report that detailed the incidents leading up to, including, and after the murder of Stephen Lawrence. The IAG was established to seek lay advice and information and to allow lay scrutiny, particularly lay minority scrutiny, of police policymaking and even operational decision making in critical incidents (Macpherson, 1999). Providing sufficient evidence of the ethical and transparent way in which the police discharge their duties must surely be regarded as a positive action for all concerned.

General Populace

Finally, and in addition to the mechanisms previously discussed, public surveys are routinely undertaken as a form of consultation (Matthews & Pitts, 2001). This was encouraged in the early 1990s by the Citizens' and Victims' Charters and by the audit commission as a preparation for policing plan formulation. In 1998, the passing of the Crime and Disorder Act meant that the police, with their partners, were bound to consult widely on local crime and disorder issues (Matthews & Pitts, 2001). These post-1998 arrangements provide opportunities for communities to hold their local police accountable. Policing is not an exact science, thus there is no one-size-fits-all solution. There are many factors that need to be taken into account, including input from local communities. Clearly, the information used by police is only as good as the source of the information itself.

Varying platforms of media reports can influence the general populace. The likes of Twitter, Facebook, and other platforms above and beyond the usual tabloids in paper form all influence the ways readers interpret a set of incidents, a phenomenon that could have an adverse influence on society (Beck, 2010). Such scrutiny by the media plays an informal but influential part in the civilian oversight of the British police. The tradition of investigative journalism in the British media has further acted as a watchdog on the police and other public bodies.

Summary

This chapter examined the importance of accountability in relation to the various police forces in the UK, as well as the policies, structures, and procedures used to ensure the most professional organizations possible. The various ethical dilemmas associated with them have been explored as well. Considering that the police service is perhaps the most intrusive organization in any free society, the ways officers conduct themselves can profoundly influence the day-to-day lives of the general populace. Thus, it is only fitting that the police service be scrutinized closely in relation to the way it conducts itself. Clearly, trustworthiness in the ways that officers conduct themselves remains a significant issue with members of the community (Kappeler & Gaines, 2009). Ensuring that police services—including the actions of individual officers—are held accountable is absolutely imperative, especially if law enforcement hopes to rebut allegations from civil, political, and media groups, while simultaneously cultivating and maintaining the public trust.

The unique structure of the 43 UK police services has created a need for comprehensive oversight and accountability. This is especially true considering the unsettling relationship between policing and the funding of police activities. Indeed, the extent to which individual police forces are monitored and, in some cases, micromanaged is dependent on whether or not they meet the government measures used to qualify their success (Grandani, 2009a). The policing targets for each fiscal year set by the Home Secretary and government undoubtedly influence how police services conduct themselves, including, in selected instances, the failure to pursue certain types of crimes, such as shoplifting and motor vehicle theft.

The tragic and untimely death of Stephen Lawrence has led to increases in professionalism, investigative accountability, and victims' rights throughout the UK police services. In addition, the forces have substantially increased community partnerships to ensure that no section of society feels underrepresented or isolated. Meanwhile, all of this has been accomplished with an increased focus on care for crime victims and suspect's rights. The enhanced professionalism, transparency, and responsiveness demonstrated by the UK's 43 police have evolved to provide a suitable model for any law enforcement agency interested in increasing accountability, ethics, and professionalism in Europe and beyond.

References

Anthony, G. (2008). *Judicial review in northern Ireland*. Oxford: Hart.

Audit Commission. (1988). *Administrative support for operational police officers*. London: Author.

Audit Scotland. (2004*). Police and fire performance indicators 2003–04: Comparing the performance of Scottish Councils*. Edinburgh: Author.

Ayling, J., Grabosky, P. N., & Shearing, C. D. (2009). *Lengthening the arm of the law: Enhancing police resources in the twenty-first century*. Cambridge: Cambridge University Press.

Barnett, H. (2010). *Understanding public law*. London: Routledge-Cavendish.

Beck, T. (2010). *User perception of targeted ads in online social networks: A theoretical and empirical investigation using the example of Facebook* (Unpublished doctoral dissertation). University of Saint Andrews, Scotland.

Brain, T. (2010). *A history of policing in England and Wales from 1974: A turbulent journey*. Oxford: Oxford University Press.

Carrabine, E., Cox, P., Lee, M., Plummer, K., & South, N. (2009). *Criminology: A social introduction* (2nd ed.). London: Routledge.

Casciani, D. (2009). BBC Q & A: What is reasonable force? *BBC News*. Retrieved from http://news.bbc.co.uk/2/hi/uk_news/6902409.stm

Colvin, M., & Cooper, J. (2009). *Human rights in the investigation and prosecution of crime*. Oxford: Oxford University Press.

Cowan, D., & Halliday, S. (2003). *The appeal of internal review: Law, administrative justice, and the (non-) emergence of disputes*. Portland, OR: Hart.

Cowper, T. J. (2000). The myth of the "military model" of leadership in law enforcement. *Police Quarterly, 3*(3), 229–246.

Crown Prosecution Service. (2005). *Crown prosecution service: Charging standards*. Oxford: Oxford University Press.

Davies, M., Croall, H., & Tyrer, J. (2010). *Criminal justice: An introduction to the criminal justice system in England and Wales* (4th ed.). Harlow, UK: Longman.

Devine, C., Hansen, C. R., Wilde, R., & Poole, H. (1999). *Human rights: The essential reference*. Westport, CT: Greenwood.

Directgov. (2011). *How police budgets work*. Retrieved from www.direct.gov.uk/en/CrimeJusticeAndTheLaw/DG_181750

Elliott, C., & Quinn, F. (2011). *English legal system* (12th ed.). Harlow, UK: Longman.

Eriksson, A. (2009). *Justice in transition: Community restorative justice in Northern Ireland*. Cullompton, UK: Willan.

Fenwick, H., & Phillipson, G. (2007). *Judicial reasoning under the Human Rights Act*. New York: Cambridge University Press.

Fielding, N. (2005). *The police and social conflict: Contemporary issues in public policy* (2nd ed.). London: Routledge-Cavendish.

Freeman, M. A. (2011). *Human rights: Key concepts*. Cambridge: Polity Press.

Gilling, D. (2007). *Crime reduction and community safety: Labor and the politics of local crime control*. Portland, OR: Willan.

Grandani, A. R. (2009a). *Criminologist blog: Statistically-led policing*. Retrieved from http://criminology.blog.co.uk/2009/11/22/statistically-led-policing-7435995/

Grandani, A. R. (2009b, November). Tricks of the TIC track. *Metline, 26–28*.

Grieve, J., Harfield, C., & MacVean, A. (2007). *Policing*. London: Sage.

Her Majesty's Inspectorate of Constabulary (HMIC). (1999). *Police integrity: Securing and maintaining public confidence*. London: Home Office.

Home Office. (2005). *Police and Criminal Evidence Act 1984: Codes of practice (s.60(1)(a), s.60A(1) and s.66(1))*. London: TSO.

Home Office. (2011). *Police grant (England and Wales): The police grant report (England and Wales) 2011/12*. London: HMSO.

Jones, B., & Norton, P. (2010). *Politics UK* (7th ed.). Harlow, UK: Longman.

Joyce, P. (2011). *Policing: Development and contemporary practice*. London: Sage.

Kappeler, V. E., & Gaines, L. K. (2009). *Community policing: A contemporary perspective* (5th ed.). Newark, NJ: Mathew Bender & Co.

Kemp, C., & Morgan, R. (1990). *Lay visitors to police stations: Report to the Home Office*. Bristol, UK: Bristol Centre for Criminal Justice.

Kleinig, J., & Zhang, Y. (1993). *Professional law enforcement codes: A documentary collection*. Westport, CT: Greenwood.

Laville, S., & Dodd, V. (2012, January). Stephen Lawrence murder: Norris and Dobson get 14 and 15 years. *The Guardian*. Retrieved from http:www.guardian.co.uk/uk/2012/jan/04/Dobson-norris-murder-stephen-lawrence/print

Macpherson, W. (1999, February). The Stephen Lawrence inquiry: Report of an inquiry by Sir William Macpherson of Cluny (Cm, 4262-1). London: HMSO.

Matthews, R., & Pitts, J. (2001). *Crime, disorder, and community safety*. London: Routledge.

Mawby, R. I. (1999). *Policing across the world: Issues for the twenty-first century*. London: Routledge.

Moreno, Y., & Hughes, P. (2008). *Effective prosecution: Working in partnership with the CPS*. Oxford: Oxford University Press.

Newburn, T. (2007). *Criminology*. Cullompton, UK: Willan.

Newburn, T. (2008). *Policing handbook* (2nd Ed.). Cullompton, UK: Willan.

Newburn, T., & Jones, T. (1996). Police accountability. In W. Saulsbury, J. Mott, & T. Newburn, (Eds.), *Themes in contemporary policing* (pp. 120–132). London: PSI.

Neyroud, P. (2003). Policing and ethics. In T. Newburn (Ed.), *The handbook of policing* (pp. 578–602). Cullompton, UK: Willan.

Neyroud, P., & Beckley, A. (2001). *Policing, ethics, and human rights*. Cullompton, UK: Willan.

Oliver, I. (1997). *Police, government, and accountability* (2nd ed.). London: Macmillan.

Sanders, A., Young, R., & Burton, M. (2010). *Criminal justice* (4th ed.). New York: Oxford University Press.

Toynbee, P., & Walker, D. (2008). *Unjust rewards: Exposing greed and inequality in Britain today*. London: Great Publications.

Walker, C., & Starmer, K. (1999). *Miscarriages of justice: A review of justice in error*. Oxford: Oxford University Press.

Waseem, S. (2005). *The independent police complaints commission: Who will guard the guardians?* Wembley, UK: Islamic Human Rights Commission.

Weaver, M. (2009, February). Stephen Lawrence: Timeline. *The Guardian*. Retrieved from http://www.guardian.co.uk/uk/2009/feb/20/stephen-lawrence-murder-timeline/print

Wilkinson, P, (2007). *Homeland security in the UK: Future preparedness for terrorist attack since 9/11*. New York: Routledge.

PART TWO

Ethical Perspectives

6

Police Misconduct and Moral Crimes Against Self

A Philosophical Analysis

Theron Bowman and Daniel Primozic

The sergeant, second in charge of the Internal Affairs Unit (IAU), was at the chief's door. "Do you have a minute?" he asked. "I have something I think you should see." The chief noticed a DVD in the sergeant's hand . . . probably not a good sign. The chief suspected he was about to see something that would result in the disciplining of an officer. He invited the sergeant into his office and slipped the DVD into his computer. "Chief, this is a business burglary scene at the XYZ Tobacco Shop that occurred this morning at approximately 3 a.m.," the sergeant announced. "I will fill you in with some of the details as the video is playing."

"Officer Smith was dispatched to the scene of this burglary," the sergeant said. "It was a busy night and when he arrived, he informed the communication center that the front glass of the tobacco shop had been broken out." He was obviously looking at a transcript of the radio transmissions obtained from the communications center. "Smith advised that he would be making entry without a back-up, but he would advise if one was needed," the sergeant continued. "He suspected a 'smash and grab' burglary, with cartons of cigarettes as the target." The sergeant paused for a moment before continuing: "Officer Smith didn't know there was a video recording unit that had been activated by the breaking of the window." The DVD was in play now, and everyone became quiet as they watched Officer Smith begin to inspect the premises.

The crunching of broken glass was obvious as Smith was observed stepping over the threshold of the broken window. The tobacco store camera also had an audio feature. Flashlight on and handgun displayed, Smith moved toward what must have been a light switch. Within seconds the lights came on. Smith moved across the front of the store in full view of the camera. He then moved off to the right and out of sight. As he came back into view, his weapon was holstered and he spoke into the radio: "Central, this building is secure. I won't need a back-up. Can you advise the ETA of the owner?" "Squad 22 (Smith's squad number), ETA is 15 minutes," came the dispatcher's reply.

The video was silent. The chief and the IAU sergeant continued watching. Officer Smith was casually walking around, looking at the various items in the little tobacco shop. Suddenly, Smith's head turned to the left. There on the counter was a rack of smokeless tobacco. While their agency had almost 500 officers, both the sergeant and the chief knew that Smith was a smokeless tobacco user. Smith approached the rack. He tilted his head as if he was trying to read the labels. Smith took a furtive look to the left and then to the right. Obviously seeing no one, he then reached to the rack and helped himself to a can of his favorite tobacco. Within several minutes, the owner entered the shop, and Smith obtained the necessary information to complete his report. He advised the owner of the actions he had taken on the scene (obviously leaving out the missing can of Skoal) and then excused himself to call back into service.

"The owner of the tobacco shop brought this DVD in about an hour ago and filed a formal complaint with IA," the sergeant commented. "Well chief, what do you think?" he asked. The chief responded by saying, "Draw up the termination papers and get us ready for the termination hearing. We're filing criminal charges as well."

As this scenario demonstrates, police misconduct, whether real or perceived, adversely impacts community trust in police officers and the police profession—yet it still occurs. Why? Do a disturbing number of crime fighters really fail to know right from wrong? Is ethical training really necessary to do the right thing? If knowledge and training deficits are the "culprits," then shouldn't "traditional" solutions be adequate? Will simply providing additional hours of ethics training not engender improvement on this front? What if we improve the selection process, ensure the department has a code of ethics and a set of core values along with very exhaustive policy manuals, and establish proficient reward and punishment systems? Unfortunately, these traditional methods of dissuading police misconduct have not eradicated the problem, and we must continue to look for new remedies.

This chapter proposes new ways of addressing the issue of police misconduct. The authors first ask, What really causes police misconduct? Next, the authors present ideas from Aristotle and Robert J. Steinberg that may hold promise for helping police to both realize and to do the right thing. Then, using the metaphor of police crime analysis of the "inner city," the authors propose a "forensic" examination of the will, charting the internal pathology of morality and rationality succumbing to their irrational and impetuous competitors. Finally, the chapter proposes a deployment strategy for fighting crimes against self in the "inner city."

_____ An Underexamined Cause of Police Misconduct

This examination of ethics begins by challenging traditional wisdom on the root causes of police misconduct. A knowledge bank account deficit in what constitutes right or wrong seems a bankrupt excuse. Perhaps it is the case that sometimes police are unaware of the right thing to do and about the impropriety of certain actions. But surely that is a minute part of the problem, one that can and must be resolved through good and solid ethics training that refocuses police on the virtues and values that together form the nobility of the work. But there also are undeveloped and underdiscussed areas that form a more complete picture of the problem of police misconduct, wherever it raises its ugly head. In what follows, the authors provide some additional elements of that more adequate picture of the problem.

One can find hints about this underexamined and understudied aspect of ethical misconduct in the ancient works of Aristotle. He provided clues as to what happens when a person who knows full well the right thing to do, yet fails to do it. Instead, that person goes forward to do what he knows to be wrong. But how, indeed, is this possible? Aristotle would call this state of affairs *akrasia*, or "weakness of will" (Kraut, 2001).

In book VII of the *Nicomachean Ethics*, Aristotle explains *akrasia* by likening it to people who "know" the right thing to do but not in a sufficient way. According to Kraut,

> Aristotle explains what he has in mind by comparing ***akrasia*** to the condition of other people who might be described as knowing in a way, but not in an unqualified way. His examples are people who are asleep, mad, or drunk; he also compares the akratic to a student who has just begun to learn a subject, or an actor on the stage (1147a10–24). All of these people, he says, can utter the very words used by those who have knowledge; but their talk does not prove that they really have knowledge, strictly speaking. (2001, para. 9)

Aristotle (1985) says this himself in the *Nicomachean Ethics*:

> Saying the words that come from knowledge is no sign [of fully having it]. For people affected in these ways even recite demonstrations and verses of Empedocles. Further, those who have just learnt something do not yet know it, though they string the words together; for it must grow into them, and this needs time. Hence, we must suppose that incontinents say the words the way that actors do. (1147a 18–24, pp. 811–812)

Therefore the "akratic" (the one of weak will) tells himself at the point of action that he should not commit this immoral action, but lets the passion, emotion, pleasure, or other less than rational temptation win him over and so commits the act he knows he should not. Although he has some knowledge that he must not commit this act, it is not yet perfected into his will. Hence, his reasoning and will are weak and vulnerable to temptation. The "weak willed" has his reason bypassed by its competitors: passion, impetuosity, emotion, pleasure, and so on (Kraut, 2001). Furthermore, his reason is so roundly defeated by its competitors that not until later does the person even realize and regret his actions. In short, what he does in the weakness of his will may not even constitute what would normally be referred to as a rational choice, conscious reflection, or decision. *Akrasia* removes this action from the realm of rationality.

When applying this ancient Aristotelian concept to police misconduct, it is not that police do not know or embrace the core values, codes, oaths, and policies of their profession and their agencies. Training that attaches police to their professional core is worthy and useful. Indeed, it should never be neglected or ignored. However, competitor desires come powerfully to the fore during moments of temptation, passion, impetuosity, and emotion (Kraut, 2001). Although inoculated with knowledge, it is during periods of lowered resistance that these competing values show their true strength by influencing the officer's actions. Providing some concrete examples that are not atypical of police experience is perhaps the best way to demonstrate this phenomenon.

Although an officer may have a sworn oath to pursue and maintain an unsullied life, situational vulnerabilities may lead to counterintuitive behavior. Here are several examples. There is a pile of money or drugs the officer believes he can take unnoticed, instead of bringing it to the department to be tagged and packaged for the evidence room. The officer knows he must treat citizens with respect and dignity—but one of those citizens just punched him in the face. Now anger and passion takes over. Calm and rational reflection of the virtues and values of policing disappear in a rather purple, quick, and affective physical overreaction that is captured on the squad car cam. The adrenaline dump that naturally occurs after a high-speed pursuit can help to yield moments of abuse of force. Some of these officers caught by the competitors of their reason regret these moments later, when the calm and untroubled waters of knowledge and self-control return. By then, it is often too late to recoup or redeem the actions they now regret. Hence, it is beneficial to dig more deeply into the specifics of Aristotle's analysis of *akrasia*.

Aristotle's Analysis of Weakness of Will

Aristotle posits that there may be a universally applicable ethical principle (described later as the major premise), and there may be a specific instance in front of us that is covered by that universally applicable principle (as described later as the minor premise). If we are using reason only and we know well the rules of logical reasoning, then that reasoning provides us with a conclusion that should form the basis of a good decision. But that is true if and only if reason solely is at play in decisions like those in ethics, and if and only if reason has no competitors like desires, pleasures, or bad habits.

Aristotle analyzes *akrasia* in terms of a "practical syllogism," and finds that practical moral reasoning could be represented in the form of a syllogism. The major premise in a practical syllogism would evoke an "ought" toward a moral action, and the minor premise would describe a particular instance of that kind of moral action. The valid logical conclusion would follow to the right kind of moral action in that particular circumstance. As Aristotle (1985) puts this in the *Nicomachean Ethics*,

> Further we may also look at the cause [of *akrasia*] in the following way, referring to [human] nature. Once belief (a) is universal; the other (b) is about particulars, and because they are particulars, perception controls them. And in the cases where these two beliefs result in (c) one belief, it is necessary in purely theoretical beliefs for the soul to affirm what has been concluded, and in beliefs about production (d) to act at once on what has been concluded.
>
> If, e.g., (a) everything must be tasted, and (b) this, some one particular thing, is sweet, it is necessary (d) for someone who is able and unhindered also to act on this at the same time. Suppose, then, that someone has (a) the universal belief, and it hinders him from tasting; he has (b) the second belief, that everything sweet is pleasant and this is sweet, and this belief (b) is active; and he also has appetite. Hence the belief (c) tells him to avoid this, but appetite leads him on, since it is capable of moving each of the [bodily] parts.
>
> The result, then, is that in a way reason and belief make him act incontinently. The belief (b) is contrary to correct reason (a), but only coincidentally, not in itself. For it is the appetite, not the belief, that is contrary [in itself to correct reason]. (1147a 25–1147b 3, p. 812)

For the sake of clarity and simplicity, a practical moral syllogism for a police officer might follow these steps:

Major Premise: All immoral and illegal (though pleasurable) temptations must be avoided to lead an unsullied, virtuous life as a police professional.

Minor Premise: What I will confront as a police officer will be many immoral and illegal (though pleasurable) temptations.

Conclusion: Therefore, I must identify and then avoid those immoral and illegal (though pleasurable) temptations.

Here the content of the major premise, a universal proposition, is gathered from training, education, habit, observation, and drill, especially in the ways in which police society defines the "good and honorable life." The minor premise emerges from an officer properly identifying the contours of the specific situation that officer is confronting and the possible alternative actions he can take in reference to it. The conclusion merely follows logically from the dictates of good reasoning.

However, as Aristotle points out, there can be a competitor syllogism that not only makes perfect logical sense, but is also informed and driven by appetite and desire, not goodness and reason, and a consideration of what is good for us in the long run. Although the logical form of the competitor syllogism is equally as valid as the practical syllogism, the content of the competitor is clearly at odds with the practical version.

Major Premise: All desires must be satisfied right now (albeit by unethical or illegal means) because my life is short, my job is tough, and my cop salary alone will not allow me to enjoy those pleasures and desires which I deserve.

Minor Premise: What I confront here and now is something that satisfies my desires now (albeit by unethical or illegal means).

Conclusion: Therefore, I must satisfy my desires now with what confronts me (albeit by unethical or illegal means) because my life is short, my job is tough, and my cop salary alone will not allow me to enjoy those pleasures and desires which I deserve.

Aside from all the psychological work that can be performed on some of the self-pity that is felt by the officer thinking in terms of this second, "competitor" syllogism, the content of the argument surely has been heard numerous times by internal affairs investigators as rationalizations for breaches of professional ethical standards and illegal acts by otherwise good police officers now taken off their career paths—or even to prison.

In the case of the second, competitor syllogism, it is not the fault of the logical form of the competitor syllogism that causes offenses against ethics and law. As Aristotle pointed out, it is the "appetite," or the officer's weakness of will, that is the culprit here (Aristotle, 1147b 3, p. 812). In short, it takes strong self-discipline, strong habit-built character, and sound common sense and wisdom concerning what is beneficial in the long run that causes the good cop to act in accordance with the first syllogism. Weakness of will that comes from a lack of self-discipline, bad habits, questionable character, and a lack of sound foresight into what is good in the long run causes the bad cop to act in accordance with the competitor syllogism. These choices show us what the officer *really* values when the chips are down and what kind of moral fiber he really possesses. Thus, as has already been indicated, though the logical form of both syllogisms are identical and are equally valid, the content of the syllogisms drive our moral decisions into two extremely opposite directions: one toward virtue and one to vice.

Cases of *akrasia* arise when the person who is making this calculation is insufficiently educated or has morality training deficiencies and, therefore, lacks a solid grasp of what is really best for him (Aristotle, 1147a 1–23, p. 811). Immoralities and errors of action can also arise if the person improperly or inadequately assesses the facts of the situation about which he must make a moral decision. Or, more to the previously emphasized point, the person simply values that which temporarily pleases more than virtuous character. But there are other proposals that we have seen for the causes of "weakness of will" that can come in handy.

_____ Other Possible Causes of Weakness of The Will

All of that moral reasoning with practical syllogisms is fine and adequate for people who already want to do the good—for people "of good will" (Kant, 2002, p. 9). But what about people who like the pleasures that come with doing the bad more than they like the virtue of doing the good? These people, it would seem, are not really helped by the syllogisms and reasoning above. Aristotle would suggest that those people who really value pleasure over virtue and doing the bad to get those pleasures need a complete education into the ultimate life benefits of virtue and rehabilitation into good and fine character habits (Aristotle, 1103a 14–26, p. 777). And this education can and often does take place in the traditional ethics in-service classroom.

Yet there are other, more contemporary thinkers, who try to wrestle with the problem of *akrasia* as well. One of these thinkers, Donald Davidson (1980), sees *akrasia* appear in cases where agents seek to fulfill moral requirements and gain the higher, more enduring happiness of so doing, but who, in the end, do not pursue the most morally defensible course of action. In short, sometimes people simply act against their better judgment because of competing temporary pleasures that they believe await them. That course of action indicates the individuals really believe that the "worse" is the better course of action, mainly because they have left out the "all-things considered" judgment. That judgment would have led them to pursue the moral high ground. For a brief moment, however, they do not know what is good for them in the long run. They focus only on what seems pleasurable for them now or in the near future. Thus, they make a judgment based on an incomplete and inadequate slice of the relevant factors for moral consideration.

Indeed, there are many interpretations in Aristotle and in many other thinkers that seek to account for why precisely the *akratic* chooses the worst course of action. But they all share a common thread—one that manifests itself as the victory of the undertrained, overbearing, morally weak will over the undertrained, underinformed, and underhabituated faculty of reason. This common thread is picked up and analyzed best in the work of Descartes.

Descartes and the Problem of the Overbearing Strength of the Will

René Descartes, the Renaissance philosopher and mathematician, was fully aware of and wrote about the vast "power differential" between the will and the intellect, reason, or, as he puts it, "the understanding" (Descartes,

1993). He declared that the will is strong and developed at birth, whereas the intellect needs a lifetime of training, strengthening, and development so that it can overcome the mistakes of the will, its desires and passions. As Descartes says,

> Next, as I focus more closely upon myself and inquire into the nature of my errors . . . I note that these errors depend on the simultaneous concurrence of two causes: the faculty of knowing that is in me and the faculty of choosing, that is the free choice of the will, in other words, the intellect and the will. Through the intellect alone I merely perceive ideas, about which I can render a judgment. Strictly speaking, no error is to be found in the intellect when properly viewed in this manner. . . . But from these considerations I perceive that the power of willing, which I got from God, is not, taken by itself, the cause of my errors, for it is ample as well as perfect in its kind. Nor is my power of understanding the cause of my errors. . . . What then is the source of my errors? They are owing simply to the fact that, since the will extends further than the intellect, I do not contain the will within the same boundaries; rather I extend it to things I do not understand. Because the will is indifferent in regard to such matters, it easily turns away from the true and the good; and in this way I am deceived and I sin. (pp. 474–475)

So how would Descartes apply this to the problem of the *akratic* falling prey to the competitor syllogism that we outlined above? How would Descartes propose that we encourage the *akratic* to run diligently along the lines of the reasonable and noble practical syllogism that would have him do the right thing and avoid doing wrong?

Descartes would tell us that the will, being stronger, more powerful, and more developed in us even from birth, will win the battle of the good versus competitor syllogism because the intellect is not as strong, powerful, and developed. The will wins that battle too often because of an underdeveloped intellect that does not perform its real function in terms of choosing (willing) according to the dictates and confines of reason (Descartes, 1993). Operating all by itself, the will takes us beyond those confines and dictates, and into error and immoral activity (what Descartes called *sin* in the quotation above).

What then would be the Cartesian remedy? The answer for him would be to develop one's intellect and reason so that it is muscular enough to rein the will into the confines of the structures of validity, logical soundness, and what is good for us in the long run (Descartes, 1993). This more fully developed intellect and reason would take into account what Davidson (1980) called the *all things considered* factors of the equation that guide our choices for action. In short, being strong and powerful enough, the intellect would perform its proper function of "policing" the will, and therefore we would make the proper moral choices. Failing that hard duty of developing our minds and intellects by education, training, discipline, planning, and vigilance, we fall prey to error and subsequent immorality. Ironically, the strength (not the weakness) of will is to blame for our errors and immoral choices and actions. So, for someone like Descartes, what Aristotle called the *weakness of will* must be strengthened and buttressed by a strong and vigorous intellect and reasoning faculty for us to choose and to do the right thing (Descartes, 1993). Nevertheless, the pursuit of developing a robust and hearty intellect in police officers tends to be overlooked in traditional ethics training because it presupposes that, because of the very nature of their jobs, these professionals require no further work in the area of critical thinking.

Yet, from what has been discussed above, the need for critical thinking *in ethics* seems quite obviously paramount, and ethics trainers can acquire some training insights from the philosophical explanations presented above. Ethics trainers who preach dictates and slogans while shaking their fingers in the faces of officers in the classroom are, at best, engaged in an exercise of absolute futility. If Aristotle, Descartes, and Donaldson are correct, trainers should instead ensure that officers develop and nourish decision making, critical reasoning skills, and sound procedures for ethical judgments. It would follow that police should be trained and drilled in those skills so that they can use them when temptations abound in real-life situations.

Also based on the previous discussion, it seems that a key to helping police do the right thing is to get their will to "listen to reason"; to choose the right version of the practical syllogism and to avoid the competitor syllogism; to choose reason and good over pleasures and unethical conduct; to help officers fashion a "good will" and eschew "ill will." But if crime fighters have not already secured the habit of making the choice for what is good for them and others, then where else can we look to help them to secure that habit of choosing wisely and not poorly? Here it is useful to take a step back, turn and look to the advice of Robert J. Steinberg.

Teaching Our Will to Listen to Reason

In his article "A New Model for Teaching Ethical Behavior," Steinberg (2009) presents some ideas that are rarely seen in the training rooms of police professionals but appear to be crucial. He begins by claiming that "what is frightening about ethical lapses is not that they happen to the ethically outrageous but that they can sneak up on just about all of us" (para. 2). This surely applies to the police, who are well intentioned but can, like the rest of us, fall prey to what Steinberg refers to as ethical *lapses*. Steinberg maintains that to do the good,

> individuals must go through a series of steps, and unless all of the steps are completed, people are not likely to behave ethically, regardless of the ethics training or moral education they have received and the levels of other types of relevant skills they might possess, such as critical or creative thinking. (2009, para. 8)

Steinberg proposes that for officers to behave ethically, they must follow the steps of his proposed eight-step model. For purposes of this discussion, only three of Steinberg's steps will be discussed.

The first step is to "recognize that there is an event to react to" or, to use language we have used above, "to make a choice about." Steinberg (2009) puts it this way:

> When people hear their political, educational, or especially religious leadership talk, they may not believe there is any reason to question what they hear. After all, they are listening to authority figures. In this way, cynical and corrupt leaders can lead their followers to accept and even commit unethical acts such as suicide bombings and murder of those with divergent beliefs. (para. 11)

In other words, officers, especially in unethical police cultures, may be so accustomed to seeing the wrong choices being made by their leaders, mentors, role models, and peers that they are not keenly aware that there is any choice at hand to be made whatsoever, let alone a moral choice. It is seen simply as the "way we do business." Or they may be so habituated by their background experience that they are similarly "asleep at the wheel." The implication is that people must be trained in a manner as to present scenarios or case studies wherein there seems to be no need for choices to be made. Cases should be presented, then, that can elicit answers that can be taken for granted and require no critical thought.

One example of such a case is extending professional courtesy to other police professionals by not issuing citations, or overlooking drunk-driving incidents, for example, by driving the officers home instead of citing their infractions or arresting the officers. Too often, police officers see such cases as having, in Steinberg's words, "nothing to question." Police regularly seem oblivious to choices when these situations are presented for moral analysis. In short, situations like this one, and their attendant choices, seem to have become the norm, taken, in many cases, as standard operating procedure.

Steinberg's (2009) second step is to "define the event as having an ethical dimension" (para. 12). This might seem like a silly thing to emphasize with adults, especially for the highly trained and essentially noble police officers charged with enforcing the morality and laws of our society. Yet, even these officers must be reminded, trained, and drilled to know when they are confronting an ethical issue. For some people in Steinberg's teaching experience, the most critical step in ethics education is working through enough "business as usual" and "taken for granted" scenarios and cases to sensitize them to the fact that there is an ethical issue, problem, dilemma, or choice to be made. Actually, increasing this ethical sensitivity may be a difficult ethics teaching challenge because some people believe they are ethically just fine. Some assume they have mastered the art of choosing and doing the right thing. Therefore, they assume there is little or nothing left to learn in this regard. Most often they are correct. However, none of us are "past masters" at this. In reality, all of us can use reminding and refinement considering the complexity of human life and the subtleties of the competitor syllogisms. This is the reason that ethics training should be repeated and reemphasized periodically in some solid form of refresher educational experiences.

Steinberg's third step is to decide that the ethical dimension is significant. As Steinberg (2009) points out,

> Perhaps they had sometimes taken what was not theirs—say, something small like a newspaper or even money they had found on the ground . . . but not see it as sufficiently significant to make a fuss. Politicians seem to specialize in trying to downplay the ethical dimension of their behavior. (para. 14)

To apply this analysis, it is necessary to revisit the issue of professional courtesy. Again, police professionals may not see this issue as significant enough to challenge, analyze, or discuss in an ethics training session. These behaviors may be ingrained in their police or organizational culture and may be *de rigueur*. They may appear to be small infractions, if at all. "Everyone has always done these things," "other professionals extend courtesies," and thus there is no "big ethical deal" here.

There is good reason to value Steinberg's insights for police ethics training. However, there are other strategies that trainers can adopt to complement their programs. Before preceding any further, however, it is important to note the following caveat. One promise that cannot be made regardless of what has already been seen above and what will now be proposed as another instrument or tool is that the educational process in ethics and the results that flow from it are foolproof or absolutely guaranteed to succeed. That promise should not be made chiefly because people will remain human and will not respond like robots to their training and education. In reality, that is a good thing, given some of the trainings that humans have undergone at the hands of the Nazi party and other similar "educational" efforts of ill repute. After all, we don't want to make "clones" of our officers, nor do we wish them to become robotic automata. Or do we? Perhaps that deserves a brief but closer look.

The Ethically Constrained Robot

Surely, it would be easier to manage a police department or agency if the officers within it were more like the proposed "ethical robots" currently being developed for our Department of Defense by researcher Ronald Arkin. Arkin seeks to make war more humane by creating armed robots programmed to make ethical decisions. Not only is this not far-fetched, but

Arkin (as cited by Devine, 2012) also thinks he has very good reason to embark on this task:

> Robots could behave better in certain situations because they aren't influenced by the emotions that can cloud a soldier's judgment. "We are not saying that we are intending to embed the full moral faculties of the human brain into a robotic system," but for a mission with a narrow objective, an ethically constrained robot could protect both soldiers and civilians in a war zone. (p. 64)

Even so, do any of us really want our police professionals (or any of our human family) to become "ethically constrained robots," despite the fact that these robots-in-development might actually have some limited use in police situations? That seems doubtful. Do any of us really want to put our laws, morality, and liberty in the power of robots that have little or no discretion, discernment, and compassion? That, too, seems doubtful. Hence, knowing that there is always a danger in allowing our ethics training to go too far in the direction of making police into robots, perhaps ethics training should be kept in the form of good adult educational models where case studies are considered through dialogue and discussion involving free exchange from human minds and hearts. In short, it seems clear that people should remain as human as possible even as they are trained to walk the narrow pathways of the good, the true, and the beautiful. Yet, there is one additional new tool for the ethical toolbox for police presented below as an experimental possibility to test in the ethics training setting.

The Forensics of Crimes Against Self in the Inner City____

To illustrate the additional experimental piece for the ethics training room, it may be useful to employ the metaphor of a typical police crime analysis of the inner city of a major metropolitan community. The metaphor of crime analysis is used because most police professionals are familiar with its use. In deploying this experimental piece of ethics training, an understanding of crime analysis will help students gain significant, meaningful, and practical results from the proposed classroom exercises that follow.

Therefore, in the same way that officers analyze where, when, what, whom, and how often a particular set of crimes occur in the physical city, participants are asked to answer the following set of "interrogation" questions to hedge against "crimes against themselves in their own *inner cities*" (or inner, moral lives):

1. What are the most typical temptations that police professionals fall prey to? *This question is ripe for good and robust, public, general discussion and dialogue from the participants themselves.* Students should arrive at some concrete answers they have heard about, seen their peers suffer from,

or perhaps even experienced themselves. However, it is advisable that the trainer has some current research and statistics ready to shape the dialogue and to arrive at answers based on real data. This exercise is quite valuable and should be given a considerable amount of time. The exercise is informative, and its public nature helps to set the stage for the more private "personal moral crime scene investigation" to follow.

2. *The second set of questions must be asked in some private way with no one else privy to the answers from participants (and the participants must be assured that these answers will be confidential and will never be accessed by anyone else but themselves).* What are your typical temptations that could lead you off the ethical course? Which are those that you are most likely to fall prey to? Which temptations to unethical conduct have you already fallen prey to in your professional life? In your personal life? What would you say your moral habit pattern is like? Where do you see ethical problems, dilemmas, or infractions most likely to arise? What situations do these ethical temptations generally arise for you? Where are they likely to arise? With whom? When have they arisen? Under what circumstances? Are they likely to arise under those conditions again? How exactly did those temptations and, if applicable, their attendant infractions take place (describe this in as much detail as possible)? How frequently did these ethical problems occur? This section is perhaps the most important self-interrogation of this proposed training method and, therefore, should be given a very healthy block of time and perhaps should even be conducted in a private place of the participants' own choosing for assurance that their responses to the questions will be private and confidential, and also so that they have the appropriate setting for deep and deadly honest reflection.

3. As a result of your interrogations concerning the first two points above, what are the ethical "hotspots" for your typical or potential "moral crimes against yourself?" What was your track record from the past? How many "crimes against self" have you already committed and in what areas? This is important because those are the most likely to be committed again if confronted with the same kinds of temptations to do the wrong thing. *Again, this should be conducted in private as was mentioned above and for the same reasons mentioned above.*

4. When you have clearly identified these potential "crime hot spots" of "crimes against yourself," you can try to assess what your values really are. You can more easily assess where you have conflicts in what you think or would like to value, and what you have sometimes really valued and which kinds of conflicts will cause you problems in the short and the long run as a person and as a professional. This will show you whether you really value virtue over immoral pleasures and temptations. Then you can make plans to avoid those areas of temptations and, if you see them coming, to leave the potential scene of the crime as quickly and completely as possible. *Again,*

this part of the session is conducted in private and must be held in a setting that will assure confidentiality.

It is recommended that before the answers to the first question are brought forward for public discussion and dialogue, participants have the opportunity to write down their answers. The responses to the remainder of the questions above should be written in journal-entry style and in the kind of classroom settings outlined above in the questions themselves.

Summary

Even after employing the traditional hedges against police misconduct like background checks, policy manuals, ethics training, FTO, PTO, and mentoring, as well as the kinds of buttresses for the intellect and reason to control and confine the unethical and immoral ranging of the human will, police professionals are only people after all, and it is doubtful that any of us wish that they become ethical robots. They have not only fine minds, intense discipline, and excellent training, but also hearts full of personal dreams, desires, and plans for themselves and for those whom they love. And because the human heart sometimes wants one thing and the human mind wants another, in a constitutional democracy, police should retain the right to choose freely. Hence, ethics training absolutely certifying that their hearts will follow their minds, or that their reasoning prowess is guaranteed to push the will in the right direction, does not take their humanity into adequate account.

Because of that, ethics training and education, even when performed optimally and excellently, should only remind and inspire the hearts of these men and women to do the right thing, not just once or on occasion, but characteristically, habitually, and almost automatically. As Aristotle and Descartes obviously tried so hard to point out in their analyses briefly presented above, the human heart (the human will) often tends to drive our intellects and our actions, and not the reverse.

This brief excursion into the causes of police misconduct offers the following suggestions as a possible remedy:

1. It may not simply be that police are unaware of the right thing to do and are totally clueless about the wrongness of certain actions they choose to take. Although that sometimes is the problem—one resolved by ethics training that refocuses police on the virtues and values that together form the nobility of their work—there are underdiscussed and underanalyzed problems that help to explain more fully the problem of police misconduct, one being the ancient problem of *akrasia,* or the weakness of will (Aristotle, 1985).

2. It is also the case that there has been a dearth of useful, practical, detailed analyses of the structures, workings, and influences of the weakness

of will, which involves looking all the way back to unlikely helpers for the police profession like Aristotle and Descartes. It may also involve looking toward equally unlikely contemporary helpers who offer more contemporary philosophical analyses like Donald Davidson.

3. As Steinberg (2009) indicates, a crucial missing step for all of us in ethical struggles is to first realize that there is a problem at hand per se, and second, that it is a problem of a significant ethical kind that will involve critical reasoning, struggle, or battle within one's self for the morally correct behavior to emerge. In other words, all people (and here, for our purposes, police professionals) should be trained in a manner that includes scenarios or case studies wherein there seems to be no real choice to be made and the answers can simply be taken for granted. Perhaps these are the very scenarios that would further benefit ethics training for police.

4. It would seem, then, that the kind of ethics training required should take the form of good and solid adult education: ethics training that presents real-life scenarios and case studies for examination, discussion, and dialogue among police practitioners who have lived through such situations or will live through them in the course of their careers. If it is undesirable to create "ethically constrained robots," then this type of adult, professional education is preferable when trying to cultivate morally noble police professionals who have ethically mature hearts and minds that will want to do the right thing.

5. Perhaps the kind of "forensic" self-examination of the potential personal hotspots for ethical and legal "crimes against self" outlined above should be tried and tested in the living laboratory of the ethics training room. Perhaps if that forensic analysis is performed well, in the right spirit, and for the appropriate purposes, it can help officers predict what their own ethical challenges might be or become during the performance of their jobs. Perhaps, therefore, it can help them think through how they, themselves, might be able to avoid choosing poorly and getting into trouble.

Perhaps what should be hoped for, after all is said and done, is something that C. S. Lewis (1955) hoped for in one of his most famous works:

> We were told it all long ago by Plato. As the king governs by his executive, so Reason in man must rule the mere appetites by means of the spirited element. The head rules the belly through the chest—the seat, as Alanus tells us, of Magnanimity, of emotions organized by trained habit into stable sentiments. The Chest—Magnanimity—Sentiment—these are the indispensable liaison officers between cerebral man and visceral man. It may even be said that it is by this middle element that man is man: for by his intellect he is mere spirit and by his appetite mere animal. . . . You can hardly open a periodical without coming across the statement that what our civilization needs is more

"drive," or dynamism, or self-sacrifice, or "creativity." In a sort of ghastly simplicity we remove the organ and demand the function. We make men without chests and expect of them virtue and enterprise. We laugh at honor and are shocked to find traitors in our midst. (pp. 234–235)

Lewis hoped for "people with chests." For the good of society and civilization, he hoped for men and women of good purpose, will, hearts, and minds: people of magnanimity, fine sentiment, and virtue. For that great hope to ever realistically materialize, perhaps the experimental training proposed above should begin with us. Perhaps we, ourselves, should be the first to fully and robustly engage the task of educating our own human hearts into a life moral excellence and integrity, whether inside or outside the police department. Perhaps we, ourselves, should be the first experimental subjects to perform our own "crime analysis" of the ethical hotspots of moral temptations unique to us so that we can avoid being ambushed by them while we live a complex and distracting contemporary life. Perhaps also we may have some credible witness in an ethics education setting where we try to teach, train, and guide. And perhaps if all of that is in place and works well, then police organizations and agencies will have a much better shot at gaining and retaining "people with chests" who are so much more than mere robots. These just may become the "chested" people of good will and character who consistently avoid choosing the competitor syllogism and choose, instead, to do the right thing. And perhaps the officer in the real-life scenario mentioned at the beginning of this chapter would forgo pinching the can of Skoal or, at very least, leave behind enough money to pay for it. It seems worth another try.

Discussion Questions

1. Explain in your own words the problem of *akrasia*. Describe it in some detail.

2. How would you describe in simple terms the "practical syllogism," especially as applied to the moral choices that face the average police officer? How would you explain the "competitor syllogism," especially as applied to the moral choices that face the average police officer?

3. From the selection presented of Robert Steinberg's thoughts, is he correct in his assessment of why people fail to behave ethically? Why or why not?

4. In your view, is there anything wrong with programming police officers in the same manner one would program "ethically constrained robots"? What, if any, are the downsides to so doing? What would some of the advantages be of doing that?

5. What do you think about the rubric of questions for self-examination that were offered in the section concerning "The Forensics of Crimes Against the Self in the Inner City?" Do you think that it would be a valuable exercise to perform in an ethics in-service for police? If so, why? If not, why not?

References

Aristotle. (1985). *Nicomachean ethics* (T. Irwin, Trans.). In S. M. Cohen, P. Curd, & C. D. C. Reeve (Eds.), *Readings in ancient Greek philosophy: From Thales to Aristotle* (pp. 870–929). Indianapolis, IN: Hackett.

Davidson, D. (1980). How is weakness of the will possible? *Essays on actions and events*. Oxford: Oxford University Press.

Descartes, R. (1993). *Meditations on first philosophy* (Donald A. Cress, Trans.). In Steven M. Cahn (Ed.), (2002), *Classics of Western philosophy* (6th ed., pp. 484–516). Indianapolis: Hackett Publishing Company.

Devine, D. J. (2012, February). Automaton army: Researcher hopes robots can make combat decisions that protect soldiers and civilians. *World Archives*. Retrieved from http://www.worldmag.com/articles/19187

Kant, I. (2002). *Groundwork for the metaphysics of morals* (A. W. Wood, Trans.). New Haven, CT: Yale University Press.

Kraut, R. (2001). Aristotle's ethics. In E. N. Zalta (Ed.), *The Stanford encyclopedia of philosophy* (Summer 2010 ed.). Retrieved from http://plato.stanford.edu/archives/sum2010/entries/aristotle-ethics/

Lewis, C. S. (1955). *The abolition of man: How education develops man's sense of morality*, New York: Macmillan.

Steinberg, R. (2009, April). A new model for teaching ethical behavior. *The Chronicle of Higher Education*. Retrieved from http://chronicle.com/article/A-New-Model-for-Teaching/36202

7

Bad Apple or Bad Barrel

Social Learning Theory as a Paradigm for Understanding Law Enforcement Misconduct

Brian D. Fitch and Christine H. Jones

According to a recent article in the *Dallas News* (Eiserer, 2012), rookie officers are introduced to the "culture of alcohol consumption at the police academy" (para. 11). Recruits drink hard and party hard with other recruits because of peer pressure and high stress levels. Many officers continue to drink throughout their careers—both on and off duty, in some cases—for the same reasons. The article goes on to report findings from a study involving Mississippi police officers that found the subjects most at risk for problem drinking were those who drank to fit in. Not surprisingly, the behaviors created by a culture of drinking have ruined an untold number of promising careers, created embarrassment for the officers and their agencies, and, in some cases, resulted in costly and widely publicized litigation. However, the need to conform to peer pressure does not stop with drinking.

A story of peer pressure and unsanctioned conduct allegedly involving members of an elite gang unit within the Los Angeles County Sheriff's Department appeared in the April 19, 2012 edition of the *Los Angeles Times*. The story, titled "Secret Clique in the L.A. County Sheriff's Gang Unit Probed," describes an investigation launched by sheriff's department officials into what appears to be a secret clique. The probe was apparently triggered by the discovery of a document suggesting the group embraces shooting as a badge of honor (Faturechi, 2012). The document purportedly described a code of conduct for the Jump Out Boys, a clique of hard-charging, aggressive deputies who gain more respect after being involved in a shooting, according to sources reported as close to the investigation. Sheriff's officials are described as notably concerned that the group represents yet another "unsanctioned clique" (para. 4.) within its ranks, a problem the agency has struggled with for decades.

In both of these examples, officers appear to be influenced by a desire to conform, regardless of the personal or professional consequences. Law enforcement agencies, however, have traditionally dismissed any relationship between social learning, conformity, and misconduct, typically labeling incidents of deviant behavior as the isolated misdeeds of a few "bad apples" in an otherwise pristine organization (Cohen & Feldberg, 1991). According to this description, a few deviant officers somehow managed to slip through a crack in the screening process and, once hired, continued to engage in illegal conduct, apparently in isolation from other members of the organization (Sherman, 1974).

The character-based explanations commonly used to rationalize police misconduct as isolated occurrences committed by a small number of socially detached officers rely on dispositional qualities, such as personality traits, personal values, and attitudes, to explain deviant behavior (Fitch, 2011). While proper values, appropriate attitudes, and certain personality characteristics are certainly important, there is no coherent body of evidence to support the idea that dispositional qualities are responsible for individual differences in moral behavior (Shermer, 2004). Indeed, research suggests that a person's moral behavior is not consistent from one situation to another—for instance, an individual who cheats in one situation may or may not cheat in another (Hartshorne & May, 1928). Similarly, there is no necessary correlation between what people say and how they act, implying that lofty moral principles, education, and religiosity often matter much less than is generally believed when examining behavior (Collins, 2000; Jordan & Monin, 2008).

Social learning theory posits a different account of police misconduct, one that relies on external variables, that is, peer associations, modeling, and reinforcers as predictors of criminal behavior (Chappell & Piquero, 2004). Proponents of this approach maintain that criminal conduct is acquired through the same processes of associative learning and modeling as other forms of behavior—and that culture plays an integral role by transmitting the normative beliefs, values, and definitions that discourage or encourage deviant behavior (Akers, 1996, 2000, 2009; Burgess & Akers, 1966). The corruption, abuse, and other forms of deviant behavior that occur in law enforcement organizations do not happen in a vacuum. Rather, police misconduct transpires in the learning context of a larger organization, "the barrel," and is influenced by peers and other important relationships that provide socialization, learning, and reinforcement (Akers, 2009).

This chapter provides an overview of social learning theory, paying special attention to four essential propositions (Akers, 2009; Burgess & Akers, 1966; Lee, Akers, & Borg, 2004): (1) differential association, (2) differential reinforcement, (3) imitation, and (4) definitions. The authors then demonstrate how these four propositions function as a general theory of police deviance, including how misconduct perpetrated by law enforcement officers is influenced by the same principles of learning as other forms of behavior. The chapter concludes with recommendations on what law enforcement administrators and supervisors can do to mitigate deviant conduct.

Social Learning Theory

The foundation of modern social learning theory can be traced to the writing of the French social theorist Gabriel Tarde (1843–1904). Tarde (1903, 1912) was interested in the social processes used to transfer ways of thinking and feeling from group to group and from person to person. Tarde theorized that deviant behavior is acquired in the same ways that popular fashions or fads pass from one group to another. In each case, behavior is acquired socially through what Tarde referred to as the three laws of imitation: (1) the law of close contact, (2) the law of imitation of superiors by inferiors, and (3) the law of insertion.

Tarde's first law holds that individuals in intimate contact with one another will imitate each other's behaviors. Thus, people have a tendency to imitate the fashions and customs of those with whom they have the closest contact. A person who is surrounded by others who engage in deviant behavior will be more likely to imitate those behaviors than the actions of others with whom he has little contact. In this way, direct association with deviant behavior is assumed to increase the likelihood of deviant conduct.

Tarde's second law suggests that behavior spreads from the top down. Young people are expected to imitate the actions of older individuals, while the socially disadvantaged members of society are expected to imitate the behaviors of the wealthy. Subsequently, crime among lower-status individuals is believed to represent an effort to imitate wealthy, successful, older members of society. Tarde suggested that people model higher-status individuals in the hope that their behaviors will secure some of the rewards associated with wealth and prestige.

Tarde's third, and final, proposition asserts that new forms of conduct "insert" themselves, superimposing onto current behaviors. In this way, existing behaviors are reinforced or discouraged. This law refers to the tendency of new, or novel, ways of behaving replacing older, more customary forms of conduct. Tarde believed that when two mutually exclusive ways of doing something come into conflict, the individual will normally favor the newer behavior.

In the 1940s, Edwin Sutherland expanded on Tarde's earlier work by introducing his theory of differential association. Sutherland posited that criminal behavior is learned through interaction with others in a process of communication. Similar to Tarde, Sutherland believed that the difference between criminals and law-abiding citizens is not a matter of character, but rather a reflection of what people have learned (Sutherland, 1939). He stated that children reared in conventional neighborhoods are more likely to acquire noncriminal behaviors, while those growing up in economically deprived areas are prone to learn and engage in criminal conduct. The theory of differential association was influenced by Tarde's early work, but Sutherland elaborated on the concept of criminal conduct being learned using nine postulates (1947, pp. 75–77). They consist of the following:

1. *Criminal behavior is learned.* Sutherland disagreed with the ideas of biological determinism and psychological pathology, as well as economic theories of crime. He believed that people must, first, be trained in crime; consequently, without prior influence an individual is incapable of criminal behavior.

2. *Criminal behavior is learned in interaction with others in a process of communication.* Sutherland believed that the communication used to transmit criminal behavior involves both verbal and nonverbal behaviors.

3. *The principle part of learning criminal behavior occurs within intimate personal groups.* Sutherland argued that intimate personal groups—such as family members, peers, and other close associates—provide the greatest influence on criminal behavior.

4. *When a criminal behavior is learned, the learning includes (1) techniques of committing the crime, which are sometimes very complicated, sometimes very simple, and (2) the specific direction of motives, drives, rationalizations, and attitudes.* Sutherland suggested that not everyone can become a criminal, but rather a person must be accepted into a group of criminals and indoctrinated into the profession.

5. *The specific direction of motives and drives is learned from definitions of the legal codes as favorable or unfavorable.* According to Sutherland, some societies are marked by definitions favorable to the laws governing society, whereas others support the violation of such legal codes. Sutherland believed that the United States consists of both definitions, which are found in varying parts of the country, thus creating a possible culture conflict with regard to favorable or unfavorable definitions.

6. *A person becomes delinquent because of an excess of definitions favorable to violation of law over definitions unfavorable to violation of law.* This is Sutherland's principle of differential association, which posits that individuals engage in criminal behavior because of more repeated contacts with criminal activity than noncriminal activity. Relatively more association with criminal behaviors translates to a greater likelihood of a person having an excess of criminal definitions compared to conforming definitions. Thus, individuals with an excess of criminal definitions will be more susceptible to new criminal definitions, while being less receptive to pro-social definitions.

7. *Differential associations vary in frequency, duration, priority, and intensity.* Sutherland proposed that if it were possible to present these modalities in quantitative form with the proper mathematical ratios, a precise description of a person's criminal behavior could be achieved.

8. *The process of learning criminal behavior by association with criminal and anti-criminal patterns involves all of the mechanisms that are involved in any other learning.* Sutherland believed that there is nothing special about criminal behavior or criminals. Rather, criminal behavior is acquired through the same processes as other forms of conduct.

9. *Although criminal behavior is an expression of general needs and values, it is not explained by those general needs and values, because noncriminal behavior is an expression of the same needs and values.* The same drives and motives that apply to criminal behavior apply to noncriminal behavior as well, which highlights why attempts to explain deviant conduct by general drives and values have not been successful.

Sutherland advanced the understanding of Tarde's earlier work by shedding more light on the psycho-social processes of learning deviant behaviors (Akers, 2009). He articulated that communication with others, including specific values, attitudes, and beliefs about deviant acts are transmitted in close social groups. It is important to note that Sutherland did not imply that mere association with criminal peers would lead inevitably to deviant behavior, a point often misunderstood by critics (Pfohl, 1994). Rather, motivational drive to commit deviant acts is attributed to the predominance of nonconforming definitions. A critical missing component, however, in Sutherland's conceptualization was the role of social learning.

Differential Association-Reinforcement Theory of Criminal Behavior

In 1966, Burgess and Akers broadened Sutherland's paradigm on deviant behavior. They believed that Sutherland's (1947) differential association theory was an important contribution to the field of criminology but lacked the social learning component of reinforcement. Burgess and Akers added the key element of social learning to Sutherland's theory and referred to their revised model as the Differential Association-Reinforcement Theory of Criminal Behavior (Burgess & Akers, 1966).

Burgess and Akers (1966) agreed with Sutherland that differential association was an essential aspect of non-normative behavior. Although they agreed on the significant role of close social groups on behavior, the social learning model devalued the impact of exposure to detailed criminal group communications and criminal definitions. Burgess and Akers viewed discriminating reinforcement for deviant behavior as the key determinant for nonconforming behavior. Similar to Tarde, they viewed imitation as another learning factor that influences criminal behavior. The reformulated paradigm proposes the following:

> The probability that persons will engage in criminal and deviant behavior is increased and the probability of their conforming to the norm is decreased when they differentially associate with others who commit criminal behavior or espouse definitions favorable to it, are relatively more exposed in-person or symbolically to salient criminal/deviant models, define it as desirable or justifiable in a situation discriminative for the behavior, and have received in the past and anticipate in the current or future situation relatively greater reward than punishment for the behavior. (Akers, 2009, p. 50)

At the core of social learning theory is the principle of differential reinforcement, which posits that a person's attitudes and observable behaviors are shaped over time by conditional rewards and punishments. Consequences provide the motivation to engage or refrain from action in a given context, not simply an excess of definitions leaned in any one direction. An individual's behavior is strengthened or weakened through the same principles of operant conditioning responsible for other forms of learning (Pfohl, 1994; Skinner, 1976). If a person anticipates greater reward than punishment for a specific behavior, it is likely that the behavior will occur (Lee et al., 2004). Akers (1996) noted that an individual's behavior could be misaligned with expected social norms if the person miscalculated the norm, was not properly socialized into the group moral standards, or did not receive proper role modeling. In most cases, however, acting to conform or engage in criminal behavior is highly reliant on whether rewards or costs outweigh the normative behavior. Thus, the anticipated consequences associated with behavior help guide one's conduct in a given context (Akers, 2009).

Similar to Sutherland's perspective on definitions, Akers believed that the individual endorses differing levels of pro-social and delinquent cognitive scripts or "definitions." He added, however, that the individual is reinforced to varying degrees for conforming or nonconforming attitudes, even without being exposed to a criminal subculture (Akers, 1996). Except in extreme circumstances, these "definitions" are viewed as a guidebook indicating how to act in specific situations to gain reward (e.g., positive group attention or satisfaction) or avoid punishment (e.g., group censure, discipline) (Lee et al., 2004). When a person's definitions are consistent with the behavior and followed by reinforcement, the same conduct is more likely to recur under similar circumstances (Akers, 1973). If the person's definitions are incongruent with his misconduct and the misconduct is reinforced and role-modeled over time, it is probable that the deviant behavior will recur and the person's definition will change to become more congruent with the deviant group norm.

Akers (2009) later added a macro-level aspect to social learning theory. He described individual deviant behavior as being a function of not only social learning principles but also the larger environmental structure. This revised, more inclusive model explained criminal behavior as being caused not only by the interaction between an individual and the group, but also by the social context and environment. Structural factors that affect social interactions include age, gender, class, family size, community location, and social positioning (Akers, 1998). Thus, the individual is viewed in the context of group norms and larger sociocultural norms that provide rules of how to behave and how not to behave based on reward and punishment contingencies. The incorporation of this broader view became the social learning and social structure theory of crime (SSSL).

According to Akers (1998), social structural variables impact the social learning variables of differential peer association, differential reinforcement, definitions, and imitation, which tailor an individual's social learning experiences and probable choice of criminal or noncriminal behavior. The social structure, social learning, and individual are separate but important components of the SSSL model that dynamically interact to influence behavior (Akers, 1985, 1996). As police misconduct occurs in the context of a larger organization, social learning theory provides a functional and comprehensive paradigm for better understanding law enforcement deviance. The concepts of social learning theory and their specific applications to law enforcement are discussed in the following sections.

Application

Social learning theory acknowledges the existence of individual factors, social group variables, and societal/cultural influences in understanding deviant behavior in the individual (Akers, 1985, 1996, 2009). Police organizations rely heavily on environmental systems to influence officer behavior. Agencies train officers to be well versed in following orders from rank, adhering to officer safety tactics, abiding by laws, following rules and regulations, and backing up partners (Kappeler, Sluder, & Alpert, 1998). In this context, it is clear that the systemic layers—peers, supervisors, unit, and department culture—strongly influence officer conduct. Hence, the social learning model captures the integral ingredients within law enforcement agencies that can contribute to individual officer misconduct.

Other key elements of social learning theory are evident in law enforcement behavior as well. In general, police officers enter the force with a standard of conduct or set of "definitions" influenced by their community/social networks (Kappeler et al., 1998). On entering the academy, recruits are faced directly with strong group norms, influential reinforcers, and competent role models. All of these aspects of social learning theory can lead an officer toward or away from misconduct. Although bad apples occasionally pass the pre-employment screening, backgrounds examination, and probationary process, many seemingly good officers exposed to the "barrel" have engaged in misconduct (Fitch, 2011).

Additionally, this theory is directly relevant to police behavior because it has sociological and psychological underpinnings that guide the analysis of various types of deviant behavior. Operant conditioning (Skinner, 1976), for example, is part of the behaviorism psychology literature and applies to all behaviors and social environments without discrimination.

It is worth noting that various aspects of the social learning model have been validated in studies examining a range of deviant behaviors. They include empirical studies on the use of alcohol in elderly and youth (Akers, 1989), smoking among adolescence (Akers, 1985), drug use in adolescence (Lanza-Kaduce, Akers, Krohn, & Radosevich, 1984), sexually deviant behavior (Akers, 1998), family violence (Wofford & Elliot, 1997), and computer crimes (Skinner & Fream, 1997). Conceptually and scientifically, the application of the social learning model to law enforcement culture and misconduct seems a logical next step.

Law Enforcement Culture

Organizational culture has been defined as a socially constructed attribute of organizations that serves as the "social glue" binding an organization together (Cameron & Ettington, 1988; O'Reilly & Chatman, 1996; Schein, 1996). It refers to the implicit values, beliefs, norms, underlying assumptions, expectations, and definitions that characterize organizations and their members—and affects the ways members think, feel, and behave (Cameron, 2008). While police officers are affected by the formal organizational culture, they are also influenced by the informal values, beliefs, norms, traditions, expectations, and definitions passed down by other members of the department.

Kappeler et al. (1998) maintains that the most dramatic change in an officer's social character occurs when he becomes part of the law enforcement occupational culture. It is important to note, however, that most larger police departments are not confined to a single, unified set of values, beliefs, and norms. Rather, they consist of differing subcultures, each sharing many values and beliefs of the larger organization, while possessing a unique set of norms and traditions that set them apart (Paoline, 2004). Depending on an officer's values and beliefs, exposure to a malignant subculture can serve to control or contribute to deviant behavior. Some police subcultures represent negative attitudes toward the public and the administration, while others possess a worldview that discourages deviant behavior (Scaramella, Cox, & McCamey, 2011).

In most cases, organizational subcultures are already in place prior to an officer joining a law enforcement agency. Depending on the amount, frequency, and duration of an officer's exposure, the behaviors of peer group members can influence the officer's attitudes, beliefs, and conduct in ways that either condone or condemn deviant behavior. Indeed, there is evidence to support the idea that officers engage in certain forms of conduct to secure and maintain peer-group approval (Chappell & Piquero, 2004). If an officer is unsure about the legality or morality of a particular behavior, he will most likely look to others who are perceived as authority figures for guidance and assurance, especially in situations defined as novel or ambiguous (Milgram, 1963, 1965, 1974).

The larger organizational culture, as well as smaller group subcultures, found within most law enforcement organizations provide a suitable model to view clearly the principles of social learning theory that contribute to police misconduct. The following sections will describe in greater detail the relationships between the social learning theory principles of differential association, differential reinforcement, imitation, and definitions, and police misconduct.

Differential Association

The central variable in social learning theory is differential association, which holds that individuals develop favorable or unfavorable definitions toward deviance through social interaction and identification with different peer groups (Akers, Krohn, Lanza-Kaduce, & Radosevich, 1979). The definitions that a person develops are then reinforced, positively or negatively, by the consequences (either real or perceived) that follow one's behavior. Furthermore, peers and salient others are believed to model the behaviors that are to be imitated (Akers, 2009).

Traditional relations between the police and the public have been described as mutually hostile and distrustful (Westley, 1970). This hostility is believed to isolate the police from the public, an attitude that fosters values of silence, secrecy, and solidarity among officers—all values which contribute to a culture that tolerates and, in some cases, can actually foster deviant behavior. The sense of social isolation experienced by many young and impressionable police officers often results in officers spending more and more time with fellow officers, especially for social purposes (Alpert & Dunham, 1997). As a result, it is often perceived as a basic necessity for officers to feel accepted by the peer group for the development of a satisfactory self-image (Conser, 1980).

Peer groups not only provide support and approval; they offer opportunities to learn deviant behaviors, as well as the values, beliefs, and rationalizations necessary to justify or excuse misconduct (Chappell & Piquero, 2004). Alpert and Dunham (1977) identify peer influence as one of the most powerful pressures operating in modern law enforcement organizations. The need for acceptance and support can create intense pressure to conform, which may involve the acceptance of deviant values and behaviors (Kappeler, Sluder, & Alpert, 2001).

Savitz (1970) measured the attitudes of police recruits toward deviance at three points in their careers. The finding indicated that as recruits graduated from the police academy to the streets, their exposure to the police subculture increased accordingly. Officers' attitudes became more tolerant concerning misconduct, with officers beginning to favor less severe forms of punishment for various categories of deviant behavior, such as accepting bribes or stealing. Thus, the heightened reliance on peer groups in police culture can create an environment whereby individual officers can become vulnerable to differential association.

Differential Rewards

The tenets of associative learning hold that behavior is a function of its consequences (Skinner, 1976). Whereas an officer's department, as well as administrators and supervisors, provide direct, formal reinforcement, an officer's informal peer group offers support, friendship, and other rewards that may be more influential than the official recognition offered by the agency. Officers who want to be accepted are more likely to adopt the beliefs, values, and behaviors of the group—even if such "manners of expression" deviate from acceptable norms (Chappell & Piquero, 2004). These attitudes and behaviors are then strengthened or weakened by the punishments or rewards (either real or perceived) that follow. Consequently, the strength of the officer's deviant behavior is a direct function of the amount, type, frequency, and probability of reinforcement (Ormrod, 2008; Sutherland, 1947).

Social learning theory posits that reward and punishment contingencies shape both a person's attitudes and overt behaviors and provide the motivation to engage or refrain from conduct at a given time and place (Akers, 2009). An individual may be willing to commit a criminal act but refrains because of the anticipated costs associated with the violation. Conversely, the perceived certainty of being rewarded for deviant conduct may be enough to motivate a person to act despite an unfavorable attitude toward such behavior (Akers, 1996). Thus, if an officer anticipates the certainty of a valuable reward for performing a deviant behavior relative to the level of punishment, he is likely to commit the act, despite the organization's ethical standards and cultural prohibitions to such an act.

Imitation

Observing a behavior that was modeled and then engaging in similar conduct is termed *imitation* (Akers, 2009). Imitation is an important element in law enforcement because most officers enter police work with little, if any, prior experience. Officers learn how to perform their jobs through direct experiences, as well as observing and imitating the behavior of their peers (Bandura, 1977, 1986). Social learning allows older, more experienced officers to transmit the beliefs, values, and norms of the group to younger, less-experienced personnel. By observing the demeanor of others, officers learn the types of behavior that are permissible in a given context, as well as the consequences associated with various forms of conduct. Hence, the ways that officers define, facilitate, and justify deviant conduct can be imitated, learned, and adopted by future generations of employees (Akers, 2000, 2009; Kappeler et al., 1998; Lee et al., 2004).

To elaborate further on imitation, a model's effectiveness is influenced by three factors, the first being *status and power*. Individuals who possess status and power in an organization are typically regarded more positively than those who do not (Bandura, 1986). Officers are more likely to imitate the behavior of models who possess prestige or influence, whether within the formal agency itself or among members of an important peer group. Indeed, the strong need for peer acceptance among many officers makes the behaviors, beliefs, and values of informal leaders a powerful tool for shaping the behavior of less-experienced officers who aspire to attain a similar level of prominence (Conser, 1980).

Competence is another important ingredient in imitation. Most people—and, by extension, most law enforcement professionals—are motivated by the pursuit of competence (Maslow, 1943). Officers are more likely to be influenced by others whom they perceive as competent (Schunk, 1987), making officers more likely to model the behaviors of experienced, capable officers regardless of the model's rank or status within the organization. Perhaps of even greater importance is the finding that a model's status or prestige in the organization tends to generalize from one form of behavior to another (Bandura, 1986), which may involve the transmission of deviant values and behaviors (Akers, 2000, 2009).

The third factor related to imitation is the *relevance of the model's behavior to the observer*. Individuals are more apt to emulate the behaviors of others whom they view as similar to themselves in some important way (Bandura, 1986). As officers tend to perform activities that are comparable to others within the peer-group, they are more likely to perceive the behaviors of peers as having greater functional value than the activities of supervisors or managers. Thus, the behaviors of salient peers often have a greater influence on an officer's performance than formal organizational dictates or supervisory conduct. If a police officer chooses to imitate role models that defy police ethics and standards, the officer could be on a path of behavior that diverges from the organizational norm of propriety.

Definitions

Social learning theory holds that people vary in the extent to which they hold delinquent or pro-social definitions that either encourage or discourage deviant behavior (Akers, 1996). The definitions a person holds provide the orientations, rationalizations, and other attitudes that label the commission of an act as right or wrong, good or bad, desirable or undesirable, justified or unjustified. The more a person's attitudes disapprove of certain acts, the less likely that person is to engage in such conduct. For example, absent any external influences, an officer who has learned and personally believes in the values of honesty, integrity, kindness, and other general beliefs that condemn lying, cheating, and stealing would be less likely to engage in misconduct (Akers, 2009). Conversely, the more an officer's attitudes approve of, or fail to condemn, deviant behavior, the greater the chances that he would engage in such acts.

It is worth noting that definitions of deviancy do not stand in direct opposition to conventional norms by defining illegal or immoral behavior as a positive good. Rather, they serve to offset conventional norms by offering justifications or rationalizations that serve to neutralize or, in some case, excuse delinquent conduct. It is not that deviant behavior is "right"; rather it is "right" under certain sets of conditions (Akers, 2009). Sykes and Matza (1957) suggested several "techniques of neutralization" used to justify deviant behavior. The following is a list of these techniques with examples specific to law enforcement:

The denial of responsibility. Insofar as a person engaging in deviant behavior can avoid responsibility, the disapproval of self and others is sharply reduced as a restraining influence. For instance, an officer who uses excessive force on a subject would seek to place blame on the other party. Thus, if the subject did not want to be the victim of excessive force, he should not have violated the law to begin with.

The denial of injury. This neutralization centers on the question of whether or not anyone was clearly hurt by an act of deviance. An officer who steals money from a suspected drug dealer can argue that because the subject obtained the money illegally, the currency does not really belong to the dealer anyway; therefore, appropriating the money does not actually harm anyone.

The denial of victim. In the event that a person accepts responsibility for a delinquent act and is willing to admit that his actions injured another, this admission can be neutralized by the fact that the injury was justified in light of the circumstances. Thus, an officer who abuses a man suspected of beating his wife may seek to justify his actions as a form of rightful retaliation or punishment for the subject's earlier act of violence.

The condemnation of the condemners. In this case, the person committing the deviant behavior shifts the focus of attention to the motives and behaviors of those who disapprove of the conduct. A detective who coerces a suspect to confess might condemn the police administration and media for failing to understand the unreasonable laws that officers are forced to obey in the performance of their duties.

The appeal to higher authorities. A person who relies on this justification sees himself as caught up in a dilemma that must be resolved, unfortunately, by violating the law. A detective who searches a pedophile's home illegally to uncover evidence of a crime would reason that the heinous nature of the offense provides ample justification for violating the law.

As Sykes and Matza (1957) note, these techniques of neutralization can be employed prospectively (before committing the deviant behavior) to forestall guilt or retrospectively (after committing the misconduct) to erase any regrets. In either case, the goal is essentially the same—to protect the individual from self-blame and the blame from others. Studies on deviant behavior have, in fact, supported the use of techniques of neutralization to rationalize or excuse criminal conduct. For example, research on white collar crime has found that corrupt individuals do not view themselves as unethical, even going as far as to explain their criminal behaviors as part of normal, acceptable business practices (Ashford & Anand, 2003). Similarly, Chappell and Piquero (2004) found in their study that officers tended to define misconduct in very narrow, conditional terms, whereas citizens defined it more broadly.

While there are no national level statistics on police deviance, it is likely that virtually every police agency has been badly bruised by some type of corruption or abuse committed by one of their own (Kappeler et al., 1998; McCafferty, Souryal, & McCafferty, 1998). The following section details strategies that are consistent with social learning theory and may help to create a culture of excellence in law enforcement agencies.

Creating a Culture of Excellence

Although it is probably safe to suggest that some instances of law enforcement misconduct are perpetrated by a small number of socially isolated officers who somehow managed to slip through a crack in the hiring process, the deviant behavior of other officers is undoubtedly influenced by the social learning principles of differential association, differential reinforcement, imitation, and definitions. And, whereas character—including certain personality traits, values, and attitudes—is clearly important, understanding and addressing police misconduct requires a more complete explanation of human behavior and motivation than is currently offered by dispositional theories (Fitch, 2011).

Social learning theory holds that group interactions, reinforcements, modeling, and definitions can influence the conduct of individual officers (Akers, 1985, 1996, 2000; Burgess & Akers, 1966). Hence, to keep officers aligned with departmental core values, prevention efforts must include the implementation of environmental strategies that create and maintain a dominant culture of proper conduct. The following interventions are based on the principles of social learning.

Differential Association

The concept of differential association informs law enforcement agencies of the dangers involved in permitting nonconforming groups of officers to emerge and possibly thrive. To prevent deviant groups from gaining power and creating a criminal norm, a strong majority of officers across all ranks must be unified in ethics at every station and bureau. In this setting, if an officer engages in misconduct, the majority group's peers and supervisors are likely to identify quickly the nonconforming conduct and intervene to change the problem behavior. A dominant culture of ethical leadership provides consistent and frequent exposures to good conduct relative to exposures to bad conduct, maintaining an environment that helps the officer remain moral in his thoughts and behavior (Weaver, 2004).

Because of the formal—as well as the equally important informal—influence accompanying the roles of field training officers, detectives, supervisors, and other lead personnel, law enforcement agencies should develop clear, specific criteria for the selection of such positions (California Commission on Peace Officer Standards and Training, n.d.). It is imperative that the selection of these and other critical positions favor officers who conform to organizational normative behaviors, support the agency's core values in both words and conduct, and demonstrate strong personal prohibitions against any and all forms of misconduct (Akers, 1996; Fitch, 2011).

Differential Reinforcement

To create an ethical organization, supervisors, managers, and administrators must make a conscious effort to recognize and reward appropriate behaviors, while confronting and correcting inappropriate conduct (Wimbush & Shepard, 1994). An environment that reinforces ethical behavior and punishes misconduct is essential for developing and maintaining a value-based organization. To help prevent differential reinforcement from undermining ethical police departments, the frequency, duration, priority, and intensity of reinforcements for good conduct must outweigh the reinforcements for deviant behavior.

Moreover, law enforcement organizations need to create a culture where officers, throughout their career assignments, are symbolically, socially, or personally reinforced for doing the right thing during the performance of their daily duties more than they are differentially reinforced for deviant conduct. In other words, officers must perceive that ethical officers get ahead and immoral officers don't—they receive punishment (Fitch, 2011). Organizational systems that have a built-in dominant culture for reinforcing ethical conduct across all ranks leaves little room to develop an excess of reinforcements and attitudes for deviant behaviors. This is especially important regarding the activities of first-line supervisors (Thomas, 2008). In addition to reinforcing appropriate conduct, supervisors must confront all levels of misconduct immediately, ensuring that deviant behavior is penalized promptly and appropriately.

Imitation

Imitation is constructively infused by law enforcement agencies beginning in the basic academy (Kappeler et al., 1998). Recruits tend to view the training staff as exemplary, senior role models, creating a natural environment whereby imitation occurs. Recruits begin to imitate the way the staff instructors think and act with positive outcomes (e.g., attention, verbal praise, not being ridiculed by a drill instructor). The dark side of imitation is activated when the same learning process of imitation takes place but the role models are engaging in misconduct rather than proprietary behaviors (Akers, 2009). Police departments that produce a majority of ethical leadership, where there are more reinforcements for appropriate behavior than not, will help prevent antisocial imitation from blossoming.

In addition to providing adequate role models, law enforcement agencies should develop and display a set of core values and mission statement. These documents, however, must represent more than hollow promises. They must form the foundation for the behavior of supervisors and managers at all levels of the organization, thus providing a clear and consistent message that good ethics is essential to an officer's success in the agency (Weaver, 2004). Employees can be surprisingly good at pointing out any inconsistencies between the organization's stated values and the conduct of supervisors and managers (e.g., supervisors minimizing the misconduct of close friends while harshly punishing other employees for the same misconduct or engaging in misconduct themselves). To be effective, core values and ethics must apply equally to employees at every level of the organization—including top executives (Webley & Werner, 2008).

Most scholars agree that integrity—defined as congruency between a person's words and deeds—is a requirement of ethical leadership (Thomas, 2008). If a department's administration expects officers to behave ethically, they must make ethics an explicit part of the leadership agenda through communication, role modeling, and the application of meaningful rewards and sanctions (Brown & Trevino, 2006). In other words, leaders must lead the way, living and breathing the values of the organization every day, as well as reward officers who do the same (Fogleman, 2001).

Definitions

Law enforcement officers enter the department with personal values and moral attitudes molded by their disposition, family, friends, neighborhood, schools, community, and society (Akers, 2009). Basic academy provides the first exposure to the police organization's ethical definitions. As the initiation from recruit to sworn officer begins, the training staff should use its status, power, and competence to refine and inspire each recruit's professional ethical definitions. Training staff should not only articulate the ethical ways to think but should also model ethical ways to behave through their daily actions, both on duty and off (Kappeler et al., 1998). Successfully transferring these cultural definitions to recruit peer leaders can go a long way toward guiding morally tenuous followers in an ethical direction. With this force of ethical presence, a few "bad apples" are not likely to gain momentum when exhibiting deviant behavior. In this authentic, value-based culture, there would be virtually very little positive gains and high risks for exhibiting antisocial behavior. A deviant peer subculture would have difficulty forming and thriving with such an excess of pro-social group associations, reinforcement for good conduct, fair corrective-discipline for misconduct, ethical group definitions, and role-modeling of values-based officer conduct.

Finally, it is important to note that while a value-based culture requires conscious effort and oversight, the ethics of most law enforcement agencies is being managed with or without the attention of top management. Neglecting ethics or even worse, behaving immorally, sends a clear message to officers that neither the agency nor its leaders care much about proper conduct. Therefore, refining and reinforcing pro-social definitions should not begin and end with academy training. Kidder (1995) suggests that ethical fitness is similar to physical fitness: Both require continuous practice. Law enforcement supervisors and managers should engage officers in frequent, meaningful discussions of ethics, as well as incorporate ethics into all forms of training. By consistently emphasizing appropriate, pro-social norms as well as accountability, reinforcing appropriate behavior, and modeling appropriate conduct, a department's administration sends a clear and consistent message that inappropriate behavior will not be tolerated, at any level of the agency (Weaver, 2004).

Summary

To mitigate misconduct effectively, law enforcement supervisors, managers, and administrators must move beyond the "bad apple" theory offered by dispositional explanations. This begins with an understanding that every officer—regardless of personality traits, personal values, and attitudes—is capable of both moral and immoral conduct (Shermer, 2004). Furthermore, social learning theory provides a critical and much needed perspective on misconduct, one that emphasizes the importance of peer associations, modeling, and consequences.

The significant role played by organizational culture—that is, the "barrel"—cannot be overstated. Only by better understanding the barrel can law enforcement agencies begin to implement policies, training, and systems better intended to address, prevent, and reduce binge drinking, unsanctioned cliques, and other forms of misconduct discussed at the beginning of this chapter. Law enforcement leaders must not only lead with value-based definitions of conduct, but also reflect those core ethical values in their day-to-day speech and behavior (Weaver, 2004). Likewise, leaders will need to inspire sworn personnel across all ranks to engage in proper behavior by reinforcing good performance and punishing deviant conduct. This means that organization administrators must consciously select and empower both supervisors and officers who live the ethical code, while leading by example.

In the end, it is imperative that police agencies believe in, and strive for, the existence of an ethical organization. The creation and maintenance of a "good barrel" will help to guide officers, with varying levels of morality, in ethical decision making and conduct. Social learning theory brings good news to law enforcement agencies: The good barrel, or ethical group environment, can create and maintain a sworn culture where the strong ethical officers pull the weak in line and together all members of law enforcement can protect and serve in ways consistent with the highest standards of ethical conduct that society expects from its law enforcement professionals.

Discussion Questions

1. What are character-based explanations of misconduct?

2. How do character-based explanations of misconduct differ from social learning theories of misconduct?

3. Describe Tarde's three laws of imitation.

4. Explain the differential association theory of criminal behavior.

5. How do the strong group norms officers learn in the academy contribute to deviant conduct?

6. What are the three characteristics of competent models?

References

Akers, R. L. (1973). *Deviant behavior: A social learning approach*. CA: Wadsworth.

Akers, R. L. (1985). *Deviant behavior: A social learning approach*. Belmont, CA: Wadsworth.

Akers, R. L. (1989). Social learning and alcohol behavior among the elderly. *Sociological Quarterly, 30*(4), 625–638.

Akers, R. L. (1996). Is differential association/social learning cultural deviance theory? *Criminology, 34*(2), 229–247.

Akers, R. L. (1998). *Social learning and social structure: A general theory of crime and deviance*. Boston: Northeastern University Press.

Akers, R. L. (2000). *Criminological theories: Introduction, evaluation, and application*. Los Angeles: Roxbury.

Akers, R. L. (2009). *Social learning and social structure: A general theory of crime and deviance*. Piscataway, NJ: Transaction.

Akers, R. L., Krohn, M. D., Lanza-Kaduce, L., & Radosevich, M. (1979). Social learning and deviant behavior: A specific test of a general theory. *American Sociological Review, 44*(4), 636–655.

Alpert, G. P., & Dunham, R. G. (1997). *Policing urban America*. Long Grove, IL: Waveland Press.

Ashford, B. E., & Anand, V. (2003). The normalization of corruption in organizations. In R. M. Kramer & B. M. Staw (Eds.), *Research in organizational behavior* (Vol. 25, pp. 1–52). Amsterdam: Elsevier.

Bandura, A. (1977). *Social learning theory*. Englewood Cliffs, NJ: Prentice Hall.

Bandura, A. (1986). *Social foundations of thought and action*. Englewood Cliffs, NJ: Prentice-Hall.

Brown, M. E., & Trevino, L. K. (2006). Ethical leadership: A review and future directions. *The Leadership Quarterly, 17*(6), 595–616.

Burgess, R. L., & Akers, R. L. (1966). A differential association-reinforcement theory of criminal behavior. *Social Problems, 14*(2), 128–147.

California Commission on Peace Officer Standards and Training. (n.d.). *Field training program*. Retrieved from http://www.post.ca.gov/field-training.aspx

Cameron, K. (2008). A process for changing organizational culture. In T. G. Cumming (Ed.), *Handbook of organizational development* (pp. 429–446). Thousand Oaks, CA: Sage.

Cameron, K. S., & Ettington, D. R. (1988). The conceptual foundations of organizational culture. In J. C. Smart (Ed.), *Higher education: Handbook of theory and research* (Vol., 4, pp. 356–396). New York: Agathon.

Chappell, A. T., & Piquero, A. R. (2004). Applying social learning theory to police misconduct. *Deviant Behavior, 25*(2), 89–108.

Cohen, H. S., & Feldberg, M. (1991). *Power and restraint: The moral dimension of police work*. Westport, CT: Praeger.

Collins, D. (2000). The quest to improve the human condition: The first 1,500 articles published in the journal of business ethics. *Journal of Business Ethics, 26*(1), 1–73.

Conser, J. A. (1980). A literacy review of the police subculture: Its characteristics, impact, and policy implications. *Police Studies, 2*(4), 46–54.

Eiserer, T. (2012, January 15). They drink when they're blue: Stress, peer pressure contribute to police's alcohol culture. *Dallas News*. Retrieved from http://www .dallasnews.com/investigations/headlines/20120115-they-drink-when-theyre-blue-stress-peer-pressure-contribute-to-polices-alcohol-culture.ece

Faturechi, R. (2012, April 12). Secret clique in sheriff's unit probed. *Los Angeles Times*, pp. A1, A15.

Fitch, B. D. (2011). Rethinking law enforcement ethics. *FBI Law Enforcement Bulletin, 80*(10), 18–24.

Fogleman, R. R. (2001). The leadership-integrity link. In R. I. Lester & A. G. Morton (Eds.), *Concepts for air force leadership* (AU-24) (pp. 39-40). Maxwell Air Force Base, AL: Air University Press.

Hartshorne, H., & May, M. A. (1928). *Studies in the nature of character: Vol. 1. Studies in deceit*. New York: Macmillan.

Jordan, A. H., & Monin, B. (2008). From sucker to saint: Moralization in response to self-threat. *Psychological Science, 19*(8), 809–815.

Kappeler, V. E., Sluder, R. D., & Alpert, G. P. (1998). *Force of deviance: Understanding the dark side of policing* (2nd ed.). Long Grove, IL: Waveland Press.

Kappeler, V. E., Sluder, R. D., & Alpert, G. P. (2001). Breeding deviant conformity: The ideology and culture of police. In R. Dunham & G. Alpert (Eds.), *Critical issues in policing: Contemporary readings* (4th ed., pp. 290–316). Prospect Heights, IL: Waveland Press.

Kidder, R. M. (1995). *How good people make tough choices: Resolving the dilemmas of ethical living.* New York: Harper.

Lanza-Kaduce, L., Akers, R. L., Krohn, M. D., & Radosevich, M. (1984). Cessation of alcohol and drug use among adolescents: A social learning model. *Deviant Behavior, 5,* 79–96.

Lee, G., Akers, R. L., & Borg, M. J. (2004). Social learning and structural factors in adolescent drug use. *Western Criminology Review, 5*(1), 17–34.

Maslow, A. H. (1943). A theory of human motivation. *Psychological Review, 50*(4), 370–396.

McCafferty, F. L., Souryal, S., & McCafferty, M. A. (1998). The corruption process of a law enforcement officer: A paradigm of occupational stress and deviancy. *Journal of the American Academy of Psychiatry and Law, 26*(3), 433–458.

Milgram, S. (1963). Behavioral study of obedience. *Journal of Abnormal and Social Psychology, 67*(4), 371–378.

Milgram, S. (1965). Liberating effects of group pressure. *Journal of Personality and Social Psychology, 1*(2), 127–134.

Milgram, S. (1974). *Obedience to authority: An experimental view.* New York: Harper Collins.

O'Reilly, C. A., & Chatman, J. A. (1996). Culture as social control: Corporations, cults, and commitment. In B. M. Staw & L. L. Cummings (Eds.), *Research in organizational behavior* (Vol. 18, pp. 157–200). Greenwich, CT: JAI Press.

Ormrod, J. E. (2008). *Human learning* (5th ed.). Upper Saddle River, NJ: Pearson Education.

Paoline, E. A. (2004). Shedding light on police culture: An examination of officers' occupational attitudes. *Police Quarterly, 7*(2), 205–236.

Pfohl, S. (1994). *Images of deviance and social control* (2nd ed.). Long Grove, IL: McGraw Hill.

Savitz, L. (1970). The dimensions of police loyalty. *American Behavioral Scientist, 13*(5–6), 693–704.

Scaramella, G. L., Cox, S. M., & McCamey, W. P. (2011). *Introduction to policing.* Thousand Oaks, CA: Sage.

Schein, E. (1996). Culture: The missing concept in organizational studies. *Administrative Science Quarterly, 41*(2), 229–240.

Schunk, D. H. (1987). Peer models and childrens' behavioral change. *Review of Educational Research, 57*(2), 149–174.

Sherman, L. W. (1974). *Police corruption: A sociological perspective.* Garden City, NY: Anchor Press.

Shermer, M. (2004). *The science of good and evil: Why people cheat, gossip, care, share, and follow the golden rule.* New York: Holt.

Skinner, B. F. (1976). *About behaviorism.* New York: Vintage Books.

Skinner, W. F., & Fream, A. M. (1997). A social learning theory analysis of computer crime among college students. *Journal of Research in Crime and Delinquency, 34*(4), 495–518.

Sutherland, E. H. (1939). *Principles of criminology* (3rd ed.). Philadelphia, PA: J.B. Lippincott.

Sutherland, E. H. (1947). *Principles of criminology* (4th ed.). Philadelphia, PA: J.B. Lippincott.

Sykes, G. M., & Matza, D. (1957). Techniques of neutralization: A theory of deviance. *American Sociological Review, 22*(6), 664–670.

Tarde, G. (1903). *The laws of imitation* (E. C. Parsons, Trans.). New York: Henry, Holt and Co.

Tarde, G. (1912). *Penal philosophy*. Boston: Little, Brown.

Thomas, J. C. (2008). Ethical integrity in leadership and organizational moral culture. *Leadership, 4*(4), 419–442.

Weaver, G. R. (2004). Ethics and employees: Making the connection. *Academy of Management Executive, 18*(2), 121–125.

Webley, S., & Werner, A. (2008). Corporate codes of ethics: Necessary but not sufficient. *Business Ethics: A European Review, 17*(4), 405–415.

Westley, W. A. (1970). *Violence and the police*. Cambridge, MA: MIT Press.

Wimbush, J. C., & Shepard, J. M. (1994). Toward an understanding of ethical climate: Its relationship to ethical behavior and supervisory influence. *Journal of Business Ethics, 13*(8), 637–647.

Wofford, M. A., & Elliot, D. (1997). A social learning theory model of marital violence. *Journal of Family Violence, 12*(1), 21–47.

8 Ethics, Enforcement, and the Prospect of Professionalism

Aaron D. Conley and Bryon G. Gustafson

I have been impressed with the urgency of doing. Knowing is not enough; we must apply. Being willing is not enough; we must do.

Leonardo da Vinci (1452–1519)

The date of the test is approaching. The subject matter is difficult. Recruits get just two chances. If they fail twice, there are no more opportunities. Both recruits and instructors feel the pressure to succeed—to validate the efforts that have been expended to prepare the next generation of law enforcement officers for public service. This is the high-stakes context for many law enforcement academies and their tests. What will recruits do to succeed? What will instructors do to help recruits succeed? Where are the ethical boundaries? Once boundaries are identified, how are ethics taught/ trained, assessed, verified, and maintained in recruits, officers, instructors, and law enforcement leaders? While most individuals in the law enforcement community will have answers to these questions, and some will assume that innate right answers should be clear, the evidence of experience might prove troubling.

Academy tests are kept under lock and key—access is restricted and test security agreements specify controls on the test content (California Commission on Peace Officer Standards and Training, 2007). Each academy has a designated staff person responsible for the tests, and instructors can review tests consistent with the security agreements and controls. After all, these tests are produced and validated by the state at significant expense and they are intended to verify requisite knowledge in future peace officers.

Academy personnel advise recruits that there is a "study guide" that they should use. Diligent recruits eager to do well heed this advice. The guide is maintained on a website provided for the recruits by the academy and each class passes on this resource. One earnest student brings the study guide to an instructor to ask about the content of a particular question and answer. The instructor sees the content of the study guide and alerts the academy administration. The study guide is real. The questions and answers—all of them—are from the actual state tests. An investigation ensues. The state gets involved. The academy is suspended. The recruits and instructional staff are questioned. In the end, however, nobody is able to say how it happened or who was responsible. It just was . . .

Readers may find this case unbelievable. A case of cheating involving nearly an entire law enforcement academy? No, many will say, it is a poorly constructed hypothetical. Law enforcement recruits are of high moral character and would not be lured in by such a thinly-veiled study guide. Beyond that, instructors in the academy are law enforcement professionals who have been through background investigations. None of the instructors would compromise their ethical standards for the sake of ensuring the success of their trainees. Professionals would know the difference between a study guide and misappropriated test questions. While this case study may seem contrived and beyond the specter of reality, its facts comport to a 2010 case involving a California law enforcement academy, and there is little reason to assume that this example in California is an isolated incident (California Commission on Peace Officer Standards and Training, 2010; Winton, 2010). Interestingly, in the aftermath of this case and others like it, California Assembly Bill 2285 was introduced to criminalize cheating on academy tests.

This case illustrates individual and group failings and organizational and institutional responses to those failings. It highlights gray areas of culpability and illustrates a systemic response. It broaches questions about how standards of behavior come to be and what an organization does when its institutionalized standards are breached. These foundational questions are explored in the next section.

Social Foundations

Social norms allow humans to coexist—albeit in varying degrees of peace and harmony. They are the basis for society and are contextualized by time and place (Durkheim, 1938). At the most coarse level, modern people normatively acknowledge the right of others to live. This foundational norm allows people to travel the world, encounter strangers, and maintain the expectation that they will not be killed for doing so. In different times and places, this would not be the norm. At a finer level, nationality or religious creed might separate people on different strata while still maintaining more foundational norms (e.g., the right to live). These norms are created as groups of individuals who present themselves through the "enactment of rights and duties" come to form social relationships (Goffman, 1959, p. 16). And so societies are born from groups of normative social relationships.

In much the same manner, people come to develop and understand ethics and law. These normative understandings are at issue in this chapter. How are ethical expectations for American peace officers—those persons who enforce society's norms—established, enculturated, and maintained? What does it mean when officers exhibit ethical failings? What should be done? Are these failures the result of individual problems with officers (e.g., inadequate selection standards or poor training) or systemic problems with law enforcement (e.g., inadequate oversight or deficient occupational norms), or are there other explanations?

This chapter begins with a review of traditional approaches to ethics generally and the formation of American law enforcement ethics more specifically. Next, it problematizes the relationship between scholarly understandings of ethics and practical enactments in law enforcement training, practice, and oversight. A discussion of alternatives and implications for the pursuit of professionalism follows, and the chapter concludes with discussion questions for further reflection on this topic.

Ethics and Enforcement

At least two overarching problems appear in the case study above. First, and most overt, is the issue of cheating—the misappropriation of answers to test questions, the misrepresentation of independent work, and the general deception associated with this case. This falls into the first category of "root sins" (Souryal, 1992, p. 192) of criminal justice that Souryal labels "Lying and deception (the most common)," "Prejudice and racial discrimination (the most infamous)," and "Egoism and the abuse of authority (the most critical)" (p. 193). Second—and the more challenging issue for this chapter and the whole of criminal justice—is the response and prescribed fix. There was an investigation to find the individual(s) responsible for the ethical breach, and, when that did not uncover a culprit, one could argue that a structural fix (i.e., the criminalization of cheating) was introduced to systematically gird against the possibility of future failings.

This second problem illustrates the commonly bifurcated view of structure versus agency. Theorists who favor structure view individual human actions as being constrained to available options within both socially constructed and lived realities. Agency theorists view individual human actions as self-directed matters of choice and will (Archer, 1995). This contrast is similar to the nurture versus nature debate, and it is not our goal to revisit what has already been done well. Many great scholars have deconstructed and reconceptualized this issue of structure versus agency. For example, Giddens' (1979) structuration theory delves well beyond the basic this-or-that argument. We advocate looking beyond just the individual or the system. Both are important and necessary.

We argue that the realistic framework of life context in which law enforcement takes place must be a factor in training, doing, and ensuring ethics. It is out of these lived realities that decisions are being made, law enforcement officers are oriented toward their communities, and ethical norms are created. As Cohen and Feldberg (1991) observed,

> Police are not recruited from the ranks of saints, and they are not identified in youth and groomed in the moral virtues, as Plato suggests they ought to be in *The Republic*. In general, American society does not channel people into future employment on the basis of temperament and moral character, and our society makes no effort to encourage any particular moral qualities in its police, though most of us would hope for honesty, courage and restraint. (p. 5)

Rather, "[p]olice are selected based on demonstrated conformity to dominant social norms and values. . . . In essence, police are selected, socialized, and placed into a working environment that instills within them an ideology and shared culture" (Kappeler, Sluder, & Alpert, 2005, p. 231). So by taking a realist approach (as opposed to an idealist approach), we avoid the downfall of thinking that structure (the system) and agency (the individual) are the key culprits. By reorienting our understanding of this ethical problem, we can stop assuming that virtuous officers/structures are binary opposites and come to realize they are two sides of the same coin. Yes, there is a tension, and in some cases one plays a larger role than another, but law enforcement ethics are still forged in the furnaces of the criminal justice system (the catch-all for our social ills/dysfunctions).

With the rest of this chapter, we argue that the *solution* is not a direct application of any ethic or ethical approach or model. Rather, solutions will present themselves when we finally acknowledge the extent to which ethics is a byproduct of the heterogeneous conglomeration that is theory and practice, education and experience, wider societal structures and attempts at systemic/agency change, community buy-in to law enforcement authority and community resistance to law enforcement abuse of authority, and the realistically complex and differing conditions of life among diverse American communities. To support this argument, the authors revisit the long-term construction of ethics as they have developed in the West and law enforcement in particular and then explore social changes that we believe necessitate one or more alternatives to the bifurcated view of individual versus institutional ethics and prescriptive models and approaches.

Foundations of Western Ethics

Socrates (469–399 BCE) tells us that knowing the good is the same thing as doing the good (Plato, 1997a). This direct link between knowing and doing is the foundation on which he explores what it means to have a just society. Socrates converses with his friends about the question, "What is justice?" In answering this question, his first conversation partner, Glaucon (circa 445–4th century BCE), asserts that justice is the advantage of the stronger. And even though Socrates will reject this aphorism, reminiscent as it is of the dictum of Mao Tse-Tung about looking down the barrel of a gun, it better captures the chasm that exists between knowing the good and actually doing it. If justice depends on force, then force is the operative principle needed to leap the chasm. Without force as an external motivation for just actions, Glaucon believes that people will not do what is right.

While Glaucon's belief that justice is the advantage of the stronger may not sit well with people with more democratic sensibilities, it can serve as a fruitful starting point for understanding some of the historical conversations about the ethics of justice and goodness. These conversations inform and enhance current trends in law enforcement ethics as practitioners wrestle with the many complex ethical issues of slippery slopes, misconduct, and full-scale corruption within policing. It is important to keep in mind that the players discussed in this section are responding to one another and do not formulate their ethics in a vacuum or without regard for their own unique historical conditions. Their responses to each other provide a rich resource from which to better understand current and future trajectories of law enforcement ethics. And yet their conclusions cannot be superimposed onto our unique ethical situations; we must determine for ourselves how to bridge the gap between knowing the good and doing the good.

The most ubiquitous approach to ethical training of law enforcement officers is character or virtue development. This approach cultivates in the law enforcement agent the ideals of "trustworthiness, respect, responsibility, fairness, caring, and good citizenship" that are necessary to serve and protect (California Commission on Peace Officer Standards and Training & Josephson, 2006, p. 16). Virtue approaches to ethics have their roots in ancient Greek philosophy as it related to questions of good citizens, guardians, and leaders. In these approaches, one can assume that justice and goodness are inextricably linked to the task of understanding ethical reasoning and action. Plato's (circa 423–347 BCE) understanding of this is indicated in the above-mentioned dialogue between Socrates and Glaucon. Yet defining what goodness or justice is tends to be a rather difficult task. To address this difficulty, Plato likens the governance of the city to the governance of the soul. Once an individual understood how to govern her soul properly, which generally required the study of philosophy to properly orient her desires away from the ego and toward the good, she would become a virtuous person.

What is more, Plato describes the ruling order of the city according to a three-tiered scheme. The *Philosophers*, led by a philosopher-king, keep society directed toward the good, by which justice is a central means. The next, lower class of citizens is the *Guardians*. These are the protectors of the city from invaders from without and disharmony from within. They must be philosophically capable of understanding and acting according to the good, and the gifted Guardians may advance to become Philosophers. The third class of people Plato calls the *Artisans*, which is a general designation for everyone else of consequence to the doing of justice (Plato, 1997b). While this structure appears orderly and oriented to the good, Plato asserts in other works that the best societies are ruled by a wise tyrant and not any democratically idealized navel-gazer. Historically, Plato used his Academy, his training school for philosophers, to "train students secretly for transformative political action" (Gilbert, 2009, p. 108). Plato himself served as a political advisor to Dionysius II of Syracuse (circa 397–343 BCE), who came to be known as a tyrant. This historical background helps illuminate that even under the best of intentions and ideals, the task of remaining consistent with ethical standards is always fraught with compromise.

Aristotle (circa 384–322 BCE), a student of Plato's Academy, provides ethicists with a fully articulated response to the relationship between knowing the good and doing it. Aristotle acknowledges that there may be many goods, or ends, that we seek, but that we must agree that certain ends are better for maintaining harmony in the social order. He states, "For even if the good of the community coincides with that of the individual, it is clearly a greater and more perfect thing to achieve and preserve that of a community" (Aristotle, 1976, p. 64). Aristotle's work on ethics—commonly known as *virtue theory*—was meant to be the precursor to his work on politics since the two are so closely related. Yet, despite these social demands, Aristotle looks to the individual to find the criteria needed to undergird a just society. Just societies are made up of virtuous individuals, and virtue is attained primarily through practice. If a person wants to be courageous, he must be put into real-life situations that require courage. As the person's moral and intellectual virtues strengthen, they become more equipped to do the good and will not stray from the straight and narrow.

While these are certainly not the only ethicists writing over the next 2,000 years, our conversation skips ahead to the industrializing and colonizing era of Europe. This historical leap is justified because it was during this period that Aristotelian virtue theory (as described above) came under great scrutiny. What is more, it was during this time period that ethics came to be approached as a rational exercise and that one could arrive at a universal standard of conduct prior to one's experience in the world. English philosopher and successor to his father as one of the executive officers of the East India Company, John Stuart Mill (1806–1873) championed a form of ethics during the 19th century where the good was defined as the greatest amount of happiness for the greatest number of people (Mill, 2001). Like Plato, Mill believed that the average person knew nothing about what was really good and therefore needed sophisticated and highly educated leaders to tell the rest of society what was in the best interest of everyone. While there may be an element of truth to his observation, we benefit by locating Mill's theory within the larger context of European colonialism. The East India Company was the largest company in the British Empire, established its own military power to protect its interests, and, with its powerful parliamentary lobby, gained extensive political and economic monopolies in both India and Britain. As the company extended its influence in India, the colonized nation, it seems that British leaders such as Mill and his father assumed the role of the highly educated leaders more capable of telling the Indian masses what their true needs were than they themselves. And the company maintained its own army to ensure that its interests could proceed uninhibited.

Mill's utilitarian ethic provided ways for ends to justify any means, so long as the two remained commensurate. It provided an alternative to the rationally derived universal ethic of Immanuel Kant (1724–1804) who wrote a few generations before Mill. Kant designed his ethic to be universally applied to any situation regardless of consequences. In its two basic formulations, he calls on every rational being to act as if he would will for that action to become a universal law and to never treat people as means but always as ends (Kant, 1998). In the first idea, we can know whether an act is ethical if we can envision everyone else doing this act without the world spinning wildly out of control. For instance, it would be an ethical act for us to help an elderly gentleman across the street because we can picture a world where everyone would do the same thing. In contrast, it would not be ethical for a medical doctor to harvest the organs of a healthy adult without his consent just because five other people would be saved as a result. If every doctor did this, our world would be gripped by a culture of fear, and nobody would trust medical practitioners. The second ethical idea of Kant is relatively self-explanatory, with the caveat that ethical actions are only directed at other humans; missing from this formulation of ethics is any mention of ethics with respect to nonhuman beings and the environment. In a large sense, both of Kant's ethical maxims assert that something is right, ethical, or moral simply because it is.

Just like with the other ethical philosophers discussed in this section, evaluation of Kant's ethic must be placed within its wider socio-political context. Like other European Enlightenment philosophers, Kant spoke eloquently about the virtues of human equality and freedom as attested by the universal nature of his ethical maxims. However, Kant's understanding of who in society is actually categorized as a rational being extends only as far as other European (predominantly White) males. Women and racial minorities, particularly Black slaves, do not fall under the universal umbrella of Kant's ethical imperatives (Mills, 2001). To restate his ethic with respect to these omissions, all rational beings (read: White and male) should act as if their own actions should become universal laws of nature, and these rational beings should always treat anyone (i.e., other rational beings) as an end and never as a means. If this assumption is correct, and indeed there is mounting evidence to support it, we might come to a better understanding as to why Kant's ethic was never used to support the abolition of slavery or challenge prevailing gender stereotypes. His ethic works wonderfully provided you fit the 18th-century criteria of a *fully rational human being.*

Each of the ethical figures discussed in this section occupies an important position in the trajectory of the Western ethical tradition. Their ideas are taught in universities as well as in many police training academies, yet on closer examination, rarely are their ideas placed adjacent to the wider social and political ideologies of their times. Telling their stories without regard for their wider historical contexts propitiates the idea that theory can operate in isolation from practice. But it is precisely in the act of telling a larger story that we begin to recognize the interconnectedness of theory and practice. A chasm will always remain between ethical training and ethical practice so long as law enforcement ethics embodies this tradition of disconnected storytelling. In the next section, the authors turn from ethical theory to practice and revisit some of the important milestones that illustrate how social and law enforcement leaders viewed and responded to ethical challenges.

Waypoints for Law Enforcement Ethics

Modern American policing began to take form late in the 19th century in the context of the ethical norms described in the previous section and amid many ethical quandaries for society as a whole (Perez & Moore, 2012). Even though the Civil War had concluded, issues of racial equality were beginning to be unveiled in new ways. Similarly, the women's suffrage movement was developing. Women who had always been more or less free found themselves lesser than Black men who, although just recently freed, already had the right to vote. In this time of development, change, and population growth, expanding police forces were fraught with problems such as theft, bribery, and general corruption among others (Harring, 1983).

Before becoming president, Woodrow Wilson (1887) decried the spoils system common throughout government and advocated a professional civil service as a systemic solution. He further proffered the politics–administration dichotomy and insisted that it was cronyism and political influence that led to graft and unethical conduct among public servants. His solution for this problem was a separation of politics from administration and the professionalization of public employees. And so began the basis for many of the systems of government in place today. Most relevant to this discourse are the effects on public employees as they relate specifically to police. Because President Wilson believed that the political and the professional aspects of government should be insulated from each other—to prevent inappropriate influence—one could argue that his efforts increased autonomy for law enforcement officers and leaders.

Before he himself became president, Teddy Roosevelt was appointed to the newly formed Civil Service Commission (advocated by Wilson) by then President Harrison in 1888 (Bishop, 1920). By all accounts, Roosevelt was a formidable reformer and was soon thereafter appointed Commissioner of the New York Police Department by Mayor Strong, where he moved to implement civil service standards (Bishop, 1920). The reforms advanced by

Wilson and Roosevelt (among others) were embraced broadly throughout the nation, and their merits were well-documented.

President Hoover's Wickersham Commission in its 1931 report further decried the influence of political forces on the police and recommended professionalism as the panacea. The prevailing logic indicated that independence from political influence would lead to right behavior (Ruchelman, 1973). Somehow police were expected to reference an internal locus of control that would appropriately guide their actions. In his 1933 article "Police Progress in the Past Twenty-Five Years," August Vollmer listed first among law enforcement achievements the creation of civil service systems and the development of police professionalization. In this way, a significant shift occurred. Unethical or corrupt policing was decided to be an outgrowth of political influence, and professionalization became the solution championed by Wilson, Roosevelt, Vollmer, and most scholars and law enforcement leaders. Interestingly, what Wilson (1887) critiqued as part of the problem may well be realized even now in the lasting nature of his solution: "Institutions which one generation regards as only a makeshift approximation to the realization of a principle, the next generation honors as the nearest possible approximation to that principle, and the next worships as the principle itself" (p. 209). To avoid unethical influences, Wilson and those who followed pushed for the professionalization of law enforcement, which necessarily led to greater autonomy for law enforcement officers and leaders.

Reform Efforts

Interestingly, today, large sectors of society fear that the increased autonomy of law enforcement leaders that was granted by this move to professionalization is now the main culprit of unethical behaviors. For example, the American Civil Liberties Union (ACLU, 1997) has repeatedly advocated the need to police the police by creating external law enforcement review boards that enhance, and in some instances create, public accountability. The ACLU claims that such measures are essential because they can help unite a city's politically organized racial minorities and the historical track records of its policing agencies. The concept of the external review board has appealed to many concerned with police conduct for decades. An early example began in Philadelphia in 1958 after a proposal and advocacy work by the ALCU (Lohman & Mismer, 1973). In practice, nominally, independent citizens are appointed by the mayor or political body (e.g., city council, county board, etc.) to consider citizen complaints against the police. The idea holds that the members of the review board are once removed from politics and separate from the police; therefore, they are independent arbiters of justice when considering (i.e., reviewing) police actions.

As the pendulum has now swung to the opposite end—from the spoils system of politically controlled police to the professional system of autonomous and potentially unaccountable police—we are faced with a conundrum.

Must we jettison the prospect of professionalization and its emphasis on agency change to compensate for the widely publicized unethical behaviors of individual officers and departments? Will the solution to law enforcement ethics be found in new efforts to reform the virtues of those few bad apples who seem to lack a baseline moral compass? Or have the centers of moral authority in our society shifted in such a way that either pendulum extreme is now proving insufficient for addressing the role of ethics in law enforcement? Turning briefly to some of the literature in law enforcement ethics provides a better sense of the current states of ethical discourses in law enforcement that will help navigate toward new solutions in the following section.

Theory, Practice, and Lived Reality

Scholarly and professional responses to law enforcement ethics—of which only a small sampling are explored here—appear to have increased notably in the past half century. Whether these responses highlight various approaches to training and education, explore possible sources of moral authority, or pick apart the elements of police environments, they all acknowledge the need for increased ethical awareness and behavior. This section highlights a few different representational responses to law enforcement ethics in an attempt to better understand the tensions that exist between the structure and the agent, or between the approaches of systemic cultures of unethical behavior and professionalism's attempt to deal with the few bad apples. Through this brief review, we get a better sense of current merits of ethical discourses as well as their shortcomings for thinking about ethics in a postmodern society.

Newburn (1999) discusses organizational structures as the leading cause of corruption that results from inadequately defined boundaries between corrupt and noncorrupt behavior. Basing his evidence on 20 years of literature on the subject from the United Kingdom, Australia, and the United States, Newburn denounces recent reform attempts that are aimed at new recruits since they assume, as did Plato, that knowing the good will lead to doing the good. Such an assumption is largely naïve and does little to change systems of corruption already in play in any given police department. Newburn's position is shared by many including Fitch (2011), Ruchelman (1973), and Kleinig (1996). Newburn follows Kleinig's careful note that corruption does not always increase along a slippery slope from minor compromise to lawlessness. He advocates instead for increasing ethical training for leadership and a more thorough integration of ethics training into every facet of police training.

Chilton (1998), Crank and Caldero (2010), and Barker (2002) stand as representatives of the human agency side of police ethics. Chilton (1998) calls for a tightening of ethical standards through a modified professionalism approach. Recognizing that traditional professional paradigms treat police as classic professionals, he seeks to integrate the larger police role as a public agent into the professional model. He argues that this integration takes root when the guiding social and moral compass is properly oriented toward the Constitution. Individual law enforcement officers must be trained to understand the moralities set by the Constitution—that is, they must develop a *constitutional conscience*. Presumably, ethical conduct will result from a better alignment or shared normativity of public interests and those of law enforcement agencies. Crank and Caldero (2010) and Barker (2002) make similar assumptions about the promotion of individual ethical conduct, albeit without the same level of nuanced analysis. Crank and Caldero advocate for what they call the *noble cause*, which

> is a moral commitment to make the world a safer place to live. Put simply, it is getting bad guys off the street. . . . It is not simply a verbal commitment . . . Nor is it something police have to learn. It's something to which they are morally committed. (p. 31)

It is not clear what factors contribute to an individual officer's ability to recognize (or know) the noble cause (or good), or even to understand whence it comes, but once he or she accesses it, ethical behavior will follow. Barker too adopts an individualist approach to ethics by calling for self-control as a primary "mechanism for controlling police unethical behavior" (p. 15). While he allows for situational variants, self-control on the part of peers and supervisors, with the help of external controls such as review boards, is the missing element of ethical policing.

Both structural and agent approaches offer important contributions to our ethical discourse. Newburn (1999) realistically recognizes that focusing on leadership will help control unethical behavior and organizational corruption rather than totally eliminate it. His emphasis on transforming departments into ethical cultures addresses an important aspect of the historical roots of corruption within policing organizations. Yet his approach falls short in at least two significant ways. First, it favors a Kantian deontological approach to ethics whereby some objective or universally recognized ethical standard is assumed and that leadership ethics must ascribe to it. But precisely where this standard comes from or how it is understood is neglected. Chilton (1998) understands that ethical standards must come from somewhere and posits the Constitution as the primary source (even though he fails to address differing interpretations of this shared social authority). Newburn's second shortfall rests in his general approach to ethical reform. By and large, he looks to solutions from within policing agencies. In other words, the burden of corruption and its solutions rest on the shoulders of law enforcement agencies. The potential shortfall of this position is that by only dealing with corruption internally, these agencies are more prone to overlook their complicity, with wider social structures of inequality and misconduct. It often takes an outside perspective for us to see our faults more clearly.

The agency examples to stemming unethical behavior explored here also have their strengths and weaknesses. Already mentioned as a strength is Chilton's (1998) attempt to posit a common source for normative moral authority within the case-law parameters of the Constitution. He also adequately tries to reconcile public interests with the professional ethics paradigm, which more effectively accounts for situational conditions. However, Chilton's vision for more ethical policing can only work well in places where, for example, minority communities are already well integrated with wider political and economic structures of their communities. Well-integrated communities already are more adept at ironing out new interpretations of the Constitution that better account for racial, gender, and other inequalities and their ethical norms reflect this (ACLU, 1997). But in communities where minority integration remains disparate, normative bases for authority will follow the well-worn patterns that contribute to police corruption. Furthermore, Chilton's agent-oriented solution and those of Crank and Caldero (2010) and Barker (2002) leaves untouched issues of how a twentysomething recruit with a General Equivalency Diploma (GED) is to behave ethically when granted autonomy to align personal ethical choices with the Constitution. Certainly, larger leadership and structural factors must be accounted for in ways that an agent-based ethic alone cannot fully capture.

Shifts in Normative Sources of Morality and Authority

Tensions in law enforcement ethics continue unabated between enacting structural reform and cultivating individual moral agents. Postmodernism has proven successful in highlighting the inefficiencies of any ethical approach to apply universally to all situations at all times. As noted in the work of Lyotard (1984), the dispersal of previous centers of authority—be they external or internal/structural or moral—has created marked shifts in societal attitudes toward the sorts of centralized authorities that law enforcement agencies represent. The solutions posed by Hoover, Wilson, Roosevelt, and others spoke to a country with firmly established moral norms. Common ethical standards in the previous century were already more or less rooted in society as a whole. One could argue that public demand for police transparency and virtue stemmed from a shared Euro-American and White moral sensibility found within socially dominant centers of authority. With a common moral authority, pushing law enforcement toward professionalism may have been an appropriate solution for addressing ethical breeches in police conduct.

The common police motto *to serve and to protect* directly applied to those who shared, supported, and drew from the wells of this normative moral authority. Those who did not were neither served nor protected in the same ways. The women's suffrage movement in the early 1900s and the civil rights movement in the 1960s provide two examples of larger challenges to Euro-American normativity that have effectively driven a wedge between what is legal from what is ethical. Chilton (1998) and the ethics curriculum of the National Institute of Ethics (n.d.) both blur the distinction between legal and ethical by calling for the Constitution, or what is "legal," to determine the boundaries of ethical behavior. In 1920, women in the United States won their rights to equal citizenship by securing the 19th Amendment, which granted them the right to vote in public elections. Prior to this, White men legally determined women's public interests. Similarly, Blacks in the United States were legally freed from institutionalized slavery in 1865 by the 13th Amendment, but in 1896, *Plessy vs. Ferguson* established legal precedent for segregating Black from White American privileges. Thus, until *Brown v. the Board of Education* in 1954 initiated the reversal of prevailing Jim Crow laws, law enforcement agencies were more or less bound to uphold the segregation of Blacks from Whites. And since this unjust obligation was legitimated as its duty, it also became its ethical norm (Lyotard, 1984).

While these two examples are etched deeply in the collective memory of the United States, they are too often neglected from discussions on ethical formations. Postmodernism provides the tools necessary for decoding and deconstructing normative sources of moral authority. All historical attempts at returning law enforcement structures and agents to a common moral source in this country must now be interpreted against the parallel stories of sexism and Jim Crow segregation, for example. These stories disrupt the dominant and prevailing Euro-American stories where White males stand as the primary benefactors of social and legal privilege. When these stories and countless others like them speak, they proclaim their own sources of authority from which they are able to distinguish properly between *legal* and *ethical*.

As a matter of fact, rather than one of judgment, the old centers of normative ethics that were rooted in common (to White males) moral values have become decentralized. For example, neighborhood rights campaigns such as the Racial Justice and Civil Rights Campaign of the Denver-based Colorado Progressive Coalition (CPC) are moving to challenge unchecked law enforcement authority. These are the conditions, especially in urban centers, in which law enforcement practices are now being tested and reviewed. The previous discussions on traditional approaches to cultivating ethical environments raise some interesting questions in light of these shifts in loci of morality and authority. Are current efforts to teach ethics to new recruits sufficiently exploring complex contexts in which ethical decisions are made or do these efforts assume that ethics is a simple matter of applying blanket universal prescriptions to every field situation? Are current structural reforms properly distinguishing between what is lawful from what is ethical in such a way that larger socio-political ideologies can be carefully considered and accounted for?

By addressing these questions and the many more that will come by interrogating historical precedent for ethical legitimation, law enforcement leaders can come to realize that ethics is an interdependent enterprise. The authors argue that on an individual level, personal lives, networks of support, and other political and economic circumstances have an equal if not greater pull on police conduct at work than does any ethical training in an academy or weekend leadership seminar like those offered by the National Institute of Ethics and the National Law Enforcement Policy Center. Police do not leave their ethics at the door when they return home after their shifts. On a structural level, law enforcement personnel generally are only as ethical as the laws they are bound by oath to uphold. In this sense, we contend that our legal system represents the baseline for justice and ethical standards rather than its zenith. Adopting a technological analogy, our legal system is like an open-source document that is continually being revised and reformatted to better suit our ever-expanding understanding of human decency and justice. The more authority and moral norms shift and decentralize, the more law enforcement must reevaluate its own loci of authority and moral foundations. If policing in a postmodern age requires the continual reassessment of its methods, policies, and practices, so too must ethical standards be continually reassessed.

Solutions

Ethics can be taught in an academy classroom, but primarily theoretically and not in such a way that will automatically translate to ethical conduct day-in and day-out in the field as is evidenced by the prevalence of the Aristotelian notion that knowing the good leads directly to doing the good (Aristotle, 1976). Ethical codes of conduct, complete with mission and vision statements, can be adopted by departments in an attempt to lift the structural cultures of unethical behavior. Similarly, leaders may receive training in fostering more ethical work places, oversight boards may be instituted to monitor misconduct, and communities can be brought in to better align their interests with police roles and expectations. Likewise, universally applying the standards of professionalism to law enforcement agencies is not the magical solution for curtailing unethical behavior. Just as Glaucon observed to Socrates, knowing the good is not the same as doing the good. How then do we cross the divide between knowing and doing the good especially as it relates to the structure/agency binary?

Available to us are a number of creative solutions that approach ethical reform from a variety of vantages. Fitch (2011), for example, calls attention to situation and psychological factors affecting ethical behavior that go largely unaddressed in traditional Aristotelian-virtue approaches. Fitch understands that peers influence one another as much if not more than superiors, which is why he advocates for the cultivation of a culture of ethics complete with mission statements, training in critical thinking, and effective systems of rewards and punishments. This focus on rewards and punishments is also emphasized by the National Institute of Ethics (n.d.), which is the nation's self-proclaimed largest resource for ethics training. The National Institute of Ethics provides extensive ethics training courses that cater to strengthening leadership skills essential for cultivating ethical department cultures. Built into their seminars is a decisive nod to psychological behaviorist B. F. Skinner, whose ideas on human motivation were based entirely on factors external to the individual's free will (Skinner, 2001). As such, the National Institute of Ethics focuses their seminars on teaching various techniques needed to prevent unethical behavior and to promote ethical behavior. While Fitch's solution deals only with the culture of a police department to the exclusion of wider social environments that press on police conduct, other training institutions such as the National Institute of Ethics deal only with external sources of motivation to the exclusion of interior standards of truth and justice.

In the end, law enforcement agencies will continue to struggle for solutions to ethical misconduct if any one or all of these measures are enacted without also addressing societal shifts in older centers of political and moral authority. The following paragraphs offer two possible avenues for better aligning law enforcement ethics with postmodern shifts in authority. We must discover where political and moral authorities are now located and understand how they are legitimated. Further, we must reevaluate the effectiveness of any one-size-fits-all approach to dealing with law enforcement ethics and seek out new localized solutions that pertain directly to individual communities across the nation.

To address ethics in law enforcement more adequately, we need to turn our attention to the wider societal trends in centers of authority. Gone are the days where we could look to things like common sense and prevailing Judeo-Christian mores to guide our collective sense of right and wrong. Even though law enforcement professionalism burst on the scene at the beginning of the 20th century as a redress for politically driven policing, the authors argue that it still remained fully reliant on the country's dominant moral conventions to legitimate its understanding of ethics. Police departments' attempts to tighten their moral laces during this period did not incorporate wider social injustices (e.g., Jim Crow laws). Given incongruities between laws and ethics, it is little wonder why ethical failings still exist in policing agencies. Social awakenings such as the civil rights movement have increased social awareness of human rights and civil liberties. These awakenings have also fostered the growth of postmodern theory, which asks important questions about who holds political and moral authority and why.

In more recent times, new modes of accountability are surfacing in the forms of social media and personal electronic devices that may prove more capable of maintaining citizen pressure for ethical behavior on law enforcement authorities. In general, citizens are using these media networks and devices to document police behavior and rapidly communicate breeches in police conduct to a global audience as was demonstrated during the University of California at Davis "pepper spray incident" in 2011 (Chappell, 2012). Bolstered and sometimes sensationalized by mass media networks, a private citizen becomes much more than a witness to police misconduct: He or she becomes a source for moral authority. What is more, the more prevalent these technologies become, the more educated the general population is becoming with respect to their rights and therefore all the more disparities are exacerbated between law enforcement and communities. For example, Police Inspector Tom Cowper states that new technologies will cause an increased demand for public security that will impact civil liberties and further stress existing tensions between police and communities (Stephens, 2005). Police officials can respond to this new center of moral authority in one of (at least) two ways. They can resist this authority and desperately seek to secure their own political authority, and therefore destroy their own moral authority by equivocating legal rightness with ethical rightness. Or they can learn from these new sources of authority and rely on them as an external motivation for practicing ethical behavior. If police officials choose this second option, they must find new ways to collaborate with their communities to better understand changing social mores and if necessary redefine police roles and functions.

Suman Kakar (1998) provides one such example based on the rubric of *community policing*. Kakar's approach explores the increasingly complex roles and functions of officers today within a postmodern context. Community policing fosters collaborations between citizens and officers that can enhance officer assumptions about who makes up the community and citizen perceptions of officers. Since police reception in individual communities is so often polarized by the actions of officers who are required to perform these complex roles and functions, Kakar hopes that such a process will humanize both officers in the minds of citizens, and vice versa.

The second solution to more ethical policing in a postmodern context is the need to reevaluate one-size-fits-all approaches to tackling police misconduct. Beginning with Kant, modern forms of ethical analysis attempt to wrap all contextual details of ethical situations under the fold of grand universal theories. The primary mode for understanding and doing ethics was largely dependent on complex theories that were tested first by the academic before they were worked out in real-life situations. According to the normative philosophical ethicists reviewed above, ethics was meant to supply a scientific—that is, unbiased and universally applicable—rubric for guiding all human actions. But as seen above, no ethic is ever devoid of a larger social context in which its rubric is fashioned. Each ethic both plays and is played by social, political, economic, and ideological norms unique to the ethicist's social context. To the extent that we continue teaching ethics to law enforcement officers while also assuming an unbiased or universal perspective, our social contexts will play us unwittingly.

Since universal theories have proven insufficient for universally resolving the tensions between knowing the good and doing it, it is little wonder that the move to professionalism in law enforcement was not sufficient for resolving the tensions between structure and agency. Police officers still engage in deceit, prejudice, or abuse of their authority (Souryal, 1992) despite decades-long progress toward professionalism. While professionalism may have been or still is a viable solution in some locations, it is not the only approach to confronting issues of ethical misconduct. We must find new ways not only to realize that ethical situations differ from region to region, but also to enact ethical approaches differently within these differing regions. Policing in Chicago is much different than policing in Sutter Creek, California. Not only are the nature and extent of crimes different; the policing agencies in each place have a different history and relationship with the communities they pledge to serve and protect. Given these discrepancies, it almost seems too obvious to call for more localized approaches to establishing and maintaining high rates of ethical conduct.

Substituting universal ethical theories and solutions with local ones may place new strains on departments already exhausted by trying to manage the host of other demands that call for their attention. While valid in its concern, the need outweighs the perceived costs. Police departments may even find community resources they never knew existed in the forms of a community's readied willingness to begin ethical reform dialogues. Such is the case, for example, in Denver, Colorado, where university students in the Denver Urban Issues and Policy class at the University of Denver and the not-for-profit CPC are raising community awareness of identified repeated problems within particular city districts. These efforts are not designed to undermine policing as an institution, but to heighten both police and public sensitivity to their issues with respect to balancing social inequalities. Yet community–police collaboration as advocated by this example and the remarks of Kakar (1998) must not be championed as the only solution to tackling ethical reforms. There may be cases where police already maintain good relations with their communities. These departments will be better served by going back to Souryal's (1992) three-tiered typology of unethical behavior to identify and address their own circumstances. It may be the case that unethical behavior can be addressed by providing more extensive psychological counseling to help officers better cope with the many stresses and traumas of their jobs.

A shift from universal to local may also be met with resistance because it tows the line with forms of moral relativism in which there are no criteria for judging between moral and immoral, just or unjust, or any other common misgiving of postmodernism (Parker, 1995). Branches of postmodern thought certainly have devolved into complete moral relativism wherein no one moral claim carries any more authority than any other. But adopting a postmodern approach does not require us also to adopt this extreme position where all things devolve into a state of chaos or anarchy. Instead, postmodern theory can be used as an aid for understanding how and where authority has been dispersed within society. Political and moral authority do not simply disappear but rather shift from place to place. No longer are social and ethical norms completely determined by traditional centralized sources. An increasingly diverse and complex society now demands an equally diverse and complex approach to law enforcement ethics.

Prospects for Professionalism

Given our deconstruction of the problems facing law enforcement ethics, the prospects for professionalism as understood by McClellan and Gustafson (2012)—the social construction of standards—are undeterred. Professions have long garnered enduring features, including educational attainment, codes of conduct and ethics, and some sort of peer review or oversight. As described throughout this chapter, many social and law enforcement leaders have advocated the structural enactment of these features of professionalism as the means toward ethical reforms. While the authors do not disagree with the merits of higher education, codes of conduct and ethics, or peer oversight and review, these are insufficient means for ensuring ethical behavior even while they are useful lenses for recognizing ethical needs. This is because knowing the good does not mean we will automatically do the good. Tactics of professionalism may well be good enhancements for law enforcement, but they are not in and of themselves a remedy.

The feature of independence or autonomous decision making prominent among professions is especially problematic for law enforcement when enacted in advance of ethical grounding. The last thing a powerful institution that is struggling with ethical conduct needs is increased autonomy because it further removes the institution from wider networks of social and political ideologies that foster inequality. And in this sense, the authors advocate ethical supports and localized reviews before broad-brush system-wide change. The authors are not, however, concerned that either of these can happen in a vacuum. Whether a matter of ethical reform or professionalization, these are socially constructed processes rooted in the discourse of countless communities and institutions. What is most important is that law enforcement and community leaders engage together to come to terms with their needs and the means for achieving them.

Summary

Policing in a postmodern age has become incredibly complex. It requires new techniques and strategies for meeting the demands of an increasingly technological and ethnically diverse society. What is clear in this brief overview and discussion of law enforcement ethics is that not all ethical decisions faced by officers are as plainly decipherable as the issue of cheating on academy exams. But even the example of cheating within training academies is not without its own complexities. The push of implementing structural reforms and pull of cultivating virtuous agents have made little progress toward any sort of universal eradication of misconduct, be it deception, discrimination, or abuse of authority. In fact, the need for a more effective ethical approach is needed now just as much as it was in 1931 when President Hoover established the Wickersham Commission and in 1975 when the International Association of Chiefs of Police hit on the Law Enforcement Code of Ethics.

Discussion Questions

Ideally this chapter will have identified areas of opportunity for enhancing ethical law enforcement practices. Further, it should also give rise to critical questions about how law enforcement personnel can go about doing good in the world. Consider the following:

1. Are there parallel professions/industries that have had struggles and learned lessons that could benefit law enforcement and community leaders? If so, what are they, and what are the lessons?

2. This chapter has argued that solutions to ethical dilemmas need to be local and contextual (within time, space, and social norms). To what extent is the same true about ethical norms or standards themselves?

3. How can we maintain national standards for ethical behavior while still allowing individual jurisdictions responsibility for establishing solutions appropriate to their own community contexts?

4. After reading this chapter, what alternative solution would you offer to the ethical dilemma presented in the introductory case study example (cheating in the law enforcement academy)?

5. We used examples from the recent and distant past (e.g., slavery) that were considered both legal and ethical then but, given today's social norms, would not be ethical or legal. What do you forecast or imagine might fall into this category now when reflected on 50 or 100 years from now? Put another way, what 2012 social norms are legal and ethical that might be illegal and unethical in the future? How does your answer relate to current hot-button issues such as immigration or protests associated with the "Occupy" movement?

6. What do you believe has been most formative for your own moral compass and where do you final moral authority? Do you draw on family roles models, religious texts, scholarly reasoning, or other sources for your inner sense of right and wrong?

References

American Civil Liberties Union (ACLU). (1997). *Fighting police abuse: A community action manual.* Retrieved from https://www.aclu.org/racial-justice_prisoners-rights_drug-law-reform_immigrants-rights/fighting-police-abuse-community-ac

Archer, M. S. (1995). *Realist social theory: The morphogenetic approach.* New York: Cambridge University Press.

Aristotle. (1976). *The ethics of Aristotle: The Nicomachean ethics.* (J. A. K. Thomson, Trans.). New York: Penguin. (Original work published circa 350 BCE)

Barker, T. (2002). Ethical police behavior. In K. M. Lersch (Ed.), *Policing and misconduct* (pp. 1–25). Upper Saddle River, NJ: Prentice Hall.

Bishop, J. B. (1920). *Theodore Roosevelt and his time shown in his own letters* (Vol. 1). New York: Charles Scribner's Sons.

California Commission on Peace Officer Standards and Training. (2007). *Basic course management guide* (6th ed.). Sacramento: California Commission on Peace Officer Standards and Training.

California Commission on Peace Officer Standards and Training. (2010). Minutes of the October 28, 2010 Meeting. Retrieved from http://post.ca.gov/Data/Sites/1/post_docs/commissionmeetings/2010/2010-10-28_minutes.pdf

California Commission on Peace Officer Standards and Training & Josephson, M. (2006). *Becoming an exemplary peace officer: An introduction to peace officer training*. Sacramento: California Commission on Peace Officer Standards and Training.

Chappell, B. (2012, April 11). Report faults UC Davis administrators, police in pepper spray incident [Web log post]. Retrieved from http://www.npr.org/blogs/thetwo-way/2012/04/11/150443916/report-faults-uc-davis-administrators-police-in-pepper-spray-incident

Chilton, B. S. (1998). Constitutional conscience: Criminal justice and public interest ethics. *Criminal Justice Ethics, 17*(2), 33–41.

Cohen, H. S., & Feldberg, M. (1991). *Power and restraint: The moral dimension of police work*. New York: Praeger.

Crank, J. P., & Caldero, M. A. (2010). *Police ethics: The corruption of noble cause* (3rd ed.). New Providence, NJ: Anderson.

Durkheim, É. (1938). *The rules of the sociological method* (S. A. Solovay & J. H. Mueller, Trans.). Glencoe, IL: The Free Press. (Original work published 1897)

Fitch, B. D. (2011). Rethinking ethics in law enforcement. *FBI Law Enforcement Bulletin, 80*(10), 18–24.

Giddens, A. (1979). *Central problems in social theory: Action, structure and contradiction in social analysis*. Berkeley: University of California Press.

Gilbert, A. (2009). Do philosophers counsel tyrants? *Constellations, 16*(1), 106–124.

Goffman, E. (1959). *The presentation of self in everyday life*. New York: Anchor.

Harring, S. L. (1983). *Policing a class society: The experience of American cities 1865–1915*. New Brunswick, NJ: Rutgers University Press.

Kakar, S. (1998). Self-evaluations of police performance: An analysis of the relationship between police officers' education level and job performance. *Policing, 21*(4), 632–647.

Kant, I. (1998). *Groundwork for the metaphysics of morals* (M. Gregor, Trans. and Ed.). New York: Cambridge University Press. (Original work published in 1785)

Kappeler, V. E., Sluder, R. D., & Alpert, G. P. (2005). Breeding deviant conformity: The ideology and culture of police. In R. G. Dunham & G. P. Alpert (Eds.), *Critical issues in policing: Contemporary readings* (5th ed., pp. 231–257). Long Grove, IL: Waveland.

Kleinig, J. (1996). *The ethics of policing*. Cambridge: Cambridge University Press.

Lohman, J. D., & Mismer, G. E. (1973). Civilian review—Philadelphia. In L. Ruchelman (Ed.), *Who rules the police?* (pp. 46–74). New York: New York University Press.

Lyotard, J. (1984). *The postmodern condition: A report on knowledge*. (G. Bennington & B. Massumi, Trans.). Minneapolis: University of Minnesota Press. (Original work published 1979)

McClellan, S. E., & Gustafson, B. G. (2012). Communicating law enforcement professionalization: Social construction of standards. *Policing: An International Journal of Police Strategies & Management, 35*(1), 104–123.

Mill, J. S. (2001). *Utilitarianism.* (G. Sher, Ed.). Indianapolis, IN: Hackett. (Original work published in 1863)

National Institute of Ethics. (n.d.) *Law enforcement and corrections.* Retrieved from http://www.ethicsinstitute.com/law_enforcement_and_corrections.html

Newburn, T. (1999). *Understanding and preventing police corruption: Lessons from the literature.* London: Home Office Policing and Reducing Crime Unit.

Parker, M. (1995). Critique in the name of what? Postmodernism and critical approaches to organization. *Organization Studies 16*(4), 553–564.

Perez, D., & Moore, J. A. (2012). *Police ethics: A matter of character* (2nd ed.). Clifton Park, NY: Delmar.

Plato. (1997a). *Gorgias.* (D. J. Zeyl, Trans.). In J. M. Cooper (Ed.), *Plato: Complete works* (pp. 791–869). Indianapolis, IN: Hackett Publishing Co. (Original work published circa 380 BCE)

Plato. (1997b). *The republic, book IV.* (G. M. A. Grube, Trans., Rev. by C. D. C. Reeve). In J. M. Cooper (Ed.), *Plato: Complete works* (pp. 1052–1077). Indianapolis, IN: Hackett Publishing Co. (Original work published in circa 360 BCE)

Ruchelman, L. (1973). *Who rules the police?* New York: New York University Press.

Skinner, B. F. (2001). *Beyond freedom and dignity.* Indianapolis, IN: Hackett. (Original work published in 1971)

Souryal, S. S. (1992). *Ethics in criminal justice: In search of the truth.* Cincinnati, OH: Anderson.

Stephens, G. (2005). Policing the future: Law enforcement's new challenges. *The Futurist, 39*(2), 51–57.

Vollmer, A. (1933). Police progress in the past twenty-five years. *Journal of Criminal Law and Criminology, 24*(2), 161–175.

Wilson, W. (1887). The study of administration. *Political Science Quarterly, 2*(2), 197–222.

Winton, R. (2010, October 16). Police classes suspended. *Los Angeles Times*, p. AA3.

9

The Psychology of Marginality

The Role of Subculture in Shaping, Developing, and Reinforcing Work Ethic

Paul Zipper and Tina Adams

On February 24, 2012, local news sources broke the story of a manhunt in Beverly, Massachusetts. An off-duty police officer had been shot twice outside a Starbucks coffeehouse and was clinging to life. Heroic civilians had quickly rendered aid to the victim. The perpetrator, who had fled the scene and was being actively pursued by members of the Beverly Police Department, was considered armed and dangerous. Within minutes of the story, however, a puzzling twist occurred. The perpetrator was identified as a fellow off-duty officer from the neighboring town of Hamilton, a 19-year veteran named Ken Nagy, who had recently been promoted to sergeant. The two apparently had a prearranged meeting at Starbucks; however, the topic of the appointment remained a mystery, as well as why one veteran police officer would shoot a fellow officer in plain sight of civilian onlookers.

The local news continued to provide periodic updates of the manhunt throughout the evening until the search eventually ended—without successfully apprehending Sergeant Nagy. Sadly, it was later reported that Nagy was found dead in his own vehicle that evening, the victim of what would eventually be ruled a self-inflicted gunshot wound. "He was a great police officer, a good investigator, well-liked by the community," Hamilton Police Chief Russell Stevens later said about Nagy. "He will be greatly missed" ("DA Credits Citizens," 2012).

With one veteran officer dead and a second in critical condition, one question remained: Why did one officer shoot another, and then choose to end his life? Nonetheless, it did not take long before details began to emerge. According to local news sources, Sergeant Nagy's wife, Katie, was employed by the Beverly Police Department, where she had worked with the victim, Officer Lantych. From his hospital bed, Lantych told investigators that in the days leading up to the shooting, he had a "moment of weakness" with Katie Nagy, but they were never intimate. The couple was in the process of divorce when Sergeant Nagy learned about the incident. It was reported that Nagy shot Lantych because of the perception of a relationship (Leighton, 2012).

As law enforcement professionals, it is critical to understand the antecedents, warning signs, and decision-making processes that contributed to this tragedy. A number of ethical and supervisory questions immediately arise. Were department supervisors or managers aware of any behavioral, emotional, or ethical problems? Was Nagy cognizant of any emotional difficulties he may have been experiencing? Were marital difficulties the primary cause of this incident, or could Nagy's behavior have been attributed to job-related stressors? Did the agency have systems or services in place to assist Nagy and others like him? And, if the answer to any of these questions, or other similar inquires, was yes, what actions, if any, were taken by supervisors, administrators, or other officers?

This chapter reviews the extant literature on marginality, including the impact of marginality on unethical behavior. The authors examine specifically the "red flags" and other behavioral warning signs of marginality, while paying special attention to the ethical dilemmas that may arise when officers experience emotional or psychological stress, particularly in those cases resulting in a ruling of unfitness for duty. The chapter further addresses the problem of marginality at three levels: the line officer, the supervisor, and the agency. The authors conclude by offering recommendations highlighting evidence-based practices that can be used to effectively identify and manage marginality.

The Officer: Candidacy and Fitness for Duty

Individual officers demonstrate their competency from the point they apply for candidacy throughout the duration of their professional careers. To be considered as a law enforcement candidate and, ultimately, as a sworn officer, every applicant must successfully complete a fitness for duty evaluation. The fitness for duty evaluation required by most law enforcement agencies demands completion of a rigorous background check, involving interviews with neighbors, friends, and past employers; a criminal records check; a credit inquiry; and a review of driver history (Fischler, 2001). Additionally, most candidates must complete a battery of tests designed to assess physical fitness, psychological well-being, verbal comprehension, and writing abilities. Applicants who successfully navigate these assessments are offered an opportunity to participate in an oral interview, often the last step before receiving a conditional offer of employment. The interview is typically conducted before a panel of high-ranking agency officials, who ask a series of questions designed to clarify any potentially damaging information uncovered during the background check. The interview also explores surrounding job knowledge, as well as responses to potential ethical dilemmas (Denton, 2009). For example: "If you stop a fellow police officer who was drunk driving, what do you do?" Not surprisingly, such scenarios focus on the candidate's potential actions and ethical decision-making processes.

Historically, fitness for duty was limited primarily to *physical* fitness (Quigley, 2008). However, law enforcement agencies have begun to recognize the need to assess *psychological* fitness as well (Fabian, 2011). As the practice has evolved, a number of methods have been developed to better assess a candidate's psychological fitness. The administration of structured assessment tools, such as personality inventories, intelligence assessments, and aptitude tests, as well as clinical interviews, may be used to further evaluate information revealed during the background investigation. This information will ultimately provide the agency with evidence to determine whether the candidate is of sound mind—that is, emotionally stable with good cognitive and judgment skills (Fischler et al., 2011). For instance, a candidate whose background investigation discloses a prior conviction for drunken driving may be eliminated from further consideration based on a perceived lack of ability to make good judgments.

The ideal psychological fitness assessment relies on three premises (International Association of Chiefs of Police [IACP], 2012). First, it is assumed that the clinical professional performing the psychological tests and clinical interview is highly qualified and capable of accurately interpreting the results of the structured tools being administered. Second, it is presumed that the clinical professional is well versed in the selection criteria and the processes used by law enforcement agencies to identify desirable candidates. Third, it is expected that there is a feedback loop between the clinical professional and the law enforcement agency. This loop should include the agency's current expectations and the clinical professional's views regarding evidenced-based practices in the fields of employee selection and retention. This system ensures the most advantageous criteria, tools, policies, and procedures available in selecting candidates who are both physically and psychologically fit (Fischler et al., 2011; IACP, 2012).

The tools used in examining psychological fitness are presumably intended to "weed out" those candidates assessed as psychologically unfit. However, within the process, there are ambiguities as criteria are not always measured as simple binary choices—in other words, as "all or none" "present or not present"—but as relative levels of strength or weakness for each criterion. There are also extraneous variables that may impact the process, for example, the reliability and validity of the tools employed, as well as the competencies of evaluating professionals (Miller, 2007). The common assumption is that individuals who decide to apply for candidacy are physically and psychologically fit. However, if the contracted evaluator in conducting his examination uncovers concern, he should feel duty bound to disclose those troubles to the agency's leadership.

While it may seem natural to assume that such disclosure commonly occurs, this may not always be the case (Davis, 1991; Kardasz, 2008). For any number of reasons—including a lack of experience, dearth of information, carelessness, or simple error—the clinical professional may miss or ignore, intentionally or unintentionally, certain warning signs. Alternatively, law enforcement administrators may fail to heed, or neglect the importance of, the results of the psychological examination (Kitaeff, 2011). Finally, a lack of disclosure may be due to errors on the part of all involved. In other words, neither the clinical professional nor the law enforcement agency sought out, or properly identified, all of the information required for the best possible decision. This may be due to both parties being unaware of the information or both having failed to understand its worth (Davis, 1991; Kitaeff, 2011).

Marginality

Despite the best efforts of many forensic psychologists, as well as the validity and reliability of the instruments used commonly to assess candidates, it can be difficult to consistently and effectively identify potentially marginal employees as the predictive validity of assessment tools can be limited (Fabian, 2011; Kitaeff, 2011). This is, in part, due to the nature of marginality itself. Marginality is perhaps best defined as exerting the minimal amount of effort needed to "pass" or to "get by"—in other words, exerting only the amount of effort necessary to prevent disqualification or disciplinary action (Iannone & Iannone, 2001). To further complicate matters, marginality can show up at any point in an officer's career. Marginality may be the product of dispositional factors, such as personality traits or temperament; psychological factors; stressors or trauma caused by the job; or, in some cases, poor supervision. In some organizations, marginality can be found at all levels, including leadership (Enter, 2006; Kouzes, Posner, & Peters, 1995). Simply put, law enforcement agencies may possess marginal officers, marginal supervisors, and marginal leadership. In any case, marginality can engender unethical behavior in both officers and supervisors. The critical point, then, is the ability to recognize marginality as a threat to the well-being and safety of the officer, supervisor, and agency. Once marginality has been identified, *it is incumbent on all involved* to begin taking steps to address and prevent marginality whenever and wherever it exists.

The Ethics of Marginality

Generally, a code of ethics guides all practices within an agency. The IACP Code of Ethics (2009) has established fundamental principles to guide the behavior of all of its members that include the following tenets: "All law enforcement officers must be fully aware of the ethical responsibilities of their position and must strive constantly to live up to the highest possible standards of professional policing" (para. 2). In addition, the code addresses the private persona of the police officer.

> Police Officers will behave in a manner that does not bring discredit to their agencies or themselves. A police officer's character and conduct while off duty must always be exemplary, thus maintaining a position of respect in the community in which he or she lives and serves. The officer's personal behavior must be beyond reproach. (para. 19)

These tenets encompass officers, supervisors, and senior leaders. An agency's code of ethics is deemed a reflection of its values and serves as a benchmark for its members. The IACP code expressly states, "Police Officers will be responsible for their own standard of professional performance and will take every reasonable opportunity to enhance and improve their level of knowledge and competence" (para. 17).

A law enforcement agency's strength is best measured by its officers' performance (Maguire, 2003). Therefore, agencies have customarily placed great importance on the selection and training of qualified applicants. While the system places considerable emphasis on the psychologist's role, too little significance has traditionally been placed on the role of supervisors, despite their direct impact on officer performance. Similarly, many police agencies place far too little value on the development of supervisory skills and continuous quality improvement (Moll, 2006). Equipping supervisors with the tools to identify and respond appropriately to the marginal behavior of employees requires that agencies invest the time, resources, and monies necessary to train supervisors in counseling, mentoring, documentation, leadership, and other skills.

However, the hiring process is not the only opportunity to screen out undesirable employees. On graduating from the academy, new officers are subject to a probationary period where the officer is once again evaluated on his ability to apply his training (Philadelphia Police Department, 2012). For those who require longer tenures of probation, the "break-in" period is typically extended. Individuals are provided with counseling and other supports to increase their readiness. Individuals who have reached this stage may, nonetheless, be terminated if they fail to meet the requirements. Appropriate supervisory training is critical at this point. If a supervisor fails to recognize and address important "red flags," or chooses to ignore such markers, the employee's marginal behavior will most likely continue—and, in many cases, deteriorate even further, exposing the officer and agency to potential litigation. In other cases, the supervisor may be part of an agency suffering a man power shortage, which has effectively adopted a "we can't afford to lose anyone" approach, or is impacted by other political constraints, such as an officer who is "politically connected," making discipline or termination virtually impossible (Enter, 2006). If the agency's leadership allows these issues to fester while failing to take the initiative to advocate for itself, those leaders are guilty of marginal behavior.

Supervisor–Subordinate Relationships

Once on the job, the relationship between the officer and his supervisor is critical, as it is at this level that ethical dilemmas and questionable behaviors first come to light (Sullivan, 2004). It is important to note, however, that the responsibility for this relationship is shared by both parties. Rather than relying solely on supervisor discretion, the subordinate who encounters a situation he feels ill-equipped to handle, anticipates the need for help in skill building, or simply feels that his overall performance is lacking is responsible for reaching out to a supervisor for guidance. Alternatively, it is the supervisor's responsibility to monitor and identify subordinates' areas of strength and weakness, especially when it is not apparent to the officer, and to work with the subordinate to develop a plan to address those needs (Schmallenger, 2009). One example of regulations stipulates that supervisors are responsible for adherence to all rules, regulations, policies, procedures, orders, and directives. More specifically, supervisors are

> [r]esponsible and accountable for the maintenance of discipline and shall provide leadership, supervision, and continuous training and serve as an example to ensure the efficiency of all operational areas . . . positively influence other members and motivate them to perform at a high level of efficiency . . . they evaluate employees in their assigned duties . . . supporting employees who are properly performing their duty, deal fairly and equitably with all employees and, when necessary correct them in a dignified manner . . . and recommend remedial or disciplinary action for inefficient, incompetent, or unsuitable employees . . . and remain accountable for any failure, misconduct, or omission by employees under their charge. (Department of State Police, 2003, p. 2)

Based on the above, it is clear that many law enforcement agencies now require their supervisors to take an active role in the oversight of subordinate employees. The goal of such policies is to hold supervisors accountable for the actions of employees under their charge. However, these mandates will have little success if supervisors are not empowered with the means to fairly and impartially evaluate their employees.

One way of addressing this problem is the Employee Evaluation System (EES) adopted by many law enforcement agencies. The overall goal of EES is to assist officers in performing their duties in a competent and professional manner. The EES system is based on the belief that constant review of performance will enhance employee professionalism and competence (Kramer,

1998). Thus, the purpose of EES is to measure performance and evaluate individuals on predetermined standards. EES recognizes outstanding performance, as well as unacceptable performance, while providing objective feedback to those evaluated. The EES applies equally to managers, supervisors, and, in this case, line officers. All groups are subject to ratings on several basic dimensions, such as knowledge, ability to follow direction, communication skills, initiative, and dependability. The EES is also equipped with an appeals process for employees who are unsatisfied with their performance evaluation.

In a situation where a member (a sworn member of the department who is rated by supervisory personnel) receives a "needs improvement" or "unacceptable" rating, the rater (an employee/member of the department who evaluates the performance of subordinate personnel) must include a statement in support of the rating (Kouzes & Posner, 2007). If the member wants to appeal his rating, he may submit a request in writing to the reviewer (the rater's immediate supervisor). The reviewer then meets with both parties and is empowered to change the rating after studying the supporting documentation. If the member is aggrieved by the decision of the reviewer, he may subsequently appeal to the superintendent. The above employee evaluation system is designed to give employees and agencies the best chance to succeed. However, for EES to work, all parties involved must take the process seriously.

Marginal Behavior and Ethical Dilemmas

In the supervisor–subordinate relationship, an ethical dilemma presents itself when the officer or his supervisor are aware of deficiencies, but choose to ignore or fail to ensure that known marginal performance is fully and effectively addressed. The dilemma is magnified when the behavior poses a risk to the citizens that law enforcement officers are sworn to protect. Miller, Braswell, and Whithead (2010) note in their discussion about police ethics that unethical behavior

[i]nvolves a broad spectrum that includes not only corruption, but also malpractice, mistreatment of offenders, racial discrimination, illegal searches and seizures, suspects' constitutional rights violations, perjury, evidence planting, and other misconduct committed under the authority of law enforcement. The consequence of such ethics violations are devastating in that they tarnish the reputation of the police department, decrease public confidence in police, and put officers at risk for retaliation by citizens when on the job. (p. 171)

There are many reasons why marginal performance is not fully and appropriately addressed. Oftentimes, a supervisor may feel that he has addressed the issue in an effective manner when, in fact, he may have approached the issue in an ineffective manner (Fitch, 2011). An example of this might involve a citizen who was issued a traffic ticket for speeding. The violator typically does not complain about receiving a traffic ticket. He may, however, file a complaint about the way he was treated. These types of complaints revolve around the motorist's perception that the officers behaved in a rude or discourteous manner. This type of complaint is typically assigned to the officer's immediate supervisor. Any time a citizen initiates a "formal" complaint, a first line supervisor and, if necessary, a manager must follow up.

The way the supervisor addresses the problem is critical to a proper resolution (Fitch, 2011; Prime Resources, 2009). The supervisor who responds by casually commenting to the officer that a citizen called to complain about the way he was treated sends the wrong message. The supervisor erroneously believes that he adequately addressed the problem by informing the officer of the complaint. However, this type of response leaves room for misunderstanding (Hess & Hess-Orthman, 2012). The officer might believe his supervisor is supportive of his actions and is just giving him a "heads up" in the event of additional fallout. He may not recognize any "informal counseling session" took place and walk away believing his actions were condoned. In his mind, his supervisor did not reprimand him. This is supported by a lack of negative consequences for his actions. In this example, neither the supervisor nor the officer has addressed the underlying issue: officer misconduct.

In this case, there seems little doubt that the officer will behave in a similar manner in the future (Fitch, 2011). On learning of a second offense, an ineffective supervisor would respond in the same manner, again missing an important opportunity to correct poor performance. Another possible scenario is that while the supervisor's approach is exemplary, the officer simply chooses to ignore the directive, especially if he believes there are no consequences for doing so. Ideally, the supervisor should follow protocol and, at the very least, engage the officer in a direct discussion about a more appropriate way to handle similar incidents in the future. If this were a one-time incident, a direct discussion may be all that is necessary (Cordner & Scarborough, 2010). However, if the officer is a repeat offender, more progressive discipline might be needed (Schroeder & Lombardo, 2006). The end result of appropriate action on the part of the supervisor is more likely to lead to a change in the officer's behavior. Selecting a "best practice" response as previously outlined allows for the following:

- Formal documentation of each incident
- Tracking and establishing a pattern of marginal behavior
- Informing management
- Referring the officer to appropriate services
- Preserving the integrity and safety of the agency and its mission

A Marginal Dilemma

A seemingly universal law enforcement benefit is the ability for officers to work "road jobs" or other paid details—that is, extra duties for paid overtime. These opportunities allow officers to supplement their incomes by making extra money working at construction sites, directing traffic for civic events, or other jobs that require a law enforcement presence. As with all law enforcement assignments, extra duty assignments involve a certain level of risk (FBI National Press Office, 2012). In response, department policy typically requires officers to wear clothing that minimizes known risks—for example, reflective clothing such as a traffic belt, vest, or raincoat with high visibility side out, as well as other duty articles. The safety benefits provided by reflective clothing are eliminated when officers fail to comply with the policy.

In an effort to ensure officer safety, supervisors are responsible for guaranteeing that officers adhere to department policy (Schroeder et al., 2006). Subsequently, supervisors may conduct inspections at these extra duty assignments or encounter their subordinates by chance and observe them not wearing reflective gear and, therefore, out of compliance with department policy. In either case, it is the supervisor's responsibility to enforce the prescribed dress code (Fitch, 2011). The agency's management may require and review monthly reports to ensure inspections are being conducted and officers are complying with the policy. This system is intended to assure that officers perform their duties in the safest manner possible; however, the success of this arrangement requires everyone involved to do their part. Having this practice adds clear expectations for officer behavior and firm consequence for noncompliance.

Marginality in the Supervisor

In the aforementioned example, the supervisor finds himself in an ethical dilemma. He wants to keep peace with his subordinates yet knows he is responsible for enforcing departmental policy. When the supervisor finds an officer who is noncompliant, he has two options. He can follow policy, make the ethically correct decision, and order the officer to put on reflective clothing. He would then be required to document the misconduct in a report to management (Schroeder et al., 2006). The marginal choice, on the other hand, is to ignore the deficiency and not make a report—a decision ripe with potential repercussions. If an officer is injured, there will certainly be an investigation. One of the first questions asked will be, Was the officer in compliance with department policy? The investigative team would determine whether or not he was wearing the mandated reflective clothing. The officer who was not wearing reflective clothing as prescribed by policy, as well as the supervisor who condoned the behavior, are both culpable for the injury.

On the other hand, the supervisor who took the initiative by documenting the officer's misconduct has recused himself and his agency from any culpability or negligence, while enhancing officer safety.

The practice of supervisors documenting misconduct only takes place when supervisors receive the appropriate level of management support. If management fails to support the supervisor's actions, the supervisor's subsequent ability to address and correct misconduct has been significantly compromised. A lack of support from management places marginality square in the lap of senior leadership (Crank & Caldero, 2011). Indeed, if management and leadership fail to enforce policies, what is the point of having such directives?

Another concern is the desire of many supervisors to address problems informally. While management must hold supervisors accountable, this means that supervisory expectations and codes of conduct must be clearly defined (Rath & Conchie, 2008). However, once a supervisor is aware of these expectations, any transgressions should be met with an appropriate management response, similar to what a supervisor would recommend for officer misconduct (Schroeder et al., 2006).

It is worth noting, however, that pressure to conform to the norms of the police subculture can significantly hamper the best efforts of supervisors and managers to correct deviant behavior. One characteristic of police subculture is an "us against them" mentality. Many officer believe that a person is either an officer (us) or not (them) (Malmin, 2012). However, within the subculture, there are even further "us versus them" divisions. For example, line officers often go to great lengths to separate themselves from "brass." Thus, anyone above the rank of line supervisor is viewed as a potential threat. This thinking can create a division between rank-and-file officers and first-line supervisors, and their supervisors (typically, agency management and senior leadership). Once an individual has assumed a management role, he is often seen by officers as someone who has forgotten the important issues affecting line officers, is unwilling to support line personnel, and is unwilling to terminate a member of his command staff (Davis, 1991; Moll, 2006; Violanti, 1999). Additionally, many of the problems associated with police subculture can be further exacerbated by the stressors common to law enforcement.

Potential Stressors Leading to Marginal Behavior

Some of the most challenging stressors that officers face can lead to termination, if not properly addressed. Consistently responding to calls for service, including homicides, child abuse, and motor vehicle accidents, can take a toll on officers' abilities to cope effectively. Over time, an officer's desire to fix the problems in his community comes face to face with the realization that he alone lacks the ability and resources to ameliorate many of these issues. In the event an officer copes poorly with this realization or receives little, if any, support, it may result in substance abuse, secondary trauma, or other mental health issues. All of this may contribute to marginal behavior, as the officer may view his circumstances as insurmountable and without a clear way out (Gilmartin, 2002). This is a pivotal time and referral to in-house resources, such as an employee assistance unit, Ombudsman, or other parts of a supportive network, is critical. According to available literature, the psychological stressors that officers face are largely unaddressed, especially as compared to efforts intended to prevent physical injury (Feemster & Collins, 2010). When marginal behavior emerges, the combination of stressors, ineffective supervision, and absent leadership can have tragic results. This potential for tragedy begs for immediate attention and intervention.

Across occupational lines, law enforcement officers are especially susceptible to alcohol abuse, with some studies estimating that one quarter of all police officers in the United States have serious alcohol problems (Moriarty & Field, 1990). While symptoms often vary, the end result of long-term abuse is often a pattern of arriving to work late or calling in "sick." The officer may ask his closest confidants to cover for him. In extreme cases, the officer may arrive for work while under the influence. Coworkers often hesitate to notify management for fear of being labeled a "rat" by their colleagues. Reporting a coworker's difficulties to the brass goes directly against the subculture, so the problem is ignored or the officer's colleagues attempt to deal with it informally as peers (Violanti, 1999). This is where the ethical dilemma presents itself. An officer who becomes aware of a coworker suffering from alcohol abuse has a responsibility to report the incident to an immediate supervisor, who is then required to address the problem formerly (Trautman, 2000). The supervisor has the additional responsibility of reporting the problem to senior leadership, who, in turn, has the duty to find a lasting solution.

As described in the opening vignette, authorities later discovered Nagy's pending divorce. Absent appropriate intervention, the situation spiraled out of control, ending in the shooting of one officer and the tragic suicide of another. As of this writing, no information has been published to indicate any "red flag" behaviors prior to the incident. However, it may be the case that such behavior, although it existed, was simply never reported.

High Stakes Consequences for Reporting

The nature of law enforcement is that violating the code of ethics is much more serious than violations in other professions (IACP, 2009). For an officer, a domestic violence complaint, drunken driving arrest, or other incident could lead to immediate suspension from duty and possible termination. A tradesman in the same predicament does not face job suspension with possible termination pending an internal investigation. In the opening scenario, Sergeant Nagy shot a fellow officer. There was also apparent marital strife between Nagy and his wife. He made the split-second decision to pull the trigger, knowing in that moment his 19-year law enforcement career was over. An individual in a different profession may not suffer the same career-ending consequence. If an individual is charged formally, once the legal process has concluded, he may have the opportunity to return to his former line of work.

It is unclear what stressors played a role in the Nagy/Lantych shooting. However, what is known is that law enforcement is a highly stressful occupation (Gilmartin, 2002; Hendricks, McKean & Hendricks, 2010; Miller et al., 2010). Hypothetically, Nagy may have been overwhelmed by the day-to-day stress of dealing with the public. His stress may have posed great risk to him, his decision-making abilities, and the safety of the citizenry. He seemingly went from "a great officer," as reported by Chief Stevens, to someone who completely decompensated. There remain a number of unanswered questions in the Nagy/Lantych incident. Were there any prior signs of coping problems or marginal behavior? What was Nagy's track record for using the employee assistance program (EAP)? It stands to reason that if Nagy was involved with the EAP, this terrible tragedy might have been avoided.

Officers face a variety of high-stress situations, many of which require highly adaptive problem-solving and coping skills. The literature recognizes the need for officers to be proficient in their conflict-resolution, crisis-intervention, and general interpersonal skills to deal with the diverse situations they encounter (Hendricks et al., 2010). However, officers also need to be equally proficient in self-care, or what has more recently become known as *officer wellness*. In the case of Sergeant Nagy, his skill level in each of these areas remains a mystery. However, research suggests that the level of training obtained by most officers in these areas is minimal—or, in other cases, altogether absent. Nonetheless, officers "are expected to make decisions and solve complicated problems" (Miller et al., 2010, p. 135). Furthermore, training in the area of stress management, emotional survival, and overall officer wellness has been virtually nonexistent in many police agencies (Feemster & Collins, 2010). Thus, it is almost certain that Nagy had very limited, if any, exposure to training in these areas. One can only wonder whether, had Nagy and other officers been routinely required to attend training in the area of self care or officer wellness, the outcome would have been different.

Gilmartin (2002) describes very effective physical safety and survival-training methods used by law enforcement agencies, but highlights the fact that many officers are "winning the battle of street survival, but fatally losing the battle of emotional survival" (p. 9). In a 2011 groundbreaking study, researchers at Harvard University found that sleep deprivation is a significant problem for law enforcement officers across the United States (Rajaratram et al., 2011; Wasserman & Moore, 1988). The results of the study, involving 5,000 officers, also revealed that these officers are 25% more likely to demonstrate uncontrolled anger toward a suspect or citizen. In a 1999 issue of the *FBI Law Enforcement Bulletin*, Violanti reported that the rate of substance abuse among police officers is double that of the general population. The 2010 Badge of Life Organization study of police suicide rates showed that the rate of suicide for police was 17:100,000 as compared to the general population at 11:100,000 (The Badge of Life Group, 2012).

Many of these problems are aggravated by the "wall of silence" historically found among members of the law enforcement subculture, causing many officers to suffer in silence (Davis, 1991; Moll, 2006). These evergrowing issues and seemingly sluggish responses by leadership raise questions about unethical behavior. Like physicians, officers take an oath to "first do no harm" (IACP, 2009). When an officer recognizes that he is overwhelmed by stress, seeking assistance is one way to ensure that he will do no harm to the public or himself by maintaining an appropriate level of mental fitness. Simultaneously, when that officer makes his needs known by asking for help or by demonstrating marginal behavior, the effective response by his supervisors must be immediate and supportive (Violanti, 1999). If Nagy had recognized that he was overwhelmed by stress and sought assistance, it could have meant the preservation of his safety and the safety of others involved in that case.

Evidence-Based Solutions

It is no secret that law enforcement has historically viewed susceptibility to stress as a form of weakness—emphasizing, instead, a "pull yourself up by your bootstraps" mentality. The agency and the public often expect superhuman effort from the officer, but forget that the officer comes from the same pool of mortals as the rest of us (Feemster & Collins, 2010; Gilmartin, 2002; Miller et al., 2010). There must be a balance between what can be reasonably expected from officers and opportunities to increase and enhance their strengths and manage their weaknesses. Psychological fitness should be the cornerstone of this approach. It is only in the last few years, however, that a movement within law enforcement agencies to recognize secondary trauma and the need for officer wellness practices and services has become part of the dialogue (Feemster & Collins, 2010).

The Selection Process

Addressing marginality begins by ensuring that the clinical professionals charged with providing psychological screening and assessment of police candidates continuously seeks to improve their skills in accurately evaluating the cognitive and emotional functioning of potential recruits. In addition, the clinical professional should provide continuous feedback to the law enforcement agency about the types of training and evaluation processes needed to ensure optimal performance and mental fitness among officers (IACP, 2012).

In the *Handbook of Police Psychology*, Kitaeff (2011) identifies the need for police psychologists or other clinical professionals charged with evaluating candidates to ensure that the structured assessment tools that are being used are valid and reliable and are specifically applicable to the field of law enforcement. Kitaeff notes that one significant limitation of the psychological screening/evaluation process is that it typically is the last part of the overall screening system and is often given little weight in hiring decisions. More importantly, the administration of the battery of psychological tests can only be completed after an offer of conditional employment. With this in mind, it is recommended that police departments confirm that staff or contracted psychologists are using evidence-based practices. It is also recommended that departments consider adopting the 2009 guidelines for Psychological Fitness for Duty Evaluations (FFDEs) put forth by the IACP. The IACP guidelines provide baseline considerations relative to when an officer should be referred for a Psychological FFDE.

Use of Policies, Procedures, and Resources to Address the Problem of Marginality

It is clear that one driving force behind exemplary police work is clear policies and procedures and the effective implementation of these guidelines by officers, supervisors, and managers (Maxwell, 2007). Additionally, policies and procedures must stay current with society's ever-changing needs. Third, law enforcement agencies must team with local, state, and federal experts in the area of stress management to develop strategies and programs to increase officer skills in maintaining wellness, stress management, and emotional survival. Fourth, agencies should develop and implement formal EAPs capable of offering professional advice and counseling (Moriarty & Field, 1990).

Employee Assistance Program

The function of an EAP is to offer assistance to law enforcement employees with occupational and personal problems that adversely affect their job performance (Moriarty & Field, 1990). An EAP should consist of highly trained peer counselors who are assigned to respond on a full-time basis. Early recognition and treatment of such problems provides benefits to the department as well as to the employee. Some of these benefits might include the retention of valued employees, especially those with specialized skill and experience, increased productivity, reduced absenteeism, and improved morale (EAP, 2012). Thus, agency leadership should strongly and consistently encourage law enforcement officers and their family members to use the services provided by EAPs (Merrick, 2011). The message must be that there is no weakness in asking for help. Rather, it is a sign of strength and resilience to do so. In addition, outcome and tracking processes must be created to ensure that programs are readily available to meet newly identified or increased need for such services (Feemster & Collins, 2010; Major Cities Chiefs Associates, Major County Sheriffs Associates, Federal Bureau of Investigation, & National Executive Institute Associates, 2012).

The Role of Supervision

Similar to the ideal selection process for recruits, the identification of officers for promotion should be approached with the same rigor (Schroeder et al., 2006). Of all the supervisory personnel in law enforcement, the success of an agency is most dependent on first-line supervisors. As reported by Froese Forensic Partners (2011), supervisors are vital in the chain of command: "Without engaged and effective supervision the connection between responsibility, performance, and accountability cannot be taken for granted. Good supervision is central to good police work" (p. 1). The foundation of a good supervisor is strong when he is selected from a pool of highly skilled and effective officers. In addition, the effectiveness of the supervisor is predicated on the orientation and ongoing training offered by the agency. Much of the available research in the area of supervisor development highlights the need for formal succession planning within departments, as well as (1) the mindfulness to identify the potential new supervisor's interpersonal strengths and areas for growth; (2) formal classroom instruction on becoming an effective supervisor; and (3) a lengthy period of application of learned skills and insights on the job, with a subsequent outcome evaluation to determine if the officer is ready and able to become a supervisor (Froese Forensic Partners, 2011; Rath & Conchie, 2008; Schroeder et al., 2006).

The research also affirms that style of supervision and quality of supervision can have significant impact on officer behavior (Engel & Worden, 2003). The National Institute of Justice, in its study of supervisory styles, illuminated four categories: traditional, innovative, supportive, and active (Engel, 2003). The traditional supervisor emphasizes strict enforcement of rules with little support of the community engagement effort that is the crux of community policing. In supervising officers, the traditional supervisor "instructs," is more likely to punish than reward, and focuses primarily on controlling officer behavior. The innovative supervisor embraces the principles of community policing and problem solving. He sees his role as establishing a positive working relationship with his subordinates, while relying mostly on coaching, mentoring, and facilitating to motivate his charge to implement new methods of policing. Supportive supervisors see themselves as protectors. More specifically, supportive supervisors view themselves as a buffer between upper management and line officers, seeking to protect their officers from unwarranted criticism and unfair discipline (Engel, 2003). Their job is to provide officers with the space necessary to accomplish their work. The active supervisor leads by example, working alongside officers while maintaining control of their behavior. The study found that while none of these styles are ideal and each has pitfalls, an active supervisory style proved to have the most influence on officer behavior, whether positive or negative. The study also found that the down side of the supportive supervisory style includes shielding officers from accountability mechanisms within the department that could lead to police misconduct.

Each of the supervisory styles has its place in law enforcement. Most effective supervisors employ a blend that draws from the strengths of all four styles (Engel, 2002). A supervisor who employs a traditional style strictly enforces the rules. This type of supervisor would be most appropriate once marginal behavior is identified. Incorporating an innovative style is necessary when trying to motivate through coaching and mentoring to eliminate marginal behavior. A supportive style is most useful once corrective action has been initiated, while an active supervisor is not to be afraid to work alongside the officer to model more appropriate behavior.

Ombudsman

Another resource to assist in managing marginal behavior is the Office of the Ombudsman. The Ombudsman provides a neutral, informal, and confidential process with the goal of resolving work-related issues (Office of the Police Ombudsman, 2012). The Ombudsman's activities are seen as a complimentary component to an agency's formally established conflict resolution system. The Ombudsman can also refer an individual to various departmental services or resources as needed or work with the individuals and others within the department to create a resolution. The communication between the Ombudsman, officer, and other levels of the agency are considered confidential. Therefore, the Ombudsman provides a safe venue to resolve conflict and address marginal behavior. It can also help provide creative solutions to decrease the influence of many negative aspects of the law enforcement subculture.

The Union

The collective bargaining association—or *union*, as they are more commonly known—has a seat at the marginality table as well. This seat comes with their responsibility to represent and act as the exclusive bargaining agent for all members of the bargaining unit and their employer (Gorman & Finkin, 2004). This representation typically includes all subject matter and procedures related to wages, hours, standards of productivity and performance, and any other terms or conditions of employment, and to all other subject matter concerning mutual aid and protection relating to employment. The union is also responsible for promoting and developing a friendly and fraternal spirit among all the bargaining unit members and their employer. In addition, the union's role is to mitigate workplace hazards (Mishel & Walters, 2003), as well as to foster goodwill with the citizens who live in their jurisdiction. One advantage often shared by union representatives is credibility. Thus, advice officered by a union representative is often taken seriously, which can make union representatives a powerful ally when dealing with marginal employees.

Accountability of Senior Leaders

The commissioner, chief, or manager within the law enforcement agency assumes the responsibility for oversight for the entire police force, including sworn officers, civilian employers, policies and procedures, and public safety (Campbell & Kodz, 2011). The assurance that active officers are both physically and psychologically fit to perform their duties rests squarely on the shoulders of these senior leaders. Relevant to the psychological functioning of active officers, these senior leaders must ensure that there are mechanisms in place that will allow managers and supervisors to quickly and accurately identify officers who are having performance issues or, more specifically, not coping well under the weight of their job duties (Walker, Alpert, & Kenney, 2001). The mechanisms used should determine the cause of the stress or poor coping, as well as provide opinions and recommendations about what interventions or services can be accessed to remedy the problems.

An effective feedback loop between department leaders and staff psychologists or contracted psychological service professionals is critical in raising the immediate awareness of officers who are having difficulties with job performance or otherwise in need of help (Phibbs, 2011). Leadership is responsible for galvanizing a rapid response using all available resources and advocating for enhancements or new services as needed to address the problem. All governmental agencies must strive for continuous quality improvement in these areas. Law enforcement agencies are not exempt from this responsibility.

An ideal strategic plan to address coping challenges among officers should, at a minimum, include the following steps:

- Ensure that the agency is committed to using evidence-based practices in the recruitment, selection, and hiring of new officers with particular attention to confirming physical *and* psychological fitness.
- Commit to continuous quality improvement in the areas of policy making and procedures. Ensure that policies and procedures are routinely reviewed and revised to match the current needs of the agency, all of its members, and the community it serves.
- Establish an EAP with access to internal services, as well as relevant community-based mental health and substance abuse service providers who have confirmed experience in working with law enforcement professionals.

- Develop and staff a Critical Incident Debriefing/Stress Management Unit.
- Ensure the availability of police psychological services for access to Psychological Fitness for Duty Evaluations as needed.
- Implement routine in-service training for managers, supervisors, and officers on officer well-being, stress management, and emotional survival strategies. Education about available community resources for officers should also be included. Training should be updated as needed to ensure that current evidence-based practices are being employed. (Feemster & Collins, 2010).

The Need for Ongoing Dialogue and Resolution

Despite an agency's best efforts, it is ultimately the officer who must decide whether or not to use services or to refuse them. What is mandatory, however, is that services be offered when a supervisor or manager perceives a potential problem (Moriarty & Field, 1990). Second, if an officer agrees to use services, any report regarding his participation and progress cannot be provided to senior leaders, managers, or supervisors without the officer's expressed informed consent, with but a few rare exceptions. If, for example, the provider has reason to believe that the officer is at risk of harming himself or another, the service provider is mandated to disclose his concern, as well as the basis (Stewart, 2003). When concerns arise, a good rule of thumb is to convene an incident review panel made up of agency leadership, staff or consulting forensic psychologist, with input from legal counsel, union representatives, and the Ombudsman. The job of the incident review committee would be to review any situation where an officer's well-being or that of the public is at potential risk.

If the officer has any reservations about the depth and scope of information that might be released to the agency or its impact on him, he can meet with the incident review committee. The committee and the officer could, then, develop a plan to allow the minimum amount of disclosure necessary to ensure that the right services are identified for the officer, the agency is assured that the individual is psychologically fit for duty, and public safety is maintained (Beety, 2010). Moving forward, the agency can work with their Ombudsman, legal counsel, and labor relations department to negotiate other situations that may be considered borderline with regard to confidentiality and develop guidelines for resolving such matters in a way that is legally sound and ethically fair.

Summary _____

Marginality is defined as exerting the minimal amount of effort needed to "pass" or to "get by"—in other words, exerting the minimum amount of effort necessary to prevent disqualification or disciplinary action (Iannone & Iannone, 2001). However, when marginal behavior is grounded in job stress, trauma, mental illness, or substance abuse, it must be dealt with immediately. If the behavior is known and little is done to respond to the problem, this can jeopardize the safety of the officer, the agency, and the public. In law enforcement, marginality can appear at any time in an officer's career (Wilson, 1978). It can also appear at any level of the agency, including line officers, supervisors, managers, and senior leadership. For any law enforcement agency to work at its optimal best, marginality must be recognized for what it is—a threat to the well-being and safety of the officer, the agency, and the public. Appropriate and effective training and supervision become essential in ensuring that officers, supervisors, and senior management understand the warning signs and the need for timely intervention (Marx, 2010). Supervisors must strictly enforce regulations, policies, and procedures, while internal and external resources must be readily available to employees suffering from stress, substance abuse, marital strife, or other stressors.

The chapter opened with the tragic case of Sergeant Nagy and Officer Lantych. This real-life situation raises many questions about missed warning signs. In addition, it points directly to the need for careful attention to the emotional well-being and psychological fitness for duty of law enforcement officers. The importance of effective stress management practices and supervision in battling marginality cannot be overstated. The likelihood of potential ethical dilemmas, subsequent declines in performance, and risks to the public are simply too great to be ignored. In the end, the timely and effective response to officers engaged in marginal behavior must be a priority for all members of the law enforcement community. Only by working together, can peers, supervisors, and counseling professionals prevent further tragedies, like the Nagy/Lantych shooting, from occurring again.

Discussion Questions

1. Complete an Internet, library, or local law enforcement agency search and review the code of ethics for law enforcement professionals for your state. Does the code address "psychological fitness"? What guidelines are included regarding officer conduct/misconduct, supervisor responsibility, and agency responsibility?

2. Do you believe that psychological fitness should be given as much weight as physical fitness in determining a "good" candidate for law enforcement? Why or why not?

3. For your state, what written policies are in place regarding Psychological Fitness for Duty Evaluations?

4. Does your state law enforcement system offer any officer wellness programs? If so, list and describe some of those services.

5. Identify a case scenario that involves marginal behavior on the part of an officer. If you were the supervisor, how would you address the situation? What resources would you access to assist you in managing the situation?

6. Using your selected scenario, what changes in policy or practice would you recommend to prevent a similar situation in the future?

References

The Badge of Life Group. (2012). *Badge of life announces 2010 police suicides figures.* Retrieved from http://www.policesuicideprevention.com/id48.html

Beety, P. (2010). *Fitness for duty exams for police officers: Timing issues, legal requirements, and practical tips.* Saint Paul: League of Minnesota Cities Insurance Trust.

Campbell, I., & Kodz, J. (2011, June). *What makes great police leadership? What research can tell us about the effectiveness of different leadership styles, competencies, and behaviors.* London: National Policing Improvement Agency. Retrieved from http://www.npia.police.uk/en/docs/Great_Police_Leader_REA .pdf

Cordner, G. W., & Scarborough, K. (2010). *Police administration* (7th ed.). New Providence, NJ: Lexis Nexis.

Crank, J. P., & Caldero, M. A. (2011). *Police ethics: The corruption of noble cause* (3rd ed.). Burlington, MA: Anderson.

DA credits citizens with saving cop. (2012, February 26). *Eagle-Tribune.* Retrieved from http://www.eagletribune.com/archive/x952193700/DA-credits-citizens-with-saving-cop

Davis, M. (1991, Summer–Fall). Do cops really need a code of ethics? *Criminal Justice Ethics, 10*(2), 14–28.

Denton, M. (2009). *Police oral boards: The ultimate guide to a successful oral board interview.* Seattle, WA: CreateSpace.

Department of State Police. (2003, May 2). *Rules and regulations: Article 3.* Boston: Massachusetts State Police. Retrieved from http://members.masstroopers.us/wp-content/uploads/2010/01/MSP-Rules-Regs.pdf

Employee Assistance Program (EAP). (2012). *Work support is just a phone call away.* Retrieved from http://www.mass.gov/anf/employee-insurance-and-retirement-benefits/coordinator-information/eap/

Engel, R. S. (2002). Patrol officer supervision in the community policing era. *Journal of Criminal Justice, 30,* 51–64.

Engel, R. S. (2003). *How police supervisory styles influence patrol officer behavior.* Washington, DC: National Institute of Justice.

Engel, R. S., & Worden, R. E. (2003). Police officers' attitudes, behavior, and supervisory influences: An analysis of problem solving. *Criminology, 41*(1), 131–166.

Enter, J. E. (2006). *Challenging the law enforcement organization: The road to effective leadership.* Ontario, Canada: Narrow Road Press.

Fabian, J. M. (2011). *Review of the handbook of psychological fitness for duty evaluations in law enforcement.* Retrieved from http://www.forensicpsychology-unbound.ws/OAJFP/Volume_3__2011_files/Fabian%20review%20of%20 Rostow%20%26%20Davis.pdf

FBI National Press Office. (2012). *FBI releases preliminary statistics for law enforcement officers killed in 2010.* Washington, DC: U.S. Department of Justice. Retrieved from http://www.fbi.gov/news/pressrel/press-releases/fbi-releases-preliminary-statistics-for-law-enforcement-officers-killed-in-2010

Feemster, S. L., & Collins, J. V. (2010, November). Beyond survival toward officer wellness (BeSTOW): Targeting law enforcement training. *The Police Chief, 77,* 34–43.

Fischler, G. L. (2001). Psychological fitness-for-duty examinations: Practical considerations for public safety departments. *Law Enforcement Executive Forum, 1,* 77–92.

Fischler, G. L., McElroy, H. K., Miller, L., Saxe-Clifford, S., Stewart, C. O., & Zeilig, M. (2011, August). The role of psychological fitness-for-duty evaluations in law enforcement. *The Police Chief, 78,* 72–78.

Fitch, B. D. (2011). The two roles of supervision. *FBI Law Enforcement Bulletin, 80*(3), 10–15.

Froese Forensic Partners, LTD. (2011). *The importance of effective supervision in law enforcement.* Toronto, Ontario: Author.

Gilmartin, K. M. (2002). *Emotional survival for law enforcement: A guide for officers and their families.* Tuscon, AZ: E-S Press.

Gorman, R. A., & Finkin, M. W. (2004). *Basic text on labor law: Unionization and collective bargaining* (2nd ed.). Saint Paul, MN: West Publishing Co.

Hendricks, J. E., McKean, J. B., & Hendricks, C. G. (2010). *Crisis intervention: Contemporary issues for on-site interveners.* Springfield, IL: Charles C. Thomas.

Hess, K. M., & Hess-Orthman, C. (2012). *Management and supervision in law enforcement* (6th ed.). Clifton, NY: Delmar Cengage Learning.

Iannone, N. F., & Iannone, M. D. (2001). *Supervision of police personnel* (6th ed.). Upper Saddle River, NJ: Prentice Hall.

International Association of Chiefs of Police (IACP). (2003). *Law Enforcement Code of Ethics by IACP.* Retrieved from http://the7thpwr.wordpress.com/2009/11/05/law-enforcement-code-of-ethics-by-iacp/

International Association of Chiefs of Police (IACP). (2009). *Psychological fitness for duty evaluation guidelines.* Denver, CO: Author.

International Association of Chiefs of Police (IACP). (2012). *Fitness for duty evaluation guidelines.* San Diego, CA: Author.

Kardasz, F. (2008). *Ethics training for law enforcement: Practices and trends.* Saarbrücken, Germany: VDM Verlag.

Kitaeff, J. (Ed.). (2011). *Handbook of police psychology.* New York: Routledge.

Kouzes, J. M., & Posner, B. Z. (2007). *The leadership challenge: Becoming a better leader* (4th ed.). San Francisco: Jossey-Bass.

Kouzes, J. M., Posner, B. Z., & Peters, T. (1995). *The leadership challenge: How to keep getting extraordinary things done in organizations.* San Francisco: Jossey-Bass.

Kramer, M. (1998, March 1). Designing an individualized performance evaluation system. *FBI Law Enforcement Bulletin.* Retrieved from http://www.highbeam.com/doc/1G1-20576395.html

Leighton, P. (2012, February 29). DA to investigate relationship between police officer, widow. *Eagle-Tribune.* Retrieved from http://www.eagletribune.com/local/x1875170346/DA-to-investigate-relationship-between-police-officer-widow

Maguire, E. R. (2003). Measuring the performance of law enforcement agencies, part I. *CALEA Update Magazine, 83.* Retrieved from http://www.calea.org/

calea-update-magazine/issue-83/measuring-performance-law-enforcement-agencies-part-1of-2-oart-articl

Major Cities Chiefs Associates, Major County Sheriffs Associates, Federal Bureau of Investigation, & National Executive Institute Associates. (2012). *Shifting the culture from avoidance to addressing police suicide.* Dallas, TX: Authors.

Malmin, M. (2012). Changing police subculture. *FBI Law Enforcement Bulletin, 81*(4), 14–19.

Marx, J. (2010, February). *Crisis intervention for police officers.* Retrieved from http://www.copsalive.com/crisis intervention for police officers

Maxwell, J. C. (2007). *The 21 irrefutable laws of leadership: Follow them and people will follow you* (10th ed.). Nashville, TN: Thomas Nelson.

Merrick, E. L. (2011, September). *The role of employee assistance programs in supporting workforce resiliency.* Washington, DC: Institute of Medicine, Committee on Workforce Resiliency Programs, Operational and Law Enforcement Resiliency Workshop.

Miller, L. (2007). The psychological fitness for duty evoluation. *FBI Law Enforcement Bulletin, 76*(8), 10–16.

Miller, L., Braswell, M., & Whitehead, J. (2010). *Human relations & police work* (6th ed.). Lone Grove, IL: Waveland Press.

Mishel, L., & Walters, M. (2003). *How unions help all workers.* Retrieved from http://www.epi.org/publication/briefingpapers_bp143/

Moll, M. (2006, Fall). Improving American police ethics training: Focusing on social contract theory and constitutional principles. *Forum on Public Policy Online.* Retrieved from http://forumonpublicpolicy.com/archivesum07/moll.pdf

Moriarty, A., & Field, M. W. (1990). Proactive Intervention: A new approach to police EAP programs. *Public Personnel Management, 19*(2), 155–162.

Office of the Police Ombudsman. (2012). *Mission.* Retrieve from http://www.spdombudsman.com/about-us

Phibbs, W. M. (2011). Analyzing organizational performance. *FBI Law Enforcement Bulletin, 80*(12), 12–19.

Philadelphia Police Department. (2012). *Hiring process.* Philadelphia, PA: Authors. Retrieved from http://phillypolice.com/careers/hiring-process/

Prime Resources. (2009). *Positive steps for addressing performance problems.* Retrieved from http://primeresources.com/Articles/PerformanceManagement/positive-steps-for-addressing-performance-problems.pdf

Quigley, A. (2008, June). Fit for duty? The need for physical fitness programs for law enforcement officers. *Police Chief Magazine, 75.* Retrieved from: http://www.policechiefmagazine.org/magazine/index.cfm?fuseaction=display&article_id=1516&issue_id=62008

Rajaratram, S. M. W., et al. (2011). Sleep disorders, health, and safety in police officers. *JAMA, 306*(23), 2567–2578.

Rath, T., & Conchie, B. (2008). *Strengths-based leadership: Great leaders, teams, and why people follow.* New York: Gallup Press.

Schmallenger, F. (2009). *Criminal justice today* (10th ed.). Upper Saddle, NJ: Pearson-Hall.

Schroeder, D. & Lombardo, F. (2006). *Management and supervision of law enforcement personnel* (4th ed.). Binghamton, NY: Gould.

Stewart, D. (2003, October). In defense of exceptions to confidentiality. *Virtual Mentor, 5*(1). Retrieved from http://virtualmentor.ama-assn.org/2003/10/hlaw1-0310.html

Sullivan, B. (2004, October). *Police supervision in the 21st century: Can traditional work standards and the contemporary employee co-exist?* Alexandria, VA: International Association of Chiefs of Police. Retrieved from http://www .policechiefmagazine.org/magazine/index.cfm?fuseaction=display_arch& article_id=1391&issue_id=102004

Trautman, N. (2000, October). *Police code of silence facts revealed.* Paper presented at the Annual Conference of International Association of Chiefs of Police, San Diego, CA. Retrieved from http://www.aele.org/loscode2000.html

Violanti, J. M. (1999). Alcohol abuse in policing: Prevention strategies. *FBI Law Enforcement Bulletin, 68* (1), 16–18.

Walker, S., Alpert, G. P., & Kenney, D. J. (2001). *Early warning systems: Responding to the problem police officer.* Washington, DC: National Institute of Justice. Retrieved from http://www.ojp.usdoj.gov/nij

Wasserman, R., & Moore, M. H. (1988). Values in policing. *Perspectives in Policing, 8,* 1–8. Retrieved from https://www.ncjrs.gov/pdffiles1/nij/114216.pdf

Wilson, J. Q. (1978). *Varieties of police behavior: The management of law and order in eight communities.* Cambridge, MA: Harvard University Press.

10 Neuropsychological Correlates of Misconduct in Law Enforcement Officers With Subclinical Post-Traumatic Stress Disorder

Amir Hamidi and Patrick M. Koga

On September 14, 2004, at 7:12 a.m., Louis Hernandez, a 34-year-old former New York City Police Department (NYPD) officer committed suicide by jumping off of a 12-story building in New York City. Two years later, his widow, Elvira, a devout Catholic overwhelmed by the double grief of her husband's death and the capital sin of his suicide, lost the custody of her two small sons to her mother, due to a severe depression worsened by poor coping with binge drinking. Officer Hernandez, a former martial arts instructor with an impeccable service record between 1994 and 2002, was never diagnosed with post-traumatic stress disorder (PTSD) or with any mental disorder.

In 2003, however, two years after the grueling work in the aftermath of the September 11, 2001 attacks as an officer of NYPD's Emergency Service Unit, Hernandez's good behavior and life began a downward spiral. In March 2003, he received a duty suspension for misconduct. Shortly thereafter, a second incident of police brutality resulted in his being fired from the job in September 2003.

After a winter spent at his grandparents' in Stockton, Hernandez returned home to New York with hopes for a new life. He landed a job as a security guard for an upscale apartment complex, but lost the position after two Middle Eastern residents complained of being frightened by his explosive temper. The summer of 2004 went equally bad for Hernandez, as he had innumerable quarrels with Elvira, including two instances of spousal battery, which were never reported. By the end of August, Hernandez had lost considerable weight and became increasingly withdrawn, morose, and silent. He would sit for hours on the balcony of his home and chain smoke in complete silence. He would slowly exhale the smoke from his cigarettes, as if in a sort of trance. On September 14, he plunged from a balcony to his death, a late casualty of 9/11 and, perhaps, of insufficient policies to prevent a silent epidemic of subclinical PTSD.

The tragic death of Officer Hernandez demonstrates the need for greater awareness of the causes, symptoms, and treatment of PTSD among member of the law enforcement community, including officers, supervisors, senior leadership, and mental health professionals. This chapter discusses the organizational and occupational stressors associated with law enforcement, including the relationship between traumatic events and PTSD. The authors further examine the symptoms and onset of PTSD, including the neurophysiological correlates of PTSD, biological responses to fear, and subclinical PTSD. Next, the authors explore the racial, ethnic, cultural, and gender determinants of PTSD. The chapter concludes with an investigation of current treatments available for PTSD patients, including cognitive processing therapy and mindfulness-based stress reduction.

Epidemiological Considerations of PTSD in Law Enforcement

In her research with men who had committed violent crimes, forensic psychologist Deirdre MacManus discovered a pattern that involved men recently returned from combat in Afghanistan and Iraq (McCleanghan, 2012). Her study, recently published and widely featured in the media, shows that one in eight Operation Iraqi Freedom/Operation Enduring Freedom soldiers has attacked someone after returning from war, with 30% of attacks involving family members. The association between serving in a combat role and being exposed to combat, and subsequent violence on return from deployment, is about two-fold. In terms of occupational and organizational stress and trauma, law enforcement work is perhaps second only to soldiering in war zones (Kop & Euwema, 2001; Violanti & Aron, 1995). If civil unrest, riots, bomb threats, shooting, and hostage crises are rare, the most trivial daily tasks—such as responding to domestic violence calls, shoplifting, and automobile accidents—involve a daily exposure to dangerous situations with potentially fatal consequences both for the perpetrator and the officer.

Some of these tragic scenarios have made headline news, like two West Memphis officers who were killed in 2010 during a traffic stop when a 16-year-old passenger exited the vehicle and opened fire with a semiautomatic rifle. In another, a Chicago Police Department officer at the end of his shift was removing gear near his car in the department's parking lot when a man ambushed the 43-year-old officer and shot him with his own weapon. The 2010 annual FBI report called *Law Enforcement Officers Killed and Assaulted* relates the story of a 62-year-old deputy sheriff in Mississippi who was shot and killed by an uncooperative suspect while responding to a "simple" domestic disturbance call. With an average of 165 line-of-duty deaths each year, or one death every 53 hours, the risk one takes simply by being a law enforcement officer is a palpable reality. In 2010 alone, 56 of the 145 officers who died in the line-of-duty were feloniously slain. According to the National Law Enforcement Officers Memorial Fund, over the last decade, there have been 53,469 assaults against law enforcement each year, resulting in 15,833 injuries (U.S. Department of Justice, 2007). In 2009, by the estimates provided by the FBI's Uniform Crime Reporting Program, 1,318,398 violent crimes occurred nationwide, which equates to 429.4 violent crimes per 100,000 inhabitants. Aggravated assaults accounted for the highest number of violent crimes, reported at 61.2%. Robbery composed 31.0%, forcible rape accounted for 6.7%, and murder accounted for 1.2% of estimated violent crimes in 2009.

The cumulative math of facing such daily hazards makes police work an occupation extremely vulnerable to PTSD with all its accompanying comorbid ills. In 2008, the RAND Corporation, Center for Military Health Policy Research, conducted a population-based study investigating the prevalence of PTSD among previously deployed Operation Enduring Freedom and Operation Iraqi Freedom (Afghanistan and Iraq) service members (Tanielian & Jaycox, 2008). Among the 1,938 participants, the prevalence of current PTSD was 13.8%. Police work is not scoring much better than active military service: 3% to 17% of police officers, too, exhibit the full spectrum of this condition (Robinson, Sigman, & Wilson, 1997). Equally worrisome, 7% to 35% of all police officers are demonstrating at any given time some PTSD symptoms, or what it is called *subclinical*, or *subclinical PTSD*.

Since both PTSD and subclinical PTSD have adverse impacts on police officers' abilities to carry out their duties, these occupational disorders may play a substantial part in officer misconduct, poor job performance, ethical violations of fiduciary duties, and personal family problems. In the United States, there are over 17,000 separate law enforcement agencies with 900,000 sworn officers serving in varying roles (Bureau of Justice Statistics, 2002). This provides a conservative estimate rate of 50,000 cases of PTSD and another 100,000 cases of subclinical PTSD. This epidemic, while perhaps exceeded in magnitude only by that experienced by the U.S. Armed Forces, is not well researched, recognized, treated, or even admitted.

Unlike the honored and dignified Odysseus of the Afghan and Iraq wars, disaster relief workers, Special Weapons and Tactics (SWAT) teams, or other emergency responders, police officers are often poorly recognized, let alone supported, by the communities which they are sworn to protect. Having to deal with hostile, angry, or aggressive residents, and constantly feeling watched and scrutinized by everybody, from alleged perpetrators' families to bypassers' iPhones, media, reviews by citizen boards, or even one's own internal affairs unit, places substantial stress on officers. In the extremes, sometimes bordering on the absurd, officers face lawsuits alleging police misconduct brought against them by criminals for wounds produced while committing a crime (Violanti & Aron, 1996).

According to Davis (2011), the following incidents are most likely to traumatize police officers:

- Witnessing the death of a law enforcement officer or viewing the body at the scene, especially when the victim was a friend or partner; trauma is often increased if the officer believed he or she should have protected the person who died, or if the dead officer was temporarily serving in place of the officer
- An officer accidentally kills or wounds a bystander, especially if the victim is a child
- An officer fails to stop a perpetrator from injuring or killing someone after the initial encounter
- Killing or wounding a child or teenager, even if the life of the officer was threatened by the person injured or killed
- Viewing the body of a child victim, particularly if the officer has children and even more so if the officer's child is the same age and sex as the victim or if the child victim is similar in some other way to the officer's child, such as appearance, clothing, toys, or school
- When a dead victim becomes personalized, rather than just an unknown body, through interaction with grieving family members or friends, or from information gained from the scene, news reports, or search warrants; continued association with the pain of survivors through an investigation and trial (and often long after) also can personalize the dead victims
- The terror of being caught in a violent riot; trauma may be increased when children are present in the crowd and the officer cannot use deadly force to defend him or herself for fear of hurting the children
- Particularly bloody or gruesome scenes; horror of the crime and the suffering of the victims
- Observing an event involving violence or murder, but not being able to intervene (i.e., "I watched him kill her. She was screaming for my help but there was nothing I could do")
- An undercover assignment in which the officer is constantly "on guard" because of the likelihood of being hurt, killed, or discovered
- When suspects who have been indicted, are being tried, or are incarcerated threaten the officer or the officer's family with violence and are deemed capable of carrying out these threats

In July 2012, a report by investigators at Florida State University and University of Windsor, Ontario, Canada, explored how alcohol abuse and PTSD influence rates of self-reported domestic violence committed by law enforcement officers. The researchers used a cross-sectional design with multiple measures and instruments. A strong correlation was found: Officers diagnosed with PTSD were four times more likely to report using physical violence; officers who reported hazardous drinking were four times more likely to report violence; and dependent drinkers were eight times more likely to report being physically violent with an intimate partner (Oehme, Donnelly, & Martin, 2012). The findings have resulted in new recommendations for training and policies to help police agencies and to reduce suffering and attrition in this population. This is the first study investigating the link between PTSD, alcohol use, and domestic violence involving law enforcement officers.

Organizational Stressors in Law Enforcement in the U.S. and Abroad

How much support had Hernandez received from his superiors and coworkers? Did his work environment contribute in any measure to his reduced resilience to traumatic stress? Although these questions have not translated into policy changes, such queries have been posed by researchers for decades. One of the early studies on police stress in Cincinnati (Kroes, Margotis, & Hurrell, 1974) asked 100 male police officers to identify major stressors in their job. They reported the courts, administration, inadequate equipment, community relations, and changing shift routines as the most bothersome aspects of their job. Surprisingly, crisis situations were the second most commonly reported stressor, only after administration.

Brown and Campbell (1990) conducted a research study that looked at organizational stressors and police operational stressors, excluding critical incidents from the study. Nine hundred fifty-four English constables participated and reported organizational stressors four times more often than police operational stressors. Staff shortages, shift work, time pressures and deadlines, lack of consultation, and communication comprised more than half of the organizational and management stressors reported by the subjects.

The findings of an investigation of organizational and management stressors and operational stressors in a Scottish police force of 700 participants reported the primary sources of perceived stress as staff shortages, inadequate resources, time pressures, work overloads, and lack of communication (Biggam, Power, & Macdonald, 1997). Just like the Scots, the Dutch police officers investigated by Kop and Euwema (2001) reported organizational aspects of the police environment more often as stressors than the nature of their police work. The results of numerous studies suggest that routine occupation stress may be a greater risk factor for traumatic stress symptoms in law enforcement officers than the risks of the job itself.

Clinical and Subclinical PTSD

What actually is PTSD? During the course of any given year, about 5.2 million Americans, aged 18 to 54, develop PTSD. This does not include the 60.7% of men and 51.2% of women who experience at least one traumatic event in which their symptoms did not meet the Diagnostic and Statistical Manual of Mental Disorders (DSM-IV-TR) (American Psychiatric Association, 2000) criteria for a full clinical diagnosis of PTSD. The trauma symptoms of this anxiety disorder are often very similar regardless of the great variety of traumatic events people may experience.

PTSD is the outcome of an intensely traumatic event, involving an actual experience or threat to self or others, accompanied by a feeling of helplessness. Symptoms of PTSD include fear, helplessness, and horror. The fundamental diagnostic criterion is significant impairment in functioning or significant clinical distress. In addition to this distress or impairment, a variety of symptoms and comorbid conditions may develop. According to the DSM-IV-TR, these symptoms are divided into three coordinates: re-experiencing the event, avoidance, and hyperarousal. The first coordinate, re-experiencing the traumatic event, includes one or more of the following symptoms: intrusive recollections of the event or events, distressing dreams, experiencing the event in the present, distress at exposure, to triggers and the body reacting to triggers. Flashbacks, nightmares, and night tremors are also common symptoms. Research indicates individuals suffering from PTSD often report intrusive recollections and nightmares. The second coordinate, avoidance, is characterized by three or more of the following symptoms: avoiding thoughts, feelings, or conversations related to the traumatic event; lack of memory about the event; decreased interest or avoidance of activities; detachment from others; limited expression of emotions; and lack of future orientation. Avoidance may occur in the form of dissociation. Feelings of isolation and alienation are common among traumatized individuals further impairing their social functioning. The third coordinate, hyperarousal, comprises two or more of the following symptoms: sleep disturbance, lack of concentration, irritability, outbursts of anger, hypervigilance, and increased startle response (American Psychiatric Association, 2000).

Individuals with PTSD may appear to be constantly on the lookout, yet at times seem unaware of their surroundings. The vacillation between re-experiencing traumatizing events and avoidance of reminders of the trauma are the defining characteristics of PTSD. In addition to common reactions for hyperarousal, such as anger, irritability, and peer and marital discord, the sometimes-extreme anger hampers one's ability to recover.

Studies indicate that trauma survivors usually develop symptoms that may lead to PTSD within hours or days of the trauma. Those experiencing delayed symptoms have postponed receiving help. Symptoms are often intensified by exposure to additional trauma. The time between the trauma and the intervention, and the severity of the symptoms are two factors that greatly impact recovery rates (Kessler, Sonnega, Bromet, & Nelson, 1995). Acute stress disorder can be diagnosed when symptoms last less than one month. Symptoms occurring immediately after the stressor and lasting less than one month may be transient and self-limited. Severe symptoms during this time increase the risk of developing PTSD (American Psychiatric Association, 2000). Active treatment for symptoms lasting one to three months may help reduce the otherwise high risk of chronic PTSD.

Anger and Hostility

A meta-analysis conducted by Orth and Wieland (2006) demonstrated a strong correlation among traumatized individuals between PTSD and anger as well as between PTSD and hostility. While anger is a diagnostic criterion for PTSD, the consistent correlation between anger and PTSD is not an artifact of measurement overlap and may play a role in the formation and maintenance of PTSD because anger functions to facilitate emotional disengagement (Foa, Riggs, Massie, & Yarczower, 1995). The research findings of a study of more than 1,000 World Trade Center rescue and recovery workers suggests that disaster workers with high levels of anger may benefit from early intervention to prevent chronic PTSD (Jayasinghe, Giosan, Evans, Spielman, & Difede, 2008). When compared over a one-year period, the participants with low levels of anger experienced fewer PTSD symptoms than those with higher levels of anger. Moreover, the individuals with higher levels of anger also had more severe symptoms of depression as well as other comorbid conditions.

Neurophysiological Correlates of PTSD

Sometimes, like menacing dark waters rising above one's head, but more often like a thunderbolt, fear arises in the amygdala, an almond-shaped brain structure lodged in a region beneath the cortex, called the *limbic system* (Yaniv, Desmedt, Jaffard, & Richter-Levin, 2004). The limbic system is the repository of our emotions, positive and negative alike, and acts like a bridge linking the mind with the body. Things that are seen, heard, smelled, touched, or tasted, become in the "mind," or cortex, cognitive constructs and representations of reality. Then various, appropriate emotions—joy, pleasure, fear, intense anxiety, hostility, anticipation, nostalgia, and so forth—are attached to that cognitive experience. This process is called *emotional encoding* (Kandel, 2004). We know things not only with our minds but with our feelings as well. Lastly, emotions become physical (body) manifestations, or corollaries of our cognitive and emotional experiences. We laugh, run or fight, freeze, hug, smile, cry, explode or relax, or pull the trigger. It is the amygdala that processes the strange noise, shadowy figure, or the hostile face, and not only triggers palpitations, nausea, involuntary urination, flight or fight, but can also suspend the works of the cortex, especially the prefrontal cortex, know to be responsible for critical thinking and executive functioning (Yaniv et al., 2004).

This process, known to psychiatrists and psychologists as *dissociation*, is largely responsible for what was termed by Veterans Administration doctors *battle mind*. Neurobiologists at the Friedrich Miescher Institute for Biomedical Research (part of the Novartis Research Foundation) in collaboration with California Institute of Technology and, later, the MIND Institute at University of California Davis School of Medicine, have been among the first to identify neural pathways and types of neurons in the amygdala which play a key role in the behavioral expression of fear and the development of subclinical and clinical PTSD (Amaral, Price, Pitkanen, & Carmichael, 1992). The authors of this chapter propose that the sequence of developing PTSD is possibly affected by the body's failure to properly reset homeostasis as a result of severe trauma.

Biological Responses to Fear

Classical conditioning, also known as *Pavlovian conditioning*, is a form of learning in which one stimulus, known as the conditioned stimulus, comes to signal the occurrence of a second stimulus, the unconditioned stimulus. After several repetitions (conditioning), the conditioned stimulus is able to elicit a conditioned response. Through classical conditioning, the traumatic event (unconditional stimulus), when paired with neutral stimuli (both external and internal), may result in the production of triggers (conditioned stimuli) of trauma-related distress (conditioned response). These lead to cognitive distortions, maladaptive beliefs, and avoidant behaviors. Our traumatic reactions and symptoms are grounded in physiological and anatomical changes in the brain. A sagital section of the brain can identify the three key components of the neuronetwork of fear (Kalat, 2012):

1. The prefrontal cortex, the place of higher cognitive functioning and for integrating our perception of reality

2. The sensory thalamus, switchboard of all incoming sensory information for a first analysis and then further processing

3. The amygdala, the ancient, reptilian part of our brain whose main function is a superfast danger appraisal and command for defensive behaviors.

In the processing of a possibly dangerous stimulus, the brain possesses a "high," cortical road, leading from the sensory thalamus up into the cortex, where the sensory stimulus we are evaluating can be thoroughly analyzed (Kalat, 2012). This pathway is slow: It can take a few seconds to analyze a new sensory stimulus. Another, alternative "low" road is a pathway that leads from the sensory thalamus directly to the amygdala. This pathway does not analyze the stimulus, but it is very fast. Within milliseconds, it fires off neurons in the amygdala, which, in turn, trigger our body's emergency response systems. In the case of a potential danger, say a hiker hearing the rattling sound of a rattlesnake while hiking in the Sierra Nevada Mountains, the cortex of the hiker confirms that the stimulus is indeed a threat. It sends signals to the amygdala that amplify the alert and triggers a fight-or-flight response. After freezing for a moment, a person will either run for his life or remain to fight. Whenever appropriate, there is an activation of both pathways in which the thalamo-amygdalic-hypothalamic tract, the "low road," will act first and get a belated validation from its slower twin, the "high road." Only three to six months later, a sagital look at this hiker's brain shows some substantial changes. The neural network that recognized the snake stimuli has been imprinted into the sensory thalamus and amygdala by the experience.

As a result, only weak signals are now sent to the cortex, while powerful signals are sent to amygdala. In fact, the cortex is now bypassed, and every time this hiker sees a vine, a coiled garden hose, or anything resembling a snake, his amygdala is triggered immediately into action so he experiences a full-fledged fight-or-flight response.

If we were to translate this into the world of a 9/11 victim, like NYPD officer Louis Hernandez, we will see that prior to 9/11, a Middle Eastern looking man was only an ordinary, neutral stimulus that would not trigger a fear response. That is because the nontraumatized brain would process the stimulus almost exclusively through a thoughtful, discriminating cortex (i.e., the high road).

After 9/11, however, an ordinary Middle Eastern face stimulus is now recognized by the brain as a fear stimulus because of Mohamed Atta, the Egyptian hijacker and one of the ringleaders of the September 11 attacks who served as the hijacker-pilot of American Airlines Flight 11, crashing the plane into the North Tower of the World Trade Center as part of the coordinated attacks. A Middle Eastern face is now no longer a neutral stimulus, but a fear stimulus due to a bypassing of the cortex. The reaction may be strictly amygdalic using the thalamo-amygdalic-hypothalamic tract (the low road). Additionally, the cortex may amplify the fear stimulus by erroneously agreeing with the amygdalic misinterpretation of an innocuous situation as a threat (Kalat, 2012). This is how Hernandez's brain operated in 2003 when he brutalized a Lebanese New Yorker after pulling him over for speeding.

Hernandez's several months of work with the NYPD Emergency Unit has created a permanent network in the amygdala, increasing its size, a finding that can be evident on an MRI. This network is hypersensitive to any incoming stimuli that resemble the stimuli that were present during this period. When any similar stimuli are perceived, it reacts with hyperspeed, immediately triggering a fight-or-flight response.

The PFC of the mind is now bypassed; the victim reacts only in a visceral, amygdalic way to any perceived threat without any inhibiting action from the anterior cingulate cortex (Amaral et al., 1992). What is worse, virtually everything is misperceived as a threat. This brain change is also responsible for the so-called *battle mind* described in traumatized soldiers and police officers.

In addition to the physical and psychological symptoms associated with PTSD, the incidence of psychiatric disorders increases with chronic PTSD (American Psychiatric Association, 2000). There is a high rate of comorbidity with PTSD. It is important to assess the onset of symptoms as they relate to traumatic experiences. This can help the clinician differentiate between PTSD and other conditions. Some conditions often confused with PTSD include traumatic head injury, concussion, delirium, and seizure disorders. Alcohol and substance abuse, along with acute intoxication or withdrawal, must also be considered in assessment. In addition, other disorders, such as factitious disorders, personality disorders, and malingering, need to be ruled out before a person is diagnosed with PTSD. In some cases, psychiatric consultation may be required because of the blurred distinction between comorbid psychiatric conditions. Comorbid disorders associated with PTSD include substance abuse or dependence, major depressive disorder, panic disorder or agoraphobia, generalized anxiety disorder, obsessive-compulsive disorder, social phobia, and bipolar disorder. Numerous studies show that PTSD consistently co-occurs with other disorders. The National Comorbidity Survey (Kessler et al., 1995) indicates approximately 84% of people with PTSD have an additional diagnosis.

Subclinical PTSD

Subclinical, or subthreshold, PTSD describes a condition in which a traumatized patient has some PTSD symptoms, but they are not severe enough to meet the DSM-IV criteria for a full PTSD diagnosis. The distress and the impairment are consistent with what is seen among individuals with a PTSD diagnosis but does not have the required number of re-experiencing, avoidance, and hyperarousal symptoms. Several studies on the psychological problems associated with active military duties have attempted to identify and measure factors that have an adverse impact on the mental health of veterans and the long-term consequences on military health care delivery systems (Asmundson, Wright, McCreary, & Pedlar, 2003; Martinez, Huffman, Castro, & Adler, 2002). Such work has assisted military planners and health care providers in mapping the thresholds of traumatic experiences from deployment to postdeployment. The problem when it comes to law enforcement is the paucity of empirical research looking at the taxonomic challenges of subclinical PTSD. When professionals rely strictly on a categorical model of psychiatric disorders, then very little attention is given to disability and impairment in individuals with insufficient PTSD symptom presentations. Subclinical PTSD may result from partial recovery from the full syndrome or from the onset of symptoms after a traumatic experience. Clinical trials and epidemiological studies rarely examine subclinical PTSD, and data is often abandoned when it fails to meet diagnostic thresholds (Pincus, Davis, & McQueen, 1999).

Research is needed to determine whether these traumatic reactions and subclinical PTSD are true precursors to the full symptomatic levels required to make a positive diagnosis of PTSD. Several studies suggest that subclinical populations warrant closer examination given the multiple stressors and potentially threatening situations to which deployed military personnel or law enforcement officers are exposed (Asmundson et al., 2003). A report by the Department of Psychiatry and Human Behavior, Rhode Island Hospital, Brown University, examined the extent to which subclinical PTSD and full PTSD are associated with impairment or distress (Zlotnick, Franklin, & Zimmerman, 2002). The findings suggest that subclinical PTSD is associated with levels of social and work impairment comparable to full PTSD. A 2010 study at Weill Cornell Medical College, Department of Psychiatry, investigated rates of subclinical PTSD and associated impairment in comparison to no PTSD and full PTSD, and prospectively followed the course of subclinical symptoms over three years. Three-thousand three-hundred and sixty workers dispatched to the World Trade Center site following 9/11 completed clinician interviews and self-report measures at three points, each one year apart. At Time 1, 9.7% of individuals met criteria for subclinical PTSD. The no PTSD, subclinical PTSD, and full PTSD groups exhibited significantly different levels of impairment, rates of current Major Depressive Disorder diagnosis, and self-reported symptoms of depression. At Time 2, 29% of the initial sample with subclinical PTSD continued to meet criteria for subclinical or full PTSD; at Time 3, this was true for 24.5% of the initial sample. The study lends credence to the clinical significance of subclinical PTSD and emphasizes that associated impairment may be significant and longstanding. It also confirms clinical differences between subclinical and full PTSD (Cukor, Wyka, Jayasinghe, & Difede, 2010).

Another recent World Trade Center (WTC) study (Pietrzak et al., 2012) examined the prevalence, correlates, and perceived mental healthcare needs associated with subclinical PTSD in police officers who participated in the rescue and recovery operation. The study, carried out by researchers at the New York/New Jersey WTC Clinical Consortium, assessed nearly 8,466 police responders who sought services from 2002 through 2008 and who completed an interview/survey as part of the WTC Medical Monitoring and Treatment Program. The findings show that past month prevalence of full and subclinical WTC-related PTSD was 5.4% and 15.4%, respectively—results comparable to those found in other studies of police responders. They also found a much higher rate of subclinical PTSD—not enough symptoms to meet the criteria for full PTSD, but that nevertheless was associated with a five times greater expressed need for mental health services, including individual counseling, stress management, or psychotropic medication, compared to those who did not meet the criteria for full or subclinical PTSD.

Police with full and subclinical PTSD were significantly more likely than controls to report needing mental healthcare (41.1% and 19.8%, respectively, versus 6.8% in trauma controls). These results underscore the importance of a more inclusive and dimensional conceptualization of PTSD, particularly in professions such as law enforcement, as operational definitions and conventional screening cut-points may underestimate the psychological burden for this population. Accordingly, psychiatric clinicians should assess for disaster-related subclinical PTSD symptoms in disaster response personnel.

More worrisome is the fact that the higher the numbers of subclinical PTSD symptoms, the greater the impairment, comorbidity, and suicidal ideation. In several research studies, the presence of subclinical PTSD symptoms increased substantially the risk for suicidal ideation even after the investigators controlled for major depressive disorder (Pietrzak et al., 2012). Given the public health implications of these findings for law enforcement officers, more efforts are needed for a timely identification of symptoms of subclinical PTSD in police officers to allow for proper early preventions and interventions.

Racial, Ethnic, Cultural, and Gender Determinants of PTSD

Bound by a number of characteristics—such as resilience, religious orientation, reliance on extended family networks, and maintenance of tight kinship bonds, and the experience of discrimination—African Americans are very sensitive to traumatic events affecting African American communities (e.g., Rodney King beating or Hurricane Katrina). African Americans compose 13.1% of the U.S. population, making them America's second largest ethnoracial minority group after Hispanics, who make up 16.7% (U.S. Census Bureau, 2011).

Most epidemiological studies have found that African Americans have lower rates of mood and substance use disorders than Caucasians (Kessler et al., 2005), but some have reported higher rates of a few anxiety disorders (e.g., simple phobia and agoraphobia) among African Americans (Zhang & Snowden, 1999). With regard to PTSD, which is also classified as an anxiety disorder, both clinical studies and epidemiological studies have reported that African Americans and Caucasians have similar rates of PTSD (Adams & Boscarino, 2005). However, a few studies have found higher rates of PTSD or PTSD symptoms among African Americans than their Caucasian counterparts.

Most prominently, the National Vietnam Veterans Readjustment Study, a nationally representative study of 1,173 Vietnam combat veterans, found that 20.6% of African American combat veterans had current PTSD as compared to 13.7% of Caucasian combat veterans (Kulka et al., 1990). Green, Grace, Lindy, and Leonard (1990) compared 145 Caucasians and 36 African American male Vietnam veterans and found higher rates of lifetime (72% versus 42%) and current PTSD (47% versus 30%) in the African American group. African Americans may differ from others in their style of coping with trauma. For example, spirituality and social support offered by churches appear to be the preferred coping strategies in some African American groups (Taylor & Chatters, 1991).

Following the September 11 attacks on the United States, a nationally representative sample of African Americans were found to be more likely than Caucasians to cope with prayer, religion, or spirituality (Torabi & Seo, 2004). However, this coping style is not necessarily protective when it comes to PTSD. For example, in one study, spirituality did not moderate the effect of exposure on PTSD symptoms in African American women who had been victims of domestic abuse (Fowler & Hill, 2004). Under some circumstances, religion and spirituality may lead people to stay in dangerous situations longer than they might otherwise (e.g., maladaptive forgiveness of perpetrators) or to avoid directly confronting the problem (e.g., waiting for God to intervene). Yet, other evidence shows that African Americans favor directly confronting problems (Broman, 1996). Thus, it would be particularly interesting to clarify the roles of spirituality, social support, and coping style in future studies of African Americans with PTSD.

Are Hispanic officers who have grown up in tough neighborhoods more resilient than their sometimes more privileged Caucasian counterparts? A study of 655 urban police officers (21% female, 48% Caucasian, 24% African-American, and 28% Hispanic) looked at ethnic and gender differences in duty-related symptoms of PTSD. The investigators used self-report measures of PTSD symptoms, peritraumatic dissociation, exposure to duty-related critical incidents, general psychiatric symptoms, response bias due to social desirability, and demographic variables, such as education, total household income, marital status, age, and years of police service. The investigators found that self-identified Hispanic officers demonstrated more PTSD symptoms than both the self-identified Caucasian and African American officers. Some of the putative factors were greater peritraumatic dissociation, lower social support, greater perceived racism, and greater wishful thinking and self-blaming, perhaps related to a religion based sense of guilt (Marmar, McCaslin, & Metzler, 2006).

Gender Variables

Contrary to expectation and, in many ways, counterintuitive, researchers found no substantial gender differences in PTSD symptoms. Such findings are of note because they replicated a previous finding of greater PTSD among Hispanic American military personnel and failed to replicate the well-established finding of greater PTSD symptoms among civilian women. Among police responders enrolled in the WTC Health Registry, PTSD was almost twice as prevalent among women as men two to three years after the 9/11 attacks. A longitudinal study of 2,940 police responders enrolled in the WTC Health Registry found that prevalence of probable PTSD doubled from 7.8% in 2003–2004 to 16.5% in 2006–2007. Female police officers were significantly more likely than male police officers to report PTSD symptoms in the first survey, but this gender difference was no longer significant in the second survey, two years later; prevalence of PTSD symptoms increased, and there was a substantial amount of co-morbidity with other mental health problems (Bowler et al., 2012). The failure to find gender differences in PTSD symptoms was consistent with similar findings in military samples (Sutker, Davis, Uddo, & Ditta, 1995). The reason may reside in the selection bias and the training common to both military and police work, which may have protected these women against the greater vulnerability to trauma found in civilian females.

Organizational Stress and Police Culture

Several studies examining the impact of organizational stressors on police performance suggest that such factors may be a great source of stress due to various structural arrangements, policies, and practices. Data analysis from a survey of 461 police officers from two large urban police agencies working patrol operations in two large urban departments in Michigan and New Jersey shows that as perceived stressors increase, work performance decreases—and that organizational stressors are significantly different from operational stressors (Shane, 2010). The findings imply the need for structural changes in police organizations. The study used the Police Stress Questionnaire (McCreary & Thompson, 2006), a 40-item questionnaire consisting of two subscales measuring operational stressors (20 job content questions) and organizational stressors (20 job context questions) on a seven-point Likert-type scale, ranging from "no stress at all" (1) to "moderate stress" (4) to "a lot of stress" (7).

Leadership and supervision showed a significant relationship with job stress and performance. Many officers have a hard time working with supervisors and managers who display inconsistent or autocratic styles, or working for supervisors who overemphasize the negative and play favorites (Robinson et al., 1997). This appears to be the most important predictor of performance and may reflect the competing differences between line officers and supervisory or management staff. Management also includes the members of internal affairs. The police subculture also feels pressured and not valued by internal affairs investigators because, as representatives of management, they must breech the solidarity and sometimes the code of silence that binds officers. When officers are confronted with an internal investigation, they receive neither guidance nor emotional or moral support from their superior officers, and sometimes experience a sense of betrayal, which may widen the gap between line officers and management (Reuss-Ianni, 1984). If organizational stress continues to be a greater source of grief for officers than police operations, the usual stress reduction and employee assistance programs may actually miss the mark. With a focus placed mostly on police operations, they may not offer helpful suggestions about how to cope with the relentless pressure generated by the organization (Chapin, Brannen, Singer, & Walker, 2008).

One source of organizational challenge for an officer is leadership and supervision. Subjective as it may be, the positive or negative impressions of supervisors regarding their subordinates reflect the organization's level of support. Rather than being treated as valuable and productive members of a supportive organization, officers may perceive a lack of leadership and supervisory support, particularly when the agency's management philosophy is autocratic and negative, increasing feelings of suspicion toward supervisors and administrators (Talarico & Swanson, 1983). Urban and larger police departments may be more likely to create impersonal environments that rely on negative discipline to elicit conformity and maximum efficiency and productivity than their smaller counterparts. When compared with the more democratic or participative management styles of smaller agencies, such bureaucracies may place a greater social distance between ranking officers and first-line officers. This may include autocratic management styles that are stressful in day-to-day operations, let alone when dealing with critical or traumatic incidents. When the organizational stress increases dramatically, the vulnerability of police officers to critical incidents increases as well (Leino, Selin, Summala, & Virtanen, 2011).

PTSD as a Cognitive Failure and Cognitive Processing Therapy (CPT)

As previously discussed, changes in the brain may cause trauma survivors to experience a combination of dissociation, hyperarousal, and re-experiencing, often resulting in a diagnosis of battle mind. The result is "psychological failure" with affective dysregulation (Kalat, 2012), a persistent emotional-cognitive incongruence, which produces cognitive distortions leading to a warped perception of reality, filled with hostility and hopelessness. Aside from psychotropic medications, such as anxiolytics, antidepressants, and antipsychotics, veterans and police officers could benefit from cognitive processing therapy (CPT), especially if preceded by training in mindfulness-based stress reduction. Whether due to dissociation, hyperarousal, or re-experiencing, the patient clearly has severe gaps between his thoughts and emotions. Based on social learning theory (Bandura, 1976), CPT was developed to help trauma survivors understand how thoughts and emotions are interconnected, as well as how their mistranslation can result in "stuck points" and subsequent PTSD. During CPT sessions, trauma survivors are guided to accept and integrate the trauma as an event that actually occurred and cannot be ignored (Kalat, 2012). While experiencing fully the range of trauma-related emotions (no dissociation), patients are taught to analyze and confront maladaptive beliefs ("stuck points") and to explore how prior experiences and beliefs affected reactions and were affected by trauma.

Trauma survivors try to make sense of and cope with trauma in three ways (Greenberg, 1995):

1. Assimilation: changing memory or interpretation of an event to fit existing beliefs
   - "I should have prevented it"
   - "It wasn't really a beating"
   - Forgetting it

2. Accommodation: changing beliefs to accept what happened

3. Overaccommodation: changing beliefs too much
   - "No Middle Eastern man can be trusted"
   - "The world is completely dangerous"
   - "Nowhere is safe"

This therapeutic modality is a transformative process administered progressively throughout 12 sessions:

- Session 1: Introduction and Education
- Session 2: Meaning of the Event (grieving can also be added here)
- Session 3: Identification of Thoughts and Feelings
- Session 4: Remembering the Traumatic Event
- Session 5: Second Trauma Account
- Session 6: Challenging Questions
- Session 7: Patterns of Problematic Thinking
- Session 8: Safety Issues
- Session 9: Trust Issues
- Session 10: Power/Control Issues
- Session 11: Esteem Issues
- Session 12: Intimacy Issues and Meaning of the Event

In the first five sessions, the therapist describes the clinical picture of PTSD, its causes, and its mechanism, as well as the three modes of processing traumatic information: assimilation, accommodation, and overaccommodation (Greenberg, 1995). The patient is taught to distinguish between natural and manufactured emotions, such as guilt and shame, and to use challenging questions to work through their "stuck points." The therapist lays out rationale and course of treatment goals: (1) accept reality, (2) change beliefs, and (3) feel emotions. The patient writes repeatedly about the meaning of the event. In Session 6, the patient has his or her "stuck points" reconsidered by using Socratic challenging questions:

- Clarification—"Tell me more" questions: "What do you mean when you say . . . ?"; "What exactly does that mean?"
- Probing assumptions—"Why" or "how" of beliefs: "How did you come to this conclusion?"
- Probing reasons and evidence—"How do you know this?"; "What evidence is there to support what you are saying?"
- Questioning viewpoints and perspectives—"How else might you look at this?"; "What would your friend or loved one say about this?"
- Analyzing implications and consequences—"Then what would happen?"; "What are the consequences of that assumption?"
- Questions about the questions—"What is the point of asking that question?"; "Why do you think you asked that question?"

In Session 7, the therapist also introduces the patterns of problematic thinking. Worksheets are also provided to identify the patient's faulty ways of thinking.

Seven patterns of problematic thinking:

1. Jumping to conclusions when evidence is lacking or even contradictory

2. Exaggerating or minimizing the meaning of an event

3. Disregarding important aspects of a situation

4. Oversimplifying events or beliefs as good/bad or right/wrong

5. Overgeneralizing from a single incident

6. Mind reading

7. Emotional reasoning

In Sessions 8–12, the patient progresses from safety issues to the meaning of the event and arrives, hopefully, at a successful resolution. The cognitive and behavioral reframing and alignment have been completed (Greenberg, 1995). Hopefully, by completing the remaining sessions of CPT, the patient will process successfully the traumatic event and return to a normal functioning.

Unfortunately, there are also some trauma patients who benefit neither from CPT nor from cognitive behavior therapy (CBT) because the cortical bypassing or the magnitude of the trauma exceeds the patient's ability to make sense of the event within an ego-based, personal framework (Molchanova & Koga, 2011). The ability of the patient to understand and cope with trauma collapses, and, in such cases, a transpersonal framework is necessary for successful processing and resolution. CBT and CPT are built on a framework of personal identity, as well as on the assumption of an egoistic structure in need of repair. Transpersonal psychotherapies extend the work beyond the ego boundaries. The self is defined not only by how it works (a mechanistic, biomedical view) but also by its worldview and belief system. A first step in this direction is to employ mindfulness-based stress reduction and mindfulness training, a method rather widely used by athletes and the military.

Mindfulness-Based Mind Fitness Training (MMFT)

Mindfulness is a mental state of full attention to present-moment experience without undue judgment, effort, or emotional reactivity (Kabat-Zinn, 1990). Mindfulness-based stress reduction (MBSR) programs are offered at medical centers around the United States to patients and community members. Originally developed in the 1980s in Boston by Kabat-Zinn (1990, 2003), MBSR has also been adapted to clinical interventions for a broad range of physical and psychological disorders, and a large body of research now suggests its efficacy in stress reduction (Lush et al., 2009). An off-shoot of MBSR, the mindfulness-based mind fitness training (MMFT, pronounced M-Fit), was created and delivered by a former U.S. Army officer with many years of mindfulness practice and training in MBSR and trauma resilience. The course matches many features of the MBSR protocol developed by Kabat-Zinn (1990).

Similar to MBSR, the course involved 24 hours of class instruction over eight weeks, with weekly two-hour meetings (on average) and a full-day silent retreat. Additionally, this new model teaches the use of mindfulness skills in a group context, integrates practices into the ongoing predeployment training, and applies these skills to counterinsurgency missions. The course builds stress resilience skills drawing on concepts from sensorimotor regulation (Ogden, Minton, & Pain, 2006), Somatic Experiencing (Levine, 1997), and the Trauma Resilience Model (Leitch, Vanslyke, & Allen, 2009), which provides specific guidance for using focused attention to re-regulate physiological and psychological symptoms following an experience of extreme stress. The MMFT, with its blending of mindfulness skills training and concrete applications in managing stress, trauma, and resilience, both in the body and in environment, might be a valuable tool for law enforcement training, not only to prevent personal subclinical PTSD but also, subsequently, for successful riot control, which might otherwise get out of hand with irreparable consequences.

Summary

Although it is impossible to know whether Officer Hernandez's tragedy could have been prevented, this chapter was written in the hope that future policies, which may have saved officer Hernandez's life, and the lives of many other officers, police, FBI, and CIA alike, will actually come to fruition. A large study conducted by the Police College of Finland, of nearly 3,000 officers, using the Police Personnel Barometer (PPB), looked at police-specific stressors to investigate the effects of these factors on police officer burnout. The four key stressors (defective leadership, role conflicts, threat of violence, and time pressure) emphasized by researchers were all statistically significant. The study introduced a new measure of stress, the Bergen Burnout Indicator, to analyze police work. The Bergen Burnout Indicator has effected national policy changes as the police administration tries to reduce the vulnerability of its officers, the incidence of officer misconduct, and subsequently, the cost of medical care and disability.

Perhaps, if similar policies would have been implemented by NYPD post-9/11, Officer Hernandez's life might not have been so tragically lost. Our intuition would need, however, to be tested in a retrospective study of police suicide that would look at the work performance evaluations and medical and mental health records over a period of at least five years preceding the suicide to find the "tipping point" when officers broke down irretrievably. It would have also been helpful for Hernandez to have had a trauma resilience screening and profiling prior to his acceptance in the police force. An Australian study (Burke & Shakespeare-Finch, 2011) on markers of resilience investigated the process of adaptation in 94 newly recruited police officers to examine the impact of a prior traumatic experience on the appraisal of potentially traumatizing incidents experienced later on the job. The researchers have noted that if the officers' personality profiles, as measured by the NEO Five-Factor Inventory, were conducive to healthy coping strategies such as positive reinterpretation of the traumatic incident, acceptance, and planning, they were more likely to cope well with traumatic incidents later, on the job. The findings appear to suggest that the successful resolution of a traumatic event prior to joining the police acts as a sort of stress inoculation, possibly facilitating positive emotional outcomes from exposure to adverse events on the job. In lay terms, the priming effect of trauma prior to joining the police force acted as a protective cushion reducing the impact of the subsequent on-duty critical stress incidents.

Such eye-opening and compelling research findings would need to translate into policy changes. No recovery from a severe burnout can take place without effecting first changes in working conditions and in police administrators' attitudes and strategies. The required actions depend on the severity of burnout. Police occupational health professionals can monitor burnout using either a Maslach Burnout Inventory-General Survey (MBI-GS) or the Bergen Burnout Indicator 15 (BBI-15). Additionally, an interview would evaluate the present situation and recent changes in work and private life, demands and resources, plus a health status examination—exclusion of physical illnesses and mental disorders, and problems in private life (Leino et al., 2011). A conference between the employee, supervisor, and occupational health service representative would help to promote concrete changes, such as admitting the problem and the need for change; strengthening resilience; letting go of impossible goals and, if necessary, temporarily letting go of work; critically evaluating individual health promoting attitudes and strategies; and planning changes to the work situation and implementing them. When the weight of an undetected subclinical PTSD lands on the fault lines of an existing severe burnout, or vice versa, the result is a disturbing synergy leading potentially to severe mental disorders, psychotic depression, pervasive hostility, explosive anger with misconduct, and, in extremis, suicide or homicide.

The lofty tenets of professional ethics do not happen in vitro or in vacuum. The answer to what happened to Officer Hernandez lies in the complex nexus of powerful determinants, such as a successful trauma inoculation or a crippling exposure; organizational stress; police culture; social stigma; cultural, religious, and spiritual beliefs; policies or lack of policies for early prevention; detection and intervention; political winds and the vagaries of resources; and, even deeper, in the synaptic recesses of our brain's hard-wired neuronetwork of fear and survival.

Discussion Questions

1. Describe the correlations between PTSD and law enforcement.

2. What types of daily hazards make police officers susceptible to PTSD?

3. Explain the differences between clinical and subclinical PTSD.

4. What causes PTSD?

5. List five symptoms of PTSD.

6. Describe common treatments for PTSD. How does each treatment method work? Which method do you believe is most effective?

References

Adams, R. E., & Boscarino, J. A. (2005). Differences in mental health outcomes among Whites, African Americans, and Hispanics following a community disaster. *Psychiatry, 68,* 250–265.

Amaral, D. G., Price, J. L., Pitkanen, A., & Carmichael, T. S. (1992). *Anatomical organization of the primate amygdaloid complex*. In J. P. Aggleton (Ed.), *The amygdala* (pp. 1–66). New York: Wiley-Liss.

American Psychiatric Association. (2000). *Diagnostic and statistical manual of mental disorders* (4th ed., text revision). Washington, DC: Author.

Asmundson, G. J. G., Wright, K., McCreary, D., & Pedlar, D. (2003). Posttraumatic stress disorder symptoms in United Nations peacekeepers: An examination of factor structure and the influence of chronic pain. *Cognitive Behaviour Therapy, 32*(1), 26–37.

Bandura, A. (1976). *Social learning theory*. Englewood Cliffs, NJ: Prentice Hall.

Biggam, F. H., Power, K. G., & Macdonald, R. R. (1997). Coping with occupational stressors of police work: A study of Scottish Officers. *Stress Medicine, 12*(2), 109–115.

Bowler, R. M., Harris, M., Li, J., Gocheva, V., Stellman, S. D., Wilson, K., et al. (2012). Longitudinal mental health impact among police responders to the 9/11 terrorist attack. *American Journal of Industrial Medicine, 55*(4). 297–312.

Broman, C. L. (1996). Coping with personal problems. In H. W. Neighbors & J. S. Jackson (Eds.), *Mental health in black America* (pp. 117–129). Thousand Oaks, CA: Sage.

Brown, J. A., & Campbell, E. A. (1990). Sources of occupational stress in the police. *Work and Stress, 4*, 305–318.

Bureau of Justice Statistics. (2002). *Census of state and local law enforcement agencies, 2000*. Washington, DC: Department of Justice. Retrieved from http://bjs.ojp.usdoj.gov/content/pub/pdf/csllea00.pdf

Burke, K., & Shakespeare-Finch, J. (2011). Markers of resilience in new police officers: Appraisal of potentially traumatizing events. *Traumatology, 17*(4), 52–60.

Chapin, M., Brannen, S. J., Singer, M., & Walker, M. (2008). Training police leadership to recognize and address operational stress. *Police Quarterly, 11*(3), 338–352.

Cukor, J., Wyka, K., Jayasinghe, N., & Difede, J. (2010). The nature and course of subthreshold PTSD. *Journal of Anxiety Disorders, 24*(8), 918–923.

Davis, N. (2011). *Law enforcement and risk for developing PTSD*. Retrieved from http://drnancydavis.com/mtp/understanding-treating-ptsd-job-related-trauma

Federal Bureau of Investigation. (2010). *Law enforcement officers killed and assaulted* (Uniform Crime Report). Washington, DC: Author. Retrieved from http://www.fbi.gov/about-us/cjis/ucr/leoka/leoka-2010/aboutleoka-2010.pdf

Foa, E. B., Riggs, D. S., Massie, E. D., & Yarczower, M. (1995). The impact of fear activation and anger on the efficacy of exposure treatment for posttraumatic stress disorder. *Behavior Therapy, 26*, 487–499.

Fowler, D. N., & Hill, H. M. (2004). Social support and spirituality as culturally relevant factors in coping among African American women survivors of partner abuse. *Violence Against Women, 10*, 1267–1282.

Green, B. L., Grace, M. C., Lindy, J. D., & Leonard, A. C. (1990). Race differences in response to combat stress. *Journal of Traumatic Stress, 3*, 379–393.

Greenberg, M. A. (1995). Cognitive processing of traumas: The role of intrusive thoughts and reappraisals. *Journal of Applied Social Psychology, 25*(14), 1262–1296.

Jayasinghe, N., Giosan, C., Evans, S., Spielman, L., & Difede, J. (2008). Anger and posttraumatic stress disorder in disaster relief workers exposed to the September 11, 2001 World Trade Center Disaster: One-year follow-up study. *Journal of Nervous and Mental Disease, 196*(11), 844–846.

Kabat-Zinn, J. (1990). *Full catastrophe living*. New York: Delta Books.

Kabat-Zinn, J. (2003). Mindfulness-based interventions in context: Past, present, and future. *Clinical Psychology: Science and Practice, 10*, 144–156.

Kalat, J. W. (2012). *Biological psychology* (11th ed.). Independence, KY: Wadsworth.

Kandel, E. (2004). The molecular biology of memory storage: A dialog between genes and synapses. *Bioscience Reports, 24*, 4–5.

Kessler, R. C., Berglund, P., Demler, O., Jin, R., Merikangas, K. R., & Walters, E. E. (2005). Lifetime prevalence and age-of-onset distributions of DSM-IV disorders in the National Comorbidity Survey Replication. *Archives of General Psychiatry, 62, 593–602.*

Kessler, R. C., Sonnega, A., Bromet, E., & Nelson, C. B. (1995). Posttraumatic stress disorder in the National Comorbidity Study. *Archives in General Psychiatry, 52,* 1048–1060.

Kop, N., & Euwema, M.C. (2001). Occupational stress and the use of force by Dutch police officers. *Criminal Justice and Behavior, 28*(5), 631–652.

Kroes, W. H., Margotis, B., & Hurrell, J., Jr. (1974). Job Stress in Policemen. *Journal of Police Science and Administration, 2*(2), 145–155.

Kulka, R. A., Schlesenger, W. E., Fairbank, J. A., Hough, R. L., Jordan, B. K., Marmar, C. R., et al. (1990). *Trauma and the Vietnam War generation: Report of findings from the National Vietnam Veterans Readjustment Study.* New York: Brunner/ Mazel.

Leino, T. M., Selin, R., Summala, H., & Virtanen, M. (2011). Violence and psychological distress among police officers and security guards. *Occupational Medicine, 61*(6), 400–406.

Leitch, M. L., Vanslyke, J., & Allen, M. (2009). Somatic experiencing treatment with social service workers following Hurricanes Katrina and Rita. *Social Work, 54,* 9–18.

Levine, P. (1997). *Waking the tiger: Healing trauma.* Berkeley, CA: North Atlantic Books.

Lush, E., Salmon, P., Floyd, A., Studts, J. L., Weissbecker, I., & Sephton, S. E. (2009). Mindfulness meditation for symptom reduction in fibromyalgia: Psychophysiological correlates. *Journal of Clinical Psychology in Medical Settings, 16,* 200–207.

Marmar, C. R., McCaslin, S. E., & Metzler, T. J. (2006). Predictors of posttraumatic stress in police and other first responders. In R. Yehuda (Ed), *Psychobiology of posttraumatic stress disorders: A decade of progress* (Vol. 1071, pp. 1–18). Malden, MA: Blackwell.

Martinez, J. A., Huffman, A. H., Castro, C. A., & Adler, A. B. (2002). Assessing psychological readiness in U.S. soldiers following NATO operations. *International Review of the Armed Forces Medical Services, 73,* 139–142.

McCleanghan, M. (2012, July 25). Violent veterans: Bringing the fight home. *The Bureau of Investigative Journalism.* Retrieved from http://www.thebureau investigates.com/2012/07/25/violent-veterans-bringing-the-fight-home/

McCreary, D. R., & Thompson, M. M. (2006). Development of two reliable and valid measures of stressors in policing: The operational and organizational police stress questionnaires. *International Journal of Stress Management, 13,* 494–518.

Molchanova, S. E., & Koga, P. M. (2011). The Civilian Mississippi PTSD Scale: A cross-cultural psychometric evaluation during the 2010 Complex Emergency in Kyrgyzstan. *Slavic University Journal, 2,* 83–91.

Oehme, K., Donnelly, E., & Martin, A. (2012). Alcohol abuse, PTSD, and officer-committed domestic violence. *Policing.* doi:10.1093/police/pas023

Ogden, P., Minton, K., & Pain, C. (2006). *Trauma and the body: A sensorimotor approach to psychotherapy.* New York: Norton.

Orth, U., & Wieland, E. (2006). Anger, hostility, and posttraumatic stress disorder in trauma-exposed adults: A meta-analysis. *Journal of Consulting and Clinical Psychology, 74*(4), 698–706.

Pietrzak, R. H., Schechter, C. B., Bromet, E. J., Katz, C. L., Reissman, D. B., Ozbay F., et al. (2012). The burden of full and subsyndromal posttraumatic stress disorder among police involved in the World Trade Center rescue and recovery effort. *Journal of Psychiatric Research, 46*(7), 835–842.

Pincus, H. A., Davis, W. W., & McQueen, L. E. (1999). Subthreshold mental disorders. *British Journal of Psychiatry, 174,* 288–296.

Reuss-Ianni, E. (1984). Two cultures of policing: Street cops and management cops. *Contemporary Sociology, 13*(4), 448–449.

Robinson, H. M., Sigman, M. R., & Wilson, J. P. (1997). Duty-related stressors and PTSD symptoms in suburban police officers. *Psychological Reports, 81*(3), 835–845.

Shane, J. M. (2010). Organizational stressors and police performance. *Journal of Criminal Justice, 38*(4), 807–818.

Sutker, P. B., Davis, J. M., Uddo, M., & Ditta, S. R. (1995). Assessment of psychological distress in Persian Gulf troops: Ethnicity and gender comparisons. *Journal of Personality Assessment, 64,* 415–427.

Talarico, S. M., & Swanson, C. R. (1983). An analysis of police perceptions of supervisory and administrative support. *Police Studies: An International Review of Police Development, 5,* 47–54.

Tanielian, T., & Jaycox, L. (Eds.). (2008). *Invisible wounds of war: Psychological and cognitive injuries, their consequences, and services to assist recovery.* Santa Monica, CA: RAND Corporation.

Taylor, R. J., & Chatters, L. M. (1991). Religious life. In J. S. Jackson (Ed.), *Life in black America* (pp. 105–123). Newbury Park, CA: Sage.

Torabi, M. R., & Seo, D. (2004). National study of behavioral and life changes since September 11. *Health Education & Behavior, 31,* 179–192.

U.S. Census Bureau. (2011). *U.S. Census 2011.* Washington, DC: Authors. Retrieved from http://quickfacts.census.gov/qfd/states/00000.html

U.S. Department of Justice (2007). *Law officers killed and assaulted, 2006.* Washington, DC: Authors. Retrieved from http://www2.fbi.gov/ucr/killed/2006/index.html

Violanti, J. M., & Aron, F. (1995). Police stressors: Variations in perception among police personnel. *Journal of Criminal Justice, 23*(3), 287–294.

Violanti, J. M., & Aron, F. (1996). Police suicide: An overview. *Police Studies, 19*(2), 77–89.

Yaniv, D., Desmedt, A., Jaffard, R., & Richter-Levin, G. (2004) The amygdala and appraisal processes: Stimulus and response complexity as an organizing factor. *Brain Research Review, 44*(2–3), 179–186.

Zhang, A. Y., & Snowden, L. R. (1999). Ethnic characteristics of mental disorders in five U.S. communities. *Cultural Diversity and Ethnic Minority Psychology, 5,* 134–146.

Zlotnick, C., Franklin, C. L., & Zimmerman, M. (2002). Does subthreshold posttraumatic stress disorder have any clinical relevance? *Comprehensive Psychiatry, 43*(6), 413–419.

PART THREE

Ethical Professionalism

11

The Ethics of Force

Duty, Principle, and Morality

Kevin A. Elliott and Joycelyn M. Pollock

"He who fights with monsters should be careful lest he thereby become a monster."

Friedrich Nietzsche, *Beyond Good and Evil*, 1886

On the evening of July 5, 2011, police officers Manuel Ramos and Joseph Wolfe responded to the Fullerton bus depot regarding a man pulling on the door handles of parked cars. According to accounts published in the *Los Angeles Times* (Winton, 2012b), the officers encountered 37-year-old Kelly Thomas. He was shirtless and, from the look of his disheveled appearance, homeless. They would later learn that Thomas had been diagnosed as schizophrenic when he was 16 years old. The officers did not pat Thomas down, but removed a backpack he was wearing and told him to sit on the curb. Officer Wolfe searched the backpack at the trunk of his patrol vehicle while Ramos stood guard over Thomas. Ramos instructed Thomas to put his legs out in front of him with his hands on his knees. Thomas appeared confused and had difficulty understanding or complying with Ramos' order as the two exchanged words.

Ramos appeared to become increasingly irritated with Thomas' failure to follow directions. Ramos eventually donned a pair of latex gloves. "Now see my fists?" he asked. "They're getting ready to fuck you up." Ramos grabbed Thomas, who was still seated, by the back of the arm. Thomas protested, pulled away, and stood up. Officer Wolfe came out from behind his vehicle to assist as Ramos drew his baton. Wolfe drew his baton as well, as Thomas moved away from the approaching officers with hands held open in a defensive position. Wolfe then swung his baton at the retreating man's legs, followed closely by a baton swing from Ramos.

231

Thomas attempted to run, but was tackled several feet away. Both officers punched Thomas numerous times, while Ramos pinned Thomas down with his body weight. Still struggling, Thomas was heard repeatedly saying that he was sorry and that he couldn't breathe. Corporal Jay Cicinelli, responding to the officers' call for help, arrived on the scene and found the officers still struggling with the pleading Thomas. He kneed Thomas twice in the head, and deployed his Taser four times. Thomas screamed in pain while continuing to yell that he was unable to breathe. At this point, Cicinelli used the butt of his Taser to hit Thomas eight times in the head and face. Thomas responded by calling for his "daddy" to help him. In fact, the last words Thomas spoke before losing consciousness forever were for his father's help.

Kelly Thomas died five days later from facial injuries, blood in his lungs, and mechanical compression of his chest that made it difficult to breathe, depriving his brain of vital oxygen (Winton, 2012a). Most of the incident was captured on video by security cameras and tape recorders carried in the officers' pockets. Ultimately, six officers were involved in the altercation that led to Thomas' death. Officers Ramos and Cicinelli have been fired and are currently awaiting trial on involuntary manslaughter charges. Officer Wolfe was fired but has not been charged with any crime. The remaining three officers have retained their jobs and have not been charged.

The beating and death of Kelly Thomas provides an illustration of the tentative relationship between society and its guardians of law and order. Ordinarily, this is a relationship based on mutual trust and respect, but sometimes that relationship goes awry. This chapter examines the use of force by police, including the roles of police and the authority granted officers in the United States and other democratic societies. The authors explore definitions of force and excessive force, department policies, and the general continuum of force, as well as pertinent case law—including the landmark *Graham v. Connor* (1989) case that set precedent for the elusive "reasonableness" standard. Additionally, the authors investigate situational factors, training, the militarization of policing, police subculture, and officer-based factors, such as the psychological and physiological effects of stress. The chapter concludes with a brief review of the major ethical systems as applied to police and coercive power.

Introduction

Americans are historically sensitive to the coercive power of government and any semblance of totalitarianism. Power and authority are fundamental concepts of political order, and police, as the agents of political power, use force as a means to control behavior detrimental to society (Wolfe, 1969). Although the application of force itself is often considered morally neutral, it can, under certain circumstances, constitute an abuse of power.

Despite the tragic death of Kelly Thomas, as well as other well-known cases of brutality, like that of Rodney King in 1991, the use of force by police officers is rare, and the use of excessive force rarer still (U.S. Department of Justice [USDOJ], 2012). Nonetheless, these cases are often so destructive to the relationship between the police and citizenry that a distorted perception of law enforcement develops, resulting in a loss of trust, costly litigation, and, in extreme cases, violence through rioting. The Los Angeles riots of 1992, also known as the *Rodney King riots*, following the acquittal of four Los Angeles Police officers, resulted in the deaths of 53 people and over $1 billion in property damage ("The L.A. Riots," 2012). The outcry over the police shooting death of Timothy Thomas in Cincinnati, Ohio produced similar results, leading to four days of rioting and to damages totaling more than $8 million. However, repercussions from the verdict did not stop there. Officers held their own form of protest following the trial by continuing to respond to emergency calls for service, but refusing to initiate proactive police work. Moreover, In the three months following the trial, civilian shooting incidents increased sixfold (Bronson, 2006; Horn, 2001). Public outcry and protests also followed the death of Amadou Diallo, who was shot in the doorway of his New York City apartment by officers after reaching for his wallet (apparently to retrieve his identification). Officers, who had mistaken Diallo for a rape suspect, fired 41 shots, hitting him 19 times. Diallo, who was not the suspect, was unarmed (Cooper, 1999). Americans remember cases of police brutality regardless of the frequency. And while many of these cases may be considered anomalies, they have, nevertheless, become part of the American psyche, significantly affecting the ways citizens think about police instances of abuse.

The Bureau of Justice Statistics estimates there are over 40 million police–citizen contacts each year, yet less than half of 1% involve the threat or application of force (USDOJ, 2012). Data published in a study by the International Association of Chiefs of Police (IACP) indicates that force was used 3.61 times for every 10,000 encounters, suggesting that force was not applied in 99.9% of all cases (IACP, 2001). As there is no standard measure for excessive force, statistical data is lacking. Given the low frequency of force, however, it appears safe to suggest that very few officer–citizen contacts result in excessive or unreasonable force. Yet, in the words of former Minneapolis police chief and past president of the Police Executive Research Forum, Robert K. Olsen, "Just one use of force incident can dramatically alter the stability of a police department and its relationship with a community" (USDOJ, 2012, p. 1).

Friedrich (1980) asserts that "police use of force is theoretically important because it involves the execution of perhaps the essential function of the state and practically important because it affects the public's attitudes and behaviors toward police and government more generally" (p. 1). The injudicious use of force by police has led not only to injury and death, but to crippling civil damages, officers convicted and sentenced to jail, and police chiefs and elected officials being removed from office (Fyfe, 1988).

Even when the application of deadly force has been justified, such incidents often polarize communities, leaving those most in need of police services the most suspicious and distrustful.

The Role of Law Enforcement

Balancing the roles of crime fighter and public servant, the men and women of American law enforcement arguably possess more power than any other governmental agent. The sworn peace officer is the only domestic agent of government with the power to take life, based solely on their discretion (Fyfe, 1988). Indeed, Bittner (1970) has argued that police are defined by their capacity to use force. The authority to use spontaneous force on other Americans is what sets them apart from every civilian and any other agent of government, including the military.

Police power is thought to originate in the "social contract," the implicit agreement between a government and its citizens, a concept developed originally by philosophers Thomas Hobbes (1588–1679) and John Locke (1632–1704). According to this model, citizens give up their right to complete freedom in exchange for protection (Cohen & Feldberg, 1991). Police are granted the power to protect with the caveat that those same powers may be used against those granting the power. Pollock (2012) uses Packer's (1968) crime control and due process models of the criminal justice system to illustrate that the police role is more often seen as a crime fighter, where controlling crime is prioritized over other duties, than as a public servant whose primary mission is public service. Despite a lack of empirical data in this area, it appears reasonable to suggest that those who subscribe more strongly to a crime fighter model of law enforcement may be more likely, under certain circumstances, to apply coercive force and, perhaps, in some cases, slide into a pattern of abusive behavior. However, before proceeding any further, it is important to define force, as well as its legal and ethical parameters.

Parameters of Force

Force is defined as the authority to use physical coercion to overcome the will of another (Pollock, 2012). Despite the negative connotations often associated with force, officers are clearly within their right to apply reasonable and necessary force in self-defense, the defense of others, in preventing escape, or in overcoming resistance during the commission of a lawful arrest. Indeed, the U.S. Commission on Civil Rights has held that "in diffusing situations, apprehending alleged criminals, and protecting themselves and others, officers are legally entitled to use appropriate means, including force" (USCCR, 2004, p. 2).

Excessive force, in contrast, is defined as that which is "greater than that required to compel compliance from a willing or unwilling subject" (IACP, 2001, p. 1). Unfortunately, defining excessive force is often much easier than actually identifying and measuring it. For example, a USDOJ research report on police use of force distinguishes between excessive force, excessive use of force, police brutality, illegal force, and force that is improper, abusive, illegitimate, or unnecessary (National Institute of Justice & Bureau of Justice Statistics [NIJ-BJS], 1999). Force labeled *improper, abusive, illegitimate*, or *unnecessary* describes mishandling a situation in opposition to procedure, expectations of the public, ordinary concepts of lawfulness, and the principle of last resort. *Illegal force* expresses force used in violation of law, whereas *brutality* refers to cruel and serious physical or psychological harm to citizens (NIJ-BJS, 1999).

One of the problems with judging the reasonableness or unreasonableness of a particular application of force is the individual judgment involved. The courts apply legal standards; law enforcement agencies apply policies; and the public is prone to emotions, often gleaned from over sensationalized, yet incomplete, media accounts of complex incidents (NIJ-BJS, 1999). Nevertheless, beginning with the landmark *Tennessee v. Garner* (1985) case, the courts have attempted to provide guidance by applying a standard of "objective reasonableness" in determining the lawfulness or unlawfulness of an officer's application of force, including deadly force.

Case Law

In *Tennessee v. Garner* (1985), the U.S. Supreme Court established standards for an officer's application of deadly force. Prior to this ruling, officers were legally justified in shooting a fleeing felon, regardless of any clear or present danger to the officer or other members of society. However, in the *Garner* case, the court ruled that officers must demonstrate probable cause to believe the suspect poses a significant threat of death or serious physical injury to the officer or others before applying deadly force. The courts have further defined an officer's application of force in *Brosseau v. Haugen* (2004) and *Scott v. Harris* (2007), as well as two other noteworthy Supreme Court rulings. In *Monnell v. New York City* (1978) and *City of Canton v. Harris* (1989), municipalities were held liable for failure to properly train officers who violated the constitutional rights of victims. While the courts have since tackled the issues of force, department policies, training, and culpability in alleged violations of constitutional rights in other cases, *Graham v. Connor* (1989) remains the most important decision in recent history.

The case began when Graham entered a convenience store for juice to quell a diabetic episode, but left quickly when he saw the line of people waiting at the checkout. A Charlotte Police Department patrol officer became suspicious on seeing Graham's quick entry and exit and, subsequently, stopped to investigate Graham and another individual as they drove away.

Graham did not resist the officer but acted erratically, running around the car before sitting down and passing out. Officers responding to the backup call handcuffed Graham; however, they ignored his pleas for sugar or to check his wallet for a diabetic card. They put him face down on the hood of the patrol car and then pushed him into the backseat of the patrol car so roughly that Graham broke his foot, as well as sustained other injuries. When the investigating officer determined that no crime had occurred, he drove Graham home and released him. In his petition for relief under the Fourteenth Amendment's due process clause, Graham sought to recover damages for injuries he sustained at the hands of police during the stop. He had sued and lost at the district and circuit court levels before the U.S. Supreme Court accepted his case for review.

Prior to this case, in allegations that an officer's application of force violated constitutional rights, courts had generally followed the "shock the conscience" test. This standard, derived from the case of *Rochin v. California* (1952), held that police are only assumed to violate substantive due process rights when their behavior is so extreme as to shock the conscience of a civilized society. In *Graham*, however, the Supreme Court held that Graham's claims were best analyzed under the Fourth Amendment, noting that arrests, detentions, and other seizures of a free citizen are best judged by relying on criteria of objective reasonableness. The court had long recognized that the right to detain and make arrests necessarily carried with it the right to threaten or use force, and that whether or not the force used was constitutional was dependent on the particular circumstances of the incident.

The Supreme Court held that the reasonableness of a police application of force "must be judged from the perspective of a reasonable officer on the scene, rather than with 20-20 hindsight" (*Graham v. Connor*, 1989, p. 490). Further, the court noted that officers are required to make quick decisions in stressful and rapidly evolving situations; therefore, the reasonableness of an officer's actions must be judged in light of the given circumstances without regard to underlying intent or motive. The court declined, however, to decide the reasonableness of the force used on Graham, remanding the case back to the lower court for a determination.

Though the Supreme Court in *Graham* ruled that reasonableness "must be judged from the perspective of the reasonable officer on the scene," it is often left to others to decide whether the officers' actions were reasonable. Thus, supervising officers, disciplinary review boards, prosecutors, grand jury members, and, in some cases, civilian juries are all left to decide reasonableness—often relying on different standards. Law enforcement agencies across the board have cited reasonableness in their force policies, yet there is still confusion over what exactly that means. Blair et al. (2011) describe the reasonable officer as "somewhat of a chimera, with no one quite able to definitively describe such an officer" (p. 327). In other words, the legal term implies definitiveness in distinguishing reasonable from unreasonable actions, a distinction that is conspicuously absent in many cases, especially after the fact when those involved may have different recollections of the incident.

Force Policy and Force Continuum

There is little doubt that *Graham v. Connor* (1989) helped shape "use of force" policies around the country. Law enforcement agencies vary in the length and depth of their force policies, but generally outline the application, reporting, documentation, and investigation of force in similar ways. One example of an agency-specific use of force policy is found in the language used by Los Angeles County Sheriff's Department (LASD). According to the agency's *Manual of Policies and Procedures*, the term *unreasonable* includes any unnecessary or excessive force. The policy directs members to use only "that force which is objectively reasonable" in light of the "circumstances presented them at the time force is applied" (LASD, 2012, p. 12). The same policy further proscribes unreasonable force, with an admonition that those who apply such force are subject to discipline and, in some cases, criminal prosecution. The authors reviewed several force policies from variously sized departments across the United States, noting that they appear to follow the same logic and definition of reasonableness as the LASD model.

Many law enforcement agencies also provide officers with appropriate guidance through the development and dissemination of a "use of force options chart" or "use of force continuum." As courts and experience have consistently pointed out, it is important to teach officers not only the appropriate application of force, including specific techniques, but also to understand when best to apply a particular category of force as determined by a suspect's behavior. Rather than requiring officers to adhere to a rank-ordered progression of responses that may result in unnecessary risk to the officer or others, force continuums employ categories of force, as well as the discretion to apply any reasonable option within that group to overcome a suspect's resistance. The categories employed generally include a suspect whose behaviors can be described as *cooperative, resistive, assaultive/high risk*, or who poses threat of "death or serious bodily injury" to the officer (e.g., see, LASD, 2012, 3-01/025.20). Many of these categories have been recently annotated with advances in less-lethal technologies, greatly expanding the number of available options, while increasing officer safety and reducing the risk of death or serious bodily injury to suspects in most cases.

Less-Lethal Technologies

Recent technological advances have provided a host of less-than-lethal force options, including the Taser and special munitions, that is, 25-mm solid rubber rounds, many of which continue to be tested in laboratory settings and in field operations. Additional options include weapons that fire nets, thermal guns that raise body temperature, electromagnetic guns that cause seizure-like responses, magnetophosphene guns that produce an effect like a blow to the head, and weapons that temporarily impact balance, visual, or auditory functions (O'Connor, 2011). One of the difficulties with deploying these technologies is deciding where they fit on the force continuum, as well as their reliability in providing less-lethal force consistently without many of the long-term effects associated with more traditional measures. Courts have been slow to approve devices beyond chemical agents without further empirical analysis to determine long-term effects and lethality.

Factors Associated With Use of Force

Police officers wield tremendous discretion in choosing where and when to apply force. Therefore, before judging a particular application of force as reasonable or unreasonable, it is important to explore the decision-making processes used by officers that ultimately led to a particular application of force. This section investigates several aspects that may influence an officer's decision to apply force, including situational and individual factors.

Situational Factors

Research indicates that persons subjected to police uses of force are more likely to live in urban communities, as well as to belong to certain populations, that is, minority, homeless, or mentally ill. Black (1976) postulates that certain groups, along with those from lower socioeconomic classes, receive more punitive treatment from police. Black and others further suggest that because society, in general, finds these individuals offensive, police, as enforcement agents for society, apply more oppressive control and punishment as a response (Herbert, 1998; Muir, 1977; Van Maanen, 1974). While there is general consensus about the types of individuals most likely to receive punitive treatment from law enforcement, theories differ as to the situational factors responsible for this relationship. For instance, rates of criminal activity are often higher in areas occupied by greater percentages of minorities, the homeless, and the mentally ill, thus police presence is more pronounced and citizen contacts are more frequent (Braga, 2001; Weisburd & Eck, 2004). Because of the higher rates of officer–citizen contact, more opportunity exists for the application of force.

Research conducted by Kania and Mackey (1977) found that the level of police violence fluctuated with the level of violence in the community. In applying theories of occupational norms and class conflict, the researchers studied the level of force applied by officers in communities per rates of homicide. Findings from their study support the hypothesis that police officers develop their job demeanor somewhat in response to the expectations of the communities where they work. Where officers work in communities with higher rates of violence, they tend to use more force in response to conflict; where violence is neither normative nor common, they respond accordingly by using less force.

One factor found to play a critical role in the application of coercive force is a suspect's demeanor. Certainly, police officers expect others to comply with their authority. Thus, the potential for coercive force increases anytime an individual chooses to resist (Engel, Sobol, & Worden, 2000). Tedeshi and Felson (1994) theorized that insubordination and disrespect for police authority might undermine police legitimacy, thus increasing the likelihood of force in an attempt to demonstrate the consequences of such actions.

Griffin and Bernard (2003) offer a different conceptualization of excessive force. Rather than relying on the inconsistent findings gleaned from efforts to identify specific individual personality traits, attitudes, or characteristics, they posit that police extralegal force is best explained via the tenets of angry aggression theory. More specifically, the chronic stressors of police work—when combined with an officer's inability to cope effectively and the social isolation that often accompanies police work—create perceptions of increased threat, as well as the aggression that naturally accompanies such pressures. They further theorize that officers may act on those stressors by directing aggressive behavior toward targets in their work environment.

The beating and subsequent death of Kelly Thomas, however, illustrates a different problem. The National Alliance on Mental Illness estimates that one of seventeen, or 6% of the population, is afflicted with serious mental disease (NAMI, 2012). In addition, there are over 30,000 suicides annually involving mentally ill victims, while it is estimated that "suicide by cop" accounts for somewhere between 10% and 40% of all law enforcement shootings nationwide. Indeed, one feature consistently associated with law enforcement's application of force, including deadly force, is mental illness. Simply put, law enforcement officers are not trained to identify, much less trained to understand or interact with, the mentally ill, often resulting in predictable, sometimes tragic consequences (Ruiz & Miller, 2004).

Race/Ethnicity

Although a lengthy treatment of police–minority issues is beyond the scope of this chapter, it is difficult to overlook such concerns when considering the application of force. Indeed, many research studies have explored the association between a suspect's race/ethnicity and force (i.e., Alpert & Dunham, 2004; Alpert & MacDonald, 2001; Garner, Schade, Hepburn, & Buchanan, 1995). Thus, while studies have established a significant correlation between resistance and force, there have been few findings to support a robust and consistent relationship between race and force after controlling for resistance and other related factors (Engel et al., 2000). For example, studies have demonstrated that Black and Hispanic officers employ force more frequently against minority suspects than White suspects. In fact, data from one study actually found that the highest levels of force involved Hispanic officers and Hispanic suspects (Alpert & Dunham, 2004).

Others have argued that the resistance offered by suspects varies, with minorities more likely to engage in greater levels of resistance, as measured on the use of force continuum, necessitating a stronger response from law enforcement. Kappeler (1997) found that police application of force was associated with the immediate threat posed by the suspect, the severity of the offense, and whether the suspect was resisting or attempting to escape. A separate study reached a similar conclusion, finding that many of the factors identified by Kappeler were themselves influenced by a host of variables, such as gender, size, and suspect demeanor, as well as the race of the officer and the number of officers present at the scene (Holmes, Reynolds, Holmes, & Faulkner, 1998). Garner and his colleagues (1995) found that officers applied force more frequently when the suspect was antagonist, involved in violent crime, a gang member, intoxicated, or known to carry weapons.

Training

Law enforcement training academies provide officers with a rudimentary knowledge and awareness of many topics with a heavy emphasis on physical fitness, defensive tactics, and weapons. Despite efforts to professionalize policing, training continually reinforces the idea that coercive power is a critical component of policing (Skolnick & Fyfe, 1993).

Over the years, law enforcement training curriculums have required greater numbers of hours for certification. In the 1960s, many departments required only a few weeks of training to become police officers, while it is not unusual for modern academies to run several months. In California, for instance, the 664 hours of instruction for basic peace officer certification covers 41 topics, yet only eight hours is spent on ethics, 16 on cultural diversity, and 12 on use of force (California Commission on Peace Officers Standards and Training, 2012). In Texas, of the state's 736 hours required for examination, only 8 hours is spent on ethics, 4 hours on problem solving and critical thinking, and 24 hours on force options (Texas Commission on Law Enforcement Officers Standards and Education, 2012). And of the 639 hours required for certification in New York, only 12 hours goes toward ethics, two to discretion, seven to force justification, and two to problem solving (New York State Division of Criminal Justices Services, 2012).

There is no question that officers need extensive training in law, firearms, physical fitness, and a host of critically relevant subject areas, but the fact remains that relatively little time is spent teaching ethics, human relations, critical thinking, problem solving, and dealing with the mentally ill. A common complaint among educators is the lack of critical thinking skills students possess as a result of instructors teaching to the tests. Officers leaving the academy may be quite adept in their use of weapons, but sorely undertrained in communication skills, critical thinking, problem solving, and the ability to deal effectively with certain populations, including the mentally ill. Indeed, with the prevalence of mental illness in the United States (NAMI, 2012), diversity of culture and language, and other traditional problems facing law enforcement, as well as the larger society, it appears reasonable to conclude that additional training in these areas could help to reduce the number of force incidents.

The Military Model

The Oklahoma City bombing, the terrorist attacks of September 11, 2001, and other recent events in American history have increased focus on homeland security, fundamentally affecting the mission of many law enforcement agencies. The enactment of the Patriot Act in 2001 and the Protect America Act in 2007 greatly expanded the powers of law enforcement to fight the "war on terror" (Pollock, 2012). The post-9/11 mission has been broadened to include not only domestic crime but also terrorism, both at home and abroad. Unlike decades past, federal, state, and local police are involved with the protection of critical infrastructure, key assets, transportation security, intelligence gathering, and border security, in addition to more traditional law enforcement duties. Indeed, evidence that certain terror groups may be working with American gangs and Mexican drug cartels has further complicated the threat (U.S. Department of Homeland Security, 2012).

While this shift in the police mission may be both necessary and desirable, the increased pressure to respond to homeland security issues has led to intensified militarization among many police agencies (White, 2006). Brown (2011) contends that this "fog of war" mentality may impair the already precarious ethical judgments of certain officers because of enhanced pressures of nationalism, stress, fatigue, and fear. What may be morally acceptable on distant battlefields is often incompatible with policing American streets, with these conflicting values pulling officers in different directions.

In addition to enhanced militarization, traditional law enforcement training relies heavily on military models of instruction, emphasizing crisp uniforms, polished boots, military decorum, physical training, marching, and stern instructors (Cowper, 2000). Similar to the psychology employed by military trainers, the general intent is to instill discipline and organizational cohesion in students, many of whom have no prior exposure to the military or other paramilitary organizations. Recruits are continuously indoctrinated into the idea that mental toughness is a key component for surviving the high stress, violent environments where much of police work occurs.

Unfortunately, the emphasis on survival, reliance on coworkers, and a jaded view of nonpolice personnel leaves little room for public service, often resulting in detachment and, in some cases, an "us against them" mentality, where anyone not directly connected with policing is viewed with suspicion (Fitch, 2011b). Indeed, few police officers survive long careers without some level of emotional detachment. The military model of policing has also led to evaluations of performance based on the number of arrests and convictions ("body counts") rather than objective determinations of the effectiveness of such procedures, that is, whether or not those efforts actually enhance community safety (Brown, 2011; Skolnick & Fyfe, 1993).

Critics of this approach—and especially the emphasis on militarization—cite a rigid, monolithic, secretive world of automatons where creative thinking is smothered and aggressive, confrontational behavior is the preferred method of operation (Weber, 1999). According to Cowper (2000), the modern military model of decision making and command is actually quite different than what is commonly understood by the public. For decades, the military services have worked to decentralize authority, empower members of the enlisted ranks and junior officers, and emphasize leadership at all levels of the organization. Rather than enforcing a strict hierarchy of command, modern military training stresses creativity, critical thinking, and intuitive skills. While it is difficult to escape the similarities between the military and law enforcement—that is, uniforms, organized rank structure, and respect for the chain of command—the missions of the military and law are actually very different.

Nonetheless, it is estimated that over 50% of sworn law enforcement officers have prior military experience or serve currently as members of the National Guard or other reserve units. Of the 120,000 Guard and Reserve soldiers activated as of 2008, over 10% were members of law enforcement (Hink, 2010). In addition, police departments throughout the nation have experienced spikes in applications from military personnel returning from active duty. Policing appears to be a natural fit for many military personnel because of similarities in training, discipline, and structure (Anderson, 2011). While the emphasis on leadership and problem-solving skills emphasized by the modern military could serve society well, there is little evidence at this point to indicate how militarization affects individual police officers.

Police Subculture

When considering situation factors, it is difficult to escape the importance of the larger police subculture on officer conduct, that is, the unspoken values, norms, and ways of doing things that influence the day-to-day decisions and actions of law enforcement professionals (Schein, 1992). Researchers have noted that police subculture endorses a unique value system, with an especially strong emphasis on loyalty, bravery, and autonomy (Crank & Caldero, 2000; Sherman, 1982), as well as, in some cases, the misuse of authority and violation of citizens' rights (Kappeler, Sluder, & Alpert, 1998; Skolnick & Fyfe, 1993). While subculture plays an important role in teaching new members the craft of policing, it frequently overemphasizes the hazards of police work, despite the relative infrequency of violent assault (Van Maanen, 1974). While officers' preoccupation with danger works to unify them, it can simultaneously separate officers from members of the public whom they are sworn to protect (Committee on Law and Justice, 1994; Kappeler et al., 1998).

An appreciation of police subculture is also important because there are instances when it may be more influential in molding young officers than their academy training or department leadership (Fitch, 2011a). This is because formal academy training is often adapted to the real world once officers begin their first assignments (Fielding, 1988). Because of the status associated with acceptance into the police subculture, peer approval may become more important than promotions or formal accolades. Many officers want to be considered part of the police family and, in some instances, will go to great lengths to obtain such an honor—a distinction that often requires unconditional loyalty, occasionally demonstrated by an officer's willingness to violate the law or department policy, including the application of coercive force.

The need for acceptance, blind loyalty, and willingness to apply coercive force may contribute to the "culture of force" identified within some departments. A recent report by the U.S. Department of Justice, Civil Rights Division, into the practices of the Seattle Police Department concluded that the agency had engaged "in a pattern or practice of using unnecessary or excessive force in violation of the Fourth Amendment" (USDOJ, 2011, p. 3). Seattle is the latest, but certainly not the only agency to be accused of similar patterns or practice. A culture of force has been found in many large U.S. cities (Human Right Watch, 1998), which is usually attributed to an absence of leadership, lack of training, and wall of secrecy, as well as normative values that endorse force as an accepted response, even without legal or policy justification.

Individual Factors

A number of studies have attempted to identify individual predictors of excessive force; however, results have been mixed (Cohen & Chaiken, 1972; Friedrich, 1980; Fyfe, 1988; Garner et al., 1995; Terrill & Mastrofski, 2002; Worden, 1995). For example, law enforcement officers are often viewed as authoritarian with aggressive personalities that may increase the potential for coercive force. Altemeyer (1998) further theorized that right-wing authoritarians tend to hold double standards on issues such as patriotic loyalty and civil rights, have higher tendencies to self-righteousness and ethnocentrism, and embrace beliefs that the world is a very dangerous place. It has also been suggested that law enforcement officers become more cynical, angry, and antisocial over time, either as a result of enculturation into negative subgroups or as an outcome of increasing distrust. A study by Carlson, Thayer, and Germann (1971) on social attitudes and personality differences did, in fact, find police officers to be more authoritarian than college students. Subsequent research by Carlson and Sutton (1975) reached a similar conclusion, finding that police science students and police officers of varying ranks and assignments were more authoritarian than a control group.

In contrast, Fenster and Locke (1973) found officers to be less neurotic than civilians, while subsequent research by Gould and Funk (1998) observed that police recruits consistently score in the normal range on the Minnesota Multiphasic Personality Inventory (MMPI). More recently, a study comparing authoritarian traits as determined by the MMPI-2 between experienced and inexperienced police officers found that both experienced and inexperienced officers tend to be psychologically healthy (Laguna, Linn, Ward, & Rupslaukyte, 2010). Indeed, the failure of researchers to uncover consistent characteristic differences between police officers and other members of society fails to support the notion that a particular personality type is attracted to law enforcement (Walker, 1999). Rather, research data seems to support the notion that police are no different than other working-class Americans (Balch, 1972; Lorr & Strack, 1994; Trojanowicz, 1971)—leading Mills and Bohannon (1980) to conclude that officers appear to be no more authoritarian or inflexible than other members of society, but instead are "bright, assertive, autonomous, self-assured, responsible, and level-headed" (p. 683).

In a study examining the effects of individual and situational variables, Friedrich (1980) found only the behavior of the suspect and public visibility to be significant predictors of force. In a separate study, Worden and Catlin (2002) concluded that a small percentage of officers are responsible for a disproportionate number of force incidents. Data from their study further indicated that those officers suffered from a lack of empathy, antisocial personality, paranoia, and cynicism, as well as a failure to assume responsibility for their actions or to learn from experience. Not surprisingly, these officers also identified strongly with the police subculture. Furthermore, younger, more inexperienced officers have been found to score higher on measures of antisocial practices (Laguna et al., 2010), as well as demonstrating a tendency to apply coercive force more frequently than older, more experienced and educated officers (Cascio, 1977; Terrill & Mastrofski, 2002). Worden (1995) further noted that officers more likely to use force adopt crime fighters as role models. These same officers often believe strongly in discretionary force, while believing that the general public either lacks appreciation or is hostile toward police.

Psychophysiology and Force Science

Many police officers undergo significant personality changes over time. They often become more self-confident and assertive, develop coping mechanisms to defend against traumatic experiences, and, of great importance, adopt a more traditionally masculine view of humanity (Anderson & Bauer, 1987). Officers frequently develop overly masculine attitudes to cope with danger and strong emotions (Reiser & Geiger, 1984). Weapons, uniforms, badges, power and authority, physical prowess, and a quasi-military environment where the majority of officers are male all contribute to a masculine persona. When provoked, insulted, or resisted, whether during a traffic stop or a long police pursuit, adrenaline surges, increasing the potential for force (Anderson & Bauer, 1987). In such cases, real or perceived threats activate the sympathetic branch of the autonomic nervous system, flooding the body with adrenaline and other catecholamines intended to help the brain and body cope with increased demands for energy and attention. When the suspect is caught, emotions may override an officer's self-control mechanisms, resulting in excessive force (Baker, 1985).

Despite the effects of training and experience, police attitudes are shaped by the perception of threats in their environment regardless of the actual risk (Skolnick, 1966). Officers' perceptions of risk may be further influenced by availability heuristics—that is, the ease with which certain events are brought to mind (Rosoff, Pontell, & Tillman, 1998). While the actual numbers of assaults, injuries, and deaths are very low, the threat of such events is continuously reinforced throughout an officer's career, beginning in the basic academy and continuing through more advanced-officer training courses (Kappeler et al., 1998). As previously discussed, officers spend a great deal of time training in self-defense, weapons, and tactics. While these skills are important for survival, the constant focus on survival creates stress that often manifests itself in isolation, paranoia, and overcoming resistance with coercive force to send a message to those who would resist and to ensure survival.

Where an officer or civilian has indeed been gravely injured or killed, especially where an officer perceived great personal risk, post-traumatic stress disorder (PTSD) may follow. Hill (1984) found that the PTSD following a traumatic event occurs in stages, including disbelief, shock, denial, and confusion. Shortly thereafter, depression typically follows. By the second week, victims of PTSD may experience nightmares, panic attacks, crying, and flashbacks. Hill found that after approximately one month, many officers developed an even stronger masculine façade, often attempting to cope with their symptoms by consuming alcohol and sleeping pills. Unfortunately, while many officers experience PTSD during their careers, few receive help, and the condition often deteriorates into alcoholism, broken families, depression, and an inability to handle stress. There is, however, no evidence that this deterioration affects an officer's decision to use force.

Because of strong emotions—as well as the cognitive, emotional, and physiological changes that accompany those emotions—it is not uncommon for officers to demonstrate only partial recall of the events surrounding a use of force or other traumatic incident. Thus, officers' memories can vary as to the precise sequence of events, as well as the type and the amount of force applied (Honig & Lewinski, 2008). Studies on police physiology have confirmed distortions in time, sound, and memory, as well as other effects, including tunnel vision, dissociation, and "automatic pilot." And, in rare cases, temporary paralysis and hallucinations have been found to occur (Artwohl, 2002).

Honig and Roland (1998) found that some level of distortion occurred in 90% of the 384 police shootings studied. The psychological and physiological effects of stress are important to understand in studying use of force for two reasons: (1) Personality changes occur because of the need for self-preservation in dangerous, often traumatic occupations; and (2) the natural physiological, cognitive, and emotional changes produced by stress often help explain an officer's poor or distorted recall of events, a phenomenon which often leads to allegations of misconduct or cover-up (Anderson & Bauer, 1987; Bumgarner, Lewinski, Hudson, & Sapp, 2006).

According to "Hick's law," a person's reaction time increases as the number of choices increase (Hick, 1952). In other words, a person's reaction time to stimuli increases by the available number of choices. While an armed suspect is usually concerned only with his personal interest (i.e., escape or escape at the expense of injuring another), an officer must consider the suspect's intent, environment, backdrop, innocent bystanders, and the legality of his actions. Despite the fact that each of these variables requires considerable cognitive resources, an officer is forced to consider each factor both individually and collectively, as well as his own safety, before deciding on a course of action—often in less than a second.

In fact, recent studies at the Force Science Institute at the Minnesota State University, Mankato and Texas State University–San Marcos, using mental chronometry to measure response times have demonstrated Hick's law. For instance, empirical evidence supports a suspect's ability to shoot and turn 180 degrees to run in less time than an officer can react and fire his weapon (Lewinski, 2000; Tobin & Fackler, 1997). Similar findings have been found with knife-wielding suspects, who can close a distance of 21 feet before an officer can draw, fire his weapon, and avoid being stabbed (Lewinski, 2005; Tueller, 1983). These findings provide important support for the reasonableness of deadly force against armed suspects, despite a public perception that the application of force in such situations is unreasonable or excessive.

Ethical Justifications for Use of Force

Police officers often enter the law enforcement with little, if any, experience in handling many of the challenges and moral dilemmas offered by police work (Fitch, 2011a). Nonetheless, officers are given vast discretionary powers and the authority to use force when needed (Skolnick & Fyfe, 1993). Many officers are profoundly influenced by normative subculture values, which, in some cases, are contrary to law and policy, especially in cases where those behaviors are positively reinforced by peer pressure (Chappell & Piquero, 2004; Fitch, 2011a). Because most officers have a strong positive image of themselves as good, caring individuals, they often attempt to justify their actions by arguing for the "greater good"—that is, society will benefit by removing a dangerous criminal from the streets.

Utilitarian ethical systems, most often credited to philosophers Jeremy Bentham (1748–1842) and John Stuart Mill (1806–1873), rely on the ends (outcomes) to justify the means (actions). Utilitarianism and other teleological systems weigh the utility and disutility of actions to determine their relative goodness (Kidder, 2003). Because crime damages not only victims but also the larger society, officers may believe it is their duty to deter criminal behavior by any means necessary for the greater good. This may be especially true for offenders who harm officers. Unfortunately, utilitarian logic relies on the erroneous belief that one can predict the outcome of a given course of action, a belief wholly void of empirical support.

Crank and Caldero (2000) describe "noble cause" policing as an ends-based commitment to doing something about "bad people." Noble cause, however, becomes corrupted when officers violate the law on behalf of personally held moral values—a notion frequently celebrated in television and movies where the protagonist operates outside the law. "Dirty Harry," a character portrayed by actor Clint Eastwood, perhaps best illustrates this concept. According to Klockars (1980), Dirty Harry inflicts pain on criminals to extract information that will ostensibly save the innocent. A strong belief in noble cause policing can increase the possibility of an officer seeing himself as above the law or as the law, instead of a servant to it. Like Dirty Harry, officers can become frustrated with legal systems that appear to favor criminals, thus ignoring the law and department policy in favor of taking matters into their own hands—a phenomenon illustrated by the video-taped beating of Rodney King.

Waddington (1999) argues that by glorifying force through the cult of masculinity, officers are better able to cope with the moral ambiguity inherent in applications of coercive force. The ethos of force is exalted in law enforcement agencies throughout the nation through the repetition of myths and stories. Younger officers hear tales regaling the virtues of employing extralegal force on criminals or other undesirable members of society, complete with concomitant rationalizations—contributing to a morally insulted police identity (Van Maanen, 1980). The application of extralegal force is further neutralized by the persona of officer as crime fighter—an image that depicts police officers as doing society's dirty work against overwhelming odds and at great personal risk. By employing this utilitarian framework, an officer is simply applying whatever amount of force is necessary to overcome a greater wrong while making society a safer place for all.

In addition to a distorted view of noble-cause policing, a distorted view of deontological justice can contribute to excessive or unnecessary force. Immanuel Kant (1724–1804) argued that offenders should receive punishment simply because they deserve it with no need to justify it as necessary for the greater good. Some officers may defend excessive force under the philosophy that offenders deserve such treatment as punishment for their crimes (accompanied perhaps by the concurrent rationale that the courts will not punish the offender appropriately). However, despite attempts to justify this view as a valid form of Kantian ethics, the underlying logic is flawed. In his writings, Kant focused on ethical duty, including the protection of all members of society. Officers have a duty to apply laws, policies, and other universal human rights equally across the board, effectively rendering any unnecessary or illegal force untenable according to the precepts of deontological ethics (Pollock, 2012). Moreover, using coercive power to punish is unacceptable because it fails to conform to universalism—the idea that standards should be applied universally to all people in similar situations, with a person's behavior in a given context serving as the prototype for the behavior of all other people under similar circumstances—and other parts of Kant's categorical imperative (Kidder, 2003).

Clearly, an officer's decision to use force, then, is based on a number of situational and individual factors, as well as an officer's moral and social reasoning. Proper ethical reasoning, however, requires exposure to an appropriately complex set of moral dilemmas (Kohlberg, 1981), as well as an appropriate level of training in decision making, critical thinking, and problem solving. Consistent with this thesis, Scharf, Linninger, Marrero, Baker, and Rice (1978) found evidence that training officers in recognizing and responding to moral dilemmas, including associated philosophical reflection and legal reasoning, may change how officers view ethics. The logical interface with force seems clear enough: Moral reasoning is a dynamic process dependent on a number of variables, each of which is further influenced by myriad factors. This conception of ethical reasoning makes sense if an officer pauses to consider how the application of coercive force is potentially dependent not only on logical reasoning, but a set of broader, underlying moral and philosophical principles.

Summary

Police officers possess significant amounts of power and authority, and use force as a means to control deviant behavior (Wolfe, 1969). The decision to use force, however, is based on the totality of inputs from myriad sources. Law, department policies, training, situational and individual variables, and ethical systems all affect an officer's decision to apply force. Nevertheless, each decision to use force has significant ethical and moral implications for the officer, his agency, and the community at large. In the end, however, it comes down to an officer choosing to follow a moral clarity, not letting emotions influence his decisions or following the immoral conduct of others, that is more likely to ensure only necessary force occurs.

The injudicious application of force has led not only to injuries and deaths, but also to crippling civil damages, officers convicted of criminal offenses, and public officials removed from office (Fyfe, 1988). Even when the application of deadly force is legally and ethically justified, such incidents have polarized communities, damaged the public trust, and left those most in need for police services suspicious and cynical. Thus, it is critical that every police officer understands the ethical, legal, and practical implication of force.

While the courts have established an objectively reasonable standard when assessing an officer's application of force, courts, disciplinary review boards, juries, and civilians often employ different standards when judging the reasonableness of an officer's actions. In an attempt to guide the actions of officers, many departments have established well-defined policies for the application, reporting, investigation, and documentation of force incidents, as well as use of force continuums. These policies and continuums describe when best to apply a particular category of force in response to a suspect's behavior (e.g., see LASD, 2012, 3-01/025.20). Nonetheless, in an attempt to increase the professionalism and objective application of force, the authors make the following recommendations.

Training

Law enforcement training currently places a strong emphasis on physical fitness, defensive tactics, and weapons, while reinforcing the necessity of coercive power (Skolnick & Fyfe, 1993). While each of these topics is of critical importance, training should be expanded significantly in the areas of ethics, critical thinking and decision making, human relations, and identifying and handling the mentally ill.

Police Subculture

Most police officers enter the profession with little, if any, prior law enforcement experience. As a result, inexperienced officers learn the profession by relying on the guidance (either direct or indirect) of senior department members (Chappell & Piquero, 2004; Fitch, 2011a). In doing so, younger officers can learn both proper (lawful and ethical) and improper (unlawful and unethical) behaviors. Thus, police management should be especially cautious in filling the roles of field training, sergeant, and detective, as each of these positions asserts considerable influence on young, highly impressionable officers who look toward the conduct of others as examples of appropriate behavior. In addition, leadership demands involvement and attention to the officers on the street, the issues they face, and the community they serve. Leadership or the lack thereof is evident in well run ethical departments and those that develop a culture of force, respectively.

Community Policing

The primary mission of law enforcement is fighting crime. However, officers and departments vary in their approach. Rather than emphasizing a crime fighter model of law enforcement, agencies should encourage and reward public service, while emphasizing community policing models and collective problem solving (Pollock, 2012). That is, in addition to encouraging and rewarding arrests, management should encourage and reward officers for working collectively with the public to create better communities.

Ethics Indoctrination

Rather than relying on a few hours of ethics training in the basic academy, law enforcement supervisors and managers should make ethics discussions an integral part of the agency's culture (Fitch, 2008). Supervisors should routinely discuss ethics—including ethical models, cognitive rationalizations, and the results of unethical conduct on officers, agencies, and communities—while paying special attention to the reasoning processes and values underlying an officer's decision.

Force Science

The human body experiences a number of cognitive, emotional, and physiological changes during stress. By educating law enforcement personnel about the kinds of changes they can expect to experience during an application of force, vehicular pursuit, or other traumatic incident, officers will be better prepared to think critically and behave reasonably, regardless of the circumstances. Moreover, a more realistic understanding of response time, available tactics, and less-lethal options should improve both officer and citizen safety during such incidents (Lewinski, 2002, 2005; Tobin & Fackler, 1997; Tueller, 1983).

Hopefully, by educating officers on critical thinking, decision making, human relations skills, tactics, and ethics, officers will better understand the wider implication of force—for the officer, his department, and society. Assaults on officers should decrease, and, with increasing officer understanding, professionalism, and tactics, tragedies like the beating and death of Kelly Thomas will hopefully no longer occur.

Discussion Questions

1. Define *discretion*, *force*, *excessive force*, and *unnecessary force*. Include the concepts that differentiate the various force terms.

2. What legal precedent defines police use of force? Discuss the general components and findings of the cases and the changes brought about to both police and society.

3. What is a force continuum? Discuss the importance of policy and its role in police use of force.

4. What is force science? Discuss key situational variables that impact use of force by police.

5. What is police subculture? Discuss how ethics and subculture affect police and use of force.

References

Alpert, G., & Dunham, R. (2004). *Understanding police use of force*. New York: Cambridge University Press.

Alpert, G., & MacDonald, J. (2001). Police use of force: An analysis of organizational characteristics. *Justice Quarterly, 18*(2), 393–409.

Altemeyer, B. (1998). The other authoritarian personality. In Mark P. Zanna (Ed.), *Advances in experimental social psychology* (pp. 48–92). New York: Academic Press.

Anderson, P. (2011, August 14). Ex-military lining up for police jobs. *The Topeka Capital-Journal.* Retrieved from http://cjonline.com/news/2011-08-14/ex-military-lining-police-jobs

Anderson, W., & Bauer, B. (1987). Law enforcement officers: The consequences of exposure to violence. *Journal of Counseling and Development, 65*(7), 381–384.

Artwohl, A. (2002). Perceptual and memory distortion during officer-involved shootings. *FBI Law Enforcement Bulletin, 71*(10), 18–24.

Baker, M. (1985). *Cops: Their lives in their own words*. New York: Pocket Books.

Balch, R. (1972). Police personality: Fact or fiction? *Journal of Criminal Law, Criminology, and Police Science, 63*(1), 106–119.

Bittner, E. (1970). The functions of the police in modern society: A review of background factors, current practices, and possible role models. Cambridge, MA: Oelgeschlager, Gunn & Hain.

Black, D. (1976). *The behavior of law*. New York: Academic Press.

Blair, J. P., Pollock, J. M., Montague, D., Nichols, T., Cumutt, J., & Burns, D. (2011). Reasonableness and reaction time. *Police Quarterly, 14*(4), 323–343.

Braga, A. M. (2001). The effects of hot spots policing on crime. *Annals of the American Academy of Political and Social Sciences, 578,* 104–125.

Bronson, P. (2006). *Behind the lines: The untold stories of the Cincinnati riots.* Milford, OH: Chilidog Press.

Brosseau v Haugen, 543 U.S. 194 (2004).

Brown, C. A. (2011). Divided loyalties: Ethical challenges for America's law enforcement in post 9/11 America. *Case Western Reserve Journal of International Law, 43*(3), 651–675.

Bumgarner, J. B., Lewinski, W. J., Hudson, W., & Sapp, C. (2006). An examination of police officer mental chronometry. *Journal of The Association for Crime Scene Reconstruction, 12*(3), 11–26.

California Commission on Peace Officers Standards and Training. (2012). *Regular basic course training specifications.* Retrieved from http://post.ca.gov/regular-basic-course-training-specifications.aspx

Carlson, H., & Sutton, M. S. (1975). The effects of different police roles on attitudes and values. *The Journal of Psychology: Interdisciplinary and Applied, 91*(1), 57–64.

Carlson, H., Thayer, R., & Germann, A. (1971). Social attitudes and personality differences among members of two kinds of police departments (innovative vs. traditional) and students. *Journal of Criminal Law, Criminology & Police Science, 62*(4), 564–567.

Cascio, W. F. (1977). Formal education and police officer performance. *Journal of Police Science and Administration, 5,* 89–96.

Chappell, A., & Piquero, A. (2004). Applying social learning theory to police misconduct. *Deviant Behavior, 25*(2), 89–108.

City of Canton v Harris, 489 U.S. 378 (1989).

Cohen, B., & Chaiken, J. M. (1972). *Police background characteristics and performance.* Lanham, MD: Rowman & Littlefield.

Cohen, H., & Feldberg, M. (1991). Power and restraint: The moral dimension of police work. New York: Praeger.

Committee on Law and Justice. (1994) *Violence in urban America—mobilizing a response.* Washington, DC: National Academy Press.

Cooper, M. (1999, February 5). Officers in Bronx fire 41 shots, and an unarmed man is killed. *New York Times.* Retrieved from http://www.nytimes.com/1999/02/05/nyregion/officers-in-bronx-fire-41-shots-and-an-unarmed-man-is-killed.html

Cowper, T. J. (2000). The myth of the "military model" of leadership in law enforcement. *Police Quarterly, 3*(3), 229–246.

Crank, J., & Caldero, M. (2000). *Police ethics: The corruption of noble cause.* Cincinnati, OH: Anderson.

Engel, R. S., Sobol, J. J., & Worden, R. E. (2000). Further exploration of the demeanor hypothesis: The interaction effects of suspects' characteristics and demeanor on police behavior. *Justice Quarterly, 17*(2), 235–258.

Fenster, C. A., & Locke, B. (1973). Neuroticism among policemen: An examination of police personality. *Journal of Applied Psychology, 57*(3), 358–359.

Fielding, N. (1988). Joining forces: Police training, socialization, and occupational competence. London: Routledge.

Fitch, B. D. (2008). Principle-based decision making for law enforcement. *Law and Order Magazine, 56*(9), 64–70.

Fitch, B. D. (2011a). Examining the ethical failures of law enforcement. In A. H. Normore & B. D. Fitch (Eds.), *Leadership in education, corrections, and law enforcement: A commitment to ethics, equality, and excellence* (pp. 3–22). Bingley, UK: Emerald Publishing Group.

Fitch, B. D. (2011b). Rethinking ethics in law enforcement. *FBI Law Enforcement Bulletin, 80*(10), 18–24.

Friedrich, R. J. (1980). Police use of force: Individuals, situations, and organizations. *The Annals of the American Academy of Political and Social Science, 452*(1), 82–97.

Fyfe, J. J. (1988). Police use of deadly force: Research and reform. *Justice Quarterly, 5*(2), 165–202.

Garner, J. H., Schade, T., Hepburn, J., & Buchanan, J. (1995). Measuring the continuum of force used by and against the police. *Criminal Justice Review, 20*(2), 146–168.

Gould, L. A., & Funk, S. (1998). Does the stereotypical personality reported for the male police officer fit that of the female police officer? *Journal of Police and Criminal Psychology, 13*(1), 25–39.

Graham v Conner, 490 U.S. 386 (1989).

Griffin, S. P., & Bernard, T. J. (2003). Angry aggression among police officers. *Police Quarterly, 6*(3), 3–21.

Herbert, S. (1998). Police subculture reconsidered. *Criminology, 36*(2), 343–369.

Hick, W. E. (1952). On the rate of gain of information. *Quarterly Journal of Experimental Psychology, 4,* 11–26.

Hill, W. R. (1984, October). Post-killing trauma, when police officers are the victims. *Law and Order,* 68–72.

Hink, J. (2010, August). The returning military veteran. *FBI Law Enforcement Bulletin.* Retrieved from http://www.fbi.gov/stats-services/publications/law-enforcement-bulletin/august-2010/the-returning-military-veteran

Holmes, S. T., Reynolds, K. M., Holmes, R. M., & Faulkner, S. (1998). Individual and situational determinants of police force. *American Journal of Criminal Justice, 23*(1), 82–106.

Honig, A. L., & Lewinski, W. J. (2008). A survey of the research on human factors related to lethal force encounters: Implications for law enforcement training, tactics, and testimony. *Law Enforcement Executive Research Forum.* Retrieved from http://www.forcescience.org/articles.html

Honig, A. L., & Roland, J. E. (1998, October). Shots fired: Officer involved. *The Police Chief. 65,* 1–5.

Horn, D. (2001, December 30). Summer of blood: Guns rule the streets. *Cincinnati Enquirer.* Retrieved from http://www.enquirer.com/unrest2001/race4.html

Human Rights Watch. (1998). *Report charges police abuse in U.S. goes unchecked.* Retrieved from http://www.hrw.org/news/1998/07/06/report-charges-police-abuse-us-goes-unchecked

International Association of Chiefs of Police (IACP). (2001). *Police use of force in America.* Retrieved from http://www.theiacp.org/Portals/0/pdfs/Publications/2001 useofforce.pdf

Kania, R., & Mackey, W. (1977). Police violence as a function of community characteristics. *Criminology, 15*(1), 27–47.

Kappeler, V. E. (1997). *Critical issues in police civil liability.* Prospect Heights, IL: Waveland.

Kappeler, V. E., Sluder, R. D., & Alpert, G. P. (1998). *Forces of deviance: Understanding the dark side of policing.* Prospect Heights, IL: Waveland.

Kidder, R. M. (2003). How good people make tough choices: Resolving the dilemmas of ethical living. New York: Fireside.

Klockars, C. (1980). The Dirty Harry problem. *Annals of the American Academy of Political and Social Science, 452*(1), 33–47.

Klockars, C. (1996). A theory of excessive force and its control. In W. A. Geller & H. Toch (Eds.), Understanding and controlling police abuse of force (pp. 1–22). New Haven, CT: Yale University Press.

Kohlberg, L. (1981). The philosophy of moral development: Moral stages and the idea of justice. San Francisco: Harper & Row.

The L.A. riots: 20 years later. (2012, April). *The Los Angeles Times.* Retrieved from http://www.latimes.com/news/local/1992riots

Laguna, L., Linn, A., Ward, K., & Rupslaukyte, R. (2010). An examination of authoritarian personality traits among police officers: The role of experience. *Journal of Police and Criminal Psychology, 25*(2), 99–104.

Lewinski, W. J. (2000, November–December). Why is the suspect shot in the back? *The Police Marksman, 25*(6), 20–26.

Lewinski, W. J. (2002, May–June). Stress reactions related to lethal force encounters. *The Police Marksman, 27*(3), 23–28.

Lewinski, W. J. (2005). Destroying myths & discovering cold facts. *Policeone.com News*. Retrieved from http://www.policeone.com/pc_print.asp?vid=102828

Lorr, M., & Strack, S. (1994). Personality profiles of police candidates. *Journal of Clinical Psychology, 50*(2), 200–207.

Los Angeles County Sheriff's Department (LASD). (2012). *Manual of policy and procedure: Use of force.* Retrieved from http://www.lasdhq.org/divisions/leadership-training-div/bureaus/mpp/3-01.pdf

Mills, C. J., & Bohannon, W. E. (1980). Personality characteristics of effective state police officers. *Journal of Applied Psychology, 65*(6), 680–684.

Monnell v New York City Department of Social Services, 436 U.S. 658 (1978).

Muir, W. (1977). *Police: Street corner politicians.* Chicago: University of Chicago Press.

National Alliance on Mental Illness (NAMI). (2012). *What is mental illness: Mental illness facts.* Retrieved from http://www.nami.org/template.cfm?section=About_Mental_Illness

National Institute of Justice & Bureau of Justice Statistics (NIJ-BJS). (1999). *Use of force by police: Overview of national and local data.* (DOJ Publication No. NCJ 176330). Washington, DC: National Criminal Justice Reference Service.

New York State Division of Criminal Justices Services. (2012). *Police officer training.* Retrieved from http://www.criminaljustice.ny.gov/ops/training/index.htm

O'Connor, T. (2011). Advanced police ethics. *Megalinks in Criminal Justice.* Retrieved from http://www.drtomoconnor.com/3300/3300lect04a.htm

Packer, H. (1968). *The limits of criminal sanction.* Stanford, CA: Stanford University Press.

Pollock, J. M. (2012). *Ethical dilemmas and decisions in criminal justice* (7th ed.). Belmont, CA: Cengage.

Reiser, M., & Geiger, S. P. (1984). Police officer as victim. *Professional Psychology: Research & Practice, 15*(3), 315–323.

Rochin v California, 342 U.S. 165 (1952).

Rosoff, S., Pontell, H. N., & Tillman, R. (1998). *Profit without honor: White-collar crime and the looting of America.* Englewood Cliffs, NJ: Prentice Hall.

Ruiz, J., & Miller, C. (2004). An exploration study of Pennsylvania police officers perceptions of dangerousness and their ability to manage persons with mental illness. *Police Quarterly, 7*(3), 359–371.

Scharf, P., Linninger, R., Marrero, D., Baker, R., & Rice, C. (1978). Deadly force: The moral reasoning and education of police officers faced with the option of lethal legal violence. *Policy Studies Journal, 7,* 450–454.

Schein, E. (1992). Organizational culture and leadership: A dynamic view. San Francisco: Jossey-Bass.

Scott v Harris, 550 U.S. 372 (2007).

Sherman, L. (1982). Learning police ethics. *Criminal Justice Ethics, 1*(1), 10–19.

Skolnick, J. (1966). Justice without trial: Law enforcement in a democratic society. New York: John Wiley.

Skolnick, J., & Fyfe, J. (1993). *Above the law: Police and the excessive use of force.* New York: Free Press.

Tedeshi, J. T., & Felson, R. B. (1994). *Violence, aggression, and coercive actions.* Washington, DC: American Psychological Association.

Tennessee v Garner, 471 U.S. 1 (1985).

Terrill, W., & Mastrofski, S. D. (2002). Situational and officer-based determinants of police coercion. *Justice Quarterly, 19*(2), 101–134.

Texas Commission on Law Enforcement Officers Standards and Education. (2012). *Basic police officer certification.* Retrieved from http://www.tcleose.state.tx.us/content/training

Tobin, E. J., & Fackler, M. L. (1997). Officer reaction-response time in firing a handgun. *Wound Ballistics Review, 3*(1), 6–9.

Trojanowicz, R. (1971). The policeman's occupational personality. *Journal of Criminal Law, Criminology and Police Science, 62*(4), 551–559.

Tueller, D. (1983). How close is too close? *The Police Policy Studies Council.* Retrieved from http://www.theppsc.org/Staff_Views/Tueller/How.Close.htm

U.S. Commission on Civil Rights (USCCR). (2004). *Coping with police misconduct in West Virginia: Citizen involvement in officer disciplinary procedures.* Retrieved from http://www.usccr.gov/pubs/sac/wv0104/wv0104.pdf

U.S. Department of Homeland Security. (2012). The U.S. Homeland Security role in the Mexican war against drug cartels: Hearing before the Subcommittee on Oversight, Investigations, and Management of the Committee on Homeland Security, House of Representatives, 112th Cong., 1st Session, March 31, 2011 (testimony of Luis Alvarez). Washington, DC: Government Printing Office. Retrieved from http://www.gpo.gov/fdsys/pkg/CHRG-112hhrg72224/pdf/CHRG-112hhrg72224.pdf

U.S. Department of Justice (USDOJ), Civil Rights Division. (2011). *Investigation of the Seattle police department.* Washington: United States Attorney's Office.

U.S. Department of Justice (USDOJ), Community Oriented Policing Services. (2012). *Use of force.* Retrieved from http://www.cops.usdoj.gov/default.asp?Item=1374

Van Maanen, J. (1974). Working the street: A developmental view of police behavior. In H. Jacob (Eds.), *The potential for reform of criminal justice* (pp. 83–130). Beverly Hills, CA: Sage.

Van Maanen, J. (1980). Beyond account: The personal impact of police shootings. *The Annals of the American Academy of Political and Social Science, 452,* 145–156.

Waddington, P. A. J. (1999). Police (canteen) sub-culture. *British Journal of Criminology, 39*(2), 287–309.

Walker, S. (1999). *The police in America: An introduction* (3rd ed.). New York: McGraw-Hill.

Weber, D. C. (1999). *Warrior cops: The ominous growth of paramilitarism in American police departments* (CATO Institute Briefing Papers No. 50). Washington, DC: CATO Institute.

Weisburd, D., & Eck, J. E. (2004). What can police do to reduce crime, disorder, and fear? *The Annals of the American Academy of Political and Social Science, 593*(1), 42–65.

White, J. R. (2006). *Terrorism and homeland security: An introduction* (6th ed.). Belmont, CA: Wadsworth.

Winton, R. (2012a, May 8). Chest compression cut off homeless man's oxygen, expert says. *Los Angeles Times.* Retrieved from http://articles.latimes.com/2012/may/08/local/la-me-0509-kelly-thomas-20120509

Winton, R. (2012b, May 8). Video portrays violent death of Kelly Thomas. *Los Angeles Times.* Retrieved from http://articles.latimes.com/2012/may/08/local/la-me-kelly-thomas-20120508.

Wolfe, R. P. (1969). On violence. *Journal of Philosophy, 66*(19), 601–616.

Worden, R. E. (1995). The "causes" of police brutality: Theory and evidence on police use of force. In W. A. Geller & H. Toch (Eds.), *And justice for all: Understanding and controlling police abuse of force* (pp. 31–60). Washington, DC: Police Executive Research Forum.

Worden, R. E., & Catlin, S. (2002). The use and abuse of force by police. In K. Lersch (Ed.), *Policing and misconduct* (pp. 85–120). Upper Saddle River, NJ: Prentice Hall.

12 Law Enforcement Interrogations

An Ethical Perspective

James L. Ruffin

Bob and Sam were arrested for the armed robbery of a convenience store. They were taken to the local precinct. At the time of arrest, neither was advised of their *Miranda* warnings, but the police asked no questions, thus no *Miranda* admonition was required. The men were separated at the precinct. Bob was asked to sit at a desk in the open squad bay, and Sam was taken to a small, glassed office on the opposite end of the room.

Bob was given a personal history form to complete. The form asked basic demographic questions, such as age, address, and birth date. Bob was still not provided his *Miranda* warnings but had not yet been questioned about the robbery. Detective Smith entered the room and placed several items on the desk. Sam looked at him anxiously. "Sam, things aren't looking too good for you right now," the detective said. "Evidence is mounting, and the best deals are given to those who come forward first." Detective Smith looked directly at Sam for a moment before continuing, "It puts me in a position to go before the judge and speak on your behalf about you having done the right thing. I would hate for your friend Bob to put this all on you." The detective left the room momentarily to "answer a telephone call." Sam's heart raced as he looked nervously around the office. On the desk, he saw a thick file labeled with his name, "Sam Turner," and a CD labeled "surveillance video." He also noticed a second file labeled "witness statements and photographs."

Detective Smith finished his call and returned to the room. He asked Sam to step over by the office window. The detective opened the blinds, allowing Sam to see his friend and accomplice, Bob, sitting at a desk, writing intently on a piece of paper. Detective Smith commented, "What do you suppose he's writing?" Sam's stomach sank. He believed Bob was spilling his guts about the robbery, possibly claiming that the robbery was all Sam's idea or that he was merely a bystander. When combined with the "surveillance video" and "witness statements and photographs," Bob's apparent cooperation with detectives was enough to convince Sam that it was time to talk.

Sam asked the detective what he would be charged with if he cooperated. "I'm sorry, Sam, but I am not allowed to speak with you about the case until you are provided your *Miranda* warnings and you waive the right to remain silent," Smith replied. Eager to be the first to cooperate, and the presumption of insurmountable evidence against him, Sam signed the *Miranda* form, waived his rights to remain silent and consult an attorney, and provided a full confession.

Little did Sam know that the "surveillance video" was blank and the files labeled "Sam Turner" and "witness statements and photographs" contained useless documents from the office paper shredder. Rather, Sam was allowed to infer that there was more evidence against him than there actually was. This, coupled with the fact that Detective Smith was prohibited from talking to him about the case until he waived his rights, was enough to lure Sam into offering a confession that he may not have otherwise provided.

This scenario, and others like it, which are played out daily across America, illustrates the commonplace use of deceit and trickery in the interrogation room. It provides a stark illustration of the way police attempt to get to the truth by lying. For example, an officer may tell a suspect that his fingerprints were found at the crime scene, that an accomplice has already implicated him, or that his DNA was found near the victim, when, in fact, no such evidence exists. Such trickery is necessary, police say, because it is a rare criminal who will confess without some persuasion (Jensen, 1998). The courts have consistently upheld the use of deceit and trickery by law enforcement so long as the tactics being used are not so insidious that they could force an innocent person to confess. Nonetheless, the debate surrounding law enforcement's use of deceit and trickery during the interrogation process remains a hotly contested topic among attorneys, scholars, and law enforcement professionals, and will likely continue to earn attention in the media and other public forms well into the future.

This chapter addresses the use of deceit and trickery in criminal interrogations, methods reserved almost exclusively to American law enforcement officers (Canter & Alison, 1999), and how members of the public and law enforcement view the use of such techniques. The chapter begins with a brief discussion on the effects of the landmark U.S. Supreme Court case *Miranda v. Arizona* (1966), which some argue may have actually promoted the use of deceit and trickery by law enforcement. Next, the author explores arguments commonly found in the courts, social sciences, and philosophy, and their impact on police practices. The author then outlines the tenets of England's Police and Criminal Evidence Act (PACE), as well as how these reforms were fueled by deep-rooted concerns about the integrity of police interviews—and what these changes may indicate for the future of American law enforcement.

The chapter concludes with a discussion on the attitudes of American police officers toward the use of deceit and trickery, as well as recommendations to improve the professionalism and public image of officers in the courts and in the public eye.

_____Miranda and the New Psychology of Interrogation

While the use of deceit and trickery have become commonplace among American police officers (Kaci & Rush, 1988), such techniques are often criticized by those in the legal professions and social sciences as psychologically manipulative (Dillingham, 1996). Many believe the Supreme Court decision in *Miranda v. Arizona* (1966), which established rigid guidelines regarding the questioning of suspects, may have actually fostered these and other manipulative techniques. The guidelines set forth in *Miranda* were in fact procedural safeguards requiring law enforcement officers to notify suspects of their guaranteed constitutional right against self-incrimination, as well as their guaranteed constitutional right to consult legal counsel prior to (and during) any questioning by law enforcement. Additional legal precedents have been established to protect against coercion and duress in the interrogation process. The new safeguards of *Miranda* created a system of checks and balances and required law enforcement officers to adjust their techniques accordingly (Leo, 1992).

Law enforcement responded to the changing demands of *Miranda* by adopting a more subtle and sophisticated psychological approach to interrogations (Gudjonsson, 1992). Trickery and deceit became the norm (Kaci & Rush, 1988), and many law enforcement officers, sponsored by their respective agencies, received training in a host of subtle techniques, such as mirroring (Skoe & Ksionzky, 1985), neuro-linguistic programming (NLP) (Dilts, 1983), verbal judo (Thompson & Jenkins, 1993), and advanced rapport-building skills (Brooks, 1989). Non–law enforcement personnel, including psychologists, psychiatrists, therapists, and communication specialists, often delivered training to officers. Instructors were tasked with teaching officers the most useful methods to obtain relevant information in the least threatening way. The training provided law enforcement with the tools necessary to obtain the most information possible while complying with the safeguards of *Miranda*.

As a result of the developing association between law enforcement and non–law enforcement professionals, a growing number of legal scholars and social scientists began to label the use of such techniques *psychologically manipulative* (Ofshe, 1989). These assertions were based on evidence that the use of such techniques creates an atmosphere of vulnerability, thus increasing the likelihood of false confessions (Kassin, 1997). Moreover, legal scholars argued that a vulnerable suspect is incapable of a truly voluntary admission or confession, regardless of the type of interrogation technique being employed. These principles, when combined with other possible vulnerabilities—such as age, intellect, mental capacity, drug and alcohol abuse, and economic status—fostered the perception that a voluntary confession may not be possible under circumstances involving psychological coercion or manipulation.

The Courts

The issue of voluntariness raised by legal scholars regarding statements and confessions is important because, in situations where *Miranda* protections are applicable, the Court, through the *Miranda* decision, provided an avenue for a waiver of rights by the suspect. However, before a suspect's admission or confession can be considered legally admissible, the suspect's choice to waive those rights must be deemed both free and voluntary. A voluntary waiver provided by a suspect sets in motion a two-pronged legal question. First, was the waiver offered voluntarily? Second, if a confession was obtained after a valid waiver, was the confession the product of coercion or duress? For example, if a person is arrested and transported to a police station for questioning, it is clearly unconstitutional to employ either deceit or trickery to obtain a *Miranda* waiver, as this would constitute a violation of the suspect's Fourth and Sixth Amendment protections. The courts have held that the use of deceit or trickery removes voluntariness at this stage of the criminal justice process. On the other hand, the Court has let stand cases where trickery or deceit were used once a voluntary waiver had been obtained. The question of voluntariness is significant because studies suggest that roughly 84% of those arrested will waive their constitutional rights as guaranteed by *Miranda* (Alschuler, 1997; Kassin, 1997). Not surprisingly, some legal scholars question whether a suspect is truly capable of voluntarily waiving his constitutional rights or providing a confession when their decision to confess is based on lies, trickery, or deceit (Jayne & Buckley, 1990; McKenzie, 1994).

The courts have provided little consistent guidance on acceptable behavior regarding the use of deceit or trickery. On the other hand, extreme forms of manipulation, which include physical abuse, torture, and extensive prolonged interrogation, have been consistently deemed inappropriate. In *Brown v. Mississippi* (1936), the Court dismissed a case involving physical abuse, calling the tactics "revolting to the sense of justice and a clear denial of due process" (p. 286). In *Spano v. New York* (1959), the Court went further and dismissed a case based on mental capacity, length of interrogation, and intelligence. *Spano* was the first case to address nonphysical practices where voluntariness may have been lessened by the use of psychological manipulation.

The Court has refused to outline those specific things needed to move a confession from a voluntary to an involuntary state. However, the Court has consistently ruled that decisions regarding the voluntariness or involuntariness of a confession must be based on "totality of the circumstances"

(*Illinois v. Gates,* 1983, p. 214). Thus, the specifics surrounding each case are judged according to a single constitutional standard. The actions of the officer and the voluntariness of the defendant are then weighed against the constitutional standard. Unfortunately, this case-by-case process leaves officers with no clear understanding of acceptable behavior.

How, then, is deceit and trickery defined? An examination of relevant case law suggests that deceptive police conduct geared toward inducing suspects' confessions falls into three categories: (1) Police misrepresentation of the facts that, if true, would give reason for the suspect to confess or not confess (*Frazier v. Cupp,* 1969); (2) police use of verbal or behavioral techniques to take unfair advantage of the emotions or beliefs of the suspect (*Spano v. New York,* 1959); and (3) police intentionally not informing the suspect of an important fact or circumstance that would decrease the likelihood of a confession (*Moran v. Burbine,* 1986). These arguments are perhaps best defined by Sasaki (1988) as

> the elicitation of a confession from a defendant by the police or their agent through deliberate distortion of material fact, a failure to disclose to the defendant a material fact, or a technique that takes unfair advantage of the defendant's emotional scruples. (p. 34)

Pre-*Miranda* due process cases documenting the Court's view of trickery have been irresolute. The Court indicated in several cases that police trickery was a factor contributing to the conclusion that a suspect's confession was involuntary (*Spano v. New York,* 1959), but the Court never indicated that the use of police trickery would be sufficient by itself to render a confession involuntary. Shortly after *Miranda,* in *Frazier v. Cupp* (1969), the Court held that a confession induced by trickery that both misrepresented the strength of the evidence against the suspect and minimized the suspect's culpability for the offense as admissible and voluntary. The Court concluded that while trickery was relevant under the due process test, it was insufficient to render the confession involuntary (White, 1998). *Frazier v. Cupp* is still the most cited U.S. Supreme Court case regarding the issue of trickery and deceit to date.

In post-*Miranda* cases, the predominant argument from legal scholars is that suspects cannot voluntarily waive their *Miranda* rights or confess if doing so is based on trickery or deceit. Weissman (1991) established a test to determine voluntariness with post-*Miranda* waivers. First, the relinquishment of the right must have been voluntary in the sense that it was the product of a free and deliberate choice rather than intimidation, coercion, or deception. Second, the waiver must have been made with full awareness of both the nature of the right being abandoned and the consequences of the decision to abandon it. Only if the totality of the circumstances surrounding the interrogation reveals both an un-coerced choice and the appropriate level of comprehension may the court properly conclude the *Miranda* rights were waived voluntarily.

The Social Scientists

To comply with the guidelines established in *Miranda*, many police officers changed their interrogation techniques to a subtler, more psychologically based format. The new techniques relied on rapport building, deceit, trickery and manipulation through pragmatic inference (Kassin & McNall, 1991). Confessions were gained by luring suspects into a false sense of security, often compared to a confidence game by critics (Leo, 1996). Deceit, trickery, and manipulation varied in scope and intensity depending on the investigating officer, the suspect, and the type of offense. Hence, crimes were maximized in capacity and penalty projections were exaggerated. The officer minimized other crimes with such statements as, "I would have done the same thing under the circumstances." Deceit and trickery may have included the officer indicating a witness who had identified the suspect or evidence against the suspect, which in fact was nonexistent (Ofshe, 1989). These kinds of statements cloud the true nature of the crime and infer to suspects that the trouble they are in is either minimal or worse than it actually is (Kassin, 1997; Kassin & Neumann, 1997).

Social scientists argue that the use of such "mind games" is tantamount to manipulation, effectively calling into question the voluntariness of a suspect's *Miranda* waiver. Critics of deceit and trickery argue that suspects are incapable of freely and voluntarily waiving their *Miranda* rights when that decision is based on inaccurate, or misleading, information supplied by the police themselves (Roppe, 1994). Psychologists claim that those techniques, coupled with a suspect's mental state—due to stress, emotional balance, IQ, or drug and alcohol abuse—effectively obviate the legality of any waiver a suspect may provide, as well as increase the likelihood of a false confession (Dillingham, 1996).

The Philosophers

The arguments provided by legal and social scientists are not inclusive; the use of trickery and deceit raises other ethical concerns as well—specifically, the strict nature of right and wrong (Brown, 1998). One argument contends that the use of lies is not good or bad in and of itself, and that good lies, those that provide benefit to someone, need not be justified (Shibles, 1985). Other justifications include lying to liars and the use of lies for the public good (Bok, 1989a), learning to lie and the effects of deception (Ford, 1996), and the ethics of fair play (Applbaum, 1999).

Bok (1989b) expounds on the issue of deception by placing lies in a justifiable context. Bok says that for deception to be justified, it must first be offered as a defensible, public statement—that is, an announcement that the communicator is willing to support openly and publicly. Second, the deception must be directed at reasonable persons, in other words, those who are fully capable of informed moral choice. If, for example, a society has openly debated the use of unmarked police vehicles and chosen to allow their use to lull speeders into a false sense of confidence, then those who chose to exceed the posted speed limit must decide whether or not to take their chances. Bok argues that the primary rationale for the use of lies or deceit is derived from the general tenets of police work. Because the state has a duty to protect the lives and property of its citizens, police (as the most visible public arm of the state) have the right to use force, trickery, and coercion when necessary to perform their function—that is, to protect citizens against those who would injure or interfere with their personal lives and property.

Communitarian, libertarian, and utilitarian perspectives differ regarding the use of trickery or deceit by police. Communitarians, for the most part, fall somewhere between individualists, who champion autonomy, and social conservatives, who advocate social order (Etzioni, 1996). Communitarians feel a good society is one that achieves a balance between social order and autonomy; thus, it is necessary to establish a set of shared values that bind and benefit the entire community. Therefore, a communitarian would likely view deception as wrong based on moral standards but support the technique if the deception benefited the community as a whole.

Libertarians champion individual rights and limited, if any, government involvement in their lives (Rothbard, 2002). Accordingly, law enforcement would be the responsibility of contracted service providers, paid for by the individual or the insurance company. This model is based on the idea that insurance companies are ultimately responsible to the victims of crime, as well as the payment of any restitution. Therefore, it is insurance companies who would ultimately benefit from such protections. Libertarians would most likely reject the use of deceit or trickery and move, instead, to arbitration between the criminal and victim, whereas an agreement would be reached based on the best individual needs for both parties.

Those operating from a utilitarian paradigm, on the other hand, strive for outcomes that bring about maximum happiness for the greatest number of people (Kidder, 1995). Each action is judged on its possible outcomes, and no action can be deemed either bad or good until the anticipated outcome is known. Using this model, trickery and deceit would probably be viewed positively. The community would see the arrest by police and subsequent conviction of the suspect as a benefit to the community as a whole, while the suspect's unhappiness would be limited to only one person.

The English Model of Investigative Interviewing

In 1984, the Police and Criminal Evidence Act (PACE) completely changed the interview and interrogation process in England and Wales. Prior to the inception of PACE, the interrogation strategies in the American and English systems were comparable. Both were adversarial in nature. Both had obtaining confessions as a primary goal.

There are several reasons why England chose to examine their interviewing practices. In the early 1980s, public attitude surveys discovered a deep-rooted concern about the integrity of the police when questioning suspects. Many citizens felt the use of threats and unfair pressures in questioning were widespread. Indeed, surveys indicated that one in 10 citizens felt the police did, in fact, fabricate evidence (Williamson, 1993). A second reason that England chose to investigate their system was a study conducted by the Royal Commission, which found that confessions in an adversarial system carried great weight. Data suggested that in approximately 13% of cases, law enforcement lacked the ability to meet *prima facie* standards without a confession. Trying to understand the importance of confession evidence, the commission began an observational research study of police questioning (Royal Commission on Criminal Procedure, 1981). The study found that police tactics often produced unreliable results and, sometimes, false confessions. Some of the factors contributing to false confessions are

1. violence or threats of violence;

2. the effects of custody;

3. psychological tactics;

4. suspects who were "at risk" and liable to make false confessions; and

5. unethical behavior on the part of police.

In addition to the factors identified above, Walkley (1983) surveyed 100 police detectives as to their preparedness to use threats or violence in the interrogation room. The results were substantial:

1. Forty-three percent agreed with the statement, "It is sometimes helpful to slap a suspect around the face."

2. Seven percent agreed with the statement, "If I think the suspect needs a good chiding to help him think about admitting an offense, then I give him one, providing all the circumstances are right."

3. Fifty-one percent agreed with the statement, "Some suspects expect rough treatment in police stations, and if it suits the circumstances, I don't do anything to allay their fears."

4. Fifty-six percent agreed with the statement, "Police officers should never use any form of violence to get the suspect to speak the truth."

5. The above dropped to 33% when the statement was presented in the form, "It is wrong to suggest physical violence toward a suspect."

Given the information above, England commissioned several studies to better understand the interrogation process, as well as the psychology of the persons being interviewed. Gisli Gudjonsson, a leading psychiatrist in London, eventually produced more than 30 studies on the subject (e.g., Gudjonsson, 1991, 1992, 1993, 1994, 1995a, 1995b; Gudjonsson, Kopelman, & MacKeith, 1999). The primary focus of the research was to identify (1) why suspects confess, (2) whether persons who confess have a psychological vulnerability, and (3) whether personality type played a role. Gudjonsson identified the following key findings:

1. The primary reason people confessed was the amount of evidence against them.

2. Younger suspects were more likely to confess than older suspects.

3. There was no difference found between trait (internal) and state (external) anxiety regarding those who confessed.

4. There was no evidence found that vulnerable people were more likely to confess than their counterparts.

5. Suspects were three times more likely to confess if they admitted to illicit drug or alcohol use within the past 24 hours.

6. Having a legal advisor present reduced the number of confessions by 20%.

Gudjonsson's findings, combined with a lagging public perception of police professionalism, the number of false confessions being obtained, and law enforcement's apparent willingness to use inappropriate tactics, prompted England to alter their system. In 1984, and revised in 1995, PACE and its Codes of Conduct were introduced to regulate the detention, treatment, and questioning of persons by the police. The new questioning process became known as Investigative Interviewing. This tactic was used in lieu of interrogation and its primary focus is that of fact-finding, not confessions (Sear & Williamson, 1999; Williamson, 1993).

The Principles of Investigative Interviewing

The first principle of Investigative Interviewing is intended to shift police focus away from a traditional prosecutorial orientation, and toward a fact-finding search for truth. This philosophical shift altered the investigator's role from one of adversary to a more neutral position when gathering information from suspects, victims, and witnesses. The second principle encouraged officers to approach investigations with an open mind, instead of the customary focus of "suspect, therefore interrogate." This principle challenges officers to conduct proper, thorough, professional investigations and collect good, solid evidence before questioning a suspect. This process relates directly to Gudjonsson's (1991) finding that the primary reason suspects confess is the amount of evidence against them. These principles allowed the police to effectively shift from interrogators to investigative fact finders.

The final principle encourages officers to be fair by emphasizing the ethical duties and responsibilities of professional law enforcement. The Investigative Interviewing model was designed to bolster police credibility in subsequent court proceedings where their actions may be questioned. This was especially important when dealing with persons who had special needs, such as low IQs, learning difficulties, or histories of drug or alcohol abuse, or others who were possibly at risk or needing special care (Sear & Williamson, 1999).

Unlike techniques still in wide use in the United States, Investigative Interviewing recommends a nonconfrontational approach with the emphasis clearly on gathering information rather than obtaining confessions. The recommended model is based on the following steps: (1) Prepare and plan for the interview; (2) engage the suspect and explain, through rapport building, the purpose of the interview; (3) obtain the interviewee's account of the circumstances; (4) close the interview by allowing the suspect to ask questions; (5) advise the suspect what will happen next; and (6) evaluate the information obtained by placing it in context with other known information (Gudjonsson, 1994).

Within the process articulated above, each interview is recorded, using either video or audiotape. This provides a permanent record of the interview that may be reviewed in judicial proceedings, particularly where police misconduct is alleged. Also, a third party, called an *appropriate adult*, is present during the interview to protect the accused against unfair interviewing tactics or to ensure that any of the suspect's vulnerabilities are not exploited (Gudjonsson, 1994).

What has taken place in England appears to be progress toward a fairer and nonaccusatorial system of interviewing (Gudjonsson, 1994). The change was necessary to quash negative public perceptions of police and to reduce the number of unreliable confessions being documented. Given the debate and constant criticism in the United States concerning society's rights versus individual rights and who is allowed to interpret them, it seems appropriate to raise the following question: Would police in the United States benefit by adopting the English model?

Police Philosophies and Practices

Without discounting the important issues articulated above, of particular interest is the perspective of law enforcement professionals regarding the use of deceit or trickery during the interrogation process. The courts, legal scholars, and social scientists have all addressed the issue of deceit in some fashion, but little has been heard from actual police officers. What are the perspectives of those who actually participate in the process of using deceit or trickery?

How do they justify their behavior? Are officers' perceptions similar to those outlined above, or do officers limit their use of deceit or trickery to certain types of criminal offenses, such as rape or robbery? Does the benefit to the community, weighted against an officer's moral or ethical standard, provide adequate justification?

Law enforcement officers are not the only occupation to face such ethical questions. A similar issue, one that centered on the justification of deceit or lying, was recently posed to members of the medical community. The study asked doctors whether they would lie on insurance forms to obtain care they believed would benefit their patients. The deception was to avoid denials and obtain treatment that insurance companies felt unnecessary and refused to cover under existing policies. The results indicated that a staggering 50% of those surveyed would lie to obtain the necessary treatment (Freeman, Rathore, Weinfurt, Schulman, & Sulmasy, 1999). In a similar study, the number of physicians who were willing to sanction deception through misrepresentation of facts increased if they felt the appeal process with insurers was longer, the appeal success rate lower, or if the health condition of the patient worsened (Werner, Alexander, Fagerlin, & Ubel, 2002).

The interesting part of this research and the reaction to it, both from within the medical community and from the public at large, is that most of those questioned believed the doctors were justified because the use of deceit would benefit the patient. Others who agreed with the use of deceit justified its use by adopting an "us against them" attitude toward the insurance industry. Thus, the question becomes, If members of the community were asked the same question regarding the use of deceit to gain a confession from a criminal suspect, would the response mirror the earlier medical studies? More specifically, is the use of deceit or trickery justified based on the best interests of the community or the removal of a criminal from society?

Within the medical community, the interviewing of suspects, or assistance provided to law enforcement regarding the interviewing of suspects, has grown tremendously given the move to a more psychologically based approach. The American Medical Association (AMA) and American Psychological Associations (APA) have put forth statements governing their members' involvement with interrogations (Behnke, 2006). The APA concludes that psychologists and physicians have an ethical responsibility to the individual under questioning, as well as to third parties and the public. The AMA emphasizes the ethical obligation to society by defining interrogation as questioning related to military or national security intelligence that is intended to prevent harm or danger to individuals, the public, or national security. Both policies are consistently driven by the "do no harm" mandate (p. 66).

Considering the range of perspectives concerning interrogation techniques, individual officers often find themselves waging a battle on several fronts: first, against members of the community who demand to be served and protected; second, against members of the social sciences who question police tactics based on their negative impact on suspects, as well as the ever-present possibility of false confessions; and finally, against members of the courts who pass judgment on police actions, procedure, and the application of law. For these reasons, officers continually feel judged by those outside the law enforcement community, effectively forcing officers to seek gratitude from their peers for a job well done (Ruffin, 2002).

Law Enforcement Attitudes on Deceit and Trickery

Before proceeding any further, and at the risk of appearing redundant, it is necessary to state the obvious. The benefits of confessions are irrefutable. Many police officers press hard and use any and all means necessary to obtain such evidence. The use of deceit is commonplace. Investigators often distort the available evidence, the credibility of witness statements, and the role of defense counsel in an effort to obtain an incriminating admission or confession. It can also be inferred from the tone used by officers that confessions bring about leniency from the courts (Kipnis, 1976), a belief often played on by police.

For these and other reasons, Newton (1998) argues for an ethical standard regarding the interview process, pointing out that most standards focus on the collection of evidence, not the ethical treatment of suspects. First, despite the wealth of legal rules concerning the criminal justice process, there are areas where police officers are left to exercise significant personal discretion. Indeed, it is during this time, when the suspect and officer interact, that there is virtually no supervision and the interaction is void of any real accountability. The lack of supervision and accountability occurs when the need for ethical conduct is at its greatest.

Second, an ethical standard is necessary to facilitate professionalism among the police services. To achieve greater professionalism, law enforcement agencies must move toward greater technical expertise, increased use of technology, and a more sophisticated manipulation of the media to resist further increases in the external regulation of police activity. To achieve these goals, Newton (1998) suggests a twofold code of ethics. First, departments should adopt a formal code of ethics, a code that is familiar to, and followed by, all members of the agency—regardless of the type of crime or offender being interrogated. Second, an informal code of ethics should be established, a code characterized by colleagues actively policing their own. Thus, an officer who witnesses a colleague behaving inappropriately during an interrogation would mentor, counsel, or apply the appropriate level of peer pressure necessary to bring the offending officer's behavior in line with the agency's formal code of ethics, effectively negating the need for outside intervention.

There has been a substantial amount of research concerning attitudes toward police, but few projects have been completed regarding attitudes of police. Many departments and individual officers have adopted the

"Oath of Honor" put forth by the International Association of Chiefs of Police, which states, in part, "On my honor, I will never betray my badge, my integrity, my character, or the public trust" (IACP, n.d.). However, questions about how the routine use of deception impacts officers' integrity and character, as well as how the public view officers' trustworthiness once it is learned that deception was used to gain a confession, have long remained unanswered.

Research on Law Enforcement Attitudes

What is missing from the previous discussions is the opinion of law enforcement officers toward the use of deceit or trickery during interrogations. Answering this question accomplishes two goals. First, it provides a voice from the practitioner's perspective; second, it offers valuable data about officers' attitudes and perspectives that can be analyzed to determine differences based on variables, such as age, gender, race, training, education, geographical location, and agency size. Moreover, the legal issues of voluntariness and coercion have shifted from the suspect's state of mind to improper influences on their freedom of choice by police (Alschuler, 1997). This shift from a focus on voluntariness to due process invites a review of police methods.

Ruffin (2002) surveyed 446 law enforcement professionals from 97 different departments, including local, state, and federal agencies. The research combined data from a 30-question survey with in-depth interviews of 16 "elite" participants who were selected specifically on the basis of their expertise to clarify information from the survey data. The survey addressed three primary questions: (1) What perceptions do officers have about their use of trickery and deceit to obtain confessions or admissions? (2) What are their perceptions about the use of trickery and deceit as its use applies to *Miranda* and the *Miranda* warnings? and (3) Do officers perceive that using trickery and deceit as a tactic that removes voluntariness from a confessions or admissions? The survey questions were later broken down into seven major sub-questions. The following outlines the study's major findings:

Sub-question 1: Do interviewing techniques change based on type of crime or type of offender? Seventy-six percent of officers surveyed believe that different interviewing techniques are required for different crimes, for example, those classified as felonies versus those classified as misdemeanors. The type of offender may also require different techniques. Of those officers surveyed, 50.4% shift to a more aggressive style when dealing with repeat offenders. Based on these results, a softer approach may or may not be taken with a first-time offender. Statistically, male officers (78.2%) are more prone to change their technique than their female counterparts (62.5%), and all races tend to agree that techniques need to change based on the type of crime.

Sub-question 2: Is the use of deceit and trickery viewed differently if used before and/or after the Miranda *warnings have been given, which may question the waiver or subsequent confession?* Seventy-one percent of officers surveyed believe that deceit and trickery are appropriate tools to obtain confessions. Officers from the Northeast and Midwest also believe that trickery and deceit are appropriate to obtain a waiver of *Miranda* rights. Fewer non-White officers support deceit and trickery as acceptable tools (17.6%) compared to White officers (74.7%).

Sub-question 3: What is the officer perception of the Miranda *warnings? Should the warnings be abolished or maintained as is?* Seventy-one percent of officers surveyed believe that *Miranda* warnings are a true safeguard for the protection of rights and should be maintained, but not at the level of a constitutional protection. Officers from departments in the Northeast tend to recognize *Miranda* warnings as a constitutional right (51%), whereas officers from the Southeast (41%) and Midwest (43%) do not. Officers from the Western region were undecided.

Sub-question 4: Is there a justification for the use of deceit and trickery, and what is the ultimate goal of the interview? Sixty-four percent of officers surveyed believe that one of the primary goals of interviews is to obtain a confession or an admission of guilt. To that end, a majority of responding officers (49.3%) believe deceit and trickery are justified if their use results in the suspect being removed from the community. Statistically, officers from larger departments are less reliant on confessions than those from smaller departments.

Sub-question 5: What are the officer perceptions of the effects of deceit and trickery during an interview? What is the effect on innocent persons, on the confession, on the image of police, and on the voluntariness of the suspect's decision to confess or waive his or her Miranda *protections?* Of the officers surveyed, 71.3% have a strong belief that people will not confess to a crime they did not commit, and 47.1% of the officers believe the use of deceit and trickery have no negative impact on police professionalism, police ethics, or on the voluntariness of a suspect to provide a valid *Miranda* waiver or confession. Education levels may impact this belief in that those with a high school or associates degree tend to not support the use of false evidence (54%), while officers with higher levels of education tend to support the use of false evidence (63%).

Sub-question 6: What are the officer perceptions on changing the current system of interviewing to a nonadversarial system? Police officers are adamantly opposed to the implementation of a nonadversarial system in the United States. Eighty-three percent of White officers feel this type of system would lower confession rates and become a barrier to accomplishing the goal of solving crimes. Non-White officers agree (64.4%), but would be more open to the nonadversarial system. A majority of responding officers (59.4%) agree that the introduction of a nonadversarial system would not increase confession rates. Those officers from departments having 100–1,000 officers are the most opposed to a new system (61.1%).

Sub-question 7: Should officers be held civilly liable for violations of Miranda? Fifty-one percent of officers surveyed do not believe they or their departments should be held civilly liable for violations of *Miranda*. The officers oppose departmental policies restricting the use of trickery and deceit (59.6%). Those officers from the Northeast (75.7%) and Midwest (63.7%) were the most likely to use deceit or trickery to obtain a *Miranda* waiver.

Based on the study results, several conclusions can be drawn that are relevant to the attitudes of law enforcement professionals toward the use of deceit or trickery during interrogation. First, it appears that police officers in the sample do not believe that it is wrong to use deceit or trickery as investigative tools, especially as it relates to *Miranda* or subsequent waivers. By failing to recognize the current trends in the social sciences and academics, officers may expose themselves and their departments to civil liability. Second, officers must realize the benefit of policing their own in regards to interrogation tactics and standards. Failing to do so may result in an officer's demise by having the court regulate their behavior.

Lastly, officers may now be faced with direct personal civil liability for violations of *Miranda*. In *McNally-Bey v. City of Santa Monica et al.* (1999), officers were sued for violations of *Miranda*. The officers claimed qualified immunity, but the U.S. District Court denied the motion. On appeal to the U.S. Court of Appeals, the court ruled that individuals who allege interrogation in violation of *Miranda* are in fact alleging a constitutional violation and officers cannot rely on training and training material to guarantee them qualified immunity. This case established *Miranda* warnings as a constitutional standard.

Each of these findings are significant given that the present research showed that officers (1) believe it is appropriate to use deceit or trickery to obtain a *Miranda* waiver, (2) fail to acknowledge that they or their department should be held liable, and (3) fail to recognize that policy should be established to govern the use of deceit and trickery.

Summary

The *Miranda* decision has, in some respects, been credited with use of trickery and deceit in criminal interrogations. These methods, practiced almost exclusively by American law enforcement, are based on an adversarial system of law, with confessions as one of the primary goals of many police interrogations. Law enforcement in the United States responded to the changing demands of *Miranda* by adopting a more subtle and sophisticated psychological approach to interrogations (Gudjonsson, 1992), which has resulted in increasing levels of criticism from the courts, social scientists, and philosophers. While other countries have carefully reexamined the methods of interrogation employed by law enforcement professionals, American law enforcement agencies have continued to pursue an adversarial system, often employing deceit or trickery to gain *Miranda* waivers and confessions.

Based on research findings in the areas of Investigative Interviewing and law enforcement officer attitudes toward the use of deceit and trickery in criminal interrogations, it appears that law enforcement agencies should establish internal polices and directives to ensure a fair, equitable, and legal interrogation process. These policies should be written with full awareness of the fact that officers frequently change their interrogation techniques based on the type of crime and/or type of offender. Supervisors who oversee criminal interrogations should recognize the emotional energy generated by crime and offender type and monitor closely the actions and techniques of officers.

The following recommendations are offered:

1. All internal departmental training programs should be reviewed to ensure that training programs are consistent with constitutional standards regarding *Miranda*, *Miranda* waivers, and voluntariness. External training programs should be held to the same standard by meeting both the constitutional standard and departmental policy.

2. Attorneys, representing each agency or department, should partner with their respective agencies to act as third-party reviewers of policy. Attorneys should review all relevant training material and, as needed, monitor internal and external training programs to ensure compliance.

3. All felony-level cases should be videotaped or audiotaped to provide protection for both the officer and suspect.

4. Law enforcement agencies should slowly begin integrating the components of Investigative Interviewing. Changing officer attitudes regarding our judicial process from an adversarial system to a nonadversarial system; moving to a fact-finding investigative interview versus the primary goal of obtaining a confession; and having a third party present to protect the suspect from overzealous police tactics.

Returning to the opening scenario, how would these recommendations have impacted Sam's decision to confess? There may have been a departmental policy prohibiting Detective Smith from using props and false evidence. Detective Smith may have received training on rapport building and fact finding versus the adversarial approach of pitting Sam against Bob and baiting Sam with false evidence. And how would the process look if Sam had a third-party advocate in the room to protect his interest? More likely than not, the end result would have been the same, a confession or incriminating statement; however, the goal would have been achieved without the potential liability and negative impact on the officer, the offender, and the department.

Discussion Questions

1. Do you think "voluntariness" is removed from a *Miranda* waiver if trickery and deceit is used as outlined in the opening scenario?

2. Do you think the courts today are more concerned with protecting individual rights or the rights of the community?

3. How would you feel if the United States adopted a nonadversarial system, such as England's, where all interviews are nonaccusatory, recorded, and witnessed by a disinterested third party?

4. Does the use of trickery and deceit impact an officer's professionalism?

5. Do you feel the *Miranda* warnings have risen to the level of a constitutional standard, whereas an individual may sue an officer for violating a constitutional right?

6. Is lying ethical for public protection? Do the ends justify the means?

References

Alschuler, A. W. (1997). Constraint and confession. *Denver University Law Review, 74*(957), 152–169.

Applbaum, A. I. (1999). *Ethics for adversaries: The morality of roles in public and private life.* Princeton, NJ: Princeton University Press.

Behnke, S. (2006). Ethics and interrogations: Comparing and contrasting the American psychological, American medical, and American Psychiatric Association positions. *American Psychologist, 37*(7), 66.

Bok, S. (1989a). *Lying: Moral choice in public and private life.* New York: Vintage Books.

Bok, S. (1989b). *Secrets: On the ethics of concealment and revelation.* New York: Vintage Books.

Brooks, M. (1989). *Instant rapport.* New York: Warner Books.

Brown, A. L. (1998). *Subjects of deceit: A phenomenology of lying.* Albany: State University of New York Press.

Brown v. Mississippi, 297 U.S. 278 (1936).

Canter, D., & Alison, L. (1999). Interviewing and deception. In D. Canter & L. Alison (Eds.), *Interviewing and deception* (pp. 3–20). Brookfield, VT: Ashgate.

Dillingham, C. (1996, October). Deception in law enforcement interrogations. *Law and Order*, 105–108.

Dilts, R. (1983). *Applications of neuro-linguistic programming* (Vol. 1). Capitola, CA: Meta Publications.

Etzioni, A. (1996). *The new golden rule: Community and morality in a democratic society.* New York: Basic Books.

Ford, C. V. (1996). *Lies, lies, lies: The psychology of deceit.* Washington, DC: American Psychiatric Press.

Frazier v. Cupp, 394 U.S. 731 (1969).

Freeman, V. G., Rathore, S. S., Weinfurt, K. P., Schulman, K. A., & Sulmasy, D. P. (1999). Lying for patients: Physician deception of third-party payers. *Archives of Internal Medicine, 159*(19), 2263–2270.

Gudjonsson, G. H. (1991). Custodial interrogation: Why do suspects confess and how does it relate to their crime, attitude, and personality? *Personality and Individual Differences, 12*(3), 295–306.

Gudjonsson, G. H. (1992). *The psychology of interrogations, confessions, and testimony.* West Sussex, England: John Wiley and Sons.

Gudjonsson, G. H. (1993). Confession evidence, psychological vulnerability, and expert testimony. *Journal of Community and Applied Social Psychology, 3,* 117–129.

Gudjonsson, G. H. (1994). Investigative interviewing: Recent developments and some fundamental issues. *International Review of Psychiatry, 6*(2–3), 237–247.

Gudjonsson, G. H. (1995a). Fitness for interview during police detention: A conceptual framework for forensic assessment. *Journal of Forensic Psychiatry, 6*(1), 185–197.

Gudjonsson, G. H. (1995b). "I'll help you boys as much as I can": How eagerness to please can result in a false confession. *The Journal of Forensic Psychiatry, 6*(2), 333–342.

Gudjonsson, G. H., Kopelman, M. D., & MacKeith, J. A. (1999). Unreliable admissions to homicide: A case of misdiagnosis of amnesia and misuse of abreaction technique. *British Journal of Psychiatry, 174,* 455–459.

International Association of Chiefs of Police (IACP). (n.d.). *The law enforcement oath of honor.* Retrieved from http://www.iacporg/policeservices/executiveservices/ professionalassistance/ethics/whatisthelawenforcementoathofhonor/presen tingthelawenforcementoathofhonor/tabid/160/Default.aspx

Illinois v. Gates, 462 U.S. 213 (1983).

Jayne, B. C., & Buckley, J. P. (1990, Winter). Interrogation alert: Will your next confession be suppressed? *The Investigator, 11–12,* 1–12.

Jensen, S. (1998). *Police using deceit to get confessions: Psychological tricks challenged in court.* Retrieved from http://articles.courant.com/1992-02-16/ news/0000205756_1_confession-suspect-cash-drawer.

Kaci, J. H., & Rush, G. E. (1988, February–March). At what price will we obtain confessions? *Judicature, 71*(5), 254–258.

Kassin, S. M. (1997). The psychology of confession evidence. *American Psychologist, 52*(3), 221–233.

Kassin, S. M., & McNall, K. (1991). Police interrogations and confessions: Communicating promises and threats by pragmatic implication. *Law and Human Behavior, 15*(3), 233–251.

Kassin, S. M., & Neumann, K. (1997). On the power of confession evidence: An experimental test of the fundamental difference hypothesis. *Law and Human Behavior, 21*(5), 469–484.

Kidder, R. (1995). *How good people make tough choices: Resolving the dilemmas of ethical living.* New York: Harper.

Kipnis, K. (1976). Criminal justice and the negotiated plea. *Ethics, 86*(2), 93–106.

Leo, R. A. (1992). From coercion to deception: The changing nature of police interrogation in America. *Crime, Law, and Social Change, 18,* 35–59.

Leo, R. A. (1996). Miranda's revenge: Police interrogations as a confidence game. *Law and Society Review, 30*(2), 259–288.

McKenzie, I. K. (1994). Regulating custodial interviews: A comparative study. *International Journal of the Sociology of the Law, 22,* 239–259.

McNally, James and Bey, James J., v. City of Santa Monica et al., 195 F. 3rd 1039 (1999).

Miranda v. Arizona, 384 U.S. 436 (1966).

Moran v. Burbine, 475 U.S. 412 (1986).

Newton, T. (1998). The place of ethics in investigative interviewing by police officers. *The Howard Journal, 37*(1), 52–69.

Ofshe, R. (1989). Coerced confessions: The logic of seemingly irrational action. *Cultural Studies Journal, 6,* 6–15.

Roppe, L. H. (1994). True blue? Whether police should be allowed to use trickery and deception to extract confessions. *San Diego Law Review, 31*(729), 4–33.

Rothbard, M. (2002). *For a new liberty: The libertarian manifesto.* New York: Macmillan.

Royal Commission on Criminal Procedure. (1981). *Report, Cmnd 8092.* London: HMSO.

Ruffin, J. (2002). *Law enforcement perspectives on the use of trickery and deceit during the interrogation process* (Doctoral dissertation). (UMI No. TX5-527-358).

Sasaki, D. W. (1988). Guarding the guardians: Police trickery and confessions. *Stanford Law Review, 40*(1593), 32–51.

Sear, L., & Williamson, T. (1999). British and American interrogation strategies. In D. Canter & L. Alison (Eds.), *Interviewing and deception* (pp. 65–81). Brookfield, VT: Ashgate.

Shibles, W. (1985). *Lying: A critical analysis.* Whitewater, WI: The Language Press.

Skoe, E. E., & Ksionzky, S. (1985). Target personality characteristics and self disclosure: An exploratory study. *Journal of Clinical Psychology, 41*(1), 14–21.

Spano v. New York, 360 U.S. 315 (1959).

Thompson, G. S., & Jenkins, J. B. (1993). *Verbal judo: The gentle art of persuasion.* New York: William Morrow and Co.

Walkley, J. (1983). *Police interrogation: A study of psychology, theory, and practice of police interrogations and the implications for police training* (Unpublished master's thesis). Cranfield Institute of Technology, London.

Weissman, J. C. (1991). Modern confession law after Duckworth v. Eagan: What's the use of explaining? *Indiana Law Review, 66*(825), 91–110.

Werner, R. M., Alexander, C. G., Fagerlin, A., & Ubel, P. A. (2002). The hassle factor: What motivates physicians to manipulate reimbursement rules? *Archives of Internal Medicine, 162*(10), 1134–1139.

White, W. S. (1998). What is an involuntary confession now? *Rutgers Law Review, 50*(2001), 52–90.

Williamson, T. M. (1993). From interrogation to investigative interviewing: Strategic trends in police questioning. *Journal of Community and Applied Social Psychology, 3,* 89–99.

13

Police Exams and Cheating

The Ultimate Test of Ethics

Alexandro Villanueva

The subject of this chapter is best introduced by a simple op-ed article, which appeared recently in the *Delaware County Daily News* (PA). In it, the editor laments how 15 members of local law enforcement agencies ended their careers in a rather odd way: They cheated on a state recertification test for peace officers. Pennsylvania's Municipal Police Officers Education and Training Commission alleged that the answers to the test were compromised, and according to the editor,

> And just like that, more than a dozen careers went up in smoke. But here's the weird part. From everything we've been told, it is almost impossible to fail this mandated Act 180 exam. In fact, if for some reason you do not pass, you get to take the test again. Given all that, why would you risk your career by allegedly cheating on the exam? (Heron, 2011, p. 5)

Throughout the United States, law enforcement agencies big and small tend to be focal points of the evening news, be it the reporting of crimes, newsworthy arrests, or allegations of misconduct by sworn peace officers. Two frequent topics of police misconduct are cheating and the abuse of executive authority, particularly in the arenas of promotional processes and decision making (Mitchell, 2011; Mondo, 2010; Ofgang, 2011). The fact that cheating can exist within a public entity, which by design is entrusted with upholding the rule of law, can be disturbing. As succinctly described by Rich Martin (2011), from the Rochester (NY) Police Department, "Leadership that allows for mediocrity to first exist and then remain, rather than demanding the highest level of conduct within a department, can create a climate ripe for misconduct" (p. 14).

This chapter repeatedly explores the all-important question of why people cheat in a variety of law enforcement settings, such as promotional examinations. The sheer number of cases presented, even by way of a cursory search, can be somewhat alarming given the prominent role law enforcement plays in many modern societies, especially in developed countries that include the United States, Great Britain, and Canada. The chapter offers a typology of cheating, a brief theoretical background of the civil service system, and a sampling of incidents that have been reported in various news media and commentaries, including social media. The chapter concludes with a set of recommendations designed to address the gravity of cheating within law enforcement settings, as well as strategies for more fair and equitable standards throughout the law enforcement promotional process.

A Rudimentary Typology

American society has historically given high marks to law enforcement, which, according to a recent national survey conducted by Gallup, identified law enforcement as one of the few institutions that received a confidence rating greater than 50% (Saad, 2010). Given that one of the primary tasks of officers is to provide sworn testimony in courts of law, evidence of unethical conduct and cheating can serve to undermine the public's general confidence in law enforcement. On the other hand, those officers who choose to cheat may experience what psychologists commonly refer to as *cognitive dissonance*— that is, a state of psychological discomfort brought on by a set of incongruent cognitions and behaviors (Festinger, 1957). For example, if a police officer who has been hired to uphold the law cheats on a promotional examination, he must find a way to rationalize his unethical behavior in a way that allows him to maintain an appropriate self-image, that of a law-abiding citizen and champion of justice. This can be accomplished by rationalizing his behavior (e.g., "I will make an excellent sergeant"), denying the legitimacy of the exam (e.g., "The testing process is unfair), blaming the testing process (e.g., "If the department doesn't want people to cheat, they should come up with a better process), or appealing to a greater good (e.g., "The department needs good sergeants and I will be one of the best") (Fitch, 2011).

There are a variety of activities that fall within the umbrella of promotional cheating, and they vary depending on the relationship between the cheater and the organization in question. A commonly reported activity is testing material security breaches, wherein cadets and in-service officers receive confidential testing information in advance of the actual examination (McCullough, 2010; Schmitt, 1994; Sherman, 2011). These incidents can involve only a handful of individuals, as in the Denver Sheriff's office (Reza, 1990; Sherman, 2011), or a small group, such as the 10 recruits dismissed from the Maryland Transportation Authority police academy (Dresser, 2011). While signing off on the dismissal of the 10 recruits, the chief of the agency, Marcus L. Brown, stated,

From day one, MDTA Police recruits are expected to uphold our core principles of honesty, integrity, dignity and dedication. I personally delivered this expectation to Recruit Class #44 at Family Night before the Training Academy started. . . . Deviation from these principles is not tolerated, and I commend the MDTA Police Command Staff for their swift and decisive actions. (Dresser, 2011, p. 11)

There are also reports of large groups, as indicated by a police certification scandal that erupted in North Carolina ("18 N.C. Officers," 2004), the infamous Naval Academy cheating scandal (Schmitt, 1994), and the Prince George County Police Academy (Ly, 2010). Other possibilities include the manipulation of the testing results themselves to achieve a predetermined result, such as allowing an idle promotional list to expire because of concerns regarding the diversity, or lack thereof, of the individuals whose names appeared on the list (Stoecker & Gendreau, 2012).

A third avenue for gaming promotional examinations exists with the offices of those who are charged with overseeing the process itself. Manipulating the testing process by advancing individuals who have failed a particular component of the examination, and then promoting them over individuals who successfully completed each phase, is one way (Diaz, 2011). Another way is for subject matter experts who develop promotional tests to participate in mentoring prospective promotional applicants, thus giving them an unfair advantage over other candidates (ABC7 News, 2010; Begin, 2011; Cory, 1979). This method, if skewed towards an identifiable group of employees, can result in rather odd demographics concerning the individuals promoted, often failing to reflect the demographics of the candidate pool (Cory, 1979).

A fourth method of steering promotional processes to a predetermined conclusion is available only to those with access to political decision makers willing to change rules. A good example of this behavior was exhibited by former sheriff Mike Carona, who lobbied the Orange County Board of Supervisors to change the eligibility requirements for executive positions within his agency, thus allowing the hiring of his campaign supporters, Assistant Sheriffs George Jaramillo and Don Haidl. Ultimately, "Team Forever" was found guilty or pled guilty to corruption and all were eventually removed from office in disgrace (Welborn, 2008).

A Note of Caution

Not every incident that makes the news is proof of a problem, but merely an illustration of its potential existence. The same is true in regard to police cheating, where allegations are constantly surfacing in the media. One example, as reported in the *San Antonio Express News*, alleged that 16 officers from the San Antonio Police Department were involved in a cheating scandal. Only when reading through the actual news article does the reader learn that the matter involved a violation of testing protocols, such as talking in line, versus actually cheating with exam material. As the chief of police, William McManus, stated,

> I think everyone jumped on the word 'cheating.' That's what garnered all the (media) attention. Cheating and violating testing protocols are two different things. One is more serious than the other. This was not about cheating and the outcome did not show cheating. . . . I spoke with each officer and we all had good conversations. Each understood how (violating procedure) could be perceived. It's about the integrity of the testing process and the integrity of the entire department coming into question. (cited in Mondo, 2010, pp. 3–8)

Given the exposure suffered by a law enforcement agency when allegations of cheating are made public, it is not difficult to understand an organization's reluctance to admit a breakdown in important personnel processes, such as promotional examinations.

In summary, the ethical issues that arise during promotional examinations can manifest themselves in a variety of ways. These include compromising and using compromised testing material, manipulating testing results, providing unfair advantages to select candidates by gaming the testing process itself, and changing the rules of the game to suit a predetermined outcome. These various practices can also be used in combination with one another, further compromising the integrity of the processes involved. Given the insidious nature of the promotional activities described above, what are the implications for those who game civil service systems to advantage their allies, and what is the impact on the ethicality of both beneficiaries and affected agency employees?

Theoretical Background

The civil service system, a ubiquitous feature in American government systems, can be found at the federal, state, and local levels. Throughout the first half of the 19th century and prior to the implementation of civil service reform, government jobs were mostly obtained via political spoils:

> The Pendleton Act was a direct response to decades of abuse of the federal civil service system since its inception in 1789. These abuses ultimately reached unprecedented proportions from the Jacksonian era to the years immediately following the Civil War, when reform groups began to champion the civil service cause and equate public service with merit. (Smith, 1983, para. 2)

Note the reference to merit, which in modern times has become synonymous with civil service systems and a foundational component of purported government operations. Even the relatively recent term *meritocracy*, according to *Merriam-Webster*, signifies a system in which the talented, rather than the wealthy or privileged, are advanced on the basis of their achievement ("Meritocracy," n.d.). Cheating, on the other hand, represents an attempt to subvert achievement through honest means—in other words, an end-run around the common understanding of merit.

Max Weber and Bureaucracy

After the Pendleton Act, and the decline of influence of Tammany Hall, the rise of bureaucracies governed by civil service rules was a prominent characteristic of public agencies in the 20th century. Max Weber (1968), the man who popularized the term *bureaucracy*, identified three principal elements of bureaucratic agencies:

1. The regular activities of the agents of the organization are defined as "official duties";

2. These duties are relatively stable, and the authority for performing them is strictly bound by rules, as is the coercive authority available for carrying them out; and

3. There are regular, established ways for assuring the continuous enactment of these duties by (and only by) those individuals who meet additional general rules or qualifications. (cited in Harmon & Mayer, 1986, pp. 70–71)

Based on Weber's concept of bureaucracy, it appears that he never contemplated the potential anarchy created by the usurpation of the rule of law by agents of an organization. Even within the framework of his writings at the beginning of the 20th century, there is a connection between stratification of duties by those who meet additional qualifications (see above). Theoretically speaking, how can an organization ensure the enactment of duties if the agents in charge of overseeing have not met the "additional qualifications"?

Given community expectations that law enforcement agencies will uphold the rule of law, the Law Enforcement Code of Ethics, in part, reads, "Honest in thought and deed in both my personal and official life, I will be exemplary in obeying the laws of the land and the regulations of my department" (cited in Payton, 1996, p. 195). The International Association of Chiefs of Police (IACP), through their Police Image and Ethics Committee, has expressed its stance on law enforcement ethics via the following statement:

There is little disagreement among law enforcement administrators that upholding professional ethics is the most critical issue facing our profession. From recruiting and selection, through promotions and assignments, to training and field activities, no other factor weaves such a powerful web through every aspect of policing. (IACP, 2011a, p. 5)

The IACP has also developed an Oath of Honor, which is currently being disseminated nationwide. The code reads as follows:

On my honor, I will never betray my badge, my integrity, my character, or the public trust. I will always have the courage to hold myself and others accountable for our actions. I will always uphold the constitution, my community, and the agency I serve. (IACP, 2011b, p. 3)

Given so much attention to formalizing core value statements, mission statements, a code of ethics, a code of honor, and the oath of office each peace officer cites when completing entry-level training, how does cheating survive in this environment? The Stanford Prison Experiment provides a striking demonstration of how ostensibly "normal" individuals from seemingly "normal" lives, can be profoundly influenced by a host of environmental factors that, under certain conditions, may influence people to engage in destructive behavior toward others without regard to their plight (Haney, Banks, & Zimbardo, 1974). Taking this notion and reframing it around individuals exploiting a promotional system to advance their careers, the destruction occurs when others are denied employment or promotions because they are testing at a presumable disadvantage.

Based on these and other findings in the fields of psychology, sociology, and management, it is not difficult to perceive how individual actors in an organizational setting can engage in unethical behavior that is rewarded when left undetected. Yet, despite this finding, all is not lost. Occasionally, officers can and do step forward and alert organizational leaders to cheating and other forms of malfeasance occurring in their organizations. In the Niagara, Ontario cheating scandal, authorities were alerted by an officer about test questions being leaked in advance of a promotional examination (Seglin, 2011).

Unfortunately, despite the sheer number of unethical incidents reported by the media involving law enforcement professionals, Adams and Balfour (2004) posit that society tends to dismiss acts of administrative evil by presuming they seldom occur, and only in rare circumstances:

A lack of attention to what we believe to be a vitally important concept can be explained by [this] understandable, yet unfortunate, tendency to lament acts of administrative evil, while dismissing them as temporary and isolated aberrations or deviations from proper administrative behavior and rational public policy. (p. 39)

In simplest terms, the fact that cheating occurs within law enforcement agencies is well documented at all levels of the organizational strata. This uncomfortable reality appears to have two distinct modes of occurrence. In the first, individuals within an organization or applicants to the organization attempt to exploit a real or perceived weakness in testing processes for their individual gain. The second, more worrisome, variation is when highly placed individuals or groups of individuals seek to game the promotional system to create or enhance their political control over an organization. This variation, by definition, is the gravest threat to the integrity of law enforcement as a profession due to its capacity to compromise the system itself, in addition to the organization involved.

When Loyalties Conflict

An often-heard phrase in law enforcement circles is that to advance, one needs to learn how to "play the game." What may sound like sage advice for newcomers represents a loaded statement for others. There is almost an air of expectation that career advancement is dependent on political patronage. Addressing this very issue, Barry Baker (2006) stated,

> The true response is that promotions in a police department is a very big deal, and competitive examinations for promotions are okay as long as there's a way to manipulate the outcome . . . the more room for manipulation the better. The simple fact is it's all about power and consolidation of power. It's okay if a police officer promoted has knowledge, but it's more important for that police officer to be known, and acceptable, to those in power. (p. 10)

There are a variety of mechanisms that have been employed by those in law enforcement leadership to consolidate or exert power. One example comes from a successful reverse discrimination lawsuit recently settled with the city of Inglewood, California. The plaintiff's attorneys noted that the defendants manipulated the promotional process to enable non-White candidates to be promoted ahead of the plaintiff, and even allowed non-White candidates to continue in the process after failing the written examination (Diaz, 2011).

Another example of allegations of power consolidation by organizational leaders comes from Cook County, Illinois, where the sheriff alleged his predecessor illegally promoted 396 deputies to the rank of sergeant, lieutenant, and captain (Mount, 1987). Similar allegations have been levied against Washington, DC's assistant chief of police, Diane Groomes, for unlawfully compromising promotional exams during staff training (Fantis, 2010), and former Providence police chief Urbano Prignano Jr. (Sorrentino, 2007).

Returning to the IACP Oath of Honor, the last sentence reads, "I will always uphold the constitution, my community, and the agency I serve" (IACP, 2011b). Note the hierarchy of loyalty implicit in this simple, yet powerful statement: constitution, people, and then organization. Acts of cheating orchestrated by law enforcement leaders to game promotional systems serve to subvert this hierarchy of loyalty, creating morally questionable motives that often fail to serve the public interest. This new hierarchy can easily read as follows: political benefactor, peers, institution. An inherent conflict of loyalty arises when these two hierarchies clash, as a beneficiary of undeserved promotions may serve to consolidate the power base of his benefactor as opposed to advancing the public's interest. Furthermore, as indicated by Adams and Balfour (2004),

> The ethical framework within a technical-rational system posits the primacy of an abstract, utility-maximizing individual while binding professionals to organizations in ways that make them into reliable conduits for the dictates of legitimate authority, which is no less legitimate when it happens to be pursuing an evil policy. (p. 153)

In essence, beneficiaries of political patronage will not hesitate to carry out the dictates from organizational authority figures, as they will substitute their own moral perspectives for those of the institution.

A slight twist to the concept of gaming promotional systems may occur when elected law enforcement leaders demand cash or campaign contributions, either directly or indirectly, through subordinates as demonstrations of loyalty. Without assessing the ability to game a particular promotional system, these efforts can run counter to expected standards of ethical conduct and prevalent laws. According to Beaudet (2011), in an investigation conducted for FOX Undercover,

> Middlesex Sheriff's Office employees routinely paid cash bribes to buy promotions and favorable treatment, nearly a dozen told FOX Undercover in interviews that revealed deep and widespread corruption inside the department.
>
> "I've been to 4–5 parties. I've seen the money counted, $2,100 in one case, $2,300 in another, and handed to the sheriff. He'd put it in his top left hand pocket and then smoke a cigar like it was normal business," one current employee told FOX Undercover. . . . FOX Undercover interviewed nearly a dozen people, mostly current and former employees, who told the same story: cash bribes were given in hundreds, even thousands, of dollars at a time to former Middlesex Sheriff James DiPaola.

The tragedy of this incident does not end with the uncovering of a pay-to-play scheme, as the just-reelected Dipaola ended up committing suicide shortly after this news became public (Beaudet, 2011).

Whistleblowers Anonymous

A relatively recent phenomenon has developed along with the expansion of social media networks. The use of anonymous blog postings to provide commentary about news, social issues, and organizational life has exploded in recent years, and the subject of this chapter is no exception. Behind the safety of anonymity, individuals who otherwise would never comment about employment issues within their organizations are now venting their anger on news websites and amateur blogs. The first example illustrating the phenomenon originates with the Washington, DC Police Department:

> Interesting! Why weren't the other "command staff officials" placed on administrative leave? Chief Lanier are you trying to control the message via damage control? Every "command official" that Assistant Chief Groomes provided the answers to should be on administrative leave and under investigation also. Chief Lanier knows she can not afford to lose Assistant Chief Groomes. The Internal Affairs Division will clear Assistant Chief Groomes of misconduct. How can Assistant Chief Groomes return as head of Patrol when she has been outed as a "cheater." Cheating goes towards integrity, honesty and ethics. (Serpico2, 2010)

As indicated previously, this blog is in reference to the actions of Assistant Chief Groomes that appeared to favor her subordinates unfairly in a promotional testing process. This caused the chief to temporarily suspend her while the investigation was ongoing. She was ultimately absolved of any wrongdoing.

Another anonymous blogger vented at the management practices of Maricopa County Sheriff Joe Arpaio, a controversial figure in law enforcement and political circles nationwide. The following comment taken from a local blog is found in an article regarding Arpaio's reelection bid:

> Sheriff Arpaio has ruled the Maricopa County Sheriff's Office with a double standard. What is good for he and his cronies, and what is good for those who work for them. Perhaps the "Hatred" shown by these disloyal people were a result of having to live and work within a once proud Sheriff's Office which has become a haven for the "Good Old Boy Gang" and for civilians who get to play copper by being posseemen? Perhaps then too this was caused by the Deputies becoming tired of Nepotism, double and triple dipping by upper echelon, and visions of being "God Like." It is a well known fact that there is an entirely different standard for the rank and file opposed to those of the Sheriff's Office in command. (BoxcarBob, 2008)

Note the recurrent theme regarding double standards: one for those who enjoy the patronage of the department head, another for those who do not. This same theme continues to resurface in allegations of cronyism, nepotism, and tokenism in law enforcement agencies throughout the nation.

This third entry was submitted in response to investigative reporting following the Providence (RI) Police cheating scandal:

> It was unfortunate that Ryan and his cohorts were not charged criminally, some of the cheaters have stayed on the job despite their

fraudulent rank, while others have escaped and receive their full pensions to this day. It would be interesting to see the list of names, of those who were called into the FBI office and the Grand Jury, I am sure that we would see some familiar faces in the current police administration. Ryan displayed a complete lack of ethics and morals which was recognized and valued by those at city hall and the police administration during that period, as a result he was able to cause the careers of many good and honest officers to wither on the vine, while those who were connected to the regime were advanced despite their lack of qualifications and ability. (Retiredguy100, 2010)

This last blog raises the intriguing question of fraudulently obtained rank. Assuming fraud is detected, what becomes of the cheater and their rank?

A close inspection of all three anonymous blogs reveals several interesting characteristics, namely, that the authors appear to have knowledge of internal organizational politics, they do not appreciate contemporary management practices, and they are pining for an overthrow of incumbent administrators. This pattern can be expected to be countered by anonymous bloggers who are or were allies to incumbent administrations and defend their actions vigorously. The question remains, given the internal turmoil suggested by these blogs and the actual public information regarding law enforcement cheating: What is the impact, both short and long term, on the agencies involved?

Political Patronage and Its Legacy

Based on the sheer number of examples of cheating provided in this chapter, one has to assume the actual number is considerably greater than what is reported for obvious reasons. Successful cheating efforts signify that individuals are occupying law enforcement positions and ranks they would not have ordinarily obtained on their own merit. Outside the burden of an occasional guilty conscious (Schmitt, 1994; Sherman, 2011), individuals do not normally turn themselves in for administrative or criminal repercussions. Not only does this run counter to the goals of a merit-based civil service system; it leaves individual organizations hampered by unqualified individuals being employed in key decision-making positions. On the other hand, individuals who honestly compete for employment and promotional opportunities can be discouraged from increasing their value to the community and the organization based on perceptions of unequal rewards (Kreitner & Kinicki, 1989).

Organizational Learning _____

Chris Argyris, a noted organizational development scholar, maintains that impediments exist which often prevent organizations from learning by failing to recognize past mistakes. By failing to recognize such shortcomings, agencies can become entrenched in defending the status quo—that is, their existing policies, procedures, and practices. As Argyris (1993) notes, "[A]n organizational defensive routing is any action, policy, or practice that prevents organizational participants from experiencing embarrassment or threat and, at the same time, prevents them from discovering the causes of the embarrassment or threat" (p. 53).

Cheating in law enforcement promotional or entry-level processes represents both dilemmas—an embarrassment if the public discovers unethical conduct, and a threat to the status quo in the dominant political group. In the instant matter of law enforcement cheating and its inimical relationship with courtroom testimony, attorney Eugene Iredale stated,

> Any act of dishonesty on an officer's part, if sufficiently serious, is relevant on cross-examination to show the person's character is poor . . . if a police officer is willing to cheat on a promotion exam, is he not by the same logic willing to shade or color his testimony on an important case if it could enhance his status for promotion? (cited in Reza, 1990, p. 13)

Given the integral part courtroom testimony plays in the criminal justice system, the mere existence of cheating within a law enforcement organization can expose a serious liability in courtroom proceedings. The fallout of a cheating scandal can reverberate through impeached testimony, new avenues for appeals on cases already adjudicated, and a loss of credibility for any member of an affected organization in sworn testimony.

Based on the examples provided in this chapter, we have seen how cheating in law enforcement organizations has provided the wherewithal for cronyism, nepotism, and tokenism to take root and influence promotional decision making. The consolidation of power in a law enforcement organization, when concentrated in a group of family and friends, can seriously undermine the legitimacy of the agency involved in that enforcing the rule of law can be difficult to achieve among those who show little regard for respecting the rule of law.

Although we have seen how cheating can facilitate tokenism (Cory, 1979; Diaz, 2011), the actual dynamics of tokenism can easily be overlooked. Tokenism provides an artificial appearance of diversity, or window dressing, which permits police leaders to consolidate power while excluding disadvantaged groups. Moreover, beneficiaries of tokenism will often adapt to the norms and values of the advantaged group, even to the point, at times, of disadvantaging their own referent group (Wright, 1991).

Nonetheless, opportunities occasionally surface that allow the organization to recast itself in a new light. One such possibility is the replacement of one top law enforcement official with another, especially when the organization in question has been the subject of scandal, media scrutiny, or public outcry. With the sudden departure of Orange County Sheriff Mike Carona amid allegations of corruption, the board of supervisors screened a number of potential contenders for the position, including current members of the department, before ultimately appointing retired Los Angeles Sheriff's division chief Sandra Hutchens as the new sheriff.

Sheriff Hutchens, concerned with the need to pursue a change in organizational culture, while at the same time preserving institutional knowledge, recruited experienced talent from both within and outside Orange County law enforcement circles (Lowe, 2008). Note that the appointment of an outsider as the agency head, followed by the diverse mixture of experience within her command staff, led to the breakup of an organizational culture in desperate need of change.

Conversely, when a sheriff is defeated in an election by another member of the same organization, the culture of that organization may continue with little, if any, change, simply a different cast of individuals performing the same functions—in other words, business as usual (Faturechi & Leonard, 2012). Likewise, the appointment of a new chief of police follows similar patterns in regard to the potential for change in organizational culture. Examples of this include the appointment of former Philadelphia Police Commissioner Willie Williams to lead the Los Angeles Police Department after the contentious departure of the long-serving former chief Darryl Gates. It wasn't until Bill Bratton that the city of Los Angeles finally reappointed a chief of police to two consecutive terms in office.

Summary

Cheating in law enforcement entry-level and promotional tests is an unfortunate reality, one that carries significant implications for the community and the organizations involved. The size of the problem is severely underreported, as successful attempts at cheating or gaming promotional systems for unethical purposes do not typically generate significant publicity. Discovery of cheating scandals usually comes in the form of individuals who were denied entry or advancement in a law enforcement organization as a direct result of others exploiting testing security weaknesses or administrative misconduct (Diaz, 2011; Mount, 1987; Sorrentino, 2007).

Left unchecked, law enforcement cheating can have a corrosive effect on public confidence, particularly given the status afforded law enforcement agencies as institutions of trust. According to a 2010 Gallup poll on confidence in institutions, law enforcement ranked the third highest in a list of 16 institutions, garnering 59% of respondents who reported a great deal or quite a lot of confidence (Saad, 2010). On a more somber note, according to the American Society for Public Administration (2012), there has been a near universal drop in trust in government around the world.

There are a number of activities that can strengthen law enforcement organizations and shield them from cheating scandals; however, these solutions cannot move forward absent acknowledgement from elected leaders that denial of potential problems is a recipe for disaster. To wit, some of these efforts should include the following:

- Enforcing laws, regulations, and policies already in place at the local, state and federal levels. Examples of these include federal Equal Employment Opportunity Commission laws, state antidiscrimination laws, and local government civil service procedures.
- Appointing external monitors to oversee testing results, looking for obvious patterns that suggest promotional processes were compromised. Similar efforts occur regularly during the administration of the College Entrance Examination Board's annual high school SAT and APT tests (Matthews, 2009).
- Enacting tough sanctions at the local level that would remove the financial incentives for cheating, such as demoting or firing individuals found guilty of the practice, and pursuing civil remedies against law enforcement executives to recoup the cost of administering new examinations.
- Eliminating financial incentives to cheat by reducing pension benefits for those who obtain rank in a fraudulent manner to their last honestly earned position.
- Creating a firewall between those charged with preparing promotional examinations and those who are engaged in coaching and mentoring prospective applicants to avoid conflicts of interest (Begin, 2011).
- Conducting a thorough audit of all promotional practices to ensure examination processes are not compromised or gamed, and that all candidates are treated equally and judged by their merit in accordance with relevant law (Villanueva, 2005).

This last recommendation is perhaps the most difficult, as promotional practices within an organization tend to be steeped in traditions that can create disparate impact among promotional candidates, even unintentionally. Such disparate impact can occur when promotional emphasis is placed on experience in units or positions that are filled based on political appointments, consent decrees, and a variety of nonperformance related measures that may skew testing results. Likewise, the capacity of an organization to detect and correct problems can be limited by their reactions to perceived embarrassments or threats (Argyris, 1993).

In short, elected officials, sheriffs, and chiefs of police need to take a proactive stance in combating cheating. Moreover, they must never assume that it cannot occur on their watch. To do otherwise is to ignore reality and face eventual accountability from a demanding citizenry. The increased level of awareness of government practices by way of social media has increased the degree of liability for government agencies for failing to take action when warranted. If left unchecked, cheating in law enforcement may very well be a new Pandora's box for the 21st century.

Discussion Questions

1. What are some of the legal implications in an uncovered cheating scandal that involves a promotional examination? Do they differ from those in an entry-level examination?

2. Are there institutional incentives to cheat? If so, can they be overcome to eliminate the potential for cheating? How?

3. In another hypothetical scenario, you are the director of personnel in a city police department. You are reviewing the results of a sergeant's promotional examination and notice an unusually large cluster of scores in the 98th percentile that correspond to individuals assigned to one particular unit. Based on your knowledge of statistics, you believe the test was compromised and the answers leaked in advance of the examination. Describe a course of action that would address competently all the issues involved.

4. Continuing the scenario described above, as you are being made aware of the magnitude of the problem, your chief of police is monitoring the city council meeting and is about to address several items on the agenda when a city council person reads out loud a printout of a news blog. In the blog, an anonymous officer claims the test was compromised and the city council member wants to know what the chief was going to do about it. What should be the chief's response to the city council? What are some of the important issues that need to be addressed, and, if left unaddressed, what might the consequences be?

5. If you were hired as a human resource consultant for promotional examinations involving sworn employees of a municipal police department, provide a brief narrative on how you would address the following topics:

   a. Test development

   b. Testing material security

   c. Proctoring examinations

   d. Assigned weights to test components

   e. Criteria for promoting candidates from test results

   f. Defending the process against a discrimination claim

References

18 N.C. officers could face suspension of police certification in cheating case. (2004, December 2). *The Associated Press*. Retrieved from http://www.policeone.com/investigations/articles/94173-18-N-C-Officers-Could-Face-Suspension-of-Police-Certification-in-Cheating-Case/

ABC7 News. (2010, November 22). Assistant police chief Dianne Groomes placed on administrative leave. *TBD Latest: What's Going Down*. Retrieved from http://www.tbd.com/blogs/tbd-latest/2010/11/assistant-d-c-police-chief-diane-groomes-placed-on-administrative-leave-4916.html

Adams, G., & Balfour, D. (2004). *Unmasking administrative evil* (Rev. ed). Armonk, NY: M.E. Sharpe.

American Society for Public Administration. (2012). Across the globe, trust in government suffers a severe breakdown. *PA Times, 35*(1), 1.

Argyris, C. (1993). *Knowledge for action: A guide to overcoming barriers to organizational change*. San Francisco: Jossey-Bass.

Baker, B. (2006). *Becoming a police officer: An insider's guide to a career in law enforcement*. Retrieved from http://www.careerpoliceofficer.com/Policeand Police/police_promotions.html

Beaudet, M. (2011, January 10). Pay-to-play at sheriff's department? Employees say cash bribes bought promotions. *Fox 25 News*. Retrieved from http://www.myfoxboston.com/story/17756030/pay-to-play-at-sheriffs-department

Begin, B. (2011, February 16). San Francisco police officer named in test-tutoring complaint. *San Francisco Examiner*. Retrieved from http://www.sfexaminer.com/local/2011/02/san-francisco-police-officer-investigated-helping-other-cops-ace-test

BoxcarBob. (2008, February 14). Re: Deputies group endorses Saban for sheriff [Web log comment]. *The Arizona Republic*. Retrieved from http://www.azcentral.com/community/swvalley/articles/0214swv-endorsement0216.html?&wired

Cory, B. (1979, March). In Atlanta (GA), a furor over cheating. *Police Magazine, 2*(2), 15–19.

Diaz, C. (2011). Reverse discrimination case over denied promotion settles. Retrieved from http://www.policeattorney.com/content/reverse-discrimination-case-over-denied-promotion-settles

Dresser, M. (2011, August 8). Transportation police oust 10 recruits in cheating scandal—misconduct follows cheating scandal at city fire department. *The Baltimore Sun*. Retrieved from http://www.baltimoresun.com/news/maryland/bs-md-police-cheating-20110808,0,6166175.story

Fantis, M. (2010). Assistant DC police chief accused of cheating. *WUSA9*. Retrieved from http://www.wusa9.com/news/local/story.aspx?storyid=120974

Faturechi, R., & Leonard, J. (2012, February 22). L.A. County to study curbing managers' solicitation of donations. *The Los Angeles Times*. Retrieved from http://www.latimes.com/news/local/la-me-county-donations-20120222,0,4729046.story

Festinger, L. (1957). *A theory of cognitive dissonance*. Stanford, CA: Stanford University Press.

Fitch, B. D. (2011). Examining the ethical failures of law enforcement. In A. H. Normore & B. D. Fitch (Eds.), *Ethical leadership in education, corrections, and law enforcement: A commitment to excellence and inclusiveness* (pp. 3–21). Austin, TX: Emerald Books.

Haney, C., Banks, C., & Zimbardo, P. (1974). Interpersonal dynamics in a simulated prison. *International Journal of Criminology and Penology, 1*, 69–97.

Harmon, M., & Mayer, R. (1986). *Organization theory for public administration*. Burke, VA: Chatelaine Press.

Heron, P. (2011, March 14). About that police cheating scandal. *The Daily Times*. Retrieved from http://www.delcotimes.com/articles/2011/03/14/opinion/doc4d 7dfc8ab45ee551829341.txt?viewmode=fullstory

International Association of Chiefs of Police (IACP). (2011a). *Focus on ethics: The Law Enforcement Oath of Honor*. Retrieved from http://www.theiacp.org/ PoliceServices/ExecutiveServices/ProfessionalAssistance/Ethics/FocusOn EthicsTheLawEnforcementOathofHonor/tabid/167/Default.aspx

International Association of Chiefs of Police (IACP). (2011b). *What is the Law Enforcement Oath of Honor?* Retrieved from http://www.theiacp.org/Police Services/ProfessionalAssistance/Ethics/WhatistheLawEnforcementOath ofHonor/tabid/150/Default.aspx

Kreitner, R., & Kinicki, A. (1989). *Organizational behavior*. Homewood, IL: Richard D. Irwin.

Lowe, P. (2008, July 23). Hutchens names command staff, mix of old and new. *The Orange County Register*. Retrieved from http://totalbuzz.ocregister.com/2008/07/23/ hutchens-names-command-staff-mix-of-old-and-new/4447/

Ly, S. (2010, October 6). Prince George's Co. police investigating alleged cheating at academy. *Fox TV*. Retrieved March 30, 2012 from http://www.myfoxdc.com/ dpp/news/maryland/prince-georges-co-police-investigating-possible-alleged-at- academy-100610

Martin, R. (2011). Police corruption: An analytical look into police ethics. *FBI Law Enforcement Bulletin, 80*(5), 11–17.

Mathews, J. (2009, September 14). Jay Mathews: Retest D.C. classes that had dubi- ous exam results in '08. *Washington Post*. Retrieved from http://www.washing tonpost.com/wp-dyn/content/article/2009/09/13/AR2009091302414 .html?hpid=sec-education

McCullough, A. (2010). 13 officers fired in cheating scandal. *Marine Corps Times*. Retrieved from http://www.marinecorpstimes.com/news/2010/05/marine_ cheating_052510w/

Meritocracy. (n.d.) In *Merriam-Webster's online dictionary* (11th ed.). Retrieved from http://www.merriam-webster.com/dictionary/meritocracy

Mitchell, J. (2011, October 1). 14 Troopers admit cheating. *The Clarion Ledger*. Retrieved from http://pqasb.pqarchiver.com/clarionledger/access/2485615781 .html?FMT=ABS&date=Oct+01%2C+2011

Mondo, M. (2010, December 30). Texas promotion exam 'cheating scandal' ends. *San Antonio Express News*. Retrieved from http://www.policeone.com/police- jobs/articles/2363068-Texas-promotion-exam-cheating-scandal-ends/

Mount, C. (1987, September 30). Sheriff sues Elrod over 396 promotions. *The Chicago Tribune*. Retrieved from http://articles.chicagotribune.com/1987-09- 30/news/8703130832_1_promotional-exams-tests-lieutenant

Ofgang, K. (2011, November 9). C.A. upholds back pay award to former O.C. assis- tant sheriff, convicted felon retains rights under POBRA, justices rule in Jaramillo case. *Metropolitan News*. Retrieved from http://www.metnews.com/ articles/2011/jara110911.htm

Payton, G. (1996). *Peace officers promotional manual*. San Jose, CA: Criminal Justice Services.

Reza, H. G. (1990, August 10). 11 officers cheat in National City promotion test: Police: Applicants for senior posts are caught in scandal, but no disciplinary action is taken. *The Los Angeles Times*. Retrieved from http://articles.latimes .com/1990-08-10/local/me-44_1_national-city-police

Retiredguy100. (2010, May 24). Re: 'Cheating scandal' documents revealed: Secret reports come to light in pension fight [Web log comment]. *Target 12*. Retrieved from http://www.wpri.com/dpp/target_12/target-12-new-details-in-police-cheating-scandal

Saad, L. (2010, February 28). Congress ranks last in confidence in institutions: Fifty percent "very little"/"no" confidence in Congress reading is record high. *Gallup Politics*. Retrieved from http://www.gallup.com/poll/141512/Congress-Ranks-Last-Confidence-Institutions.aspx

Schmitt, E. (1994, January 13). An inquiry finds 125 cheated on a naval academy exam. *New York Times*. Retrieved from http://www.nytimes.com/1994/01/13/us/an-inquiry-finds-125-cheated-on-a-naval-academy-exam.html?pagewanted=all&src=pm

Seglin, D. (2011, January 13). Niagara police officers caught cheating on exam. *CBC News: Canada*. CBC. Retrieved from http://www.cbc.ca/news/canada/story/2011/06/13/niagara-police-test.html

Serpico2. (2010, November 19). Re: Assistant D.C. Police Chief Diane Groomes placed on administrative leave [Web log comment]. *TBD*. Retrieved from http://www.tbd.com/blogs/tbd-latest/2010/11/assistant-d-c-police-chief-diane-groomes-placed-on-administrative-leave-4916.html

Sherman, D. (2011, May 18). Denver's undersheriff investigating allegations of cheating on deputy exams. *9news*. Retrieved from http://www.9news.com/news/article/198957/339/Undersheriff-investigates-cheating-on-exams

Smith, T. (1983). 1883–1983: One hundred years of the civil service act. *The Rutherford B. Hayes presidential center publication*. Retrieved from http://www.rbhayes.org/hayes/content/files/Hayes_Historical_Journal/1883-1983_one_hundred_years_of_the_civil_service_act.htm

Sorrentino, M. (2007, June 20). Police cheaters don't deserve pensions. *The Boston Phoenix*. Retrieved from http://thephoenix.com/Boston/News/42244-Police-cheaters-dont-deserve-pensions/

Stoecker, J., & Gendreau, L. (2012) New Haven police officers sue for promotions: Several black firefighters said they are being discriminated against. *NBCConnecticut*. Retrieved from http://www.nbcconnecticut.com/news/local/New-Haven-Police-Officers-Sue-for-Promotions--136801103.html

Villanueva, A. (2005). *Leadership diversity in law enforcement* (Unpublished doctoral dissertation). University of La Verne, La Verne, CA.

Weber, M. (1968). Bureaucracy. In G. Roth & C. Wittich (Eds.), *Economy and society* (pp. 956–958). Los Angeles: University of California Press. (Original work published 1921)

Welborn, L. (2008, July 9). Carona was a paranoid egomaniac, former friend tells FBI. *The OC Register*. Retrieved from http://www.ocregister.com/news/carona-67985-haidl-fbi.html

Wright, S. C. (1991). *Responding to intergroup discrimination: An analysis of tokenism*. (Unpublished doctoral dissertation). McGill University, Montreal, Quebec.

14 Henry Louis Gates and Racial Profiling

What's the Problem?

Bernard E. Harcourt

I studied the history of racism. I know every incident in the history of racism from slavery to Jim Crow segregation. . . . [But] I haven't even come close to being arrested. I would have said it was impossible.

Henry Louis Gates Jr., July 22, 2009 (in Thompson, 2009)

On July 16, 2009, Professor Henry Louis Gates Jr. was arrested and handcuffed on the front porch of his home in Cambridge, Massachusetts, by Sergeant James Crowley of the Cambridge Police Department on a charge of disorderly conduct.[1] Sergeant Crowley was responding to a 911 call reporting a possible break-in at Professor Gates' home. Sergeant Crowley and Professor Gates had verbal exchanges. Professor Gates provided Sergeant Crowley with his Harvard University identification card. The two men continued to have verbal exchanges. Shortly thereafter, Sergeant Crowley arrested Professor Gates on the charge of creating a public disturbance. Professor Gates was handcuffed at his home and transported to a Cambridge police station, where he was booked and photographed, and detained for approximately four hours.

A few days later, on July 22, 2009, President Barack Obama commented on the arrest of Professor Gates during a prime-time news conference

---

[1]Henry Louis Gates' narrative of the incident, communicated through his attorney, Charles Ogletree, is available at *The Root* here: http://www.theroot.com/views/lawyers-statement-arrest-henry-louis-gates-jr. Officer Crowley's narrative of the incident is communicated in his arrest report concerning the incident, which can also be found online.

concerning health care reform. In response to a question about the incident, President Obama stated that

> number one, any of us would be pretty angry; number two, that the Cambridge police acted stupidly in arresting somebody when there was already proof that they were in their own home. And number three, what I think we know separate and apart from this incident is that there is a long history in this country of African-Americans and Latinos being stopped by law enforcement disproportionately. That's just a fact. ("Obama's Fifth News Conference," 2009, p. 12)

While all charges against Gates were ultimately dismissed, the incident served as a stark reminder of America's long struggle with issues of race and crime. This chapter outlines recent and historical data on racial profiling, as well as the rationale underlying the use of statistical discrimination, otherwise known as *profiling*, by law enforcement agencies throughout the nation. It examines the adverse effects of statistically determined policing on crime (in many instances, actually increasing crime rates) despite the best intentions of law enforcement to police in the most efficient and effective means possible. Next, it discusses the potential detrimental consequences of profiling on profiled populations, namely, the possible "ratchet effect" on employment, education, family, and social outcomes. The chapter concludes with a model of policing based on randomization that promotes principles of justice while more accurately reflecting the demographics of the offending population.

Introduction

In August 2008, Ian Ayres of Yale University—one of the leading law and economics scholars in the country—published a study on racial profiling by the Los Angeles Police Department (LAPD) (Ayres, 2008). Ayres analyzed data obtained from over 810,000 "field data reports" collected by the LAPD from July 1, 2003 to June 30, 2004 (field data reports are completed whenever a police officer makes a pedestrian or motor vehicle stop). Ayres found that there were more than 4,500 stops per 10,000 African American residents, whereas there were only 1,750 stops per 10,000 White residents. In two neighborhoods, Central and Hollywood, Ayres actually found that "there were more stops of African-Americans in one year than there were African-American residents, meaning that the average number of stops per resident was greater than one" (p. 5).

Ayres controlled his findings for variables, such as the rate of violent and property crime, and found that the disparity was not the result of different crime rates in different areas—the stop rate per 10,000 residents was 3,400 stops higher for Blacks than Whites, and more than 350 stops higher for Hispanics than Whites. Once stopped, Blacks were 29% more likely to get arrested than Whites, and Hispanics were 32% more likely. Police were 127% more likely to frisk or pat down stopped Blacks than stopped Whites, and 43% more likely to do so for Hispanics. While minorities were more likely to be stopped and then searched once stopped, the results of these searches were less productive than comparable searches with White residents (Ayres, 2008). Searched Blacks were 37% less likely to be found with weapons than searched Whites, 24% less likely to be found with drugs, and 25% less likely to be found with other contraband. Similarly, searched Hispanics were 33% less likely to be found with weapons, 34% less likely to be found with drugs, and 12% less likely to be found with other contraband. The race of the stopping officer also mattered—the disparities found decreased when the officer was of the same race as the person who was stopped.

In April 2008, the American Civil Liberties Union (ACLU) of Arizona released a study analyzing the first full year of data on highway traffic stops collected under a settlement agreement with the Arizona Department of Public Safety—the period spanned July 1, 2006 to June 30, 2007 (ACLU of Arizona, 2008). The analysis revealed that patrol officers searched African Americans, Hispanics, and Native Americans at a higher rate than Whites or other minorities. Blacks and Hispanics who were stopped by police were searched 10% of the time, and Native Americans 13% of the time. In contrast, Whites, Asians, and Middle Easterners were searched around 3% to 5% of the time. The study found no evidence to support such differential treatment by race—on average, 34% of Whites searched were found with contraband, while only 22% of Hispanics searched were found with contraband. Blacks were found with contraband at similar rates as Whites (38%), but were twice as likely to be searched. Middle Easterners, who were searched at slightly higher rates than Whites (5%, compared to the 4% search rate of Whites), were found with contraband only 24% of the time. Additional evidence of differential racial treatment was found in the disparity of stop duration by race. Overall, minorities were held for longer periods during police stops, excluding stops that involved searches.

In a follow-up study commissioned by the Arizona Department of Public Safety using an additional six months of data, the researchers found that, conditional on being stopped, racial disparities existed in the outcome of the stop, even after controlling for other explanatory factors (Engel, Cherkauskas, & Smith, 2008). Whites were more likely to receive warnings (44.6% of stops) than Blacks (41.3% of stops) and Hispanics (only 33.6% of stops). In contrast, Hispanics and Blacks were more likely to be cited than Whites (48.9% for Hispanics, 48.1% for Blacks, and 43.4% for Whites). Hispanics, Blacks, and Native Americans were all significantly more likely to get searched or arrested. Whites were arrested only 2.1% of the time, while Native Americans were arrested 5.4% of the time, Blacks 4.2% of the time, and Hispanics 3.9% of the time. Hispanics were searched at an 8.6% rate, Blacks at 7.5%, Native Americans at 6.9%, and Whites at

3.3%. All results were statistically significant at the .001 level (pp. 53–54). Analysis of the percentage of searches that successfully found contraband showed that for nonconsent discretionary searches, searches of Hispanics had the lowest success rates (37.5%); in comparison, the success rates were 52.9% for Native Americans, 50.4% for Whites, 50.0% for Blacks, and 46.4% for other races.

In February 2009, the state of West Virginia issued its "traffic stop study" final report for 2008 (Haas, Turley, & Sterling, 2009). The state found that, on average, Blacks were 1.64 times more likely to be stopped by police than Whites, and Hispanics were 1.48 times more likely to be stopped than Whites. Blacks and Hispanics were also more likely to be searched than Whites, with the rate of being searched at 10.64% for Blacks, 10.24% for Hispanics, and 4.32% for Whites. While the rates of being stopped and searched were higher for minorities, the contraband "hit rates" (the rate at which contraband is found in a search) were lower. The hit rate for Blacks was 43.11%, 30.23% for Hispanics, and 47.17% for Whites. Finally, the rates of receiving a citation or getting arrested were higher for Blacks (57.34%) and Hispanics (60.92%) than for White drivers (46.52%). Similar results were found on data at the county and agency level.

In mid-2009, Alexander Weiss and Dennis P. Rosenbaum of the University of Illinois at Chicago Center for Research in Law and Justice issued the 2008 annual report on traffic stops for the state of Illinois—the fifth annual traffic stop report based on data collected annually starting in 2004 required under state law due to allegations of racial profiling. Weiss and Rosenbaum (2009) found that minority drivers were around 13% more likely to get stopped than White drivers. Once stopped, minorities were around 10% more likely to receive a citation. Specifically, 64% of Blacks were cited, 69% of Hispanics, 65% of Asians, and 70% of Native Americans, compared to 58% of Whites. In terms of searches, Hispanic drivers were 2.4 times more likely to be subjected to a consented search than White drivers, and Black drivers 3 times more likely. While minorities were about 2.5 times more likely to be searched than Whites, they were less likely to be found with contraband. Searches of White drivers turned up contraband 24.4% of the time, while searches of minorities did so only 15.1% of the time—in other words, police were searching minorities more even though searches of Whites found contraband 1.6 times more than searches of minorities (pp. 12–13).

These reports extend a long and consistent history of studies documenting racial profiling in American policing across the country. Earlier in 2007, for instance, the RAND Corporation had issued a report on racial disparities in the stop, question, and frisk practices of the New York City Police Department (NYPD) (Ridgeway, 2007). Using data on street encounters between NYPD officers and pedestrians in 2006, the RAND Corporation found that officers frisked Whites less than they frisked similarly situated non-Whites (29% of stops, compared to 33% of stops). Although search rates were roughly the same across races, at 6% to 7% (the study notes that in Staten Island, the search rates of minorities was significantly greater), officers successfully recovered contraband less from minorities than similarly situated Whites. Specifically, the success rate for Blacks was 5.7%, 5.4% for Hispanics, and 6.4% for Whites (pp. xii–xiv). And a year earlier, in 2006, the Northeastern University Institute on Race and Justice had issued a report on traffic stop disparities in Rhode Island (Farrell & McDevitt, 2006). The study found, *inter alia*, that minorities were subjected to searches at over twice the rate compared to Whites (13.6% for minorities, 6.3% for Whites). Limiting the data to only discretionary searches (searches not incident to a lawful arrest) still found minorities being searched at twice the rate of Whites, with minorities being searched at 5.9% and Whites being searched at 2.9% (pp. 68–70). While minorities were searched at twice the rate as Whites, the productivity of searches was less for minorities than Whites. For discretionary searches, Whites had a 26.5% hit rate, while minorities had a 22.3% hit rate (p. 78).

More recently, on June 30, 2009, the ACLU released its report to the U.N. Committee on the Elimination of Racial Discrimination: *The Persistence of Racial and Ethnic Profiling in the United States* (ACLU, 2009). The report catalogued the independent and ACLU-based evidence of racial profiling in 22 states and the federal government, describing in an intricate and detailed 98-page report all the evidence for racial profiling by state and local law enforcement. The report concluded that both data and anecdotal evidence revealed that minorities in the United States are being subjected to racial profiling in spite of the numerous public statements by state and federal government officials that the practice of racial profiling should end. Anecdotal examples of racial profiling—such as the illegal deportation of a cognitively impaired U.S. citizen from Los Angeles because officials did not believe he could possibly be a citizen (p. 46) or Detroit police officers accused of conducting bare-hand searches of genitals on a number of young Black males (p. 56)—were supported by analyses of state level data from Minnesota to California finding consistent patterns of racial minorities being overstopped, oversearched, and overfrisked in comparison to Whites (pp. 41–68).

Nevertheless, the problem of racial profiling did not make headline news. Or rather, it did not make headline news until shortly after July 16, 2009, the day that Professor Henry Louis Gates Jr. was arrested and handcuffed on the front porch of his Harvard home. It was only then that the media began to pay attention. It was only then that the matter got to the White House.

The Persistence of Racial Profiling

This prologue raises three sets of questions. First, why is racial profiling so pervasive in American policing and patrolling? Why do practically all the analyses seem to reveal disproportionate enforcement on African Americans and Hispanics, especially given the often lower hit rates on searches? Second, why does it take the wrongful arrest of a respected and dear member of an elite community to focus the attention of the country on such a deeply scarring and pervasive problem in policing and social relations? Why does racial profiling only matter and become a national issue when "one of us" or a renowned person is the victim? Third, did Sergeant Crowley engage in racial profiling when he questioned and ultimately arrested Professor Gates? Did racial profiling infect the incident on July 16, 2009? Let's consider these questions in reverse order.

Without doubt, the issue of racial profiling infected the encounter between Sergeant Crowley and Professor Gates. Professor Gates explicitly mentioned the topic of racial profiling during the encounter and accused Sergeant Crowley of treating him differently because of his race. Sergeant Crowley had been hand-picked by the former police commissioner, Ronny Watson, to teach a class on racial profiling and taught that class for five years at the Lowell Police Academy (Lavoie, 2009). Unquestionably, Sergeant Crowley was aware of the racial dimensions of the encounter. Racial profiling was explicitly "on the table" in the incident.

It is, however, far more difficult to conclude without further investigation— and it may, ultimately, be impossible to resolve this to the satisfaction of a social scientific evidentiary standard—that Sergeant Crowley himself knowingly engaged in racial profiling. (Implicit bias *during that incident* would be equally, if not more, difficult to prove *ex post* given the contested facts of the encounter.[2]) Although race was inscribed throughout the encounter, and although it is impossible to discuss the incident today without reference to contemporary race relations, it is difficult to ascribe explicit or intentional profiling to Sergeant Crowley without further evidence.[3]

Using the "swap-the-race-of-the-suspect" approach that Banks (2001) advocates in the Fourth Amendment context—and that seems entirely appropriate in this case—it is hard to imagine that Sergeant Crowley would have arrested a White Harvard professor of equal stature or status, such as Professor Harvey Mansfield of the Government Department. However, it is also hard to believe that Professor Mansfield would have protested the police presence and questioning so vehemently—and in that sense, again, it

---

[2]We are all familiar with the most recent research on "implicit bias" and with the IAT—the "Implicit Association Test" (https://implicit.harvard.edu/implicit/demo/; well described for those who are less familiar here http://www.washingtonpost.com/ac2/ wp-dyn/A27067-2005Jan21?language=printer). Several researchers, including Thierry Devos and also Mahzarin Banaji at Harvard, have recently done fascinating work on implicit bias in relation to the recent election of President Obama (see Devos & Gaffud, 2008). They conclude, "Ethnicity and national identity may play a larger role than often realized in how political candidates are perceived and, more broadly, in American politics. The present findings have intriguing implications for the role that the media and political campaigns may have on the outcome of presidential elections."

[3]This is, incidentally, another problem with the constitutional treatment of racial profiling, which requires evidence of intentional discrimination.

is impossible to extricate race from the encounter, on *both* sides of the incident. If one were to substitute race and racial relations with, for instance, antipolice or anti-authority sentiment (e.g., with the anti-Vietnam or anti–Iraq War protest movements), it would not be inconceivable that a Cambridge police officer would have arrested a White Harvard professor who was vehemently confronting and challenging the officer's authority. One can imagine other axes—other than race—that could possibly have triggered an excessive, perhaps even personal or overly emotional reaction on the part of an arresting police officer in the heat of a confrontation.

It is, on the present record, hard to rule out the possibility that Sergeant Crowley may have arrested Professor Gates because he (Sergeant Crowley) irrationally lost his temper in response to the accusations and challenge to his authority, or, alternatively, that he made the arrest to minimize a likely police complaint. In other words, Sergeant Crowley may have believed that Professor Gates was going to file a police complaint against him and decided to make the arrest as a way to delegitimize any possible complaint—given that police complaints in cases where there has been an arrest are viewed as more dubious than those where there has been no criminal activity charged.

Now, would Sergeant Crowley have acted differently, in any respect whatsoever, if Professor Gates had been White? At each minute juncture of the encounter, might there have been a difference—say, in the way the sergeant introduced himself, asked for identification, responded to the challenge, positioned his body, or looked at Professor Gates? No one can say for certain without further evidence, but the suspicion remains that racial stereotyping on the part of Sergeant Crowley—as well as police stereotyping on the part of Professor Gates—played a role in the encounter. That is the author's hunch—but, of course, that also says something about the author. What is absolutely clear and uncontestable is that *race* played a dominant role in the encounter—on both sides of the encounter—and that it inextricably colors the way that all individuals interpret the event. It is clear that Professor Gates *believed* that he was being profiled. It is also clear that Sergeant Crowley *understood* that he was being accused of racial profiling. Both the incident and the interpretations of the incident are laced with race.

This, then, brings us to the other two questions. Why did it have to take the arrest of a well-respected member of an elite community like Harvard University to resuscitate the issue of racial profiling and to draw the attention of the national media? As President Obama said, correctly, during his first intervention in the affair, "there is a long history in this country of African-Americans and Latinos being stopped by law enforcement disproportionately. That's just a fact" ("Obama's Fifth News Conference," 2009, p. 12). An avalanche of studies over the past few years has documented racial profiling in practically all the states of the Union. Why is it that we pay so little attention to the flood of studies? And why have we not, by now, implemented proper legal remedies for racial profiling? Why is there no adequate legislation? And why is racial profiling so pervasive?

What's the Problem?

The reason is that racial profiling is just another form of statistical discrimination and that, today, we have all come to embrace statistical discrimination as efficient and entirely justified whenever there are, in fact, group-based differences in behavior or factual disparities. We all, today, play the odds. That's how we have come to lead our lives. We have become statistical creatures, and we live our lives daily based on statistical discrimination. Whether it is labeled *stereotyping*, *generalizations*, or *profiling*, that's how we operate in all dimensions of our daily life. It makes life much more manageable, incredibly more efficient—in fact, it's simply impossible to succeed in our competitive world without using forms of statistical discrimination. We do it all the time on exams, in our research, in our daily practices, and in every aspect of our working environment. When one adds to that the fact that most Americans and most criminologists believe that there are statistical differences in the rates of "street crime" offending along race lines, there is every reason to engage in racial profiling. It's simply second nature—and, tragically, the truth is, most Americans do it all the time on the street.

One way to eliminate racial profiling, then, would be to eradicate the commonly held belief that young African American males commit street offenses at a higher rate than others. In certain contexts, there may be good evidence for that; so, for instance, much of the profiling on the highways is aimed at uncovering illicit drugs, and the national statistics on drug use do not reveal significant differences as between races (Harcourt, 2007a). But there has been a long and controversial debate throughout the 20th century on the question of the racial composition of street crime offenders (Langan, 1985; Tonry, 1995).[4] The real trouble here is that there is sticky and persistent evidence for statistical disparities in offending along race lines because of the way that we define crime. We tend to define *crime* as "street crime," as the public acts associated with the drug trade, robbery and violence, and thus in a way that correlates with low-income, urban neighborhoods with certain identifiable demographics. The police do not focus on embezzlement or fraud, but on the types of crimes that take place on the street, in public—and, as a result, the statistics, however faulty, continue to draw connections between race and "ordinary" crime.

There is, however, a better way to address racial profiling, and that is to make people understand that statistical discrimination is entirely misguided in policing and criminal justice because of the feedback effects; to demonstrate that statistical discrimination is counterproductive even to the law enforcement objectives of reducing crime, and that statistical discrimination leads us astray in policing. Two things in particular undermine statistical discrimination in the criminal justice context. First, if we assume rational choice assumptions, statistical discrimination is likely to be counterproductive

---

[4]Given that criminal justice data are predominantly generated by policing, law enforcement, and corrections agencies, there is a natural skew in the evidence—it is itself, in all likelihood, infected by racial profiling.

to the ultimate objective of law enforcement and cause more crime. Under the conservative assumption that the targeted population (the population with higher offending) is less responsive to policing than the nontargeted population, statistical discrimination is likely to have perverse effects on the law enforcement objective. Second, if we do not assume rational action, statistical discrimination is going to lead to a ratchet effect on members of the profiled population with highly detrimental consequences on their employment, educational, familial, and social outcomes that is likely going to result in counterproductive effects on crime.

This may sound technical, and I do hope to make it a lot clearer in the following pages. But what it suggests, overall, is that the real problem with racial profiling is not only the racial harm. It is not only the fact that an innocent victim, such as Professor Gates, is deeply injured and harmed because of the color of his skin. The problem extends beyond the issues surrounding race. The problem extends to all forms of profiling or statistical discrimination that involve a feedback loop. In other words, the heart of the problem in racial profiling is not only the racial or ethnic dimension. Like Lani Guinier and Gerald Torres's metaphor of the miner's canary, the racial dimension of profiling is what makes us *see* the problems with statistical discrimination more generally.

Let me borrow then from Guinier and Torres' (2005) book, *The Miner's Canary: Enlisting Race, Resisting Power, Transforming Democracy.* Just like the canary, whose distress is a warning that the air in the mine is poisoned, the troubling aspect of race in the debate over racial profiling points to the larger problems of statistical discrimination. Race is the first place where we see the poison, but it is a poison that affects everyone else. Like the canary in the coal mine, the trouble surrounding racial profiling alerts us to the problem with the use of statistical discrimination more generally. The mathematics of profiling and the overlooked detrimental costs to the profiled populations affect all profiling techniques, whether they focus on race or recidivism, gender or sexual orientation, national origin, or other classifications. We may, as a society, decide to apply less scrutiny to some of these classifications than to others, but the effects are the same. The problem, it turns out, is with statistical discrimination *tout court*.

The Problems With Statistical Discrimination

For most of us, racial profiling is simply wrong.[5] Practically none of us, though, believes that *statistical* discrimination is wrong. That is the key

---

[5]In fact, prior to 9/11, there was near unanimity among politicians, at least at the level of public statements, that racial profiling was wrong. You may recall that President George W. Bush denounced racial profiling on the grounds that "[a]ll of our citizens are created equal and must be treated equally" (quoted in Mosher, Miethe, & Phillips, p. 183); and former President Bush's FBI Director, Robert Mueller, similarly declared that "[r]acial profiling is abhorrent to the Constitution" (see Albert Alschuler, 2002, p. 163, n. 3, citing 147 Cong Rec S 8683 [Aug. 2, 2001]).

tension in the racial profiling debate that has allowed the issue to percolate without any end in sight.

The central problem is that, today, with the exception of racial profiling, the general public and most academics are *entirely comfortable* using the kind of generalizations, stereotypes, and profiles based on group traits that underlie racial profiling. The public supports the use of statistical discrimination across the policing and law enforcement spectrum in the United States—and perhaps across all other domains. To most everyone, it is a matter of plain common sense. In fact, it is exactly what we are willing and happy to do in practically all other contexts, especially in the context of recidivism or other "known" differentials. As a result, statistical discrimination permeates policing and punishment in the United States today—from the use of the IRS Discriminant Index Function to predict potential tax evasion, to the drug-courier and racial profiles to identify suspects to search at airports and on the highways, to risk-assessment instruments to tag violent sexual predators, prediction instruments increasingly determine individual outcomes in policing, enforcement, sentencing, and correctional practices.

The problem has been aggravated by recent economic studies. A number of economists have begun working on econometric models of profiling, using racial profiling as their lead example, and have reached the conclusion that disproportionate stops of racial minorities may not necessarily reflect invidious discrimination on the part of the police, but may be consistent instead with an honest and good faith effort to increase the success rate of searches—to engage in efficient policing on the basis of statistical discrimination. So long as the differences in offending rates between minorities and majorities are not spurious, these economists assert, searching a disproportionate number of minorities is only demonstrably problematic (racist) if the rate of successful searches of minority suspects is *lower* than the rate of successful searches of White suspects. Otherwise, disproportionate searches of minorities are consistent with policing efficiency and do not prove invidious bias.[6]

If statistical discrimination is efficient, if it saves money and reduces crime, then what could possibly be wrong with it? The fact that there are innocent victims, such as Professor Gates, is in some sense inevitable. It is impossible to implement a policy without Type 1 and Type 2 errors. There

---

[6]Others defend the rise of the actuarial in more general terms—while carving out specific exceptions for generalizations based on race, gender, or sexual orientation. Frederick Schauer, in his book *Profiles, Probabilities, and Stereotypes* (2003), offers a generalized, but nuanced, defense of actuarial reasoning. "In this book," Schauer explains, "I defend the morality of decision by categories and by generalizations, even with its consequent apparent disregard for the fact that decision-making by generalization often seems to produce an unjust result in particular cases" (p. ix). Schauer defends the type of nonspurious generalizations that form the basis of many stereotypes and profiles on the ground that they tend to be prudent and efficient, and, in many cases morally appropriate.

will always be innocent victims—persons who are suspected but not guilty—as well as persons who are guilty but not suspected. That is inevitable. In fact, statistical discrimination seeks to minimize those errors by targeting the more likely suspects.

If there is a problem with racial profiling, then, it has to be with the fundamentals of statistical discrimination. Barring that, no one will ultimately change his or her behavior. And the thing is, there are real problems with statistical discrimination where the use of such methods have feedback effects on the interested parties. Let's turn, then, to the two greatest problems.

Statistical Discrimination Is Likely Counterproductive to Law Enforcement

Let's first assume a rational choice framework and presume, with many economists, that individuals are responsive to the cost of policing. On the assumptions of rational action theory, statistical discrimination promotes efficiency through deterrence: Assuming that potential offenders respond rationally to the probability of being apprehended and punished, then the use of statistical discrimination to target law enforcement on members of a higher-offending group will both (1) decrease the offending rates of those higher-offending group members because it will increase their cost of deviant behavior, and (2) increase the efficiency of the police in detecting crime and apprehending offenders—or increase the efficiency of the sentencing authorities in meting out punishment and deterring future offending. In its purest form, the economic model of crime suggests that the government should target members of higher-offending groups until the point where that group's offending rate has fallen to the same level as the general population. At that point, the government maximizes the effectiveness of its law enforcement practices by both detecting the maximum amount of crime and maximally reducing offending among the higher-offending group.

Drawing on the groundbreaking work on tastes for discrimination by the Nobel laureate economist Gary Becker (1996), a group of economists has developed econometric models of profiling (e.g., see Borooah, 2001; Dominitz & Knowles, 2005; Hernández-Murillo & Knowles, 2003; Knowles, Persico, & Todd, 2001; Persico, 2002). The models would apply to any form of profiling, but they are being developed in the specific context of racial profiling in large part because there is a lot of new data on police practices broken down by the race of the person stopped. The goal of the models is to test police behavior to distinguish between efficiency and racial animus in policing; that is, the purpose is to test whether a situation involving potentially disproportionate searches of minority motorists reflects, on the one hand, efficient discrimination—or what is called *statistical discrimination*—that results from the police desire to maximize the number of successful searches of suspects, or, on the other, raw racial prejudice.

The fact that police disproportionately search minority suspects is not, in itself, proof of racism, these economists contend. What matters, instead, is the rate of successful stops or searches—in other words, stops or searches that lead to arrest or that discover contraband. This is most frequently referred to as the *hit rate*—the rate at which police interventions are successful in detecting criminality. And the models of racial profiling suggest the following: When the hit rates are the same across racial or ethnic lines, the police are not bigoted in their searches because they have no incentive to search more or fewer suspects of any particular race. At equilibrium, the police have achieved a racial balance, though perhaps one with a racial imbalance at its heart, that they are unwilling to change on the basis of race—unless, of course, they have a taste for discrimination.

Accordingly, when the data reveal equal hit rates between different racial groups, these economists conclude that the disproportionate searches of minority suspects do not reflect a taste for discrimination, but rather an attempt to maximize successful searches. When the data reveal lower hit rates for minority suspects, these economists reason that bigotry against minority suspects explains the disparity. And when the data reveal higher hit rates for minority suspects, these economists conclude that reverse racism is at play—in other words, bigotry against White suspects.

The trouble is, this argument rests on a crucial assumption that is unfounded and likely wrong in many circumstances, namely, that the different groups react similarly to a change in policing. This is referred to, in more technical jargon, as the relative *elasticity of offending to policing*—or *comparative elasticity*, for short—of the two groups. The elasticity of offending to policing is the degree to which changes in policing affect changes in offending. So, for instance, if the IRS targets—to take a nonracial category—car dealers for audits of their tax returns, as they did in the mid-1990s, we expect that there will be less tax evasion by car dealers (assuming full information). We assume that their tax evasion is elastic to policing and will fall with the enhanced scrutiny. It is the elasticity that reduces the offending of the targeted group—those identified by the actuarial method. But even if we assume elasticity of offending to policing among car dealers, society as a whole will only benefit from their decrease in tax evasion if the *nonprofiled groups* do not begin to evade their tax burden more, in absolute numbers, because they feel immune from scrutiny—in other words, because of their elasticity to reduced enforcement. Accountants and bankers, for instance, may realize that they are less likely to be audited and may therefore cheat a bit more on their taxes. What matters, then, is the *comparative elasticity* of the two groups—profiled (car dealers) and nonprofiled (accountants and bankers). If the targeted group members have lower elasticity of offending to policing—if their offending is less responsive to policing than other groups—then targeting them for enforcement efforts will likely increase the overall amount of crime in society as a whole because the increase in crime by accountants and bankers will exceed the decrease in crime by car dealers.

Naturally, the economists are right that profiling on a nonspurious group trait that predicts higher offending will maximize the law enforcement goal of detecting criminal activity and, if we buy the premises of rational action theory, will decrease crime among the higher-offending group. But this will only improve society and increase the general welfare of society if it has the effect of decreasing overall crime in society, and this will only happen if the members of the higher-offending targeted group have the same or greater elasticity of offending to policing. The overall effect on crime in society will depend entirely on the relative elasticity of the two groups to the profiling. If, on the other hand, the targeted population is less responsive to the change in policing, then the profiling will increase overall crime in society.

In effect, the problem with the economic model of racial profiling is that it does not properly specify what counts as "success" for purposes of a highway drug interdiction program. The models assume that a nonracist police officer seeks to maximize the rate of successful searches that discover drug contraband. That, however, is simply the wrong objective. The proper goal for the police is to minimize the social cost of crime—in this case, to minimize the transportation of drug contraband on the highways and the social cost of policing. And the fact is, under certain identifiable conditions, minimizing the social costs of crime is at odds with maximizing search success rates. Under certain conditions, statistical discrimination leads to higher overall social costs associated with the profiled crime and the costs of searches.

To model police behavior properly, then, we have to focus not on maximizing search success rates but on minimizing the costs associated with the profiled crime, including the social costs of the crime itself and of the policing technique. Let me, then, propose a model—one that is more rigorous and more accurately describes the goal of crime reduction. While this model is presented in greater detail in the book, *Against Prediction: Profiling, Policing, and Punishing in an Actuarial Age* (Harcourt, 2007a), let's sketch the outline here again.

The first objective of the model, naturally, is to minimize the costs to society that are produced by the profiled crime. For purposes of notation, let $r \in \{M, W\}$ denote the race of the motorists, either minority or White. Let Pop_r denote the representation of each racial group in the total population. Let O_r denote the offending rate of each racial group. Let D denote the social loss associated with one instance of the profiled crime, namely, the transportation of illicit drugs on the highway. Let I_r denote the rate at which motorists are being searched. O_r (defined as the internal rate of offending for each group) is a function of I_r and so will be noted accordingly.

In more technical terms, then, the cost to society associated with the profiled crime can be captured by the following expression:

$$D \, [\, O_M (I_M) \, Pop_M + O_W (I_W) \, Pop_W \,] \tag{1}$$

The second objective is to minimize the social costs associated with searching motor vehicles for contraband. For purposes of notation, let Q denote the cost associated with one instance of a police search. In more technical terms, the cost to society associated with the searches of automobiles can be captured by the following expression:

$$Q\,[\,I_M\,Pop_M + I_W\,Pop_W\,] \tag{2}$$

To minimize the total costs to society, we would need to take the derivative of the total cost function, denoted as C_r, which would be a function of I_r and would contain both equations (1) and (2). The total cost function can be expressed as follows:

$$C_M(I_M) + C_W(I_W) = D[O_M(I_M)Pop_M + O_W(I_W)Pop_W]$$
$$+ Q[I_M\,Pop_M + I_W\,Pop_W] \tag{3}$$

Using partial differentiation to resolve separately for the two racial groups, if we were to minimize the social costs, it would produce the following:

$$C'_r(I_r) = D[O'_r(I_r)Pop_r] + Q\,Pop_r \tag{4}$$

Rewriting the equation, we obtain the following:

$$-\,[Q\,/\,D\,] = O'_r\,(I_r) \tag{5}$$

Since we are assuming that Q and D are the same for White and minority motorists—that is, we are assuming nonracist police officers—minimizing total social costs produces the following first order condition:

$$O'_M\,(I_M) = O'_W\,(I_W) \tag{6}$$

Since $O'_r\,(I_r)$ is the slope of O_r at point I_r, or $[\,\partial\,O_r\,/\,\partial\,I_r]$, we can rewrite this first-order condition as follows:

$$\frac{\partial O_M}{\partial I_M} = \frac{\partial\,O_W}{\partial\,I_W} \tag{7}$$

We can rewrite this as follows, multiplying both sides by 1:

$$\frac{\partial O_M}{\partial I_M}\,\frac{I_M}{O_M}\,\frac{O_M}{I_M} = \frac{\partial O_W}{\partial I_W}\,\frac{I_W}{O_W}\,\frac{O_W}{I_W} \tag{8}$$

Given the definition of elasticity and using E_r to denote elasticity, the first-order condition can be expressed as follows:

$$E_M \frac{O_M}{I_M} = E_W \frac{O_W}{I_W} \qquad (9)$$

This first-order condition must be satisfied to minimize the total social costs associated with the illicit transportation of drug contraband on the highways. As is clear from the equation, whether the condition is satisfied will depend on the comparative elasticities, natural offending rates, and search rates. It is possible to construct a 3 x 3 table to identify the conditions under which the police should search different racial groups at different rates. The following table (Table 14.1) summarizes the nine findings:

The two shaded cells represent situations where racial profiling may *increase* total social costs. In the case where minority motorists have lower elasticities of offending to policing and higher natural offending rates, and similarly where minority motorists have higher elasticities but lower natural offending rates, racial profiling may increase overall social costs depending on the relationship between the relative offending and search rates.

The foregoing underscores the myopia of an efficiency analysis that looks solely for equal hit rates and elides elasticities and offending differentials. As the model makes clear, minimizing the costs to society will entail a distribution of searches between White and minority motorists that will depend on the comparative elasticities of offending to policing and on the relative natural offending rates. In other words, the equilibrium point is not defined by the equality of hit rates, but instead depends on comparative elasticities and the relationship between offending and search rates. As a result, the focus of the analysis should turn on the size and characteristics of the group of persons at the margins who are most likely to be influenced one way or the other to carry illicit drugs on the highway for personal or commercial purposes.

Table 14.1 Police Searches Under Different Conditions

	$E_M = E_W$	$E_M < E_W$	$E_M > E_W$
$O_M = O_W$	$I_M = I_W$ (No Racial Profiling)	$I_M < I_W$ (Profile Whites)	$I_M > I_W$ (Profile Minorities)
$O_M > O_W$	$I_M > I_W$ (Profile Minorities)	$I_m < I_w[O_M/O_W]$ (Not Clear)	$I_M > I_W$ (Profile Minorities)
$O_M < O_W$	$I_M < I_W$ (Profile Whites)	$I_M < I_W$ (Profile Whites)	$I_M > I_W[O_M/O_W]$ (Not Clear)

The bottom line is that criminal profiling may be entirely counter-productive to the crime-fighting goal—and in fact, several economists, including Persico (2002), Dominitz and Knowles (2005), and Manski (2006), have begun to recognize this. In a subsequent paper, written four years after developing the original Knowles, Persico, and Todd model (2001), Dominitz and Knowles (2005) acknowledge that "policies that are optimal under [the hit-rate maximization hypothesis] can actually lead to maximization of crime" (p. 4). Dominitz and Knowles now specifically recognize that the traditional assumptions about offending rates "are not sufficient to allow inference of racial bias from observation of search rates and hit rates, when police are known to minimize crime" (p. 16). As a result, we need to know more about comparative elasticities and offending rates as between different groups in society before engaging in actuarial policing.

The bottom line is that the use of statistical discrimination may well increase crime in society. Racial profiling will only reduce total crime depending on the relationship between comparative elasticities and offending rates of the two groups. If minority motorists have lower elasticity, racial profiling may well increase overall profiled crime. The problem, then, with the narrow definition of efficiency—maximizing search success rates—is that it may effectively mask racial prejudice. If a police officer or police department engages in disproportionate searches of minority motorists to maximize the success rate of searches and pays no attention to the consequences on long-term trends in the transportation of drug contraband—or, if we as modelers and policymakers focus on narrow efficiency—then the police may endorse a scheme of racial profiling that may in fact promote more crime in the long term. The police may promote, whether intentionally or unwittingly, a policy that discriminates on the basis of race and increases overall crime. That would not be efficient. To the contrary, it would in effect be racially prejudiced.

What is most troubling in all this, of course, is that there are good reasons to suspect that minority and White motorists may have different elasticities of offending to policing and that the elasticity of minority motorists may be less than that of White motorists. Elasticity is going to depend in large part on the existence of legitimate work alternatives, and, as the work of Wilson (1996) demonstrates, there is a deep and complex relation between work opportunities, race, and the inner city. Even the economists developing the racial profiling models recognize this. Persico (2002), in fact, suggests that, as a theoretical matter, the elasticity for African Americans may be less than for Whites because they may have fewer job opportunities and therefore fewer alternatives to crime—which seems eminently right. As Persico explains, "the amount of criminal activity—and hence also the elasticity of crime to policing—depends on the distribution of legal earning opportunities" (p. 1474). This may affect the transportation of illicit drugs and the substitutability of drug couriers.

In other words, there is no good reason to assume that the higher-offending group is as responsive to policing as the lower-offending group. The two groups do, after all, have different offending rates—otherwise the police would be profiling on a spurious trait. Whether the different offending rates are due to different socio-economic backgrounds, to different histories, cultures, or education, nonspurious profiling rests on the nonspurious assumption that one group of individuals offends more than another, holding everything else constant. If their offending is different, then why would their elasticity be the same? If they are, for instance, offending more because they are socio-economically more disadvantaged, then it would follow logically that they may also have less elasticity of offending to policing because they have fewer alternative job opportunities. The bottom line, then, is that there is every reason to believe that nonspurious racial profiling would actually *increase* crime in society.

There are two final points regarding this first problem with statistical discrimination. First, some economists will respond that this argument is technically accurate with regard to *existing* profiling techniques, but that the existing techniques are only error prone insofar as they do not incorporate a measure of the comparative responsiveness of the different populations. Though technically accurate, they suggest, this first problem should not undermine our faith in the efficiency of profiling techniques when they are properly administered. The correct use of statistical discrimination is "always efficient in theory" (Margalioth, 2008).

This is entirely right at the *theoretical* level. There is no question that if we had perfect information on the comparative elasticities and offending rates of the two groups at the margin, then we could administer statistical discrimination efficiently and ensure that there are no negative effects on crime. The table above demonstrates that well: If we knew the exact comparative elasticities, offending, and internal search rates, then we could determine whether and whom to profile perfectly efficiently. In this sense, at the level of *pure theory*, the use of statistical discrimination is indeed always efficient.

The problem, however, centers on the importance to place on the theoretical versus the actual. The fact is, we do not have any data on comparative elasticities, and, until now, the social scientists who have been working on these actuarial instruments have never paid any attention to comparative elasticities. From the very first prediction tool onward, researchers have based their instruments on comparative offending rates as the outcome measure. From Ernest Burgess, who developed the very first prediction tables implemented in the 20th century, to the DEA agents who developed the drug-courier profile in the 1970s to the most up-to-date sexual offender risk assessment instruments—all of the profiling instruments are based on offending differentials only. In other words, throughout the 20th century and now into the 21st, statistical discrimination is tied to differences in offending rates. The research—practical and theoretical—has never measured comparative elasticities. The result is that, today, we know effectively nothing about comparative elasticities.[7]

The pure theory of statistical discrimination is so divorced from our current state of knowledge and from our existing profiling techniques that the more meaningful conclusion to draw is that our use of statistical discrimination is likely inefficient in practice.

Second, it is important to emphasize that this critique of racial profiling plagues all instances of statistical discrimination in the criminal justice context, including the sentencing context. The case of parole prediction, it turns out, works in exactly the same way as racial profiling: Overall crime in society would increase if the elasticity of the recidivists is lower than the elasticity of the first-time offenders—which we could easily assume if they do in fact have different offending rates. The intuition, again, is simple: Recidivists are a small minority of the population, and they may in fact be less responsive to punishment; if so, first-time and one-time offenders may engage in more criminal behavior overall due to the comparatively reduced cost of crime, and their offending may outpace any gains achieved with regard to the recidivists. Again, this assumes the rational action model. It assumes that individuals will commit more crime if the relative cost of crime declines. But the result is exactly the same, and the consequences equally troubling: Depending on comparative elasticities, the use of statistical discrimination, whether at sentencing or in policing, may *increase* overall crime in society.

Statistical Discrimination Likely Causes a Ratchet Effect

What if we do not believe in rational action theory and are not prepared to assume that individuals are elastic to policing? Surprisingly, the case is even stronger for racial profiling. If you have two inelastic groups with

---

[7]It is only very recently that researchers have even begun to consider the implication of comparative elasticities to profiling. At the theoretical level, Nicola Persico raised the possibility of inefficiency in an article in 2002, but only recently have comparative elasticities begun to be included in the mathematical models (see Bjerk, 2007; Blumkin & Margalioth, 2006; Dominitz & Knowles, 2005; Harcourt, 2004). At the empirical level, Avner Bar-Ilan and Bruce Sacerdote have a working paper from 2001 that explores the comparative responsiveness to an increase in the fine for running a red light along several dimensions—finding that the elasticity of red light running with respect to the fine is larger for younger drivers and drivers with older cars," equivalent for drivers "convicted of violent offenses or property offenses," and smallest, within Israel, for "members of ethnic minority groups" (2001, pp. 1–2). In addition, Paul Heaton had a 2006 working paper on the effect of eliminating racial profiling policies in New Jersey on the offending of minorities; however, the policing intervention in New Jersey involved no de-policing of Whites, so there is no proper way to assess how the elasticity of black offenders compared to that of Whites (see Heaton, 2010). The bottom line is that we still do not know anything about real comparative elasticities in the United States.

different offending, it will always be more efficient to profile on the higher-offending group: You will always get more bang for your buck. This feeds into the incapacitation argument for profiling: If the police stop and search more motorists who are more likely to be transporting drug contraband, they will detect and punish more drug couriers. Incapacitation theory tells us that there will simply be more detection of crime—and, correlatively, fewer undetected drug-couriers on the highways. In short, statistical discrimination here helps incapacitate more offenders with the same resources, and even more offenders with even more resources. And this, of course, is a good thing.

But all good things come at a price, and the key question is, at what price? An evaluation along these lines, naturally, calls for cost-benefit analysis. Here, then, let us assume the cost-benefit approach and the goals of law enforcement—let's enter the utilitarian framework—and analyze the overall picture. When we do that, it turns out, there is one particular cost that is generally overlooked—overlooked in large part because it focuses on the guilty more than on the innocent—and that likely outweighs the benefits of profiling. This is the *ratchet effect*.

Under normal conditions, the use of accurate statistical discrimination (under conditions of no elasticity) will have a distortive effect on the targeted population, a distortion that ultimately operates as a ratchet. The distortion occurs when successful profiling produces a supervised population that is disproportionate to the distribution of offending by racial group. To give a rapid illustration, if the targeted population represents 25% of the *overall* population, but 45% of the *offending* population—in other words, targeted persons are offending at a higher proportion than their representation in the general population and the profiling is nonspurious—then if law enforcement profiles the targeted population by allocating, say, 45% of its resources onto the targeted population, the resulting distribution of offenders will be approximately 67% targeted and 33% nontargeted individuals. This too can be demonstrate with equations, illustrations, and graphs (Harcourt, 2007a). The disparity between targeted persons representing 45% of actual offenders but 67% of detected offenders represents a distortion that has significant negative effects on the minority population. This distortion will produce a ratchet if law enforcement then relies on the evidence of the resulting correctional traces—arrests, convictions, supervision—to reallocate future law enforcement resources. How serious the distortion and ratchet effect will be depends, again, on subtle variations in offending rates. But some distortion is inevitable.

The reason, in essence, is that when we profile, we are essentially sampling more from a higher-offending population. Instead of sampling randomly—which would net a proportional representation of the offending population—we are sampling in greater numbers from the pool of higher offenders, and thereby skewing our sample results. Somewhat counterintuitively, the only way to produce a prison population that mirrors the offending population is to sample randomly from the general population—to engage in essentially random searches, or random audits, or random policing. Barring that randomness, our results will be distorted.

The logic of the ratchet in the policing context is simple: If the police dedicate more resources to investigating, searching, and arresting members of a higher-offending group, the resulting distribution of arrests (as between profiled and nonprofiled persons) will disproportionately represent members of that higher-offending group. The basic intuition is that policing is like sampling: When the police profile higher offenders, they are essentially sampling *more* among members of the higher-offending group. Instead of sampling randomly, which would be the only way to achieve a proportional representation of the offending population, the police are sampling in greater numbers from within the higher offender group, thereby skewing the sampling results in favor of higher offenders.

The distortive effect of criminal profiling on the new carceral population will produce a ratchet whenever law enforcement relies on the evidence of correctional traces—arrests or convictions—to reallocate future law enforcement resources. And the fact is, given the paucity of reliable information on natural offending rates, law enforcement often does rely heavily on arrest, conviction, and supervision rates in deciding how to allocate resources. As Peter Verniero (Verniero & Zoubek, 1999), former Attorney General of New Jersey, explained,

> To a large extent, these statistics have been used to grease the wheels of a vicious cycle—a self-fulfilling prophecy where law enforcement agencies rely on arrest data that they themselves generated as a result of the discretionary allocation of resources and targeted drug enforcement efforts. (p. 68)

This accelerates the imbalance in the prison population and aggravates the secondary impact on the profiled population.

The Costs of the Ratchet

What the ratchet effect does is to disproportionately distribute criminal records and criminal justice contacts, with numerous secondary implications for members of the profiled group in terms of their education, employment, and family lives. Disproportionate criminal supervision and incarceration reduces work opportunities, breaks down families and communities, and disrupts education. The pernicious effects of overrepresentation of African Americans in our prisons—especially among incarcerated felons—have been detailed and documented by many scholars (e.g., see Cole, 1999; Meares, 1998; Roberts, 1999; Tonry, 1995; Wacquant, 2005; Western, 2006). Widespread conviction and incarceration affect not only the targeted individuals but also the communities from which they are drawn—producing feedback effects on them and others. Drawing on insights from the Chicago school of urban sociology—specifically, on the social disorganization theory of Shaw and McKay (1969)—Meares (1998) describes well the devastating effects of high incarceration on the convict and on his community, on "the vitality of families, the life chances of children left behind, and the economic circumstances of African-American communities" (p. 206). Meares writes,

> The status of "convict" severely compromises the released felon's ability to make investments in human capital. A released convict may perceive further investment in human capital to be useless because he may understandably reason that sinking money and time into education and training will not overcome the stigma of a felony conviction on a job application. When he makes the decision to refrain from further investment, he weakens existing relationships he has with people who will be less likely to depend on him, because his ability to provide them with benefits through interaction is compromised. Additionally, the individual who decides not to make further investments in education, skills and training cuts himself off from potential useful relationships with others who have no incentive to form relationships with him. . . . The basic point is this: all unemployed populations are not equal, and any incremental increase in the proportion of convicts among the unemployed population of the ghetto portends incrementally worse consequences for the vitality of the community. (pp. 209–210)

Lower employment opportunities not only harm the released prisoner on reentry, but also erode the social fabric of the community. The deadly combination of prison and unemployment that Bruce Western (2006) details in his book *Punishment and Inequality in America* fuels a cycle of detrimental consequences for the community that then feedback on the community members. These include "fewer adults to monitor and supervise children," resulting in "increased opportunities for children to become involved in delinquency and crime," more broken families, and deepening poverty, all of which produce severe disruptions in African American communities (Meares, 1998, pp. 206–208).

The ratchet also contributes to an exaggerated general perception in the public imagination and among police officers of an association between being African American and being a criminal—between, in Roberts's (1999) words, "blackness and criminality" (p. 805). Roberts discusses one extremely revealing symptom of the "black face" of crime, namely, the strong tendency of White victims and eyewitnesses to misidentify suspects in cross-racial situations. Studies show a disproportionate rate of false identifications when the person identifying is White and the person identified is Black. In fact, according to Johnson (1984), "[T]his expectation is so strong that Whites may observe an interracial scene in which a White person is the aggressor, yet remember the black person as the aggressor" (p. 949). The black face has become the criminal in our collective subconscious. "The unconscious association between Blacks and crime is so powerful that it supersedes reality," Roberts (1999) observes: "[I]t predisposes Whites to literally see Black people as criminals. Their skin color marks Blacks as visibly lawless" (p. 806).

This, in turn, further undermines the ability of African Americans to obtain employment or pursue educational opportunities. It has a delegitimizing effect on the criminal justice system that may encourage disaffected youths to commit crime. It may also erode community–police relations, hampering law enforcement efforts as minority community members become less willing to report crime, to testify, and to convict. The feedback mechanisms, in turn, accelerate the imbalance in the prison population and the growing correlation between race and criminality.

Again, it is important to emphasize that the ratchet effect, while extremely troubling in the case of race, is not only troubling because of race. Again, race serves as the miner's canary, but it is vital to see the fundamental problem (the lack of oxygen). The ratchet is an abstract mechanism that can be equally troubling in other contexts. The very same problem plagues the profiling of persons with prior criminal records, with a very similar, detrimental effect on recidivists who are reentering society—what is termed *recidivist criminality*. What the ratchet effect does here is to accentuate the symbolic meaning of prison and incarceration: It compounds the perception that being a former prisoner means that the convict is more likely to reoffend. To be sure, there may well be a correlation. Again, as in all the cases in this chapter, there is an assumption that the prediction is correct. The statistical correlation is presumably reliable, not spurious. What the ratchet does, though, is aggravate that precise correlation: Whereas prior offenders may represent, hypothetically, 40% of the offending population, profiling prior offenders will result in their representing, again hypothetically, 65% of the prison population. This differential represents a ratchet with heavy symbolic meaning. It means that the general public will tend to think that prior offenders are even more prone to future criminality than they really are. And this will have devastating effects on the possibilities and the reality of reentry.

It is what makes reentry so terribly hard on prior felons; it is what reduces their employment opportunities and their ability to reintegrate into society. It is what renders them suspicious to us all. Less trustworthy. The first to investigate when a crime is committed—the first to suspect when something is missing. It is what makes it even harder for someone returning from prison to go back to school, to find a job, to make friends, to be trusted. And this too feeds a vicious cycle. As Sampson and Laub (1993) observe, imprisonment has

> powerful negative effects on the prospects of future employment and job employment. In turn, low income, unemployment, and underemployment are themselves linked to heightened risks of family disruption.

Through its negative effects on male employment, imprisonment may thus lead indirectly through family disruption to increases in future rates of crime and violence. (p. 225)

What Is Really Going On? Estimating the Impact of Racial Profiling

The problems of racial profiling, then, are problems of statistical discrimination *writ large*. To what extent are these problems being actualized? Is there a ratchet effect today? Are the different groups elastic to policing, and, if so, is the profiling increasing crime in society? What do we know about what is really going on, then? Unfortunately, the new data on police searches from across the country do not provide reliable observations on the key quantities of interest necessary to answer these questions precisely—specifically, the data do not contain measures of comparative offending or comparative elasticity. Nevertheless, it is possible to make reasonable conjectures based on both the best available evidence and conservative assumptions about comparative offending rates and elasticity.

As demonstrated in Chapter 7 of *Against Prediction* (Harcourt, 2007a), "A Case Study on Racial Profiling," based on reasonably conservative assumptions including, first, relatively low elasticity of offending to policing, second, slightly lower elasticity of offending to policing for minority motorists, and third, slightly higher drug-transportation rates among minority motorists, it is fair to infer that racial profiling on the highways may *increase* the total number of persons transporting drug contraband on the roads. From equation (9) above, we know that racial profiling will increase crime if the ratio of White elasticity to minority elasticity is greater than the ratio of minority offending to White offending—in other words, if the elasticity differential is greater than the offending differential. Given the paucity of evidence on both relative elasticities and offending, any conclusion is tentative, but under conservative assumptions, racial profiling on the roads probably increases the profiled crime.

Racial profiling on the highways also probably has a significant distortion effect on the profiled population. From the earlier analysis of the basic racial profiling models, it is clear that the police may have to subject a disproportionate number of minority motorists to criminal justice supervision to equalize offending rates. In all likelihood, this is exactly what is happening in the extensive data from Maryland. It is hard to imagine, even if we assume that minority motorists are offending at a higher natural rate than White motorists, that minority offenders represent 60% of all offenders under natural conditions of offending (i.e., if the police are engaged in color-blind policing). After all, 84% of motorists in Maryland found with drugs had trace or personal-use amounts, and 68% had trace or personal-use quantities of marijuana only; and the survey data seem to suggest that personal consumption of drugs is relatively even across racial lines. Even if we assume that all the other 16% of seizures—those seizures involving large hauls of drugs—consist entirely of minority motorists,[8] then minority offenders would still represent only approximately 31% of offenders.[9]

The most likely explanation for the disjunction between this extreme hypothesized offending differential in Maryland (30/70) and the actual apprehension differential under present conditions of racial profiling (60/40) is that, if we assume elasticity, it takes a lot of profiling to bring the hit rates down to the same level. The result is a significant imbalance in negative contact with the police—whether the seizure of drug contraband results in a fine, an arrest, probation, or imprisonment. This represents a distortion effect that has a significant cost to minority families and communities.

In the end, if we make reasonably conservative assumptions from available evidence, it becomes clear that racial profiling on the highways probably does *not* reduce overall crime, but on the contrary *increases* it, and probably contributes significantly to a ratchet effect in society. And the available data from the criminal justice system is entirely consistent with this informed speculation. During the 20th century, African Americans represented a consistently increasing proportion of the new and overall supervised population. Since 1926, the year the federal government began collecting data on correctional populations, the proportion of African Americans newly admitted to state prisons has increased steadily from 23.1% to 45.8% in 1982. It reached 51.8% in 1991, and stood at 47% in 1997.[10] The result has been a steadily increasing rate of incarceration for African Americans: In 1997, 6.84% of African American adult males were incarcerated in this country, up from a little over 3.5% in 1985 and in sharp contrast to less than 1% of White males.[11] The overall effect can be visualized in Figure 14.1.

Naturally, there is no evidence that these trends verify the ratchet effect. They are merely consistent with a ratchet effect operating in the U.S. criminal justice system against African Americans.

---

[8]Note that this would be an unreasonably conservative assumption. A more reasonable assumption from the Maryland data is that approximately 84% of the dealer population is African American (see Gross & Barnes, 2002, p. 703).

[9]Assuming that 18% of the motorists are minorities, if minorities and Whites offend at the same rate with regard to 84% of the offenses (personal use seizures) and minorities comprise all of the other 16% of the offenders, then minority motorists represent 31.12% of all offenders. (The equation is $(18/100 * 84/100) + (16/100 * 1) = .1512 + .16 = .3112$).

[10]The data are drawn from several sources. For statistics from 1926 to 1982, see Langan (1985); for statistics from 1985 to 1989, see U.S. Bureau of Justice Statistics (1997, Table 1.16); for statistics from 1990 to 1997, see U.S. Bureau of Justice Statistics (2000, Table 1.20).

[11]Maguire and Pastore (2001, Table 6.2); U.S. Bureau of Statistics (2000, Figure 1). For excellent discussions of these trends, see Tonry (1995, pp. 28–31, 56–68). See also Schiraldi and Ziedenberg (2002).

Figure 14.1   State and Federal Prisons and Jail Population Ratios by Race

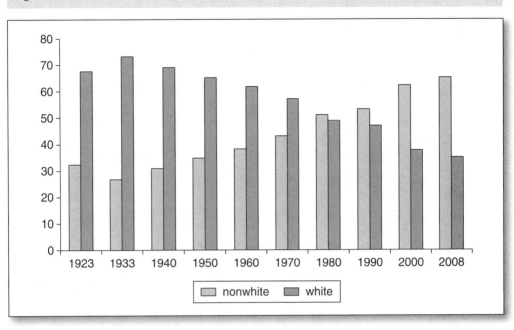

The Real Solution: Axing Statistical Discrimination, Embracing Chance

The real solution to racial profiling, then, is not racial sensitivity training or classes on racial profiling at police academies. I do not mean to belittle these efforts, but they will have little effect if police officers and the general public still believe, as they mostly do today, that statistical discrimination is natural and right, and that young African American and Hispanic males offend on the street at higher rates than others. No amount of counterintuitive training is going to significantly reduce racial profiling, especially not in split-decision, emergency situations.

Instead, we need to start understanding that statistical discrimination, where there are feedback loops, is counterproductive and probably increases street crime over the long term. That it undermines, rather than promotes, the law enforcement objective of reducing crime. Even on very conservative assumptions entirely consistent with rational choice theory, the use of profiling is probably self-defeating: Given the reasonable possibility that offending differentials go hand-in-hand with different elasticity to policing, there is good reason to believe—again, from a rational action perspective—that statistical discrimination will increase rather than decrease the overall amount of crime in society. And where there is uncertainty about offending and elasticity differentials, the use of statistical discrimination will aggravate social disparities. The problems set forth in this paper reflect problems with statistical discrimination more generally—not just with specific types of stereotyping or profiles.

What, then, should we do? Surprisingly, the answer is that we should randomize policing to a far greater extent (for further, see Harcourt, 2007b; Harcourt, Harel, Levy, O'Hear, & Ristroph, 2009). Since the police cannot seek consent to search every car that speeds over the limit, it should use mechanisms that effectively randomize over the speeding population—for example, by seeking consent from every tenth driver stopped or, say, from every person driving between 85 and 90 miles per hour. Randomization may strike you as odd at first, but it is in fact simply a mechanism to extract discretion—and racial prejudice—from the process of selecting persons to search. It is merely a mechanical way to eliminate discretion. It is the best way to take discretion out of policing *without* undermining the goal of police efficiency and *while* promoting principles of justice. Randomization, it turns out, is the only way to achieve a carceral population that reflects the offending population, and it is the only way to avoid the counterproductive effect on crime rates.

Randomization in the policing context is simply a form of random sampling and has all the virtues of random sampling. On the highways, it is the only way that the police would obtain an accurate reflection of the offending population. What randomization achieves, in essence, is to neutralize the perverse effects of statistical discrimination, both in terms of the possible effects on overall crime and of the other social costs.

Randomization translates into different practices in policing and other criminal justice contexts. In the policing context, though, randomization is relatively straightforward: On the highway, the state patrol could deploy random numerical ordering to seek consent to search cars or to stop cars that are speeding. Randomization is already a feature of our law in a number of other areas. It should become part of policing.

Summary

Race has always played a key and disturbing role in the history of statistical tools and methods. The first parole prediction instrument, developed in 1927 by Ernest Burgess at the University of Chicago, included the race and nationality of the father as one of twenty-one factors that predicted success or failure on parole (Harcourt, 2007a). The Illinois Board of Paroles in 1933 implemented Burgess' model and, as a result, race was used expressly as one factor in the "prognasio" that served as the basis for the decision whether or not to parole an inmate. This continued for many decades. In fact, when California began using a parole prediction instrument in the 1970s, it used an actuarial device that relied on race. The first California "Base/Expectancy Score" narrowed in on race and only three other factors: prior commitments, offense type, and number of escapes (Simon, 1993, p. 173).

Race is also what motivates our disgust with racial profiling. It is, without doubt, the issues surrounding race and racial discrimination that bother us most in the incident leading to the arrest of Professor Gates—not the problems with any abstract notions of statistical discrimination. The mug shot of Professor Gates is haunting because it reminds us of our peculiar institutions, of Apartheid, of "Blackness and criminality"—not because of mathematics, partial differentiation, or comparative elasticities. It is racial discrimination that concerns us when we identify racial profiling.

And yet, the problem with racial profiling is precisely the misguided use of statistical discrimination in situations where there are potential feedback effects. The problem is that our customary and ordinary forms of rationality, our "odds reasoning," our daily uses of statistical discrimination, are leading us astray. Race is the miner's canary that signals—or should signal—the larger problems of statistical discrimination and profiling. And until we properly understand the problems of statistical discrimination writ large, I fear that we will make little progress on racial profiling.

Discussion Questions

1. What is statistical discrimination? How does it differ from racial profiling?

2. In what ways does statistical discrimination permeate policing?

3. What is meant by *elasticity of offending to policing*?

4. How can criminal profiling be entirely counterproductive to police work?

5. How can randomized searches help eliminate statistical discrimination while increasing seizures of contraband?

References

Alschuler, A. (2002). Racial profiling and the Constitution. *University of Chicago Legal Forum, 2002,* 163–269.

American Civil Liberties Union (ACLU). (2009). *Persistence of racial and ethnic profiling in the United States: A follow-up report to the U.N. committee on elimination of racial discrimination.* Retrieved from http://www.aclu.org/pdfs/human rights/cerd_finalreport.pdf

American Civil Liberties Union (ACLU) of Arizona. (2008). *Driving while black or brown.* Retrieved from http://www.acluaz.org/sites/default/files/documents/ DrivingWhileBlackorBrown.pdf

Ayres, I. (2008). *Racial profiling and the LAPD: A study of racially disparate outcomes in the Los Angeles police department.* Retrieved from http://www.aclu-sc .org/issues/police-practices/racial-profiling-the-lapd/

Banks, R. R. (2001). Race-based suspect selection and colorblind equal protection doctrine and discourse. *UCLA Law Review, 48,* 1075–1124.

Bar-Ilan, A., & Sacerdote, B. (2001, December). *The response to fines and probability of detection in a series of experiments* (NBER Working Paper No. 8638). Cambridge, MA: National Bureau of Economic Research.

Becker, G. (1996). *Accounting for tastes.* Cambridge, MA: Harvard University Press.

Bjerk, D. (2007). Racial profiling, statistical discrimination, and the effect of a colorblind policy on the crime rate. *Journal of Public Economic Theory, 9*(3), 521–545.

Blumkin, T., & Margalioth, Y. (2006). Targeting the majority: Redesigning racial profiling rules. *Yale Law & Policy Review, 24,* 317–345.

Borooah, V. K. (2001). Racial bias in police stops and searches: An economic analysis. *European Journal of Political Economics, 17,* 17–37.

Cole, D. (1999). *No equal justice: Race and class in the American criminal justice system.* New York: The New Press.

Devos, T., Ma, D. S., & Gaffud, T. (2008). *Is Barack Obama American enough to be the next president? The role of ethnicity and national identity in American politics.* San Diego, CA: San Diego State University. Retrieved from http://www-rohan.sdsu.edu/~tdevos/thd/Devos_spsp2008.pdf

Dominitz, J., & Knowles, J. (2005). Crime minimization and racial bias: What can we learn from police search data? *Economic Journal, 116*(515), 368–384.

Engel, R., Cherkauskas, J. C., & Smith, M. R. (2008). *Traffic stop analysis study: Year 2 final report.* University of Cincinnati Policing Institute. Retrieved from http://www.azdps.gov/agreement/pdf/DPS_Year_2_Data_Report_2008.pdf

Farrell, A., & McDevitt, J. (2006). *Rhode Island traffic stop statistics data collection study 2004–2005.* Boston, MA: Northeastern University Institute on Race and Justice.

Gross, S. R., & Barnes, K. Y. (2002). Road work: Racial profiling and drug interdiction on the highway. Michigan Law Review, 101(3), 651–754.

Guinier, L., & Torres, G. (2005). *The miner's canary: Enlisting race, resisting power, transforming democracy.* Cambridge, MA: Harvard University Press.

Haas, S. M., Turley, E., & Sterling, M. (2009). *West Virginia traffic stop study: Final report.* Criminal Justice Statistical Analysis Center. Retrieved from http://www.djcs.wv.gov/SAC/Documents/WVSAC_Traffic_NEWOverviewofState wideFindings2009.pdf

Harcourt, B. E. (2004). Rethinking racial profiling: A critique of the economics, civil liberties, and Constitutional literature, and of criminal profiling more generally. *The University of Chicago Law Review, 71,* 1275–1381.

Harcourt, B. E. (2007a). *Against prediction: Profiling, policing, and punishment in an actuarial age.* Chicago: University of Chicago Press.

Harcourt, B. E. (2007b). Post-modern meditations on punishment: On the limits of reason and the virtues of randomization (a polemic manifesto for the twenty-first century). *Journal of Social Research, 74*(2), 307–346.

Harcourt, B. E., Harel, A., Levy, K., O'Hear, M. M., & Ristroph, A. (2009). Randomization in criminal justice: A criminal law conversation. In P. Robinson, K. Ferzan, & S. Garvey (Eds.), *Criminal law conversations* (University of Chicago Law & Economics, Olin Working Paper No. 471; University of Chicago, Public Law Working Paper No. 267; Marquette Law School Legal Studies Paper No. 09-26). Retrieved from http://ssrn.com/abstract=1428464

Heaton, P. (2010). Understanding the effects of anti-profiling policies. *Journal of Law and Economics, 53*(1), 29–64.

Hernàndez-Murillo, R., & Knowles, J. (2003). Racial profiling or racist profiling? Testing aggregated data. *International Economic Review, 45*(3), 959–989.

Johnson, S. L. (1984). Cross-racial identification errors in criminal cases. *Cornell Law Review, 69,* 934–987.

Knowles, J., Persico, N., & Todd, P. (2001). Racial bias in motor vehicle searches: Theory and evidence. *Journal of Political Economics, 109*(1), 203–232.

Langan, P. A. (1985). Racism on trial: New evidence to explain the racial composition of prisons in the United States. *Journal of Criminal Law & Criminology, 76*(3), 666–683.

Lavoie, D. (2009, July 23). Cop who arrested black scholar is profiling expert. *Associated Press.* Retrieved from http://www.timesfreepress.com/news/2009/jul/23/cop-who-arrested-black-scholar-profiling-expert/

Maguire, K., & Pastore, A. L. (2001). *Sourcebook of criminal justice statistics, 2000.* Albany, NY: Hindelang Criminal Justice Research Center.

Manski, C. (2006). Search profiling with partial knowledge of deterrence. *Economic Journal, 116*(515), 385–401.

Margalioth, Y. (2008). Looking at prediction from an economics perspective. *Law and Social Inquiry, 33*(1), 235–242.

Meares, T. L. (1998). Social organization and drug enforcement. *American Criminal Law Review, 35*(2), 191–227.

Mosher, C. J., Miethe, T. D., & Phillips, D. M. (2002). *The mismeasure of crime.* Thousand Oaks, CA: Sage.

Obama's fifth news conference. (2009, July 22). *New York Times.* Retrieved from http://www.nytimes.com/2009/07/22/us/politics/22obama.transcript.html?pagewanted=1&ref=politics

Persico, N. (2002). Racial profiling, fairness, and effectiveness in policing. *American Economic Review, 92*(5), 1472–1497.

Ridgeway, G. (2007). *Analysis of racial disparities in the New York police department's stop, question, and frisk practices.* Santa Monica, CA: RAND Corporation.

Roberts, D. E. (1999). Foreword: Race, vagueness, and the social meaning of order-maintenance policing. *Journal of Criminal Law & Criminology, 89*(3), 775–836.

Roberts, D. E. (2004). The social and moral costs of mass incarceration in African American communities. *Stanford Law Review, 56*(5), 1271–1305.

Sampson, S. L., & Laub, J. H. (1993). *Crime in the making: Pathways and turning points through life.* Cambridge, MA: Harvard University Press.

Schauer, F. (2003). *Profiles, probabilities, and stereotypes.* Cambridge, MA: Harvard University Press.

Schiraldi, V., & Ziedenberg, J. (2002, September 1). Cellblocks or classrooms? The funding of higher education and corrections and its impact on African-American men. *Justice Policy Institute.* Retrieved from http://www.justicepolicy.org/research/2046

Shaw, C. R., & McKay, H. D. (1969). *Juvenile delinquency and urban areas: A study of rates of delinquency in relation to differential characteristics of local communities in American cities.* Chicago: University of Chicago Press.

Simon, J. (1993). *Poor discipline.* Chicago: University of Chicago Press.

Thompson, K. (2009, July 22). Scholar says arrest will lead him to explore race in criminal justice. *Washington Post.* Retrieved from http://www.washingtonpost.com/wp-dyn/content/article/2009/07/21/AR2009072101771.html?hpid=artslot&sid=ST2009072301777

Tonry, M. (1995). *Malign neglect: Race, crime, and punishment in America.* New York: Oxford University Press.

U.S. Bureau of Statistics. (1997, June). *Correctional populations in the United States, 1995.* Retrieved from http://bjs.ojp.usdoj.gov/index.cfm?ty=pbdetail&iid=744

U.S. Bureau of Statistics. (2000, November). *Correctional populations in the United States, 1997.* Retrieved from http://bjs.ojp.usdoj.gov/index.cfm?ty=pbdetail& iid=2316

Verniero, P., & Zoubek, P. H. (1999, April 20). *Interim report on the state police review team regarding allegations of racial profiling.* The State of New Jersey, Department of Law & Public Safety, Office of the Attorney General. Retrieved from http://www.state.nj.us/lps/intm_419.pdf

Wacquant, L. (2000, August). The new 'peculiar institution': On the prison as surrogate ghetto. *Theoretical Criminology, 4,* 377–389.

Weiss, A., & Rosenbaum, D. P. (2009). *Illinois traffic stops statistics study 2008 annual report.* University of Illinois at Chicago Center for Research in Law and Justice, 2009. Retrieved from http://www.dot.state.il.us/travelstats/ITSS%20 2008%20Annual%20Report.pdf

Western, B. (2006). *Punishment and inequality in America.* New York: Russell Sage.

Wilson, W. J. (1996). *When work disappears: The world of the new urban poor.* New York: Vintage.

PART FOUR

Ethical Challenges

15 Leading Within the Era of Superagencies

Recruiting, Educating, Inspiring, and Retaining the Post-9/11 Generation of Officers

Kelly W. Sundberg

Over the course of two days in June 2010, the city of Toronto hosted the fourth meeting of the G-20 (a group consisting of government leaders from 19 of the world's leading economies and a representative of the European Union). Despite the fact that prior G-20 summits resulted in violent protests, and knowing some of the world's highest profile leaders would be in attendance, the Toronto Police Service (in conjunction with the Royal Canadian Mounted Police, Ontario Provincial Police, and neighbouring municipal police services) only commenced their security planning in February 2010—four short months prior to the event (Morrow, 2011). As identified in the June 2011 *Toronto Police Service After-Action Review*, inadequate time for planning, lack of specialized training, and deficits in issues management led to a number of officer conduct complaints and a high level of public dissatisfaction with how the police handled this international event (Toronto Police Service, 2011).

As observed by Ontario Ombudsman André Marin, the conduct of police during the Toronto G-20 Summit represented one of the worst compromises of civil liberties in Canadian history (DiManno, 2010). In total, 1,118 members of the public were arrested, 39 citizens and 97 police officers injured, two police officers criminally charged for excessive use of force, and another 121 disciplined for misconduct (Mackrael, 2012; O'Toole, 2011; Toronto Police Service, 2011). Additionally, in August 2011 the Ontario Superior Court allowed a $45 million class-action lawsuit to proceed, exposing the

Toronto Police Service to one of the largest civil actions against police in Canadian history (Small, 2011). In short, the June 2010 G-20 Summit in Toronto demonstrated how a lack of leadership, training, and an apparent unhealthy organizational culture can cause the legitimacy and reputation of one of Canada's largest and most historic police services to be significantly compromised as a result of unethical conduct on behalf of police in only two short days.

The fallout from the G20 summit illustrates the importance of appropriate leadership, training, and organizational culture—phenomena that have assumed new levels of prominence in the aftermath of 9/11 among law enforcement organizations throughout the Western world. Traditionally, law enforcement agencies have focused primarily on maintaining the peace through service to the community, administration of domestic law, and the protection of citizens and property. Since 9/11, these traditional responsibilities have come to include duties associated with the combating of terrorism and transnational crime (Brown, 2011). Additionally, with the advent of the Internet, mobile telecommunications, social media, and an increased propensity for citizens to take litigious actions against government officials they feel have violated their rights, law enforcement officers have had to become professionals who are highly ethical and transparent in all their activities (Wilson & Grammich, 2009). Citizens expect officers to be experts in every facet of policing, empathetic and sensitive during all their interactions, and responsive to the unique needs of their increasingly diverse and informed stakeholders. From the frontline officer to senior commander, society demands contemporary policing professionals not only to serve and protect, but also to be vigilant and responsive to contemporary threats of global terrorism and crime—all while being well-educated and informed champions of social justice (Wilson & Grammich, 2009). To meet these increasingly high expectations, today's law enforcement organizations must recruit and develop personnel of exceptional character who are well educated, dedicated to their duties, and skilled in their policing profession.

This chapter explores how in the years subsequent to 9/11, police leadership, ethics, professionalism, and accountability have risen to the forefront of academic, government, and public discourse. The importance of professionalism and ethical policing has become especially pronounced among federal policing professionals who have become members of large, consolidated, and specialized organizations tasked with new counterterrorism duties in addition to their traditional policing and regulatory responsibilities. Since 9/11, most Western democracies (most notably the United States, Canada, and the United Kingdom) have amalgamated their once independent customs, immigration, and agricultural inspection services into large border and national security policing agencies (and increasingly security intelligence). The aim of integrating these once separate services into a single, unitary agency was primarily to promote and maintain international migration, trade, and commerce, while enhancing protections against threats of terrorism and transnational crime (Winterdyk, & Sundberg, 2010).

Resulting from the emergence of these new multifaceted border security agencies, governments have had to meet the challenges associated with establishing single organizational cultures based on those of their legacy agencies, and to recruit highly skilled officers who embrace these new cultures, are adaptable to diverse new policing mandates, and also ensure they remain flexible and responsive to risks and threats in a manner that reflects high community expectations. By drawing on established management and organizational behavior scholarship, and through a reflection on historic lessons learned, this chapter affords insight into how today's post-9/11 superagency leaders can meet these significant challenges.

The North American Border Security Superagency Era

On October 8, 2001, in direct response to the 9/11 terrorist attacks, then U.S. President George W. Bush allocated over $56 billion to establish the Department of Homeland Security (DHS)—an umbrella superagency that consolidated 22 once separate agencies into seven sub-agencies having more than 210,000 employees (Hobijn & Sager, 2007). Specific to this chapter, contemporary leadership challenges faced by the two DHS sub-agencies of Customs and Border Protection (CBP) (including the Border Patrol) and Immigration and Customs Enforcement (ICE), along with the Public Safety Canada sub-agency of the Canada Border Services Agency (CBSA), will be reviewed.

Both the CBP and ICE were created on March 1, 2003 as a means of advancing America's border and national security strategies. These two sub-agencies combine once separate border services into two amalgamated organizations primarily responsible for customs, immigration, and agricultural inspection either along the border, domestically, or abroad (Heyman & Ackleson, 2010). The CBP constitutes the former U.S. Customs, Immigration, and Agriculture departments' ports-of-entry (POE) operations; ICE is the amalgamation of these same departments' inland enforcement components. By 2005, three short years after being established, the CBP had over 40,000 employees with an annual budget of approximately $6.2 billion (Koslowski, 2011). Today, the CBP has significantly increased in size, having approximately 60,000 employees with an annual budget around $11.4 billion. When combined with ICE, the DHS has nearly 80,000 personnel with annual budgets exceeding $17 billion tasked with administrating and enforcing America's border security strategy (Haddal, 2009).

Because of Canada's proximity and relationship with the United States, the 9/11 terrorist attacks also had a profound impact on Canadian federal policing strategy. It is no coincidence that on December 12, 2003, only a few short months after the United States created the CBP and ICE, then Canadian Prime Minister Paul Martin announced the establishment of what today is known as Public Safety Canada (Winterdyk & Sundberg, 2010). Public

Safety Canada (PSC), like the DHS, consolidates once separate federal law enforcement agencies into a single overarching organization—namely, the Royal Canadian Mounted Police, Canadian Security Intelligence Service, Canada Border Services Agency (CBSA), National Parole Board of Canada, Firearms Centre, and Correctional Service of Canada. Of particular note-worthiness is that when PSC was formed, so was the CBSA.

Of the six sub-agencies under PSC, the CBSA is the only newly created organization. With over 10,000 staff formally from the Canada Customs and Revenue Agency, Citizenship and Immigration Canada, and the Canadian Food Inspection Agency, the CBSA became Canada's third largest federal law enforcement agency (Winterdyk & Sundberg, 2010). The primary focus of the CBSA is to protect Canada's borders; administer customs, immigration, and agriculture inspection laws; and contribute actively to Canada's counter-terrorism and transnational policing strategy—roles that were only periph-eral within the legacy customs and immigration departments.

In light of these two major post-9/11 bureaucratic developments on each side of the Canada/U.S. border, there is great value in examining the leader-ship, ethical challenges, and operational successes the CBP, ICE, and CBSA have had to face. All three agencies have been tasked with developing new organizational cultures that respect the legacies of their founding agencies, attracting new personnel who are capable of addressing new responsibilities and duties, and fulfilling border and national security duties in manners which ensure flexibility and prompt responsiveness to risks and threats asso-ciated with transnational crime and terrorism (Brown, 2011; Wilson & Grammich, 2009). Considering the speed at which these new agencies were established, there is little question CBP, ICE, and CBSA leaders have had to become highly skilled and capable in their ability to promote change, man-age transition, and establish organizational cultures that inspire and pro-mote ethical success.

With any major organizational transition and change, pitfalls and criti-cism can be expected. Critics of the DHS have argued that the superagency is overly bureaucratic, burdened with turf wars between members from the legacy agencies, and lacking in a structure that promotes strategic planning and sound policy development ("Fighting Terrorism," 2005). Cognizant of these organizational problems, in 2005, the DHS embarked on a massive reorganization with the aim of increasing its operational effectiveness, enhancing public confidence, eliminating redundancies, and further develop-ing an organizational culture that unites its over 200,000 personnel with a single vision, mission, and mandate (Brattberg, 2012). At the core of this reorganization was the development of frontline leadership abilities.

Likewise, Canada's relatively new superagency (in particular the sub-agency of the CBSA) has also been criticized for becoming too big too quick, resulting in inefficiencies and organizational culture challenges (Winterdyk & Sundberg, 2010). Despite billions of dollars being spent on post-9/11 security reforms and initiatives, in the early years of PSC, little improvement was realized in relation to enhanced border and national security. As observed by the Hon. Colin Kenny, Senator (Le Parti libéral du Canada) and chairman of the Senate Standing Committee on National Security and Defence, "[T]he money [spent on security] is inadequate and a sense of urgency [on behalf of the Government of Canada towards security improvements] is missing" (Geddes & Gillis, 2005, p. 21). As with the DHS critics, Senator Kenny identified serious organizational culture concerns within PSC—in particular, within the CBSA. Responding to this criticism, both the PSC and the CBSA have taken great effort to rebrand their images and further develop the leadership capacities of their frontline leaders; both focused on building an elevated ethos among personnel and advancing a culture that respects the history of their legacy agencies.

Reflecting on the 1968 Unification of the Canadian Forces

Despite nearly a decade passing since the creation of the CBP, ICE, and CBSA, many critics maintain these agencies are unresponsive, bloated bureaucracies offering little to enhanced border security (Winterdyk & Sundberg, 2010). In the United States, the advent of the DHS represents the largest government reorganization of federal departments since the mid-1940s when former President Harry S. Truman established the Department of Defence, Central Intelligence Agency, and National Security Council (Kahn, 2009). For Canada, the creation of PSC (including the CBSA) constitutes the largest government reorganization of federal departments since the 1968 unification of the Canadian Army, Royal Canadian Navy, and Royal Canadian Air Force into the Canadian Forces (Hopper, 2011). In both the American and Canadian contexts, the creation of the DHS and PSC (including their sub-agencies) involved sweeping government agency reforms, all with the aim of creating more effective and responsive agencies unified under consolidated command and control structures.

Based on the commonly accepted supposition that unified command and control allows for greater efficiencies in military, intelligence, policing, and disaster management operations (Maniscalco & Christen, 2011), policymakers in the United States and Canada quickly responded to the events of 9/11 by creating new consolidated law enforcement and security intelligence agencies based on longstanding established ones. Although infrequent, the wholesale reforming of government agencies in the face of international threats is not new. Governments faced with addressing natural disasters often will create ad hoc centralized command and control systems to coordinate emergency and rescue services. Moreover, police from various jurisdictions often will form joint force operations when addressing criminal threats such as gang violence. Although less common, governments faced with emerging security and crime threats will create entirely new agencies specifically focused on confronting global crime concerns—two examples include the 1972 reform of the U.S. Bureau of Alcohol, Tobacco, and

Firearms to address increasing concerns surrounding the domestic and international illegal weapons trade (while also addressing violations associated with the manufacturing and sale of alcohol and tobacco products), and the 1973 creation of the U.S. Drug Enforcement Agency to address organized drug smuggling within the United States and abroad.

Late-1960s Canadian military reforms also provide an example whereby existing government organizations were consolidated in an attempt to address an emerging global threat—namely, the increasing military aggression of the Soviet Bloc nations. Having to maintain its commitments to Cold War military efforts through its membership in the North Atlantic Treaty Organization (NATO), while at the same time being fiscally challenged in its ability to maintain a well-trained and equipped military, Canada needed to reorganize its armed forces in a manner that minimized costs and maximized effectiveness. As such, in 1968 the Government of Canada unified its historically small, minimally funded, and limited capacity army, navy, and air force into what today is known as the Canadian Forces (CF). This decision was based in part on the recognition that Canada was too small a nation to maintain separate military branches that were globally mobile (Shaw, 2001).

Just as in the post-9/11 era where policing agencies had to shift (in part) from being community-focused public service organizations to becoming globally aware intelligence-led paramilitary ones, in the 1960s, Canada's armed forces needed to shift focus from its historic wartime combat role to one principally focused on peacekeeping and humanitarian missions. In short, the creation of the CF represented Canada's shift from being an active combat force to being peacekeepers (Merdinger, 2000). With this shift in operational focus came a need for a wholesale reform of the CF's culture.

Reflecting on the changing nature of Canada's military role in the late 1960s (i.e., its primary role as a peacekeeping force), military personnel from the legacy branches were cross-trained to perform a multitude of functions (land, naval, and air). Additionally, a single military support structure was established to supply, administer, and support the whole of Canada's military, and a single uniform and rank structure was also adopted to reflect the CF's new unified vision (Shaw, 2001). Although most agree these efforts successfully generated costs savings in relation to the acquisition of arms and equipment, allowed for a more focused and coherent application of Canada's new peacekeeping mandate, and afforded greater flexibility and utility in the conducting of peacekeeping and humanitarian missions, there is also agreement that unification resulted in low morale and infighting among members of the legacy branches, and caused a significant reduction in recruitment and retention (Department of National Defence [Canada], 1980).

Drawing on the example of the CF, and recognizing the parallels existing between post-9/11 federal law enforcement superagencies in the United States and Canada, challenges associated with the creation and transition of organizational cultures can be explored. From this, lessons learned and best practices can be identified. Change is innate within any social structure, including military, security/intelligence, and policing organizations. To meet the many challenges associated with change, governments around the world often have had to restructure their public institutions with the goal of having them "work better and cost less" (Johnson & Leavitt, 2001, p. 129). However, it is only those organizations that accept the inevitability of change, commit to developing a cohesive culture, and invest in the leadership development of their frontline personnel and leaders that eventually realize the great benefits change can provide. Conversely, organizations that fail to identify change, and that ignore the human factor associated with it, ultimately fail in realizing an improvement over their previous situation (Shields, 1999). As will be discussed, the CF represents an organization that failed to adequately address change, resulting in dire consequences and national embarrassment.

By reflecting on the shortfalls and challenges faced by the CF through the lens of contemporary organizational behavior and leadership scholarship, historic insight into the challenges associated with the unification of government organizations can be achieved. Although the creation of the CF, CBP, ICE, and CBSA were similar in design, the motivations were somewhat different—the CF was focused on maximizing resources allocated to a national military so as to maintain international obligations while minimizing government expenditures, and the CBP, ICE, and CBSA on maximizing resources allocated to an emerging and elusive threat from globally mobile terrorist groups. In essence, the CF was created more out of need; the CBP, ICE, and CBSA, out of necessity.

Many organizations that undergo significant restructuring often take an ad hoc approach to their human resource strategy and often fail to implement comprehensive changes in their human resource practices (Shields, 1999). Through the late 1960s to the early 1980s, the CF experienced an erosion of its organizational culture, an elimination of traditional symbols, and a significant decline in morale (Merdinger, 2000). Evidence also suggests that the CBP, ICE, and CBSA all initially neglected to address the importance human factors play in transitional success (see Department of National Defence [Canada], 1980; Kahn, 2009; Shaw, 2001; Winterdyk & Sundberg, 2010). Unfortunately, during their initial years, this neglect caused the CBP, ICE, and CBSA each to experience low morale, decreased effectiveness, and ethical challenges—issues that since appear to have been resolved. As will be illustrated in the case of the CF, unintended consequence from transitional shortfalls can have serious and long-lasting negative impacts.

With the 1968 creation of the CF came a significant psychological impact on tens of thousands of military personnel from the three legacy military branches. Once proud traditions and cultural icons were eliminated in favour of a single uniform, a unified command structure, and shared resources (Ayton, 1996). The majority of criticism of the 1968 amalgamation stems from the Government of Canada's failure to consider the psychological impact that cultural change would have on Canada's military personnel (Newman, 1983). Although many agreed that the concept of amalgamation made economic sense, several military leaders warned the political elite that such a transition could pose a major culture shock to the rank-and-file members from the traditional branches (Ayton, 1996). Moreover, recruits who joined the new CF would potentially become pushed and pulled into existing tensions between longstanding members from the former branches.

Rear-Admiral William Landymore, along with seven other admirals and a half-dozen air marshals and generals, appealed to then National Defence Minister Paul Hellyer to reconsider his decision to create a single military force (Newman, 1983). These military leaders feared that unification would strip the traditional cultures of the former military branches and cause a decrease in morale among their personnel. During the final meeting of military leaders and the Minister of National Defence prior to unification, Landymore asked Hellyer, "Give me one reason, one fact, one objective of yours—one way in which unification is going to make our armed forces more efficient and more economical." "Just wait," Hellyer replied, "Every country in the world will copy us" (Newman, 1983, p. 42). To date, no other nation has adopted the unified CF model, and in fact, this model has been viewed by the U.S. Department of Defence as a gross failure in military reform (Merdinger, 2000).

The Failure of the Combined Forces Initiative

The amalgamation of Canada's traditional military branches caused a gradual confusion between various layers of the organization and inhibited the successful development of a new CF culture (Merdinger, 2000). It also created an environment where new members to the CF became vulnerable to historic inter-branch infighting. The CF's failure to prepare personnel for change created diminished morale that resulted in operational ineffectiveness (Ayton, 1996). Landymore stated,

> It is the supreme irony of the Canadian defence situation that, literally, the only clear-cut political decision on defence policy any government has made in the past twenty years was on unification of the armed forces—and it has been a disaster. (Newman, 1983, p. 37)

Shaw (2001) identified that the Government of Canada's failure to consider the recommendations of its key stakeholders, and instead proceed along a purely political track in its creation of the CF, resulted in a lack of buy-in by CF personnel into the new organization's values and culture—a grave error in any cultural development process (Charlesworth, Cook, & Crozier, 2003; Kouzes & Posner, 2002). Resulting from the Government of Canada's neglect, the CF went through a decade of diminished morale and loss of seasoned leaders, and also developed an international reputation as being an ill-prepared and incapable military force (Merdinger, 2000).

Lacking its seasoned leadership, the CF lost its unified focus, and corps subcultures superseded the force's overall mission, vision, and goals. In short, Canada went from being one of the best-equipped and professionally trained military services in the world during the 1940s and 1950s to a force barely capable of meeting its domestic obligations let alone its international ones (Shaw, 2001).

The most pronounced example of how a failure on behalf of the CF's leadership to recognize the human factors associated with change and transition is that of the Canadian Airborne Regiment (Régiment aéroporté canadien). Formed in 1968 and comprising personnel from a variety of military regiments and branches, the Canadian Airborne Regiment was meant to be a mobile response brigade capable of ad hoc combat and peacekeeping deployments that reinforced Canada's role within NATO and United Nations' peacekeeping and humanitarian missions (Winslow, 2008). The Canadian Airborne Regiment fast became a highly autonomous group within the CF with a distinct subculture, which often was at odds with CF's new peacekeeping mandate. Resulting in part from this cultural disconnect, in 1992, two paratroopers from the Canadian Airborne Regiment, who were deployed to Somalia on a United Nations peacekeeping mission, tortured and murdered 16-year-old Shidane Arone (Stewart, 1992).

This incident, which has come to be known as the *Somalia Affair*, exemplified the significant and longstanding ethical, leadership, and professional shortcomings that had plagued CF since its inception. Resulting from media coverage of Shidane Arone's murder, news reports and television footage of Canadian Airborne Regiment members participating in demeaning, violent, and racist initiation rites began to surface. Outraged by the highly unethical and unprofessional conduct of its military, the Canadian public demanded the Government of Canada to investigate. As a result, in 1997, the findings of the Somalia Commission of Inquiry was publicly released, which revealed that Canada's elite military "peacekeeping" force had engaged in rape, torture, and murder—all stemming from a violent and racist subculture that had developed within the regiment (Razack, 2000). In response, the Government of Canada disbanded the regiment and launched an across-the-board review of CF's leadership, management, and operations.

The failure of CF to clearly communicate its vision of change and transformation among its rank and file, attain buy-in of its new peacekeeping-focused organizational culture, and educate its personnel on professional and ethical conduct ultimately resulted in the CF being viewed domestically and internationally as an unprofessional, corrupt, and untrustworthy organization (Shaw, 2001). As with any breach of trust, it has taken over a decade for the CF to regain its reputation—yet, even today, the Somalia Affair remains fresh among many Canadians (Bercuson, 2009). Yet, what is perhaps most discerning about the Somalia Affair is that even before the tragic murder of Shidane Arone, the Government of Canada had attempted (unsuccessfully) to address widespread dissatisfaction with the CF.

The Fyffe Report

In the late 1970s, the Canadian Minister of Defence commissioned the Task Force on Review of the Canadian Forces—commonly referred to as the *Fyffe Report* after the task force chairman, Greg Fyffe. This report outlined a number of suggestions on how the government could improve low morale, unprofessionalism, and unethical conduct among CF personnel. Fyffe wrote, "Clearly, a lesson evident from the recommendations was that integration and unification had gone too far, and fast enough, in its desire to ensure a common identity" (Bailey, 2002, p. 34). Fyffe acknowledged the motivation for amalgamating the CF was logical on a political level; however, he believed it lacked a frontline analysis of how change would affect personnel on a cultural and emotional level. Tragically, although the Minister of Defence commissioned the report and accepted its recommendations, it was not until the aftermath of the Somalia Affair that these recommendations where fulsomely implemented. The important lesson learned from the Fyffe Report is that commissioning a study to address observed organizational concerns, yet failing to take timely and sincere efforts to implement recommendations, can have dire, unintended and unforeseen consequences. Since the Fyffe Report, and in light of the Somalia Affair, the CF has implemented a number of reforms that have resulted in positive cultural change—most notably training and education programmes aimed at developing service unity, ethical and professional conduct, and buy-in of the CF's vision, mission, and goals (see Bailey, 2002; Bercuson, 2009; Razack, 2000).

By learning from the CF experience, other government organizations that have undergone significant change (such as the CBP, ICE, and CBSA) can avoid the shortcomings experienced by the CF leadership. Of course, the CF case is not meant to provide an exact parallel to the advent of the CBP, ICE, and CBSA; rather, it is meant to provide an example whereby potential risks associated with the management of change and organizational amalgamation can be identified. In the case of the CF, a failure to address issues at a frontline level ultimately resulted in lowered morale, diminished recruitment, infighting, as well as a loss of institutional respect and legitimacy (Bercuson, 2009; Shaw, 2001).

Specific to the issues that will be addressed in the remainder of this chapter, the ability of the CF to effectively manage, mobilize, and, most importantly, develop the ethos and leadership capacity of their personnel was significantly disadvantaged because of poor high-level decision making. Yet, despite these disadvantages, the frontline leaders of the CF were still able to persevere in their efforts. Today, these once frontline CF leaders are now senior commanders in what has become a highly respected and effective military service. The shame of the Somalia Affair has mostly lifted, and Canada can once again take pride in its role as a respected peacekeeping force. Not since World War II has the CF had as high a level of morale among its ranks as today. Moreover, recruitment is at an all-time high, incidents of misconduct are at an all-time low, and the CF once again is a respected member within NATO (Horn, 2009).

Effectively Communicating and Implementing Change

Having a comprehensive and effective communications strategy is imperative in any organization, regardless of its size or history, or whether it is public or private, for- or not-for-profit (Johnson & Leavitt, 2001; Kouzes & Posner, 2002). Communication is the basis of building trust, expressing thoughts, and, most importantly, conveying the importance of ethics and professionalism. Through communication, we develop emotional, physical, and intellectual bonds, and also convey expectations, beliefs, and understanding (Kouzes & Posner, 2002; Maxwell, 1995). By openly and frequently communicating an organization's vision, mission, and goals, leaders are able to reinforce their own personal expectations of professionalism and ethics, as well as those of their organization.

Effective leaders need to identify mediums through which information, ideas, and goals can be conveyed. Without these mediums, leaders are unable to affect change, develop culture, create vision, or achieve their organizational goals (Giuliani, 2002; Kouzes, 2003). The lack of comprehensive communication on behalf of leaders can seriously inhibit an organization's ability to effectively transform and effect change—ultimately risking collapsing from within (Shields, 1999). As discussed in the example of the CF, poor communication of overarching vision, mission, and goals allowed an unhealthy subculture to develop, and organizational legitimacy and reputation to be seriously damaged.

As was the case for CF, and today in the CBP, ICE, and CBSA, organizational transition, as opposed to change, is not a choice but rather a natural progression (see Bridges, 1986). Organizational leaders need to focus on the anticipated outcome and not attempt to control the transition. It is up to these leaders to plot the course for change, accept transition as a temporary phenomenon, and encourage their members to steer the organization toward its ultimate goal with the aim of sustained success (Fullan, 2001; Kouzes & Posner, 2002). To promote sustainability or organizational success, leaders must always seek out and develop new leaders from within the organization and empower managers to promote both the personal and professional development of their personnel—open and sincere communication is a critical component to this endeavor (Fullan, 2001).

In the aftermath of 9/11, law enforcement leaders have had to communicate how their roles have evolved from being local/regional in focus to being global in scope. Gone are the days when a frontline officer simply had to understand the nuances of the community they served; today, these officers need to understand how global forces can impact their local responsibilities. As identified by Brown (2011), post-9/11 officers can become ethically torn between their sworn duty to protect and serve the community in compliance with the Constitution, while, on the other hand, being called to arms in the "war on terror" (p. 651). As a result, officers may become conflicted in their loyalty to serving the community and with their role (as minute as it may be) in fighting the war on terrorism. Considering this, it is imperative that today's law enforcement leaders communicate through both words and actions that these potential conflicts can be overcome through the application of ethical and professional decisions that respect domestic legal restraints. At the end of the day, by acting ethically and professionally in the execution of their sworn duty of serving and protecting their community, offices will gain respect and legitimacy from their stakeholders by demonstrating through actions the fundamental tenets of democracy and virtues of freedom.

Creating, Sustaining, and Evolving Organizational Culture

Creating, sustaining, and evolving a healthy and rich organizational culture is key to recruiting, educating, inspiring, and retaining highly effective and adaptable law enforcement personnel. Culture brings people together in a manner that promotes the vision, mission, and goals of an organization, ultimately giving it legitimacy and status. Without adhering to culture, an organization's progressive success will be significantly inhibited (Johnson & Leavitt, 2001; Shields, 1999). Organizations that fail to identify the cultural needs of their stakeholders can expect deceased efficiency, lower morale, and inhibited service delivery. However, what is worse, they also risk ethical violations on behalf of their members (Charlesworth et al., 2003; Kouzes & Posner, 2002). Conversely, an organization having a healthy organizational culture will find that others wish to join them. For law enforcement organizations, this has a twofold impact—not only will members of the public find a career with their agency as being attractive, but the whole of the public will value the agency as an important and legitimate public service as well.

Culture is established through leadership that is grounded in shared values of a specific constituency (Kouzes & Posner, 2002; Maxwell, 1995; Yukl, 2002). When leaders identify the need for change, they must formulate a plan that will effectively and transparently communicate their vision and, in turn, promote culture (Henderson & Venkatraman, 1999; Kouzes, 2003). Leadership is the catalyst for developing culture and sound management practices that ensure continued cultural development (Fullan, 2001). There is little question that had the CF paid more attention to its frontline leaders, afforded them development opportunities, and supported their efforts to communicate change and transformation, the tragedy of the Somalia Affair would not have occurred and they would not have had to spend a decade regaining public support and approval.

Leaders within the CBP, ICE, and CBSA all have the opportunity to learn from the CF example, and work to develop their own unique and cohesive organizational cultures. By acknowledging the history and traditions of their legacy agencies, building on past and current successes, and learning from initial transitional failures, the CBP, ICE, CBSA (along with other post-9/11 law enforcement organizations) will gain the unique opportunity to create new traditions and culture based on a foundation of ethics and professionalism. Moreover, by interweaving the tenets of ethics and professionalism throughout their emerging cultures, these new superagencies will negate the risk of corrupt subcultures from emerging within. A significant benefit of investing in the creation of a healthy culture is that intelligence and other information needed by officers to achieve their law enforcement goals will be more openly and freely available by their respective stakeholders.

Educating

The efficient transfer of institutional knowledge from one generation of officers to the next is paramount to achieving sustained organizational success (Henderson & Venkatraman, 1999). To achieve this transfer, organizations must establish themselves as learning organizations that capitalize on technology and encourage interaction between personnel at all levels (Kouzes & Posner, 2002). Specific attention must also be given to the diversity that exists among individual members (Lancaster & Stillman, 2002). Leaders must identify the different learning styles that exist among their personnel and develop learning plans that accommodate these differences. This effort can be very difficult considering the vast differences that exist among today's multigenerational workforce.

As observed by noted economist and demographer Professor David Foot, today's modern workforce is composed of three principal generational cohorts, each having unique learning and social characteristics: Baby Boomers (born between 1947 and 1966), Busts (born between 1967 and 1979), and Echos (born 1980 and 1995). As Foot (2007) observes, although learning and cognitive development are very much dependent on individual genetics, how we are socialized to learn is to a great degree dependent on the generational cohort to which we belong. Baby Boomers (which constitute the largest cohort) have mostly been educated in a traditional face-to-face classroom setting where they were expected to memorize information and accept what was taught to be conclusively the truth. On the other hand, those of the Echo (or Gen Y) generation (which are the second largest cohort) are very much reliant on the Internet to obtain knowledge, often are educated through virtual learning mediums, and are very comfortable in challenging the knowledge of their educators. In between these two groups (and constituting the smallest of the three cohorts), is the Busts (or Gen X) generation, who have become attuned to learning both in a traditional and contemporary setting, and also straddle the learning styles of both the Baby Boomers and Echos.

The challenge organizational educators and trainers face is finding innovative and effective means to transfer knowledge between these three unique cohorts. This effort can be incredibly challenging for organizations, such as today's superagencies that have tens, and even hundreds, of thousands of personnel. Yet, despite the immense expense, effort, and challenging logistics that come with educating large numbers of diverse learners, organizations that fail to invest in education and training can risk the same shortfalls associated with poor communication and unhealthy culture; after all, effective communication and the development of healthy organizational culture both rely on leaders and personnel alike being educated and trained.

One way organizations can become learning organizations is through the hiring of professional educators and application of educational technologies (Brown, LeMaster, & Swisher, 2001). Although costly at first, such an investment can help ensure its members are fully aware of their organization's professional expectations, have the skills needed to effectively perform their duties, and, most importantly, have the ability to convey institutional knowledge among existing generational cohorts of personnel as well as future generations. Failure of government to accept the importance of adapting sound educational programs and technologies can greatly hamper future transitional challenges and operational imperatives (Foot, 2007).

Specific to the development of ethics and professionalism among the various generational cohorts of law enforcement personnel, leaders much also understand that each cohort conceptualizes ethics and professionalism in a different way. As such, great effort must be taken on the part of law enforcement leaders, educators, and trainers to convey consistent moral principles, expected professional practices, and governing behaviors they expect and demand from all their personnel (Brown et al., 2001). Additionally, information and knowledge must be communicated in a multitude of mediums that respect generational and individual learning differences. The benefit of investing in such an approach is that once in place, this system will become a core component in the organization's recruitment, in-service, and leadership education and training regimen—providing a central portal through which information, knowledge, skills, and culture can be developed in a coherent, consistent, and organization-wide manner.

Recruiting and Retaining Excellent Officers

As observed by Roswell (Georgia) Police Department Chief Dwayne Orrick (2012), "[S]upervisors who micromanage, fail to provide positive reinforcement, and are quick to criticize their staff generally compel individuals to leave agencies" (p. 23). Reflecting on Chief Orrick's observation, these supervisors would be ones with limited communications skills and a misunderstanding of their organization's cultural norms, and who have not received the requisite education needed to be inspirational, developmental, and respected leaders. Agencies having supervisors such as those described by Chief Orrick will not only lose valuable and skilled officers, but will also likely miss out on the opportunity to attract new ones. Considering the costs associated with the selection of new recruits and the reputational damage that can ensure from losing quality (yet unhappy) officers to other organizations, it behooves senior leaders to view the ongoing selection and development of their frontline leaders as a crucial part of their overall recruitment and retention strategy.

When a law enforcement agency achieves excellence in its communications, culture, and education, the recruitment and retention of excellent officers becomes instinctive and effortless. To this end, law enforcement agencies that are viewed by the public and other stakeholders as being champions of ethical and professional best practices, and whose personnel openly express their pride in service and membership within the agency, will inspire others to join these ranks. People want careers within organizations where they feel valued, respected, and encouraged (Kouzes & Posner, 2002). Additionally, people want to belong to organizations that are respected by the whole of society and are viewed as being champions of social justice, ethical in their activities, and professional in their operation—this is especially true for those seeking to join a law enforcement agency (Orrick, 2012).

The first step law enforcement agencies (especially new superagencies) need to take in enticing excellent recruits, is to showcase their inspiring, healthy, and attractive organizational culture. Considering the budgetary impediments facing many agencies, and considering the new cost-effective mediums through which many of today's youth frequently communicate (in particular, social media sites), agencies have a new opportunity to showcase their culture in a way that speaks to the next generation of officers. Irrespective of how this culture is communicated, potential recruits nonetheless will be attracted to organizations that promote a healthy, cohesive, and inspiring culture. Second, agencies need to formulate their selection process in a manner that encourages those who already emulate the desired tenets of their respective organizational culture to achieve success within the application process (Johnson & Leavitt, 2001). The key aspect of this strategy is to attract recruits who have the ability to embrace the agencies' culture, and most importantly, help develop this culture in a meaningful and positive way—after all, recruits eventually become leaders. Third, recruit selection criteria should include both an ability to perform the hard skills needed in law enforcement, as well as identify a desire and aptitude to achieve personal and professional success as a leader and role model within the community. Finally, great effort needs to be taken to ensure those who join an agency are of the highest ethical character, are focused on service to society, and possess the ability to think critically and make sound, ethical decisions.

As intuitive as this advice may be, many of today's law enforcement agencies face significant fiscal restraints, have limited pools of qualified candidates to draw from, and are in increasing competition with other agencies to attract new officers. Adding to these challenges, the profession of law enforcement has become more challenging with new threats of terrorism and transnational crime. Yet, those agencies that fail to invest in both recruitment and retention due to budgetary and logistical challenges often find they spend more in addressing civil litigation as a result of officer misconduct, lose legitimacy among their stakeholders due to diminished responsiveness, and eventually see a rise in the level of violence and crime within their community because of ineffective policing practices (Wilson & Grammich, 2009). Considering this, the most cost-effective and successful approach to recruitment and retention is to create, develop, and maintain a healthy organizational culture, promote and encourage learning, and ensure frequent and open communication.

Summary

As in the case of the CF, frontline leaders within the legacy agencies of the CBP, ICE, and CBSA have the opportunity to reflect on past failures and successes with the goal of creating new traditions and establish vibrant and heralded cultures that unify officers in the protection of sovereignty and promotion of social justice, law and order, and freedom from the plights of transnational crime and terrorism. To this end, the leaders of today's super-agencies must recruit and retain officers of the highest character, ethics, and professionalism. Through an acceptance that human capital constitutes the most important element of a successful law enforcement agency, today's superagencies will become examples other policing organizations follow. There is little question that today's law enforcement agencies face significant challenges in regard to recruiting and retaining highly capable personnel; however, they nonetheless retain the principal responsibility for safeguarding society from an increasing threat from terrorism and transnational crime.

Taking from the experience of the Canadian Forces, the leadership of today's superagencies cannot afford to forgo investing in human capital. It is not enough to simply create new organizations tasked with addressing contemporary threats—as evident in the case of the Canadian Airborne Regiment, this in itself can cause must greater harm than what was politically intended. In every regard, a commitment to ensuring a healthy, inspiring, and encouraging organizational culture stands as the foundation for not only recruitment and retention, but also the maintaining of an agency's legitimacy and effectiveness. Today's superagency leaders must capitalize on the multitude of experience and capacities of their generational cohorts of employees; they must also promote ongoing learning and celebrate ethical, professional behavior, critical thinking, and decision making. Finally, today's law enforcement leaders must themselves lead by example and demonstrate through their own conviction, resolve, and ethical conduct that success is achievable irrespective of current economic and global challenges. There is always a light at the end of the proverbial tunnel in times of change and conflict; it is the task of policing leaders to ensure they have taken every possible step to negate the possibility this light is not cast by an oncoming locomotive.

Discussion Questions

1. Describe how the terrorist attacks of 9/11 resulted in a paradigm shift to occur within the policing profession.

2. What are some of the common generational challenges police leaders can expect to face when managing diverse personnel?

3. How could the Canadian Forces have better managed its transition so as to mitigate a decrease in morale?

4. What steps can frontline leaders of today's superagencies take to best promote a healthy organizational culture reflective of the agencies' missions, visions, and goals?

5. In your view, and reflecting on past examples, what will be the major challenges associated with police recruitment and retention in the next decade?

References

Ayton, D. G. (1996, November). Getting Canada's armed forces back on track. *The McGill Reporter, 29*(11), 1–3. Retrieved from http://reporter-archive.mcgill.ca/Rep/r2906/war.htm

Bailey, K.W. (2002, May 6). *Integration and unification equals jointness in 21st century Canadian forces* (Unpublished master's thesis). Canadian Forces College, Kingston, ON.

Bercuson, D.J. (2009). Up from the ashes: The re-professionalization of the Canadian forces after the Somalia affair. *Canadian Military Journal, 9*(3), 31–39.

Brattberg, E. (2012, March 15). Coordinating for contingencies: Taking stock of post-9/11 homeland security reforms. *Journal of Contingencies and Crisis Management, 20*(2). doi:10.1111/j.1468-5973.2012.00662.x

Bridges, W. (1986, Summer). Managing organizational transition. *Organizational Dynamics, 15*(2), 24–34.

Brown, C. A. (2011). Divided loyalties: Ethical challenges for America's law enforcement in post-9/11 America. *Case Western Reserve Journal of International Law, 43*(651), 652–675.

Brown, R., Jr., LeMaster, L., & Swisher, S. (2001, June). Training the correctional force of today and tomorrow. *Corrections Today, 63,* 120–121.

Charlesworth, K., Cook, P., & Crozier, G. (2003, November). Leading change in the public sector: Making the difference. *Management Services, 47*(4), 12–15.

Department of National Defence [Canada]. (1980, March 15). *Task Force on the Review of Unification of the Canadian Armed Forces: Final report* (IRC: 355.30971 C35). Ottawa, ON: Government of Canada.

DiManno, R. (2010, December 8). DiManno: Make it right, Chief Blair. *The Toronto Star Online.* Relieved from http://www.thestar.com/news/crime/article/903363--dimanno-make-it-right-chief-blair

Fighting terrorism: Imagining something much worse than London. (2005, July 14). *The Economist.* Retrieved from http://www.economist.com/node/4174486

Foot, D. (2007). Changing demographics: Marketing and human resource trends in a global economy. In T. Wesson (Ed.), *Canada and the new world economic order* (pp. 238–259). Toronto, ON: Captus Press.

Fullan, M. (2001). *Leading in a culture of change*. San Francisco: Jossey-Bass.

Geddes, J., & Gillis, C. (2005, July 18). How safe are we? *Maclean's Magazine, 21*.

Giuliani, R. W. (2002). *Leadership*. New York: Miramax Books.

Haddal, C. C. (2009, April 9). *Border security: Key agencies and their missions* (CRS Report No. RS21899). Retrieved from http://www.dtic.mil/cgi-bin/GetTRDoc?AD=ADA500430

Henderson, J. C., & Venkatraman, N. (1999). Strategic alignment: Leveraging information technology for transforming organizations, *IBM Systems Journal, 38*, 472–484.

Heyman, J., & Ackleson, J. (2010). United States border security after 9/11. In J. A. Winterdyk & K. W. Sundberg (Eds.), *Border security in the Al-Qaeda era* (pp. 37–75). Boca Raton, FL: CRC Press.

Hobijn, B., & Sager, E. (2007, February). What has homeland security cost? An assessment: 2001–2005. *Current Issues in Economics and Finance, 13*(2). Retrieved from http://www.newyorkfed.org/research/current_issues/ci13-2.pdf

Hopper, T. (2011, August 15). "Royal" returns for Canada's armed forces. *The National Post*. Retrieved from http://news.nationalpost.com/2011/08/15/royal-returns-for-canadas-armed-forces/

Horn, B. (Ed.) (2009). *Fortune favours the brave: Tales of courage and tenacity in Canadian military history*. Toronto, ON: Dundurn Press.

Johnson, G., & Leavitt, W. (2001, Spring). Building on success: Transforming organizations through an appreciative inquiry. *Public Personnel Management, 30*(1), 129–136.

Kahn, L. H. (2009, June 9). The problem with the Department of Homeland Security. *Bulletin of the Atomic Scientists*. Retrieved from http://www.thebulletin.org/web-edition/columnists/laura-h-kahn/the-problems-the-department-of-homeland-security

Koslowski, R. (2011, February). *The evolution of border controls as a mechanism to prevent illegal immigration* (Migration Policy Institute Report). Retrieved from http://www.migrationpolicy.org/pubs/bordercontrols-koslowski.pdf

Kouzes, J. M. (Ed.) (2003). *Business leadership: A Jossey-Bass Reader*. San Francisco: Jossey-Bass.

Kouzes, J. M., & Posner, B. Z. (2002). *The leadership challenge*. San Francisco: Jossey-Bass.

Lancaster, L., & Stillman, D. (2002). *When generations collide: Who they are, why they clash, how to solve the generational puzzle at work*. New York: Harper.

Mackrael, K. (2012, April 5). Cost of G20 police review expected to double. *The Globe and Mail*. Retrieved from http://www.theglobeandmail.com/news/national/toronto/cost-of-g20-police-review-expected-to-double/article2393826/

Maniscalco, P. M., & Christen, H. (2011). *Homeland security: Principles and practices of terrorism response*. Sudbury, MA: Jones and Bartlett.

Maxwell, J. C. (1995). *The winning attitude: Developing the leaders around you: becoming a person of influence*. Nashville, TN: Thomas Nelson.

Merdinger, S. E. (2000, Autumn–Winter). Recipe for failure: Centralization and US joint forces command. *Joint Force Quarterly, 23*(4), 15–19.

Morrow, A. (2011, June 23). Toronto police were overwhelmed at G20, review reveals. *The Globe and Mail*. Retrieved from http://www.theglobeandmail.com/news/national/toronto/toronto-police-were-overwhelmed-at-g20-review-reveals/article2073215/

Newman, P.C. (1983). *True north: Not strong and free*. Toronto, ON: McClelland and Stewart.

Orrick, D. (2012, January). Recruiting during the economic downturn. *The Police Chief, 79*, 22–24.

O'Toole, M. (2011, June 10). Officer charged with assault causing bodily harm from G20 summit. *National Post*. Retrieved from http://news.nationalpost.com/2011/06/10/officer-charged-with-assault-causing-bodily-harm-from-g20-summit/

Razack, S. (2000, February). From the "clean snows of Petawawa": The violence of Canadian peacekeepers in Somalia. *Cultural Anthropology, 15*(1), 127–163.

Shaw, G. D. T. (2001, July). The Canadian armed forces and unification. *Defense Analysis, 17*(2), 159–174.

Shields, J. L. (1999, April). Transforming organizations: Methods for accelerating culture change processes. *Information Knowledge Systems Management, 1*(2), 105–115.

Small, P. (2011, August 30). Judge allows one G20 class action lawsuit to seek certification, while staying a second one. *The Toronto Star Online*. Retrieved from http://www.thestar.com/news/crime/article/1047030--judge-allows-one-g20-class-action-lawsuit-to-seek-certification-while-staying-a-second-one

Stewart, B. (1992, December 8). Somalia: Culture, chaos, and clans. *Prime Time News Report–Canadian Broadcasting Corporation*. Retrieved from http://rc-archives.cbc.ca/programs/587-4302/page/7/

Toronto Police Service. (2011, June). *Toronto Police Service after-action review: G-20 Summit, Toronto, Ontario, June 2010*. Retrieved from http://www.torontopolice.on.ca/publications/files/reports/g20_after_action_review.pdf

Wilson, J. M., & Grammich, C. A. (2009). *Police recruitment and retention in the contemporary urban environment: A national discussion of personnel experiences and promising practices from the front line*. Santa Monica, CA: RAND Corporation. Retrieved from http://www.rand.org/pubs/conf_proceedings/2009/RAND_CF261.pdf

Winslow, D. (2008). Misplaced loyalties: The role of military culture in the breakdown of discipline in two peace operations. *Canadian Review of Sociology, 35*(3), 345.

Winterdyk, J. A., & Sundberg, K. W. (Eds.). (2010). *Border security in the Al-Qaeda era*. Boca Raton, FL: CRC Press.

Yukl, G. (2002). *Leadership in organizations* (5th ed.). Upper Saddle River, NJ: Prentice Hall.

16 Implementing Democratic Policing Reform

Challenges and Constraints in Three Developing Countries

Cyndi Banks

It is not possible to forget, not after they did to us what they did when they dragged us out of the jeepney. At the barangay centre, I was struck here, here, here and here (points to various parts of his body; some spots still exhibited signs of severe bruising) with their batons. They broke one of my legs and then they took us to the CIG (Criminal Investigation Group section of the local police station). We were forced to crawl all over the CIG while being beaten over our backs. They electrocuted our heads (apparently with stun guns), beaten and abused every time we were interrogated. All the time my leg was broken. I refused to talk because every time I tried to say something, the beatings happened. These beatings went on for about a week. Our bodies were full of bruises and my face swelled. They did not give us medical treatment. One of their favorite forms of beating was to hit the back of your knees very hard (hahampasin ka sa alulud.) The police were also telling us that if we each gave them 50,000 pesos, they would let us go free. (Varona, 2011, p. 187)

Introduction

Inevitably, the commanding role that policing plays in the maintenance of the rule of law, in justice systems, in police and citizen interactions, and in resource allocation,[1] calls attention to the need for appropriate standards of conduct. The account of police brutality in the Philippines set out above illustrates how the powers entrusted to law enforcement can be abused, especially when there is no effective civilian oversight of policing or genuine accountability. While many police organizations worldwide operate under systems that prescribe ethical policing standards, law enforcement bodies in developing states often lack ethical codes or any training or instruction in ethical issues or in ethical dilemmas that affect policing.

International organizations and the international community have established a number of global norms associated with ethical law enforcement, including norms formulated under the auspices of United Nations organizations. Universal norm creation goes hand in hand with the shaping and diffusion[2] of discourses and practices that collectively make up the concept of "democratic policing"[3] by members of the donor community who finance and support police reform[4] projects in developing and transitional states, and by others such as consultants who specialize in police reform, and academics whose field is policing or security.

---

[1]As Clegg, Hunt, and Whetton (2000) note, "very high proportions of criminal justice personnel are police officers and very high proportions of criminal justice expenditure are devoted to policing, in all countries" (p. 3).

[2]Hills (2008, p. 220) argues that the transferability of police practices is always assumed and that contextual assessments are not prioritized. She calls for researchers to map the development of specific police forces over time and for studies of the political economy of policing.

[3]Before the notion of democratic policing was developed, police reform projects tended to focus on developing "professionalism" in policing (and many U.S. projects still follow this approach). Professionalism, as an alternative to the insular occupational culture of policing found in all states, focuses instead on impartiality, accountability, specialist knowledge and ethical standards in police work (Brogden & Shearing, 1993, p.108). It implies replacing traditional police culture with a culture of professionalism (Chan, 1996, p. 232), but it is a technocratic approach that fails to address the purpose of policing or its governance. As Neild (2001) suggests, professionalism reflects a Western perspective to policing based on "high-tech, information-driven policing" (p. 22). Pino and Wiatrowski (2006, p. 55) argue that teaching ethics within the professional policing model can be regarded as an admission that the professional model has failed to meet its objective of ensuring professionalism.

[4]Hills (2008) comments that police reform is seen not only as a key element in democratization but also in conflict prevention and poverty-reduction strategies, and this has aided in the internationalization of policing discourse and practice (p. 215). Hills points out that there is now "an international police-reform industry" (p. 220). As Bayley (2006) observes, during the 1990s, international assistance for police reform became a "substantial industry for the international community collectively as well as for many, primarily, first world countries" (p. 9).

These discourses, designed by Western policing experts, consultants, and academics,[5] embody the paradigm of good policing and include elements of police governance intended to ensure public accountability and oversight of police, and to promote the concept of community policing. Consequently, through the medium of police reform projects, developing states may be the recipients of both global standards designed to ensure ethical policing and elements of police reform projects that promote oversight and accountability of police to the community. In both cases, appropriate standards of conduct are the outcome of policy transfers from developed to developing states. As Neild (2001) notes, most donor policing interventions are focused on police recruitment, training at all levels, disciplinary codes and practices, building and strengthening leadership, providing infrastructure and resources, putting in place management information systems, and increasing technical capacity. More recently, police and community relations have become very prominent, along with modes of accountability such as police review boards and complaints boards.

Global norms and standards[6] either directly address police conduct through stipulations about prohibited behavior or they may more indirectly attempt to regulate conduct by prescribing the procedures and practices for proper governance and oversight of policing action. In the latter case, accountability and oversight may scrutinize police conduct after a law enforcement event has occurred in the expectation that the lessons learned through oversight will not only ensure accountability for police wrongs but also avert similar incidents in the future because the decision of the oversight body is publicized within a police service. Accordingly, in this case, global norms provide a framework and mechanism for maintaining ethical standards of conduct.

---

[5]Marenin (2007, pp. 181–182) refers to this group of policing experts as *transnational policymakers* and makes the point that the policing discourses that are disseminated rely on the experiences and the practice of Western policing agencies. Hills (2008, p. 220) notes that a number of specialist policing journals publish work on police reforms and that other material can be located in conference and workshop proceedings and reports written for donors. Most police advisers are retired or seconded officers and most publications are policy driven or descriptive in nature.

[6]The idea of prescriptive international normative standards is well expressed by the United Nations Office on Drugs and Crime (UNODOC) as, "Laws set the framework in which police are to operate, and international law sets the framework for national legislation." In another elaboration of the concept, Article 8, paragraph 2, of the *United Nations Convention Against Corruption*, provides that "in particular, each State Party shall endeavor to apply, within its own institutional and legal systems, codes or standards of conduct for the correct, honorable and proper performance of public functions."

This discussion begins with an explanation of the concept of democratic policing and then explores some of the current international norms relating to police conduct. An assessment follows of how those norms, as "best practices" embodied in the concept of democratic policing, have been applied in some selected states through police reform projects and to what degree of success.[7] To add context, the social, historical, and the political economy of policing in the selected developing states and the scope and content of police reform projects in those states will also be explored. In designing and implementing police reform projects, Western constructs of policing, including international norms, standards, and best practices, are often confronted by local policing constructs that originated in colonial times but have survived into the postcolonial period. Overcoming the constraints of colonial and postcolonial policing models and transforming them into democratic policing models presents many challenges, especially in terms of reshaping local police cultures. Transformation may be less problematic, however, in smaller postconflict states with a low population where civil conflict has effectively devastated the local policing model.

Democratic Policing

According to Trebilcock and Daniels (2008), police reform did not generally form part of the efforts to strengthen the rule of law in developing states until the last 15 years. In fact, United States legislation, in the form of the Foreign Assistance Act, prohibited U.S. agencies from training police and it was only in the late 1980s that this prohibition began to be eased.

In many developing states, police have traditionally been regarded as protectors of the interests of the state rather than protectors of citizens. In Latin America, police have been subordinated to the military in the context of guerrilla challenges to the power and authority of the state. Accordingly, in Central and South America, the separation between military power and police power has become distorted as both the police and the military have concentrated on regime protection to the detriment of basic crime prevention and law enforcement functions (Hinton, 2006). Violence and crime, toleration for corruption in public offices, and lack of political commitment to police reform have constrained the development of service-oriented police forces in this region. For example, describing the failure of police reforms in Argentina and Brazil, Hinton observes that "old patterns of patronage, clientelism, impunity, and rule by fiat" continue to thrive even after the overthrow of military dictatorships and the election of reformist Presidents (p. 194). The Latin American tradition of "policing only the lowest rungs of

---

[7]Pino and Wiatrowski (2006, p. 77) point out that it is the international character of policing norms and standards that gives them credibility and renders them morally persuasive to national governments. They are not the norms or practices of local police departments in the United States or Europe.

state and society" is indicative of the disconnect between the government and the people (p. 200).

In Africa, oppressive and authoritarian colonial policing practices, committed to protecting the colonizers from the colonized, have continued to dominate post-independence policing because the colonial model of policing is still the standard in most African states. According to Hills (2008), "most police in most African countries are fundamentally unchanged from what they were ten years ago" (p. 216). In the postcolonial period, inherited colonial police systems are often perceived to have questionable legitimacy because of their origins (Chiabi, 2005), and African policing systems tend still to be centered on order and control rather than crime prevention and justice (Hills, 1996). In considering issues of design and implementation of police reforms in Africa, therefore, it is always necessary to consider the historical and social context within which the police operate (Arthur & Marenin, 1996).

In Eastern Europe, following the breakup of the Soviet empire, the inherited police forces of newly emergent states were shaped by a history of oppression employed as a tool of the Communist Party. For example, in the then East Germany, the police force of 60,000 officers was placed under the authority of the Secretary-General of the Communist Party (Jobard, 2004). In the former Yugoslavia, the militia was regarded as unprofessional and uneducated, and as a military organization employed in eavesdropping and maintaining files on enemies of the state (Ivkovic, 2004). Police reform efforts in the developing and post-Soviet worlds have, therefore, faced different challenges according to historical and political and socio-economic legacies. Yet, as Trebilock and Daniels (2008) note, a common theme exists in policing in these states: "Police were alienated from citizens because of the exclusive focus of the police on securing social order and defending ruling interests" (p. 109). In sharp contrast to the Soviet legacy for policing, the earliest international norm of policing—the *UN Code of Conduct for Law Enforcement Officials 1979*—asserts that the role of police is to "serve the community" (Office of the United Nations High Commissioner for Human Rights [OHCHR], 1979).

Many police forces in countries within the former Soviet Union continue to experience corruption despite extensive efforts of reform. For example, in Hungary, a survey conducted in 2000 of public perception indicated that the traffic police and the customs authority were the most corrupt state institutions (Dimovne, 2004). The most typical form of police corruption was police collecting bribes from small businesses. In Bulgaria, despite the adoption of codes of ethics since 1999, police investigations are intentionally suspended, and police inaction is sometimes deliberate, revealing links between police and criminal organizations (Shopov 2004). In Macedonia, part of the former Yugoslavia, "endemic corruption," low police salary levels, and the absence of a democratic policing culture continue to limit the pace of change (Yusufi, 2004). According to Robertson (2004), Russia "has yet to achieve the reforms considered necessary for the development of democratic policing, in particular, responsiveness, accountability, defense of human rights, and transparency" (p. 289). She suggests that the militia culture continues to be sustained in day-to-day policing practices and is not countered by training focused on democratic policing because new recruits acquire the militia culture after a few years in the police.

Contemporary interventions aimed at reforming police draw on international norms and standards of policing constituting best practice in policing worldwide and have adopted the term *democratic policing* to describe the purpose of such interventions. Explanations and definitions of the term are a work in progress, but there seems to be an overall consensus among academics and other policing experts on the elements that comprise this concept.

Some policing experts argue that the central principles of policing should be the notions of protecting human rights and furthering justice. These conceptions link democratic policing to a democratic society (Alderson, 1998; Palmiotto, 2001; Wiatrowski, 2002; for these, see Pino & Wiatrowski, 2006). As Neild (2001) puts it, "democratic policing . . . exists in a symbiotic relationship with democratic government" (p. 23). Respect for people's human rights and dignity is said to be central to the issue of public confidence in the police (Neyroud, 2003). Adopting the same focus on human rights and dignity, Manning (2005) describes democratic policing as policing that "eschews torture, terrorism and counterterrorism; is guided by law; and seeks minimal damage to civility" (p. 23). Pino and Wiatrowski (2006, pp. 83–86) have suggested that democratic policing should incorporate the following principles:

- The rule of law: the notion that laws and institutions established by law originate through a process that is democratic and that individual and organizational conduct and disputes are regulated and resolved by application of the rule of law.
- Legitimacy: the concept that people and institutions exercise authority according to the explicit purposes of the law and social institutions. The foundation of legitimacy is the consent of the governed.
- Transparency: the extent to which government operations such as policing are conducted openly and visibly so that citizens are always aware of government actions.
- Accountability: the guarantee that institutions and persons having authority always remain responsible to citizens and to elected or appointed leaders for their action and inaction. It also implies that a capacity to measure performance exists.
- Subordination to civil authority: The police will never be a law unto themselves and, in the public interest, will always remain accountable to a civil authority.

The authors suggest these principles are fundamental to the notion of democratic policing and would necessarily be included in any ethical standards in policing. However, these principles do not include responsiveness to citizens, which is commonly perceived as an essential element in democratic policing.

Call (2000) agrees with Pino and Wiatrowski (2006) that one element of democratic policing is that police are situated under civilian rather than military control and proposes, that other primary elements include the police providing a public service while adhering to human rights standards, and that police are ethnically plural and nonpartisan. Bayley (1985) proposes that democratic policing is grounded in the values of responsiveness and accountability and that the degree to which policing can be evaluated as democratic can be assessed by comparing the ratio of police responses to service calls from the public to forms of police work instigated through the chain of command.

One United Nations explanation of democratic policing focuses on service delivery (responsiveness to the public) and fairness or nondiscrimination in the application of the law. The United Nations International Police Task Force in 1996, assisting in police reform in Bosnia-Herzegovina, concluded that "the police force of a democracy is concerned strictly with the preservation of safe communities and the application of criminal law equally to all people, without fear or favor" (cited in Stone & Ward, 2000, p. 14). The following basic principles were identified by this 1996 policing mission:

- Police must function in accordance with the law.
- Police conduct must be regulated by a professional code of conduct.
- The highest priority of policing is the protection of human life.
- Police must serve the public and are accountable to the public and must communicate their actions to the public to establish the legitimacy of police action.
- A central focus of policing is the prevention of crime.
- Police must act in such a way as to respect human rights.
- Police must act in a nondiscriminatory manner.

Marenin (2007) argues that a basic consensus on the principles that constitute democratic policing now exists. The fundamental police responsibility is argued to be the protection of human rights, and this translates into the following goals:

Accountability, professionalism and legitimation, supported by specific policies which will lead to their achievement: non-partisanship and impartiality in the application of law; representativeness in the composition of police personnel; personal integrity sought through proper recruitment, training and promotion and sanctioning procedures; transparency of all operations which are not based on specifically and legitimately protected information; sensitivity to the diversity of social identities, cultural interests and non-dominant values in society; responsiveness to societal demands and norms; an orientation to public service; and a commitment to the rule of law. (p. 180)

Democratic policing has been critiqued for assuming that the dispersal of Western discourses and practices on policing will be effective in developing states, especially postconflict states, and for prioritizing reform over effectiveness. As Ellison (2007) puts it, "[P]olice democratization will do little to enhance citizen safety without some parallel effort to enhance police capacity and political steps to ameliorate the structural conditions of crime" (p. 233). Murphy (2007) similarly notes that research has shown that Western policing models are "often inappropriate, seldom sustainable and usually ineffective, and are sometimes harmful to the interests of local citizens and communities" (p. 258). It is therefore critical that indigenous policing responses are developed that can respond to local circumstances and conditions. In translating this critique into actual reform practice, Murphy argues that policing interventions that focus on professionalism to develop police capacity to prevent, detect, and prosecute crime ought to have priority if democratic reforms, including community policing, are to gain traction, especially in postconflict states.

Police reform practitioners tend to agree with academic analysis on the content of democratic policing. For example, in its publication *Anticorruption and Police Integrity: Security Sector Reform Program*, USAID (2007) calls for a focus on democratic policing with "reform strategies that emphasize accountability, transparency, and professional practices" and "greater responsiveness to communities" (p. 13). As well, articulating a more bureaucratic standpoint, democratic policing practices are stated to include "improving standards, selection, training, and salaries" and "performance indicators and well-defined job descriptions (that) will support merit-based systems for assignment and promotion" (p. 13). USAID also calls for all officers to become familiar with and to understand ethical codes and standards and police codes of ethics.

In discussing the implementation of democratic policing, Pino and Wiatrowski (2006) include the need to educate police on ethics and police integrity because, in their view, this will set moral operational standards of conduct. In the European policing context, the Patten Report 1999, detailing recommended democratic policing reforms in Northern Ireland, called for a new code of ethics that incorporated the European Convention on Human Rights and for extensive human rights training for officers (p. 172).

Global Norms and Standards Relating to Democratic Policing

The elements of democratic policing include codes of ethics, which, as foundational documents, can provide part of the framework within which policing is undertaken in a state. Codes of ethics are a mechanism for promoting professionalism within a police service. Codes can explicitly declare the types of conduct deemed unacceptable and can also offer a vision of the objectives police are attempting to achieve. When ethical standards are clearly understood by all personnel within a police force, wrongdoing is easily recognized, and, hopefully, appropriate action is taken. Moreover, personnel should feel hesitant to act unethically when all coworkers and superiors understand the wrongfulness of such an act. Finally, those who have acted unethically are more likely to be held accountable in an environment where ethical standards are declared and promoted. One major critique of ethics codes is that they emphasize acts prohibited on ethical grounds, but they rarely declare the obligations of police.

Ethics codes in policing, like other globalizing justice discourses based on Eurocentric models, have migrated to the developing world as features of development assistance projects in which planned interventions are to be implemented with the aim of building country capacity to administer justice and enforce the rule of law. Since codes of ethics commonly incorporate international standards of conduct intended to protect and promote human rights during the process of law enforcement, they aim to guide and shape the interaction between the police officer and the citizen. In this way, the purpose is to deliver responsive and effective policing in accordance with international standards. This, of course, assumes that every law enforcement officer is aware of such standards and has the skills, knowledge, and material means, as well as the administrative support, necessary to implement them. As noted above, these conceptions of democratic policing have been shaped by transnational actors, largely from the Western police agencies, and are widely accepted as the standard for democratic policing (Marenin, 2007).

It is possible to evaluate or audit police conduct against codes of ethics and sets of principles to ensure convergence with standards protecting human rights. Ethics statements and standards provide an important benchmark against which action can be judged (Clegg, Hunt, & Whetton, 2000). Rules expressing these standards must therefore focus on the officer–citizen interaction, on the command and management of law enforcement agencies, and on the accountability and external supervision of the police. The most prominent international norms are contained in the following instruments.[8]

United Nations Code of Conduct for Law Enforcement Officials 1979

In 1979, the General Assembly of the United Nations adopted the Code of Conduct for Law Enforcement Officials (OHCHR, 1979). It recognizes the key role that police play in protecting human rights and guaranteeing equal treatment under the law. The UN Economic and Social Council adopted the Guidelines for the Effective Implementation of the Code of Conduct for Law Enforcement Officials in its resolution 44/162 in 1989. The guidelines state that effective mechanisms need to be established to

---

[8]This is not an exhaustive list.

ensure the internal discipline and external control as well as the supervision of law enforcement officials. As well, the guidelines require that provision be made for the receipt and processing of complaints against law enforcement officials made by members of the public.

The Basic Principles on the Use of Force and Firearms by Law Enforcement Officials 1990

These principles were adopted by the Eighth United Nations Congress on the Prevention of Crime and the Treatment of Offenders, August 27 to September 7, 1990 (OHCHR, 1990). The Basic Principles are to be taken into account by governments within the framework of their national legislation and practice. Governments and law enforcement agencies are to adopt and implement rules on the use of force and firearms against persons by law enforcement officials. Ethical issues associated with the use of force and firearms are to be kept under review.

A basic principle is that police shall apply nonviolent means before resorting to the use of force and firearms. They may only use force and firearms where other means prove to be ineffective. Governments are to ensure that arbitrary or abusive use of force or firearms is punished as a criminal offense. Intentional lethal use of firearms is only permitted when strictly unavoidable to protect life. The circumstances in which firearms may be used are limited to self-defense or in defense of others where there is an imminent threat of death or serious injury; to prevent the commission of a serious crime involving grave threat to life; and to arrest a dangerous person or prevent his or her escape when less extreme means will not serve this stated purpose. The use of force and firearms in policing unlawful assemblies and in policing persons in custody or detention is specified in negative terms. In terms of police training, the guidelines require that special attention be given to police ethics and human rights and to alternatives to the use of force and firearms. Finally, reporting and review procedures seek to hold accountable police who employ force or firearms, including holding superior officers responsible, access to judicial process, and the making of detailed reports of incidents.

Optional Protocol to the Convention against Torture and Other Cruel, Inhuman or Degrading Treatment or Punishment 2006

Article 1 of the Optional Protocol contains a significant police oversight mechanism by requiring that a practice be followed of making regular visits to places of police detention and to places where police interrogate suspects (OHCHR, 2006). The visits should be made by independent international and national bodies to places where people are deprived of their liberty, to prevent torture and other cruel, inhuman, or degrading treatment or punishment. The provision is clearly directed at preventing police misconduct in relation to the treatment afforded to detainees.

Standard Minimum Rules for the Treatment of Prisoners, United Nations Rules for the Treatment of Women Prisoners and Non-Custodial Measures for Women Offenders (the Bangkok Rules), and Body of Principles for the Protection of All Persons under Any Form of Detention or Imprisonment

These instruments set out basic principles associated with treating detainees with dignity (OHCHR, 2010a, 2010b, 2010c). They require states to make known places of detention and the identities of custody and interrogation officers so as to facilitate accountability. The Body of Principles, dating back to 1988, also includes a requirement for places of detention to accept a system of external visits similar to that provided for under the Optional Protocol to the Convention Against Torture and Other Cruel, Inhuman, or Degrading Treatment or Punishment. In addition, the Body of Principles provides detainees with the right to make a complaint to the authorities responsible for the administration of the place of detention and to higher authorities and, when necessary, to appropriate authorities vested with reviewing or remedial powers, and also to bring the complaint before a judicial or other authority in case it is rejected or inordinately delayed. As well, the Body of Principles states that whenever the death or disappearance of a detained or imprisoned person occurs during his detention or imprisonment, an inquiry into the cause of death or disappearance shall be held by a judicial or other authority, either on its own motion or at the instance of a member of the family of such a person or any person who has knowledge of the case. Such an inquiry can also be held if someone dies shortly after having been detained; the findings can be made available on request.

Global Standards to Combat Corruption in Police Forces/Services, adopted by the International Criminal Police Organization (INTERPOL)

The aim of these standards is to ensure that police possess high standards of integrity and promote and strengthen the development of "measures needed to prevent, detect, punish, and eradicate corruption in the police forces/services within its national boundaries and to bring to justice police officers and other employees of police forces/services who are corrupt" (INTERPOL, n.d.-a, p. 3). The Global Standards call for the establishment of a mechanism such as an oversight body to monitor the above-mentioned systems and measures and their adequacy. The standards include a provision authorizing the INTERPOL General Secretariat to monitor their implementation in member countries.

European Code of Police Ethics, 2001

This code clearly promotes democratic policing stating that the main purposes of the police in a democratic society governed by the rule of law are

- to maintain public tranquility and law and order in society,
- to protect and respect the individual's fundamental rights and freedoms,
- to prevent and combat crime,
- to detect crime, and
- to provide assistance and service functions to the public.

The principles of this code state that national laws relating to the police should accord with international standards to which the country is a party and must be clear and accessible to the public, and that the police should be subject to the same legislation as ordinary citizens. In relation to accountability, the code requires that a state make police accountable to the state, the citizens, and their representatives. As well, state control of the police must be apportioned between the legislative, executive, and the judicial powers; public authorities must ensure effective and impartial procedures for complaints against the police; and accountability mechanisms, based on communication and mutual understanding between the public and the police, are to be promoted (European Code of Police Ethics, 2001b).

Member states must develop codes of ethics for police based on the principles set out in the code. Specifically, police training must include practical instruction on the use of force and limits with regard to established human rights principles. A detailed set of guidelines applies to operational policing covering the use of force, prohibition on torture and inhuman treatment, and actions to be impartial and nondiscriminatory; moreover, all police personnel must oppose all forms of police corruption. Police conducting investigations and arresting or detaining persons are subject to specific duties and prohibitions. An explanatory memorandum to the code (European Code of Police Ethics, 2001a) explains the importance and intent of a code of ethics for police stating, for example, "In terms of its possible influence upon police practice, a police code of ethics recommends best practice for the police, and is a specialized version of habitual, every day, common sense principled conduct" (para. 6).

Interpol Code of Conduct for Law Enforcement Officers

The Code of Conduct sets out principles intended to guide law enforcement officers' conduct (INTERPOL, n.d.-b). The code does not seek to restrict police discretion but "to define the parameters of conduct within which that discretion should be exercised."

Community Policing

Community policing in its various manifestations is an important element in democratic policing, but it will not be discussed in detail. In essence, there is no single model of community policing; rather, the notion is that the public should play an enhanced role in securing public safety. This means that police have the responsibility to devise ways in which to associate the public with law enforcement (Skolnick & Bayley, 1988). Community policing may be defined or explained in different ways, but in the developing country context, South Africa is a useful example. The South African Police Service's 1997 *Community Policing: Policy Framework Guidelines* (cited in Clegg et al., 2000, p. 41) states the core elements of community policy to be

- service orientation—police respond to the public;
- partnership—a problem solving cooperative relationship;
- problem solving—identifying and analyzing the causes of crime and devising ways to address it;
- empowerment—joint responsibility; and
- accountability—police are accountable to the community through agreed processes.

Precisely how these elements are connected together and whether they will produce the desired outcomes will depend on the circumstances of each country. However, as noted by Clegg et al. (2000), studies reveal that community policing can be successful if it is treated as a core function of policing and not simply added on to other functions, and where there exists a long-term and sustained commitment to its practice. Some reasons why community policing initiatives do not succeed in developing states are revealed in the following:

[I]t seems doubtful if Community Policing, as currently practiced, has yet to lead to any substantive change in the public image of the UPF. Indeed the obstacles to a full realization of the benefits of Community Policing in Uganda remain formidable. In discussion with police and non-police sources alike we found clear signs that the police regard community policing primarily as a means of instructing local populations, rather than listening to them. They thus learn less than they might, whilst doing little to mitigate their authoritarian image. (Clegg et al., 2000. p. 44)

Global Police Reforms

This section examines police reform activities in a number of developing states to highlight the challenges in instituting democratic policing in such areas. This section will focus on policing in the Philippines, Nigeria, and Sierra Leone. Policing reforms must, of course, be situated within the overall political, social, and historical contexts of the country concerned, and the domestic policing model must be understood within that same context. Understanding the historical trajectory of policing in the states reviewed here is crucial to gaining an appreciation of how the encounter between the domestic policing model and the new democratic policing interventions plays out. Ideally, reformers would also have a thorough understanding of the political economy of policing in a particular developing state before designing a police reform project for that state.

Policing in the Philippines

With a current population of about 94 million, a centralized police force of about 130,000 (U.S. Department of State, 2010), and an archipelagic land mass comprising some 7,000 widely separated islands, policing in the Republic of the Philippines presents many challenges. The Philippines has suffered two colonial occupations: under the Spanish for 333 years and, for about 50 years, under the United States. The colonial legacy includes the country's policing institutions. During the colonial period and the lengthy postcolonial dictatorship of Ferdinand Marcos from 1965 to 1986, the police were employed as a tool of authoritarian rule (Varona, 2011). Under Spanish rule, policing took the form of a paramilitary force based on the Spanish Guardia Civil. During the U.S. occupation, police were trained to fight insurgents against U.S. rule, and following independence in 1946, the then Philippine Constabulary retained its principal function of suppressing resistance to government rule. The Philippines National Police (PNP) was created under the 1987 Constitution and was explicitly declared to be a civilian force.

The PNP nevertheless remains a largely paramilitary force and sustains a police culture associated with militarism (Varona, 2011). It has yet to overcome its nondemocratic policing heritage despite having promulgated ethical standards that set a democratic and accountable way forward. Torture and serious human rights violations by PNP are a long-standing issue, and torture has continued to be reported in criminal investigations. Ethical violations involving police violence observed and recorded by Amnesty International (2003) in the Philippines by PNP members include

- the use of electric shocks;
- the "water cure," which involves tying a piece of cloth over a detainee's face and then pouring water over it slowly to induce suffocation;
- beatings with fists, rifle butts, or batons wrapped in newspaper or other material (a technique known as *mauling*);
- the insertion of rifle bullets between a suspect's fingers and then squeezing the fingers;
- the application of chili pepper on suspects' eyes or genitals; and
- the use of psychological methods, such as the placing of gun muzzles against a suspect's head or mouth while threatening to open fire while guns are actually discharged close by.

As well, police have been implicated in criminal acts including the kidnapping of wealthy businessmen in collusion with criminal gangs (Brown & Wilson, 2007). According to a report by the Immigration and Refugee Board of Canada (2006), "police officers are frequently named as suspected gunmen" in cases involving violence against journalists (para. 4). According to the U.S. Department of State's 2010 Human Rights Report, Philippines, "Members of the PNP were regularly accused of torture, soliciting bribes, and other illegal acts" (p. 8).

Police corruption, together with corruption and graft at all levels within public service agencies, is widespread. In the Philippines, corruption began during the Spanish conquest because low salaries in the colonial bureaucracy encouraged the sale of public offices. During the period of U.S. occupation beginning in 1898, corruption was brought under control because salaries were raised, but following World War II, corruption again became a serious problem extending throughout the public service. Quah (2004) traces the anticorruption strategies promoted by presidents, including the creation of numerous anticorruption boards and commissions, and notes that during the time of President Marcos from 1965, corruption "reached an all-time high" (p. 61). In all, Quah identifies seven laws and 13 anticorruption agencies since the 1950s. In Quah's view, anticorruption strategies and laws have not worked in the Philippines because there is no political will to enforce them. Moreover, low salaries paid to public servants and police mean that bribery and graft will flourish in the absence of any effective antigraft policing systems. As he puts it, "Junior policemen are paid such low salaries that they are forced to live in the slums with other criminal elements" (p. 76). According to information collected by the Immigration and Refugee Board of Canada (2006), the chief director of the PNP admitted in 2003 that corruption was a problem within the PNP; that police on traffic duty often sought bribes from drivers; and that extortion, arrest, and kidnapping were among the illegal acts committed by police. The U.S. Department of State reported in 2010 that the PNP "suffered from a widely held and accurate public perception that corruption remained a problem" (p. 22).

On paper at least, PNP officers are subject to strict codes of conduct requiring that ethical standards be applied. For example, in 1995 the PNP published the *Philippine National Police Ethical Doctrine Manual.* Western law enforcement agencies would be surprised to find that the standards determined there for the PNP are derived from a distinctly moralistic and religious foundation. Thus, for example, the doctrine is said to "provide moral and ethical guidance to all PNP members" who must internalize the core PNP values which are stated to be "Love of God, Respect for Authority, Selfless Love, Service for People, Sanctity of Marriage and Respect for Women, Responsible Dominion and Stewardship over Material Things, and Truthfulness" (Directorate for Human Resource and Doctrine Development, 1995, pp. 4–5, 16). As Varona (2011) notes, in the PNP, "ethics management methods largely focus on the use of religious mechanisms to improve individual police morality as part of the effort to improve police ethical conduct" (p. 109).[9]

Chapter III of the manual containing the doctrine lists 15 articles that explain and define standards of conduct. As well as referring to a "commitment to democracy" and a "commitment to public interest," the ethical standards enumerated include morality, judicious use of authority, integrity, justice, humility, and orderliness and perseverance. In addition, the manual incorporates standards concerning a wide range of behaviors not usually found in policing ethics rules, including appropriate table manners, manner of walking, the personal appearance of police personnel, and social graces required of PNP members (Directorate for Human Resources and Doctrine Development, 1995, pp. i–ii, 1–15, 17). Again, this demonstrates that the range of conduct considered to be within the boundaries of "ethical" is far broader than is generally found in police codes of ethics.

Having a code of ethics that extends to an entire manual (each doctrine is elaborated in some detail) seems problematic in terms of the police internalizing the standards and norms. As well, according to Varona (2011), it is unlikely that the doctrine is the product of a participatory process within PNP because it takes the form of an order or directive from management. It is also significant that the PNP performance evaluation system does not attach the same weight to adherence to ethical standards of policing as to other factors.[10] Bayley (2006) argues that policing agencies should include educational programs as part of a set of policing reforms that "stress the norms of lawfulness, human rights, and individual dignity . . . [and] enact concise codes of ethics to replace the usual lengthy and detailed disciplinary regulations (and) provide training in ethics that involves illustrations from the rough-and-tumble of active service" (p. 61). Thus, simply publishing a detailed set of ethical standards is clearly not adequate to internalize them.

The close link between moral and ethical conduct and religious or spiritual faith and practice may be related to the cultural expression of social and political resistance to colonialism and overbearing leadership. However, if police consider themselves as moral agents, they may seek to justify extrajudicial activity as an appropriate response to action they consider to be immoral. For example, police in Cebu City told Varona (2011) they had carried out extrajudicial executions of suspected criminals because they considered that the lengthy justice process and the fact that criminals were better

---

[9]A U.S. police trainer of police in the Philippines explained to Varona (2011, p. 114) that he found numerous references to God and religion (in the PNP Code of Ethics, among others) as the basis for ethical behavior in the PNP, which he would not find in an American police institution. As a result, the American trainer had to make adjustments to materials he had designed for his ethics course.

[10]For example, while a maximum of 25 points can be awarded for "work management," only a maximum rating of 10 is provided for "personal qualities," which is defined to include adherence to ethical standards (Varona 2011, p. 87).

armed than police meant ethical standards could be ignored, especially when the criminals themselves applied no such standards. Accordingly, when police act unethically within the PNP, this is explained and understood by PNP as revealing an individual's absence of morality or spirituality. The PNP operational response to unethical police conduct is to strengthen the individual police officer's moral and spiritual capability through interventions by priests, ministers, and imams of the PNP Chaplain Service. These individuals are required to participate actively in internalizing the Ethical Doctrine (Directorate for Human Resource and Doctrine Development, 1995, p. 39, Manual Chapter VI, Section 2). One Catholic chaplain explained the logic of this virtue-based approach as, "The more you are God-centred, the more you are effective and less prone to commit misdemeanors and abuses" (Varona, 2011, p. 128). Nevertheless, officers, as opposed to chaplains, may take a more secular view and see applying improved discipline as the correct approach to ethical violations. As one officer from the Directorate for Police-Community Relations explained to Varona,

> When it comes to the management of the ethical conduct of personnel, the first thing needed is, uh, discipline. This is in addition to professionalism. Discipline is the key to an ethical PNP. After discipline comes their (meaning PNP personnel) well-being. (p. 143)

Respondents to a survey conducted by Varona (2011) believed that police discipline, and therefore ethical standards, could be improved through enforcing penalties for violations of discipline rules, by consistently applying disciplinary standards, and through PNP leaders setting examples. A police expert, member of an ICITAP training team[11] took the following view:

> There is nothing wrong with the PNP Ethical Doctrine on paper. It is even far more developed than similar doctrines in other countries. The issue is not what is on paper, but that something is probably lost between what's on paper and what happens on the street. (p. 145)

In assessing why violations of the Ethical Doctrine occur the same ICITAP police instructor believed that "[t]here are some institutional and cultural issues that drive ethics problems in the PNP. Filipino society is generally tolerant of minor bribes, and minor bribes lead to bigger bribes" (Varona, 2011, p. 162). He also believed that the likelihood of unethical conduct by police was far greater in rural areas because the risk of getting caught was far less.

---

[11]ICITAP is the International Criminal Investigative Training Assistance Program of the U.S. Department of Justice that "works with foreign governments to develop professional and transparent law enforcement institutions that protect human rights, combat corruption and reduce the threat of transnational crime and terrorism" (ICITAP, n.d.).

Democratic Policing Reforms—Philippines

According to Varona (2011), the PNP is currently implementing the latest in a series of long-term reform strategies. The Integrated Transformation Program (ITP) is now considered the PNP's "roadmap for a long term and lasting reform" (p. 197). It was initially designed for implementation over the period 2005 to 2015 and is to be financed by the Philippine Government and through grants of foreign assistance. According to the ITP, citizens will be empowered by gaining knowledge of their rights, and they are to be encouraged to participate in the development and implementation of local peace and order plans.

In relation to strengthening police ethics, the ITP contains provisions for capacity building for police officers, for values formation, and for spiritual programs intended to help police internalize appropriate values (Varona, 2011). However, efforts to internalize ethical codes may not in themselves produce ethical policing, and it is generally agreed that multiple strategies must be pursued. For example, while he agrees that ethical codes can be a mechanism for minimizing corruption, Newburn (1999) stresses the critical role of police managers in providing positive role models. Similarly, Bayley (2006) observes that "sustained and committed leadership by top management, especially the chief uniformed officer, executive, is required to produce any important organizational change" (p. 56). Consequently, it seems that codes of ethics need to be supported by all levels of police management and that simply facilitating internalization of the code will not adequately address corruption in the PNP. As Bayley aptly observes, "Resistance to reform is the rule rather than the exception. What foreigners regard as obstacles to reform, locals may find useful, such as corruptible police officers and politically subservient judges" (p. 96).

Varona (2011) administered a survey to PNP members that revealed that low police wages and benefits are much of the cause of the corruption that PNP officers engage in. Some respondents explained that PNP members attempt to supplement their low salaries by gambling, and that if salaries were increased and other benefits provided—such as for housing, basic needs, and assistance with education expenses for dependents—corruption in the PNP would be eliminated. As it is, police financial management effectively ensures that in some affluent parts of the country, police are well provided for, but in the poorer areas, police have few resources and depend on local political patronage. One solution to the low-wage issue is suggested by USAID's 2007 *Anticorruption and Police Integrity* report, which notes that petty police corruption can be addressed by giving pay increases to the worst-paid lower ranks and reducing differentials between senior officers and patrolmen.

Transparency International (2008) surveyed the extent to which selected institutions in the Philippines were perceived to be corrupt. On a scale of 1 (not at all corrupt) to 5 (extremely corrupt), Filipino respondents reported that they viewed the Bureau of Customs as the country's most corrupt agency, with a score of 4.4. The PNP and the Bureau of Internal Revenue shared the same score of 4.1, making them perceived to compete for the status of the second most corrupt agency.

Community policing is one area of democratic policing where attempts have been made to civilianize the PNP and emphasize service and responsiveness to the public. The results have been mixed. According to a study by Pilar et al. (2001), the PNP Reform Act 1998, providing for the reform and reorganization of the PNP, explicitly recognizes the concepts of civilianization and community policing. As noted above, the boundary between police and the military in the Philippines has always been blurred. The PNP, as now constituted, was not established by law until 1990, even though the 1987 Constitution declares there shall be only one police force, which shall be civilian in character and controlled by a national police commission. Personnel in PNP are trained at the Philippine Public Safety College, which offers training courses in "civilianization of uniformed personnel" and a "community immersion program." The latter focuses on a close relationship between PNP and the local community with the aim of keeping the community informed about policing activities and building public safety through public cooperation with the community and police acting in partnership.

Pilar et al. (2001) note that police headquarters has demonstrated a "lingering reluctance" to the concept of community policing. For example, one police internal memorandum states, "Community policing is a developing philosophy and may need modifications for the Philippine setting. . . . [T]o be sure, it is an addition to and not supposed to be a substitute for the traditional police tactics for crime prevention" (p.167), revealing that community policing is far from being accepted as a mainstream function within PNP. Other research cited by Pilar et al. reveals that

- community policing is regarded within PNP as a special project that could not be correlated with mainstream police functions;
- while it improved police visibility and response time, it did not receive total community support;
- community policing initiatives were perceived as police led and not community led; and
- operational issues arising out of community policing had not been addressed.

Police appear to resist community policing because it is seen as opposed to, and as challenging, the military-like police culture.

Citizens have also expressed reservations about this form of policing because the PNP is regarded as not acting in good faith but, rather, as lacking "integrity, competence, and discipline" (Pilar et al., 2001, p. 171). Both police and citizens acknowledge a disparity between what is perceived as the ideal police (under the community policing concept) and the real police (based on both police and citizen experiences). Nevertheless, according to this study, both police and citizens have a positive attitude toward the need for PNP to transform its values, principles, and conduct to more closely reflect the need to serve the community.

The People's Law Enforcement Board exercises civilian oversight over the PNP. The board investigates and adjudicates cases of complaints involving the PNP, and each municipality has at least one board (de Guzman & Frank, 2004). De Guzman and Frank found in their study that the boards were perceived by PNP to have an effect on officer behavior and to influence police policies. Complainants did not, however, register the same effect on police. Possibly, this can be explained by the fact that the boards usually find that police have acted properly. Internal police investigations by the Internal Affairs Unit of PNP are described by the U.S. Department of State (2010) as "largely ineffective."

In the Philippines, police violence and corruption continue to dominate accounts of PNP conduct within and outside the country. The strength of the centralized police force shows a police to population ratio of 139, far below European levels, where 60% of European states have levels of between 200 and 400 (Aebi et al., 2010) and do not face the difficulties of policing over 7,000 islands. Clearly, the PNP remains a militarized force resistant to community policing initiatives and with an institutional culture that tolerates serious police violence. Leadership that will model ethical policing is lacking both at senior and middle levels, and corruption is rife. There seems little political commitment to changes in policing. Although PNP has launched various improvement interventions to democratize its policing model, there is no evidence of success. In fact, PNP police culture, like that of pre-apartheid South Africa, is wholly embedded in a host culture of corruption, violence, and patronage networks. To a significant extent, the present status of PNP can be traced back to its origins under Spanish rule and to political developments in the country when the police have been used to project the power of the state and to enrich the elites. As Chan (1996) points out in her analysis of police culture, researchers often underestimate "the power of the field," that is, "the social, economic, legal, and political sites in which policing takes place" (p. 130). A political economy of policing would no doubt show the links and connections between elites, political patrons, and the police, and how power is routinely exercised for their benefit and protection.

While the PNP maintains some of the elements of democratic policing, such as a detailed code of ethics and a form of community policing, democratic policing standards are not internalized in the rank and file or in leadership because no regular education or training interventions are conducted. Instead, developing virtuous conduct has become the domain of police chaplains who see strengthening religious belief as the key to ethical policing. As with many police forces, resource constraints influence policing to the extent that corruption is an outcome of minimal salaries. No radical overhaul of the public service salary structure, including the PNP appears to have been conducted to see how limited resources can be applied most effectively to minimize public service corruption. All in all, the prospects for the future development of democratic policing in the Philippines appear bleak. It is hard to see how policing can be transformed without some radical changes in the systemic corruption that saturates the country in the same way that sweeping changes overthrew pre-apartheid forms of policing in South Africa.

The constraints of the colonial and postcolonial policing legacy and transforming the PNP into a democratic policing model has been challenging in the Philippines, particularly in the challenge of reshaping local police cultures. Similar, but even more complex challenges face another developing nation, that of Nigeria.

Policing in Nigeria

The African state of Nigeria has been the recipient of considerable donor assistance for police reform, especially from the United Kingdom, the former colonial power.[12] The policing environment in Nigeria is extremely challenging, as the country is large and populous,[13] and the society is characterized by violent crime, poverty, unemployment—especially among poor youth—and competition for land. Multiple social strains arise from political, religious, and ethnic tensions (Hills, 2008). One challenge was that it was only in 1999 that the country returned to democratic rule after a series of military regimes had been in power since independence from Britain in 1960.

In Nigeria, as for many African colonies of Britain, "British colonial policy . . . required that the police operate both as a civil law-enforcement agency and as a quasi-military organization supporting those in power and suppressing civil disorder" (Hills, 1996, p. 279). In Nigeria, as for Ghana, "the exercise of policing was forceful, often repressive, frequently arbitrary, and adjusted to the nature of complainants and victims, whether they were native or white colonialists" (Arthur & Marenin, 1996, p. 170). As Pino and Wiatrowski (2006) point out, the paramilitary style of policing common in Africa means that police–community relations are characterized by violence and repression and that policing is often employed as an instrument of state violence with complete impunity.

---

[12]According to Adebayo (2004, p. 111) the Nigeria Police Force had a strength of 312,000 in 2004. Improvements in promotion and salary have also been implemented since 1999. Hills (2008, p. 216) notes that Nigeria's police have received millions of pounds and U.S. dollars for technical assistance and training programs, and refers to a force of 325,000. The UK Department for International Development (DFID) is currently operating a modest program that ends in 2015 of only 490,000 pounds, only a minor proportion of which relates to security sector reform (see DFID, n.d.).

[13]Nigeria is the most populous country is Africa with an estimated population of 170 million in 2012 (CIA, 2012).

During the colonial period in Nigeria, police performed a variety of functions, including detecting and investigating crime, providing escorts for residents and other officials, prosecuting offenses, guarding prisons and prisoners working outside the prison in labor gangs, serving summonses and executing warrants, patrolling, and suppressing slave raiding (Alemika & Chukwuma, 2000). Police training emphasizes drill and physical exercise, and the training model at senior levels is the Northern Ireland Police—a force trained itself to resist rebellion against the British presence there (Nwankwo, Mbachu, & Ugochukwu, 1993). Police participated in colonial wars and punitive operations as a paramilitary force and were accustomed to using batons, rifles, and revolvers to suppress those opposing colonial rule. The first police force was established in 1861, and the modern Nigeria Police Force was created in 1930 (Igbinovia, 2000). The paramilitary nature of the police has fashioned a hierarchical and authoritarian institution. Lower ranks show great deference to their superiors, and officers lack the capacity to motivate subordinates (Adebayo, 2004).

Following the end of the colonial period, Nigeria suffered periods of protracted military rule under which constitutions were suspended, and special military tribunals were constituted under which citizen's rights were not properly protected under any form of rule of law. Military rule generated increased police violence and corruption, which the military regimes condoned (Alemika & Chukwuma, 2000). Politicians in power used police as a tool to oppress their political opponents, and military rule had the effect of elevating the police culture of violence toward citizens to the level of state policy. As Alemika and Chukwuma point out, "The purpose and methods of policing in colonial and post-colonial Nigeria are similar because, at the fundamental levels, the political and economic structures of both eras are similar" (p. 35). According to Nwankwo et al. (1993), the alienation between police and the public that existed during the colonial times "was intensely aggravated by a post-independence history of corruption, mismanagement, and general misuse in attempts to settle personal and political scores" (p. 4). Today, according to Hills (2008), the Nigeria Police Force is widely regarded as one of the most corrupt institutions in a society characterized by violence, corruption, and ethnic conflict.

In their study of the root causes of police violence in Nigeria, *Police–Community Violence in Nigeria*, Alemika and Chukwuma (2000) analyzed the incidence, extent, and pattern of violence by the Nigerian police. The researchers defined violence for their study as constituting homicide, torture (especially in relation to police interrogation), and brutality applied in police–citizen contacts for law enforcement purposes, including the use of excessive force and the lethal use of firearms, including the extrajudicial executions of suspects and sometimes of innocent citizens. Hills (2008) also found that police abuse of power in Nigeria includes "torture, brutality, extrajudicial killings, deaths in custody, corruption and intimidation" (p. 219).[14] Police misconduct is seldom inquired into, and confessions compose the basis of some 60% of prosecutions.

Alemika and Chukwuma's (2000) study reveals that it is common for police in Nigeria to employ violence against citizens. The most usual form of police–citizen interaction occurs on highways, most frequently where police erect traffic checkpoints (referred to by citizens as *toll points*) and conduct stop-and-search operations (p. 8). Hills (2008) also points out that most drivers arrive at checkpoints with a 20 naira[15] note in hand. During such incidents, police may beat and kick citizens and restrain them without good cause with handcuffs and leg chains. Police special task forces assigned to patrol highways and cities are known to carry out summary executions to keep the incidence of armed robbery in check (Alemika & Chukwuma, 2000). The Alemika and Chukwuma study found no citizen support for police, and that citizens complained of physical and verbal assault and harassment and violation of rights. Police overreactions in controlling industrial disputes have caused student demonstrations, public processions, and demonstrations against unpopular government policies. The authors report that police frequently resort to vigilantism.

Human Rights Watch, in its report on Nigeria in January 2012, highlights police human rights violations: "As in previous years, the undisciplined Nigeria Police Force was implicated in frequent human rights violations, including extrajudicial killings, torture, arbitrary arrests, and extortion related abuses" (p. 2). Acts of police corruption include police soliciting bribes from victims as an incentive for them to investigate crimes but also demanding bribes from suspects to cease investigations. According to Nwankwo et al. (1993), the bail process has also been corrupted because police regularly require money be paid to them to secure bail, despite signs in police stations prominently declaring, "You do not have to pay or bribe the police for bailable offences" (p. 47).

Nevertheless, some positive action is being taken to counter police abuse and establish accountability. Human Rights Watch (2012) reports that in

---

[14]Extrajudicial killing, also known as *self-policing* and *vigilantism*, can include activities such as:

- "lynching, which involves citizen's action against another citizen presumed to have committed a crime or violated some social norm; it may or may not result in the victim's death;
- justice-makers (*justicieros* in Brazil) who assassinate criminals and alleged trouble makers and who may be off duty police/military or civilians;
- death squads or semi-formal para-military and para-police groups;
- armed revolutionary political groups in areas under their control" (Clegg et al., 2000, p. 57).

[15]*Naira* is the local currency. Approximately 157 naira = 1 U.S. dollar (http://themoneyconverter.com/USD/NGN.aspx).

July 2011, the attorney general brought criminal charges against five police officers, including three assistant commissioners, for extrajudicial killings that took place in 2009. However, no such action has been taken to prosecute police for the unlawful killing of more than 130 persons in November 2008 during sectarian violence. Neild (1999) notes that the lower ranks of the police are largely illiterate, and some have criminal records, and that a 1986 reorganization of the police included the dismissal of 160 officers for serious disciplinary and criminal acts.

While offering a bleak perspective on the future development of the Nigeria Police Force, Igbinovia (2000) perceives the dominant features of Nigerian society remaining constant and therefore sees little scope for any radical change in policing. Consequently, he suggests that "ethnic conflict, religious intolerance, political instability, student unrest, and crime" will shape the future role of police which will, therefore, continue to be "complex and ambiguous" (p. 539). Igbinovia sees Nigeria following the British policing model because training and technical assistance continue to be provided by the United Kingdom, albeit with seemingly no impact in terms of democratic policing. He foresees an uninterrupted pattern of militarization with promotion from the ranks ensuring that graft and corruption will be sustained; a national police force rather than decentralization; and increased pressure on police through population growth and urbanization.[16] Only minor improvements can be expected in police operations, and crime, especially violent crime, is likely to increase and remain beyond police control. Overall, insufficient resources will be allocated to safety and security. Police will continue to be affected by political direction and control. More positively, police will become better educated and will cease to live in isolation from the population in barrack accommodations.[17]

Exploring the records of two recent inspectors general of police, Hills (2008) concludes that neither tried to address internal police corruption; both promoted community policing but at the same time accepted a policing culture that thrived on graft, bribe taking, and corruption; both promoted community conflict resolution while still relying on paramilitary elements to oppress dissidents; and, according to this account, both revealed the superficiality of their reform programs using the language of democratic policing while "they accommodated Nigerian realities" (p. 231). It is noteworthy in this context that the expressed purpose of the community policing program was to introduce "a culture of excellence in service provision," to enhance individual officer accountability for their performance, and to place "ethical policing" at the core of all personnel and organization development programs (p. 228).

---

[16]According to Igbinovia (2000, p. 543), a 1998 World Health Organization survey has projected Nigeria's population to reach 329 million by 2025.

[17]The practice of housing police in barracks was introduced in colonial times so that police could be easily mobilized in emergencies (Nwankwo et al., 1993, p. 70).

Hills (2008) proposes a dialectic approach to reform projects in Nigeria—an interactive process "best described as a waltz; one step forward is followed by one step sideways or backwards," but stresses that reform projects can make a difference to policing "albeit of a localized and temporary nature" (p. 217). Nigeria has a robust civil society advocating reform, and many groups and individuals have offered solutions. According to the Network on Police Reform in Nigeria (www.noprin.org), 46 NGOs are working on police reform in the country, including on the issue of police–community relations. Nevertheless, according to Hills, policing reform in Nigeria resembles a waltz in that it is dependent on political development so that the election of a new president or the appointment of a new inspector general as police commander can and does interrupt or displace interventions and donor policies. Consequently, public statements about police reform by politicians and senior police officers may be understood more as responses to political pressures and strains than genuine commitments to reform.

According to Hills (2008), the primary role of the police in Nigeria continues to be enforcing decisions taken by the political elite, maintaining public order, undertaking paramilitary operations, and carrying out regulatory activities. The inspector general of police (who himself exercises inordinate power over the police) is appointed and dismissed by—and is only accountable to—the president. Thus, as Hills puts it, "policing is always guided by presidential calculations," and overall, "democratic reform in an environment such as Nigeria's is invariably superficial, localized and temporary" (p. 227).

In Nigeria, unlike the Philippines, policing has had the benefit of numerous projects of reform and substantial funding, but again, the policing model and the police culture are products of an enduring historical legacy that used policing to protect and further the interests of those in power, whether colonial officials or, subsequently, politicians and military leaders. The police culture is seemingly resistant to reform, and there is no genuine political commitment to advance the democratic policing agenda. "Democratic reform requires the active support of the police at many levels and at least the acquiescence of politicians and the public," notes Bayley (2006, p. 96). "Obtaining 'buy-in' is probably the most often cited lesson of security assistance." It seems that in a chaotic society such as Nigeria, social control and policing lack a coherent framework and structure, and citizens are oppressed by police and obliged to secure their own security and safety. Consequently, both citizens and police engage in vigilantism, police respond to the dictates of politicians rather than perform basic policing tasks, and crime is beyond control.

Like the Philippines, the social, economic, and political context in which policing is located adversely affects the policing model, and corruption is pervasive. Democratic policing may have gained a toehold but appears to be unsustainable in view of the fractured nature of society. The future state of security in the country seems perilous when a force of some 325,000 police in a centralized structure cannot ensure safety and security. The variance between the Philippines and Nigeria lies in the former possessing a degree of social cohesion, whereas Nigeria is plagued not only by high crime, corruption, and a militarist police force, but also with ethnic tensions, an ever-increasing population, and fragile governance structures. Both countries reveal the critical importance of understanding the political economy of policing before undertaking any democratic policing reforms.

Policing in Sierra Leone

Civil unrest during the 1990s and early 2000s in Sierra Leone was associated with a period of almost constant conflict and brutality. From a population of 6 million, 50,000 were killed, and 500,000 became refugees.[18] There is no space here to provide a detailed account of events or causes of that civil strife, but poor governance, poverty, and authoritarian rule with inequitable distribution of resources all played a part (Horn, Olonisakin, & Peake, 2006).

Sierra Leone was a British colony from 1808 until 1961 when it gained independence. During the colonial period, policing was abusive in nature (Ebo, 2006). The current police force has its origins in the Sierra Leone Frontier Police and was established following the founding of the capital, Freetown, in 1808. By 1889, colonial jurisdiction was being exercised over the provinces known as the Hinterland, and police authority was extended there. For five years after independence, the army, police, judiciary, and civil service functioned with a degree of professionalism (Fayemi, 2004). However, under the lengthy one-party rule of Siaka Stevens from 1968 until 1992, the police were tribalized, and oppressive policing and corruption were the norm. The security sector focused on state and regime security (Baker, 2006). Ebo (2006) observes that before the civil war, the security sector was largely ethnically based and that ethnicity, party political affiliations, and interpersonal connections rather than professional performance determined the outcome of recruitment and promotion.

Police reform financed by the United Kingdom began in 1998 with a range of interventions to build skill and capacity in the Sierra Leone Police (SLP) (Horn et al., 2006).[19] From 1998 to 1999, a small team of police officers from Canada, Sri Lanka, the United Kingdom, and Zimbabwe began a reform process but this was interrupted in 1999 due to civil conflict. This team followed a strategic approach and the SLP produced a policing charter stressing the role of police in ensuring the safety and security of citizens rather than protecting the state (Thomson, 2007).

---

[18]The 10-year war in Sierra Leone concluded in January 2002 (Baker, 2006, p. 26).

[19]The aim was to restore the police force to its pre–civil war strength of 9,500 (Baker, 2006, p. 33).

During the next reform phase, from 1999 to 2002, a new philosophy of policing was introduced, and a wide range of initiatives undertaken to build up police capacity and skills (Horn et al., 2006). An assessment for the UK Department for International Development (DFID) reported the SLP to be "not effective," especially since the military controlled most of the capital. There was a need to establish the SLP "as the primary force for maintaining law and order" (Horn et al., 2006, p. 115). The new philosophy was centered on "local needs policing," a mode of community policing intended to replace the highly centralized system in place at that time. Under this concept, local police partnership boards were set up in a partnership between police and the community. According to Baker (2006), these boards "are little more than intelligence gatherers for the police" (p. 40). He doubts they will have an impact of police accountability. In later research, Baker (2008) seemingly revises his view to some extent, evaluating the boards as being valued by the community but nevertheless constituting "essentially a police-led initiative to ease their lack of intelligence or manpower" (pp. 23, 40). Family support units were established to improve services to victims of sexual assault and domestic violence (Horn et al., 2006). Using on-the-job mentoring, advisers built the capacity of SLP and its professionalism. Both DFID advisers and UN Civilian Police (CIVPOL) officers undertook this work. According to Baker (2006), the 170 CIVPOL staff came from 17 different countries, and many lacked adequate skills for the task. CIVPOL officers may come from states that do not practice democratic policing. Deficiencies at the senior level remained in strategic planning and budgeting.

The next phase of reform ran from 2002 to 2006. In April 2004, the Security Sector Reform (SSR) program in Sierra Leone, including both police and the military, was cited as an example of good practice in SSR in the OECD Development Assistance Committee (Horn et al., 2006). Organizational structures, systems, and resources were now in place, and SLP managers took over day-to-day policing, including the position of inspector general previously filled by a British expatriate police officer. Despite these positive advances, some observers expressed reservations about the capacity of the police. For example, the International Crisis Group reported in 2004, "There are serious questions about the capacity of Sierra Leone's police to manage internal security. . . . Nor have the security forces yet earned civilian confidence" (cited in Thomson, 2007, p. 11). In 2005, DFID commenced a Justice Sector Development Program covering the entire justice sector, resulting in a dramatic reduction in DFID funding support for SLP (Horn et al., 2006).

The SLP now has a paramilitary wing comprising about 3,800 officers, known as the Operational Support Division (OSD), who wear camouflage uniforms and carry arms (Baker, 2006; Horn et al., 2006). OSD officers are hired out to commercial organizations to provide protective services and receive a premium above their wages (Baker, 2006).

Internal police conduct can be investigated by the Complaints Discipline and Internal Investigations Department. An external police complaints board is also planned for 2012. Despite these accountability measures, Baker (2006) reports that 80% of the public claim that traffic police demand money from drivers.

Senior management in SLP has benefitted from management training in the United Kingdom, but one report suggests that while senior police are able to plan and conceptualize strategically, middle and lower ranks significantly lack policing skills and adopt an insular view of the policing function.[20] Baker (2006) agrees that it is open to doubt whether new strategic concepts and practices can be transferred to lower levels under the local unit commanders, and doubts that the new basic training course is sufficient to significantly improve lower ranks performance.

Overall, however, the improvements in management, in resources, and in training for lower ranks, together with the improved relations between police and citizens and the enhanced perception of the police as a force responsive to and protective of citizens, show what can be achieved.[21] Denney (2011), citing interviews with a leader of market women and with bicycle taxi riders observes that "police are widely recognized as being more effective and reliable" and as "partners in development" and that while corruption remains, "the majority of the population no longer lives in fear of police brutality" (p. 287). As Denney points out, in terms of development, however, the country is making little progress, being ranked last of 179 countries in the 2007–2008 UN Development Program Report. The security–development nexus perspective maintains that development will follow once security is established, but Denney observes that the newly created security in the country has failed to satisfy this contention, suggesting that the causal link is more problematic than is assumed.

Nevertheless, Baker (2006) remains unconvinced that fundamental weaknesses in the strength of the force, the sustainability of what has been accomplished given the country's lack of resources, and the ongoing issue of police corruption (as well as corruption within the other parts of the justice system) can ever be fully corrected. Ebo (2006) also characterizes the gains from postconflict reconstruction in security sector reform as "fragile" and points to the need for more work to be done to improve governance. He notes that police salaries continue to be low, fuelling petty corruption, and that police continue to be implicated in crimes ranging from extorting money from small traders to more serious crimes. Most commentators

---

[20]Personal communication, James Baker, specialist Justice Delivery Adviser, in a DFID Access to Justice team (in country from January to March 2012), based on interviews undertaken by him with actors in the justice sector.

[21]Denney (2011) describes the work of the UK in reforming the security sector in Sierra Leone as "impressively comprehensive" (p. 284).

agree that lack of resources[22] severely affects the operational side of policing, while the strengths lie in the strategic and policy making areas at senior management.

Sierra Leone, unlike the Philippines and Nigeria, is a small country with a police force of only around 12,000. With a population of about 6 million, Sierra Leone immediately presents a more manageable challenge in terms of police reform. Possessing the same kind of colonial policing background as Nigeria, Sierra Leone nevertheless maintained a stable, albeit authoritarian and corrupt government for many years until the advent of civil war in 1999. During the rule of Siaka Stevens, the police were put to the service of the state, but since 1999, a different trajectory has shaped the policing model. The virtual disintegration of the police during the civil war greatly affected policing as it effectively deconstructed police culture, thus permitting forms of democratic policing to find space, supported by successive democratic policing reforms. Leadership training, strategic planning (at top management levels), and community policing represent the strengths of the police as compared to its pre-1999 structure and operations. Now however, with the virtual cessation of British aid to the police and a shift to supporting the justice sector as a whole, police have ceased to enjoy the resources associated with democratic policing projects. Even when reform aid ceased, corruption was an issue within the police and seems never to have been directly addressed through measures such as public service pay reform or supplements to police salaries.

Sierra Leone is a poor country with very limited resources, and police reform, while benefitting top management in terms of training and, to a lesser extent, leadership, has not adequately addressed the capacity building needs of middle management and lower ranks. Thus, it can be argued that police culture appears to have become fragmented with a technocratic professional policing model operating at top management level and a more traditional corruption-based politically directed model at middle and lower levels. Petty corruption through collection of fines from motorists and the like remains firmly entrenched and wages continue to be set at very low levels. Police tend to adapt to the immediate environment, and, as Marenin (1998) aptly puts it, "if they are underpaid they will use their uniform and guns to extract resources; if they are offered bribes by the poor and threatened by the well-off, they will respond as self-interest dictates" (p. 160).

Thus, while there has been a shift away from the historical legacy of policing, considerable democratic reform work remains to be done, and in the absence of further support from the international community, there is a real likelihood that the gains achieved to date will be dissipated. Oversight

---

[22]For example, for 2011, SLP received only about half of the budget it requested from government. The authorized strength of the SLP is now 12,000 (SLP Review of Capabilities, Horn and others, March 2011, p.18).

of policing remains weak, and there is no distinct program to minimize police corruption. The democratic policing principles embodied in international norms and standards may be well understood at the top of the force but overridden by the middle and lower levels working in the streets.

Police Culture

Western models of policing and international standards and best practices—embodied, for example, in universalist codes of ethics for law enforcement—are disseminated to the developing world as elements of the "democratic policing" project. These projects are confronted by the policing structures and police institutional cultures found in recipient states that are often the outcome of colonial policing policies and practices sustained into the postcolonial period. In local policing models, such as in the Philippines, Nigeria, and Sierra Leone, police cultures are often at variance with the democratic policing model, and the challenge for reformers includes overcoming the many constraints to democratization. How can constraints be overcome? This is achieved (or not) through a process of negotiation over time between the host state and the donor state. Bayley (2006) points out, "There is universal agreement among scholars as well as foreign assistance practitioners that democratic reform takes a long time—five years at least, more likely ten or more" (p. 90). Additionally, democratic police reform is "a difficult, sensitive and unpredictable undertaking" (p. 23).

While practitioners of police reform scarcely mention police institutional culture, police culture has long been a focus of academic police studies.[23] As Marenin (1998) points out, police studies uniformly show that

> police cultures exist, are strong and entrenched, guide discretion, and are shaped largely by the contingencies of their work. . . . Any reform which ignores the power of existing cultures and the ability or willingness of the police to shape their own work cultures is simply rhetorical tinkering and pious hope. (p. 159)

Accordingly, to succeed in effecting change, democratic policing reforms must be embedded in police cultures. To fully explain "police culture," however, is a much larger undertaking, but for purposes of this chapter, it represents a dimension integral to the workings of a police institution that comprises the attitudes, values, and norms of that institution (Banks, 2013). Manning (1989) describes it as "accepted practices, rules and principles of

---

[23]Marenin (1998) observes that in his experience in attending conferences and workshops on police reform, "Almost no-one seemed to be familiar with the literatures on the police. There was much discussion about the police, of course, as if they were a black box almost, devoid of organizational and personal dynamics, interests and goals, but there was little discussion of police from the inside" (p. 159).

conduct that are situationally applied and generalized rationales and beliefs" (p. 360).

In analyzing aspects of police culture in the West, researchers have identified values that police infuse into their interactions with the public, including

- a police focus not simply on the crime committed but also on the nature of the suspect, including aspects such as demeanor, race, age, social class, and the extent to which a person cooperates with police;
- never hesitating to use force when a threat is perceived, including threats to police authority and control;
- loyalty to one's colleagues, which is paramount;
- lying and deception, which are seen as necessary actions to ensure criminals are caught;
- accepting gifts from the public—a practice that recognizes the dangerous nature of police work and is thereby justified; and
- always viewing citizens with suspicion. (Banks, 2013, pp. 19–20)

As Chan (1996) puts it, "police culture has become a convenient label for a range of negative values, attitudes and practice norms among police officers," whose "informal working rules can subvert or obstruct policing reforms initiated at the top, or law reforms imposed externally" (p. 110).

Changing police culture within a reform process is extremely challenging. For example, research into police forces in the West tends to show that because pressures associated with policing remain the same, police culture does not alter over time (Loftus, 2010). This may be because the values associated with police culture are deeply embedded in officers' value systems from the start. Accordingly, some argue that newly recruited officers bring to their police academy and to on-the-job training a set of values based on class and socialization that mirror the elements of police culture. It follows that those elements will necessarily be sustained once a new officer is fully on the job (Crank & Caldero, 2010, p. 66).

There is scant detailed research on police culture in developing states with the exception of South Africa.[24] The characteristics of pre-apartheid policing culture in South Africa illustrate the kinds of barriers encountered by reform efforts. As noted by Brogden and Shearing (1993), despite political commitment, changes in the law, and the adoption of a community policing model, many observers perceived the South Africa Police (SAP) culture to be a major constraint to the transformation of the policing model into a democratic policing model. For example, Marks (2003) shows how the Durban Public Order Police (previously, under apartheid, the Riot Unit) was one of the most brutal units within the SAP. Following police reforms,

---

[24]In many respects, South Africa is a developed state but "developing state" is a statistical and economic construct. Thus, according to the *International Monetary Fund World Economic Outlook Report 2012* (IMF, 2012), South Africa is a developing economy, as are the Philippines, Nigeria and Sierra Leone.

while behavioral changes did occur within the unit, situational demands and features operated to subvert reform as some police in the unit sometimes reverted to the pre-apartheid police culture of brutal policing perceiving themselves to be "fighting a war" against high levels of crime in the townships and valuing only "hard-hitting methods" of crowd control. Marks, therefore, argues that no fundamental change in values had taken place and that changes in police conduct in crowd control were merely a response to command instructions.

In describing the SAP culture, Brogden and Shearing (1993) draw attention to the military structure of the SAP and to "a police culture of enormous brutality" (p. 41). The police culture operated within a framework that prioritized serving the interests of the white minority in sustaining their supremacy over the black majority. As Brogden and Shearing show, the pro-apartheid historical account of the origin of South Africa includes the defense of Afrikaner civilization against "the Black Danger" and this was manifested in police culture especially in rural areas by the "kick, shoot and hammer mentality which brooks no cheekiness from Blacks" (p. 44). The police culture was of such potency and weight that even black police were trapped within it, making jokes, and speaking and writing like Afrikaners. Police culture was in turn sustained by the national ideology operating as a kind of "host culture" located in the values of Afrikanerdom that created apartheid. Brogden and Shearing explain how policing was linked to religion to render policing a sacred mission. The SAP Code of Honor, for example, commits a police officer to "acknowledge(s) the honor and sovereignty of God" and to affirm that "I educate myself in the service of God and my country." Police violence became a sacred mission and the police "chosen people within a chosen people" (p. 49).

Summary

This chapter has explored local policing models in the Philippines, Nigeria, and Sierra Leone with the aim of gaining an understanding of how their policing models were shaped by the past and how they operate now. As noted here, comprehending these policing models includes focusing on the institutional police cultures in these countries, drawing on whatever research is available. In this way, it is possible to gain an appreciation of the likely challenges to reform and a better realization of how some interventions have succeeded and others failed. Police violence and corruption continue to dominate accounts of police conduct in the Philippines. Police remain a militarized force with an institutional culture that tolerates serious police violence, and there is little commitment to change at any level. In Nigeria, the policing model and the police culture are products of a historical legacy that used policing to protect and further the interests of those in power then and in the modern day. Police culture is also resistant to reform, and there is little political commitment to a democratic policing model. Social control and policing lack coherence and citizens are oppressed by police and must resort to safeguarding their own security and safety.

The differences between the Philippines and Nigeria seems to be attributable to the lack of social cohesion in Nigeria, which is plagued not only by high crime, corruption, and a militarist police force, but also with ethnic tensions. Both countries reveal the importance of understanding the political economy of policing before undertaking any democratic policing reforms. In the much smaller and poorer nation of Sierra Leone, police reform has failed to adequately address the capacity building needs of middle management and the lower ranks. Police culture is fragmented so that the top management level employ a technocratic professional policing model, while the poorly paid middle and lower ranks adapt to their immediate environments and operate a more traditional corruption-based politically directed model.

As Neild (2001) has noted, "[R]espectful policing is effective policing" (p. 34). Thus, in police reform projects, international norms, standards, and best practices need to be presented as relevant and operationally effective tools for police, not only strategically but on the street as well. International standards and best practices aim at ensuring that police respect human rights. Police practices that violate basic rights will serve only to alienate police from society, and police will come to rely on coercion, fear, and intimidation. The arguments for incorporating international standards into all policing models are therefore easily discerned, but, as noted above, challenges to reform efforts stemming from police institutional culture will be formidable. As well, in many countries, the legacy of past policing models will be a fundamental element in those cultures. Overcoming institutional barriers to reform requires a properly paced long-term reform project. Police reform is an iterative process, not the mere adoption of an overseas policing model without regard to the "specificities of the context" (Brogden & Shearing, 1993, p. 123) but rather a dialectic or ongoing dialogue about what works in a given context. The account of police violence in the Philippines at the beginning of this chapter reveals the immense challenges involved in changing police practices and police culture to ensure respect for citizens' human rights.

Once democratic policing reforms are adopted and internalized within a policing unit, appropriate best practice internal and external accountability systems, such as effective internal investigation systems and external police complaints institutions, must be in place to ensure reforms are monitored and sustained. Above all, the political economy of policing in a country must be studied and exposed so that every dimension of the policing model is understood and grasped. This will help to ensure that behavioral change is not merely dutiful but is also "accompanied by adequate structural change and change in basic assumptions and values" (Marks, 2003, p. 256). Policing is not an activity isolated from the society in which it occurs and the socio-economic context of policing will necessarily constitute the framework within which police reforms will either succeed or fail.

Discussion Questions

1. What challenges are faced by police reformers attempting to introduce democratic policing reforms?

2. To what extent does the concept of democratic policing incorporate international norms concerning policing and police ethics?

3. Explain how the discourse of democratic policing is transmitted to Third World countries.

4. What commonalities exist between the policing models in the three developing countries discussed in this chapter?

5. What methods or processes have police reformers found to be the most effective in introducing democratic policing?

6. What is meant by "the political economy of policing," and why is it important in police reform efforts?

References

Adebayo, D. (2004). Perceived workplace fairness, transformational leadership and motivation in the Nigeria police: Implications for change. *International Journal of Police Science and Management, 7*(2), 110–122.

Aebi, M. F., Aubusson de Cavarlay, B., Barclay, G., Gruszczyn´ska, B., Harrendorf, S., Heiskanen, et al. (2010). *European sourcebook of crime and criminal justice statistics, 2003–2007* (4th ed.). The Hague: Boom Juridische Uitgevers. Retrieved from http://www.europeansourcebook.org/chapter_1/1a2.doc

Alemika, E. E. O., & Chukwuma, I. C. (2000). *Police–community violence in Nigeria.* Lagos, Nigeria: Centre for Law Enforcement Education (CLEEN).

Amnesty International. (2003). *Philippines: Torture persists—appearance and reality within the criminal justice system.* Retrieved from http://www.amnesty.org/en/library/asset/ASA35/001/2003/en/76cb1b2b-d75f-11dd-b024-21932cd2170d/asa350012003en.pdf

Arthur, J. A., & Marenin, O. (1996). British colonization and the political development of the police in Ghana, West Africa. In C. B. Fields & R. H. Moore Jr. (Eds.), *Comparative criminal justice: Traditional and nontraditional systems of law and control* (pp. 163–181). Long Grove, IL: Waveland Press.

Baker, B. (2006). The African post-conflict policing agenda in Sierra Leone. *Conflict, Security, and Development, 6*(1), 25–49.

Baker, B. (2008, March). Community policing in Freetown, Sierra Leone: Foreign import or local solution? *Journal of Intervention and Statebuilding, 2*(1), 23–43.

Banks, C. (2013). *Criminal justice ethics: Theory and practice* (3rd ed.). Thousand Oaks, CA: Sage.

Bayley, D. H. (1985). *Patterns of policing: A comparative international analysis.* New Brunswick, NJ: Rutgers University Press.

Bayley, D. H. (2006). Changing the guard: Developing democratic police abroad. Oxford: Oxford University Press.

Brogden, M., & Shearing, C. (1993). *Policing for a New South Africa*. London: Routledge.

Brown, L., & Wilson, P. (2007). Putting the crime back into terrorism: The Philippines perspective. *Asian Journal of Criminology, 2*(1), 35–46.

Call, C. T. (2000). *Pinball and punctuated equilibrium: The birth of a "democratic policing" norm?* Draft Paper Prepared for the Annual Conference of the International Studies Association, March 16, 2000, Los Angeles, California.

Central Intelligence Agency (CIA). (2012, October 16). *The World Fact Book: Nigeria*. Retrieved from https://www.cia.gov/library/publications/the-world-factbook/geos/ni.html

Chan, J. (1996). Changing police culture. *British Journal of Criminology, 36*(1), 109–134.

Chiabi, D. (2005). Police in developing countries: The case of Cameroon. In C. B. Fields & R. H. Moore Jr. (Eds), *Comparative and international criminal justice: Traditional and nontraditional systems of law and control* (pp. 278–298). Long Grove, IL: Waveland Press.

Clegg, I., Hunt, R., & Whetton, J. (2000, November). *Policy guidance on support to policing in developing countries*. Swansea: University of Wales.

Crank, J. P., & Caldero, M. A. (2010). *Police ethics: The corruption of noble cause*. Burlington, MA: Anderson.

de Guzman, M. C., & Frank, J. (2004). Using learning as a construct to measure civilian review board impact on the police: The Philippine experience. *Policing: An International Journal of Police Strategies & Management, 27*(2), 166–182.

Denney, L. (2011). Reducing poverty with teargas and batons: The security-development nexus in Sierra Leone. *African Affairs, 110*(439), 275–294.

Department for International Development (DFID). (n.d.). *UK Aid: Justice for All Programme*. Retrieved from http://projects.dfid.gov.uk/project.aspx?Project=114161_

Dimovne, E. K. (2004). Hungarian police reform. In M. Caparini & O. Marenin (Eds.), *Transforming police in central and eastern Europe: Process and progress* (pp. 65–92). Münster, Germany: LIT.

Directorate for Human Resource and Doctrine Development. (1995). *Philippine national police ethical doctrine manual*. Retrieved from http://pnp.gov.ph/main/index.php?option=com_joomdoc&task=doc_details&gid=22&Itemid=112

Ebo, A. (2006). The challenges and lessons of security sector reform in post-conflict Sierra Leone. *Conflict, Security, and Development, 6*(4), 481–501.

Ellison, G. (2007). Fostering a dependency culture: The commodification of community policing in a global marketplace. In A. Goldsmith & J. Sheptycki (Eds.), *Crafting transnational policing: Police capacity-building and global police reform* (pp. 203–242). Portland, OR: Hart.

European Code of Police Ethics. (2001a). Explanatory memorandum relating to the recommendation Rec (2001) of the committee of ministers to members on the European Code of Ethics. Retrieved from http://www.legislationline.org/documents/action/popup/id/8007

European Code of Police Ethics. (2001b). *Recommendation Rec(2001)10 of the committee of ministers to member states on the European code of police ethics*. Retrieved from http://www.legislationline.org/documents/action/popup/id/8007

Fayemi, J. K. (2004). Governing insecurity in post-conflict states: The case of Sierra Leone and Liberia. In A. Bryden & H. Hänggi (Eds.), Reform and reconstruction of the security sector (pp. 179–205). Münster, Germany: LIT; Geneva Centre for the Democratic.

Hills, A. (1996). Towards a critique of policing and national development in Africa. *The Journal of Modern Africa Studies, 34*(2), 271–291.

Hills, A. (2008). The dialectic of police reform in Nigeria. *Journal of Modern Africa Studies, 46*(2), 215–234.

Hinton, M. S. (2006). The state on the streets: Police and politics in Argentina and Brazil. Boulder, CO: Lynne Rienner.

Horn, A., Gordon, M., & Albrecht, P. (2011). *Sierra Leone police: Review of capabilities.* (Unpublished report to Department for International Development). London: DFID.

Horn, A., Olonisakin, F., & Peake, G. (2006). United Kingdom-led security sector reform in Sierra Leone. *Civil Wars, 8*(2), 109–123.

Human Rights Watch. (2012, January). *World report 2012: Nigeria.* Retrieved from http://www.hrw.org/world-report-2012/world-report-2012-nigeria

Igbinovia, P. E. (2000). The future of the Nigeria Police. *Policing: An International Journal of Police Strategies and Management, 23*(4), 538–554.

Immigration and Refugee Board of Canada. (2006, August). Philippines: Reports of corruption and bribery within the police force; government response; frequency of convictions of members of the police force accused of criminal activity (2004-2006). Retrieved from http://www.unhcr.org/refworld/docid/45f147971a.html

International Criminal Investigative Training Assistance Program (ICITAP). (n.d.). *About ICITAP.* Retrieved from http://www.justice.gov/criminal/icitap/

International Monetary Fund (IMF). (2012). *International Monetary Fund world economic outlook report 2012: Growth Resuming, dangers remain.* Retrieved from wwwimf.org/external/pubs/ft/weo/2012/pdf/01/pdf/text.pdf

INTERPOL (n.d.-a). The fight against corruption: Global standards to combat corruption in police forces/services. Retrieved from http://www.interpol.int/Crime-areas/Corruption/INTERPOL-Group-of-Experts-on-Corruption

INTERPOL (n.d.-b). *INTERPOL code of conduct for law enforcement officers.* Retrieved from http://www2.ohchr.org/english/law/codeofconduct.htm

Ivkovic, S. K. (2004). Distinct and different: The transformation of the Croatian police. In M. Caparini & O. Marenin (Eds.), *Transforming police in central and eastern Europe: Process and progress* (pp. 195–220). Münster, Germany: LIT

Jobard, F. (2004). The lady vanishes: The silent disappearance of the GDR police after 1989. In M. Caparini & O. Marenin (Eds.), *Transforming police in central and eastern Europe: Process and progress* (pp. 45–64). Münster, Germany: LIT.

Loftus, B. (2010). Police occupational culture: Classic themes, altered times. *Policing and Society, 20*(1), 1–20.

Manning, P. K. (1989). Occupational culture. In W. G. Bailey (Ed.). *The encyclopedia of police science* (pp. 360–364). New York: Garland.

Manning, P. K. (2005). The study of policing. *Police Quarterly, 8*(1), 23–43.

Marenin, O. (1998). United States police assistance to emerging democracies. *Policing and Society: An International Journal of Research and Policy, 8*(1), 153–167.

Marenin, O. (2007). Implementing police reforms: The role of the transnational policy community. In A. Goldsmith & J. Sheptycki (Eds.), *Crafting transnational policing: Police capacity-building and global police reform* (pp. 177–202). Portland, OR: Hart.

Marks, M. (2003). Shifting gears or slamming the brakes? A review of police behavioural change in a post-apartheid police unit. *Policing and Society: An International Journal of Research and Policy, 13*(3), 235–258.

Murphy, C. (2007). The cart before the horse: Community oriented versus professional methods of international police reform. In A. Goldsmith & J. Sheptycki (Eds.), *Crafting transnational policing: Police capacity-building and global police reform* (pp. 243–262). Portland, OR: Hart.

Neild, R. (1999). *From national security to citizen security: Civil society and the evolution of public order debates.* Montreal, Canada: International Center for Human Rights and Democratic Development.

Neild, R. (2001). Democratic police reforms in war-torn societies. *Conflict, Security and Development, 1*(1), 21–43.

Newburn, T. (1999). *Understanding and preventing police corruption: Lessons from the literature.* London: Home Office Research, Development and Statistics Directorate, Policing and Reducing Crime Unit. Retrieved from http://tvernedra .ru/Pretotvkorvpolice.pdf

Neyroud, P. W. (2003). Policing and ethics. In T. Newburn (Ed.), *Handbook of policing* (pp. 578–602). Cullompton, UK: William.

Nwankwo, C., Mbachu, D., & Ugochukwu, B. (1993). *Human rights practices in the Nigerian police.* Lagos, Nigeria: Constitutional Rights Project.

Office of the United Nations High Commissioner for Human Rights (OHCHR). (1979). *United Nations code of conduct for law enforcement officials: General assembly resolution 34/169 of 17 December 1979.* Retrieved from http://www2 .ohchr.org/english/law/codeofconduct.htm

Office of the United Nations High Commissioner for Human Rights (OHCHR). (1990). *The basic principles on the use of force and firearms by law enforcement officials.* Retrieved from http://www2.ohchr.org/english/law/firearms.htm

Office of the United Nations High Commissioner for Human Rights (OHCHR). (2006). *Optional protocol to the convention against torture and other cruel, inhuman, or degrading treatment or punishment.* Retrieved from http://www2 .ohchr.org/english/law/cat-one.htm

Office of the United Nations High Commissioner for Human Rights (OHCHR). (2010a). *Body of principles for the protection of all persons under any form of detention or imprisonment.* Retrieved from http://www.un.org/documents/ga/ res/43/a43r173.htm

Office of the United Nations High Commissioner for Human Rights (OHCHR). (2010b). *Standard minimum rules for the treatment of prisoners.* Retrieved from http://www2.ohchr.org/english/law/treatmentprisoners.htm

Office of the United Nations High Commissioner for Human Rights (OHCHR). (2010c). *United Nations rules for the treatment of women prisoners and noncustodial measures for women offenders (the Bangkok rules).* Retrieved from http://www.un.org/en/ecosoc/docs/2010/res%202010-16.pdf

Pilar, N. N., Resullida, M. L. G., Lopez, J. P., Mariano, M. G., Santos, G. M., & Honorio, F. F. (2001). Civilianization and community-oriented policing in the Philippines. *Arms and Militaries, 16*(2), 143–180.

Pino, N. W., & Wiatrowski, M. D. (2006). Implementing democratic policing and related initiatives. In N. W. Pino & M. D. Wiatrowski (Eds.), *Democratic policing in transitional and developing countries* (pp. 99–128). Burlington, MA: Ashgate.

Quah, J. S.T. (2004). Democratization and political corruption in the Philippines and South Korea: A comparative analysis. *Crime, Law, and Social Change, 42*(1), 61–81.

Robertson, A. (2004). Police reform in Russia. In M. Caparini & O. Marenin (Eds.), *Transforming police in central and eastern Europe: Process and progress* (pp. 289–304). Münster, Germany: LIT.

Shopov, V. (2004). Democratic government and administrative reform: The transformation of policing in Bulgaria. In M. Caparini & O. Marenin (Eds.), *Transforming police in central and eastern Europe: Process and progress* (pp. 131–146). Münster, Germany: LIT.

Skolnick, J. H., & Bayley, D. H. (1988). Theme and variation in community policing. *Crime and Justice: A Review of Research, 10,* 1–37.

Stone, C. E., & Ward, H. W. (2000). Democratic policing: A framework for action. *Policing and Society, 10*(1), 11–45.

Thomson, B. (2007). *Sierra Leone: Reform or relapse? Conflict and governance reform.* Retrieved from http://www.chathamhouse.org/sites/default/files/public/Research/Africa/reportsierraleone0607.pdf

Transparency International. (2008). *2008 bribe payers index.* Retrieved from http://www.transparency.de/uploads/media/BPI_2008_REPORT-1.pdf

Trebilcock, M. J., & Daniels, R. J. (2008). *Rule of law reform and development: Charting the fragile path of progress.* Cheltenham, UK: Edward Elgar.

United Nations Office on Drugs and Crime (UNODOC). (2004). *United Nations Convention Against Corruption.* Retrieved from http://www.unodc.org/unodc/en/treaties/CAC/

U.S. Department of State (2010). *Human rights report: Philippines.* Retrieved from http://www.state.gov/j/drl/rls/hrrpt/2010/eap/154399.htm

USAID. (2007, May). USAID program brief: Anticorruption and police integrity: Security sector reform program. Washington, DC: Author.

Varona, G. (2011). *Towards improving ethics and governance in the Philippines national police: A critical systemic review* (Unpublished doctoral dissertation). Flinders University, Adelaide, South Australia.

Yusufi, I. (2004). Macedonia's police reform. In M. Caparini & O. Marenin (Eds.), *Transforming police in central and eastern Europe: Process and progress* (pp. 221–238). Münster, Germany: LIT.

17

The Tarnished Badge

Police Off-Duty Misconduct

David C. Massey

What causes police off-duty misconduct? Police officers are exposed to many stressors related to their dangerous duties. The life span of those choosing the profession is shorter than personnel choosing other careers (Ortmeier & Davis, 2012), and both divorce (Goldfarb, 2004) and suicide rates are higher (Bennett & Hess, 2007) than what is found in the general population. Never before have police been under such intense scrutiny, as the emerging electronic media of today can document and publicize off-duty misconduct as well as on-duty misconduct (Lovell, 2003). Police leadership must cultivate an atmosphere in their agencies where off-duty misconduct will not be condoned, yet provide assistance programs to employees that may prevent misconduct, due to the stressful nature of policing.

In the author's first tenure as a police chief, in a large resort police department, he soon learned that off-duty misconduct by police was not just an occasional diversion. A veteran police officer, intoxicated and off duty, was involved in a hit-and-run traffic accident, which injured two pedestrians. His subsequent arrest was even more tragic, when it was learned that a fellow off-duty officer had asked, yet failed, to take his vehicle keys from him at a local nightclub just prior to the accident, despite his obvious intoxication. Luckily for the suspect officer, the pedestrians were not seriously injured; yet the exemplary career of this officer was forever ruined with his arrest and termination of employment.

This and a series of subsequent off-duty misconduct cases over the years lead the writer to examine more deeply the problem of stress in the law enforcement profession. What is it about our profession or culture that seems to promote off-duty misconduct by some of our members?

What can we, as police leaders, do to proactively address this problem in the media-driven age we live in?

Off-Duty Misconduct in the Media Age

The city of Pittsburgh settled four misconduct lawsuits in 2010, with two of those suits involving officers who were off duty, or moonlighting, at the time the incidents occurred. In 2011, two more settlements were made, both for off-duty misconduct (Smydo, 2011). One of the settlements, for $40,000, involved a citizen who was accidentally shot by an off-duty officer during a tussle that was prompted by the officers' belief that the victim had assaulted him earlier in the evening. In 2010, the Mayor of Pittsburgh, angered by allegations of off-duty misconduct by city police, said that public employees should "clean up their act," noting that efforts by his administration to discipline employees are often stymied by state law (Lord & Gurman, 2010).

Off-duty misconduct by police is not confined to Pittsburgh. Over the years, the media has publicized a series of high-profile cases. An off-duty New York City police officer was charged with manslaughter in the drunk-driving traffic accident that resulted in the deaths of a pregnant woman, her sister, and her four-year-old son in Brooklyn (Mazulli, 2001). In San Francisco, three off-duty officers attacked two men and fled the scene in a truck. The San Francisco Police Department began both criminal and administrative investigations into the conduct of the three off-duty officers and also the possible misconduct of numerous other officers in connection with the involvement and handling of the incident ("Police Disciplinary Charges," 2007).

In Chicago, as Ford and Washburn (2003) relate, jurors awarded $1 million in a federal lawsuit against the Chicago Police Department over an alleged beating by an off-duty officer. The plaintiff's attorney stated that the Chicago Police Department's internal disciplinary process at the time of being designed to "exonerate" off-duty police accused of attacking other citizens. During the trial, he presented evidence that during a two-year period, of 73 internal police department investigations of improper use of force by off-duty officers, only one resulted in arrest.

Similarly, officers from the Hartford, Connecticut Police Department liked to drink beer after work, in uniform, in a parking lot behind police headquarters. The *Hartford Courant* related that during one particular drinking session, an intoxicated officer fired nine shots at three unoccupied cars and was charged with unlawful discharge of a firearm, among other criminal counts ("Conduct Unbecoming," 1993). The police department acknowledged that police "occasionally shared a few beers in the lot when they got off-duty" (p. C10), and the Police Chief said he will, "discourage drinking in the lot and try to persuade officers to use the departmental gym to work off stress.

Off-Duty Abuse of Police Powers

High-profile off-duty misconduct cases do not always revolve around violence. Wallman (2009) presented a case involving 28 south Florida police officials, including captains, majors, undercover officers, and the department spokesperson, in which they guarded, off duty, the home of a prominent local attorney while federal agents say he ran a $1 billion Ponzi scheme! He was the only person in the department's history to have permanent round-the-clock police protection at his home.

Investigative reporting by the media can uncover patterns of abuse by off-duty officers that also relate to the nonenforcement of speeding laws. A *Florida Sun Sentinel* investigation revealed that police officers are not cited for speeding off duty, like ordinary citizens (Kestin, Maines, & Williams, 2012). Speeding off duty, the article alleged, routinely goes unchallenged unless someone complains, and punishment can be as slight as a verbal or written reminder to obey the speed limit. Their investigation also revealed that during the period of 2004–2010, at least 320 law enforcement officers across Florida were involved in crashes blamed on speeding. Only 37 officers were charged with speeding, or 12% of the total. In contrast, 55% of citizens who were speeding at the time of their crashes were ticketed.

Delving further into the numbers, this same investigative team found that a dozen Fort Lauderdale cops were caught driving 80 to 100 miles per hour, off duty. All received only a reminder to obey the traffic laws. One sergeant, who was caught driving 86 to 95 miles per hour 10 times during a six-week period, received a one-day suspension from duty as discipline.

Even the moral conduct of off-duty police officers can come under media scrutiny. The Vernal, Utah Police, in a highly publicized case, according to Winslow (2008), suspended an officer for having an adulterous affair with a married county sheriff's deputy. The Vernal Police had earlier responded to the home of that deputy on a report that her husband was threatening suicide. The six-month suspension from duty of the Vernal officer for disciplinary reasons provoked a public outcry.

One county sheriff asked, "Should we be in the business of disciplining police officers who engage in adulterous activities off-duty?" The public safety director asked, "To what extent should the government be involved, when the conduct isn't criminal?" The police chief responded, "We (the police) are held to a higher standard and I don't think we should apologize for it" (p. A3).

Increasing Mistrust of Law Enforcement

With each new headline of misconduct, mistrust of law enforcement increases, police–community relations suffer, and the reputation of good, hardworking, and ethical law enforcement professionals and their organizations become tainted (Kinnard, 2007). Miller and Davis (2008) state that public attitudes toward police misconduct appears highly susceptible to the influence of the media, a fact that should not be surprising given the way media coverage tends to focus more on law enforcement misconduct than the sometimes abstract examples of effectiveness or responsiveness. Perception of the community cannot be ignored in contemporary society, according to Kinnard (2007), since this is evidenced by the proliferation of the video camera and news media. Every action is subject to review, not only by police administrators and colleagues, but also by the public at large.

Even though citizens do not witness every police action that occurs from day to day, they do watch television and pay attention to other media outlets. Bennett and Hess (2007) point out the strength of media influence when they state that approximately one third of regular television programming deals with some aspect of the criminal justice system. According to Miller and Davis (2008), the perception of police misconduct, but not so much their effectiveness or responsiveness, is associated with news consumption. This applies both to experiences of bad news about the police in the previous month and respondents' patterns of news consumption, with "highbrow" news consumers more likely to see the police as prone to misconduct, other things being equal.

To better illustrate the particular strength of media influence, a 1996 incident involving the conduct of several off-duty officers in Indianapolis, known as the *Downtown Police Brawl*, requires further examination. The off-duty officers, all of whom were White, were accused of being rowdy and intoxicated, using racial and sexist slurs, reportedly battering two males (one African American and one White), and then arresting them (Chermak, McGarrell, & Gruenewald, 2006). The officers involved in this incident had earlier been with the chief of police and the mayor at a minor league baseball game.

The initial police account was that the officers were not at fault and were simply reacting to rowdy and disorderly conduct on the part of citizens when they made their arrests. As the media began focusing on this incident, they discovered a number of discrepancies in the case and located several independent witnesses who labeled the officers as aggressors. Ultimately, the incident caused the chief of police to resign, and several officers were later charged criminally and terminated. There is evidence to suggest that consuming the news *did* affect the attitudes about the guilt of these officers at their criminal trial—that is, the more a citizen read the newspaper, the more likely he or she was to believe the officers involved were guilty (Chermak et al., 2006). Whites who consumed the news were more likely to perceive the officers involved as a "few bad apples," whereas African Americans familiar with the case were more likely to generalize and think the officers' behavior was representative of other officers in the department.

Developing a working relationship with the media can help during a crisis (Chermak et al., 2006). Police departments must be prepared to respond to such events because they have the potential to undermine any public relations and community policing efforts. Thus, it is important for police departments to evaluate their relationships with media organizations and how best to use the media as a mechanism to communicate department goals and objectives, as well as make an effort to provide full accounts when crisis events occur.

The Indianapolis Police Department was later able to frame the Downtown Police Brawl incident as an unfortunate occurrence, involving a few bad apples, positioning itself toward repairing public relations damage caused by the event. Results of this effort appear to have been somewhat successful (Chermak et al., 2006).

Police Culture and Stress

As Dean and Gottschalk (2011) relate, sometimes the idealism of joining the police to do something worthwhile for the community can become diluted by too many negative experiences with the public, too little job satisfaction, and too much bureaucracy. Under such circumstances, idealism can be fatally ruptured, and police deviance takes up residence in the space where idealism used to live. Police work is the second most stressful job in the United States (the first is inner-city high school teacher) (Ortmeier & Davis, 2012).

Perin (2007) states that many elements of law enforcement contribute to stress reactions, including shift work, pending retirement, negative public perceptions, unsupportive management, and physical ailments. When these are compounded or aggravated by personal problems, such as strained relationships, financial hardship, and substance abuse, police officers can find themselves under immense stress. All of these variables contribute to a shorter life span for police officers. In the United States, average life expectancy for men is a little over 74 years, and a little over 80 years for women. For police officers with 10 to 19 years on the job, life expectancy is just 53 to 66 years (Ortmeier & Davis, 2012).

Alcohol abuse and domestic violence can be off-duty byproducts of police work. Indeed, there is evidence to suggest that some police officers are drawn to alcohol as a coping mechanism (Johnson, Todd, & Subramanian, 2005). For example, they may drink to diminish the intensity of pain or guilt resulting from pent-up anger, acts committed or witnessed, or failure to prevent tragedy. Unfortunately, there is a dearth of high-quality empirical data on patterns of abuse in police officers, despite the fact that anecdotal evidence suggests alcohol abuse and dependence are a significant concern in this population, with earlier studies estimating that up to 25% of officers have serious problems with alcohol (Ballenger et al., 2010).

In a study of a large urban police sample (852 officers) in Australia, it was reported that 48% of male officers and 50% of female officers said they drank excessively or engaged in binge drinking, or hazardous or harmful drinking in the past three months (Richmond, Wodak, & Kehoe, 1998). A later study of a large sample of officers (712 officers) in an urban American police agency found that approximately 11% of males and 16% of females had engaged in at-risk levels of alcohol use during the previous week, while over one third of male and female officers reported a binge drinking episode at some time during the last month (Ballenger et al., 2010).

Risk factors that make a police family vulnerable to stress include limited knowledge of police work, conflict between job and family priorities, and isolation felt by the officer and spouse (Bennett & Hess, 2007). The national divorce rate is 50%, but research shows police officers suffer a substantially higher divorce rate, with estimates ranging between 60% and 75% (Goldfarb, 2004). Apart from the fact that most families will not "air dirty laundry" with the police, domestic violence by law enforcers has escaped detection primarily because of officers' strong adherence to a code of secrecy, commitment to camaraderie, and resistance to internal intrusion (Johnson et al., 2005).

Many risk factors associated with domestic violence are conspicuously present within the police culture, including isolationism, exposure to violence, job burnout, authoritarianism and control, and substance abuse (Johnson et al., 2005). In contrast to the other negative factors, however, authoritarianism and control are considered by some officers to be necessary for effective policing, while many find alcohol use desirable for camaraderie. "No agency can afford the negative ramifications that come with a domestic abuse incident by one of their own," stresses Graves (2005). "An insufficient or complete lack of investigation increases risk of civil litigation stemming from unaddressed domestic violence issues involving agency personnel" (p. 108).

Most effective in exposing the code of secrecy that protects police domestic abusers has been the Omnibus Consolidated Appropriations Act of 1996 (also known as the *Lautenberg Amendment*). This retroactive law prohibits individuals (including law enforcers) convicted of misdemeanor domestic violence offenses from owning or using firearms (Johnson et al., 2005). A conviction of domestic violence under this act will bar an officer from possessing a firearm, which will effectively sever employment (Raterman, 2001).

The breakup of relationships, alcohol, family problems, and stress all contribute to the high rate of police suicide, about 30% higher than what is found in the general population (Bennett & Hess, 2007). Every year, about 150 officers are killed in the line of duty in the United States (D'Antonio, 1999), but more than twice that number commit suicide. Evidence suggests that police officers are eight times more likely to take their own lives than to be killed by a criminal in the line of duty (Ortmeier & Davis, 2012).

Post-Traumatic Stress Disorder (PTSD) and Police _____

One of the most important occupational hazards of police work is frequent exposure to traumatic incidents and the resulting risks of developing post-traumatic stress disorder (PTSD) (Ballenger et al., 2010). A strong body of evidence suggests that rates of alcohol use disorders are significantly higher in individuals with PTSD, compared with trauma-exposed individuals without PTSD. Javidi and Yadollahie (2012) define PTSD as an anxiety disorder brought about by exposure to unexpected extreme traumatic stress. Exposure to extraordinary events, especially those having the potential to cause or threaten death or serious disability, can result in short-term psycho-physiological responses (i.e., nausea, bowel release, fainting, and hyperventilation) and long-term effects (chronic anxiety, mood disorders, insomnia, and emotional numbness) (Johnson et al., 2005).

Not all individuals who experience extreme sudden trauma acquire PTSD; however, some 60.7% of men and 51.2% of women experience at least one potentially traumatic event in their life (Javidi & Yadollahie, 2012). While the overall prevalence rate of chronic PTSD is estimated at 4%, the prevalence rate among police, fire, and emergency service workers is estimated at anywhere from 5% to 32%. Perhaps the greater recent example of mass trauma among emergency personnel occurred during the World Trade Center Disaster (9/11). Approximately 5,000 police officers responded within the first two days, and more than 25,000 worked at ground zero, the morgues, or the Staten Island landfill (Dowling, Moynihan, Genet, & Lewis, 2006). Moreover, at least 68% of the officers reported at least one disaster-related symptom still current some 15–27 months after the attack. Of those interviewed, more than 5,700 officers (20%) reported such significant difficulties in response to the attack that they were advised to seek further assistance.

Police are also more likely than civilians to acquire PTSD as a result of a direct assault or from being threatened with death by guns, knives, or other instruments, according to B. Green (2004). He noted that in the civilian population, the most common cause of PTSD is a motor vehicle accident. While the "acting as if the trauma is re-occurring" symptom is most marked in military combat veterans, there is a trend for police to be more likely to have this symptom, perhaps indicating the quality of the trauma police now face—partway between civilian and military combat experience. About 84% of those suffering from acute PTSD may have comorbid conditions, including alcohol or drug abuse; feeling shame, despair, or hopelessness; physical symptoms; employment problems; divorce; and violence, which made life harder (Javidi & Yadollahie, 2012).

The Blue Wall of Silence

Despite all of the stressors inherent in law enforcement, there is often reluctance on the part of many police officers to admit problems or reveal misconduct. D'Antonio (1999) feels that there is a kind of natural selection that makes cops lousy at seeking help. The kind of men who gravitate to police work, he opines, tend to believe in the cowboy code: A man doesn't talk about his problems; he does what he has to do. Confessing weakness is hard for many men, and it's especially hard in a paramilitary world that values stoicism.

Although contemporary U.S. policing has a rich and well-documented history, replete with paradigmatic shifts over time due to cultural changes and historical events, of particular import is the emphasis on officers' loyalty to one another (Shockey-Eckles, 2011). Loyalty is an important moral virtue for police—it sits with other instrumental virtues such as courage, integrity, and pride (Richards, 2010). Police solidarity can often be a virtue (Miller, 2010). It enables officers to cooperate with one another and to stand solid in the face of danger and successfully discharge their duties. It also reinforces the individual capacity for physical courage, including preparedness to die in the service of others. And it generates a willingness to help other police when they most need help. In some cases, however, an officer's loyalty can be seriously misplaced.

Misplaced Loyalty

Police solidarity, known as *the Blue Wall*, is often perceived by members of mainstream society as an impenetrable fortress whereby contemporary police officers protect their own—including those who engage in misconduct—beneath a code of secrecy (Shockey-Eckles, 2011). Among some police officers it is also known as the *code of silence*, which means that a police officer is not expected to uncover any misconduct he has noticed in the organization (Kaariainen, Lintonen, Laitinen, & Pollock, 2008).

According to Richards (2010), misplaced loyalty often begins with those complaints that do not involve serious criminal conduct. This may involve turning a "blind eye" to police misconduct, on and off duty, in a way that favors the police officer over the civilian complainant. His research states that this paradigm reveals a police organization that is socially cohesive, relatively insular, hierarchical, and subject to legitimate authority.

D. Green (2002) relates that in the case of criminal occurrences, officers are able to remember the most trivial detail and have the ability to recall it months or years later when it comes time to testify in court proceedings. In misconduct cases against police, however, officers suddenly have amnesia or Alzheimer's disease. They can't recall or don't remember. Incidents are unclear, and they are unsure if they were even present. Equally, they were not observant and didn't notice improper activity.

D'Antonio (1999) believes that even under the best of circumstances, cops have powerful tribal instincts. They socialize with other cops, drink at cop bars, work out in cop gyms, and even live in cop neighborhoods. Law enforcement officers are seen as authority figures in their communities, and, as such, people deal with them differently and treat them differently (Bennett & Hess, 2007). Wearing a badge, a uniform, and a gun makes a law officer separate from other members of society. Many officers report a feeling of always being on duty, and the difficulties of blending into society. As a result, many police officers tend to socialize with other officers, both on and off-duty (Rees & Smith, 2008).

Approximately one third of regular television programming deals with some aspect of the criminal justice system. The distorted view of law enforcement as portrayed by the media means that many citizens have unrealistic expectations of what law enforcement officers can actually do (Bennett & Hess, 2007). Unfortunately, the hypervigilance necessary in police work reinforced by a perceived hostility or lack of appreciation from the community often creates an "us versus them" attitude. "Them" not only includes civilians, but often the "top brass" (particularly in large departments), who sometimes create organizational goals which are insensitive to the patrol officers' street realities and their personal needs (Johnson et al., 2005).

Ethical Conduct and Management's Responsibility

Criticisms of police practice are invariably couched in moral terms; even the all-important rule of law is rooted in a moral consensus or association, and police officers' most challenging task is that of maintaining appropriate levels of integrity in an organization that is permeated, indeed, constituted by, moral requirements, including principled loyalty (Richards, 2010). Few professions demand as much moral fiber as policing. Indiscretion, easily overlooked in other political arenas, brings shame and mistrust in the field of law enforcement (Stephens, 2006).

Police are subject to moral temptations not typically found in other professions (Miller, 2010). Consider detectives in drug enforcement. They are exposed to drug dealers prepared to offer large bribes to have an officer "do nothing." Arguably, the conjunction of extraordinary powers with enhanced temptation justifies setting higher minimum standards of moral character for police than many other professions.

Historically, police officers have been held accountable for improper activities committed both on and off duty. In spite of changing societal values that have tempered the abilities of employers to hold employees accountable for conduct outside of work, sworn offers continue to be held accountable for certain types of off-duty conduct (Raterman, 2001). This off-duty regulation can even extend to limiting an employee's rights to free speech and association. As Bulzomi (1999) relates, as an employer, the government has an interest to achieve its goals as effectively and efficiently as possible. When an employee's speech undermines this role, the courts can elevate what typically is an employer's subordinate interest in controlling speech into a significant one.

Law enforcement organizations may also have constitutional authority to regulate employee's off-duty associational activities, including off-duty sexual conduct, when it involves a supervisor–subordinate relationship or association that impacts adversely an employee's ability to perform the job or otherwise materially impairs the effectiveness and efficiency of the police department (Bulzomi, 1999). Numerous court rulings have upheld an officer's dismissal for off-duty conduct or circumstances that caused a negative impact on the agency and its mission. As long as there is a rational nexus of the employee's behavior to the employee's job, public safety employers can sanction objectionable off-duty conduct (Raterman, 2001).

Ethics Starts at the Top

Because ethical conduct has always been the cornerstone of policing, communities expect proper behavior from their public servants (Glensor & Stitt, 1998). In an organization that needs to possess integrity, such as a police organization, the pervasive ethos or spirit—that is, the culture—should be conducive to high performance, both technically and ethically (Miller, 2010). Law enforcement leaders must create a culture of ethics within their organization. The organization must ascribe to a mission statement and a clear set of operating values that represent more than hollow promises but, rather, establish standards for employees' behavior at all levels and illustrate that ethics play a crucial role in an officer's success in the agency (Fitch, 2011).

Kinnard (2007) states that poor police conduct tends to begin at the top of any organization. Reasons for this may vary. In some cases, it may be something outside one's professional work life that impacts one's behavior on the job. If a supervisory officer is ignoring police rules, officers under his charge could observe this, begin to think that such behavior is the norm, not consider policies important, and eventually disregard them altogether. In at least one study, an especially strong relationship was found between the lack of exemplary behavior on the part of managers and (1) favoritism within the organization (2) discrimination, and (3) sexual harassment, gossiping, bullying, and falsely reporting in sick (Huberts, Kaptein, & Lusthuizen, 2007).

As Huberts et al. (2007) state, of all the measures that can be taken to prevent integrity violations, the behavior of management remains the most important. Several scholars, as well as practitioners, argue that leadership is the key variable influencing the ethics and integrity of employees. Cartwright (2010) echoes this theme, by stating that agency executives set the tone for what constitutes acceptable behavior. Leaders must not only model appropriate actions but also ensure that personnel who cross ethical lines face appropriate consequences; otherwise, unethical behavior will increase.

Role Modeling

Role modeling by executives and supervisors is important and especially significant in limiting unethical conduct in the context of interpersonal relationships. Employees seem to copy a leader's standards of integrity in their daily interactions with others (Huberts et al., 2007). If a leader talks about how vital and necessary ethical behavior is, but behaves in ways that suggest it is alright to cut corners or bend rules, subordinate personnel will almost certainly emulate the leader's actions, not the leader's words. Nothing demoralizes personnel more than a leader who talks about the importance of ethical behavior, but turns around and "lowers the standard" for themselves or others (Henry, 1998).

As Field and Meloni (1999) state, it is the ethical responsibility of law enforcement executives to present a clear, concise set of expectations for their employees. This begins when the officer is hired, for it is at that point the administrator should portray a realistic description of organizational philosophies, such as honor, respect, integrity, values, accountability, and a willingness to accept responsibility for one's misconduct and mistakes. There should be no question in an employee's mind, prior to employment, that he or she will be held accountable for their conduct. As Fitch (2011) says, instead of expecting that officers possess a firmly engrained set of values (good or bad) when they enter the police force, managers must remember that all officers have the potential to act virtuously; however, when the work environment allows misbehavior either implicitly or explicitly, the potential for abuse skyrockets.

Disciplining Off-Duty Misconduct

Law enforcement embraces higher individual and organizational standards than most professions. Discipline builds organizational prestige by sustaining effective organizational performance and preserving spirit. Its goal is internal order and individual accountability with an emphasis on discovering the truth based on a solid framework that respects the needs of the public, the agency, and the employee (Field & Meloni, 1999). Discipline acts as a catalyst supporting the necessary change. It targets the conduct, not the individual; discipline is certain, swift and proportionate; and employees know with certainty that any form of intentional misconduct will be disciplined.

Bennett and Hess (2007) state that, like McGregor's Theory X and Theory Y, lessons learned from a hot stove should be present in effective discipline. When a person touches a hot stove (violates a rule or regulation), the burn (punishment) is immediate, is consistent (it happens every time), and is impartial (it is the same for everyone). Further, the severity of the burn depends on the length of time the stove and victim remain in contact, as well as the heat of the stove.

The proportionality of the discipline to the offense is important. As Miller (2010) puts it, it is conducive to a punitive culture when minor unethical conduct on the part of subordinates, once exposed, is harshly punished in the service of a police management hell-bent on demonstrating a tough anticorruption stance to the political masters and the public at large, when a more remedial or development approach would be more appropriate. Such a punitive culture actually reinforces the blue wall of silence, particularly among lower echelon officers. D. Green (2002) argues that appropriate action should take place based on the seriousness of the officers' activity and frequency once misconduct is identified. The specific act of misconduct, the employees involved, and any knowledge of similar acts should be considered as well. He feels discipline should be progressive and positive. The initial step in minor infractions should begin with counseling and the development of a plan for improvement.

The key to disciplining off-duty conduct, according to Raterman (2001), is finding a sufficient nexus between the off-duty conduct and the duties and responsibilities of the sworn officer. The clearest case for sanctioning off-duty conduct is where an officer is arrested off duty for a crime. Both on and off duty, a sworn employee, one who has the duty to uphold the law by virtue of an oath, may be held accountable for unlawful actions. Officers with the power of arrest are especially accountable.

In most law enforcement agencies, the off-duty arrest of an officer may well serve as the sole basis for administrative charges against the officer. Often, if the employing agency conducts an independent inquiry into the incident, it will find other areas of concern to the agency. Generally, it is best if internal affairs investigators conduct some amount of independent inquiry (Raterman, 2001).

Conduct Unbecoming

Not every off-duty conduct violation fits neatly into established rules and regulations. Often, police agencies use the charge of "conduct unbecoming an officer" as their catalyst for action. Martinelli (2007) states that conduct unbecoming an officer is a charge used in policy to discipline officers for behavior that violates an agency's policies and expectations. The officer's perceived deviant behavior usually does not fit perfectly into an agency's rules and regulations, so administrators charge the offending officer with conduct unbecoming. It is used as a catchall charge. Yet defining conduct unbecoming requires an approach similar to U.S. Supreme Court Justice Potter Stewart's attempt to define pornography in 1964—we'll know it when we see it.

We can assume that if officers clearly know the ethical rules of professional conduct, and if they have a feeling that the administration investigates and disciplines rule violations fairly and impartially, they are able to trust the administration. Furthermore, according to the theory of police culture, trust in the administration means a weakening of the "code of silence" (Kaariainen et al., 2008). Openness in an organization decreases the likelihood of employee misconduct (Huberts et al., 2007). In an open organization, employees can be honest about mistakes, ask for advice when confronted with integrity-related issues, discuss integrity dilemmas, and report deviant behavior.

Establishing rapport with officers can also be an important aspect of reducing stress (Bennett & Hess, 2007). Law enforcement managers can provide both positive reinforcement and constructive criticism if there is a foundation of respect and communication. They should keep in close touch with their subordinates and recognize the symptoms of stress. If an officer shows such symptoms, the manager should be ready to assist and reduce, to whatever extent possible, the level of stress. Sometimes, employees can benefit by simply having someone to talk with. If counseling or psychological assistance is needed, it should be provided or information forwarded regarding local sources of assistance (Perin, 2007).

Leadership Challenges

Police leaders must also be concerned that they are not hiring officers from other police agencies with a proven record of prior off-duty misconduct. Shockey-Eckles (2011) cautions against a phenomenon in the police world known as *officer shuffle*. This refers to the ease with which disreputable officers are able to move across jurisdictions, thus maintaining their police certification and continuing to serve in law enforcement. These officers, referred to as *gypsy cops* or *rogue officers*, place communities at risk, while often tainting the image of all law enforcement. Most problematic when considering the presence of gypsy cops is that they often bring with them the old mindsets, behaviors, and personality traits that have long been the trademarks of their careers. The rogue cop who is forced to move between departments or across jurisdictions due to acts of malfeasance calls into question the professionalism of all.

Facilitating this problem is the fact that no standardized criteria for licensure revocation exist across jurisdictions. This, at least in part, contributes to the grave disparity among the quality of officers serving in different states. It also opens the door for those who have been decertified in one state to find employment in another (Shockey-Eckles, 2011). As Carter (2006) relates, police supervisors know that 20% of the officers cause 80% of the problems. Time and again, the same officers are the focus of disciplinary actions.

Generational changes in the workforce present new challenges as well. "Generation X," a generation infused with values created by computer games, mass media, television, and entertainment industries, has begun to enter law enforcement (Field & Meloni, 1999). Traits attributed to them, such as placing self above the organization, demands for immediacy, a fixation for making money, and career success at any cost, may impact the future effectiveness and efficacy of traditional disciplines. In the final analysis, however, ethical conduct resides within the individual. As Mills (2003) relates, it is indeed a universal truth that people are responsible for their own behavior and actions of individuals. Aristotle suggested that a person who exhibits responsibility is one who intends to do the right thing, has a clear understanding of what the right thing is, and is fully cognizant of other alternatives that might be taken (Field & Meloni, 1999).

Proactive Management to
Reduce Off-Duty Misconduct

Maher (2008) relates that police managers and administrators have historically reported the view that police corruption and misconduct represent the individual moral defects of a few police officers, rather than resulting from systematic problems throughout the organization. This administrative view, often referred as the *bad apple theory* of police misconduct, suggests that police deviance and misconduct are isolated; a single rotten apple in a barrel of good apples, and has been the subject of much criticism in recent years. As Fitch (2011) relates, law enforcement agencies must strive to recruit, hire, and train only those who demonstrate strong moral values *before* they enter the academy. Yet, despite this, even a department's best efforts will not prevent instances of police misconduct from garnering attention.

When there is a desire to reduce the potential for misconduct and litigation, writes Kinnard (2007), the initial formation of policies and procedures is central for successful implementation of any central mechanism to address those issues. Martinelli (2007) argues that educating officers on the content of departmental policies and the organization's expectations behind those policies is critical. Discussing off-duty problems for which others have been disciplined can only benefit an agency and can supply a chief with an ample due-process defense in civil court. Failing to educate officers on the organization's definition of off-duty misconduct leaves the door open for juries to answer for themselves the meaning behind the policy and its implementation.

In addition to educating employees, police administrators and supervisors have a legal duty to ensure that police officers under their command are mentally and emotionally fit to perform their duties, and failure to do so can result in significant civil liability and serious consequences to the employer (Fischler, 2011). For example, in a case involving an off-duty New York police officer who shot his wife and himself, the city was found negligent because, in part, the officer "was never identified as a problem officer, despite his displaying many of the signs that should have flagged him as having mental or emotional problems" (p. 72). The court held that a law enforcement department must take reasonable precautions to hire or retain officers who are psychologically fit for duty. The doctrine of official immunity may not be invoked to protect an agency from allegations of vicarious liability, involving negligent retention.

Therefore, Perin (2007) warns that police departments need to become more aware and learn more about certain mental health disorders like PTSD. When there is a critical incident, they need to have peer support and psychological counseling available. Police agencies must have the appropriate professionals helping the officers cope with what they witnessed and what they had to do in the performance of their job. Police officers in crisis often seek help from their peers, and, in every department, a few individuals who prove adept in helping others are turned to repeatedly (Finn & Tomz, 1998).

Support Services

Law enforcement agencies should capitalize on the natural abilities of select employees to provide assistance by establishing peer-support programs. In doing so, they provide training to increase the effectiveness of natural peer helpers, while marketing their services so that as many individuals as possible become aware of the program's availability. Organized peer-support programs also help agencies choose the right individuals to meet the needs of employees in trouble. A number of law enforcement agencies currently use peer supporters to help employees prevent and deal with stress. According to Finn and Tomz (1998), peer-supporter programs prove especially appropriate for assisting officers involved in shooting incidents and officers with drinking problems. Many peer supporters are recovering alcoholics who can link fellow officers with detoxification programs, inpatient treatment, and Alcoholics Anonymous groups.

Critical incident stress debriefing (CISD) is another effective way to prevent or reduce stress. In CISD, officers who experience a critical incident, such as a mass disaster, a traffic collision that results in multiple deaths, or a murder, are brought together as a group for a psychological debriefing soon after the event. A trained mental health professional leads the group members as they discuss their emotions and reactions. This allows officers to vent and realize their reactions are not abnormal; rather, they are responding normally to abnormal situations (Bennett & Hess, 2007).

When management becomes concerned over an officer's reaction to stress, they may order the officer to undergo a fitness for duty examination (FFDE). Fischler (2011) defines FFDE as a "formal, specialized examination of an incumbent employee that results from:

1. Objective evidence that the employee may be unable to safely or effectively perform a defined job; and

2. A reasonable basis for believing that the cause may be attributable to a psychological condition or impairment." (p. 72)

Assisting the police family members by educating them on the stressful nature of police work can also be helpful. As Ortmeier and Davis (2012) state, many police academies' curricula now include training for family members. Known as *family programs*, *significant-other training*, or *police-spouse seminars*, these programs aim to educate police officers' families about the nature of police work, including how shifts work, what police jargon means, what salaries and benefits their loved ones share, and what types of incidents, individuals, and equipment officers deal with. Additionally, some departments have ride-along programs, which enable family members to observe police officers in action. Developers hope to demystify the police profession so spouses can work on overcoming stress that might interfere with healthy personal relationships.

Summary

Professionalism, by definition, involves belonging to a profession and behaving in ways that are consistent with professional standards (Carter, 2006). Managing risk in a police department includes minimizing officer off-duty misconduct that results in a loss of manpower hours, litigation costs, settlement payouts, and jury awards. For every off-duty misconduct case, one can conclude that hours of internal investigation, paperwork, disciplinary hearings, and court appearances resulted in an appellate body reviewing that officer's alleged misconduct (Martinelli, 2007).

It is important to remember that the public's ethical expectations of police do not stop when they go off duty. The moral and ethical conduct of police officers is held to a higher standard than other occupations—as well they should be. As enforcers of the law, police are expected to fairly and impartially administer the law during their tour of duty. Just as importantly, they are expected to model ethical behavior not only while working, but also in their personal lives, off duty.

Ethical leadership is critical to define clearly what off-duty conduct is acceptable to the organization. As Huberts et al. (2007) relate, three of the most cited qualities of ethical leadership in relation to integrity violations of employees are

1. role modeling of managers through setting a good example for employees;

2. strictness of managers applying clear norms and sanctioning misbehavior of employees; and

3. openness of managers to discuss integrity problems and dilemmas.

Police agencies must change from a posture of being *reactive* to off-duty misconduct, to being *proactive* in the recognition that stressors in the police profession may contribute to off-duty misconduct. Ortmeier and Davis (2012) believe that to mitigate dangerous levels of stress for officers, police agencies must excel at stress management by putting in place a blend of prevention, training, and intervention programs for all employees. These programs include peer-support programs and mandated critical incident stress debriefing for all major traumatic events. When officers' off-duty conduct evidences mental health issues, mandatory mental health evaluations known as *fitness for duty evaluations* may be needed as well.

Nor should these preventive programs be confined to larger police agencies. As Oliver and Meier's (2004) study indicates, small-town and rural police agencies can benefit from stress intervention programs as well. Among the factors that contribute to stress in smaller agencies are the "fishbowl" environment, in which officers police the people they know; limited resources; lack of training; and the general boredom of inactivity.

Early warning systems allow a police organization to control its assets successfully. To defend a police agency in a negligence suit, it must be illustrated that there exists an interaction between policy and control within the organization (Kinnard, 2007). Another preventive tool for leaders to consider in mitigating potential off-duty misconduct is recruitment.

Considering that exposure to traumatic incidents is inevitable in police work, B. Green (2004) suggests that police agencies should sift recruits according to potential resilience to stress.

Justification for organization change to address the problem of off-duty misconduct is required by two phenomena in law enforcement: public confidence and legal parameters. The police have a responsibility of legal authority that requires them to maintain the trust of the public. Mere reports of off-duty misconduct by police officers often cause citizens to lose confidence in the police. Ethical leadership is required to address both the cause and effect of off-duty misconduct.

In the case of the off-duty police officer who was arrested and terminated for leaving the scene of a personal injury accident, the present writer immediately prepared a press release on the incident and informed the public. There was naturally a concern that this incident would tarnish the reputation of the department. While the writer was feeling very alone in his office, the phone rang and a citizen stated that he wanted to *thank* the writer for publishing this event, because he knew how hard it was to release this information, but he knew it was the most ethical thing to do. He was comforted to know that he had an honest police department, not afraid to admit its mistakes.

Discussion Questions

1. What types of conduct would constitute off-duty misconduct?

2. What is "conduct unbecoming an officer"? When is it applicable?

3. What is the blue wall or code of silence in law enforcement?

4. What causes post-traumatic stress disorder in police officers, and how serious a problem do you believe it has become?

5. As a police manager, what are some proactive programs your department could implement to reduce stress within your agency?

6. Ultimately, who has the moral responsibility for acting ethically off duty?

References

Ballenger, J. F., Best, S. R., Metzler, T. J., Wasserman, D. A., Mohr, D., Liberman, A., et al. (2010). Patterns and predictors of alcohol abuse in police officers. *The American Journal on Addictions, 20*(1), 21–29.

Bennett, W., & Hess, K. (2007). *Management and supervision in law enforcement.* Belmont, CA: Wordsworth Thompson Learning.

Bulzomi, M. J. (1999). Constitutional authority to regulate off-duty relationships. *FBI Law Enforcement Bulletin, 68*(4), 26–32.

Carter, L. (2006). Measuring professionalism of police officers. *The Police Chief, 73*(8), 8–10.

Cartwright, G. (2010). Maintaining ethical behavior. *FBI Law Enforcement Bulletin, 79*(8),10–14.

Chermak, S., McGarrell, E., & Gruenewald, J. (2006). Media coverage of police misconduct and attitudes toward police. *Policing: An International Journal of Police Strategies and Management, 29*(2), 261–281.

Conduct unbecoming police officers. (1993, September 27). *Hartford Courant,* p. C10.

D'Antonio, M. (1999, November). Men in blue. *Men's Health,* 72–78.

Dean, G., & Gottschalk, P. (2011). Continuum of police crime: An empirical study of court cases. *International Journal of Police Science and Management, 13*(1), 16–28.

Dowling, F., Moynihan,G., Genet, B., & Lewis, J. (2006). A peer-based assistance program for officers with the New York City Police Department: Report of the effects of September 11, 2001. *The American Journal of Psychiatry, 163*(1), 151–153.

Field, M., & Meloni, T. (1999). Constructive police discipline: Resurrecting the police spirit. *Law and Order, 47*(5), 85–91.

Finn, P., & Tomz, J. (1998). Using peer supporters to help address law enforcement stress. *FBI Law Enforcement Bulletin, 67*(5), 10–18.

Fischler, G. (2011). The role of psychological fitness-for-duty evaluations in law enforcement. *The Police Chief, 78*(8), 72–76.

Fitch, B. D. (2011). Rethinking ethics in law enforcement. *FBI Law Enforcement Bulletin, 80*(10), 18–24.

Ford, L., & Washburn, G. (2003, May 3). Man gets $1 million in attack by officer: His attorney says cops given free reign. *Chicago Tribune,* pp. A1, A21.

Glensor, R., & Stitt, B. (1998). Ethical considerations in community policing and problem solving. *Police Problem Solving, 1*(3), 19–34.

Goldfarb, D. (2004). The effects of stress on police officers. *Speech to Union Delegates.* Retrieved from http:/www.heavybadge.com/efstress.htm

Graves, A. (2005). Law enforcement involved domestic abuse. *Law and Order, 53*(11), 108–111.

Green, B. (2004). Post-traumatic stress disorder in UK police officers. *Current Medical Research and Opinion, 20*(1), 101–105.

Green, D. (2002). Ethics: Problem employees in smaller agencies. *Law and Order, 50*(10), 96–99.

Henry, M. (1998). Unethical staff behavior. *Corrections Today, 60*(30), 112–117.

Huberts, L., Kaptein, M., & Lasthuizen, K. (2007). A study of the impact of the leadership styles on integrity violations committed by police officers. *Policing: An International Journal of Police Strategies & Management, 30*(4), 587–607.

Javidi, H., & Yadollahie, M. (2012). Post-traumatic stress disorder. *The International Journal of Occupational and Environmental Medicine, 3*(1), 2–9.

Johnson, L., Todd, M., & Subramanian, G. (2005). Violence in police families: Work–family spillover. *Journal of Family Violence, 20*(1), 3–12.

Kaariainen, J., Lintonen, T., Laitinen, A., & Pollock, J. (2008). The "code of silence": Are self-report surveys a viable means for studying police misconducts? *Journal of Scandinavian Studies in Criminality and Crime Prevention, 9,* 86–96.

Kestin, S., Maines, J., & Williams, D. (2012, February 13). Speeding cops get special treatment, Sun-Sentinel investigation finds. *Florida Sun-Sentinel,* pp. A1, A3.

Kinnard, B. (2007). Exploring liability profiles: A proximate cause analysis of police misconduct: Part 1. *International Journal of Police Science and Management, 9*(2), 135–144.

Lord, R., & Gurman, S. (2010, May 6). Mayor scolds public safety force: "Clean up," says Ravenstahll over recent allegations of off-duty conduct. *Pittsburgh Post Gazette,* pp. A1, A6.

Lovell, J.S. (2003). *Good cop/bad cop: Mass media and the cycle of police reform.* Monsey, NY: Willow Tree Press.

Maher, T. (2008). Police chiefs' views on sexual misconduct. *Police Practice and Research, 9*(3), 239–250.

Martinelli, T. (2007). Minimizing risk by defining off-duty misconduct. *The Police Chief, 74*(6), 12–20.

Mazulli, J. (2001, May 6). Alcohol not a new problem for NYPD. *New York Daily News,* pp. A1, A6.

Miller, J., & Davis, R. (2008). Unpacking public attitudes to the police: Contrasting perceptions of misconduct with traditional measures of satisfaction. *Journal of Police Science and Management, 10*(1), 9–22.

Miller, S. (2010). Integrity systems and professional reporting in police organizations. *Criminal Justice Ethics, 29*(3), 241–257.

Mills, A. (2003). Ethical decision making and policy: The challenge for police leadership. *Journal of Financial Crime, 10*(4), 331–335.

Oliver, W., & Meier, C. (2004). Stress in small town and rural law enforcement. *American Journal of Criminal Justice, 29*(1), 37–56.

Ortmeier, P., & Davis, J. (2012). *Police administration: A leadership approach.* New York: McGraw-Hill.

Perin, M. (2007). Police suicide. *Law Enforcement Technology, 34*(9), 8–16.

Police disciplinary charges timely filed. (2007). *Police Department Disciplinary Bulletin, 15*(1), 4–5.

Raterman, M. (2001). Police discipline for-duty conduct. *Police Disciplinary Bulletin, 9*(1), 2–4.

Rees, B., & Smith, J. (2008). Breaking the silence: The traumatic circle of policing. *International Journal of Police Science and Management, 10*(3), 267–279.

Richards, N. (2010). Police loyalty redux. *Criminal Justice Ethics, 29*(3), 221–240.

Richmond, R., Wodak, A., & Kehoe, L. (1998). How healthy are the police? A survey of life factors. *Addiction, 93*(11), 1729–1737.

Shockey-Eckles, M. (2011). Police culture and the perpetuation of the officer shuffle: The paradox of life behind the "blue wall." *Humanity and Society, 35*(3), 290–309.

Smydo, J. (2011, January 23). Payouts increase for lawsuits that allege police misconduct. *Pittsburgh Post-Gazette,* pp. A1, A5.

Stephens, N. (2006). Law enforcement ethics do not begin when you pin on the badge. *FBI Law Enforcement Bulletin, 75*(11), 22–24.

Wallman, B. (2009, November 15). High-ranking police officers guarded over Rothstein. *South Florida Sun-Sentinel,* pp. A1, A3.

Winslow, B. (2008, December 11). Off-duty conduct of police is sticky issue: Salt Lake Telegram. *Deseret News (Salt Lake City, Utah),* pp. A1, A3.

18

Public Information in the Age of YouTube

Citizen Journalism and the Expanding Scope of Police Accountability

Jarret S. Lovell

Who is a journalist? It's a tantalizing question, but it's hardly worth asking anymore. We're All Journalists Now."

Ann Cooper (2008, p. 45)

Simon Glik never anticipated that he would be arrested for using his cellular-phone camera in public. Yet in October 2007, that is precisely what happened. Glik was walking near the Boston Common when he noticed three police officers scuffling with a man on a park bench in an apparent drug arrest. Hearing a bystander exclaim to the officers, "You're hurting him," Glik—himself a lawyer—decided to put the camera application on his phone to use and record the police–citizen encounter. But after police apprehended the drug suspect and placed him into custody, they quickly turned their attention toward Glik and his cell phone, which they knew contained an account of their behavior that afternoon. Relying on a state wiretap law that makes it a crime to record audio without second-party consent, the police confiscated the phone and arrested Glik on charges of illegal electronic surveillance (Griffin, 2011; Rowinski, 2010).

The use of state wiretap laws to arrest citizen journalists who document police behavior has become something of an emerging trend. In December 2008, a Boston man was arrested after he filmed officers using what he believed to be unnecessary force to break up a party (Rowinski, 2010). In

2010, a Maryland motorist was charged with violating state law after he posted to YouTube footage of his own traffic stop captured by his helmet camera ("Our View on Cops and Cameras," 2010). In June 2011, a woman was arrested in Rochester, New York after she filmed a traffic stop from her own front lawn. Having just read an article about Black drivers being disproportionately stopped by the police, she decided to record the encounter once she noticed that the driver of the stopped car was Black and the traffic officers were White (Sledge, 2011). These are but a few examples of police arresting individuals for engaging in what has come to be known as *citizen journalism.*

Citizen journalism is a model of news reporting that calls on everyday people to play an active role in the collection, analysis, and dissemination of public information (Bowman & Willis, 2003). It is a practice highly reliant on the use of mobile media technology, such as cellular phones and Flip cameras, to create a visual or verbal account of events that are then distributed to the public through social media websites like YouTube, Facebook, or Twitter, as well as through countless blogs. Sometimes referred to as *participatory media,* those who champion citizen journalism note its potential to democratize news reporting. This is because citizen journalism shifts power away from government, which serves as information gatekeepers, and toward everyday people who can inject into the public discourse issues of concern otherwise excluded from news headlines (Antony & Thomas, 2010). At the same time, citizen journalism loosens the public's dependence on mainstream media to hold public officials accountable. Now, anyone with access to social media can disseminate information that challenges official narratives and questions the ability of political actors to govern. For these reasons, officials who typically benefit from their ties to establishment media find citizen journalism a challenge to their political legitimacy.

While still in its infancy, citizen journalism has already proven to be a powerful force for police accountability by bringing to the public what are often unseen police practices—such as the police use of manual force, the deployment of the Taser gun and other less-than-lethal weaponry, and protest policing. This ability of citizen journalism to use social media to expand the scope of information about officials democratizes law enforcement, leading to fruitful analysis of police procedures. Like all new media, then, citizen journalists and the social media websites they use are catalysts for police accountability, and they may even contribute to long-term organizational and strategic reform.

This chapter explores the impact of citizen journalism and social media on contemporary policing. It argues that if used correctly and ethically, citizen journalism is a force for police accountability that can contribute to meaningful police reform. This is because police are like other political figures that must routinely monitor their public image and alter their behavior according to feedback they receive (Lovell, 2003). As media imagery constructs an image of law enforcement on a routine basis, this chapter begins with a discussion of how these images shape the behavior of political figures. Next, it provides a brief overview of media and police reform. With the history of "mass" media closely paralleling that of the "modern" police force, we can see how changes in media technology bring to the public new information about police practices, leading to strategic and organizational change. Among these key changes is the incorporation of media specialists into the police organizational framework. The goal of these specialists is to routinely monitor the police public image and work with media to create news stories that reflect positively on the police agency. The emergence of citizen journalism and social media technology, however, disrupts the traditional news-making process and circumvents the role of law enforcement as filters in the crime-related news-making process. This chapter therefore concludes with a discussion of citizen journalism and its impact on the police image. As all new media have expanded the scope of information about police services, they have also contributed to the quality of these services. So, too, must contemporary law enforcement work with citizen journalism and recognize the technology of social media as a positive force for police accountability.

Media and Public Behavior

One of the defining features of modern society is the extent to which media actually shape political behavior. This occurs through a process known as *reflexivity* (Giddens, 1990). Reflexivity represents a process wherein people alter their behavior according to the evaluations they received about their conduct. Often, this reshaping of behavior is anticipatory and based on presumptive responses. That is, individuals and organizations plan future behavior according to past evaluations. For public officials, these evaluations stem from public opinion polls shaped by media coverage of their daily actions, and this feedback either sparks change in their overall performance, or it reinforces good performance. Media, therefore, serve as a political force that shapes not only public opinion but also public behavior.

To understand the influence of media on public behavior, one must recognize the interrelationship between media technology and social legitimacy. In his landmark publication *Understanding Media*, Marshall McLuhan (1964) described the technologies of media as extensions of the senses and of the body. Radio serves as an extension of the ears, allowing sounds that are miles away to be heard as if the origin of the sound was standing in the same room as the listener. Similarly, microphones (a technology on which radio is dependent) serve as extensions of the vocal chords. The camera lens may be conceptualized as extensions of the eyes, bringing into focus that which might otherwise not have been seen. Finally, recordings (whether audio or video) are extensions of the mind since they preserve a record of an event when our memory might otherwise fail to recall specific details. Historian Daniel Boorstin (1992) has noted that it was only with the invention of recording devices that the phrase "no comment" first became a response by political figures to press inquiries. With a permanent record to which voters could refer, many leaders felt it best not to comment at all! Clearly, by serving as extensions of the senses, media have the ability to bring to the fore that which would otherwise remain unseen, unheard, or forgotten. For political figures and celebrities, media can be intrusive, revealing to the public that which public figures would prefer to have remained hidden. It has become a modern necessity for public figures to engage in reflexivity and restructure their behavior to meet the demands of mediated society.

When reviewing contemporary policing, a number of agency-specific social, political, and budgetary factors influence the nature, shape, and ultimate success (or failure) of police administration. Media are among the factors that play a crucial role in shaping contemporary policing. Each day, police performances appear prominently in newspaper headlines, on nightly news broadcasts, and now increasingly on social media websites such as YouTube. So prominent are law enforcement in media that content analyses of the news have shown that crime stories receive nearly three times the coverage as the president, Congress, or the economy, with news coverage of criminal justice focusing primarily on police practices (Graber, 1980). Now with the increased availability of news through 24-hour cable channels and online news sites, stories of police work continue to proliferate (Surette, 2011).

As police are public features regularly featured in the news, media coverage of police work contributes to police reflexivity (Manning, 1997). Since the public does not have routine, daily interaction with police, it learns about police practices primarily via media. Each day, crime "beat" reporters, camera crews, newsroom editors, and now increasingly citizen journalists serve as extensions of the senses and play a significant role in constructing a police image. This image in turn influences public opinion about police practices. Operating under the protection of the First Amendment and using their "fourth estate" mandate, some of the images news media project are critical of law enforcement, calling into question the level of police professionalism as well as the quality of services officers provide. Editorials may even project interpretations of police work and call for immediate reform. Police officials wishing to maintain their organizational legitimacy and a level of favorable public support have little choice but to alter their behavior to address the news images portrayed. In essence, then, police today understand that who they are is largely a product of the media (Perlmutter, 2000). Agencies wishing to maintain favorable public support for their law enforcement practices must monitor coverage of police in the media and alter their performances accordingly.

New Media and Police Reform

Although the police organization is often resistant to change (Zhao, 1996), the emergence of new media at key points in the history of policing has helped to usher in periods of significant police reform. It is interesting to note that the rise of the mass media closely parallels the rise of the first modern American police forces, with both making their initial appearances during the 1830s and 1840s. Moreover, as is explained below, each era of police reform was in part precipitated by advances in media technology that revealed limitations in law enforcement practices and threatened the legitimacy of police work. New media, then, exert a powerful influence on police practices and contribute to cycles of police reform.

Early American policing (1830–1931) was marked by corruption as it became connected with political machines (Reiss, 1992). When the first departments became fixtures of American cities during the mid-19th century, the prevailing police strategy at the time called for close and personal ties to the community and a decentralized organizational structure. While this allowed police to become integrated into neighborhoods, the lack of oversight over officers allowed for police inefficiency, disorganization, and corruption (Kelling & Moore, 1988). Police personnel were political appointees, and this led to partisanship both in the enforcement of laws and in the monitoring of elections. The latter half of the 19th century therefore found big city police departments ruled by political machines and special interests where inefficiency, police corruption, and involvement in vice became unfortunate realities (Reppetto, 1978).

During this same period, advances in printing technology made periodicals cheaper and therefore accessible to the working class for the first time (Shapiro, 1968). With the introduction of the steam press in 1804 came a new period of output, accessibility, and affordability as the new technology substituted steam power for human muscle (Davidson, Boylan, & Yu, 1976). What resulted was the creation of the "penny" press periodicals, named for their low cost and news content geared toward the masses. Recognizing its readership as those at the bottom of the social hierarchy, one of the favorite themes of the "pennies" was crimes of the elite. This meant that much of the content of these periodicals revealed manipulation of the government by the rich and powerful. It also meant that the style of reporting was sensational, perhaps serving as a template for what would later become tabloid journalism. Still, at a time of widespread government corruption, the pennies did much to democratize journalism, and they established a foundation for muckraking journalism—a more serious type of reporting that would reveal the inadequacies of early American police work.

Muckraking journalism emerged in the early 20th century and was a populist trend in news reporting that catered to the masses by exposing the improprieties of the politically connected. Subsequently, not a few publications highlighted the malfeasance of local law enforcement that was widespread at the time. For example, in 1907, *Cosmopolitan* reported that the New York Police were accepting bribes in return for failing to enforce city restrictions on poolrooms. It accused the police of "standing publicly as partner in and sponsor for the most widespread and destructive form of vice known to the city" (Flynt, 1907/1971, p. 331). In 1909, *McClure's Magazine* noted that "the purchase of the police in Chicago . . . is freely and frankly for sale to the interests of dissipation" (Turner, 1909/1964, p. 400). These are but a few of the stories of early policing disseminated to the masses through the power of the press. Indeed, for some 15 years, these popular news journals pushed for political and social change. In doing so, they exposed to the public what they largely already knew: Early American policing was in desperate need of reform.

In time, the early 20th century saw a number of reformers calling for change in the management of policing, and advances in printing technology allowed newspapers providing extensive coverage of reformer demands to reach a wide audience. The culmination of this new era in reporting resulted in the formation of the National Commission of Law Observance and Enforcement, which published recommendations for a new model of policing in its *Wickersham Commission Reports* on the police (1931/1968). The new model of law enforcement was to be a more bureaucratic and hierarchically structured police organization with increased officer oversight (Walker, 1977). Commonly referred to as the *professional era*, departments adopted new hiring standards and better training for officers. They also increased their reliance on the squad car and radio technology, they incorporated a rigid paramilitary structure into the police organization, and they limited officer discretion, all to increase officer accountability—a marked contrast to the lack of officer oversight and lack of professionalism during the early years of policing.

By the 1960s, the strategies adopted by the reform movement were firmly entrenched, yet many of the rigid policies contributed to the already growing tension within the nation. For instance, the strict enforcement of laws and limited officer discretion led to the aggressive policing of civil rights and antiwar protesters, many of whom were gaining the sympathy of the American public. At the same time, the rise of television news, coupled with domestic unrest, did much to undermine the image of police. Certainly, those within the civil rights movement were quite fond of their newfound power in television, for it exposed to the nation the brutality of segregation and— worse—the brutality of law enforcement who were complicit in its maintenance. At the same time, television also called into question the policing of protesters opposed to the war in Vietnam by adding a new dimension to the language of politics and war. Meyrowitz (1986) argues that in print and on radio, terms such as *enemy*, *ally*, *communist*, and *freedom fighter* can more easily go unchallenged since readers and listeners lack the kind of visual information that conveys a shared humanity. With words now accompanied by visuals, images of police officers using their batons against the public "did not make good press to say the least" (Geller, Nimocks, Goldstein, & Rodriquez, 1994, p. 7).

Almost from its inception, then, the television news broadcast became a national mirror reflecting social instability that police appeared incapable of managing in a professional manner. Largely due to images of law enforcement that were playing on television, calls for reform were swift. During the late 1960s and early 1970s, a number of government reports called on law enforcement to soften their dependence on reactive policing and preventive patrol and to adopt a more community-oriented approach of problem solving through community partnerships. These reports also made explicit mention of the power of media to construct a police image, and they criticized law enforcement for operating without concern for their media image. For example, the National Advisory Commission on the Causes and Prevention of Violence (1969) noted that police were both "inexperienced in dealing with civil disorders" as well as communicating with media, leaving reporters with the task of sorting out "fact from rumor" (p. 107). In 1973, the National Advisory Commission on Criminal Justice Standards and Goals advocated that police agencies begin to incorporate media into their organizational and strategic framework by adopting a policy of routinely presenting information to the media, rather than merely responding to media inquiries.

Recognizing the limitations of reactive policing and the paramilitary structure on the creation of a favorable media image, police began to adopt a more "community-oriented" face of law enforcement based on proactive problem solving, increased officer discretion, and police–citizen partnerships (Kelling & Moore, 1988). Following these reports, police departments across the nation began reforming their approach to dealing with members of the press, adopting a more proactive position on media communication rather than one that found police responding to media inquires somewhat defensively. To achieve this end, police agencies during the 1980s established media relations units staffed by police Public Information Officers (PIOs). These officers serve as liaison between the police agency and the press and act as the media spokespersons for the department (Lovell, 2001). They may also participate in the news-making process by penning agency-related news releases, by serving as quotable news sources that reporters can call on, and by feeding reporters with possible news stories.

When the history of police is understood, the end of the 20th century marked an acknowledgment of the media "as part of the policing apparatus" (Ericson, Baranek, & Chan, 1989). Police now recognized that a favorable image in the news contributes to the overall quality of police performance, and police began actively working to construct a positive image of law enforcement. To achieve this end, police PIOs began to establish close ties to establishment media. Police realized that by serving as information gatekeepers, they could take an active role in the creation of news and in a more favorable police-media image. Participation in daily news-making process therefore became a central component in maintaining the legitimacy of contemporary law enforcement practices.

Police and the News-Making Process _____

On any given day, law enforcement is featured prominently in the news. Police are the most visible representatives of government, and they likely have a familiarity with the local community that is unmatched by even the top leaders in city government (Lipsky, 1980). For this reason, law enforcement officials are frequently called on by reporters to comment on local events and (Lovell, 2006) to serve as authoritative news sources regarding community happenings. Routinely, then, police are able to maintain a level of control over news stories regarding crime and its prevention by actively serving as news sources.

The news media are source driven, and news sources are the lifeblood of reporters. Sources represent authoritative voices that can provide reporters with quotable information at a moment's notice. Because news organizations require journalists to provide accounts of community events on a routine basis (Tuchman, 1978), reporters are highly dependent on, and cooperate with, government officials—including police—who compose the bulk of news sources and who provide the necessary news accounts (Gans, 1979). To ensure a constant supply of news items and authoritative sources, journalists maintain a database of names and viewpoints for both news and editorials that may be readily accessed at any given point in the news-making process. This journalistic dependence on public officials works to the benefit of government agencies by affording them privileged status in the marketplace of ideas, allowing them to frame news events according to their organizational needs (Bennett, 1990).

Police are routinely key participants in the news-making process, and they represent primary sources for the production of crime news (Barak, 1988; Chermak, 1995; Chibnall, 1981; Fishman, 1980; Sherizen, 1978). As a result, they maintain privileged status as the key definers of the crime problem (Hall, Critcher, Jefferson, Clarke, & Roberts, 1978). News organizations are dependent on the police for a constant supply of crime information that composes a large portion of the daily news. In turn, police organizations are dependent on the news media to publicize crimes, to request public cooperation with investigations, and to lobby for additional law enforcement resources (Lovell, 2003). Contrary to what many officers believe, this frequent and direct access that police have to the media often works to the advantage of law enforcement, which typically receives favorable coverage in the news. In fact, studies of crime news reveal that police receive more favorable coverage than either the criminal courts or corrections (Chermak, 1998; Graber, 1980).

With PIOs now part of the organizational framework of most police agencies, law enforcement no longer have wait for a call from reporters to participate in the news-making process. In fact, research into the daily responsibilities of PIOs (Lovell, 2001, 2003) suggests that police often use their close ties to reporters to create a more favorable image of their agency. Some examples of news stories that have originated from police agencies include: a father–son team working together at the same department; an arrangement between a community college and the local police whereby students restore retired vehicles for police use as custom vehicles; an off-duty officer who saved a diner's life. Such stories allow PIOs to frame the police positively as everyday members of the community, a practice which certainly benefits law enforcement. But these stories also aid local news outlets who are in constant need of news "filler" on slow news days.

While the norms of news production and the need for government sources typically favor the police, the dynamics of the news-making process shift during times of nonroutine news events, such as accidents or scandals. During times when government officials are the subjects of a news story, they may be reluctant to provide commentary (Ericson et al., 1989). This creates a news hole, and alternative voices that lack habitual access to the media are often brought to the forefront by reporters. These alternate voices now serve as the primary news sources, and the quotes they provide may challenge the official, government narrative of events. It is during times of controversy and scandal when established government sources lose their hegemony over the interpretation of events, and when new voices pose a threat to the legitimacy and authority of public officials (Bennett, 1990).

Because police organizations are not immune to scandal, on those occasions when police become the subject of a story, reporters may turn to alternate voices to serve as the primary news sources, especially when police make themselves unavailable for comment. For example, Lawrence (1996) examined news coverage of police use of force in the *Los Angeles Times* between 1987 and 1992 to study the impact that two prominent media stories had on reporter reliance on police as sources. She found that victims, their families, attorneys, witnesses, and community groups became key sources during such news events, and that these sources often provided challenges to official interpretations of police misconduct.

To be sure, one of the reasons for reporters' shift to nonpolice voices during times of controversy is the reluctance of police to provide commentary when police themselves become the story. When faced with unfavorable media coverage, police agencies have traditionally adopted a reactive approach to dealing with news reporters by withholding facts, cutting off access to reporters, or establishing a level of organizational secrecy (Ericson et al., 1989). The increased prominence of PIOs within the police organization has improved the accessibility of police as sources during times of scandal. PIOs can build on their longstanding relationships with news reporters to try to manage or contain a story, or they can at the very least respond to allegations stemming from alternate news voices in an attempt to paint a more favorable image of police practices.

With the rise of mobile and social media technology, however, public information is increasingly bypassing the traditional news-making process, as citizens are no longer purely the recipients of news but are also now those reporting it (Bowman & Willis, 2003). For police, this new media paradigm translates into a diminution of influence over the content of crime-related news, especially news about law enforcement practices. Under this new model of news making, footage of police using force against the public can be disseminated directly by the public through social media websites, with bloggers and commentators posting their own interpretations of news events. Simply put, with citizen journalism and social media, the traditional news-making process no longer applies, and police no longer maintain privileged status as the creators, gatekeepers, and framing of police-related news and information.

Citizen Journalism and Social Media

In November 2011, some 20 journalists covering the arrests of Occupy Wall Street (OWS) activists across the country were themselves arrested for not having what law enforcement officials considered to be "official" or legitimate press accreditation. According to a report by the Committee to Protect Journalists (Rafsky, 2012), "[P]olice repeatedly refused to acknowledge as a journalist anyone who did not have what they considered to be official accreditation, leaving freelancers and new media journalists particularly vulnerable" (para. 2). With the nature of media and information technology changing faster than perhaps any other sector of society, determining who among a crowd of protesters is a journalist can be difficult, though it must be emphasized that most of those arrested at the November OWS event did have press credentials or other forms of documentation identifying them as press. Still, the arrests point to the defining feature of news reporting under the new media paradigm of citizen journalism, namely, that press credentials or not—everyone today is a journalist.

"[F]reedom of the press," writes Ann Cooper (2008) in the *Columbia Journalism Review*, "now belongs not just to those who own printing presses, but also to those who use cell phones, video cameras, blogging software, and other technology to deliver news and views to the world" (p. 45). It is a sentiment echoed by the First Circuit Court of the United States when Simon Glik—the lawyer turned citizen journalist mentioned at the beginning of the chapter—challenged his arrest in court. The justices first dismissed his case by noting that wiretap laws apply to the recording of *private* conversations and not public events. Police behavior, the court noted, falls within the scope of public events. Perhaps more importantly for any discussion of citizen journalism, the court next rejected attempts by the police to draw a distinction between citizens acting as journalists on the one hand, and the establishment press on the other. "The public's right of access to information," the court ruled, "is coextensive with that of the press" (Griffin, 2011, para. 6). It was an important acknowledgment by the government that the definition of "press" has expanded.

The practice of citizen journalism and the ubiquity of social media websites pose several challenges for public officials wishing to police their public image by exerting an influence on the news. First, citizen journalism is a markedly different practice of news reporting that is neither dependent on government information nor on establishment media to disseminate information. If establishment media has traditionally been thought of as the fourth estate that would hold government accountable, then Ward and Wasserman (2010) suggest that citizen journalism is best thought of as a "fifth estate," referring to groups that not only influence the public sphere but that also hold the establishment press accountable by covering events overlooked by or ignored by mainstream journalism. Citizen journalism is therefore unlike traditional journalism in that it adheres to a "bottom-up" or grassroots model of news production. Rather than information originating from the powerful and reaching the masses, in many instances, information stems from the people and works its way to those at the top of the political hierarchy. Not only does this render the public liberated from their role of passive consumers of news; it also liberates the public from government news gatekeepers, or at a minimum it makes them less dependent on others to decide what is newsworthy (Lewis, Kaufhold, & Lasorsa, 2010).

With social media making the public less dependent on government and the journalists with whom they are closely aligned for information, citizen journalists can themselves cast a spotlight on government malfeasance and serve as a force for accountability, and this poses a second challenge to the legitimacy of those in power, for it places them as recipients—rather than as makers—of the news. In the Middle East, citizen journalists have used their ware to question the legitimacy of autocratic governments or to bring an end outright to some of the most repressive of regimes (Hamdy, 2009; Kouddous, 2011). By using social media technology, these journalists have been able to disseminate information faster than governments were able to suppress it (Hamdy, 2009). This allowed for a public discussion of issues that the establishment media avoided—such as feminism or the monarchy. When governments finally responded, these same citizen journalists posted video footage of repressive state actions to social media websites. Once the information taboo was broken, it created a climate wherein the mainstream press felt more comfortable taking risks, and it began to feature what were previously uncovered topics. Here is how one Egyptian blogger explained it: "When us bloggers began to post videos, that [sic] gave courage to traditional journalists to cover the story as well" (cited in Kouddous, 2011, para. 7).

In other global regions, too, social media have been a powerful source of government accountability. Text-message reporting proved pivotal in holding the Kenyan government accountable during its 2007 presidential election. Early poll results reported from journalists using the messaging technology on their cell phones suggested that the opposition candidate was clearly on the way to victory. So when the incumbent was declared the winner, the election was quickly called into question. When the election announcement triggered violence in the streets, the government began to censor the media by banning live coverage of events as well as commentary on news broadcasts. It could not, however, reach text-message reporting, which filled the real-time information void by circumventing government control (Rhodes, 2009).

The challenges of increased accountability posed by citizen journalism in "closed" nations also pose challenges to authority in more open or democratic societies. This has been especially true at the local level of governance where police officers are the most visible of government agencies. As street-level bureaucrats who carry out and enforce the policies of municipalities (Lipsky, 1980), the police find themselves the frequent targets of citizen journalists, and footage of police practices is routinely made available to the public through social media websites. Many times, this footage is later picked up by establishment media. When this occurs, police are no longer framing the news and its interpretation but are instead merely reacting to it the best they can.

One of the earliest and most famous instances of citizen journalism and police accountability took place in early 1991. George Holliday was standing on the balcony of a nearby building when he videotaped the beating of motorist Rodney King at the hands of four police officers taking place on the street below. The events featured on his 81-second videotape (which he delivered to the media) not only shook up the Los Angeles Police Department; they also sparked a national dialogue on issues of racism, police abuse of force, and the need for community policing, bringing about a era of police reform (Lovell, 2003). In Seattle 1999, cellular phones and "open" publishing websites (such as Indymedia) played a crucial role in the coordination and dissemination of information among various protest constituencies who questioned the fairness of the World Trade Organization (Gillham & Marx, 2000; Kidd, 2003). Moreover, video footage captured by ordinary citizens during the several days of protest challenged the official narrative of a restrained response by law enforcement (Freidberg & Rowley, 2000). The availability of this citizen-captured footage resulted in the resignation of the police chief and an investigation into the city handling of the event. More recently, the beating death of a mentally ill homeless man by police in a Southern California suburb was ignored by establishment media until the victim's father snapped a photo of his son's unrecognizable face and sent it to a community blogger. It was *only* then that the story of the victim—Kelly Thomas—became international news, it was *only* then that the extent of law enforcement mental illness training became questioned, and it was *only* then that a second degree murder charge was brought against one of the officers involved in the beating (Moxley, 2011). All of this because of an image sent to a citizen journalist.

A final challenge posed by citizen journalism and social media reporting centers on the question of journalistic ethics and standards among the new breed of reporters. Ward and Wasserman (2010) define *ethics* as "norms and practices intended to guide the conduct of group of people, such as members of a profession" (p. 276). They note that traditionally journalists have operated within a "closed" system of ethics where the guidelines are "intended for a relatively small group of people" (p. 277). This insulated reporters from allegations that their coverage was influenced by special interests and increased public confidence that the news was objectively reported. Citizen journalism and social media are reshaping media ethics, creating a more open system where those practicing journalism may not be familiar (or concerned) with the ethical canons of the profession. Returning to the presidential election in Kenya, while text-messaging served as an important check on the government, it was also used to spread rumors and to cultivate intolerance and fear, adding to the level of violence in the streets (Rhodes, 2009).

Closer to home, observers and practitioners of citizen journalism, such as Robert Cox of the *Media Bloggers Association*, suggest that bloggers "are going to be intentionally provocative" because they "rely on hyperbole, sometimes" (cited in Cooper, 2008, p. 46). David Hazinski (2007), a correspondent for NBC News, actually criticized the term *citizen journalist* in an opinion piece appearing in *The Atlanta Journal-Constitution*. Saying that someone is a citizen journalist "is like saying someone who carries a scalpel is a 'citizen surgeon'," he went on to add, "Information without journalistic standards is called gossip."

It is certainly true that absent ethical standards, citizen journalism and social media have the potential to spread misinformation and false allegations. This may be especially problematic with social media coverage of law enforcement practices since the public often hold misconceptions about police (Roberg, Novak, Cordner, & Smith, 2012). But this simply means that police must do a better job informing the public about police practices, especially during times when police are the targets of critical news coverage. Where police have traditionally avoided providing comment in the media during times of accident or scandal, we have seen that alternate voices dominate news commentary. With commentary now increasingly stemming from blogs and social media sites, police now have little choice but to inject themselves into the media spotlight when they become the story, or else lose all public legitimacy. This may require that police use the media to own up to their missteps when headlines are bad, and promote their successes when headlines are good. To that end, police may also choose to "develop more interactive and participative communication strategies" of their own while making more use of social media themselves (Copitch & Fox, 2010, p. 44). Simply put, police wishing to maintain public legitimacy must not avoid citizen journalism and social media; they must embrace it or fall victim to it.

Summary

Like all new media technology, citizen journalism and social media contribute to police accountability. Virtually anyone with a cellular phone and a personal computer can disseminate information about police performance to the World Wide Web, thereby creating a dialogue where questions about such issues as police training, use of force, and police professionalism can be publicly debated. Unfortunately, some police agencies have not taken warmly to being held more accountable to the public they serve, and the method by which some agencies in the United States have addressed citizen journalism resembles those used in nondemocratic countries. So while Egyptian blogger Alaa Abdel Fattah was seized by government officials and imprisoned for 45 days for publishing information and opinion on a blog (Kouddous, 2011), in the United States, citizens who record police–citizen encounters and post this footage online are being arrested and threatened with prison sentences ranging from 15 to 75 years (Kelly, 2011). To be fair, it is doubtful that on-the-scene officers in the United States improvised the application of state wiretap laws against citizen journalists on their own. More likely, instruction on the use of such laws came from higher up in the police organization—suggesting that the arrest of citizen journalists to pre-vent police images from higher up in the police organization, or worse in city or state government. There is something disconcerting about public officials who celebrate the spread of citizen journalism abroad while taking steps to silence it at home.

Today, citizen journalism and social media websites represent the new news-reporting paradigm. The potential of social media to bring images of policing directly to the public without first passing through the government and establishment media filters understandably represents a new challenge to law enforcement. Unfortunately, police and public officials have been slow or simply unwilling to accept the citizen journalism/social media para-digm. Yet, with social media now ubiquitous, law enforcement must learn to conduct their work as if "we're all journalists now," for, as Simon Glik reminds us, in many ways we are.

Discussion Questions

1. What are citizen journalism and social media? How do they differ from more traditional modes of journalism and media?

2. What is meant by "accountability"? How does citizen journalism con-tribute to police accountability?

3. In what ways have new media shaped the nature of contemporary polic-ing? Cite historical examples.

4. Police often complain that the news media portray law enforcement unfavorably. Is this a fair complaint? Explain. What role if any do police play in contributing to their media image?

5. What are some of the ethical issues raised by the practice of citizen jour-nalism? What are some of the ethical issues raised by police trying to suppress its practice?

References

Antony, M. G., & Thomas, R. J. (2010). This is citizen journalism at its finest: YouTube and the public sphere in the Oscar Grant shooting incident. *New Media & Society, 12*(8), 1280–1296.

Barak, G. (1988). News making criminology: Reflections on the media, intellectuals, and crime. *Justice Quarterly, 5*(4), 565–567.

Bennett, W. L. (1990). Toward a theory of press-state relations in the United States. *Journal of Communication, 40*(2), 103–125.

Boorstin, D. J. (1992). *The image: A guide to pseudo-events in America.* New York: Vintage.

Bowman, S., & Willis, C. (2003). *We media: How audiences are shaping the future of news and information.* The Media Center. Retrieved from http://www .hypergene.net/wemedia/weblog.php?id=P36

Chermak, S. (1995). *Victims in the news: Crime and the American news media.* Boulder, CO: Westview Press.

Chermak, S. (1998). Police, courts, and corrections in the media. In F. Y. Bailey & D. C. Hale (Eds.), *Popular culture, crime and justice* (pp. 87–99). Belmont: CA: Wadsworth.

Chibnall, S. (1981). The production of knowledge by crime reporters. In S. Cohen & J. Young (Eds.), *The manufacture of news: Deviance, social problems and mass media* (pp. 75–97). Beverly Hills, CA: Sage.

Cooper, A. (2008, September–October). The bigger tent: Forget who is a journalist; the important question is, what is journalism? *Columbia Journalism Review,* 45–47.

Copitch, G., & Fox, C. (2010). Using social media as a means of improving public confidence. *Safe Communities, 9*(2), 42–48.

Davidson, W. P., Boylan, J., & Yu, F. T. C. (1976). *Mass media: Systems and effects.* New York: Holt, Rinehart, and Winston.

Ericson, R. V., Baranek, P. M., & Chan, J. B. L. (1989). *Negotiating control: A study of news sources.* Toronto: University of Toronto Press.

Fishman, M. (1980). *Manufacturing the news.* Austin: University of Texas Press.

Flynt, J. (1971). Corporation and police partnership with criminal pool-rooms. In H. Swados (Ed.), *Years of conscience: The muckrakers* (pp. 328–331). New York: World Publishing. (Original work published 1907)

Freidberg, J., & Rowley, R. (2000). *This is what democracy looks like.* New York: Big Noise Films.

Gans, H.J. (1979). *Deciding what's news: A study of CBS evening news, NBC nightly news, Newsweek, and Time.* New York: Vintage Books.

Geller, W., Nimocks, R., Goldstein, H., & Rodriguez, M. (1994). Four decades of policing in Chicago. *Police Forum, 4,* 4.

Giddens, A. (1990). *The consequences of modernity.* Stanford, CA: Stanford University Press.

Gillham, P. T., & Marx, G. T. (2000). Complexity and irony in policing and protesting: The world trade organization in Seattle. *Social Justice, 7*(2), 212–236.

Graber, D. (1980). *Crime news and the public.* New York: Praeger.

Griffin, M. (2011, September 26). First circuit affirms right to record the police. *Harvard Civil Rights–Civil Liberties Law Review.* Retrieved from http:// harvardcrcl.org/2011/09/26/first-circuit-affirms-right-to-record-the-police/

Hall, S., Critcher, C., Jefferson, T., Clarke, J., & Roberts, B. (1978). *Policing the crisis: Mugging, the state, and law and order.* New York: MacMillan.

Hamdy, N. (2009). Arab citizen journalism in action: Challenging mainstream media, authorities, and media Laws. *Westminster Papers in Communication and Culture, 6*(1), 92–112.

Hazinski, D. (2007, December 13). Unfettered citizen journalism too risky. *Atlanta Journal-Constitution,* p. A23.

Kelling, G. L., & Moore, M. H. (1988). *The evolving strategy of policing.* (Perspectives on Policing No. 4). Washington, DC: National Institute of Justice.

Kelly, L. (2011, January 28). 75-year prison sentence for taping the police? The absurd laws that criminalize audio and video recording in America. *Alternet.* Retrieved from http://www.alternet.org/rights/149706/75-year_prison_sentence_for_taping_the_police_the_absurd_laws_that_criminalize_audio_and_video_recording_in_america/

Kidd, D. (2003). The independent media center: A new model. *Media Development, 50*(4), 7–11.

Kouddous, S.A. (2011). *Citizen journalism paves the way in Egypt.* Pulitzer Center. Retrieved from http://pulitzercenter.org/node/10235

Lawrence, R. G. (1996). Accidents, icons, and indexing: The dynamics of news coverage of police use of force. *Political Communication, 13,* 437–454.

Lewis, S. C., Kaufhold, K., & Lasorsa, D. L. (2010). Thinking about citizen journalism: The philosophical and practical challenges of user-generated content for community newspapers. *Journalism Practice, 4*(2), 163–179.

Lipsky, M. (1980). *Street-level bureaucracy.* New York: Russell Sage Foundation.

Lovell, J. S. (2001). *Police performances: A study of police organizations and media relations.* Ann Arbor: University of Michigan Press.

Lovell, J. S. (2003). *Good cop/bad cop: Mass media and the cycle of police reform.* Monsey, NY: Willow Tree Press.

Lovell, J. S. (2006). *More Effective Media Relations for Law Enforcement.* Boston: Quinlan Publishing Group.

Manning, P. K. (1997). *Police work: The social organization of policing.* Prospect Heights, IL: Waveland Press.

McLuhan, M. (1964). *Understanding media: The extensions of man.* New York: New American Library.

Meyrowitz, J. (1986). *No sense of place: The impact of electronic behavior on social behavior.* New York: Oxford University Press.

Moxley, S. (2011, August 4). Fullerton stands up for Kelly Thomas: Businessman/blogger Tony Bushala isn't letting anyone forget Kelly Thomas' brutal death at the hands of Fullerton police. *OC Weekly.* Retrieved from http://www.ocweekly.com/2011-08-04/news/moxley-confidential-kelly-thomas-tony-bushala-friends-for-fullertons-future/

National Advisory Commission on the Causes and Prevention of Violence. (1969). *Mass media and violence* (Vol. 11). Washington, DC: U.S. Government Printing Office.

National Advisory Commission on Criminal Justice Standards and Goals. (1973). *The police.* Washington, DC: Government Printing Office.

National Commission on Law Observance and Enforcement. (1968). *Report on lawlessness in law enforcement* (NCLOE Publication No. 11). Montclair, NJ: Patterson Smith. (Original work published 1931)

Our view on cops and cameras: When citizens film police, it shouldn't be a crime. (2010, July 14). *USA Today*. Retrieved from http://www.usatoday.com/news/opinion/editorials/2010-07-15-editorial15_ST_N.htm

Perlmutter, D. D. (2000). *Policing the media: Street cops and public perceptions of law enforcement*. Thousand Oaks, CA: Sage.

Rafsky S. (2012). *Accreditation disputes at center of U.S. arrests*. Committee to Protect Journalists. Retrieved from http://cpj.org/blog/2012/02/accreditation-disputes-at-center-of-arrests-in-us.php

Reiss, A. J., Jr. (1992). Police organization in the twentieth century. In M. Tonry & N. Morris (Eds.), *Modern policing* (pp. 51–97). Chicago: University of Chicago Press.

Reppetto, T.A. (1978). *The blue parade*. New York: The Free Press.

Rhodes, T. (2009). *In text-message reporting: Opportunity and risk*. Committee to Protect Journalists. Retrieved from http://cpj.org/search.php?cx=0026 35367788333464843%3A1kfp8mbluhy&cof=FORID%3A9&ie=UTF-8&q=in-text+message+reporting%2C+opportunity

Roberg, R., Novak, K., Cordner, G., & Smith, B. (2012). *Police and society*. New York: Oxford University Press.

Rowinski, D. (2010). Police fight cellphone recordings. *Boston.com*. Retrieved from http://www.boston.com/news/local/massachusetts/articles/2010/01/12/police_fight_cellphone_recordings/

Shapiro, H. (1968). *The muckrakers and American society*. Boston: D.C. Heath.

Sherizen, S. (1978). Social creation of crime news: All the news fitted to print. In C. Winick (Ed.), *Deviance and mass media* (pp. 203–224). Beverly Hills, CA: Sage.

Sledge, M. (2011). Rochester woman arrested after videotaping police from her own front yard. *Huffington Post*. Retrieved from http://www.huffingtonpost.com/2011/06/22/emily-good-arrested-videotaping-police-rochester_n_882122.html

Surette, R. (2011). *Media, crime, and criminal justice: Images, realities, and policies*. Belmont, CA: Wadsworth.

Tuchman, G. (1978). Making news by doing work: Routinizing the unexpected. *American Journal of Sociology, 79*(1), 110–131.

Turner, G. T. (1964). The city of Chicago: A study of the great immoralities. In A. Weinberg & L. Weinberg (Eds.), *The muckrakers* (pp. 389–407). New York: Capricorn. (Original work 1909)

Walker, S. (1977). *A critical history of police reform: The emergence of professionalism*. Lexington, MA: Lexington Books.

Ward, S. J. A., & Wasserman, H. (2010). Towards an open ethics: Implications of new media platforms for global ethics discourse. *Journal of Mass Media Ethics, 25,* 275–292.

Zhao, J. (1996). *Why police organizations change: A study of community-oriented policing*. Washington, DC: Police Executive Research Forum.

Index

About the Authors _____

Tina Adams, Ph.D., is a licensed psychologist and has been working in the mental health services field for over 15 years. Dr. Adams is formally trained as a clinical and forensic psychologist. She received her master's and doctoral degrees from the California School of Professional Psychology (currently known as Alliant International University). Dr. Adams has experience as a child and family therapist, school psychologist, court clinician, and director of court clinic services. She also has expertise in psychological assessment. Over the course of her career, she has routinely worked with criminal justice professionals, including police, attorneys, judges, and probation officers. She has also served as the clinical director for the Worcester West Area Office for the Massachusetts Department of Children and Families. Presently, she is an associate professor of criminal justice at the Worcester State University. Her previous work experience includes a post as the statewide manager of Juvenile Forensic Services for the Massachusetts Department of Mental Health/Forensic Services Division. She has also served on many interagency groups and task forces, including the Massachusetts Juvenile Firesetting Stakeholders Group led by the Massachusetts Department of Fire Service and the Massachusetts Attorney General's Office, as well as the Massachusetts Governor's Juvenile Justice Advisory Council. In addition, she has experience in training criminal justice professionals in the area of critical incident response.

Cyndi Banks, Ph.D., is a professor of criminology and criminal justice, and associate vice-provost and associate dean of University College at Northern Arizona University. She is internationally recognized for her work as a criminologist in Papua New Guinea, Bangladesh, Myanmar, Iraq, Sudan, East Timor, and Iraqi Kurdistan in international children's rights, juvenile justice reform, and rule of law police. She has published widely on comparative and cultural criminology, international children's rights, indigenous incarceration, and criminal justice ethics. She has authored seven books, including *Criminal Justice Ethics* (3rd ed., Sage, 2013) and *Alaska Native Juveniles in Detention* (Edwin Mellen, 2008), and is soon to publish *Youth, Crime, and Justice* (Routledge, 2013).

Theron L. Bowman, Ph.D., is police chief at Arlington (TX) Police Department. He led the regional public safety efforts for the 2010 NBA All-Star Game, 2010 and 2011 MLB World Series games, as well as the 2011 NFL Super Bowl. Chief Bowman created and led an internal workgroup that explored and later created a statistically significant predictive geospatial algorithm that accurately explained more than 70% of residential burglaries in a city of 370,000 people. He serves as a commissioner for the Commission on Accreditation for Law Enforcement Agencies. Chief Bowman has received the Police Executive Research Forum's Gary P. Hayes Award and the John Ben Shepperd Public Leadership Institute Outstanding Local Leader Award. Chief Bowman received three degrees from the University of Texas at Arlington, including a doctorate in urban and public administration. He is a graduate of the FBI National Academy, the FBI National Executive Institute, and the Senior Management Institute for Police.

Gary G. Collins, Ph.D., is professor of psychology and associate dean of graduate programs for the School of Behavioral Sciences at California Baptist University. He served as a peace officer in Mill Valley, CA and Ventura, CA before becoming a licensed clinical psychologist in 1976. In addition to his clinical practice, Dr. Collins has accumulated more than 30 years of experience in law enforcement psychology for police and fire service agencies, providing assessment for employment applicants, Fitness for Duty evaluation, threat assessment, Critical Incident Stress Debriefing, and hostage negotiation. Dr. Collins also served as the primary researcher for three metropolitan agencies in Southern California in studies focused on the use of psychological instruments in the selection of peace officers and public safety dispatchers, and the prediction of burnout among police officers.

Aaron D. Conley, Ph.D., is an undergraduate instructor for the Department of Religious Studies at Regis University in Denver, Colorado where he teaches courses in ethics, philosophy of religion, and other topics related to religion and social change. He holds a doctorate in religion and social change from the University of Denver and the Iliff School of Theology. Dr. Conley has developed and taught graduate classes at the Iliff School of Theology on violence in religious thought and practice, restorative justice, and the relationships between history, memory, and group identity. He worked for six years building houses with Habitat for Humanity of Metro Denver. During this tenure at Habitat, he collaborated with many different community stakeholders, including public safety officers, officials from local jurisdictions, financial donors, and countless volunteers to build the future of families in need. This experience with Habitat breathes life into Dr. Conley's personal and academic pursuits.

Kevin A. Elliott, M.P.A., is a veteran of the U.S. Army, former firefighter, water survival instructor, and retired detective-sergeant from the Los Angeles County Sheriff's Department where he was a recognized expert in gangs, narcotics, and behavioral analysis. Mr. Elliott was also a senior robbery/ assault investigator and worked cases for LASD Homicide and NYPD Cold Case Squad. He had major cases featured on the Today Show, the Leeza Show, and American Justice. He is currently a corporate security director and subject matter expert for Toyota Motor Corporation, specializing in strategic security, emergency response, and crisis management. Mr. Elliott has been an adjunct faculty member and a lecturer for several American universities lecturing in contemporary problems in policing, criminal investigations, gangs, and workplace violence. He is board certified in strategic security management, holds a bachelor of science in criminal justice from the University of Texas at El Paso, and a master's in public administration from California State University–Northridge. He is currently pursuing a doctor of philosophy degree at the School of Criminal Justice, Texas State University.

Brian D. Fitch, Ph.D., is a lieutenant and a 30-year veteran of the Los Angeles County Sheriff's Department. He has worked a variety of assignments, including custody, field operations, investigations, training, and administration. Dr. Fitch is the former director of the Los Angeles County Sheriff's Department Education-Based Incarceration program, as well as lead facilitator for the agency's Deputy Leadership Institute curriculum. Dr. Fitch holds faculty positions at California State University–Long Beach, as well as Southwestern Law School. He has received several awards from the Los Angeles County Sheriff's Department including 2010 Exemplary Service Award, 2010 Meritorious Service Award, and 2007 Leadership Award. Dr. Fitch has trained more than 5,000 law enforcement professionals throughout the United States and abroad, in leadership, supervision, ethics, leadership, and communication. He currently teaches ethics, decision making, and motivation in the leadership programs sponsored by the Los Angeles Police Department, Los Angeles Fire Department, and California Police Officer's Association. Dr. Fitch has published more than 30 articles and book chapters, and is the co-editor of two prior volumes: *Education-Based Incarceration and Recidivism: The Ultimate Social Justice Crime Fighting Tool* (Information Age, 2012) and *Leadership in Education, Corrections, and Law Enforcement: A Commitment to Ethics, Equity, and Excellence* (Emerald Books, 2011).

Ana M. Gamez, Ph.D., is an associate professor of psychology and practicum director of a forensic psychology graduate program for the School of Behavioral Sciences at California Baptist University. She is also a law enforcement psychologist for the Los Angeles County Sheriff's Department. She has accumulated eight years of teaching experience in university settings, including California State University–Long Beach, National University, and Los Angeles Sheriff's academy. Prior to becoming a psychologist, she spent almost nine years working as a custody assistant for the Los Angeles County Sheriff's Department. Dr. Gamez teaches graduate-level courses in police psychology, forensic psychology and law, crisis intervention and brief psychotherapy, advanced psychopathology and criminality, statistics, research methods, and forensic mental health. She also teaches ethical decision making to law enforcement professionals. Dr. Gamez is a licensed psychologist who provides critical incident stress debriefings, officer-involved shooting debriefings, and individual and couples therapy to law enforcement personnel.

Attilio R. Grandani, Ph.D., is a fellow at Bramshill Police Staff College, Hook, Hampshire, England. He has written numerous articles for police journals, including *Metline*, *Jane's Police Review*, and *The Investigator*. He is the national and international academic lead for offences taken into consideration (TIC), and is currently engaged in a doctorial research program observing offending from the offender's perspective. He has conducted many research studies, some of which include Closed Circuit Television (CCTV) and its influence on volume crime offences, and TIC policy and processes in the United Kingdom. He has many academic qualifications, including policing, risk and security management, and criminology and criminal justice. He is a member of the Worshipful Company Of Security Professionals (WCOSP), which is a livery company located within the city walls of Old London, and a lecturer on the specialist subject of criminology and associated disciplines. He is a member of the Criminal Justice Matters (CJM) group, London.

Bryon G. Gustafson, Ph.D., is a bureau chief with the California Commission on Peace Officer Standards and Training (POST) and also holds a lecturer appointment at the University of Colorado Denver. He currently directs POST's research team and oversees standards and evaluation for California peace officers and dispatchers. Previously, Gustafson was police lieutenant and executive officer of the Sutter Creek (CA) Police Department. He is a graduate of the 218th FBI National Academy, holds a Ph.D. in public affairs from the University of Colorado Denver, a Pi Alpha Alpha M.P.A from the University of Southern California, and a magna cum laude B.S. in psychology from Excelsior College.

Amir M. Hamidi, Ph.D., is resident agent-in-charge for the Department of Justice, Drug Enforcement Administration, Sacramento District Office. He directs the operations of various domestic and international law enforcement programs, including state and local task forces, intelligence units, fiscal units, technical units, chemical diversion units, tactical diversion units, administrative units, and other investigative programs in 34 counties. Dr. Hamidi was previously assigned as an inspector to the Office of Professional Responsibility and as Pacific Region Organized Crime Drug Enforcement Task Force coordinator, as well as a supervisory special agent for the High Intensity Drug Trafficking Area Transportation Task Force. Dr. Hamidi is an expert in national security projects and is often called on for consultation and assistance by federal agencies. He has been tasked with providing training to the FBI Joint Terrorism Task Force, and state and local agencies in the area of international terrorism and Middle Eastern affairs. Dr. Hamidi serves as a board member on the scientific advisory board of Veteran, Immigrant, and Refugee Trauma Institute of Sacramento (VIRTIS, a research organization focused on PTSD).

Bernard E. Harcourt, Ph.D., J.D., writes on contemporary critical theory and punishment practices, and on political economy and legal theory, and teaches at the University of Chicago, where he is the chairman of the Department of Political Science, the Julius Kreeger Professor of Law and Criminology, and professor of political science. He is the author most recently of *The Illusion of Free Markets: Punishment and the Myth of Natural Order* (Harvard, 2011), and the coeditor, with Fabienne Brion, of the forthcoming French and English editions of Michel Foucault's *Mal faire, dire vrai: Fonction de l'aveu en justice* (Louvain and Chicago, forthcoming). He is the author of several other books, including *Against Prediction: Profiling, Policing, and Punishing in an Actuarial Age* (Chicago, 2007), which won the Gordon J. Laing Prize from the University of Chicago Press in 2009; *Language of the Gun* (Chicago, 2005); and *Illusion of Order* (Harvard, 2001). He also founded and edits an interdisciplinary journal called *Carceral Notebooks*. Harcourt earned his bachelor's degree at Princeton University and holds his Ph.D. in political science and law degree from Harvard University. Before joining the faculty at the University of Chicago, he taught at Harvard, NYU, and the University of Arizona, and has also taught at the École des Hautes Études en Sciences Sociales and Université Paris X–Nanterre.

Christine H. Jones, Psy.D., received her bachelor's degree in economics at the University of California, San Diego. She received her doctorate in clinical psychology from Pepperdine University. She has worked and trained at the Greater Los Angeles Veterans Administration, the University of Southern California, Loyola Marymount University, Mount St. Mary's College, the University of San Diego, and Aetna Employee Assistance Program. Dr. Jones has worked in consulting, crisis management, critical incident post-interventions, clinical treatment, training, prevention/outreach, and organizational consultations. Her professional areas of interest include organizational leadership, ethics, law enforcement family stresses, intimate relationship resilience, trauma, suicide prevention, and evidence-based treatments. She is a member of the Association for Behavioral and Cognitive Therapies, the International Association of Chiefs of Police, and the American Psychological Association– Division 18 (Psychologists in Public Service).

J. J. Klaver, Ph.D., has been a special agent with the FBI for more than 22 years. Dr. Klaver began his career in the Indianapolis Division, Gary Resident Agency, and now works in the Philadelphia Division. He has handled investigations across the broad spectrum of the FBI's jurisdiction and responsibilities, was the Philadelphia Division's public affairs and media relations coordinator, and serves currently as a supervisory special agent there, overseeing media relations, community outreach, training, special agent applicant recruiting, and crisis management. Dr. Klaver has a B.A. in sociology and an M.B.A., both from Tulane University, and a Ph.D. in organization and management from Capella University.

Patrick Koga, M.D., M.P.H., is a former college teacher and mentor to hundreds of police officers at the Union Institute, Sacramento campus. Dr. Koga received his education and training at the University of Medicine and Pharmacy, Timisoara, Romania, and Tulane School of Public Health and Tropical Medicine, New Orleans, United States. His work focuses on the disparity gap in mental health services for traumatized veterans, refugees, and immigrants. Dr. Koga currently serves as an associate clinical professor of public health at University of California–Davis School of Medicine; and a researcher at UC Davis Center for Healthcare Policy & Research. His past appointments include professor and director of Trauma Center, Institute of Transpersonal Psychology, Palo Alto; medical director, Romanian Community Center of Sacramento; visiting professor of psychiatry, Cambridge, England; clinical associate professor of psychiatry, Tulane School of Medicine; associate adjunct professor, Tulane School of Public Health and Tropical Medicine; and medical director, Samaritan Counseling Center of Greater Sacramento. Over the past 10 years, Dr. Koga has given over 100 invited talks, presentations, and workshops in the United States, Africa, and Europe on PTSD. Dr. Koga is also the president of Veteran, Immigrant, and Refugee Trauma Institute of Sacramento (VIRTIS, a research organization focused on PTSD).

Jarret Lovell, Ph.D., is associate professor in the Division of Politics, Administration and Justice at California State University, Fullerton. His academic interests focus on civil disobedience, social protest, mass media, and police accountability. He is the author of several scholarly articles as well as two books: *Good Cop/Bad Cop: Mass Media and the Cycle of Police Reform* (Willow Tree, 2003), and *Crimes of Dissent: Civil Disobedience, Criminal Justice, and the Politics of Conscience* (NYU, 2009). He is currently researching the subjects of activism in repressive political climates, as well as how the justice system investigates and prosecutes cases of cruelty and abuse toward animals. He lives in Orange County, California.

David Massey, Ed.D., has 37 years of law enforcement experience, 21 of which have been as chief of police. Dr. Massey was the first person to advance through the ranks of the Ocean City Police Department from seasonal police officer to chief, as well as the first department member to attend the FBI National Academy. As chief of police, he implemented many new programs and concepts, including establishment of a SWAT unit, a computer-aided dispatch and records-management system, a vehicular mobile data system, a bike patrol unit, and a computerized crime analysis component (COMPSTAT). The department won numerous community policing awards, including a National League of Cities Community Policing Award for its Reducing Alcohol Availability to Minors (RAAM) community-wide program. After retiring from the Ocean City Police Department in 2002, Dr. Massey was appointed chief of police of the Ocean Pines Police Department in 2003. Chief Massey possesses a bachelor of science degree in education from Salisbury University, a master of science degree in public administration from Wilmington University, and a doctoral degree in education from Wilmington University.

Randolph B. Means, J.D., is an attorney with more than 30 years of full-time experience as a legal and risk management trainer and advisor to American law enforcement. After serving as a military officer, he then attended law school at the University of North Carolina and went on to become a department head at a state law enforcement training center, where he also advised and trained the State Bureau of Investigation. He then served for nearly 10 years as in-house counsel to the Charlotte Police Department. Long time legal and risk management instructor for the International Association of Chiefs of Police, he has been a speaker at 10 of its annual international conferences and at multiple annual conferences of the FBI National Academy Associates and Public Risk Management Association. He has appeared on the FBI Training Network and taught at the Federal Law Enforcement Training Centers, east and west. His work has been mentioned in the *Wall Street Journal*, discussed on *60 Minutes*, and featured on the Law Enforcement Television Network. He is author of the popular book *The Law of Policing in America* (Labor Relations Information System, 2007) and more than 60 published articles, and writes the "Law and Risk Management" column for *Law & Order* magazine. Past head of the International Association of Police Legal Advisors, Mr. Means' teaching and consulting work has taken him to every state, Canada, and Great Britain, and he has taught more than a quarter million law enforcement officials. He has provided consulting services to hundreds of law enforcement agencies, including some of the largest in the country.

Luann P. Pannell, Ph.D., is the director of police training and education for the Los Angeles Police Department (LAPD). She is responsible for the evaluation of all LAPD training curricula to ensure relevancy, and compliance with state and federal criteria and department policy. She researches best practices in police training and adult learning to continually advance training and to identify the best delivery methods for accelerated learning, retention, behavior change, and organizational change. Stemming from this research, Dr. Pannell led the team responsible for the complete redesign of the LAPD Academy in 2008. Dr. Pannell teaches regularly in LAPD schools, as well as consults in the selection and training of instructors. Dr. Pannell received an M.A. and Ph.D. in clinical psychology from the School of Psychology at Fuller Seminary in Pasadena, as well as an M.A. in theology and cross-cultural studies. She served for two years as the co-chair of the

INTERPOL Group of Experts on Police Training (2009–2011). During her 12 years with the LAPD, she has written articles and presented at psychological conferences on the relationship between exposure to community violence and psychological distress, the collaboration between mental health professionals and law enforcement, and improving training outcomes for law enforcement.

Joycelyn M. Pollock, Ph.D., J.D., received her doctorate in criminal justice at the State University of New York at Albany. She also obtained a J.D. at the University of Houston, and passed the Texas Bar in 1991. Dr. Pollock is a professor of criminal justice at Texas State University–San Marcos, and has taught at the Houston Police Academy and the Bill Blackwood Law Enforcement Management Institute. She is a past recipient of the Fulbright Teaching Fellowship, and Senior Scholar Justice Award from the Open Society Institute. In 2007, she was awarded the Bruce Smith Award from ACJS for outstanding contributions to the field of criminology, and in 2008, she was awarded the Distinguished Alumni Award from the State University at Albany, School of Criminal Justice. Dr. Pollock is the author of nine books, including *Ethical Dilemmas and Decisions in Criminal Justice* (Cengage, 2012).

Daniel T. Primozic, Ph.D., is associate director of the Institute for Law Enforcement Administration at the Center for American and International Law, where he is charged with leading the Center for Law Enforcement Ethics, with teaching and developing courses in ethics and in leadership, and with editing *The Ethics Roll Call* and *The Journal of Law Enforcement Leadership and Ethics*. Prior to his current position, Dr. Primozic served as the dean of liberal and fine arts at Santa Fe Community College after having worked as chair and associate professor of the Department of Philosophy at Elmhurst College. He later also founded and headed the Elmhurst Institute for Business Ethics. He has spoken nationally and internationally; published journal articles, book chapters, scholarly monographs, scholarly newsletters, and book reviews; edited *Dialogue*, the international honor society undergraduate and graduate journal in philosophy; published his own book, *On Merleau-Ponty* (Wadsworth, 2001); and is now writing about the ethics of C. S. Lewis and about the philosophy of Abraham Lincoln.

James L. Ruffin, Ph.D., has spent the past 26 years employed in both federal and state law enforcement agencies. He is currently a senior special agent group supervisor with the Bureau of Alcohol, Tobacco, and Firearms in Dallas, Texas. Dr. Ruffin earned his bachelor's and masters of science degrees in criminal justice from the University of Southern Mississippi. He later completed a masters of arts and a doctor of philosophy in human development from the Fielding Institute in Santa Barbara, California. Dr. Ruffin has been honored as a Life Fellow from the American College of Forensic Examiners and holds Diplomat status with the American Board of Law Enforcement Experts.

Greg Seidel, B.A., is a graduate of Randolph Macon College and several law enforcement institutions, including the FBI National Academy. He served the Bureau of Police in Petersburg, Virginia, for over 25 years, ultimately commanding its Investigative Division, its Office of Internal Affairs, and part of its patrol function. Captain Seidel has also served as a deep undercover narcotics detective, SWAT team leader, and training officer. Captain Seidel is a licensed polygraph examiner and a certified instructor in firearms, chemical munitions, police cyclist, and fitness. He has received more than 40 formal awards from local and federal agencies, including the Combat Cross and Purple Heart. He is the lead subject matter expert for the national distance-learning courses on use of force and officer survival endorsed by the Commission on Accreditation for Law Enforcement Agencies and the FBI National Academy Associates, and a contributing expert for their national courses on ethics and emotional intelligence. His articles have been published in a variety of professional journals. Captain Seidel is now the director of training for the Thomas & Means Law Firm, a police training and consulting group, where he teaches nationally and internationally in human relations, ethics, and leadership.

Kelly W. Sundberg, Ph.D., is an associate professor and serving chair for the Department of Justice Studies at Mount Royal University. He holds a bachelor of arts in political science from the University of Victoria, a master of arts in justice and public safety leadership and training from Royal Roads University, and a doctorate in criminology from Monash University. Since 2011, Dr. Sundberg has served as the alternate nongovernment representative to the United Nations for the Academy of Criminal Justice Science. His research, conference presentations, and publications principally focus on issues concerning border and national security, internal immigration enforcement, as well as transnational crime. Prior to joining Mount Royal University, Dr. Sundberg served in a number of enforcement and investigative positions with what today is the Canada Border Services Agency. During his 14 years with the CBSA, he received a number of commendations for his meritorious service to the public. Dr. Sundberg is actively involved with law enforcement training and development initiatives throughout Canada, the United States, and Australia.

Alexandro Villanueva, D.P.A., is a 27-year veteran of the Los Angeles County Sheriff's Department. Dr. Villanueva has worked a number of assignments, including training, field operations, and custody. He is a military veteran, who enlisted in active duty in the U.S. Air Force and completed his service as a commissioned officer in the California National Guard. His experiences working with hierarchies of law enforcement and the military served to enrich his perspective on career development, diversity, and equality. Dr. Villanueva's professional experience includes serving as a law enforcement union president and organizer, and as an advocate for banning indoor smoking in county jails. He is a former adjunct professor in the Criminal Justice

Department at California State University–Long Beach, and has taught recruits in the Sheriff's Academy. A firm believer in lifelong learning, Dr. Villanueva holds a doctorate in public administration from the University of La Verne, a masters of public administration from California State University–Northridge, a bachelor of science in liberal studies from Regents College, the University of the State of New York, and an associate of arts degree from San Bernardino Valley College.

Paul Zipper, Ph.D., CFI, has been with the Massachusetts State Police for 25 years. He serves currently as the station commander for the state police in Newbury. Prior to becoming a station commander, Dr. Zipper was assigned to the State Police Fire and Explosion Investigation unit for 20 years. His work with the Lawrence Arson Task Force, which began in 1992, brought him national (and international) attention. He has lectured in Australia, Canada, and the United Kingdom. Dr. Zipper served as a technical advisor with the U.S. Fire Administration through the National Fire Academy in the development of an interview/interrogation and courtroom testimony course. He is currently working with the International Association of Chiefs of Police in delivering juvenile interview and interrogation training. Dr. Zipper is a contributing author of the text, *Firesetting in Children and Youth: A Multidisciplinary Practical Handbook* (Academic Press, 2002). He is also coauthor of an article titled "Children and Arson: The Importance of Early Intervention in Juvenile Fire Setting," published in the *FBI Law Enforcement Bulletin*. Dr. Zipper is also the recipient of the Medal of Merit, the highest award bestowed on sworn personnel, for his work on the "Bomb Components Bill," currently one of the most comprehensive explosive-related statutes in the country.

⑤SAGE research**methods**

The essential online tool for researchers from the world's leading methods publisher

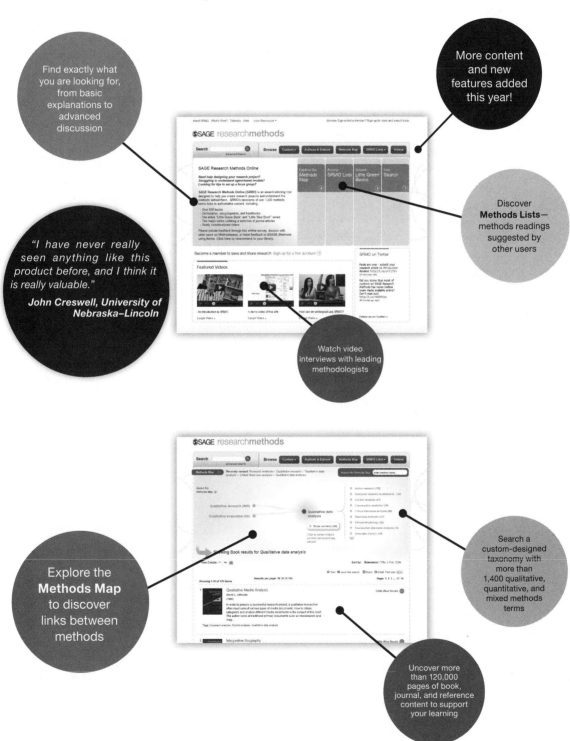

Find exactly what you are looking for, from basic explanations to advanced discussion

More content and new features added this year!

Discover **Methods Lists**— methods readings suggested by other users

"I have never really seen anything like this product before, and I think it is really valuable."

John Creswell, University of Nebraska–Lincoln

Watch video interviews with leading methodologists

Explore the **Methods Map** to discover links between methods

Search a custom-designed taxonomy with more than 1,400 qualitative, quantitative, and mixed methods terms

Uncover more than 120,000 pages of book, journal, and reference content to support your learning

Find out more at
www.sageresearchmethods.com